The author

Jacqui McDowell is a CPAG author, living in Edinburgh. She works as a freelance consultant, writer and trainer.

Acknowledgements

The author would like to thank Jon Blackwell and Kate Pawling for their thorough and meticulous hard work in checking the text and for making available their considerable experience in this difficult field. A huge debt is owed to the authors of previous editions of the book: Alison Garnham, Emma Knights, Simon Cox and Jon Blackwell.

Thanks are due to Nicola Johnston for editing and managing the production of the book. Thanks also to Katherine Dawson for compiling the index and Paula McDiarmid and Hayley Merrick for proofreading.

Many individuals at the DWP and CSA contributed to this edition, checking text, answering queries and discussing contentious points. It would be impossible to name each personally; to all the staff who helped, thank you for your time, attention to detail and patience.

As always, we acknowledge the enormous contribution of those who contact CPAG with comments on the book and information about families involved with the CSA.

Jacqui McDowell
June 2004

The law described in this book was correct at 1 June 2004.

Contents

Part 1   Introduction
Chapter 1   Introduction to the child support scheme   3
1. An outline of the scheme   3
2. Using the *Child Support Handbook*   6
3. Issues for parents and advisers   7

Part 2   Getting started
Chapter 2   The Child Support Agency   11
1. What is the Child Support Agency   11
2. Communicating with the CSA   13
3. CSA standards of service   17
4. Complaints about the CSA   18

Chapter 3   Who is covered by the scheme   23
1. The duty to maintain   23
2. Parent   23
3. Qualifying child   26
4. Person with care   28
5. Non-resident parent   29
6. Relevant child   30
7. Welfare of the child   31
8. Family   32
9. Habitually resident in the UK   33
10. The role of the courts in child maintenance   34
11. Existing 'old rules' cases   39

Chapter 4   Applications   43
1. Who can apply to the CSA   43
2. How to apply to the CSA   47
3. Withdrawal/cancellation of an application   52
4. Multiple applications   54
5. Existing 'old rules' cases   56

Chapter 5   Parents treated as applying   62
1. What happens when a parent is treated as applying   62
2. Opting-out   68
3. Harm and undue distress   70
4. Reduced benefit decisions   75
5. Existing section 6 'old rules' cases   83

v

Chapter 6 Information	87
1. Information-seeking powers	87
2. Contacting the non-resident parent	94
3. Parentage investigations	99
4. Further investigations	110
5. Duty to disclose changes	113
6. Disclosure of information by the CSA	114
7. Existing 'old rules' cases	117

Part 3   New rules maintenance

Chapter 7 The 'new rules' maintenance calculation	125
1. Maintenance calculation rates	125
2. Net income	132
3. Shared care	140

Chapter 8 Variations in 'new rules' cases	160
1. Grounds for variation	160
2. Applying for a variation	173
3. Procedure	174
4. The decision	180

Chapter 9 Conversions	191
1. When do 'old rules' cases convert to the 'new rules'	191
2. The conversion calculation and transitional phasing	193
3. The conversion decision	199
4. The Linking rules	202
5. Revision, supersession and appeal	207
6. Conversion, benefits and collection	212

Part 4   Old rules formula

Chapter 10 The 'old rules' formula in outline	219
1. A rigid formula	219
2. The five steps of the 'old rules' formula	221
3. Minimum child maintenance	223
4. 'Old rules' non-resident parents on certain benefits	224
5. Special cases	227

Chapter 11 The maintenance requirement: Step 1 of the 'old rules' formula	229
1. What is the maintenance requirement	229
2. How much is the maintenance requirement	230
3. Both parents are non-resident	232
4. More than one non-resident parent	233

Chapter 12	Exempt income: Step 2 of the 'old rules' formula	238
1. What is exempt income		238
2. How much is exempt income		239
3. Housing costs		241
4. Pre-April 1993 property settlements		249
5. Travel-to-work costs		253
6. Second families		255

Chapter 13	Assessable income: Step 3 of the 'old rules' formula	261
1. What is assessable income		261
2. What is net income		262
3. Calculating assessable income		281

Chapter 14	Proposed maintenance: Step 4 of the 'old rules' formula	286
1. What is proposed maintenance		286
2. How much is proposed maintenance		287
3. The 50 per cent calculation		289
4. The additional element calculation		291
5. Maximum child maintenance		296
6. Both parents are non-resident		298
7. More than one person with care		300
8. Divided family		305
9. More than one non-resident parent		306

Chapter 15	Protected income: Step 5 of the 'old rules' formula	310
1. What is protected income		310
2. Basic protected income		313
3. Total protected income		315
4. What is the maintenance payable		317
5. Change of circumstances		321

Chapter 16	Shared care under the 'old rules'	326
1. What is shared care		326
2. Care shared by separated parents		328
3. Care shared between a parent and another person		337
4. Care shared between two people who are not parents		341
5. Three persons with care		341
6. Care provided in part by the local authority		342
7. The maintenance requirement is met in full		342

Chapter 17 Departures under the 'old rules' 347
1. Grounds for departure 348
2. Applying for departure 358
3. Procedure 359
4. Considering departure 362
5. The departure direction 364

Part 5 Decisions and beyond
Chapter 18 Maintenance decisions 381
1. Making the initial maintenance decision 381
2. Default maintenance decisions 384
3. Notification of decisions 386
4. Court order phasing of calculations 387
5. When the first maintenance calculation begins 388
6. When a calculation ends 391
7. How a calculation affects benefit 394
8. Taxation of child maintenance 398
9. Existing 'old rules' cases 398

Chapter 19 Revision and supersession 413
1. Changing decisions 413
2. Revision 416
3. Supersession 420
4. Test case rules 427
5. Existing 'old rules' cases 430

Chapter 20 Appeals 434
1. Appeal tribunals 434
2. Procedure 437
3. Oral hearings 444
4. Decisions 447
5. Child support commissioners 450
6. Existing 'old rules' cases 454

Chapter 21 Collection and enforcement 458
1. Payment of child maintenance 459
2. Collection of other payments 466
3. Arrears 467
4. Deduction from earnings orders 477
5. Enforcement 483
6. Existing 'old rules' and conversion cases 489

Part 5 Decisions and beyond
Appendix 1 Useful addresses 497

Appendix 2	Income support premiums	502
Appendix 3	Child support 'old rules' formula	507
Appendix 4	Statutes	515
Appendix 5	Information and advice	517
Appendix 6	Books and reports	519

The terms we use

Use of 'she' and 'he'
As nine-tenths of people with the care of a qualifying child are women, we use 'she' to describe the person with care. We therefore use 'he' to describe the non-resident parent.

However, the law applies in the same way if the person with care is a man or the non-resident parent is a woman.

We recognise that in a small minority of cases the non-resident parent will be the mother and the parent with care the father. But clarity requires that we use 'she' for the person with care and 'he' for the non-resident parent.

Use of 'second family'
We use the term 'second family' loosely to describe the situation where a parent of a qualifying child (in our examples, usually the non-resident parent) also has children with a different partner. This could in fact be a third or fourth family, or even a first family where, for example, a married man remains with his wife despite having a child by another woman.

Use of 'step-child'
We use the term 'step-child' to describe the child of a person's partner, whether or not they are a married couple.

Abbreviations

CAU	Child support appeals unit
CSA	Child Support Agency
CSAC	Child Support Agency centres
CTB	Council tax benefit
CTC	Child tax credit
DCI	Departmental Central Index
DEO	Deduction from earnings order
DWP	Department for Work and Pensions
HB	Housing benefit
ICE	Independent Case Examiner
IMA	Interim maintenance assessment
IS	Income support
JSA	Jobseeker's allowance
LSB	Local service bases
PC	Pension credit
SPC	Satellite processing centre
WTC	Working tax credit

Child support rates 2004/05

Many assessments in force during this year will have been calculated on the basis of earlier years' rates.

Dependent children's personal allowance
Under 19 £42.27

Adult's personal allowances
Single £55.65
Couple* £87.30
* This is only used in the protected income calculation

Premiums
Family £15.95
Disabled child £42.49
Carer £25.55
Disability (single) £23.70
Severe disability (single) £44.15
The following premiums are only used in the protected income calculation (in addition to those listed above):
Disability (couple) £33.85
Severe disability
    couple (if one qualifies) £44.15
    couple (if both qualify) £88.30
Pensioner/Enhanced/Higher Pensioner
    single £49.80
    couple £73.65

Child benefit
For only or eldest child (lone parent rate)* £17.55
For other only or eldest child £16.50
For other children £11.05
* *Only for lone parents with transitional protection – see CPAG's Welfare Benefits and Tax Credits Handbook for details.*

Child support
Minimum payment of child maintenance (old rules) £5.60
Contribution towards child maintenance deducted from
income support (old rules) £5.60

Minimum payment of child maintenance (new rules) £5.00
(In some circumstances half this amount can be deducted)
Benefit penalty £22.26

Income tax (pa)
Personal allowance £4,745
Married couple's allowance £2,210
Blind person's allowance £1,560

National insurance contributions
Gross weekly earnings
Lower earnings limit £79.00
NICS are 11% on earnings between £91 and £610

Bands of taxable income
Lower rate – 10% £0-£2,020
Basic rate – 22% £2,021-£31,400
Higher rate – 40% over £31,400

Part 1
Introduction

Chapter 1

Introduction to the child support scheme

This *Handbook* deals with the child support scheme in 2004/05.
   This chapter covers:
1. An outline of the scheme (below)
2. Using the *Child Support Handbook* (p6)
3. Issues for parents and advisers (p7)

1. An outline of the scheme

The child support scheme was created on 5 April 1993 by the Child Support Act 1991. On 3 March 2003 it was substantially amended by the Child Support, Pensions and Social Security Act 2000. This introduced:
- a new method of calculating child maintenance;
- changes to the way parents with care on certain benefits are treated, including the introduction of a child maintenance premium;
- changes relating to collection and enforcement; *and*
- consequential amendments relating to revisions, supersessions, appeals and other areas.

Existing cases at 3 March 2003 may not be affected by all of the new provisions for some time. Some provisions relating to persons with care on benefit apply immediately; however, this does not include the child maintenance premium. Existing cases with a maintenance assessment will be referred to as 'old rules' while those worked out under the new scheme will be referred to as 'new rules'. Existing cases will convert to the new scheme at a future date, known as C Day. At the time of writing, no date has been set for conversion, however, current legislation means that this could be up to April 2005. However, some cases may convert earlier. For more on conversions, see Chapter 9.
   The main features of the child support scheme are:
- a Child Support Agency (CSA) to assess and enforce child maintenance and enforce its payment;

Chapter 1: Introduction to the child support scheme
1. An outline of the scheme

- the use of a standard mechanism to set the level of that child maintenance; *and*
- special rules for parents claiming certain benefits and caring for children not living with their other parent to be treated as applying for child maintenance or face a reduction in benefit.

The CSA deals with applications from both benefit claimants and non-claimants. It has taken over both the liable relatives work of the Department for Work and Pensions (DWP) and the role of the courts in setting child maintenance (although some old court orders continue to exist – see Chapter 4 – and in some specific situations new court orders can be made – see Chapter 3).

Some work has been transferred from the CSA to the DWP (see Chapter 5), under the 'closer working initiative'. The CSA is also trying to improve the way it operates (see Chapter 2).

Responsibility for child maintenance

The 1991 Act starts with the principle that both parents of a child have a duty to contribute to the maintenance of that child.[1] This liability is met when a non-resident parent makes payments of child maintenance assessed under the formula.[2] This duty applies whether:
- the child is living with the other parent or someone else;
- the child is living with a lone parent or with a married or unmarried couple; *or*
- the child's parents are on benefit or not.

However, the duty only has effect once an application is made to the CSA (see Chapters 4 and 18).

The 1991 Act introduced new terms into the language of relationship breakdown and child maintenance. These have been amended under the 2000 Act:[3]
- a parent who does not live with her/his own child is a **non-resident parent**;
- where a parent is a non-resident parent, the child is a **qualifying child**;
- the person with whom the child is living and who provides her/him with day-to-day care is the **person with care**;
- if a person with care is also a parent of the qualifying child, s/he is a **parent with care**;
- a child living with the non-resident parent, for whom they or any new partner receive child benefit, is a **relevant child**.

For details see Chapter 3.

Parents with care may be treated as applying for child maintenance if they claim certain benefits (see p5). Other persons with care and parents not in receipt of such a benefit have a choice about whether to apply for child maintenance.

Chapter 1: Introduction to the child support scheme
1. An outline of the scheme

The Child Support Agency

The CSA is the body set up by the Secretary of State for Work and Pensions to administer the child support scheme. It is responsible for the calculation of child maintenance payments and their collection where requested. This includes tracing non-resident parents and investigating parents' means. Information can be obtained from a number of sources (see Chapter 6). Powers under the child support scheme are currently held by CSA staff acting with the authority of the Secretary of State for Work and Pensions (see p11). We refer simply to the CSA in this *Handbook*. Where there is a discretion, the CSA must have regard to the welfare of any child likely to be affected (see p31).

For details of the CSA, see Chapter 2.

Parents with care claiming benefits

The 1991 Act places special obligations on parents with care getting income support (IS) and income-based jobseeker's allowance (JSA). Such parents can be treated as applying for child maintenance when they claim benefit. This means firstly, that they authorise the Secretary of State to take action to recover maintenance; secondly, they must co-operate by giving the information needed to pursue the non-resident parent; and thirdly, they may be asked to take a DNA test.[4] However, a parent may ask the Secretary of State not to act – ie, opt out.[5] A parent who opts out without good cause may have their benefit reduced. Good cause means that there are reasonable grounds for believing that if maintenance were pursued or the parent with care were to give the required information/take a DNA test, there would be a risk of her, or any children living with her, suffering harm or undue distress.[6] The Secretary of State has given the DWP responsibility for good cause interviews and decision making via the Jobcentre Plus.

For details of the rules relating to parents treated as applying, see Chapter 5.

Calculating maintenance

Child maintenance is worked out using rules set down in the legislation. Until all existing cases (ie, from before 3 March 2003) are converted to the new scheme there will be two methods of working out maintenance.

For existing cases, maintenance assessments are made using a five-stage formula, which is complicated (for details, see Chapter 10). The formula is based on IS benefit levels. It does not take into account the actual expenses of parents and children, other than housing costs. However, an application can be made for departure from the standard formula in certain circumstances (see Chapter 17).

For new cases, maintenance calculations are made using one of four rates (for details see Chapter 7). The calculation is based on the income of the non-resident parent. The calculation may be varied in certain circumstances (see Chapter 8).

Existing cases that convert to the new scheme may have special rules applied to how their maintenance is worked out (see Chapter 9).

Chapter 1: Introduction to the child support scheme
2. Using the *Child Support Handbook*

2. Using the *Child Support Handbook*

This *Handbook* covers the child support scheme in England, Wales and Scotland as at June 2004. Chapters contain the provisions relating to the new scheme with a separate section relating to anomalies or differences for existing 'old rules' cases. Separate chapters detail how maintenance is worked out under the 'old' and 'new' rules. Although there are some references to earlier changes, for full details of the scheme in previous years consult earlier editions. Developments during the year will be covered in CPAG's *Welfare Rights Bulletin* (see Appendix 6), and the next edition of this *Handbook*. We do not cover the scheme in Northern Ireland, but the rules are very similar (see p12).

This book is a guide to the scheme for parents and their advisers. It has a detailed explanation of the law and an outline of CSA procedures. We also include practical advice and tactics for dealing with the CSA and challenging decisions.

Structure of the book

This Part offers an outline of the scheme and explains how to use this *Handbook*. Part 2 introduces the CSA and its service, and explains the key principles and terms of the child support scheme. It covers the pre-calculation dealings with the CSA, such as making applications and providing information. The rules regarding parents treated as applying and the role of the Jobcentre Plus (eg, in good cause decision making) are also covered. Once all the information is available, the amount of maintenance can be worked out – Part 3 does this under the 'new rules' and Part 4 under the 'old rules'. The transitional rules relating to conversion of existing cases to the new scheme are also covered (Chapter 9). Part 5 covers the CSA activities which follow the formula calculation – decisions, reviews, appeals, collection and enforcement.

The appendices contain CSA addresses, information about useful reference materials, an explanation of income support premiums, and calculation sheets for 'old rules' cases. For benefit rates, see pxii.

The best way to find the information you need is to use the index at the back of the book.

Footnotes

At the end of each chapter are the footnotes. These contain the legal authorities and other sources of information which support the text, and some further information. Parents and advisers can quote the reference to the CSA if the statement in the text is disputed. Appendix 7 explains the abbreviations used in the footnotes with information on how to get hold of the sources.

Some footnotes refer to the online guidance material provided to CSA staff. These are only guidance and are *not* law. Guidance for Jobcentre Plus staff is contained in the *Guidance and Procedure* (GAP) volumes and associated circulars.

This *Handbook* includes references to relevant caselaw, in particular child support commissioners' decisions (see p453).

3. Issues for parents and advisers

Here we review briefly some of the more common problems experienced by persons with care and non-resident parents and with which advisers may be able to help. In most child support cases there are two parties with conflicting interests so representatives may find themselves in an adversarial situation.

Other problems arise from the CSA's interpretation of the law. In some cases there may be an argument that the CSA has wrongly interpreted the law and an adviser may be able to mount a test case. However, in many cases only a change in the law itself would solve the problem.

One major concern is the **poor standard of adjudication by the CSA**. Although this is improving, it is important to seek revision/supersession (see Chapter 19) and then appeal (see Chapter 20) where there is any doubt about the facts used or the application of the law.

Another common complaint is **delay** at all stages of the CSA's work, beginning with dealing with the application and continuing through to collection and enforcement. Concern about **protection of personal information** (see p114) leads to two kinds of complaints: first – mainly from persons with care – that they are not told what is happening with the case in relation to the other party; second – mainly from non-resident parents – that personal information is given to the other party, either in the notification of a decision (see p386) or in appeal papers. It is worth warning parents that application/enquiry forms are routinely included in appeal papers and therefore the other party will see that information if the case goes to appeal. Indeed, some parents may appeal simply to obtain the information they need to check the CSA's decision. If parties are concerned that information could be used to locate them, they should ask that it remains confidential (see p439).

In the past, problems for parents with care on benefit have stemmed largely from the policy requiring them to co-operate with the CSA rather than the way it is implemented. Even though the rules have changed, many parents with care may continue to accept the benefit penalty without giving any information about why they do not wish to pursue child maintenance. These parents should be encouraged to explain any 'harm or undue distress' (see p70) that might result if an application were made for child maintenance, as they may be able to show 'good cause' for opting out. Jobcentre Plus visiting officers interview parents with care about good cause. Decision makers in the Jobcentre Plus also decide whether or not to impose a reduced benefit decision. Where appropriate, parents with care should be encouraged to appeal and supported in the presentation of their cases. In the meantime, they may choose to opt in to avoid cuts in their benefit (see

Chapter 1: Introduction to the child support scheme
3. Issues for parents and advisers

p82). They should also be reassured that they can make representations to the Jobcentre Plus and appeal without the non-resident parent being informed. Parents who opt out and offer no reasons to support this are likely to be visited by fraud officers. They should understand that they are always entitled to opt out and accept instead the benefit penalty. Also, negotiating a maintenance arrangement with the non-resident parent is lawful, but any payments received by a benefit claimant must be declared to the Jobcentre Plus.

The CSA's effectiveness at working out and collecting maintenance depends to some extent on whether the non-resident parent is employed or self-employed. Its reluctance to investigate the non-resident parent's income results in the calculations of some self-employed non-resident parents being too low (see p270). However, its powers to impose a deduction from earnings order on employed parents without needing to go to court (see p477) makes it easier to recover assessed maintenance in those cases.

Delay in making a calculation means there will be **initial arrears** (see p468) so non-resident parents should consider making voluntary payments in the meantime which can be set against arrears arising later. If the **assessment is too high** but there are delays in altering it, the CSA may permit lower payments to be made until the revised calculation is done (p470).

Notes

1. **An outline of the scheme**
    1 s1(1) CSA 1991
    2 s1(2) and (3) CSA 1991
    3 s3 CSA 1991 as amended by Sch 3 para 11 CSPSSA 2000
    4 s6 CSA 1991 as substituted by s3 CSPSSA 2000; s46 CSA 1991 as substituted by s19 CSPSSA 2000
    5 s6(5) CSA 1991 as substituted by s3 CSPSSA 2000
    6 s46 CSA 1991 as substituted by s13 CSPSSA 2000

Part 2
Getting started

Chapter 2
The Child Support Agency

This chapter covers:
1. What is the Child Support Agency (below)
2. Communicating with the CSA (p13)
3. CSA standards of service (p17)
4. Complaints about the CSA (p18)

1. What is the Child Support Agency

The Child Support Agency (CSA) is a government 'next steps' agency which is part of the Department for Work and Pensions (DWP). It is responsible for collecting information about and tracing non-resident parents, and calculating, collecting and enforcing child maintenance.

The CSA is not mentioned in child support law. The 1991 Act gives powers to the Secretary of State but these powers are normally exercised by CSA staff. The CSA Chief Executive issues guidance to CSA staff and is responsible to the Secretary of State for the administration of the CSA. The DWP retains responsibility for child support policy issues. The Secretary of State can appoint CSA staff as inspectors. They have power to enter premises and make enquiries, to inspect documents and question people. For details, see p112. The Secretary of State can authorise individual CSA staff to represent the CSA in certain types of child support cases in a magistrates' or sheriff's court (see Chapter 21).

There are procedures for challenging and changing CSA decisions (see Chapter 19) and for appealing some sorts of decisions (see Chapter 20). There are also procedures for complaints about those CSA decisions which cannot be appealed (see p18). Wherever a decision maker has a discretion, s/he must take into account the welfare of the child (see p31).

DWP staff are responsible for identifying child support cases with the CSA where a parent with care claims income support or income-based jobseeker's allowance. The CSA then determines what, if any, action may be needed – eg, gathering information, conducting 'good cause' interviews and making decisions regarding reduced benefit decisions (see Chapter 5). This work is carried out by Jobcentre Plus staff.

Chapter 2: The Child Support Agency
1. What is the Child Support Agency

The 1991 Act set up a single scheme for the UK, but there is a separate child support agency for Northern Ireland, accountable to its Department for Social Development. Its powers are the same as the CSA in Great Britain. Great Britain and Northern Ireland are each referred to as 'territories' and there are reciprocal arrangements between them (see p382). There is a Child Support Agency centre based in Belfast which assesses cases for England and Wales: this centre is not part of the Northern Ireland CSA.

CSA offices

The CSA is divided into six regional business units (see Appendix 1), each with one **Child Support Agency Centre** (CSAC) and other local offices. Each business unit is allowed some independence about how it distributes work amongst its different offices. This means CSA organisation varies from region to region and in some areas a case may be dealt with by the CSAC from the start, while in others the same sort of case would only be passed to the CSAC after the child maintenance is worked out.

Due to regional variations it is difficult to give precise advice about what to expect and how to deal with problems. If no level of the CSA seems to be taking responsibility for a case, complain to the CSAC (see p18). The CSAC responsible for a case is determined by the parent with care's address. Where a non-resident parent has qualifying children living with different persons with care, the case is dealt with by the CSAC of the person with care who first applied for child support. Staff at the CSACs are responsible for case work after the first payment has been received from the non-resident parent. They are divided into the following teams:[1]

- **New Client teams** – progress applications through tracing, contact with the applicant and non-resident parent, calculate child maintenance, determine straightforward variation applications, set up payment accounts and monitor payments until a regular payment pattern is established. They are also responsible for any reviews while they are working on the case as well as paternity issues.
- **Maintain Compliance teams** – take over cases once the pattern is established, monitor payments, deal with delays and shortfalls, keep the calculation up to date, deal with changes and revise the rates due, negotiate and pursue arrears.
- **Enforcement teams** – deal with cases where formal debt enforcement action is needed, where paternity cases need to be pursued and where information needs to be pursued via inspectors.
- **Specialist teams** – Additional Trace, Appeals, Parliamentary Business Units, Senior resolution teams and Special Cases teams (self-employment).

Most CSA staff work at a regional centre. However, the CSA has **satellite processing centres** (SPCs) which undertake calculation work. The initial work on most cases, such as registering applications and gathering evidence, should be done from these SPCs. All field work should be done from a small number of **local** service bases (LSBs), based at local Jobcentre Plus offices. LSBs carry out the face-to-face interview work of the agency. Each LSB is attached to a CSAC, with which any difficulties should be raised.

2. Communicating with the CSA

In the past the main problems of communicating with the CSA have been:[2]
- long periods during which clients do not hear from the CSA and therefore suspect inactivity;
- lack of a specific reply to specific written or telephone enquiries;
- telephone calls promised to be, but not, returned;
- difficulties getting through to a member of staff who can help;
- inaccurate information provided; *and*
- unwanted contact or telephone calls from the CSA.

It is intended that the new staff structures and computer systems within the CSA will improve the management of case work and this in turn should improve contact and communication with customers.

Representatives

Anyone dealing with the CSA can appoint a representative to act on her/his behalf.[3] If the representative is not legally qualified, written authorisation is needed from the client. This can be provided at any time. The representative can complete any forms, provide information to and seek information from the CSA in writing and over the telephone and, where requested by the client, receive all correspondence from the CSA.[4] Payments of child maintenance will be sent to the client unless requested otherwise.

A representative, especially one experienced in dealing with the CSA, may find it easier to obtain information and the required action than a parent can. For example, where a representative is involved and a full reply to a written enquiry is not possible within the target of ten days (see p17), CSA staff are instructed to resolve complaints within 20 days.[5] If this is not resolved within 20 days the CSA will agree a resolution plan with the client as to how to resolve the complaint. See Appendix 5 for where to find independent advice.

Representatives with legal authority to act (ie, a person with power of attorney, a receiver or a mental health appointee/Scottish mental health custodian) are entitled to act for the CSA client in every respect, including receiving any payments, without authorisation.[6]

Writing to the CSA

To avoid disputes later, it is best to put information in writing to the CSA and to keep copies of correspondence. Include the reference number in any letter and

Chapter 2: The Child Support Agency
2. Communicating with the CSA

mark both the envelope and the letter for the attention of the relevant field office or Chils Support Agency centre (CASC). The agency has a commitment to acknowledge letters received within two days either by letter or telephone call. If a response to a specific enquiry is not received this should be followed up by telephone. See p18 for complaints.

Posting of documents

Documents posted by the CSA are usually treated as sent on the day of posting (excluding Sundays and Bank Holidays).[7] If more than one document has to be sent, or has to be sent to more than one person, and they are sent on different days, then they are treated as posted on the later or latest date.[8] When a document is sent to the CSA by post it is treated as having been sent on the day the CSA receives it.

In 'old rules' cases, documents are treated as posted on the second day after the day of posting,[9] or where more than one is sent on different days to more than one person – on the latest date.[10] Documents can be treated as sent earlier if there was unavoidable delay.[11]

Telephone contact with the CSA

The CSA's preferred method of contact is by phone.[12] Staff are trained on how to conduct telephone interviews and scripts are offered for a variety of situations. Some staff work outside normal office hours and may ring in the evening or at weekends. A direct line for the staff member dealing with the case should be printed on CSA correspondence. If a telephone call is inconvenient, the CSA should agree a convenient time to discuss the problem or to deal with it by post, if the person wishes it.

The CSA has a national enquiry line (08457 133133) for general enquiries during office hours. The staff do not have access to case information, so can only answer general questions such as 'Would a change of earnings of £x be likely to change the assessment?' However, they are able to transfer a caller through to either the appropriate case worker or case team where the named individual is not available.

Telephoning the CSAC

If no telephone number has been given on the correspondence, each CSAC has a client helpline (see Appendix 1), sometimes known as the call-handling section.

The person who takes the call has access to the child support computer system and should be able to give a progress report on the case. The person taking the call will attempt to forward the query to the team which is currently dealing with the case. If s/he is unable to pass the call directly, s/he will arrange a telephone call back to the client. If the call is not returned within the promised time, telephone again and ask to be put through to the relevant section:

Chapter 2: The Child Support Agency
2. Communicating with the CSA

- the New Client team – if awaiting or querying a calculation (whether on initial application, revision or supersession), queries about the maintenance account, method and timing of payment and DNA testing;
- the Maintain Compliance team if notifying the CSA of a change of circumstances;
- the Enforcement team if enforcement or other formal action is underway;
- the customer service section for complaints. Complaints are either dealt with by the relevant team or the Parliamentary Correspondence Unit (if the query is from an MP or for the Chief Executive). If they refuse to take a complaint, a complaint can be made against them.

Citizens' Advice Bureaux have access to a direct dialling service for people they are advising, but this is not available to the public.

Make a brief note of what was said, and with whom, together with the date. If the information is important, ask for confirmation of the information to be sent. The CSA should follow up the telephone call with a letter confirming the points that have been made so that no misunderstanding can arise. The CSA is unlikely to write and confirm a telephone conversation, however a record of the call will be made. This will not be a tape recording – only calls on the national enquiry line and client helpline are recorded, although these are deleted after 14 days. Staff should give at least their first names and their position.[13] Although this is a commitment made in the charter (see p17) some staff try to avoid giving their name. If necessary, remind them of the charter and then ask to speak to the customer service section. If the member of staff agrees to take some action but fails to do it within the stated time, follow this up again by telephone, asking to speak to the particular named member of staff and, if this fails to produce the desired result, write to the section supervisor. If the case warrants it, copy the letter, marked 'complaint', to the customer services manager.

Online contact with the CSA

The CSA website has a calculator for estimating child maintenance under the 'new rules' and general information about the Agency. There are also online forms that can be completed, printed off, signed and returned to the Agency. There is limited use of email to gather information and pursue case work due to issues of confidentiality. This means emails may be sent to the CSA but they will not reply by email.

Contact with satellite processing centres/local service bases

Satellite processing centres (SPCs) are likely to contact parents at home by telephone (see p14). A direct telephone line should be printed on SPC correspondence, but if there is no telephone number at all, the local CSAC can be called (see p14 and Appendix 1 for addresses). Staff at the local service base (LSB)

Chapter 2: The Child Support Agency
2. Communicating with the CSA

may also telephone and interview people at their office, a more convenient Jobcentre Plus office or at home.

Requesting an interview

A parent may request an interview and should do so for a problem which s/he feels cannot be resolved by telephone/writing. This face-to-face contact is provided by the LSB for the whole agency so, even if the enquiry involves actions taken by the CSAC/SPC, any interview would be carried out by a local staff member.

The request for an appointment should be made to the office dealing with the case. If it is not clear which office is presently responsible, or if the SPC/LSB does not respond, the request should be made to the CSAC. The request should outline the problem, so that the interviewing officer can be briefed, if necessary, by the CSAC. It is therefore usually better to request an appointment in advance rather than turning up at the office. If no response is received to the request for an interview, the CSAC manager should be contacted and if that fails, a complaint made (see p18).

Where the local officer is unable to provide the information requested, check that it is information which can be disclosed (see p114) and then repeat the request in writing. However, where advice has been given by the interviewing officer, written confirmation should be requested straight away if necessary, as s/he may not keep a full record of the conversation. The interviewing officer will record any information given by the client but the decision on what information is used in the calculation is made by the specific case officer. In some cases, the interviewing officer may enter data onto the computer system during the interview; a print-off of this should be provided. A record should always be made of the contact.[14]

Interview at CSA request

Sometimes the CSA requests an interview – eg, where paternity is disputed (see p95) or it is a more appropriate way of gathering information due to an individual's special needs.[15] Interviews are not compulsory, but it may be to the parent's advantage to attend. The LSB can be asked to arrange an interpreter or disabled access and about facilities for young children. A parent may request a home visit instead of an interview at the Jobcentre Plus office.

Where possible, the CSA will arrange the interview or visit by phone.[16] A visit will involve two officers only in particular circumstances, for example, where there is a potentially violent person in the household or the parent wants to tape the interview.[17] Early morning and evening visits can be conducted by staff on the way to and from work. The CSA also occasionally makes weekend visits or, where a client works shifts, arranges to see her/him at her/his place of work. However, while out-of-business hours interviews may be arranged, this may cause delays in arranging for a member of staff to attend at the requested time. Guidance suggests un-notified visits can be made if the decision maker thinks it is reasonable and likely to result in greater co-operation, for example where a notified visit to a non-resident parent has failed (see p95) or there may be potential violence.[18] Interviewing officers wear name badges in the office and carry identity cards when visiting.

Travelling expenses

Travelling expenses for attending an interview at the request of the CSA can be refunded. A refund is only given to a person on income support or income-based jobseeker's allowance who has had to travel to the office on essential business[19] – eg, s/he was asked to attend. However, these payments can also be made to someone who calls at the office uninvited because the matter could not be dealt with by telephone or letter.[20] Field officers are advised to consider whether the person has difficulties with reading or writing, communicating by letter or telephone, a good command of English and access to a telephone.[21]

No refund will be made for the first pound of a fare or for amounts of less than 10 pence.[22] The whole fare will, however, be met for a second or subsequent call within the same week (Monday to Sunday). Fares of a companion, child or interpreter can also be met in certain circumstances – eg, the child would have been left alone.[23] Refundable fares are based on the cheapest return fare by public transport or the cost of petrol up to the equivalent of public transport costs, or actual costs – including taxi fares – where public transport is unavailable or the person is disabled.[24] Proof of fares is requested only if someone is suspected of being untruthful.[25] Payment is made through the Jobcentre Plus by cash or girocheque.[26]

3. CSA standards of service

Performance targets are set for the CSA by the Secretary of State and published each year in the CSA business plan. The full list is available from the CSA. However, a few Secretary of State targets for 2004/05 are:
- accuracy – the most recent decision for all assessments checked in the year to be correct to the nearest penny in at least 78 per cent of cases;
- client satisfaction – 98 per cent of clients surveyed to be satisfied with the service;
- correspondence – 70 per cent of letters to be replied to in 10 working days;
- cash compliance – to collect 68 per cent of child maintenance and arrears due to be paid through the CSA's collection service.

The CSA has reviewed its service standards. The current standards that remain, as either internal targets or measures are:[27]
- to have payment arrangements in place within six weeks;

Chapter 2: The Child Support Agency
3. CSA standards of service

- to pay maintenance to parents with care (or their bank or building society) within 10 working days of receiving it from the non-resident parent;
- to answer a general enquiry telephone call within 20 seconds during normal working hours;
- to reply to a letter within 10 working days of receiving it;
- to see a client arriving in the office for a booked appointment within 10 minutes of the appointment time;
- CSA staff to always give their name on the telephone, wear name badges when meeting clients in the office and show identity cards when making a home visit;
- to resolve complaints within 20 working days of receipt;
- to issue customer account statements within 40 working days of the request;
- to make payments to a person with care within 90 working days of an application.

4. Complaints about the CSA

There are procedures of revision, supersession and appeal allowing the parties to challenge certain CSA decisions (see Chapter 19). Judicial review may also be possible (see p415). However, there are other procedures for complaints about the way in which matters have been handled. A complaint may be about delay, poor administration, rudeness, sexist, racist or other derogatory remarks, breach of confidentiality or lack of enforcement action. A complaint can lead to action and/or compensation.

A complaint about Jobcentre Plus staff acting under child support law can be made to the Jobcentre Plus. Further information on complaints about the Jobcentre Plus and other DWP Agencies can be found in CPAG's *Welfare Benefits and Tax Credits Handbook*.

To make a complaint, follow these steps until the desired response is obtained (see Appendix 1 for addresses).

- Write to the customer services manager in the CSAC, or LSB, marking both the letter and the envelope as a complaint. Once the details of the complaint have been entered onto the computer system an acknowledgement will be issued automatically.[28] A full reply should be sent within 20 working days (see above).
- If the response is inadequate or agreed action is not carried out, write to the CSAC manager with details of the complaint.
- If that does not work, write to the CSA Chief Executive. Explain the problem simply, if possible enclosing a copy of the letter written to the customer services manager, a covering note explaining why the response was not satisfactory and, where necessary, a list of events in date order.

It can be helpful to complain to the local Member of Parliament (MP), especially if the Chief Executive's office is approached and there is a delay in receiving a reply. MPs can be written to at the House of Commons, London SW1A 0AA or seen at their local surgeries.

The MP may write to the CSA for an explanation. The CSA is committed to respond to complaints within 20 working days, or provide a progress report.[29] If an immediate response is required, MPs can call a telephone hotline to the CSA. There is a special section in the CSA dedicated to queries from MPs. The MP can also refer cases of maladministration to the Independent Case Examiner or the Ombudsman.

If the complaint concerns the legislation and the policy behind the legislation, an MP should be asked to raise the issue with the minister.

The Independent Case Examiner

The Independent Case Examiner (ICE) acts as an impartial referee where the client is not satisfied with the CSA Chief Executive's response to a complaint. The ICE takes on cases where:
- the applicant has already used the CSA's own complaints procedure;
- less than six months have passed since the Chief Executive's reply;
- the Ombudsman is not involved in the case; *and*
- the complaint relates to the way in which the CSA has handled the case (including exercising any discretion – see p18) rather than a criticism of the legislation itself.

The ICE does not deal with complaints about the Jobcentre Plus – eg, reduced benefit decisions. For information on complaints about the Jobcentre Plus see CPAG's *Welfare Benefits and Tax Credits Handbook*.

Complainants can go direct to the Ombudsman, but the Ombudsman's office will usually encourage individuals to use the ICE first.

Complaints must be made in writing with as much relevant information as possible, including:
- name, address, date of birth and daytime telephone number;
- CSA reference number (if known) and the CSA office the complaint relates to;
- details of the complaint (eg, a copy of letters to the customer services manager and the Chief Executive);
- details of the CSA's response (eg, a copy of the replies from the customer services manager and the Chief Executive); *and*
- what the applicant wants the CSA to do to settle the complaint (eg, compensation – see p20).

After collecting all the relevant information from both parties, the ICE tries to settle the complaint. If this fails, a formal report is made with recommendations. The CSA has agreed to follow the recommendations in all but exceptional circumstances. Cases in which the recommendations are not followed are reported anonymously in the ICE's annual report. The ICE aims to deal with cases in an average of 34 weeks. For the address, see Appendix 1.

The Ombudsman

If the reply from the Chief Executive or the ICE is not satisfactory, the next step is to complain to the Ombudsman, via the local MP. The Parliamentary Commissioner for Administration (commonly called the Ombudsman) investigates complaints made by MPs against government departments. The Ombudsman's office sends a leaflet about their procedure to the complainant. If the complaint is investigated, the MP will be sent a full report. If the Ombudsman finds that someone was badly treated, s/he will recommend an apology and possibly compensation. The investigations can also lead to revised CSA guidance on procedures.

The CSA should respond to the Ombudsman within six weeks of receiving a submission on all new complaints or a draft report on the conclusion of an investigation.[30] However, the full investigation will take many months and quite often over a year.

Claiming compensation

In January 2001 a temporary compensation scheme was introduced. It only applies to non-resident parents who have accrued arrears due to unreasonable delay by the CSA. For further details, see Chapter 21.

Where a parent has lost out because of the way the CSA has operated the child support scheme, a claim for compensation or special payment should be considered. There are two main categories of special payment:
- extra statutory – ie, due to defective legislation or loss of statutory entitlement;
- ex-gratia – ie, due to actual financial loss, delay or consolatory payments.

Examples of circumstances where the CSA may consider a special payment are as follows:
- Delayed issue of a maintenance application form (MAF) or maintenance enquiry form (MEF). These forms should be issued within one month unless further enquiries are necessary before the issue of a MEF in which case the form must be issued within two months. For cases where there is already a court order in existence the MEF must be issued within four months. (For cases that pre-date April 1996 see earlier editions of this *Handbook*.) The CSA will not make a payment if it has acted reasonably and the delay is due to the non-cooperation of either party.
- Delay in assessing child support maintenance – advance payment of maintenance.
- Delay in reviewing child support maintenance liability.

Chapter 2: The Child Support Agency
4. Complaints about the CSA

- Delay or error in enforcement.
- Incorrect suspension of a court order where the CSA had no jurisdiction.
- Where a non-resident parent is wrongly identified.
- Loss of child support maintenance where there has been a court order in force during the period concerned.
- Situations where there is a measurable financial loss because of CSA error – eg, bank charges, postal charges.
- For instances of gross inconvenience, gross embarrassment and breach of confidentiality, and severe distress.
- Delay in forwarding maintenance to the parent with care.

This list is not exhaustive.

Any redress should include an admission of error and public arrangements for fair and reasonable compensation which restore the claimant to the original position s/he would have been in but for the maladministration. There is, however, no right of appeal against a refusal to award a special payment.

The first step is to write to the customer services manager explaining the full sequence of events and detailing the resulting loss. The manager should forward the claim to the Special Payments Unit of the CSA. If there is no satisfactory response, write to the Chief Executive of the CSA, with a copy to the government minister with responsibility for child support, at the DWP (see Appendix 1). It is useful to obtain the support of the MP. Even in cases where the DWP is currently very unlikely to pay any compensation, it may be worth requesting compensation in order to register a protest.

If compensation is not forthcoming, the claim can be repeated to the ICE (see p19). In addition, legal advice could be sought on the merits of taking the CSA to court.

Chapter 2: The Child Support Agency
Notes

1. What is the Child Support Agency
1. CSA Operational Vision Reforming Child Support 2001, p11-17

2. Communicating with the CSA
2. DWP, National Survey of Child Support Agency Clients, The Stationery Office 2001
3. Reg 22 CS(MCP) Regs
4. Third Party Representative
5. Post April 2002
6. s99 Mental Health Act 1983; s94 Mental Health (Scotland) Act 1984; s44 Court of Protection Rules 1994 (SI No.3046); Third Party Representatives
7. Reg 2 CS(MCP) Regs
8. Reg 2 CS(MCP) Regs
9. Reg 1(6) CS(MAP) Regs
10. Reg 1(8) CS(MAP) Regs
11. Reg 1(6)(a) and (7) CS(MAP) Regs
12. Using the telephone to contact the client
13. What you can expect from us
14. Record decision of FTF interview
15. Face to face overview
16. Contacting the client to arrange the appointment
17. Deciding to accompany the FTF officer
18. Deciding to notify the client
19. Part 6 para 290 FTFG
20. Part 6 para 310 FTFG
21. Part 6 para 311 FTFG
22. Part 6 para 320 FTFG
23. Part 6 para 340 FTFG
24. Part 6 para 350 FTFG
25. Part 6 para 330 FTFG
26. Part 6 paras 360-70 FTFG

3. CSA standards of service
27. Post April 2002

4. Complaints about the CSA
28. Add complaint detail dialog
29. Post 2002
30. CSA Business Plan 1995/96

Chapter 3
Who is covered by the scheme

This chapter covers:
1. The duty to maintain (below)
2. Parent (below)
3. Qualifying child (p26)
4. Person with care (p28)
5. Non-resident parent (p29)
6. Relevant child (p30)
7. Welfare of the child (p31)
8. Family (p32)
9. Habitually resident in the UK (p33)
10. The role of the courts in child maintenance (p34)
11. Existing 'old rules' cases (p39)

1. The duty to maintain

Both parents of a **qualifying child** (see p26) are responsible for maintaining her/him.[1]

The CSA can only require a **non-resident parent** (see p29) to pay child maintenance for a qualifying child. A **parent with care** (see p29) cannot be required to pay child maintenance for the child for whom s/he is caring, unless s/he is treated as a non-resident parent because s/he provides care for less time than someone else or, in some cases, for the same amount of time (see Chapter 16).

The CSA can only make a calculation if the person with care, non-resident parent and qualifying child meet the **habitually resident in the UK rules** (see p33).

2. Parent

A parent is a person who is in law the mother or father of the child.[2] This includes:
- a biological parent (see below for human-assisted reproduction);
- a parent by adoption;[3]

23

Chapter 3: Who is covered by the scheme
2. Parent

- a parent under a parental order (used in surrogacy cases).[4]

If a child was conceived by artificial insemination or *in vitro* fertilisation:
- the mother is the woman who gave birth to the child (wherever in the world the insemination or fertilisation took place),[5] unless an adoption order or parental order (used in surrogacy cases) is made;[6] *and*
- the father is the man who provided the sperm, unless:
  – where the method was insemination before 1 August 1991 *and* the child was born in England or Wales after 3 April 1988, the father is the mother's husband, unless he did not consent to the insemination;[7]
  – where the method was insemination or fertilisation after 31 July 1991, the father is:[8]
    – the mother's husband, unless he did not consent to[9] or died before insemination;[10] *or*
    – if that was during licensed treatment services provided for the mother and a man, that man.[11] This does not apply to a woman inseminated/fertilised outside the UK.[12] It is not clear whether the man must also have received treatment[13] or need only have attended with the woman.[14]

This means that where an unmarried woman self-inseminated the donor is the father.

Where a person denies being the parent of a child, the CSA must *assume* that the person is a parent of the child in the following situations, unless the child has subsequently been adopted by someone else (see 'adoption order' below):[15]
- in England, Wales or Northern Ireland, a declaration of parentage or, in Scotland, a declarator of parentage, is in force about that person;[16]
- a declaration under section 27 of the 1991 Act has been made about that person;
- in Scotland,[17] England and Wales,[18] the person is a man who:
  – was married to the mother at any time between the child's conception and birth; *or*
  – acknowledged his paternity *and* was acknowledged by the mother *and* was named as the father on the birth certificate issued in the UK;
- the person is a man who was found to be the father by a court in England or Wales in proceedings under certain legal provisions (see Appendix 4). The court decision usually states the legal provision under which it was made;[19]
- the person is a man who was found by a court in Northern Ireland to be a father in proceedings under similar legal provisions to those in Appendix 4;[20]
- the person is a man who was found by a court in Scotland to be the father in any action for affiliation or aliment;[21]
- the person is a man who refuses to take a DNA test, or where the results of the test show that he is the father (even if he refuses to accept it);[22]

Chapter 3: Who is covered by the scheme
2. Parent

- where certain types of fertility treatment have been carried out by a licensed clinic and the person is treated as a parent of the child under sections 27 or 28 of the Human Fertilisation and Embryology Act 1990.[23]

These rules apply even if paternity was not disputed in the proceedings.[24]

If none of the above applies, the CSA cannot make a calculation until parentage is admitted by a person or decided by a court.

An **adoption order** means that the child's biological parents (including anyone assumed to be a biological parent under the rules above) are no longer in law that child's parents.[25] This means that the liability of a biological parent to maintain her/his child ends on adoption and the parent(s) by adoption become the only people liable to maintain the child.

A person who, in England and Wales, has parental responsibility under the Children Act 1989 or, in Scotland, has parental rights and responsibility under the Children (Scotland) Act 1995, is not a parent for child support purposes just because of that.[26] A step-parent (except one assumed to be a parent under the rules above) cannot be required to pay child support maintenance, but the courts could order maintenance (see p37).

A foster parent is not a parent for child support, but s/he is a person with care if s/he has day-to-day care of a child who lives with her/him, except where the child has been placed with her/him by a local authority (see p28).

Parentage disputes

Where the parent with care does not name the other parent, or where the alleged other parent disputes parentage, the CSA investigates to identify and, if possible, show that the alleged other parent is assumed to be a parent under the rules above (see pp94 and 99). If the alleged non-resident parent disputes that those rules apply (eg, he says the person named in the court order is someone else), he can appeal against the CSA decision. This appeal is dealt with by a magistrate's/sheriff's court rather than by an appeal tribunal (see also pp99 and 437).[27]

However, if the alleged non-resident parent accepts that those rules apply, but disputes the correctness of the court order referred to by the CSA (ie, the court was wrong to name him as the father), he cannot dispute parentage through the CSA appeals system. Instead, he should consider applying to the court to set aside its order and/or making a late appeal against it.

If no one is assumed to be the other parent under those rules, the CSA usually tries to arrange voluntary DNA testing or applies to court for a declaration of paternity (see p105). A section 6 parent with care may face a reduced benefit decision if she refuses DNA testing (see p75).

Chapter 3: Who is covered by the scheme
3. Qualifying child

3. Qualifying child

Child support maintenance is only payable for a **qualifying** child. A child is only a qualifying child if one or both of her/his parents are non-resident parents (see p29).[28] However, a child only counts as a qualifying child when working out maintenance if the parent with care has applied or been treated as applying to the CSA for maintenance for her/him.[29]

'Child' is defined in the Acts (see below) but, generally, a person for whom child benefit is being paid counts as a child for child support purposes.

A child is defined as a person:[30]
- under 16;
- 16-18 years old and receiving full-time, non-advanced education (see below); or
- 16/17 years old and registered for work or youth training (see p27).

Even if a person falls into one of these groups, s/he is *not* a child if s/he is, or has been, married. This applies even if the marriage has been annulled or was never valid – eg, s/he was under 16.[31]

If a person is not a child, the courts may still be able to order maintenance – eg, a dependent child at university (see p37).

Full-time, non-advanced education

A course is **non-advanced** if it is up to A-level or higher level Scottish Certificate of Education (this includes a Scottish certificate of sixth year studies and a national diploma or certificate from BTEC or ScotVEC). Courses of degree level and above (including DipHE, Higher National Diploma, or a Higher Diploma or certificate from BTEC or ScotVEC) count as advanced education.[32]

The child must attend a recognised educational establishment (such as a school or college) *or* the education must be recognised by the Secretary of State.[33]

The CSA must treat a child as receiving **full-time** education if the child attends a course where weekly contact time is more than 12 hours.[34] Contact time includes teaching, supervised study, exams and practical or project work which are parts of the course. It does not include meal times or unsupervised study, whether on or off school premises.

Where a child is not attending such a course (eg, where contact is for less than 12 hours) the CSA must look at all the facts and decide if the education is full time.

After leaving school or college, a child still counts as being in full-time education until the end of a fixed period after s/he leaves. The end of this period is called the **terminal date**[35] and it coincides with the beginning of the next school term. A school leaver still counts as a child for child support up to the

Chapter 3: Who is covered by the scheme
3. Qualifying child

Sunday following this date unless s/he is 19 before that date, in which case it is the Sunday following the Monday before the 19th birthday.[36]

Time of leaving school	Terminal date
Christmas	First Monday in January
Easter	First Monday after Easter Monday
May/June	First Monday in September

If a child is under school leaving age when s/he leaves school, s/he is treated as leaving school on the date s/he reaches that age. The terminal date is the next one after that date.[37] If a child is entered for an external examination before s/he leaves school, the terminal date is the first one that follows the last exam.[38]

If s/he does any paid work of 24 hours or more a week before the terminal date, s/he no longer counts as a child unless the work is temporary and expected to end before the terminal date.[39]

Breaks in full-time education

Someone at school or college still counts as a child if there is a temporary break in full-time education.[40] It does not matter whether they are under or over 16 when education is interrupted.

Any break must be reasonable in the particular circumstances of the case. The break can be up to six months or, if it is due to physical or mental illness or disability of the child, longer. The break must not be likely to be, or in fact be, followed immediately by a period on Work-Based Training for Young People (Skillseekers in Scotland), or by education because of the child's job.[41]

16/17-year-olds not in full-time education

A 16/17-year-old who is no longer at school or college full time still counts as a child for child support if s/he is registered for work or youth training, but has not actually started either work or Work-Based Training for Young People (Skillseekers in Scotland).[42] This lasts for the **extension period** (see below). S/he still counts as a child if s/he does paid work so long as it is *either* for less than 24 hours a week *or* is temporary and expected to end before the end of the extension period.[43]

A 16/17-year-old entitled to income support or income-based jobseeker's allowance in her/his own right does not count as a child in this situation.[44]

The extension period begins on the day the person would otherwise stop being treated as a child (usually the terminal date – see p26). The date it ends depends on the terminal date. If the terminal date is after the end of the relevant extension period, there is no extension period.

Extension periods for 2004/05 are:[45]

27

Chapter 3: Who is covered by the scheme
3. Qualifying child

Terminal date	Extension period ends
12 September 2004	2 January 2005
9 January 2005	3 April 2005
10 April 2005	3 July 2005
11 Septembner 2005	1 January 2006

4. Person with care

A person with care is the person with whom the child has her/his home (see p29) and who usually provides day-to-day care (see below) for the child.[46] The person with care need not be the parent nor an individual but could, for example, be an organisation such as a children's home.

A person with care *cannot* be:[47]
- a local authority;
- in England and Wales, someone looking after a child placed with her by a local authority under the Children Act 1989, *unless* she is the child's parent and the local authority allows the child to live with her under that Act;[48]
- in Scotland, someone looking after a child who has been boarded out by a local authority under the Social Work (Scotland) Act 1968.[49]

There may be more than one person with care of a particular child.[50]

Day-to-day care

Day-to-day care is not defined in the Acts. It should be taken to have its ordinary, everyday meaning. A person who is responsible for a child's daily routine may be providing day-to-day care even if some things are done by another person – eg, a childminder.

Day-to-day care is defined in the shared care regulations.[51] It means care of at least 104 nights per year on average.[52] The average is usually taken over a 12-month period ending with the **relevant week** (see p264). Alternatively, the amount of care can be averaged over another period that, in the CSA's opinion, is more representative of the current care arrangements (see p326).[53]

Even though the definition of day-to-day care in the shared care regulations does not apply to the Acts, the CSA uses this definition when considering whether a person is a person with care under the Acts.[54] If this makes a difference, it is important to argue that the ordinary meaning of day-to-day care should be used, rather than the definition in the regulations.

For example, a mother on night shifts leaves her son in the care of grandparents for 22 nights a month. She decides what he will eat and when he will go to bed, and each morning she dresses him and takes him to school. Using the 104 nights average, she does not provide day-to-day care, but, using the ordinary meaning of those words, she is the principal provider of day-to-day care.

In two situations, the care actually being provided does not matter. Where a child is placed with her/his parents by a local authority under the Children Act 1989 (Children (Scotland) Act 1995), the parents are treated as providing day-to-day care under the Act.[55] Where a child is a boarding-school boarder or a hospital inpatient, the person who would otherwise provide day-to-day care is treated as providing day-to-day care under the Act.[56]

There may be no one with day-to-day care and no one treated as a person with care. For shared care under the 'new rules' see p140, and for under the 'old rules' see Chapter 16.

Home

The person with care must have a home with the child. A home is the physical place where the child lives. It is different from a household (see below).[57] Where a child has her/his home is usually clear. A child may have more than one home.[58]

Parent with care

A parent with care is a person with care who is also a parent (see p23) of a qualifying child (see p26).[59] There are special rules for a parent with care who claims income support or income-based jobseeker's allowance.[60]

A parent with care may be treated as a non-resident parent, see p329.

5. Non-resident parent

A non-resident parent is a parent (see p23) who is not living in the same household (see below) as his child, and the child has her/his home with a person with care[61] (see p28) – eg, where the parents of a child have separated. A parent with care who shares care may be treated as a non-resident parent (see p329).[62] If the non-resident parent begins living in the same household as the parent with care, the calculation immediately ceases to have effect.

Both parents can be non-resident parents, in which case they can both be required to pay child maintenance (see p341).[63]

Household

'Household' is not defined in child support legislation. A household is something abstract, not something physical like a home (see p29). It is either a single person or a group of people held together by social ties.[64] In many cases, whether people are members of the same household is obvious. Where it is not obvious whether several people share a household, the following factors should be considered:[65]

Chapter 3: Who is covered by the scheme
5. Non-resident parent

- whether they share the same physical space – eg, a house or flat;
- whether they carry out chores for the benefit of all of them (eg, cooking, shopping, cleaning).

No settled intention about future arrangements is necessary for a household to exist.[66] The meaning of 'household' has also been considered in family and social security cases. Caselaw may be used for child support purposes.[67] (For the social security caselaw see CPAG's *Welfare Benefits and Tax Credits Handbook*.)
Guidelines from the caselaw are:
- there can be two or more separate households in one house;[68]
- one or more members of a household can be temporarily absent from the home without ending their membership of the household;[69]
- there does not need to be a relationship like marriage for people to share a household – eg, two sisters can form a household.[70]

In social security law, a person can only be a member of one household at a time.[71] However, for child support cases, previous guidance from the DWP stated that 'where the person divides his time equally between households we would consider that he is a member of each household'.[72] This argument may be particularly important for shared care arrangements (see p328). Where there is a polygamous marriage there may be several partners in one household or several households.[73]

Advisers should be careful when arguing that a supposed non-resident parent shares a household with a parent with care on benefit. A decision by the CSA or an appeal tribunal that the couple share a household for child support purposes may lead the Jobcentre Plus to decide that the couple share a household for benefit purposes.

CSA staff are advised that 'household' and 'home' are different concepts and that a single home may contain a number of households.[74]

6. Relevant child

A relevant child is a child other than the qualifying child for whom the non-resident parent or their partner receives child benefit.[75] This can include a child who does not live with the parent all the time – eg, because they are at boarding school or there is a shared care arrangement for them.

Where this relevant child is cared for by a local authority either for part or all of the time, they will continue to count as a relevant child if the non-resident parent or their partner receives child benefit for them.[76]

The number of relevant child(ren) has significance in the calculation of child maintenance.

Relevant non-resident child

'Relevant non-resident child' is a term used by the CSA to refer to a particular child of the non-resident parent for whom an application for child maintenance cannot be made because the non-resident parent is liable to pay maintenance under a court order for the child.[77] In simple terms, this is a child who would have been considered a qualifying child if an application could be made for child support maintenance for them.

The number of relevant non-resident child(ren) has significance in the calculation of child maintenance.

7. Welfare of the child

Whenever the CSA or Jobcentre Plus is making a discretionary decision about a case, they must take into account the welfare of any child likely to be affected by the decision.[78] This also applies to an appeal tribunal and the child support commissioners, but only where the tribunal or commissioner is making a decision that could have been made by the CSA or Jobcentre Plus (for other decisions, see below).

Many decisions involve choosing between alternatives, such as whether a person is habitually resident or not, but these are not discretionary decisions. A person has a discretion only if, once s/he has decided what the facts of a case are and what the law requires, s/he still has a choice about what decision to make.

Examples of discretionary decisions are: whether to make a reduced benefit decision; collection and enforcement of maintenance, including making a deduction from earnings order (DEO); or to revise or supersede a decision.[79] Only the welfare of a child counts (see definition of a child on p26). However, it is not only 'qualifying children' or those named in the maintenance application that count. Any child likely to be affected by the decision counts[80] – eg, a child of the non-resident parent's new family, known under the 'new rules' as a relevant child, or another child of the non-resident parent who does not live with them.

'Welfare' includes the child's physical, mental and social welfare. For example, if a DEO would prevent a non-resident parent from visiting a child, that child's emotional welfare may be affected. However, a DEO may mean the parent with care has more money coming in, which may improve the child's physical and social welfare.

In the case of a reduced benefit decision, where there is no risk of harm or undue distress (see p70) the welfare of the child(ren) must be considered.[81] Previous caselaw indicates that this may not stop a decision being made unless there is a special factor – eg, the age or health of a child or the parent with care.[82]

The 1991 Act describes the welfare of children as 'a general principle'.[83] The High Court has said that considerable weight should be given to this welfare

Chapter 3: Who is covered by the scheme
7. Welfare of the child

principle.[84] However, because there is usually no discretion about whether to make a calculation (or 'old rules' assessment), or about the amount of maintenance due, there are only a limited number of cases in which welfare of a child can make a difference. CSA and Jobcentre Plus guidance reminds staff to consider the welfare of any children likely to be affected when making any discretionary decision.[85] Staff are told that they do not need to make enquiries about the welfare of the child, but must take into account any evidence they have.[86] This means that it is important that the CSA/Jobcentre Plus is given full details at the earliest stage about the effect a decision may have on a child's welfare. Where a decision has been made in ignorance of its effect on a child, the CSA/Jobcentre Plus should be asked to reconsider.

Guidance points out that welfare of the child must be balanced with the benefits of the receipt of maintenance and the purpose of the Acts, which is that non-resident parents support their children.[87] This means that the financial consequences of enforcement for the non-resident parent's children will not usually be enough to stop enforcement. Guidance suggests that welfare of the child will only make a difference in unusual situations.[88] Examples of when welfare of the child may affect the decision all relate to sick or disabled children. For example, where a child in the non-resident parent's household has a disability and requires an expensive special diet not provided for by the NHS, in deciding to enforce the full amount under a DEO the decision maker may decide to enforce at a reduced rate to ensure that the parent can afford the diet required by the child. Previous guidance gives another example, where the family have a Motability car paid for by disability living allowance, the CSA in deciding whether to apply to court for a disqualification from driving, would consider the welfare of the child if the non-resident parent was the designated driver.[89] CSA staff are instructed to record how the welfare of the child has been taken into account in a discretionary decision.[90] Persons affected may want to ask for these reasons, if they have not already been given to them. A decision can be challenged by judicial review (see p415). Where an appeal tribunal or child support commissioner makes a discretionary decision which the CSA could not make (eg, whether to adjourn a hearing), the welfare of the child must still be considered, because it is legally relevant to the discretion.[91]

8. Family

Family is defined as a married or unmarried couple or a single person where at least one member of the couple, or the single person, has responsibility for a child who lives in the same household.[92] **'Married couple'** means a man and a woman married to each other and living in the same household (see p29). It includes polygamous marriages (see CPAG's *Welfare Benefits and Tax Credits Handbook* and *Migration and Social Security Handbook*). **'Unmarried couple'** means a man and woman who are 'living together as husband and wife' (see CPAG's *Welfare Benefits and Tax Credits Handbook* for caselaw). The children living with a couple or lone parent do not have to be biological or adopted children to count as family members. Foster children are not included. A person under 16 cannot be a member of a married or unmarried couple.[93]

Lesbian and gay partners do not count as a couple. A lesbian or a gay man caring for a child is considered a lone-parent family, even if s/he has a partner. This rule may change if challenged under the Human Rights Act 1998.[94]

9. Habitually resident in the UK

The CSA cannot make a maintenance calculation unless the person with care, non-resident parent and qualifying child are all habitually resident in the UK,[95] or the non-resident parent lives abroad but is employed by the civil service, the armed forces, a UK-based company, a local authority or the NHS (including Trusts).[96] The requirement for the person with care to be habitually resident does not apply if that 'person' is an organisation.[97]

The UK means England, Scotland, Wales and Northern Ireland (including coastal islands like the Isle of Wight). It does not include the Isle of Man or the Channel Islands.[98]

Habitual residence is covered fully in CPAG's *Migration and Social Security Handbook*.

For child maintenance where a person is not habitually resident in the UK, see p38.

Meaning of habitually resident

'Habitually resident' is not defined in the Acts. CSA guidance indicates it should be interpreted in accordance with existing caselaw.[99] This says that a person is habitually resident if s/he is ordinarily resident and has been for an appreciable period of time.[100] A child support commissioner has decided that, for child support purposes, habitual residence is to be considered bearing in mind that the purpose of child support is the social need to require non-resident parents to contribute to the maintenance of their children.[101] Ordinary residence means 'residence for a settled purpose'.[102]

While each case is different and a decision has to take into account all of the person's circumstances and intentions, some of the most important factors to consider are:[103]
- the person's normal centre of interest or connections to a particular place;
- the length, continuity and purpose of residence in the UK;
- the length and purpose of any absence from the UK; *and*
- the nature of the person's work.

Chapter 3: Who is covered by the scheme
9. Habitually resident in the UK

If the non-resident parent is employed by the civil service, the armed forces, a UK-based company, a local authority or the NHS (including Trusts) he will be deemed habitually resident.[104]

Caselaw also gives the following guidelines:
- a person can habitually reside in more than one country or in none;[105]
- habitual residence can continue during an absence from the UK;[106]
- a person cannot be habitually resident if s/he has never been here;
- a person who leaves the UK intending never to return to reside will stop being habitually resident in the UK on the day s/he leaves;[107]
- a person held in a country against her/his will may not be habitually resident there, even after long residence (but see 'Children' below);[108]
- a person unlawfully in the UK probably cannot be habitually resident.[109]

A person returning to the UK after an absence may have remained habitually resident in the UK during her/his absence.[110] A child support commissioner has said that, when deciding whether a person has ceased to be habitually resident in the UK for child support purposes, the emphasis is on the nature and degree of past and continuing connections with the UK and intentions for the future.[111]

Children

For a child, habitual residence depends on where the parent or person with parental responsibility lives. Where there are two such people who live apart, one parent should get the consent of the other parent to a change in the residence of the child, otherwise the child may be considered to have been abducted. Where there is only one person with parental responsibility the child's residence changes with that person's.[112]

If a child has been abducted, s/he is considered still to be resident with the person with whom s/he was living with lawfully before, unless that person later agrees to the move.[113] Agreement might be assumed if that person does not act.[114] However, where a child is of sufficient maturity, her/his views may prevail in a child abduction case.[115]

10. The role of the courts in child maintenance

CPAG recommends seeking legal advice about any court proceedings. The following is not intended to be a comprehensive guide to the law.

The courts cannot make or vary an order for periodical payments of child maintenance where the CSA has jurisdiction to make a calculation if an application were made.[116] The CSA has jurisdiction where the child is a qualifying child and all the relevant parties (child and parents) are habitually resident in the UK. This applies even if the CSA *would not* in fact make a maintenance calculation.[117]

Chapter 3: Who is covered by the scheme
10. The role of the courts in child maintenance

However, courts have the power to make certain orders in relation to maintenance – eg, consent orders, orders in relation to special expenses or where the young person is no longer considered a child by the CSA. Courts can also vary orders, unless a maintenance calculation has been made – ie, an order was made on or after 3 March 2003 that has been in force for less than a year or the order was made before that date and the person is prevented from making a voluntary application.[118]

The situation regarding **consent orders** is complex. A consent order is an order made by the court with the written consent of both parties. It is legally binding and can be enforced like any other court order and cannot be changed by one party without the court's permission. This prevents an application to the CSA unless the parent with care is treated as applying (see Chapter 5). A consent order is useful where one party wants to prevent the other from voluntarily applying to the CSA in the future. However, where the order is made after 3 March 2003 this may only prevent an application for up to one year. Parents who want a consent order can agree with each other what should go in it, but should seek assistance from a solicitor or law centre to turn that agreement into a draft order to be submitted to the court. This is because a consent order needs to be made as part of a formal application to the court and to refer to the family law provisions under which it is made. The wording of the order is important – eg, a consent order containing an order to provide maintenance for the parent with care and undertakings to provide maintenance for the children may not prevent a calculation by the CSA.[119] However, in some circumstances it will be right to interpret both undertakings and orders as a whole without any distinction.[120]

From 3 March 2003 a section 4 or 7 application (see pp44 and 45) cannot be made if there is in force:[121]
- a written maintenance agreement made before 5 April 1993 (see p45);
- an order made before 3 March 2003; *or*
- an order made after 3 March 2003 that has been in force for less than a year.

The child support scheme does not change the court's powers in relation to other aspects of relationship breakdown – eg, contact and residence orders, spousal maintenance, property division and related parentage disputes (for which see p25).

A CSA decision refusing to make a calculation can be appealed to an appeal tribunal (see Chapter 20). A court ruling that it has no jurisdiction can be appealed or judicially reviewed (see p415).[122] No case should be outside the jurisdiction of both the CSA and the courts.

If a court order is cancelled because it was made by mistake when a CSA calculation was in force, any payments made under the order are treated as payments of child support maintenance.[123]

If a court order ceases to have effect because of a maintenance calculation, but the Secretary of State revises the decision and decides no maintenance is

35

payable as the previous decision was made in error, the court order revives and any child support maintenance already paid counts as paid under that order.[124]

The courts also deal with appeals about parentage (see p25).

If the CSA has jurisdiction

Until a CSA calculation is made

Even where an application could be made to the CSA (but has not been), an agreement for periodical payments for a child (in Scotland, aliment) can be entered into.[125] However, any clause included which claims to prevent anyone from applying to the CSA is void.[126] Anyone who considers they would get a better deal from an agreement than under the maintenance calculation may wish to try to enter into one. If it is made into a consent order (registered agreement in Scotland) after 3 March 2003 it only stops a party to the agreement from voluntarily applying to the CSA for one year from the date it was made (see p45).[127]

The court can also use its powers to vary an existing agreement (whenever made) by *increasing* periodical child maintenance due under that agreement,[128] but not by *adding* a requirement to pay periodical child maintenance, unless the parties consent in writing.[129] A person who does not want to apply to the CSA, or who is waiting for a CSA decision, can go back to court to increase (or reduce) maintenance. This is especially important if it is unclear whether the CSA has jurisdiction (eg, the agreement does not clearly meet the rules for preventing a section 4 application), so that the level of child maintenance is reconsidered quickly by the court and not left unchanged until any CSA decision is finally made.

Effect of a maintenance calculation on existing court orders and agreements

When a maintenance calculation is made, any existing court order or maintenance agreement either ceases to have effect or has effect in a modified form in relation to periodical payments (see below).[130] The existence of a court order or agreement may mean that the amount of the calculation is 'phased in' (see p387). Where there is a court order, the CSA may make a maintenance calculation following a section 6 application, or a section 4/7 application that is made where the order was made after 3 March 2003 and has been in force for more than one year.

These rules apply even to 'clean break' orders/agreements. There are conflicting court decisions on whether the child support scheme (or changes made to it) allows the court to re-open the capital/property part of such an order.[131] The arrangement may be self-adjusting to address the effect of any maintenance calculation which may be made. This could mean a legal charge on the transferred home so that the non-resident parent could recover any sums paid under the child support scheme from the transferred asset.[132] It could also mean an order that the non-resident parent top up any future calculation to a certain total amount of maintenance.[133]

If a child maintenance calculation is made for all of the children still covered by a **court order**, that order ceases to have effect on the effective date of the calculation – ie, two days after the calculation is made (see p389).[134] Where the order includes provisions for additional maintenance such as education or training expenses of a child, or for a disabled child's special needs, only the elements for periodical maintenance for a qualifying child should cease to be in force. Where the order is made solely for these additional expenses the order remains in force.[135] Parts of the order for matters other than periodical maintenance for the children named in the calculation (eg, other children, spousal maintenance) remain in force.[136]

In Scotland, if the CSA ceases to have power to make a calculation with respect to a child, then the original order revives from the date it ceases to have that power.[137] The same is not explicitly stated for England and Wales, which means that the original order does not revive when CSA involvement ceases. However, it could be argued that it should apply since the court order has not been revoked but simply ceased to have effect for the duration of a maintenance calculation. As the original order does not revive, this means that a new agreement and consent order will need to be negotiated. Where this is no longer possible, a parent may have no other option than to use the CSA to calculate and enforce child maintenance.

Maintenance agreements are unenforceable from the effective date (see p400) of the calculation.[138] Again, this only affects the part of the agreement to pay periodical maintenance for the children named in the calculation. The agreement remains unenforceable until the CSA no longer has the power to make a calculation.[139] Any court order made for children *not* covered by the assessment can be backdated to the date of the maintenance calculation.

Notifications

As well as notifying the parties about the calculation (see p386), the CSA must notify the court in which the order was made or registered.[140] Similarly, where a court makes an order which affects or is likely to affect a maintenance calculation, the relevant officer of the court (see p91) must notify the CSA of this if s/he knows a calculation is in force.[141]

Additional maintenance

Even where the CSA has jurisdiction, the courts can still make an order for:[142]
- maintenance for stepchildren of the non-resident parent – ie, children who were accepted by him as members of his family when they used to live with him;[143]
- maintenance for expenses of a child's education or training for a trade, profession or vocation;[144]

Chapter 3: Who is covered by the scheme
10. The role of the courts in child maintenance

- maintenance to meet expenses of a child's disability – a child counts as disabled if s/he is getting disability living allowance (DLA) or does not get DLA but is blind, deaf, without speech, or is substantially and permanently handicapped by illness, injury, mental disorder or congenital deformity.[145] The courts may even extend payments beyond the child's 19th birthday;[146]
- spousal maintenance;
- maintenance from the person with care;[147] *and*
- child maintenance in excess of the maximum worked out under child support rules.[148]

The courts can backdate these maintenance orders to the effective date (see p400) of a maintenance calculation, if the application is made within six months of that date.[149] Backdating is at the court's discretion and can ensure that other maintenance is in step with child support.

The courts' power to make a lump-sum award for a child will not be used to provide regular support for the child, but only to meet a need for a particular item of capital expenditure – eg, acquiring a home.[150]

If the CSA has no jurisdiction

If the CSA does not have jurisdiction (eg, because one parent or the qualifying child is not habitually resident in the UK) the court may make and vary a maintenance order. In addition, where there is a pre-3 March 2003 court order for child maintenance, a post-3 March 2003 order which has been in effect for less than a year, or a pre-April 1993 agreement (see p45), the courts have the power to vary such orders and agreements.[151]

In the past, many courts used calculations under the 'old rules' CSA formula as guides when setting levels of child maintenance. It is likely this practice will continue using the 'new rules' calculation, so parents seeking variation of an order or agreement can ask their solicitors to prepare a calculation. A High Court judge has said of the 'old rules' scheme 'that the formula figure is strongly persuasive, although not binding'.[152] The courts also have the power to enforce orders and agreements, including those made by other countries' courts.[153]

Where a section 4 application cannot be made because of a pre-April 1993 written maintenance agreement (see p45), the courts cannot make an order or revive one, except with the parties' consent (see p34).[154]

Although the courts can revoke child maintenance orders, this is not usually done simply to allow an application to be made to the CSA.[155] If revocation is being considered advice should be sought on the likely child maintenance calculation.

In England and Wales applications for maintenance are made to the family proceedings (magistrates) court, the county court or High Court. In Scotland they are made to the sheriff court or Court of Session.

Where a maintenance calculation is cancelled because one of the parties moves abroad (see p393), an application for maintenance can be made to the court. If the application is made within six months of the end of the maintenance, the order can begin from that date.[156]

11. Existing 'old rules' cases

In existing 'old rules' cases most of the definitions and provisions are identical to those in the new scheme. In this section we outline the differences.

In 'old rules' cases, references are to the legislation prior to the changes brought into effect on 3 March 2003. This means the Child Support Act and Maintenance Arrangements and Jurisdiction Regulations prior to amendments listed in the references and the Maintenance Assessment Procedure and Maintenance Assessments and Special Cases Regulations apply. For full coverage see the 2002/03 edition of this *Handbook*.

Terminology
Absent parent is used instead of non-resident parent.
Maintenance assessment is used instead of calculation.

Definitions
Child is defined in the Maintenance Assessment Procedure Regulations.[157]
Day-to-day care is defined in the Maintenance Assessment and Special Cases Regulations.[158]
Family is defined in the Maintenance Assessment and Special Cases Regulations as a married or unmarried couple, or single person where at least one member of the couple or the single person has day-to-day care or any children living with them.[159]

Court jurisdiction

The legislation on court jurisdiction in 'old rules' cases is identical to 'new rules' apart from the post-3 March 2003 orders. In addition, where a maintenance assessment is made for children covered by a court order (ie, in a section 6 case) the order ceases to have effect two days after the assessment is made.[160]

Chapter 3: Who is covered by the scheme
Notes

Notes

1. **The duty to maintain**
   1. s1(1) CSA 1991

2. **Parent**
   2. s54 CSA 1991 'parent'
   3. s39 AA 1976; s39 A(S)A 1978; s26(2) Case A CSA 1991
   4. s30 HF&EA 1990; s26(2) Case B CSA 1991
   5. s27(3) HF&EA 1990
   6. ss27(1) and 29(1) HF&EA 1990
   7. s27 Family Law Reform Act 1987 came into force on 4 April 1988 (there was no equivalent provision for Scotland). The father of a child born before that date is always the man who provided the sperm: *Re M* (Child Support Act: Parentage) [1997] 2 3 FCR 383, [1997] 2 FLR 90, [1997] Fam Law 536. s49(4) HF&EA 1990 came into force throughout Great Britain on 1 August 1991.
   8. s29(2) HF&EA 1990
   9. s28(2) HF&EA 1990; *Re CH* (Contact: Parentage) [1996] 1 FCR 768, [1996] 1 FLR 569, [1996] Fam Law 274
   10. s28(6) HF&EA 1990
   11. s28(3) HF&EA 1990
   12. Because such a clinic would not have a UK licence: *U v W (A-G intervening)* [1997] 3 WLR 739, [1997] 2 CMLR 431, [1997] 2 FLR 282
   13. *Re Q* (Parental Order) [1996] 2 FCR 345, [1996] 1 FLR 369, [1996] Fam Law 206
   14. *Re B* (Parentage) [1996] 3 FCR 697, [1996] 2 FLR 15, [1996] Fam Law 536
   15. s26 CSA 1991
   16. Under s56 Family Law Act 1986, Article 32 Matrimonial & Family Proceedings (Northern Ireland) Order or s7 LR(PC)(S)A 1986
   17. s26(1) CSA 1991 Case E and s5(1) LR(PC)(S)A 1986
   18. s26(1) CSA 1991 Cases A1 and A2
   19. s26(1) CSA 1991 Case F(a)(i) in 'relevant proceedings' under s12(5) Civil Evidence Act 1968 or affiliation proceedings
   20. s26(1) CSA 1991 Case F(a)(i) in 'relevant proceedings' under s8(5) Civil Evidence Act 1968 (Northern Ireland) or affiliation proceedings
   21. s26(1) CSA 1991 Case F(a)(ii) in affiliation proceedings
   22. s26(1) CSA 1991 Case A3
   23. s26(1) CSA 1991 Case B1 as inserted by s15 CSPSSA 2000
   24. *R v Secretary of State for Social Security ex parte Shirley West*, unreported, 30 April 1999, Johnson J, CO/568/1998
   25. s54 CSA 1991 'parent'; 'adopted' in Part IV AA 1976, or, in Scotland, Part IV A(S)A 1978
   26. s3(4) CA 1989; s3(3) Children (Scotland) Act 1995
   27. Arts 3 and 4 CSA(JC)O; Art 3(1)(s) and (t) C(AP)O

3. **Qualifying child**
   28. s3(1) CSA 1991
   29. Sch 1 Para 10C CSA 1991
   30. s55(1) CSA 1991
   31. s55(2) CSA 1991
   32. Sch 1 para 2 CS(MCP) Regs; CCS/12604/1996
   33. s55(1)(b) CSA 1991
   34. Sch 1 para 3CS(MCP) Regs
   35. Sch 1 para 5(3) CS(MCP) Regs
   36. Sch 1 para 5(1) CS(MCP) Regs
   37. Sch 1 para 5(2) CS(MCP) Regs
   38. Sch 1 para 5(6) and (7) CS(MCP) Regs
   39. Sch 1 para 5(5) CS(MCP) Regs
   40. Sch 1 para 4(1) CS(MCP) Regs
   41. Sch 1 para 4(2) CS(MCP) Regs
   42. s55(1)(c) CSA 1991; Sch 1 para 1 CS(MCP) Regs
   43. Sch 1 paras 1(1)(b) and 6 CS(MCP) Regs
   44. Sch 1 para 1(3)(b) CS(MCP) Regs
   45. Sch 1 para 1(2) CS(MCP) Regs

4. **Person with care**
   46. s3(3) CSA 1991
   47. s3(3)(c) CSA 1991; reg 21 CS(MCP) Regs
   48. s23(5) CA 1989
   49. s21 Social Work (Scotland) Act 1968
   50. s3(5) CSA 1991
   51. Reg 1(2) CS(MCSC) Regs

Chapter 3: Who is covered by the scheme
Notes

52 Reg 1(2) CS(MCSC) Regs 'day to day care' (a)
53 Reg 1(2) CS(MCSC) Regs 'day to day care' (b)
54 Deciding principal provider of day to day care
55 Reg 13 CS(MCSC) Regs
56 Reg 12 CS(MCSC) Regs
57 R(IS) 11/91
58 Reg 1(2) CS(MCSC) Regs
59 s54 CSA 1991
60 s6(2) CSA 1991

5. Non-resident parent
61 s3 CSA 1991
62 Reg 8 CS(MCSC) Regs
63 s1(3) CSA 1991
64 *Santos v Santos* [1972] 2 WLR 889, [1972] All ER 246, CA
65 Household
66 CCS/2318/1997
67 Household
68 CSB/463/1986
69 R(SB) 4/83
70 R(SB) 35/85
71 R(SB) 8/85
72 Letter to CPAG from DSS, 8 December 1992
73 Household
74 Household

6. Relevant child
75 Sch 1 Para 10C CSA 1991
76 Reg 10 CS(MCSC) Regs
77 Reg 11 CS(MCSC) Regs

7. Welfare of the child
78 s2 CSA 1991
79 When to consider the Welfare of the Child
80 CCS/1037/1995 para 11; Welfare of the child – General Principles
81 Para 170 IS/GAP Circular 02/02 (revised) 00/02; Vol 10 App 8 IS/GAP
82 CCS/1037/1995 para 13
83 Heading to s2 CSA 1991
84 *R v Secretary of State for Social Security ex parte Biggin* [1995] 2 FCR 595, [1995] 1 FLR 851
85 When to consider the Welfare of the Child; Vol 10 App 8 IS GAP
86 How to make a Welfare of the Child decision; Vol 10 App 8 IS GAP
87 General principles; Vol 10 App 8 IS GAP
88 Vol 4 Welfare of the Child paras 205 and 207 CSG
89 How to make a Welfare of the Child decision

90 How to make a Welfare of the Child decision: This is replicated throughout DWP guidance
91 *Wednesbury Corporation v Ministry of Housing and Local Government (No.2)* [1966] 2 QB 275, [1965] 3 WLR 956, [1965] 3 All ER 571, HL

8. Family
92 Reg 1(2) CS(MCSC) Regs; reg 1(2) CS(MASC) Regs
93 CFC/7/1992
94 Under Article 1 of Protocol 1 and Article 14 unjustified discrimination in respect of property (which may include child support assessments) is prohibited.

9. Habitually resident in the UK
95 s44(1) CSA 1991
96 s44(2A) CSA 1991; reg 7A CS(MAJ) Regs
97 s44(2) CSA 1991
98 Sch 1 Interpretation Act 1978; definition of United Kingdom
99 Deciding on habitual residence
100 *Nessa v Chief Adjudication Officer*, CA, [1998] 2 All ER 728, [1998] 2 FCR 461, [1998] 1 FLR 879, [1998] Fam Law 329 applying *Re J (A Minor) (Abduction: Custody Rights)* [1990] 2 AC 562, [1990] 3 WLR 492; [1990] 2 All ER 961, [1991] FCR 129, [1990] 2 FLR 442, [1991] Fam Law 57, HL; *Cruse v Chittum* [1974] 2 All ER 940; *Brokelmann v Barr* [1971] 3 All ER 29; *Langford v Athanassoglou* [1948] 2 All ER 722
101 R(CS) 5/96; CCS/7207/1995
102 *Shah v Barnet* LBC [1983] 2 AC 309, [1983] 2 WLR 16, [1983] 1 All ER 226, HL per Lord Scarman
103 Deciding on habitual residence
104 s44(2A) CSA 1991; reg 7A CS(MAJ) Regs
105 Deciding on habitual residence
106 *Lewis v Lewis* [1956] 1 WLR 200, [1956] 1 All ER 375
107 *Re J* (A Minor), see note 100
108 *Shah v Barnet LBC; Re Mackenzie* [1940] 4 All ER 310
109 *Shah v Barnet LBC*
110 R(CS) 5/96
111 R(CS) 5/96
112 *Re J* (A Minor), see note 100
113 *Re M* (Minors: Residence Order: Jurisdiction) [1993] 1 FCR 718, [1993] 1 FLR 495, [1993] Fam Law 285, CA
114 *Re A* (Minors: Abduction: Acquiescence) [1992] 2 WLR 536, [1992] 1 All ER 929, [1992] 2 FCR 97, [1992] 2 FLR 14, [1992] Fam Law 381, CA

Chapter 3: Who is covered by the scheme
Notes

115 *Re M* (A Minor) (Abduction: Child's Objections) [1995] 1 FCR 170, [1994] 2 FLR 126, [1994] Fam Law 366, CA

10. The role of the courts in child maintenance

116 s 8(1) and (3) CSA 1991
117 s8(2) CSA 1991
118 s8(1) and (32) CSA 1991
119 CCS/316/1998; CCS/8328/1995
120 CCS/316/1998
121 s4(10) and s7(10) CSA 1991; reg 2 CS(A:PD) Regs
122 rr8.1(2)-(6), 10.24 and 10.25 Family Proceedings Rules; Order 37 r6 CCR 1981; rr6 and 7 FPC(CSA)R
123 Reg 8(2) CS(MAJ) Regs
124 Reg 8(1) CS(MAJ) Regs
125 s9(2) CSA 1991
126 s9(4) CSA 1991
127 s4(10) and 7(10) CSA 1991; reg 2 CS(A:PD) Regs
128 s9(6) CSA 1991 (applies unless a calculation is made in an s6 case, when the agreement becomes unenforceable)
129 ss9(5) and 8(5) CSA 1991
130 s10(1) and (2) CSA 1991
131 *Crozier v Crozier* [1994] 1 FLR 126; *Mawson v Mawson* [1994] 2 FLR 985
132 *Smith v McInerney* [1994] 2 FLR 1077. However, an arrangement like this might be void under s9(4) CSA 1991 because it would 'restrict the right to apply for a maintenance assessment', though the commissioner in CCS/2318/1997 thought not.
133 See the arrangement in CCS/2318/1997
134 Reg 3(2) CS(MAJ) Regs
135 Reg 3(3) CS(MAJ) Regs
136 Reg 3(2) CS(MAJ) Regs
137 Reg 3(4) CS(MAJ) Regs
138 Reg 4 CS(MAJ) Regs
139 Reg 4(3) CS(MAJ) Regs
140 Reg 5(1) CS(MAJ) Regs
141 Reg 6 CS(MAJ) Regs
142 s8 CSA 1991
143 MCA 1973 or, in Scotland, FL(S)A 1958, 'child of the family'
144 s8(7) CSA 1991
145 s8(8) and (9) CSA 1991

146 Sch 1 para 3(2)(b) CA 1989. In *C v F* (Child Maintenance) [1997] 3 FCR 405 the court held that where s8(1) CSA 1991 applies, s8(8) CSA 1991 limits this power to children aged under 19. However, this seems to be wrong because the fact that CSA 1991 only applies to those aged under 19 can hardly prevent an order being made under CA 1989 for a person aged over 19.
147 s8(10) CSA 1991
148 s8(6) CSA 1991
149 s29(7) MCA 1973; s5(7) DPMCA 1978; Sch 1 para 3(7) CA 1989 as amended by Sch 3 paras 3,5, and 10 CSPSSA 2000 respectively
150 Sch 1 CA 1989; *Phillips v Pearce* [1996] 2 FLR 230
151 ss8(3A) and 9(6) CSA 1991; *McGilchrist v McGilchrist* [1997] SCLR 800
152 *E v C* (Child Maintenance), [1996] 1 FLR 472
153 MO(RE)A 1992
154 s8(3) and (3A) CSA 1991
155 s8(4) CSA 1991; *B v M* (Child Support: Revocation of Order) [1994] 1 FLR 342, [1994] 1 FCR 769, [1994] Fam Law 370
156 s29(7) MCA 1973; s5(7) DPMCA 1978; Sch 1 para 3(7) CA 1989

11. Existing 'old rules' cases

157 Sch 1 CS(MAP) Regs
158 Reg 1(2) CS(MASC) Regs 'day to day care'
159 Reg 1(2) CS(MASC) Regs 'family'
160 Reg 3(2(a)), (5) and (6) CS(MAJ) Regs

Chapter 4
Applications

This chapter covers:
1. Who can apply to the CSA (below)
2. How to apply to the CSA (p47)
3. Withdrawal/cancellation of an application (p52)
4. Multiple applications (p54)
5. Existing 'old rules' cases (p56)

1. Who can apply to the CSA

Any person with care (see p28) or non-resident parent (see p29) can apply to the CSA for child maintenance, unless barred by an existing maintenance arrangement (see p45).[1] In Scotland, children who are aged 12 or over can apply to the CSA under section 7 of the Child Support Act 1991 for child maintenance, provided no application has been made/treated as made by the person with care or the non-resident parent.[2]

Where there is more than one person with care of a qualifying child and at least one, but not all, of them has parental responsibility for the child, only those persons with parental responsibility can apply for maintenance.[3] For example, where a child is cared for partly by her/his mother who has parental responsibility, and partly by her/his grandmother, who does not have parental responsibility, only the mother can apply to the CSA. Parental responsibility has the same meaning as in the Children Act 1989 and the Children (Scotland) Act 1995. Parents who were married to each other when the child was born automatically have parental responsibility which continues even if they divorce.[4] Where the parents are not married, the mother can make a formal agreement giving the father parental responsibility.[5] The courts can also give parental responsibility to a person or persons (including a non-parent) who apply/ies for it.[6] From 1 December 2003, in England and Wales, if an unmarried father's name appers on the birth certificate, he has parental responsibility (this is not retrospective). It is inteded that similar provisions will apply in Scotland but this has not come into force yet.

Chapter 4: Applications
1. Who can apply to the CSA

Section 6 applicants

Section 6 of the 1991 Act applies to *parents* (and not other persons) with care who claim or are on income support (IS) or income-based jobseeker's allowance (JSA), even if someone else claims one of these benefits for them.[7] Such a parent can be treated by the Secretary of State as having applied for a maintenance calculation and recovery of maintenance from the non-resident parent, unless she requests the Secretary of State not to act.[8] A benefit penalty can be imposed for making such a request without good cause (see p83). In this *Handbook*, such parents are known as section 6 applicants. A court order or maintenance agreement does not prevent such an application being made.[9]

Neither a non-resident parent nor another person with care can make an application for child maintenance where the parent with care or her partner is receiving IS/income-based JSA, even if she requests the Secretary of State not to act.

Section 4 or 7 applicants

Section 4 of the 1991 Act applies to parents with care not on IS/income-based JSA and to any person with care who is not the parent of the qualifying child. Section 7 applies to children in Scotland. An application for maintenance is voluntary but may be prevented by an existing maintenance arrangement or court order (see below). In this *Handbook* these are called section 4 or 7 applicants. Such applicants are called private clients by the CSA and their applications called voluntary applications. People within this group can instead make a voluntary maintenance agreement and even apply to court for a consent order (see p35).

A written maintenance agreement

A written maintenance agreement for a child prevents a section 4 or 7 application (see above) for that child.[10] Maintenance agreement means a written agreement for making or securing the making of periodical payments of maintenance (or aliment in Scotland) to or for the benefit of a qualifying child.[11] An agreement only counts for this purpose if it:[12]
- was made before 5 April 1993. The Act does not require that it was actually in force before 5 April 1993, and allows the agreement to be varied after that date;
- is in writing. This can include an agreement made in correspondence headed 'without prejudice'.[13] While it need not be formal or prepared by lawyers, a spoken agreement is not enough, even if payments were made;[14]
- is an agreement. An offer that is never accepted in writing does not constitute a written agreement.[15] An undertaking made in court proceedings can be an agreement;[16]
- is made by the non-resident parent. The Act does not require that the person with care is a party to the agreement. A commissioner has decided that an agreement between the non-resident parent and the qualifying child does not

count.[17] CSA guidance suggests the agreement should be between the parents or their representatives;[18]
- is for periodical payments. An agreement to pay mortgage interest charges and fuel bills as they fall due can count, even though the amounts to be paid are not written down and are not at even intervals;[19]
- is for the benefit of the child(ren). The child need not be named in the agreement and an agreement to pay the mortgage for the home where they live counts as for the benefit of those children;[20]
- is 'in force'. An agreement to pay only a nominal amount counts.[21] An agreed change to the arrangement may mean the original agreement is no longer in force.[22]

A maintenance order

A maintenance order made by a court before 3 March 2003 prevents a section 4 or 7 application for the child(ren) concerned.[23] Where the order was made after 3 March 2003 and has been in force for less than one year no application may be made.[24] A court order only counts for this purpose if it:
- requires the making or securing the making of periodical payments of maintenance (or aliment in Scotland) to or for the benefit of a qualifying child.[25] Orders for payment of costs of education or training of the child, or because the child is disabled, or to 'top up' a maintenance, all count as maintenance orders.[26] Such top-up orders may be made in addition to any liability worked out by the CSA. For details of these, see p37. Because an order only prevents an *application* to the CSA, an order made *after* the application does not stop the CSA making a calculation (old rules assessment) or revising or enforcing an existing one. A court order directing capital payments (ie, not periodical payments) does not count as an order.[27] The wording of the order is important – eg, a consent order with provision for maintenance of the parent with care and undertakings to provide maintenance for the children may not prevent an application;[28]
- is in force. A commissioner has decided that an order is only 'in force' if it has a practical effect.[29] In that case, the agreement was made when the children were living with the parent with care, but they had then moved to live with the non-resident parent.[30] On the other hand, an order is in force where some undertakings or arrangements, such as for residence of the child, are still in effect, even though there is no further liability for maintenance payments,[31] or the liability for child maintenance under the order has not yet begun.[32] Where a court decides that it has no power to either vary or enforce an order, an application can be made to the CSA;[33]
- is made under one of certain legal provisions (see Appendix 4).[34] The order usually states the legal provision under which it was made.

Chapter 4: Applications
1. Who can apply to the CSA

A person who cannot apply to the CSA because of an agreement/order can, instead:
- ask the court to vary or enforce the amount of maintenance under the order or agreement (see p36);
- where there is an agreement, agree with the other party to end the maintenance part of the agreement or even unilaterally break the agreement, so it is no longer in force;
- where there is an order, ask the court to revoke it so that a CSA application can be made (but see p38);
- if she is a parent with care, claim IS/income-based JSA (see p62). However, if benefit is refused before a CSA calculation is made, then the Secretary of State will cease to treat the application as having been made because a court order or written maintenance agreement exists.[35] Where a non-resident parent believes that the parent with care has made a benefit claim to obtain access to the CSA, he may want to delay providing information until the benefit claim has been determined, but should explain to the CSA why he is doing that.

The CSA announced in 1995 that people with court orders or agreements would, at a future date, be allowed to use the CSA's collection and enforcement service for amounts due under those orders/agreements.[36] This commitment has only been met for those where child support maintenance is being collected (see p466).

Figure 4.1: Summary of who can apply to the CSA

Is there a pre-1993 written maintenance agreement? → Yes → There cannot be a voluntary application under s4, by a person with care or non-resident parent, or s7, by a child in Scotland. However, if a parent with care claims IS/income-based JSA the CSA has jurisdiction.

↓ No

Is there a consent order or, in Scotland, a registered minute of agreement? (These may still be obtained.) → Yes → [same as above]

↓ No

Applications may be made to the CSA under s4, by a person with care or absent parent, and s7, by a child in Scotland.*
However, if a parent with care claims IS/income-based JSA the CSA will require her to authorise pursuit of maintenance.

* Alternatively, the parties may make an informal arrangement or draw up a written agreement that may be formalised into a consent order, or in Scotland, registered in the Court of Session.

2. How to apply to the CSA

Applications under the 'new rules' need not be in writing.[37] In some cases the Secretary of State may direct that the application must be in writing, in which case a form may be provided. Where the Secretary of State issues a form or requests information this must be provided within 14 days unless s/he is satisfied that there was unavoidable delay.[38] In practice, the application procedures will be slightly different depending on whether the individual is a section 4, 7 or 6 applicant.

Section 4 and 7 voluntary applications

Section 4 and 7 applications may be taken orally or in writing.[39] This means applications can be made over the phone, in person, or on an application form sent to the applicant by the CSA or downloaded from the CSA website. Note that downloaded forms must be signed and returned by post to the CSAC. Signing the form confirms that the information given is correct. This is important; since there are penalties for knowingly providing false information (see p93).

In practice, a person with care's section 4 application will normally be taken by phone (or at a face-to-face interview). The information given can be entered onto the computer system as the call/interview is taking place. Applicants will be sent/given a printout of the information and they may contact the CSA to amend this. There is no need to sign and return the printout.

Where a person with care claims income support (IS) or income-based jobseeker's allowance (JSA) they may choose to opt in – ie, claim for child maintenance.[40] In these cases the Jobcentre Plus will arrange an interview with the person with care. The visiting officer will complete a child maintenance administration form with the person to gather the information to pursue maintenance (see p62).

A section 4 non-resident parent or section 7 applicant can apply over the phone but instead of the data being entered onto the computer a child maintenance application form may be sent to them or the form may be completed over the phone and sent to them to check. The application form completed is slightly different than that completed by a person with care but the information sought is comparable. There is no time limit for the return of the form – if it is not returned there will be no effective application (see p51).

If the Secretary of State requests further information or reissues the application for child maintenance form, the information requested should be provided within 14 days.[41] Where this does not occur and the Secretary of State is not satisfied that there was unavoidable delay this may delay the date of an effective application (see p51) or where no information is received cancel the application (see p52).

Chapter 4: Applications
2. How to apply to the CSA

The application for child maintenance form

This form may be used to gather information to pursue maintenance. It includes sections on:
- personal details – name, address, national insurance number, date of birth, phone numbers (home, work, mobile) and the best time to phone, armed forces service number;
- child(ren) being applied for – name, date of birth, national insurance number if over 16, who gets child benefit for the child, maintenance arrangements, shared care arrangements (or local authority care);
- does the non-resident parent know they are being named as the parent;
- child's education (if between 16 and 19) – school/college, course, type of course, hours a week;
- local authority details (where child is cared for by them);
- non-resident parent details – name (other names), address or last known address and when they lived there, national insurance number, date of birth, employment details (job, employer and contact details), phone number (home, work, mobile), whether the parent is the father or mother of the child;
- does the non-resident parent know where the applicant lives;
- payment details – preferred method and frequency, bank details (name, address, sort code, account number), post office details where payment by giro cheque is preferred;
- representative details – name, address, phone number (home, work, mobile) and the best time to phone. If the representative is not a solicitor, power of attorney, Scottish Mental Health Custodian, Mental Health Appointee or Receiver the applicant must sign the client authority declaration on the form;
- further information – a blank page to add other relevant information.

Copies of any court order or written maintenance agreement and representative's authority (eg, power of attorney document) will be returned.

Signing the form confirms that all the information given is correct and complete. This is important since there are penalties for knowingly providing false information see (p93).

Section 6 applications

A parent with care is treated as having applied for child support maintenance when they claim IS/income-based JSA or it is claimed on their behalf. This is known as a section 6 application.[42] This includes situations where the partner of the parent with care makes the claim. However, a claim for a child who is a parent with care is not included.

In this section for ease of reference we will refer to IS claims. However, similar provisions relate to income-based JSA claimants.

48

Chapter 4: Applications
2. How to apply to the CSA

A parent with care who claims IS is issued form A1 and a leaflet on maintenance for children. This advises them that their claim for benefit is also a claim for child support maintenance. Child support legislation states that a request may be made at any time to the Secretary of State to cease acting in relation to child support – this is known as opting out.[43] There is a section on the A1 where the parent may indicate that they want to opt out. Both the A1 and the leaflet state that if the parent believes they have good cause for opting-out of the application they should explain their reasons. The wording of the A1 and leaflet implies that opting out may only occur where there is good cause. This is **not** the case.

A parent with care does not have to have good cause to opt out. If she does not want the CSA to act she may state on the A1 that she wants to opt out or make a formal statement – eg, 'I request, under s6(5) of the Child Support Act 1991, the Secretary of State cease all action under s6(3) of the Child Support Act 1991'.[44] This will prevent any further action in relation to child support maintenance. This request can be made at any time (see p68).

Where a parent has indicated on the A1 that she has good cause or requested to opt out, a good cause interview will be arranged. This will normally be at the same time as the new claims visit (see p64).

Where the parent has not indicated good cause or made the request to opt-out on the form she may still opt-out at any time – eg, at the visiting officer's new claims interview or at any later stage. A good cause interview will then be carried out by Jobcentre Plus visiting staff. A Jobcentre Plus decision maker will consider the case and where good cause is not accepted a reduced benefit decision may be imposed (see p75).

Where the parent wants to pursue child support maintenance the new claims visiting officer will complete a child maintenance administration form with the parent at the interview. The completed form will be forwarded to the CSA. Where the child maintenance administration form cannot be completed at the visit the form must be completed and forwarded to the Jobcentre Plus within 14 days. In some cases the CSA may indicate that a completed child maintenance administration form is not required – eg, there is a calculation (old rules assessment) currently in force and there are no new qualifying children or non-resident parents.

The parent can request 14 days to consider her position at the new claims/good cause interview.[45] After this time the process will continue as appropriate – eg, good cause interview, completion of the child maintenance administration form.

There may be a few parents with care who have been on IS continuously since 1993 who have not yet been approached about child maintenance; they can request an application form. The Jobcentre Plus should arrange for a form to be issued by a visiting officer.

Chapter 4: Applications
2. How to apply to the CSA

Claims for a child who is a parent with care

Where a claim for benefit is made which includes a parent with care who is under 16, or defined as a child for benefit purposes, the young parent is not treated as applying for child support maintenance under section 6 (see p48). This is because the young parent is unable to make an application for IS/income-based JSA in her/his own right. However, s/he may make a voluntary application under section 4.

Applications with more than one non-resident parent

In section 4 and section 7 cases, the applicant can choose which non-resident parent they wish to apply to for child support maintenance. Thus an application may be made for maintenance from some but not all non-resident parents. A section 6 applicant will be treated as applying for maintenance from all the non-resident parents of qualifying children unless she requests the Secretary of State not to act – ie, opt out. This request can be made generally against all of the non-resident parents or in relation to a specific non-resident parent. Whether the request is made against one or all non-resident parents, the section 6 applicant will still be subject to a good cause interview and face a reduced benefit decision where good cause is not established (see Chapter 5).

When to apply

There are no time limits for making an application to the CSA. One can be made as soon as someone becomes a person with care or a non-resident parent, or at any later date. However, liability to pay child maintenance usually runs from the date that the non-resident parent is notified and that cannot occur until an effective application (see p51) is received by the CSA. This means that delaying the application may delay the start of liability. There is no provision for applications in advance – eg, before the birth of a baby.

A benefit penalty can be imposed on a section 6 applicant who opts out without good cause or does not provide information to pursue maintenance, but only by using the full procedures, including the right of appeal (see p83).[46]

Any parent with care on IS since April 1993 who has not yet been contacted about child maintenance but who wishes to apply, can do so at the CSA's discretion. She cannot make a voluntary application under section 4,[47] but the CSA has agreed to take such cases on under section 6 at the request of the parent with care.[48] As the Jobcentre Plus deals with the issue of maintenance administration forms to section 6 applicants, the parent should contact them to request a form. A gateway/case intervention interview should be arranged by a Jobcentre Plus visiting officer to issue the form. If there is any difficulty, parents should contact the CSA, who will be able to advise them on how to proceed.

Refusal to accept an application

The CSA may not accept an application – eg, because it believes an existing maintenance agreement prevents a section 4 application or that it does not have jurisdiction. If this happens, the would-be applicant should write to the CSA explaining why s/he believes s/he is entitled to apply and asking for a written CSA decision. If a written decision is issued, s/he can try to appeal this to a tribunal (see Chapter 20). If this does not work or if the CSA refuses to respond in writing, a complaint (see p18) and/or judicial review (see p415) should be considered.

Effective applications

Only an effective application allows the CSA to make a maintenance calculation. An application is effective if it is made by phone or in writing according to the Secretary of State's direction.[49] All applicants must provide information to enable the non-resident parent to be identified and traced, and the amount of child maintenance payable by him to be calculated and recovered (see Chapter 6).[50] If a section 6 applicant does not provide the information, she may suffer a reduced benefit decision (see p83). If a section 4 or 7 applicant does not supply the information, the CSA may refuse to process an application because it is not effective (see p52).

The CSA may ask the applicant to provide further information or evidence to make an effective application; this may be done over the phone or in writing. The CSA may issue an application for child maintenance form to the applicant. Where a form has been previously sent to the applicant, this may include issuing a further form. Where the information or evidence is received within 14 days of the request, it takes effect from the date the earlier application was treated as received by the CSA (see p14).[51]

For section 6 applicants the application is treated as made in relation to the claim for benefit. The relevance of this date is only important in relation to determining the effective date in special circumstances (see p400). To gather the information needed to pursue maintenance, the Jobcentre Plus will complete a child maintenance administration form with the parent with care and forward this to the CSA. The Jobcentre Plus will have conducted any further interviews and made any necessary decisions about good cause where the parent with care has opted out or failed to provide information requested (see Chapter 5).

Once an effective application has been made (or treated as made), any other relevant person (non-resident parent or person with care) is informed of the application either by phone or in writing.[52] The relevant person will be asked to provide information to enable the maintenance calculation to be made. This can be done over the phone or the person may be asked to complete a form. This form is known as a child maintenance enquiry. Non-resident parents will be informed of the effective date of the calculation and rules on default maintenance decisions at the same time as they are informed of the application.[53] The CSA cannot refuse

Chapter 4: Applications
2. How to apply to the CSA

to deal with an effective application, even if it considers that processing it would be against the welfare of the children concerned.[54] For refusal to accept an application, see p51.

For delays in dealing with applications, including where the non-resident parent is not co-operating, see p382.

Amending the application

An application can be amended at any time before a maintenance calculation is made, but not to take into account a change which occurs after the effective date (see p400) of a calculation.[55] For details of this and of changes after the effective date, see p383.

3. Withdrawal/cancellation of an application

Requests to cease acting by the applicant

An applicant or parent treated as applying may request that the Secretary of State cease acting on her/his application for child maintenance.

This request is straightforward in a section 4 or 7 application, but a section 6 parent may be subject to a good cause interview and reduced benefit decision. The request by a section 6 parent is known as opting out (see p68).

The CSA cannot refuse this request by the applicant or parent treated as applying.[56] The request can be made at any time, whether or not a calculation (or old rules assessment) has been made. For more on cancelling calculations, see p392.

Requests to cease acting can be made by phone or in writing to the CSA office processing the application, to the CSAC if it is not clear which office has responsibility, or to the Jobcentre in section 6 cases.

Withdrawal/cancellation of an application by the Secretary of State

The Secretary of State may withdraw/cancel an application before a calculation is made where the:
- applicant in a voluntary application does not provide information;
- qualifying child dies; *or*
- income support (IS)/income-based jobseeker's allowance (JSA) ceases.

The applicant in a voluntary application does not provide information

According to CSA guidance, a case involving a voluntary application can be closed if insufficient co-operation is received from the person with care.[57] However, if the applicant is the non-resident parent and the person with care does not want maintenance, then, if the aplication is not withdrawn, it will not be cancelled, but no maintenance can be collected and passed on to the person with care.[58]

Cases can be cancelled only where no 'effective application' has been made (see p51). Where there is an effective application, a decision must be made and notified, even if it is a decision not to make a calculation (see p384). If an effective application is cancelled against the wishes of the applicant, advice should be sought.

The qualifying child dies

Where a qualifying child dies before a calculation has been made, the application is treated as if it had never been made with respect to that child.[59] If the child was the only child named in the application, any calculation ceases to have effect. Otherwise, any calculation is superseded because of a change of circumstances (see p421).

Withdrawal/cancellation when benefit ceases

A section 6 application (see p44) can be cancelled without a request from the parent with care if the claim for benefit is refused or withdrawn before the calculation.[60]

If the parent with care stops claiming IS or income-based JSA, (or it stops being claimed for her), where a calculation has been made this will continue unless the parent requests that the Secretary of State cease acting.

Where the calculation has not been made the Secretary of State may treat the application as withdrawn or cancel the application – but still make a calculation.

The Secretary of State will check whether there is a maintenance agreement or order in force. Where there is an agreement/order that could have prevented a section 4 application the Secretary of State will treat the application as never made – ie, withdrawn.[61] The parent (and non-resident parent where appropriate) will be notified of this decision.[62] The parent will not need to request withdrawal, but where there is uncertainty over whether or not the agreement/order is in force the parent should request the Secretary of State to cease acting.

Where no agreement or order is in force which could have prevented a section 4 application the Secretary of State will write to the parent asking her if she wishes the application to be treated as a section 4 application.[63] The parent will be given one month to reply. If the parent does not reply, or requests the Secretary of State to cease action, the application will be cancelled.

If the non-resident parent has already been contacted and an effective date set then a maintenance calculation will be completed. The non-resident parent will have a liability to the Secretary of State for maintenance for the period between the effective date and the cancellation of the application.

Chapter 4: Applications
3. Withdrawal/cancellation of an application

Short-term or fraudulent benefit claims

The Jobcentre Plus treats all parents who claim IS/income-based JSA as having applied for child maintenance (unless the parent opts out), including where the application is made by the parent's partner, however short-term the benefit claim and irrespective of allegations from the non-resident parent that the benefit claim is fraudulent.

Allegations of fraud are referred to the fraud section for investigation (see p78) but do not hold up the CSA's processing of a section 6 case. Since benefit *is* being paid, the CSA cannot consider whether the parent with care *should* be being paid.[64]

4. Multiple applications

Where more than one application for child maintenance is made in respect of the same qualifying child, only one can go ahead.[65] Only an effective application (see p51) counts.[66] If a calculation has not yet been made, the applications are either treated as a single application or one is selected to be considered (see below).[67] For applications made after a calculation has been made, see p56.

The decision on whose application goes ahead only determines which applicant has the power to withdraw an application or to request a cancellation of any resulting calculation. It does not affect the outcome of any calculation or have any effect on who is liable to pay any resulting child maintenance. Information included on any competing applications can be taken into account by the CSA.

If an application with priority is made by an applicant in Northern Ireland, the CSA there (see p382) deals with the application.[68]

Before a calculation has been made

The rules below apply unless a request is received to cease acting in relation to all but one of the applications.[69]

Same person applies more than once

If a person applies under either section 4 or section 6 and then applies again under the same section before a calculation is made, both applications are treated as if they were the same application.[70]

If a parent with care applies under either section 4 or section 6 and then again under the other section before a calculation is made, the applications are treated as a single section 6 application where the parent with care is still treated as applying under section 6.[71]

Where more than one section 7 application is made by the same child in Scotland and maintenance has not yet been calculated, it counts as a single

54

application so long as it is made in respect of the same non-resident parent and person with care.[72]

More than one applicant

The CSA decides which application to deal with as follows:[73]

Applicants	Priority application
Only one person with care	
Person with care and non-resident parent	Person with care
Person with care or non-resident parent applies following an application under section 7 by a child in Scotland	Person with care/non-resident parent
More than one qualifying child applies under section 7 in relation to the same person with care and non-resident parent	Elder or eldest child
Both parents are non-resident parents and both apply	Treated as a single application
More than one person with care	
Parent with care makes a section 6 application, and a person with care (with parental responsibility or parental rights) makes a section 4 application	Parent with care (in fact, the other person with care is not entitled to make a section 4 application where the parent with care is on IS/income-based JSA – see p44)
More than one person with care with parental responsibility (or, in Scotland, parental rights) applies under section 4, and one person is treated as a non-resident parent for calculation purposes (see p328)	Person with care not treated as a non-resident parent
More than one person with care applies under section 4 and none of the applicants has parental responsibility/ rights, or all do and either none can be treated as a non-resident parent, or even after one of the applicants has been treated as a non-resident parent under the calculation, there is still more than one application	The principal provider of day-to-day care (see p28) in the following order of priority: the person who gets child benefit for the child(ren); the person who, in the CSA's opinion, is the principal provider of day-to-day care.

55

Chapter 4: Applications
4. Multiple applications

If the applications are treated as a single one under these rules, that application covers all the children named in either, and the effective date (see p400) is set by the application which was made first.[74]

Where more than one person with care applies and each application refers to different children, then the CSA treats the application it deals with as covering all the children mentioned in all applications.[75] Where the same person with care does not provide the principal day-to-day care for all the qualifying children mentioned in the applications, then separate calculations are made in relation to each person with care.[76]

Once the calculation is in force

No section 4 application can be made if a calculation is in force in response to an application treated as made under section 6.[77] A calculation in force in relation to a section 4 person with care does not prevent the Secretary of State making a new calculation where a parent with care is treated as applying under section 6.[78] Once a calculation is in force, any subsequent application for maintenance under the same section of the Act in respect of the same person with care, non-resident parent and qualifying child(ren) will not be dealt with.[79] It may, however, be treated as a request for supersession (see p421).

Applications for additional child(ren)

Where there is an existing calculation and there is an application for additional child(ren) of the same non-resident parent cared for by the same person with care, this is a relevant change of circumstances and a new calculation is made which supersedes the existing calculation.[80]

5. Existing 'old rules' cases

The rules on applications and orders of priority decisions made before 3 March 2003 are covered in the 2002/03 edition of this *Handbook*. Here we summarise the main differences between the schemes and clarify how decisions are made where there are multiple applications under the old and new rules and highlight when new applications after 3 March 2003 can trigger conversion of the existing case to the 'new rules'.

Main differences between old and new scheme applications

The principal differences between the old and new schemes applications are that under the 'old rules':
- applications had to be made on a maintenance application form;
- section 6 parents with care were required to co-operate and authorise pursuit of maintenance unless they could show good cause. Where good cause could

not be shown a reduced benefit direction could be made. Such parents may now request the Secretary of State to cease acting (see p68);
- where a parent with care's benefit claim ceased before a maintenance assessment had been made and there was no court order/maintenance agreement in force, there may be some maintenance liability to the Secretary of State even if the parent with care requested that no further action is taken. This is because an effective date may already have been set and the non-resident parent will have a liability from the effective date to the date of withdrawal. In addition, when the benefit claim ceased the parent will have been asked if they wish the application to continue as a section 4 application and asked to reply within 28 days.

Multiple applications before and after 3 March 2003

Where no assessment is in force

Where no assessment is in force there are transitional provisions for determining how to proceed if there is an existing application under the 'old rules' and a further application is made under the 'new rules' in respect of the same person with care, non-resident parent or qualifying child.[81] These determine whether the applications are treated as a single application or only one is to be proceeded with, as shown below:

Person with care applies under s6 (or s4) of the 'old rules' then under s4 (or is treated as applying under s6) of the 'new rules'	Treated as a single application
Non-resident parent applies under the 'old rules' and 'new rules' in relation to the same qualifying child	Treat as a single application
Child in Scotland applies under s7 of 'old rules' and then under s7 of the 'new rules'	Treated as a single application
Person with care applies under s6 or s4 of the 'old rules' or s6 of the 'new rules' and the non-resident applies under s4 of the old or new rules	Person with care's application has priority
Child in Scotland applies under s7 of the 'old rules' and a 'new rules' application is made by either the person with care or non-resident parent	Person with care or non-resident parent's application has priority

Chapter 4: Applications
5. Existing 'old rules' cases

More than one child applies under s7 either under the 'old' or 'new' rules in relation to the same person with care and non-resident parent	The application of the elder or eldest child has priority
Parent with care applies under s6 of the 'old rules' and a person with care (who has parental responsibility applies under s4 of the 'new rules'	Parent with care's application has priority
More than person with care with parental responsibility applies, one under s4 of the 'old rules' the other under s4 of the 'new rules', and one person is treated as a non-resident parent for calculation/assessment purposes	The application of the person with care not treated as a non-resident parent has priority
More than one person with care applies (as above) but none has parental responsibility or all do and either none can be treated as non-resident parents, or even after one of the applicants has been treated as a non-resident parent for the calculation/assessment, there is still more than one application	The application of the principal provider of day-to-day care in the following order of priority: the person who gets child benefit for the child(ren), otherwise the person who in the CSA's opinion is the principal provider of day-to-day care

Whether the case is proceeded with as a 'new rules' or 'old rules' case then depends on the effective date of the application being progressed or whether a maintenance assessment was previously in force in relation to the same person with care, qualifying child(ren) and non-resident parent. If an assessment was in force within the previous 13 weeks then the application is treated as an application for a maintenance assessment regardless of whether the effective date of the application is before or after 3 March 2003.[82]

Where a maintenance assessment is in force

Where a maintenance assessment is already in force and an application is made or treated as made under the 'new rules' in relation to the same person with care, qualifying child(ren) and non-resident parent, the calculation application will not proceed.[83]

Where there is an existing assessment and there is an application for an additional child(ren) of the same non-resident parent cared for by the same person with care this is a relevant change of circumstances and a new assessment is made which supersedes the existing assessment.[84]

New applications which trigger conversion of an existing case

Existing cases will continue to be dealt with under the 'old rules' until C Day, unless there is a related decision that causes an early conversion to the 'new rules'.[85] In many cases these will be triggered where there is a new application by another person that involves either the non-resident parent or parent with care in the existing assessment. In addition, parents who form new partnerships with people on benefit or partners who each have maintenance but move onto benefit may be affected. The full list of situations where a conversion will occur is as follows:[86]

- a maintenance calculation is made in respect of a person who is a relevant person (person with care or non-resident parent) in the existing assessment whether or not in relation to a different qualifying child;
- an application is made or treated as made that would result in a maintenance calculation but there is an assessment in force, the non-resident parent in the new application is the non-resident parent in the existing case but the person with care in the new application is a different one from that in the existing case;
- a maintenance calculation is made in relation to person A who is a partner to person B who has a maintenance assessment, they are in receipt of IS or income-based JSA, and A and B are either both persons with care or non-resident parents;
- a maintenance assessment is in force in relation to person C and a maintenance calculation is in force in relation to person D, either C or D are in receipt of IS or income-based JSA, C and D are either both persons with care or both non-resident parents and then C and D become partners;
- a maintenance assessment is in force in relation to person E and a maintenance calculation in force in relation to their partner F. E and F are either both persons with care or both non-resident parents and then they become entitled to IS or income-based JSA as partners.

When an existing case converts to the 'new rules', transitional phasing may apply. For more information on conversion, see Chapter 9.

Chapter 4: Applications
Notes

1. Who can apply to the CSA
1. ss4(1) and 6(1) CSA 1991
2. s7(1) CSA 1991
3. ss5(1) and 54 'parental responsibility' CSA 1991
4. s3(1) CA 1989; C(S)A 1995
5. s4(1)(b) CA 1989; C(S)A 1995
6. ss4(1)(a) and 5(6) CA 1989; C(S)A 1995
7. s6(1) CSA 1991
8. s6(3-5) CSA 1991
9. s9(3) CSA 1991; CCS/12806/1996; CCS/12598/1996
10. ss4(10)(a) and 7(10) CSA 1991
11. s9(1) CSA 1991
12. ss4(10)(a) and 7(10) CSA 1991; Written maintenance agreements
13. CCS/12767/1996
14. CCS/12797/1996
15. CCS/11052/1995
16. CCS/8328/1995 paras 12-13
17. CCS/2908/1995
18. Written maintenance agreements
19. CCS/8328/1995 paras 3 and 14
20. CCS/8328/1995 paras 15-16
21. CCS/12849/1996
22. CCS/8328/1995 paras 21-22
23. ss4(10)(a) and 7(10)(a) CSA 1991; reg 2 CS(A:PD) Regs
24. s4(10)(aa) and s7(10)(b) CSA 1991; reg 2 CS(A:PD) Regs
25. s8(11) CSA 1991
26. Otherwise s8(6)-(8) CSA 1991 would be unnecessary
27. CCS/4741/1995, upheld by the Court of Appeal in *AMS v CSO* [1998] 1 FLR 955
28. CCS/316/1998
29. R(CS) 11/94
30. R(CS) 4/96 CCS/3127/1995
31. CCS/4741/1995
32. CCS/11364/1995
33. Reg 9 CS(MAJ) Regs; Maintenance orders
34. s8(11) CSA 1991; reg 2 CS(MAJ) Regs. Provisions repealed before 1 April 1980 are not listed.
35. s 11(3) CSA 1991
36. Improving child support, 1995, para 4.3

2. How to apply to the CSA
37. Reg 3(1) CS(MCP) Regs; New Application
38. Regs 3-4 CS(MCP) Regs
39. Reg 3(1) CS(MCP) Regs
40. A1 Form; paras 24-27 IS Gap Circular 02 (revised)
41. Reg 3(4) and (5) CS(MCP) Regs
42. s6 CSA 1991
43. s6(5) CSA 1991
44. s6(5) CSA 1991
45. para 145 IS/GAP Circular 02 (revised)
46. s46 CSA 1991
47. s4(10)(b) CSA 1991
48. DSS Press Release, 1 November 1993; Improving child support, 1995
49. Reg 3(2) CS(MCP) Regs
50. ss 4(4), 6(7) and 7(5) CSA 1991
51. Reg 3(4) CS(MCP) Regs
52. Reg 5(1) CS(MCP) Regs
53. Reg 3(2) CS(MCP) Regs
54. R(CS) 4/96; CCS/14/1994; CCS/17/1994 and CCS/16535/1996
55. Reg 3(6-7) CS(MCP) Regs

3. Withdrawal/cancellation of an application
56. ss4(6) CSA 1991 and 6(5) CSA 1991
57. Failure to provide requested information
58. PWC does not wish to co-operate
59. s11(3) CSA 1991
60. s11(3) CSA 1991
61. s11(3) CSA 1991; s4(10) CSA 1991
62. s11(5) CSA 1991
63. s11(4) CSA 1991
64. *Secretary of State for Social Security v Harmon, Carter & Cocks* [1998] 2 FLR 598, CA

4. Multiple applications
65. s5(2) CSA 1991
66. Sch 2 paras 1, 2 and 3 CS(MCP) Regs
67. s5(2) CSA 1991; reg 4 CS(MCP) Regs; Sch 2 CS(MCP) Regs
68. Sch 1 para 6 CS(NIRA) Regs
69. Reg 4(2) CS(MCP) Regs
70. Sch 2 para 1(1) CS(MCP) Regs
71. Sch 2 para 1(2) CS(MCP) Regs
72. Sch 2 para 2 CS(MCP) Regs
73. Sch 2 para 3(1) CS(MCP) Regs; Multiple applications; Multiple applications table

Chapter 4: Applications
Notes

74 Reg 4(3) CS(MCP) Regs
75 Sch 2 para 3(12) CS(MCP) Regs
76 Sch 2 para 3(13) CS(MCP) Regs;
   Multiple applications
77 s4(9) CSA 1991
78 s6(12) CSA 1991
79 Sch 2 para 4 CS(MCP) Regs;
   Assessment/Calculation already made
80 Relevant change in circumstances

5. Existing 'old rules' cases
81 Sch 3 CS(MCP) Regs
82 Reg 28(1) CS(TP) Regs
83 Sch 3 para 4 CS(MCP) Regs
84 Sch 2 para 6(1) CS(MAP) Regs
85 Reg 3 CSPSSA (Comm12)O; reg 15 CS(TP) Regs
86 Reg 15 CS(TP) Regs

Chapter 5
Parents treated as applying

This chapter covers:
1. What happens when a parent is treated as applying (below)
2. Opting-out (p68)
3. Harm or undue distress (p70)
4. Reduced benefit decisions (p75)
5. Existing section 6 'old rules' cases (p83)

All 'good cause' decision making on claims of income support (IS) or income-based jobseeker's allowance (JSA) by parents with care are made by the DWP. This is carried out by Jobcentre Plus staff.

These provisions apply to all parents with care who claimed IS or income-based JSA after 3 March 2003, though there are special provisions for those applying within 13 weeks of an old rules case being in force (see p203).

In 2004/05 parents on IS or Income-based JSA who have personal allowances and premiums relating to children will transfer onto child tax credit. This may make some better off as maintenance is ignored when working out tax credits.

These provisions do not apply to parents when they transfer from IS or income-based JSA to pension credit (PC) or claim PC.

1. What happens when a parent is treated as applying

A parent

When a parent with care claims income support (IS) or income-based jobseeker's allowance (JSA) or it is claimed on her behalf, she may be treated as applying for child support maintenance.[1] This includes situations where the partner of the parent with care makes the claim. However, where a claim is made for a child or young person who is a parent with care, the child is not treated as applying for child maintenance (see p63).

The parent with care may be treated as applying even where there is an existing maintenance agreement or court order in force.

Chapter 5: Parents treated as applying
1. What happens when a parent is treated as applying

A parent with care may believe she has good reasons for not pursuing maintenance, as it would cause the parent or any children living with her undue harm or distress (see p70). This is known as good cause. In this situation, the parent with care should opt out and give her reasons at the good cause interview.

A parent does not need to show good cause to opt out and she may opt out at any time. However, a good cause interview will be arranged when a parent opts out (see p68).

Opting-out means that all action on working out and pursuing maintenance ceases.

Unless the parent with care opts out (see p68) she will be required to provide all the information she has, which will enable the Secretary of State to:[2]
- identify and trace the non-resident parent;
- calculate the amount of maintenance due by non-resident parent;
- recover the amount due by the non-resident parent.

A parent with care is only expected to provide information 'so far as she reasonably can'.[3] If there is a reason for not giving the information requested, she should say so to help avoid a reduced benefit decision. Parents with care who do not know the name of the father should have their word accepted unless their evidence is self-contradictory or inherently improbable (see p72). Jobcentre Plus staff are reminded that if the relationship was casual, information on the non-resident parent may be sparse.[4]

Information is gathered at the new claims interview, arranged by the Jobcentre Plus (see p64). The visiting officer has guidance on collecting information in different circumstances – eg, where the parent cannot provide the non-resident parent's full name.

The Jobcentre Plus decision maker will then examine any reasons for good cause and whether the parent has complied, as far as she reasonably can, with the requirement to supply information. If they decide there are no good reasons for opting-out or failure to supply information, a reduced benefit decision may be made (see p75).

Where there is a dispute or uncertainty over the identity of the non-resident parent the parent with care may be asked about DNA testing (see p105). Where she refuses DNA testing she will be interviewed by Jobcentre Plus staff and if good cause cannot be shown a reduced benefit decision may be made (see p75).

Young parents with care

A young parent with care will not be treated as applying for child maintenance if a claim is made for her because she is too young to claim IS/income-based JSA in her own right. However, a young parent may still be able to make a voluntary section 4 application for child maintenance (see p44).

Chapter 5: Parents treated as applying
1. What happens when a parent is treated as applying

Income support/income-based jobseeker's allowance new claims visit

A new claims visit will normally be arranged by the Jobcentre Plus at the parent's home. The visit will normally be arranged with 48 hours of the claim, or if benefit has already been awarded, within 10 working days.

Notification of the visit will normally be by phone or in writing.[5] If it is the claimant's partner who is the parent with care, the claimant is told that the parent with care must be at the interview. Where this is the case the parent with care may request that the interview be conducted at the Jobcentre Plus.[6] If the parent with care wishes to be interviewed alone or have a representative present, the visiting officer should consider moving the interview to another day.[7] If the parent with care is not the claimant the interview can be arranged at the Jobcentre Plus office.[8]

Each case will be checked with the CSA to determine if any action needs to be taken in relation to child support maintenance.[9] The CSA will decide if it is an 'old rules' or 'new rules' case. Even where there is no entitlement to IS/income-based JSA or the claim is defective or withdrawn there may still be CSA interest in the case.[10] The visiting officer will also have information on whether good cause has been accepted before a reduced benefit decision (or 'old rules' reduced benefit direction) is made.[11]

At the new claims visit, the visiting officer will deal with any outstanding issues in relation to the benefit claim and take any action in relation to child support. This can include:

- gathering information to pass to the CSA to decide whether a claimant (or her partner) is a person with care;
- completing a maintenance administration form to gather information needed to pursue maintenance (see p65);
- carrying out a good cause interview if the parent with care has opted out, regardless of whether or not good cause has been indicated on the benefit claim form (see p68).

In all cases the visiting officer must:[12]

- explain the advantages of receiving maintenance and stress the benefits;
- explain the child maintenance premium that allows up to £10 of maintenance to be ignored when working out benefit entitlement.

If the parent has or claims good cause, the visiting officer must check she has received and understood leaflet CSL100. This explains opting-out, good cause procedures and reduced benefit decisions[13] and should have been issued before the interview. If it has not been issued, the visiting officer should give CSL100 to the parent.

The parent with care may request time to think things over. This can occur at any time – eg, while a maintenance administration form is being completed or a good cause interview is being conducted. The visiting officer will normally

Chapter 5: Parents treated as applying
1. What happens when a parent is treated as applying

arrange another visit in 14 days.[14] If the parent then fails to provide information, opts out or gives reasons for good cause she will be given a four-week period to provide reasons for opting-out or a reduced benefit decision may be made (see p75). Parents with care who are uncertain about their position should seek advice before a visit or ask for extra time. If the parent with care is put under pressure, or extra time is refused, a complaint can be made (see p18).

The visiting officer will compile a report on information given by the parent with care which was not included on the maintenance administration form, including information on good cause where this was provided, why more time was requested and a note on general welfare issues, particularly those relating to the child(ren).

Information from, or suspicions aroused at, a new claims visit can be used to begin fraud investigations (see p78).

Completing the maintenance administration form

The visiting officer has guidance on completing the maintenance administration form.[15] The form is divided into sections and gathers information on:
- personal details about the parent with care – eg, other names, mobile phone number, best times to contact;
- if she wants to use the collection service – the method and frequency of payments which she prefers, including relevant bank details;
- representative details (see p13);
- qualifying child(ren's) details – eg, parents' names, date of birth, is the non-resident parent registered as the parent or does he know he is considered to be the parent, does the child stay overnight with anyone else (or local authority), has anyone else received maintenance in the last eight weeks for the child. If the CSA already has information on the qualifying children, information will only be requested on additional qualifying children;
- non-resident parent details – eg, name, address (or last known address and when they lived there), date of birth, national insurance number, previous names used, details of any benefits he may be claiming, details of any employer, business details if he is self-employed. The parent with care may be asked further questions to add helpful information (see p66). The form also asks if the non-resident parent knows the parent with care's address;
- existing maintenance arrangements – eg, court orders (where and when it was made, whether it covers all or only some of the children), written maintenance agreement, any other maintenance arrangement (whether or not this is being paid, the amount and frequency of any maintenance being paid), whether there is a pre-93 property/capital transfer;
- other information which may be useful – eg, to trace the non-resident parent, or details of payments the non-resident parent makes to third parties for fuel bills or school fees. This information may be passed to the non-resident parent in the event of an appeal.

65

Chapter 5: Parents treated as applying
1. What happens when a parent is treated as applying

When the parent with care signs the form she is declaring that all the information she provided is correct and complete. It is a criminal offence to fail to provide information when required, or knowingly provide false information, and penalties may be imposed (see p483). In practice, if the parent with care fails to provide information she may have a reduced benefit decision imposed rather than a penalty.

Staff at the Jobcentre Plus may then access the computer interface with the CSA to update/enter the information gathered on the form onto the system. The form will also be sent to the CSA. The CSA will continue processing the application.

Additional questions to help identify and trace the non-resident parent

Where the parent wants to pursue maintenance but states she does not know the identity of one or more of the non-resident parents, visiting officers are encouraged to probe for information. Examples of issues that could be discussed are:[16]

- Does the parent have any documents – eg, wage slips that may show the non-resident parent's national insurance number?
- Are there any other addresses at which the non-resident parent lived in the past, which may help in tracing him?
- Where and under what circumstances did she meet the non-resident parent?
- Did she know the non-resident parent or did they have any mutual friends?
- Does she or the qualifying child have any contact with the non-resident parent?
- If the non-resident parent is not named on the birth certificate is anyone else? (The visiting officer may ask to see the birth certificate.)
- Does the non-resident parent know he is considered to be the parent?
- Is the qualifying child's surname the same as the parent with care? If not – why?
- Is she certain the non-resident parent is the parent?

Where the non-resident parent is not a spouse or the parent with care is unable to fully identify the non-resident parent's name and address there are suggested questions the visiting officer may ask. DWP guidance indicates that these may be of use when the CSA is establishing paternity. The visiting officer may ask them at the new claims interview if the:

- parent with care names more than one possible non-resident parent;
- non-resident parent is not aware of the child's existence and not named on the birth certificate;
- non-resident parent is named on the birth certificate but is not aware of the child's existence;

Chapter 5: Parents treated as applying
1. What happens when a parent is treated as applying

- non-resident parent is aware of the pregnancy but not the birth and is not named on the birth certificate.

Suggested questions include:[17]
- What is the forename/middle name/surname/nickname of the non-resident parent?
- Where did he live – was he a local?
- Did he have distinguishing accent?
- Did he live with family or friends?
- Did the parent with care ever go back to his place?
- Describe him – height, build, hair length and colour?

Written record of the interview

The record of the interview contains:[18]
- notes of the answers the parent with care gave to background questions;
- a statement outlining the parent with care's evidence – she is asked to sign this; *and*
- a report of the interview which includes any facts not included in the statement and the officer's comments on the parent with care's demeanour (eg, she was distressed).

A parent may not provide a statement or co-operate at the interview. There is no compulsion on her to provide one, but if she does not a reduced benefit decision may be made.

Where the parent with care gives reasons for opting-out, shows good cause or is unable to provide information the visiting officer should write this down word for word in the statement. When the parent signs the statement, she is agreeing that it 'is a true and complete record of what I have said in this interview'. It is therefore very important that time is taken to read it thoroughly so that any changes or additions can be made before it is signed. Although visiting officers are told that the parent should sign the statement in every case, if there is a dispute about the wording or the emphasis, she should not do this but ask that her specific concerns be recorded. She could offer to provide a summary of her answers instead. Whether or not the parent with care does sign the statement at the interview, a copy can be requested from the visiting officer for future reference.

The visiting officer forwards the parent's statement and her/his own report as the written record to the Jobcentre Plus decision maker for a decision on whether:
- the parent has given all the information it is reasonable for her to provide; *or*
- there are reasons for good cause.

If the parent with care wants to provide any further information or comments, she should send them to the Jobcentre Plus as soon as possible after the interview. This is particularly important if the interview went badly or she wants to provide

67

Chapter 5: Parents treated as applying
1. What happens when a parent is treated as applying

further information to assist the decision maker. The Jobcentre Plus does not send her the visiting officer's report, though she should see it if a reduced benefit decision is eventually made and appealed (see p439), or she makes a request under the Data Protection Act.

2. Opting-out

A parent with care on income support (IS)/income-based jobseeker's allowance (JSA) may request the Secretary of State not to act in relation to child support maintenance.[19] This request is known as **opting-out**. and may be made even where it is:
- the partner of the parent with care who has claimed benefit; or
- a case with an 'old rules' maintenance assessment or a claim for good cause was being dealt with at 3 March 2003.[20]

The Secretary of State must cease all action when a request to opt out is made.

The request may be worded as a request to opt out or a request that the Secretary of State cease acting. In addition, the request to opt out need not be in writing and may be made to the Jobcentre Plus who will pass the information on to the CSA. Parents who are concerned may wish to contact the CSA direct.

Where the reason given for the request is because:[21]
- she is no longer the parent with care of a qualifying child; or
- IS or income-based JSA is no longer claimed by or for her, or paid to or for her,

the CSA will cease all action and there will be no further Jobcentre Plus intervention.

Where no reasons are given for opting-out or the parent indicates reasons for good cause the CSA will cease all action immediately. The Jobcentre Plus will carry out a good cause interview and may make a reduced benefit decision where good cause is not upheld.

Good cause interview

A good cause interview may be carried out:
- at the same time as the new claims interview; or
- at a further interview if a request for 14 days' thinking time is made at the new claims visit (see p64); or
- at any other time when a parent with care opts out, regardless of whether or not reasons for good cause are given; or
- when a good cause decision is being reconsidered (see p74); or

68

Chapter 5: Parents treated as applying
2. Opting-out

- where a reduced benefit decision has been in force for three years and a decision needs to be made whether to make and impose a further reduced benefit decision.

A parent with care who opts out does not have to show good cause to stop the Secretary of State acting in relation to child support maintenance. However, she may face a reduced benefit decision if good cause is not shown (see p75).

Good cause is where there is a risk of the parent with care, or any children living with her, suffering harm or undue distress (see p70). Where a parent with care is trying to show good cause she should seek independent advice to prepare for the interview (see Appendix 5). She may want to arrange for a friend or adviser to be present. As well as support, their presence may help stop the interviewer from asking inappropriate questions. She should think about how she is going to answer the officer's questions. This may involve writing down points she wants to make.

A full good cause interview may not be required where the parent is:[22]
- in a women's refuge or safe house. She may provide written reasons and a supporting letter from a case worker stating they believe there is a risk of harm or undue distress;
- claiming rape or incest as the reason for good cause, this was previously accepted, her circumstances have not altered and she still does not wish to apply for maintenance (see p74);
- claiming good cause on a repeat claim in the six-month linking period (see p74).[23]

A female interviewing officer can be requested, and should be provided if the interview covers particularly sensitive issues, such as rape.

Visiting officers are given training and guidance on interviewing skills, and on how to prepare for and conduct a good cause interview.[24] The visiting officer takes notes of the interview. There is nothing to stop a parent with care from interrupting, asking questions, taking notes or even taping the interview. A complaint can be made if an interview is conducted in an inappropriate way (see p18).

The visiting officer should ensure that the parent:[25]
- understands that the visiting officer only conducts the interview and does not make the good cause decision;
- is told that the information she gives is given in strictest confidence.

The interviewing officer should ask questions to build up so-called 'pen pictures' of the family and non-resident parent:[26]
- The history of the relationship – how long did the relationship last? Did the couple live together? When did they separate? Is there a court order for maintenance?

69

Chapter 5: Parents treated as applying
2. Opting-out

- Contact since break-up – when was the last contact with the non-resident parent? Has contact been regular? What have relations been like since the separation?
- The non-resident parent's contact with the child(ren) – how often does he see the child(ren)? Does he have contact rights? What is the current relationship between them? Does the child know who her/his father is?
- The non-resident parent's current situation: where is he? Does he have a new partner/other children? Is the new partner aware of the parent with care and her child(ren)? Is he self-employed and if so, does the parent with care have details of his business?

The visiting officer will try to establish the risk of harm or undue distress by asking:[27]
- what the parent understands by these;
- why the parent thinks good cause applies;
- why the parent believes there would be a risk of harm or undue distress;
- what does the parent think the non-resident parent's reaction would be.

This is the parent with care's opportunity to show the risk of harm or undue distress (see below) and of any possible effect on the welfare of any child(ren) (see p31). The parent with care could have made a list of the points she wishes to make. This also helps in checking that the written statement is correct and complete (see p67). She may be able to supply supporting evidence (see p73) – eg, in the case of past violence.[28]

The visiting officer will include the statement in the written record of the interview (see p67) which is forwarded to the decision maker for a decision on whether to accept good cause or make a reduced benefit decision.

3. Harm and undue distress

The risk of harm and undue distress is referred to as good cause. This section explores the meaning of the risk of harm and undue distress and how a parent with care may support a request to opt out with good cause reasons.

What is a risk of harm or undue distress

It is a *risk* of harm or undue distress that is relevant: there is no need for anything actually to have taken place in the past.[29] There do not even need to have been threats. There need only be a real risk that harm will arise.[30] The fear does not have to be of the non-resident parent, but must be as a consequence of the parent with care:[31]
- being treated as applying;

Chapter 5: Parents treated as applying
3. Harm and undue distress

- providing sufficient information to pursue maintenance;
- taking a DNA test.

A risk of harm or undue distress caused by an unrelated event (eg, one of the parties moving in with a new partner or an ongoing contact or residency dispute), is not relevant. However, hostility around such issues is an important part of assessing whether the above actions would cause harm or undue distress. The risk could arise from a fear of violence from a new partner so long as this is the result of the parent with care being treated as applying, providing information or taking a DNA test.[32]

For distress to be sufficient, it must be 'undue', but there is no such qualification in relation to harm, so *any* harm is sufficient. Harm is not limited to physical harm but includes psychological or emotional harm.

Meaning of terms

These terms are not defined in child support legislation and therefore are taken to have their ordinary English meaning.[33]

'**Harm**' means to hurt, injure, or damage.

'**Undue**' means not suitable, improper, unreasonable, excessive, unjustifiable, disproportionate, illegal, or going beyond what is appropriate, warranted or natural.

'**Distress**' means strain, stress, pressure, anguish, pain, damage, danger, affliction affecting body, spirit or community, or exhausted condition under severe physical strain; distress might also mean 'lack of money or comforts'.

Child support commissioners have decided that:
- if the children were likely to be distressed if their father's visits ceased or were curtailed, then it would probably follow that such distress would be undue;[34]
- there was a risk of undue distress to an older daughter who knew her father but not that he had another family. The appeal tribunal had accepted the argument that the risk could be disregarded because total confidentiality could be ensured by serving papers and carrying out the assessment without the non-resident parent's wife and family finding out;[35]
- a tribunal was entitled to exempt a parent with care (from the requirement to co-operate under the 'old rules') on her written evidence that CSA activity would probably result in all contact ceasing between the non-resident father and son. Relations were already strained and the father's new wife resented the contact.[36]

'Risk of harm or undue distress' covers a wide range of situations – eg, where a step-parent has been accepted as the father, or where a couple are having a trial separation and hope to be reconciled in due course. This is borne out by the range

Chapter 5: Parents treated as applying
3. Harm and undue distress

of decisions which have been given in the past, although the majority are accepted as having a fear of violence or abuse.

Where a child was conceived as a result of rape or sexual abuse, visiting officers are instructed to handle these situations with 'extreme tact', and 'great care and sensitivity'. However, they are reminded that the parent with care may not want to free the non-resident parent from the responsibility to provide support for his child. In the case of a risk of violence, staff have to ask the reasons for fearing violence in order to decide whether there are reasonable grounds for the fear (see below).[37] Decision makers have to consider both the risk of physical harm resulting from actual violence and the risk of undue distress caused by a well-founded fear or the receiving of threats.

Reasonable grounds

The decision maker must consider whether there are **reasonable grounds** for believing there is a risk of harm or undue distress.

Providing evidence of reasonable grounds

The Government accepts that corroboration of a parent with care's own evidence is not necessary:[38]

> While corroborative evidence in support of a parent's claim of good cause will be welcome, it will not be essential. A social security commissioner's decision sets out the presumption which applies in similar circumstances for benefit decisions, namely that the person concerned is telling the truth, unless there are strong grounds for thinking otherwise. The Government thinks it is right to follow such an approach for child maintenance . . . We will be able to consider the circumstances of every single case specifically. A lone parent has the right to expect that – unless it is inherently implausible – her story will be believed, if she expresses her fears to the Agency. Supporting evidence will be helpful but it will not be essential.

This is repeated in guidance to Jobcentre Plus staff.[39] However, this guidance may be undermined by the emphasis on detecting fraud. Where fraud or collusion with the non-resident parent is suspected, the Jobcentre Plus decision maker may unreasonably refuse to believe the parent with care unless there is independent evidence to support her case. If this happens, the Jobcentre Plus should be asked to say why they consider the parent's evidence 'inherently implausible'.

Appeal tribunals have to give reasons for disregarding a parent's evidence, and any failure to do so can be appealed to a commissioner.[40]

In some cases, while acknowledging that a parent has genuine fears of harm or undue distress the Jobcentre Plus decision maker may not agree that these fears are realistic (see p70). The parent with care knows the people involved and their history and therefore is likely to be able to anticipate their reactions, while the decision maker does not. It is therefore important for the Jobcentre Plus to explain why they consider the fear is fanciful, and to show that their decision is not based on rumour or unfounded opinion.

What counts as evidence

Evidence may be provided orally or in writing. If the decision maker does not agree that there are reasonable grounds, any evidence given orally at an interview or over the telephone should be sent in writing during the next four weeks, and expanded upon where possible. Written communication should suffice unless the decision maker needs further information, in which case a visiting officer will be asked to contact the parent.[41]

Supporting documentation

The parent with care is generally asked to produce documentary evidence, where it exists, to corroborate her own oral or written evidence.[42] However, it is recognised that not all parents will be able to provide information and this should not prejudice their case for good cause. Evidence could be a police, medical or social work report – eg, after an incidence of violence. It could be a statement from someone who knows the family and the situation – eg, a teacher, religious or community leader, youth worker, neighbour, friend or relative. It could be a statement from the parent's caseworker in a refuge.[43] The statement should, where possible, give that person's recollection of previous events, or assessment of the attitudes or mental state of anyone involved and explain why the parent and/or child(ren) would be likely to suffer harm or undue distress.

The Jobcentre Plus has no power to approach third parties to request information about the risk of harm or undue distress (see p87). However, the parent with care could give her permission for them to contact a third party on her behalf. She may prefer instead to do this herself and obtain any specific information the Jobcentre Plus needs.

The decision on good cause

Decision-making staff have to weigh all the information and evidence available – written and oral – in making the decision.[44] Staff are encouraged to 'err on the side of caution when making good cause decisions'.[45] We take this to mean that they should not take risks where harm or undue distress is involved, and that the parent with care is given the benefit of any doubt. The decision maker should be able to show that all relevant evidence and factors have been taken into account.[46]

The welfare of the child is always considered where good cause is not accepted for the parent with care.[47]

When good cause is accepted the decision maker must also decide whether to set a date for reconsideration of good cause.[48] In some cases good cause may be accepted indefinitely.

The parent will be notified in writing of the decision on good cause and any date set for reconsideration.[49]

Reconsideration of good cause

A good cause decision made after 3 March 2003 may be reconsidered at any time.[50] (This includes where the decision was made in relation to the welfare of the child.[51]) The decision maker may set a date, any time up to three years from the date of the decision, to reconsider the case.[52] A reconsideration may be triggered earlier than this if there is a change in circumstances that indicates reconsideration is appropriate – eg, the parent with care has the non-resident parent's baby.

In some circumstances the decision maker may decide it is **not** appropriate to reconsider the decision, and accept good cause indefinitely – eg, where the qualifying child was conceived due to rape, incest or sexual abuse.[53]

When a good cause decision is to be reconsidered a further visit will be arranged. The parent will be asked if she still does not wish to apply for child maintenance, and if not, to give her reasons for maintaining the request not to act.[54] In practice, this is a further good cause interview. The visiting officer and the decision maker will have information on the reason good cause was accepted previously but the parent must remake the case for good cause. It will not be sufficient for the parent to state that her reasons have not changed (unless this is due to rape/sexual abuse); the visiting officer must complete a fresh statement to support good cause. This means showing that there is a current risk of undue harm or distress. Visiting officers and decision makers are reminded that circumstances may have changed so that the original reasons for good cause being accepted are no longer valid[55] – eg, if the relationship between the parent with care and non-resident parent have improved or the parent with care has a new partner and there is no longer a risk of violence.

Further benefit claim where good cause was accepted previously

Where 'good cause' has been accepted previously, visiting officers are informed of this before the new claims interview.[56] They are not given the evidence that was produced last time or the reasons *why* good cause was accepted. In all cases, the parent will still be reminded of the benefits of receiving maintenance at the new claims interview even if they are opting-out with good cause reasons.

There are two situations where 'good cause' can be accepted automatically, so long as the parent's circumstances have not changed and she still does not wish to pursue maintenance. These are:
- where a parent with care is making a repeat claim within six months of a previous claim where good cause was accepted and she states at the visit that her circumstances have not changed since the date of the last decision.[57] This is known as the six-month linking period;
- where good cause was previously accepted due to rape or sexual abuse.[58]

In each of these cases a full good cause interview will not be conducted. However, in the latter case, the parent will have to state that rape or sexual abuse is the reason. A visiting officer must accept this statement.

In all other cases the visiting officer will undertake a full good cause interview and gather information for the decision maker. The decision maker will then make a decision based on this current information. This decision may be different from a previous decision. This does not mean that previous threats are irrelevant, merely that the parent must ensure she gives full details, as no other information will be available.

If good cause was accepted previously because a tribunal or commissioner allowed the parent's appeal against a reduced benefit decision (or 'old rules' benefit penalty), and circumstances have not changed, advice should be sought to challenge a subsequent decision on a further claim not to accept good cause. An appeal can be brought against any reduced benefit decision (see p82).

4. Reduced benefit decisions

A reduced benefit decision is considered by a Jobcentre Plus decision maker where a parent with care who is treated as applying for child maintenance:[59]
- opts out (whether or not giving reasons to be considered as good cause) (see p68);
- fails to provide sufficient information to pursue maintenance;
- refuses to take a DNA test (see p105).

A reduced benefit decision will not be made if the decision maker is satisfied that:
- there is good cause – ie, the parent, or any children living with her, would suffer 'harm or undue distress' (see p68) as a result of being treated as applying, providing information or taking the DNA test, as appropriate;[60]
- the welfare of the child would be affected (see p31).[61]

Where these reasons are accepted a good cause decision can be reconsidered at a later date and a different decision made (see p74). There are some situations where even if good cause and the welfare of the child are not accepted, the reduced benefit decision cannot be imposed (see p77).

The reduced benefit decision process

After the new claims/good cause interview the decision maker will review the written record and other evidence available.
On the basis of this s/he may:
- accept good cause/welfare of the child if relevant and notify the parent;[62]
- issue a written notice requiring the parent to provide reasons within four weeks.[63]

Chapter 5: Parents treated as applying
4. Reduced benefit decisions

Before issuing the notice the Jobcentre Plus checks whether the benefit award continues.[64] If it does not and there has been no further claim for benefit then no further action may be taken by the Jobcentre Plus. Unless the parent has opted-out, the CSA may contact the parent – eg, to ask for further information to identify or trace the non-resident parent (see p87).

Where written notice is issued by the Jobcentre Plus, the four-week period given to supply reasons begins on the day the notice is given or sent to the parent with care.[65] This time limit can be extended in special circumstances – eg, if she is in hospital.

The parent need not give further reasons for opting-out in writing (ie, she may provide them over the phone or at interview) unless directed by the Secretary of State.[66]

After the four-week period the decision maker will re-examine the case and consider any reasons supplied. Where s/he cannot be satisfied regarding good cause/welfare of the child a reduced benefit decision may be made. There are certain circumstances in which a reduced benefit decision cannot be given (see p77).

The parent will be sent written notification of the decision to either:
- accept good cause/welfare of the child;[67] *or*
- make a reduced benefit decision.[68]

Where a parent with care has opted-out and good cause has been accepted, the Secretary of State may reconsider the case at any time (see p78).[69] This also applies where good cause was not accepted but the reason a reduced benefit decision has not been made is the welfare of the child.[70]

When a reduced benefit decision is made the appropriate benefit payment office will be notified.[71] This notification will state:
- the date from which the reduced benefit decision will take effect (see p79);[72]
- the amount of the reduced benefit decision – ie, standard or modified (see p77).[73]

A reduced benefit decision will apply for 156 weeks (three years).[74] At the end of this period a further reduced benefit decision may be made (see p82).

Where a reduced benefit decision has been made the parent with care may later provide further information or reasons regarding good cause or the welfare of the child. This will trigger a reconsideration of the reduced benefit decision by the Jobcentre Plus. The decision maker may decide to accept good cause or that the welfare of the child is affected and revise or supersede the previous decision.

For the circumstances in which a reduced benefit decision cannot be imposed see pp77 and 80, and ceases to be in force, see p81.

Chapter 5: Parents treated as applying
4. Reduced benefit decisions

The standard and modified amount of the reduction

The standard amount of the reduced benefit decision is 40 per cent of the income support (IS) personal allowance for an adult aged 25 or over, even where the parent is under 25.[75] Any fraction of over half a penny is rounded up, and any of half a penny or less is disregarded.[76]

For 2004/05 this means that the parent's IS/income-based jobseeker's allowance (JSA) will be reduced by £22.26 a week.

When the benefit rates are uprated in April, the amount of the reduction also increases. The level of the reduction goes up from the next benefit week following the date of the uprating.[77]

If applying the reduced benefit decision would reduce the amount of benefit to nil or to below the minimum payment for that benefit, then the amount is modified to leave the minimum amount payable.[78] The minimum payment is 10 pence for IS and income-based JSA, except where the parent is receiving IS under the trade disputes provisions, when it is £5.[79] The penalty cannot be deducted from any other benefit which may be payable with IS (eg, incapacity benefit) or with income-based JSA (eg, contribution-based JSA). Any period for which the penalty cannot be paid in full (or at all) because of these rules still counts as a period serving the penalty.[80]

Test case rules (see p427) apply to reduced benefit decisions as they did to 'old rules' reduced benefit directions and to Jobcentre Plus decisions to impose the benefit penalty.[81]

See p79 for when the reduction begins and p80 for when it ends.

When can the reduced benefit decision not be imposed

There are certain circumstances where even though good cause/welfare of the child do not apply a reduced benefit decision cannot be imposed. These are:[82]
- where the parent with care, or her partner, is paid IS/income-based JSA that includes a disabled child premium, a disability premium or a higher pensioner premium (this applies even if it is the partner who has the disability);
- where the parent with care, or her partner, is paid an award of child tax credit that contains an element for a disabled child or young person with a disability;
- where the parent has claimed good cause and she, or her partner, made a claim for IS/income-based JSA for a qualifying child but benefit is not paid for the child as there is a dispute over the child benefit for the child.[83]

Where an appropriate premium ceases to be paid or the parent with care is awarded child benefit, the reduced benefit decision can be imposed.

Where one of the premiums is awarded retrospectively, and should have been payable on or before the reduced benefit decision was made, the reduced benefit decision is cancelled.[84] However, if it only becomes payable after the date of the decision it remains in force.

Chapter 5: Parents treated as applying
4. Reduced benefit decisions

Reconsideration of a reduced benefit decision

Where a reduced benefit decision has been made the parent with care may later provide further information or reasons regarding good cause/welfare of the child. This will trigger a reconsideration of the reduced benefit decision by the Jobcentre Plus.

Where the parent has opted in, the reduced benefit decision will cease from the beginning of the benefit week in which the parent stated she wished to opt-in.[85] The legislation refers to this as withdrawal of her request to opt-out.

Where the decision maker decides to accept good cause or that the welfare of the child is affected, the decision may be revised, if it is within the time limit; otherwise the decision is superseded. This supersession will take effect from the first day in the benefit week in which the parent provided the information which enabled the good cause/welfare of the child decision to be made.[86]

Benefit fraud referrals

Jobcentre Plus staff refer cases to the Benefit Fraud Investigation Services for benefits fraud investigation where:
- the parent with care does not provide information about the non-resident parent, but they suspect that she is in contact with the father;
- a reduced benefit decision is imposed without any contact from the parent with care;[87] *or*
- a parent with care provides no information and 'readily accepts' the reduced benefit decision (this appears to cover cases where the parent with care opts out but does not offer any evidence of good cause or states from the outset that she is prepared to accept a reduction).[88]

In addition, the CSA aims to work closely with the Jobcentre Plus to identify and deter collusive cohabitation, fictitious desertion and other types of benefit fraud. This includes:
- systematic referral of suspected benefit fraud to the Jobcentre Plus, including allegations of benefit fraud made by third parties (often the other parent);
- a fraud liaison officer in each Child Support Agency Centre (CSAC – see p12) to provide a source of advice for staff, scrutinise fraud referrals and forward them to the Jobcentre Plus, monitor progress of investigations and provide feedback to staff;
- the appointment of a fraud awareness officer in each CSAC to educate staff; *and*
- routine closer working with the Jobcentre Plus.

Although the CSA is informed of the outcome of the Jobcentre Plus investigation, this information cannot be passed on to the third party who made the allegation (see p115).[89]

See p93 for the possible effects of giving false information to the CSA.

Chapter 5: Parents treated as applying
4. Reduced benefit decisions

Only one reduced benefit decision at any one time

Only one reduced benefit decision can be in force at any one time in relation to a parent with care.[90] This applies to a parent with care of children by different non-resident fathers who refuses to pursue any of them. Even if she pursues one but not another, a reduced benefit decision can be imposed.

See p80 for what happens to the reduced benefit decision if a parent with care stops claiming benefit and subsequently re-claims.

Additional qualifying child

If a parent with a reduced benefit decision becomes the parent with care of another qualifying child (ie, the child is born to her or moves into her home), the parent will be treated as applying for child support maintenance. If she opts out, fails to provide information or take a DNA test and good cause/welfare of the child cannot be accepted, a reduced benefit decision may be made.

If a reduced benefit decision is in force when the further one is made, the original reduction stops and the further reduction starts the day after the original reduction ceases to be in force.[91] The new reduction is applied for a period of 156 weeks.[92] The further reduction only covers the additional child(ren) not named in the first direction. Where the further reduction ceases to be in force (see p80), but the original reduced benefit decision would not have ceased to be in force, the reduction continues until 156 weeks have been served in total.[93] A further reduced benefit decision may be made.

When does the reduction start

Once a reduced benefit decision has been issued, the Secretary of State supersedes the relevant benefit award to or for the parent with care, and the reduction is made from the first day of the second benefit week following any such supersession.[94]

If a recent benefit claim has been made, it should be processed as normal and not held up while a decision is made about whether or not to impose a reduced benefit decision.

Income support and jobseeker's allowance claimants

IS and income-based JSA are paid for seven-day periods running from the day of the week payment is made. This is known as a benefit week. A benefit week overlaps two calendar weeks (for more details, see CPAG's *Welfare Benefits and Tax Credits Handbook*). If a claimant's benefit week changes, the reduced benefit decision can be modified slightly. The reduction lasts for between 155 and 156 weeks, finishing on the last day of the benefit week which ends before the 156-week period is up.[95]

The reduction is imposed even where the parent has other deductions from benefits (but, for the minimum benefit payable, see p84).

79

Chapter 5: Parents treated as applying
4. Reduced benefit decisions

Reduction deferred until the next order book

IS claimants are normally paid by order book (rather than girocheque). Where a parent with care is paid by order book and a reduced benefit decision would result in a small change to her benefit (ie, because of the minimum payment rule – see p77), the reduction can be deferred until later – eg, the next order book.[96] Any change in IS of less than 50 pence a week can be deferred up to the date when the claimant comes off benefit, or a week after the date of the last order in the book, whichever comes first.[97]

When does the reduction stop

A reduced benefit decision normally lasts for 156 weeks, but it can be brought to an end before the full period has been served in certain circumstances. A reduction can:
- be suspended (see below) – the reduction stops for a period, but the suspended portion then has to be served unless more than 52 weeks has passed;
- cease to be in force (see p81) – the reduced benefit decision stops being in force from a specified date and cannot be resurrected;
- be revised or superseded (see Chapter 19) or appealed (see p82).

The Jobcentre Plus must notify the parent with care in writing that the reduction has stopped, or in certain cases, been suspended.[98] This notice does not apply to cases where the direction is suspended because a parent goes into hospital or care home, or where it is suspended because benefit has stopped.

At the end of the 156-week period a further reduced benefit decision may be made and imposed (see p82).

Suspension of a reduced benefit decision

An reduced benefit decision can be suspended and, if appropriate, reinstated in the following situations:
- the benefit claim ceases;
- the claimant is no longer a parent with care; *or*
- the parent goes into hospital or a care home.

Benefit claim ceases

If the parent with care comes off IS or income-based JSA the reduction is suspended.[99] If she re-claims within 52 weeks, then the suspended part of the reduction can be applied to the new benefit award.[100] The parent will be sent notification that unless she opts in or provides reasons supporting good cause within 14 days the remainder of the reduced benefit direction will be imposed.[101] Where the parent opts in or gives reasons a visit will be arranged to complete a maintenance administration form or good cause interview.[102] The decision maker will consider the evidence and decide whether or not to reapply the reduction.

Chapter 5: Parents treated as applying
4. Reduced benefit decisions

If the parent provides no reasons or the decision maker cannot accept good cause/welfare of the child, the reduction benefit decision again comes into operation at the end of the 14 days. The remainder of the 156-week reduction starts from the first day of the second benefit week following this decision.[103]

After 52 weeks off benefit, the reduction ceases to be in force – ie, lapses.[104] Where the parent concerned opts out on a new claim, a new reduced benefit decision can be made and the reduction imposed for 156 weeks.[105]

Claimant no longer a parent with care

Where the one and only child covered by a reduction ceases to count as a child, or the parent stops being the person who looks after the child(ren), the reduction is suspended from the last day of the benefit week in which this change occurs.[106] For example, if a child goes to live with someone else or leaves school, the reduction is lifted from the end of the week this happens. A parent with care should tell the Jobcentre Plus of any relevant changes and if the reduction is not lifted, she should ask for a supersession of the reduced benefit decision (see p420).

If the child starts to count as a child again, or the parent resumes the care, then the unexpired portion of the reduction again applies to the benefit award.[107] On the other hand, where the reduction has been suspended for 52 weeks, it will lapse if no relevant benefit is in payment at that time.[108] If later the same person becomes a parent with care again, claims a relevant benefit and opts out, a new reduced benefit decision may be made.

Parent goes into hospital or a care home

If a parent with care goes into certain types of accommodation or care, then the amount of her family's IS or income-based JSA is worked out differently (see CPAG's *Welfare Benefits and Tax Credits Handbook*). This applies to people in care homes or independent hospitals, or people provided with a care home service or independent health care service. If a reduced benefit decision is given or is in operation, it is suspended if the parent's benefit calculation is modified in this way.[109] Where a suspension has lasted for 52 weeks, the direction will lapse and cannot be re-applied.[110]

When a reduced benefit direction ceases to be in force

A reduced benefit decision ceases to be in force if:[111]
- the parent with care withdraws the request to opt out. The reduction ceases from the first day in the benefit week the parent states she is opting in;[112]
- the parent complies with the requirement to provide information. The reduction ceases from the first day in the benefit week the parent provided the information;
- the parent consents to a DNA test. The reduction ceases from the first day in the benefit week the parent agrees to take the test;[113]

81

Chapter 5: Parents treated as applying
4. Reduced benefit decisions

- the Secretary of State accepts that there are reasons for good cause/welfare of the child. The reduction ceases from the first day in the benefit week the parent provided sufficient information to accept good cause;[114]
- a section 7 qualifying child for whom the reduced benefit decision is in force makes an application and a calculation is made for all the qualifying children concerned. The reduction ceases from the end of the benefit week in which the information is received enabling the calculation to be made;[115]
- the Jobcentre Plus decides for another reason to revise or supersede the reduced benefit decision and to end it (see pp416 and 420).

Although not stated explicitly in the legislation, when a parent moves onto pension credit (PC) from IS or income-based JSA the reduction will cease, as the provisions on being 'treated as applying' do not extend to PC.

Further reduced benefit decision after three years

At the end of the three-year reduced benefit decision, the parent with care will be given the opportunity to provide information to pursue child support maintenance.[116] She will be asked to opt in, take a DNA test, or provide information or reasons for good cause within four weeks.[117] If she responds, a visit is arranged and either a maintenance administration form is completed or a good cause interview is conducted. At the end of the four-week period the decision maker will then decide whether or not to make a further reduced benefit decision.

The new reduced benefit decision will begin on the day after the previous reduced benefit decision ceases.[118] This process is repeated after each three-year period.[119] This means that a parent with care may be subject to a reduced benefit decision for many years.

Appeals

A parent with care can appeal to an appeal tribunal against a reduced benefit decision, or against a decision on revision or supersession (see Chapter 19).[120] For details of appeals, including time limits, see Chapter 20.

The reduced benefit decision stays in force pending the appeal tribunal's decision. A parent with care who wants to challenge the refusal to accept good cause, but cannot afford the reduction could appeal and then:
- provide further information to enable supersession;
- opt in, provide information or take a DNA test as appropriate in the circumstances.

The reduction then stops, but the appeal proceeds.

Supersession

In some cases where a parent has a pending appeal against a reduced benefit decision, the Jobcentre Plus may supersede it – eg, because the parent provides information that supports good cause/welfare of the child. In this case the reduced benefit decision stops, but only from a later date. The parent must consider whether to withdraw the appeal, or continue to get the reduced benefit decision overturned for the whole period (and so have the deducted benefit repaid). When deciding whether to continue the appeal, the possible gain through benefit being repaid should be weighed against the possibility that if the tribunal dismisses the appeal, the Jobcentre Plus may look again at its decision to supersede. If an appeal is lost and this happens, seek further advice.

Appeal and opt in
Where a parent with care takes this course of action she should explain that she is only opting-in, providing information or taking the DNA test under protest until the tribunal decides the question of harm or undue distress, and that she still believes she has good cause but cannot afford a benefit reduction. Although a calculation may then be made, she at least has an appeal where she can dispute the refusal to accept good cause/welfare of the child.

This course of action is not without risk. The parent may still opt out at a later stage and would be given four weeks to provide reasons for opting-out.

Outcome of the appeal
If the tribunal allows an appeal from the original reduced benefit decision or from a revision of it, the reduced benefit decision ceases to have effect from its start and all benefit deducted is paid to the parent with care.

If the tribunal allows an appeal from a supersession decision to impose or not to cease a reduced benefit decision, the reduced benefit decision ceases to have effect from the date that supersession decision should have had effect and benefit deducted from that date is paid.

5. Existing section 6 'old rules' cases

This means a case where the old section 6 rules applied prior to 3 March 2003[121] and includes cases:
- where a maintenance assessment has been made;
- where a reduced benefit direction has been made and a benefit penalty imposed;
- where good cause was accepted before 3 March 2003;
- going through the 'old rules' good cause process at 3 March 2003.

Parents with a maintenance assessment
Parents with a maintenance assessment will continue to have their maintenance assessed under the 'old rules' until:

Chapter 5: Parents treated as applying
5. Existing section 6 'old rules' cases

- the case converts to the 'new rules' at the case conversion date or earlier (see p191);
- the parent opts out and then it will be treated under the 'new rules' as a request to cease acting and the procedures may result in a reduced benefit decision.[122]

In all of these cases where a parent with care opts out they will be dealt with under the new procedures as explained in this chapter and good cause may be accepted or a reduced benefit decision made and imposed. The parent may just decide she no longer wants the child maintenance via the CSA or she may have new family circumstances (eg, a baby by another non-resident parent from whom she fears violence) that give good cause for opting out or raise concern for the welfare of the child.

Where a parent opts out and then opts in to try to force an early conversion to the new scheme, this will not occur if there has been a maintenance assessment in force within the previous 13 weeks.

Parents with a reduced benefit direction and benefit penalty

In these cases benefit will continue to be reduced but it will be treated as if made under a reduced benefit decision.[123] At the end of the three-year period a further reduced benefit decision may be imposed.

If the parent provides information to pursue maintenance then the case will be dealt with as a 'new rules' case and a maintenance calculation carried out.

Where the parent provides information supporting good cause or the welfare of the child, a reconsideration of the decision will take place. The case will be dealt with under the 'new rules' and procedures. This means that where good cause is accepted that decision may be subject to reconsideration.

Parents where good cause has been accepted before 3 March 2003

In these cases there will be no change and a decision will not be reconsidered. However, where the parent ceases to claim and then reclaims benefit, though good cause may be accepted automatically (due to the six-month linking rule or special cases rules regarding showing good cause) when her/his good cause is accepted, it may be subject to reconsideration at a later date because the parent has gone through the new procedure.

Chapter 5: Parents treated as applying
Notes

Notes

1. **What happens when a parent is treated as applying**
   1. s6 CSA 1991
   2. s6(7) CSA 1991
   3. s6(7) CSA 1991
   4. para 9 App 3 IS/GAP Circular 02/02 (revised)
   5. App 7 G&CI
   6. Vol 1 para 10822 IS GAP and para 9501 G&CI
   7. Vol 1 para 10822 IS GAP and para 9501 G&CI
   8. Vol 1 para 11140 IS GAP
   9. paras 48 and 57 IS/GAP and App 2 Circular 02/02 (revised)
   10. paras 60, 61 &63 IS/GAP Circular 02/02 (revised)
   11. paras 112, 141 and 181 IS/GAP Circular 02/02(revised)
   12. para 142 IS/GAP Circular 02/02 (revised)
   13. para 144 IS/GAP Circular 02/02 (revised)
   14. para 145 IS/GAP Circular 02/02 (revised)
   15. App 3 IS/GAP Circular 02/02 (revised)
   16. App 3 IS/GAP Circular 02/02 (revised)
   17. App 3 IS/GAP Circular 02/02 (revised)
   18. paras 9760, 10190 and App 7 IS GAP

2. **Opting-out**
   19. s6(5) CSA 1991
   20. Reg 31 (4&7) CS(MCP) Regs
   21. s6(9-10) CSA 1991
   22. paras 139 &140 IS/Gap Circular 02/02 (revised); para 9420 and App 7 G&CI
   23. para 140 IS/GAP Circular 02/02 (revised)
   24. Vol 1 para 10820 IS GAP; para 9200 G&CI
   25. App 5 and App 7 G&CI
   26. App 7 G&CI
   27. App 7 G&CI
   28. App 7 G&CI

3. **Harm and undue distress**
   29. s6(7) CSA 1991
   30. CCS/1037/1995
   31. s46(3) CSA 1991
   32. CCS/7559/1999
   33. Shorter Oxford English Dictionary; The Concise Oxford Dictionary
   34. CCS/1037/1995
   35. CCS/12609/1996
   36. CCS/15109/1996
   37. App 7 and App 11 G&CI
   38. Alistair Burt MP, Under-Secretary of State for Social Security, Hansard, 22 June 1992; DSS press release (92/191), 24 November 1992. The social security case referred to is R(SB) 33/85.
   39. App 7 G&CI
   40. CCS/12092/1996
   41. para 9422 G&CI
   42. App 7 G&CI
   43. para 9420 G&CI
   44. Vol 10 para 34530 IS GAP
   45. IS Good cause training materials
   46. Vol 10 paras 34550 and 34570 IS GAP
   47. Vol 10 paras 34525, 34682 and App 10 IS GAP
   48. para 156 IS/GAP Circular 02/02 (revised)
   49. s46(4) CSA 1991
   50. s46(6) CSA 1991
   51. para 158 IS/GAP Circular 02/02 (revised)
   52. para 159 IS/GAP Circular 02/02 (revised)
   53. paras 157 IS/GAP Circular 02/02 (revised)
   54. para 166 IS/GAP Circular 02/02 (revised)
   55. para 155 IS/GAP Circular 02/02 (revised)
   56. para 114 IS/GAP Circular 02/02 (revised)
   57. para 9301 G & CI: para 140 IS/GAP Circular 02/02 (revised)
   58. Vol 10 para 34514 and App 7 IS GAP

4. **Reduced benefit decisions**
   59. s46(1) CSA 1991
   60. s46(3) CSA 1991
   61. s2 CSA 1991
   62. s46(4) CSA 1991
   63. s42(2) CSA 1991; reg 9 CS(MCP) Regs
   64. Vol 10 para 34530 IS GAP
   65. Reg 2 CS(MCP) Regs
   66. s46(9) CSA 1991

Chapter 5: Parents treated as applying
Notes

67 s46(4) CSA 1991
68 s46(7) CSA 1991
69 s46(6) CSA 1991
70 para 158 IS/GAP Circular 02/02 (revised)
71 para 199 IS/GAP Circular 00/02
72 s46(8) CSA 1991
73 Regs 11 and 12 CS(MCP) Regs
74 Reg 11(2) CS(MCP) Regs
75 Reg 11(2) CS(MCP) Regs
76 Reg 20 CS(MCP) Regs
77 Reg 11(7) CS(MCP) Regs
78 Reg 12 CS(MCP) Regs
79 Regs 26(4) and 27(2) SS(C&P) Regs; reg 87A JSA Regs
80 Vol 10 paras 34792 and 35060 IS GAP
81 ss28ZA and ss28ZB CSA 1991
82 Reg 46(50) CSA 1991; reg 10 CS(MCP) Regs
83 para 175 IS/GAP Circular 02/02 (revised)
84 Vol 10 para 34850 IS GAP
85 para 186 IS/GAP Circular 02/02 (revised)
86 para 187 IS/GAP Circular 02/02 (revised)
87 Vol 1 para 1111 IS GAP
88 paras 11270-72 G & CI
89 Fraud and failed escalation FAQs
90 Reg 11(8) CS(MCP) Regs
91 Regs 11(4) and 17(2) CS(MCP) Regs; reg 7B(15) SS&CS(DA) Regs
92 Regs 11 and 17(2) CS(MCP) Regs
93 Reg 17(4) CS(MCP) Regs
94 Reg 11(3) CS(MCP) Regs
95 Reg 11(6) CS(MCP) Regs
96 Reg 11(5) CS(MCP) Regs
97 Reg 26(2) SS(C&P) Regs
98 Reg 19 CS(MCP) Regs
99 Reg 13 CS(MCP) Regs
100 Reg 13(3) CS(MCP) Regs
101 Reg 13(6) CS(MCP) Regs; para 182 IS/GAP Circular 02/02 (revised)
102 para 184 IS/GAP Circular 02/02 (revised)
103 Regs 13(5) and 11(3) CS(MCP) Regs
104 Reg 13(2) CS(MCP) Regs
105 para 205 IS/GAP Circular 00/02
106 Reg 18(1) CS(MCP) Regs; reg 7B(16) SS&CS(DA) Regs
107 Reg 18(3) CS(MCP) Regs
108 Reg 18(2) CS(MCP) Regs
109 Regs 14 and 15 CS(MCP) Regs as amended by reg 5(3)CS(MA)(No2) Regs 2003
110 Regs 14(3) and (15(3) CS(MCP) Regs as amended by reg 5(3) CS(MA)(No2) Regs 2003
111 Reg 16 CS(MCP) Regs; reg 7B(11) SS&CS(DA) Regs
112 Para 186 IS/GAP Circular 02/02 (revised)
113 para 188 IS/GAP Circular 02/02 (revised)
114 Reg 7B(12) SSCS(DA) Regs; para 187 IS/GAP Circular 02/02 (revised)
115 Reg 7B(14) SSCS(DA) Regs
116 para 178 IS/GAP Circular 02/02 (revised)
117 para 180 IS/GAP Circular 02/02 (revised)
118 para 180 IS/GAP Circular 02/02 (revised)
119 para 179 IS/GAP Circular 02/02 (revised)
120 s20(1)(c) and (2)(b) CSA 1991

5. Existing section 6 'old rules' cases
121 s6 CSA 1991 before substitution by s3 CSPSSA 2000
122 Reg 31(4) CS(MCP) Regs; para 319 IS/GAP Circular 02/02 (revised)
123 Reg 31(6) CS(MCP) Regs

Chapter 6
Information

This chapter covers:
1. Information-seeking powers (below)
2. Contacting the non-resident parent (p94)
3. Parentage investigations (p99)
4. Further investigations (p110)
5. Duty to disclose changes (p113)
6. Disclosure of information by the CSA (p114)
7. Existing 'old rules' cases (p117)

1. Information-seeking powers

The CSA has wide powers to obtain information from (among others) parents, employers, local authorities and the Inland Revenue.[1] In addition, the CSA can appoint inspectors who have extensive powers to obtain information (see p112). Staff at the regional Child Support Agency Centres (CSACs – see p12) ask for information by telephone, those at local service bases (LSBs – see p12) also conduct face-to-face enquiries. As far as possible information is gathered by telephone, with clear guidance on when and how this should be conducted.[2]

This chapter explores how the CSA exercises its powers. However, the Jobcentre Plus may seek information under child support legislation – eg, when making decisions about good cause and the reduced benefit decision (see Chapter 5).

When the CSA can ask for information

All applicants are under a duty to provide information to identify and trace a non-resident parent, and calculate and collect maintenance.[3] The information may also be required to verify whether information already gathered is correct.[4]

In many cases all the information needed will be collected by phone. Applications need not be in writing but where they are requested an application for child maintenance form is provided. A section 6 parent with care is treated as applying and therefore a maintenance administration form is completed with her to gather the information needed. Further information may be required to make an effective application.

Chapter 6: Information
1. Information-seeking powers

Where information is not provided, a section 4 or 7 application may be treated as withdrawn (see p52) or a section 6 applicant may have a reduced benefit decision imposed. It is a criminal offence to fail to provide or knowingly provide false information (see p93).

After an application has been made the non-resident parent will be contacted, usually by phone, to notify them of the application and gather information.[5] In some cases a face-to-face interview may be arranged or, where there is no phone number, a form called the 'child maintenance enquiry' is issued. The child maintenance enquiry form can be used to gather the information needed to calculate and collect maintenance (see p97).

Information can only be requested if it is necessary to:[6]
- decide whether there is a qualifying child, non-resident parent or person with care in relation to an application;
- decide whether the CSA has jurisdiction – ie, the qualifying child, non-resident parent, and person with care are all habitually resident in the UK (see p33);
- decide whether a written maintenance agreement made before 5 April 1993 is in force or a court order made before 3 March 2003 or after 3 March 2003 which has been in force for one year (see p44);
- decide which application has priority (see p54);
- decide, where there is more than one person with care, if they have parental responsibility for a qualifying child (see p55);
- identify a non-resident parent (see p99);
- trace a non-resident parent (see p94);
- determine who is in receipt of child benefit either for a relevant child or qualifying child where a parent may be treated as a non-resident parent in shared care situations (see Chapter 16);
- calculate the amount of child maintenance;
- identify how much is payable under a court maintenance order;
- collect child support maintenance or maintenance under a court order from a non-resident parent;
- decide whether to enforce a CSA calculation or other maintenance through the courts (see p483);
- work out or collect interest on arrears (see p476);
- identify any proceedings for a court maintenance order;
- verify whether information already gathered is correct.[7]

See p89 for who can be required to give information and p93 for the effects of failing to provide it.

Chapter 6: Information
1. Information-seeking powers

What information can the CSA ask for

CSA references to information include evidence such as statements and documents. The legislation does not specify any restrictions on the kind of information the CSA can ask for, only on the purpose for which it is needed. Instead, the regulations give as examples issues on which the CSA can require information:[8]

- the habitual residence of the person with care, the non-resident parent and any child covered by the application to determine jurisdiction (including where the individual works for a relevant employer abroad);
- the name and address of the person with care and non-resident parent, their marital status, and the relationship of the person with care to any child covered by the application;
- the name, address and date of birth of any child covered by the application, the child's marital status and any education the child is undergoing;
- where there is more than one person with care:
  - who has parental responsibility (or parental rights in Scotland) for any qualifying child, *and*
  - how much time is spent by that child with each person with care;
- where parentage is disputed, whether someone can be assumed to be a parent (see p23) and if not, who is the parent of a child (a section 6 parent can be asked to take a DNA test[9]);
- the name and address of any current or recent employer of a non-resident parent and the gross earnings derived from any such employment;
- where the non-resident parent is self-employed, the address, trading name, gross receipts and expenses, any other outgoings of the trade or business and taxable profits;
- any other income of the non-resident parent;
- how much is paid or payable under a court maintenance order or maintenance agreement;
- anyone who lives in the same household as the non-resident parent, their relationship to them and to each other, and the date of birth of any child of those people;
- details and statements of any account in the name of the non-resident parent, including bank and building society accounts;
- whether a person counts as a qualifying child for the purposes of child support (see p26);
- information needed to decide whether a calculation should end (see p403).

Who has to give information to the CSA

Information can be required from the people listed on pp90-92. It can only be required from a person who has that information in her/his possession or can reasonably be expected to acquire it.[10] Information can also be given to the CSA

Chapter 6: Information
1. Information-seeking powers

when there is no obligation to provide it – eg, from a relative, neighbour, GP or landlord. However, any such voluntary disclosure of information made without the permission of the person(s) concerned could break professional codes of practice, civil contracts or the Data Protection Act 1984, depending on the circumstances. Information supplied to the CSA can give rise to a libel action.[11] For disclosure by the CSA, see p114.

The relevant persons

The person with care, a non-resident parent (or a parent treated as non-resident for the purposes of the calculation) and in Scotland, a child applicant, must provide the information on p89 if requested.[12]

Someone who denies parentage of a child

Someone who denies parentage of a child named in a maintenance application can be required to give information *only* if it is needed:[13]
- to decide whether or not all the relevant persons are habitually resident in the UK and therefore whether the CSA has jurisdiction to make a calculation; *or*
- to identify a non-resident parent.

This means, for example, that where the CSA only wants to identify a person as the non-resident parent, employment details would not normally be necessary and so should not be requested until parentage is established.

Employers

The current or recent employer of the non-resident parent can be required to give information *only* if it is needed to:[14]
- identify a non-resident parent;
- trace a non-resident parent;
- calculate child maintenance;
- collect child support maintenance, interest or arrears of maintenance under a court order from the non-resident parent; *or*
- decide whether to pursue a garnishee or charging order.

An employer of an alleged parent can only be required to provide information to identify and trace that parent.[15]

The same rules apply where the employer is the Crown.[16]

Companies or partnerships

A company or partnership for whom a non-resident parent has had a contract for services with may be required to provide information but *only* if it is needed to:[17]
- trace a non-resident parent; *or*
- calculate child maintenance.

This means, for example, a self-employed IT consultant could be traced through companies for which he provides a service and his income investigated.

Accountants

The person who acts as the non-resident parent's accountant, or who has done so in the past, can be required to give information *only* where it is needed to:[18]
- trace a non-resident parent;
- calculate child maintenance;
- collect child support maintenance, interest or arrears or maintenance under a court order from the non-resident parent; *or*
- decide whether to pursue a garnishee or charging order.

Court officials

The following court officials can be required to give information.[19] In England and Wales:
- the senior district judge of the High Court Family Division or, at a district registry, the district judge;
- the district judge of a county court or the chief clerk or other officer who may be acting on her/his behalf;[20]
- the justice's chief executive for a magistrates' court.

In Scotland:
- the Deputy Principal Clerk of Session of the Court of Session;
- the sheriff clerk of a sheriff court.

Court officials can be required to give information *only* where there is or has been a court maintenance order, or an application for such an order has been made but not determined, and the information is needed to:[21]
- identify how much is payable under a court maintenance order;
- collect child support maintenance or maintenance under a court order;
- identify any proceedings about a court maintenance order;
- decide whether there is in force either a pre-April 1993 maintenance agreement (see p44) or a maintenance order made after 3 March 2003 which has been in force for a year; *or*
- decide, if there is more than one person with care, whether they have parental responsibility for the qualifying child.

Crown employees

Some Crown employees can be required to give information but *only* when it is needed to trace the non-resident parent[22] – eg, officials of the prison services or DVLA staff.

Chapter 6: Information
1. Information-seeking powers

Government benefit departments

Any DWP agency may give information held for benefits purposes to the CSA.[23] This may involve, for example, the use of national insurance records or child benefit records.

Local authorities

Local authorities may be required to give information but *only* if it is needed to:[24]
- decide whether there is a qualifying child, non-resident parent or person with care in relation to an application;
- identify a non-resident parent;
- trace a non-resident parent;
- calculate child maintenance;
- collect child support maintenance, interest or arrears or maintenance under a court order from the non-resident parent; *or*
- decide whether to pursue a garnishee or charging order.

This applies only to the local authority for the area where one or more of the following resides or used to reside:
- the person with care;
- the non-resident parent;
- the parent treated as non-resident;
- the alleged non-resident parent; *or*
- in Scotland, a child applicant.

This means the CSA may require a local authority to give information concerning housing benefit or council tax benefit – eg, the parent's bank account details if held in relation to council tax direct debit.[25]

The Inland Revenue

The Inland Revenue can be required to disclose the current address or details of the current employer of a non-resident parent to the CSA.[26] Where the parent is self-employed this also includes the taxable profits, gross receipts and expenses.[27] Any information disclosed must not go any further than authorised CSA staff, unless it is about civil or criminal proceedings under the 1991 Act. However, where information is obtained under the Social Security Administration Act 1992, no such restriction applies. Information may also be obtained under the Tax Credits Act 1999.[28] Information is taken from records held in connection with the assessment and collection of income tax. It is unlawful for the Inland Revenue to give the CSA any other information.[29]

When information must be supplied

Where information is requested to make an effective application (eg, by the re-issue of a child maintenance application or maintenance administration form or

Chapter 6: Information
1. Information-seeking powers

request for further information) the information must be supplied in 14 days.[30] No deadline is specified for the provision of information in other circumstances only that it must be provided as soon as reasonably practicable in the circumstances.[31] In practice the CSA allow seven days when making a calculation and one month in the case of revision/supersession.[32] See p14 for when a document is treated as sent and received.

Not giving information and giving false information

If a person fails to provide information there are a range of consequences s/he will face:
- if she is a section 6 parent (see p44), a reduced benefit decision may be imposed (see p75);
- if she is a section 4 applicant (see p44), her application may not be processed (see p51);
- if he is a non-resident parent, a default maintenance calculation may be made; *and*
- a criminal fine of £1,000 may be imposed.[33]

If there is a good reason why the information cannot be provided the offence will not apply.[34] In addition, where a parent with care has a reduced benefit decision imposed the fine will not apply.[35] However, a non-resident parent who fails to return a child maintenance enquiry form or provide information may have both a default maintenance decision and a fine imposed. This also means that where a non-resident parent makes a section 4 application and the parent with care fails to provide information s/he can be fined, though this would be extremely rare.

Where the person knowingly provides false information, or allows it to be provided, this is also a criminal offence.[36] The CSA can go to court and a fine of up to £1,000 can be imposed. This is paid to the court, not the CSA.

The CSA must notify the person that it is a criminal offence to refuse to supply or knowingly supply false information.[37] All forms and requests issued contain this notification to ensure the fine may be pursued.

Where a parent fails to give information, the CSA may ask another person for that information – eg, a parent's employer or accountant. As they are required to give information, the criminal sanctions apply. This gives the CSA greater powers to investigate and pursue other sources of information. In the past a commissioner has twice criticised the CSA for failing to seek information from other sources when the parent does not return a form despite reminders,[38] and commented that between the child's mother and the father's employer there should have been sufficient information to enable the CSA to calculate the non-resident parent's income with reasonable precision. The person approached may provide inaccurate but convincing information – eg, one parent may give details about the other's self-employed earnings which are too high; the second parent would then need to persuade the CSA of the real figures. Another commissioner decided that as no

Chapter 6: Information
1. Information-seeking powers

indication is given in the legislation about the extent of evidence for self-employed earnings, this is left to the discretion and commonsense of CSA staff or an appeal tribunal; in this case, the tribunal was entitled to estimate the non-resident parent's net earnings on the basis of documentary evidence provided by the parent with care.[39] However, since that decision the legislation has been amended to allow the CSA to obtain details of self-employed earnings from the Inland Revenue (see p92).

Disputing the information required

Where the CSA/Jobcentre Plus requires information:
- not relevant to the reason for the request;
- of a very different kind from the examples given in the regulations;
- from a person who cannot be required to give it; *or*
- when the CSA has enough information to make a full calculation,

the request should be queried. Where the CSA/Jobcentre Plus insists, refusal or a challenge to the request (see p415) should be considered. If a person in this situation refuses to give information, in order to avoid a penalty s/he should explain that decision, preferably in writing. A complaint could also be made (see p18).

2. Contacting the non-resident parent

If the person with care has given the non-resident parent's telephone number and the non-resident parent is named on the birth certificate and is aware of the existence of the child, he is contacted by phone.[40] Where the telephone number is not known a child maintenance enquiry form may be issued (see p97). The date of contact is the date liability for child maintenance usually starts – this is known as the effective date (see p400). In some cases under the old scheme there were long delays in setting the effective date and the person with care could be due compensation. It is intended that there will be few delays in setting the effective date in new scheme cases. However, where this occurs due to CSA error the parent may be able to ask for compensation (see p20).

Tracing the non-resident parent

The CSA can use its information-seeking powers to identify and trace the non-resident parent. The responsibility for tracing non-resident parents lies primarily with the New Client Team (see p12).[41] There is also an Additional Trace Team to deal with more difficult cases – eg, to pursue tracing via the Inland Revenue.

Only those persons and agencies listed on p90-92 can be required to provide information. CSA staff are advised to use the following sources of information when tracing a non-resident parent:[42]

- the applicant;
- another party;
- the telephone directory or directory enquiries;
- the Departmental Central Index (DCI) – this DWP computer network gives access to national insurance and DWP records;[43]
- the Common Enquiry Service – this gives access to other DWP computer systems, such as those for income support or jobseeker's allowance;[44]
- the Inland Revenue – for an address of a current employer (see p92);[45]
- the National Insurance Contributions Office, where the non-resident parent is employed or self-employed;[46]
- the army, navy, airforce or Ministry of Defence if the non-resident parent is serving in, or recently discharged from, the forces;[47]
- the Prisoner Location Service, Scottish Prison Service, Northern Ireland Prison Service;[48]
- employers, past and present.[49] The request for information is usually faxed to an (ex)employer. It does not have a CSA logo and the return envelope is marked to a confidential box number rather than the CSA. If the employer does not supply the information, the CSA telephones them to find out the reason, and if the employer appears to be deliberately unhelpful, an inspector may be appointed;
- local authorities – this method may only be used after attempts have been made to gather information from the non-resident parent;[50]
- DVLA/DVLNI – this method may only be used where all else has failed and there are special procedures for referring enquiries.[51]

Finding a confident address

An address is considered confident if the information on the DCI (see above) matches exactly the non-resident parent's full name, date of birth and that address, and there is no information which suggests that the non-resident parent is not living there.[52] If the DCI gives the non-resident parent the same address as the person with care, this is not considered confident. Where it is not possible to trace the person the CSA may suspend action for 12 months.

Information from the person with care

If the person with care has not given an address for the non-resident parent, she is contacted by telephone (or where this is not possible, by letter) and, if she does not know the address, she is asked to give any information that could help trace the non-resident parent:[53]
- middle name(s) and any other names he may be known by;
- other addresses he may have lived at;
- his place of work, and any previous employers;
- the name and address of his accountant;
- any benefit claims made; *and*

- if he has a car, the registration or make, model, colour and other details.

In addition, a face-to-face interview may be arranged. At this the person with care may be asked to confirm a potential address or provide further information to allow a trace to be made. CSA procedures do not detail the types of questions asked, but Jobcentre Plus guidance on completing an administration form suggests asking where they met, how she contacts him in an emergency or for a description of him. A parent may be asked to give a recent photograph of the non-resident parent where DNA testing may be involved. She is asked to bring any relevant documents, such as a marriage certificate or expired passport, and is warned that the CSA may contact friends and relatives with whom the non-resident parent may be living. The CSA must preserve confidentiality where this occurs and should not disclose CSA interest.

At the interview the person with care is asked other detailed questions, such as:[54]

- if she and the non-resident parent ever lived together, and if so, about the arrangements for paying the bills;
- whether they ever separated before and if so, where did the non-resident parent go then;
- whether the non-resident parent has any contact with the child(ren);
- whether he has ever lived or worked in any other areas;
- his parent's names and addresses, and whether anyone else in the family has the same name as the non-resident parent;
- whether the non-resident parent knows of the child, whether he is likely to deny paternity, and how the CSA is likely to be received by him on a visit;
- whether he has any other children and, if so, who they are; *and*
- for a description and registration number of his car.

The Jobcentre Plus may have asked many of these questions of a section 6 parent at the new claims interview (see Chapter 5). Contact by the CSA is only likely where additional trace action is required – eg, to obtain details of the non-resident parents car or where parentage is disputed.

The Jobcentre Plus will already have made a decision on whether the parent has provided all the information it is reasonable for her to supply (see Chapter 5). A referral back to the Jobcentre Plus will only be made where the parent with care refuses to take a DNA test or a DNA test/declaration of parentage (declarator of parentage in Scotland) indicates an alleged non-resident parent is not the parent and therefore details of a further non-resident parent are required.[55]

Suspending tracing action

If all the above are unsuccessful in tracing the non-resident parent, action can be suspended, usually for a year.[56] The person with care is notified of this. Where the national insurance number has been traced, the National Insurance Contributions

Chapter 6: Information
2. Contacting the non-resident parent

Office is asked to let the CSA know of any new information in the meantime. If new information is received or at the end of the year, the parent with care is still on benefit, trace action will be carried out again, beginning with a DCI check. A person with care who is not on benefit but wants to receive maintenance should check that the CSA takes this further action.

Initial contact with the non-resident parent

Once an effective application (see p51) has been made or is treated as made, the CSA must give notice of that to any person(s) with care, the non-resident parent and any person treated as a non-resident parent, other than the applicant, as soon as reasonably practical.[57] The CSA will attempt to phone a non-resident parent to notify them of the application and gather information.[58] Where it is not possible to phone and the non-resident parent is aware of the child, a child maintenance enquiry form may be issued. If the parent is unaware of the child or not named on the birth certificate, the CSA will try to arrange a face-to-face interview.

There are special rules for young non-resident parents (see p99).

During the initial phone call information will be checked to confirm the identity of the individual before proceeding.[59] The non-resident parent may be asked questions to confirm jurisdiction and whether they accept parentage.

The parent may be asked for confirmation of any court orders or information needed to make a maintenance calculation. If the parent is willing to give the information but is unable to proceed with the call they can either call the CSA back or have a child maintenance enquiry form issued.[60]

Where the non-resident parent agrees to call the CSA back when they have the information he will be allowed seven days to return the call.

When the CSA has all the information that is needed to calculate maintenance a print out will be sent to the parent as confirmation.[61] There is no need to sign and return this. Once the print out is issued the parent has seven days to correct any information, after this has elapsed a maintenance calculation may be made if there is sufficient information to do so.

The child maintenance enquiry form

The CSA intends that all or most of the information needed to work out maintenance will be provided or collected over the phone. This means a child maintenance enquiry form will only be issued when the non-resident parent requests it or there has been no co-operation by the non-resident parent. If the non-resident parent does not know he is an alleged non-resident parent, a face-to-face interview should be arranged.

In simple terms, a form cannot be issued unless:
- a 'confident' address for the non-resident parent is established (see p95);
- an alleged non-resident parent is aware that he is considered to be the father of the child;

Chapter 6: Information
2. Contacting the non-resident parent

- an alleged non-resident parent is at least 16 years old, or under 19 and still treated as a child (however, a statement of paternity is sought – see p99).

When a child maintenance enquiry form is issued the parent is allowed 14 days to return it.[62] This is not regulated by legislation, so it is up to the CSA to determine what is a reasonable length of time in the circumstances, this may mean the CSA only allow seven days or phone the parent after this period of time to check when the information will be returned.

A non-resident parent who is a prisoner may be issued a form when the prisoner identification number and prison address are known.[63] If the prisoner does not know that his is the alleged father the CSA may contact him by phone.

Even where a form is issued the non-resident may instead choose to phone in the information.

Any notice sent to a non-resident parent must tell him the effective date (see p400) of any calculation to be made, and inform him about default maintenance decisions (see p384).[64]

The child maintenance form asks for information on the following:
- personal details – name, address, other names used, phone number (work and mobile), national insurance number, date of birth, best contact times;
- do they accept paternity for all or some of the qualifying children named;
- income support/income-based jobseeker's allowance details if this is claimed by or for them;
- student details if appropriate – ie, college, course, qualification, full or part time status (evidence is requested);
- child(ren) who live with them – ie, date of birth, national insurance number (if appropriate) who gets child benefit for the child (evidence is requested);
- details of any shared care, average per week and any other special arrangements;
- employment details – title, employer (name, address and phone number), start and end dates (if appropriate);
- income details – frequency of pay, gross pay, bonus, expenses (pay slips are requested);
- self-assessment form or tax calculation notice if the parent is self employed;
- tax credits in payment;
- other income – eg, pension;
- other payments made to a personal or private pension;
- collection details – when they want collection, bank details such as account number and sort code. Direct debit is the preferred method but standing order, deductions from wages, transcash or bank giro credit are also available;
- representative details, name address, phone number (work and mobile) and best contact times (signed authorisation is needed in certain circumstances);
- further information;
- declaration; *and*

- parents are informed that failure to provide the information requested or knowingly providing false information is a criminal offence (see p93).

Information given can be amended at any time before a calculation is made, but not about changes after the effective date.[65] For changes after the effective date, supersession should be sought.

If the form is returned fully completed and no indication is made that paternity is denied, the CSA assumes that the alleged non-resident parent accepts paternity. A commissioner has decided that where a parent disputes that he is non-resident and maintains that he has day-to-day care of the child (see p28), this is not a proper reason for refusing to return the form (this decision was made in reference to the 'old rules' maintenance enquiry form).[66]

Young non-resident parents

A face-to-face interview must always be arranged with a young non-resident parent – ie, one under 16 years of age or between 16 and 19 but still treated as a child.[67] They will be asked to confirm parentage but no calculation can be made until they cease being treated as a child. An adult must be present at the interview.

Where the non-resident parent is between 16 and 19 and no child benefit is being paid for them, a series of questions will be asked to establish if they are a child.[68] They can be classed as a child if they are:
- in full time non-advanced education, ie child benefit is still payable for them;
- registered for work or youth training with an education authority, DoFEE, MOD or similar Euopean body; *or*
- working temporarily for 24 hours or more per week due to end before the terminal date.

The young person is no longer treated as a child, if they are under 18 and:
- in employment after the terminal date;
- in paid work-based training or Skillseekers; *or*
- on IS or Income-based JSA.

3. Parentage investigations

Where parentage is denied, a maintenance application cannot be decided unless the CSA can assume parentage (see p23). In the vast majority of cases, it is a non-resident father disputing paternity. Paternity is also investigated where there is some doubt about it (eg, more than one possible father is named). However, in section 6 cases, the parent with care may already have been asked to identify the most likely father (see Chapter 5).

Paternity investigations can take place pre- or post-calculation. For example, an alleged non-resident parent may deny paternity on the initial phone contact

Chapter 6: Information
3. Parentage investigations

or on a child maintenance enquiry form (see p97). The dispute can be about one or all of the qualifying children. The CSA can proceed with the calculation, or collection in post-calculation cases, for those children for whom paternity is accepted or can be assumed while investigations are taking place for others.

In pre-calculation cases if a presumption of parentage cannot be made the CSA cannot make a calculation until paternity has been resolved. For details of when paternity may be assumed see p23. The CSA will carry out investigations to determine if paternity may be assumed or established. This may involve interviewing both the non-resident parent and person with care; this may also include interviewing the other parent. The CSA may seek a DNA test or court action to establish paternity (though this is unlikely given the presumptions and consequences of failure to take DNA tests). Court action may also be pursued by the person with care or alleged non-resident parent at any time.

In post-calculation cases the non-resident parent may dispute paternity through seeking a revision. If the CSA has been able to assume paternity (see p23), they should first consider whether the non-resident parent:[69]

- is tying to avoid paying maintenance – eg, where a default maintenance decision has been made; *or*
- has discovered information to make him doubt paternity – eg, the parent with care tells him he is not the father.

Where the presumption of parentage was based on:[70]
- a positive DNA test result;
- adoption;
- fertility treatment;
- a declaration/declarator of parentage that is still in force and the child has not been adopted;
- a declaration under section 27 of the 1991 Child Support Act;
- treating him as the father due to section 28 of the Human Fertilisation and Embryology Act 1990,

the decision is not revised and the non-resident parent is advised that they may apply to the courts for a declaration/declarator of parentage.[71] A decision to refuse to revise may be appealed, however paternity may only be established by the court (see p108).

In all other cases the non-resident parent will be asked to provide evidence.[72] Documentary evidence is preferred. Where the evidence is a previous negative DNA test or declaration/declarator of parentage this will be sufficient proof. The calculation will be cancelled and any payments made refunded.[73] The person with care may be re-interviewed to identify another alleged non-resident parent, in section 6 cases this will be carried out by the Jobcentre Plus (see Chapter 5).

It is not sufficient in post-calculation cases to simply deny paternity, evidence must be given to raise doubt – eg, the parent with care was having another relationship when the child was conceived.[74] Where a doubt is raised the parent with care will then be contacted by phone or in a face-to-face interview for her comments on the non-resident parents evidence. Where the parent with care:
- accepts that there may be doubt about paternity, a DNA test may be offered;
- disputes the non-resident parents evidence, the decision will not be revised. The non-resident parent will be advised to obtain a DNA test or declaration/declarator of non-parentage; the CSA will not offer a DNA test in this case.[75] They will also be informed of their right to appeal to a court.

In cases where doubt is raised the collection of child maintenance will be suspended during the parentage investigation.[76]

Interviews where parentage is disputed

Interviews can be carried out by phone or face-to-face. Where paternity is denied after initial contact or the issue of a child maintenance enquiry form, the parent with care may be interviewed first in order to establish the case to be put to the alleged non-resident parent: in other cases sufficient information may already be available to contact the non-resident parent first. However, both parties are interviewed before being offered DNA tests (see p108) and, even if the parent with care has already been interviewed or paternity assumed she may be re-interviewed to see how she responds to the alleged non-resident parent's version of events.[77] If the parent with care has already filled in a paternity statement she will only be re-interviewed if the alleged non-resident parent introduces new evidence.

In the case of a face-to-face interview if the interviewee does not want to come to the LSB (or another local Jobcentre Plus office if that is closer), s/he can be interviewed at home or at a friend's or relative's house.

If the parent with care or alleged non-resident parent is under 16 or under 19 and treated as a child, their parent or guardian must consent to the case progressing.[78] The young person must have a face-to-face interview at home in the presence of a parent or guardian.[79] A calculation is not made, but a paternity statement is required for future use – ie, action is suspended until the young person ceases to be a child and then a calculation may be made.[80]

If an alleged non-resident parent is of no fixed abode and is claiming incapacity benefit, the Jobcentre Plus is asked to assist in training.[81] In the past it was suggested that they make an appointment for an interview when he next collects his benefit; however, this is not made clear in current guidance.

It is not compulsory to attend any interview, but see p90 for who can be required to provide what information. See p16 for interview facilities, and p17 for travel expenses for attending an office interview.

Chapter 6: Information
3. Parentage investigations

Interview with an alleged non-resident parent

When the non-resident parent is unaware of the qualifying child a face-to-face interview may be arranged to notify them of the application (see p101). Staff were reminded in previous guidance that the allegation of paternity may come as a shock and that if the alleged non-resident parent's reaction suggests that he needs time to consider what he has been told, the interview should be suspended and continued about a week later. However, current guidance does not reflect this so an alleged non-resident parent may wish to ask for time to consider things.

When paternity is denied the alleged non-resident parent will be asked if they have documentary or verbal evidence that they are not the parent.[82] The alleged non-resident parent's evidence is recorded word for word on a paternity statement.[83] There are specific questions to ask in cases where fertility treatment was used.[84] The alleged non-resident parent may ask for further time to obtain evidence, seven days are usually allowed to provide this further evidence.

Where documentary evidence cannot be supplied the person with care may be interviewed to gather their evidence. Where no evidence can be provided to assume paternity the case may progress to DNA testing.

CSA guidance suggests that interviewing officers ask non-resident parents for the following details:[85]

- whether or not the alleged non-resident parent knew the mother at the time of conception;
- whether he had sex with the mother and if so over what period of time;
- whether contraceptives were used;
- how long the relationship lasted and whether he lived with the woman concerned as husband and wife;
- whether or not he has had any contact with the child(ren);
- his reasons for thinking that he is not the father; *and*
- any other information which might support his view.

These questions are in guidance only. The non-resident parent need only answer these questions where he denies paternity and the information is needed to decide if he is the father.

The alleged non-resident parent is sent information about disputing parentage and about the reduced-cost DNA test (see p105) before the interview. At the interview he may be asked if he would be prepared to take it and, if so, pay for it.[86]

If the alleged non-resident parent accepts paternity, a child maintenance form is completed at the interview or, if there is not enough time, a paternity agreement form. This information may be input onto the computer system directly.[87]

Interviewing officers take notes and after the interview (including a telephone interview), two reports are completed.[88] One is a 'factual' report and the other is an 'opinion' report. Interviewing officers are instructed not to put these titles on the reports.[89] The factual report is completed and signed by the interviewing officer as a statement of what was said in a form which could be used in court as evidence.[90] If the non-resident parent wishes to make a statement, this is taken down verbatim by the interviewing officer and added to the factual report.[91] The opinion report contains the interviewing officer's impressions, recommendations and views of the alleged non-resident parent.[92]

If the non-resident parent does not attend an interview, the interviewing officer attempts to arrange another, and if he does not attend the second one, the officer arranges a home visit. The CSA may phone or write to the parent with care for a full statement for use in court proceedings.[93] In some cases an unannounced visit will be made to the alleged non-resident parent, this will be decided by the face-to-face manager at the LSB.[94]

Interview with a parent with care

Where someone has been named as the parent of a qualifying child and denies it, the CSA contacts the parent with care to tell her of this and explain the procedures which follow.[95]

The parent with care is asked if she has documentary evidence so that the CSA could assume parentage – eg, birth certificate, marriage certificate, DNA test, court declaration/declarator of parentage.[96] The parent may ask for more time to provide evidence, in which case seven days are usually allowed for her to provide the evidence.

If no evidence can be provided to assume paternity the parent with care is asked if she is willing to take a DNA test (see p105).

Initially, she is questioned to get enough detail about her relationship with the alleged non-resident parent at the time of conception to establish whether he could be the father.[97] This is often done over the telephone. However, the parent may prefer to have a face-to-face interview.[98]

The CSA may ask for the following details:[99]
- the place the child was born and whether the pregnancy was full term;
- was the alleged non-resident parent present at the birth;
- whether the man is named as the child's father on the birth certificate and if so, whether and why paternity is now being denied;
- when and where she first met the father and in what circumstances;
- when and where sex first took place, how often, and over what period;
- whether contraceptives were used by either of them at or about the probable time of conception;
- her address at the time the child could have been conceived;
- the date of her last period before the date of conception;
- when she first discovered that she was pregnant and whether she told the man about it and if so, when and where, and what words the man used in reply and whether there were any witnesses;
- why she did not tell him, if she did not, and whether anyone else did – if so, what was his reaction and can she provide the name and address of this person;

Chapter 6: Information
3. Parentage investigations

- whether she had sexual intercourse with anyone other than the father in the three months before or after the date of conception, what the dates were and whether contraception was used;
- whether she and the alleged non-resident parent ever lived together and, if so, when and at what address and why the relationship broke up;
- whether she considered them to be a couple at the time the child was conceived;
- if she was married at the time the child was conceived, the date of the marriage, whether she was separated from her husband and the date of separation, or whether she was living with another man;
- if she was living with her husband or he visited her during the relevant period, by reference to some event, the dates when she last had sex with him, and when she last met him before the child was born;
- has the alleged non-resident parent ever acknowledged the child;
- has he ever paid any maintenance;
- is there, or has there ever been, any contact with his family;
- whether she has any letters, postcards, birthday cards, etc, from him and whether she can identify his handwriting;
- if the alleged non-resident parent has made certain allegations, whether she can refute them – eg, if he has named another possible father, whether she can give details of any relationship;
- whether there is anyone else who can say that she was associating with the father at a time when the child could have been conceived, when she was obviously pregnant, or after the child was born;
- whether anyone else could say that she was regularly meeting the father on a social basis;
- whether anyone else was present when the man admitted responsibility for her pregnancy or paternity of the child, or behaved as if he were responsible;
- whether she has any photographs of him; *and*
- whether she is willing to give evidence in court.

Where a person considers the question(s) inappropriate, she should ask the interviewer the point of the questions. If the interviewer insists, the person with care could ask to end the interview so that she can consider whether to give the information requested. She can ask the interviewer to write down the questions and the reason for them. If at the interview, or later, she refuses to answer any of the questions, she should indicate that she has given all the information that is necessary to trace and identify the father. See p81 for refusal to give information.

If the parent with care provides any other relevant information this is recorded word for word on the parentage statement.[100] A paternity statement will be drafted at the face-to-face interview where the parent refuses to take a DNA test, one will also be prepared and sent to the parent where this occurs on a phone interview. The parent can refuse to sign this and have her reasons recorded. The parent may ask for a copy of the parentage statement or reasons for failing to sign the statement. This statement is added to the report of the interview and can be used in court proceedings (see p108).

Interviewing a person with care who is not the mother

Where both parents are non-resident and an alleged non-resident parent continues to deny paternity after an interview, the person with care may be interviewed.[101] The questions depend on the person with care's relationship with the alleged parents – eg, a mother or sister is likely to know the length of the relationship between the parents. She is asked for the addresses of both parents, and any letters or cards from them. She is also asked why she is looking after the child(ren), whether there is any documentation regarding the care arrangements and whether she gives her consent for the child(ren) in her care to undergo a DNA test (see below) if she has parental responsibility. A statement is prepared if the case is to go to court.[102]

DNA testing

DNA testing involves taking a blood sample from the parent with care, alleged non-resident parent and qualifying child. The test establishes the genetic fingerprint of the individual and is virtually conclusive.

DNA testing is used in cases where parentage cannot be presumed and the parties involved give consent. In cases where the CSA has applied to court for a declaration/declarator of parentage the court may order DNA testing.

The CSA has special arrangements with a private testing agency called LGC Ltd, where reduced testing rates may apply. There are special rules that apply where the alleged non-resident parent wishes to arrange his own test.

Consent

Where there is a dispute about parentage, both the parent with care and the alleged non-resident parent are asked to agree to a DNA test. Written consent must be obtained before a test can be made.[103] In the case of the parent with care this is a signed declaration to allow disclosure of her name and address to the DNA testing company. In the case of the alleged non-resident parent consent is recorded on the interview report. Where the qualifying child is under 16 the parent or guardian must give consent.

Refusal to take the test will have the following consequences:
- section 6 parent with care refuses to take the test herself – a reduced benefit decision may be made (see p75);[104]
- section 6 parent with care refuses consent for the qualifying child to take the test – the CSA may take court action to get a declaration/declarator of parentage. However, the DWP child support policy department indicate that this may only be considered in 'old rules' cases. It also states that a reduced benefit decision should not be made;[105]

Chapter 6: Information
3. Parentage investigations

- alleged non-resident parent – may be assumed to be the parent (see p23);[106]
- non-resident parent already assumed to be the parent – CSA refuses to revise the calculation;[107]
- section 4 parent applicant refusing consent for themselves and/or a qualifying child – the case may be closed;[108]
- section 7 applicant whose parent or guardian refuses consent – there is no procedural guidance, however DWP child support policy department indicates that action may be taken to get a declaration/declarator of parentage.

The reason for any refusal must be explored.[109] The DNA test usually involves giving a small blood sample; some individuals may object to this on religious or medical grounds – eg, recent cancer treatment, blood transfusion or haemophilia. A mouth swab can be offered as an alternative to the blood test. In this case all the other parties will be tested in the same way.

Where the alleged non-resident parent agrees to the test but fails to attend the appointment, parentage will be assumed unless there are good reasons – eg, he was in hospital, did not receive test notification or was ill. Where the person with care fails to attend a reduced benefit decision may be made or the case may be closed.

Paying for the DNA test

The CSA offers discounted tests to alleged non-resident parents, these are known as voluntary cases.[110] The cost varies depending on the number of people tested, for 2004/05 the fee is £238.69 for testing three people in voluntary cases. The alleged non-resident parent must agree to the results being passed to the CSA. Alleged non-resident parents pay the discounted fee direct to LGC Ltd (the independent testing agency). This service may be offered to non-resident parents in section 4 and 7 applications (see p44).[111]

In cases where the court directs the DNA test to be taken, the non-discounted fee is charged. Rates vary according to the number of people tested; in 2004/05 the non-discounted cost of a test for three people is £286.26.

Where the alleged non-resident parent is found not to be the parent, a full refund of the cost of the test is made, as long as the parent with care confirms that the photograph of the person who attended for the test is the person she named as the father.[112]

If the alleged non-resident parent says he cannot afford to pay for the test in advance, the CSA may pay for the test initially if the alleged non-resident parent agrees to accept the results and to recoup the fee should it show that he is the father.[113] Where the alleged non-resident parent still refuses to take the DNA test parentage may be assumed (see p23).

The CSA can recover the costs of the test from the alleged non-resident parent where the test does not exclude him from being the parent and:[114]

- he does not now deny that he is the parent; or

- a court has now made a declaration that he is a parent (in Scotland, a declarator of parentage).

There are no refunds of travelling expenses for attending a DNA test.[115]

Alleged non-resident parent arranges private testing

An alleged non-resident parent may arrange the test himself either through LGC Ltd or another agency, in the meantime the CSA may still assume parentage if the CSA test has been refused.[116] In this case there would be no discount or CSA non-discounted rate offered. The full fee is approximately £450 and it may not be refunded if the test proves negative.

The test must be carried out by an approved agency and proper security measures must be in place, otherwise even where the test is negative the CSA and court may not accept the result.

Tests must involve the mother; a test with only the alleged non-resident parent and the qualifying child will not be accepted. The CSA will not provide the address of the parent with care to the alleged non-resident parent or the independent testing company. If the parent with care does not consent to such a private test no action can be taken against her.

DNA test results

The test results take about 12 weeks, but most of this time is used for arranging for the samples to be taken. The results are normally sent to the parent with care, the alleged non-resident parent and the CSA.[117]

Where the alleged non-resident parent is shown to be the parent, the CSA will follow up the notification by phone call. During this, information may be gathered to make the calculation or a child maintenance enquiry form may be issued.[118] (If a form has been issued earlier, the date of liability for child maintenance relates to that first contact – see p400.) If the alleged non-resident parent still does not accept paternity, he will have to take court proceedings to obtain a declaration/declarator of non-parentage. The CSA may make a calculation or refuse to revise because a positive DNA test is grounds to assume parentage.

Where the DNA tests confirm that the alleged non-resident parent is not the father, the parent with care is re-interviewed to confirm that the person tested was the non-resident parent.[119] Where this is not the case further action may be taken – eg, regarding fraud if he sent some one else to be tested or to pursue further tracing where the wrong person has been traced. Where the identity is confirmed any calculation is cancelled and any payments made are refunded, or where no calculation has been made the case closes. The parent with care may be re-interviewed about any other possible non-resident parent.[120] If the parent with care is a section 6 parent, the Jobcentre Plus will do this.

Chapter 6: Information
3. Parentage investigations

Preparation for court proceedings

When all possible action and investigation have been completed, a CSA supervisor decides whether to apply to court for a declaration of parentage (in Scotland, declarator of parentage), or to suspend the case for 12 months (see p110).[121] CSA guidance indicates that court action should be rare given the increased grounds on which to assume parentage. Examples of situations where court action may be possible include:[122]

- a section 6 parent with care refuses consent for a qualifying child to take a DNA test;
- a DNA test is inconclusive;
- cases involving fertility treatment where the alleged non-resident parent denies he gave consent to the treatment;
- in post-calculation cases where the parent with care disputes the non-resident parent's non-conclusive evidence – in this instance the non-resident parent must raise the action (the CSA may not be involved in this action but may be informed of the outcome).

Where the CSA is going to take court action a file is compiled detailing gestation periods, interviews, statements, phone calls, correspondence, investigations and other documentary evidence including exhibits such as a birthday card from the alleged non-resident parent to the child.[123]

If the CSA decides not to take court action, the person with care may initiate court action. The parent with care or non-resident may raise court proceedings at any time.

If a case is to go to court, a proceedings file is prepared by the CSA.[124] A copy of the child's full birth certificate is obtained from the Registrar if the parent with care cannot supply one.[125] Where the parent with care has mentioned potential witnesses (see p105) – eg, to confirm that she and the alleged non-resident parent were in a relationship at the time of the conception – a record is made of the witnesses' names and addresses.[126] In Scotland, two written statements have to be obtained at this point. Two witnesses are needed to attest to the sexual nature of the relationship otherwise the case cannot proceed to court.[127] In Scotland, such files are referred to the solicitors' office at the Scottish Office (Office of the Solicitors to the Advocate General for Scotland), and, in England and Wales, to the solicitors' branch of the DWP (Sol B2).[128] In England and Wales, unless the solicitor advises that the case should not go ahead, the application proceeds for a declaration of parentage that may be heard under lay representation. This means that a local CSA officer, known as the court presenting officer, presents the case to court.[129] Where the case is complex or contentious a solicitor will be present. In Scotland, the solicitor presents the case.[130]

The hearings

The CSA *or* the person with care can apply to court for a declaration/declarator of parentage. However, if the CSA is willing to do so, the person with care should normally not also apply, because she would probably have to pay her own legal costs (and those of the alleged non-resident parent) if she loses (see p110). If the CSA suspends the case (see p108), but the person with care wants to go to court herself, she should consider taking legal advice.

The hearing normally takes place in the alleged non-resident parent's area, unless the alleged non-resident parent knows the parent with care's address or both parties and the court agree to it being held in the person with care's area.[131]

The first court hearing is known as a directions hearing; this is an informal hearing where the parties produce the documentary evidence and the clerk to the court (a similar preliminary hearing is heard by the sheriff in Scotland) arranges procedure, including directions for DNA tests.[132] There is no legal obligation for the alleged non-resident parent and parent with care to attend. However, in England and Wales, if the alleged non-resident parent does not attend, the court may adjourn the hearing and ask the CSA (or, if it is her application, the parent with care) to serve notice of the hearing on him in person.

Only the courts have the power to order blood tests – including DNA tests (see p105) – in any civil proceedings in which paternity is an issue.[133] If convinced that blood testing would be against the child's interests, the court should not order it.[134] A court can direct that blood tests be used to ascertain whether or not a party is excluded from being a parent of the child, but cannot force anyone to give a blood sample, though it can overrule a child's lack of consent if it believes it is in the child's interests.[135] However, the court may draw its own adverse inferences if s/he fails to comply, depending on all the circumstances of the case.[136] For example, the fact that s/he may have taken an earlier, if inconclusive, blood test does not prevent the courts from drawing an adverse inference now that DNA testing is available.[137] Courts can only order DNA or blood testing where a party applies for it and agrees to pay. However, if that party wins the case, the court will usually order the losing party to pay costs, which can include the costs of any test. In Scotland, if an alleged non-resident parent takes action for a declaration of non-parentage or illegitimacy and the CSA does not defend the action; no expenses can be awarded against the CSA.[138]

In England and Wales, if DNA tests have been directed, a second informal hearing is arranged with the clerk once the result is obtained: if it is negative, the CSA withdraws the case.[139] If the result is positive, and the alleged non-resident parent admits he is the father, a full hearing before the magistrates takes place, if possible, on the same day. In other cases, notice of a full hearing at a magistrates'/sheriffs' court is sent to all parties. The magistrate (or sheriff in Scotland) then considers whether to make a declaration/declarator of parentage on the available evidence.

Chapter 6: Information
3. Parentage investigations

Outcome of the court proceedings

When a declaration/declarator of parentage is issued, the CSA treats these cases as priority and where no calculation has been made contacts the non-resident parent by phone to gather the information needed to make a calculation.[140] If the court finds that the person is not the parent, the parent with care is approached to establish if there a different alleged non-resident parent may be named.[141] In the case of a section 6 parent this will be carried out by the Jobcentre Plus and there may be further consideration of a reduced benefit decision (see p75). In other cases unless the parent can name an alternate alleged non-resident parent the case may be closed.

The court can order any party to pay some or all of the legal costs of another party. Usually, the losing party is ordered to pay the other parties' costs. However, an order for costs cannot normally be made against a party who is legally aided. In addition to the costs of any test, the CSA usually asks the court to order the losing party to pay towards its own presentation costs – eg, solicitors fees and witnesses costs.[142]

Suspending a case

The first decision to suspend a case is made by a CSA decision maker (see p108). A decision may be made to suspend the debt, for up to 12 months, where paternity is being disputed after a calculation (old rules assessment) has been made.[143] Following investigation a CSA decision maker considers whether to authorise DNA tests, court action, a further suspension or case closure. If new information is received at any time, the case is reconsidered. Therefore, persons with care who are anxious to have the case resolved should send any further evidence to the CSA. A person with care who wishes action to continue could complain (see p18).

A person with care may also initiate court proceedings herself. The CSA should explain to the person what action is required and tell her about the costs involved.[144]

4. Further investigations

Apart from the enquiries dealt with above, the CSA may make further enquiries when considering an application, revision or supersession. In practice, the CSA normally makes no further investigation where:
- parentage is accepted; *and*
- information is provided to make a calculation – ie, via phone or relevant form; *and*
- any documents requested are provided – eg, copy of maintenance agreement, payslips, tax calculation notice.

Even where one parent challenges the details provided by the other, the CSA may be reluctant to make any further enquiries unless the parent can provide evidence to trigger a revision/supersession. Enquiries are normally made by telephone, if possible.

The need for evidence

Corroboration of evidence – other evidence to support what the CSA already has – is not requested unless the evidence the CSA has is self-contradictory, improbable, or contradicted by other evidence.[145] For example, where a self-employed parent says s/he has not worked for six months, that is normally accepted without any written evidence.

Evidence includes documentary, written and oral information.[146] CSA staff are advised to weigh carefully any direct, indirect or hearsay evidence. CSA guidance says that hearsay evidence (ie, evidence from one person of what another person has told her/him, or of what s/he has read) is of limited value – eg, a report from a parent with care that a non-resident parent's earnings have increased by £20 a week may be sufficient evidence to consider supersession, but insufficient to base a new calculation on.[147]

Verifying information

Verification of housing costs ('old rules') and earnings is routinely sought by the CSA.[148] However, if every effort to obtain verification of the earnings has failed, the amounts provided are accepted as long as they are reasonable. Verification of other benefits, income and costs (needed to make an 'old rules' assessment) is only sought where the amounts appear to be disproportionate or there is another reason to doubt them.

CSA staff are advised that where verification is required, it should be written evidence corroborating information already held.[149] CSA staff can request evidence in the form of formal documents and signed statements but wherever possible collect information by phone and then seek written confirmation if necessary.[150]

Verification of earnings from a non-resident parent's employer is only requested if the employee cannot provide it (see p90).[151] Where verification details remain outstanding, CSA staff are advised to consider making a default maintenance decision or a maintenance calculation using the available evidence.[152] A parent and any employer who fails to provide information when requested may also be liable for criminal sanctions (see p93).

Verification of self-employed earnings is dealt with at the CSAC by a special section, and evidence of income is requested.[153] If not supplied, attempts will be made to obtain the information through phone calls, the accountant, companies or partnerships the parent works with or for, face-to-face interview, inspector's visit or a request to the Inland Revenue for self-assessment details where all other means to obtain the information have failed.[154] Criminal sanctions may apply

Chapter 6: Information
4. Further investigations

where those required to provide information have failed to do so – eg, the parent's accountant (see p91).

Where the CSA does not investigate

In some cases, the CSA fails to investigate to the satisfaction of one party. Except where one parent believes that the other should not be entitled to income support (IS) (see p415), this situation does not usually arise until the calculation is made because the parent with care is only then notified of the non-resident parent's income (see p386). If at any stage a person believes that the CSA ought to make more enquiries, the CSA should be asked to do so. The most effective way is to phone the CSA explaining all the information the person has, asking what enquiries have already been made and suggesting further enquiries. Reference should be made to the CSA's power to require information (see p87) and use an inspector to conduct investigations (see below). Where the CSA refuses to say what steps have been taken or to make further enquiries, judicial review may be possible (see p415). An appeal tribunal can make enquiries as soon as an appeal is made (see p440). The tribunal has more powers than the CSA and it may be easier to persuade it to use them.

A person who is dissatisfied with CSA enquiries can also make their own enquiries and pass the information to the CSA – eg, a person with care applying for a court order for spousal maintenance (see p37) may obtain information about the non-resident parent's income.

The inspectors

The Secretary of State can empower the CSA to appoint inspectors to obtain information required under the 1991 Act.[155] The inspectors are permanently appointed and are no longer tied to investigations on a specific case.[156] In the past, inspectors were appointed only rarely.[157] The inspector must have a certificate of appointment,[158] which must be produced when entering premises.[159]

Certificates will be issued by the Chief Executive and the inspector will be an existing CSA employee based at an LSB. The LSB manager would then be required to maintain appropriate records – eg, the address/title of the places to be visited, and details of the person(s) from whom the CSA wants information.[160]

If an office in Great Britain needs to appoint an inspector in Northern Ireland, or the other way around, an inspector can be appointed there.[161]

Powers of inspectors

Inspectors have the power to enter premises (except those used only as a home)[162] to make enquiries and to inspect documents.[163] Premises can include vehicles, aircraft, moveable structures and offshore installations.[164] The power to enter premises does not include any power to enter by force. Premises include ones where:[165]

- the non-resident parent is or has been employed;
- the non-resident parent carries out or has carried out a trade;
- there is information held by someone whom the inspector has reasonable grounds for suspecting has information about the non-resident parent acquired in the course of their own trade, profession, vocation or business.

An inspector can question any person aged 18 or over found on the premises s/he has entered[166] and request all such information and documents s/he might reasonably require from:[167]
- an occupier of the premises;
- an employer or employee working there;
- anyone else whose work or business is based at those premises;
- an employee or agent of any of the above.

An inspector can enter Crown premises in order to obtain information as long as the Queen is not in residence. Crown employees or anyone carrying out Crown functions on the premises can be questioned and asked for information in the same way as anyone else.[168]

The powers of the inspectors are set out in the 1991 Act, and are not limited by the regulations on information. However, no person is required to give any evidence or answer any question that might incriminate her/him or their spouse.[169] Deliberately delaying or obstructing an inspector carrying out her/his duties is an offence. Failing or refusing to answer a question or to provide evidence requested is an offence, unless there is a good reason for not doing so.[170] The maximum fine for such an offence is £1,000.[171]

A solicitor is entitled to claim privilege as regards information about a client's confidential affairs and can refuse to give information. Also, the CSA has given assurances that the powers of inspectors will not be used in relation to other representatives, except where information is required from an employer about an employee. CSA guidance used to suggest that inspectors would only be used when employers or the self-employed refuse to supply information, or when calculations are being enforced, however current guidance is less specific. Staff should consider using an inspector when there are problems obtaining information.[172]

There are clear directions regarding further investigations where there are suspicions of fraud or misrepresentation.[173]

5. Duty to disclose changes

There is no general duty to volunteer information about any changes of circumstance to the CSA. However, there are some changes which must be notified. These only apply to a person with care and only when a calculation has been made, including a nil rate. No other person has a duty to disclose any change of circumstance.

A person with care has a duty to tell the CSA if she believes that a calculation has ceased to have effect because:[174]
- the person with care, non-resident parent or qualifying child has died;
- the person with care, non-resident parent or qualifying child is no longer within CSA jurisdiction – ie, habitually resident in the UK or working for a relevant employer and treated as habitually resident (see p33);
- the non-resident parent is no longer a non-resident parent of the child or, if there is more than one, all the children named in the calculation – eg, because the child is adopted;
- a child no longer counts as a child, or as a qualifying child (see p26); or
- she has stopped being a person with care in relation to the child or, if there is more than one, all the children named in the calculation.

The person with care is required to give the reasons for her belief in writing. She may be required to give further information for a decision to be made.

The person with care is not required to inform the CSA until the change has taken place. There is *no* duty to disclose information to the CSA *except* in the circumstances described above and where the CSA has the right to request the information – eg, a non-resident parent does not have to disclose a change of income. This is different from the position for social security claims, where there is a continuing duty to disclose any relevant change.

For the effect of not disclosing information, see p93.

6. **Disclosure of information by the CSA**

In the course of their investigations, CSA staff collect a lot of information and evidence about people affected by maintenance applications. Some forms of disclosure are part of the CSA's duties, such as giving information to courts, tribunals, the DWP or local authorities. Each party to a maintenance calculation must be given details of how the calculation has been worked out (see p386). The CSA may disclose information given to it by one party to a calculation to another party to explain:[175]
- why an application for child maintenance or for revision or supersession has been rejected; or
- why an application cannot proceed or why a calculation will not be made; or
- why a calculation is cancelled or ceases to have effect; or
- how a calculation has been worked out; or
- why a decision has been made not to arrange for, or to stop, collection of child maintenance; or
- why a particular method of enforcement has been used; or

- why a decision has been made not to use or to stop using a deduction from earnings order (see p477) or a liability order (see p483).

The parties to an assessment are the person with care, the non-resident parent and a child applicant in Scotland. Where one of those people has died, a person appointed to represent that person or a personal representative handling a revision/supersession or appeal for one of those people is also a party.[176] Any request for the above information must be made in writing to the CSA, giving reasons, but the CSA can provide the information without a request.[177]

The CSA must not disclose a person's address or other information which could reasonably be expected to lead to that person being located. This disclosure can only be made when the person concerned has given written permission to that effect to the CSA. (This does not apply where a case is appealed – see p439.) Also, the CSA must not disclose information which could reasonably be expected to lead to the identification of any person, other than a person with care, non-resident parent, person treated as non-resident or qualifying child.[178]

The CSA can disclose any information it has to an appeal tribunal or a court, where that disclosure is for proceedings under the child support or benefits legislation and the information is that which is required under the regulations.[179] In practice, in a child support appeal, CSA papers are included in the CSA submission sent to each party (see p439). The CSA can also disclose information to a court which has made, varied or revived a maintenance order or agreement where that information is required in relation to those proceedings or other matters arising from them.[180] The CSA can also disclose information it has to local authorities for their use in administering housing benefit or council tax benefit.[181] However, this excludes information obtained form the Inland Revenue in relation to tracing and the earnings/self-assessment details of the self-employed. Otherwise, information cannot be given to third parties without written permission of the person to whom it relates (see p116) – see above for dealings with representatives. Any unauthorised disclosure of information is a criminal offence (see p116).

Anyone wishing to see a copy of the information on her/him held on the CSA's computers records can apply in writing to the CSA. Under the Data Protection Act 1984 this information must be supplied within 40 days. If anyone has concerns about the collection, retention, accuracy or use of this information, the Data Protection Registrar can be contacted.

Disclosure within the CSA

There is no specified general power to allow all information to be transferred within the CSA. However, CSA guidance indicates information may be disclosed to other staff – eg, re-suspensions, revisions, multiple or linked applications.[182] Disclosure outside this (eg, to an officer 'trawling' through files looking for references to a particular person) would be unlawful.

Chapter 6: Information
6. Disclosure of information by the CSA

Disclosure to other government departments

The CSA can disclose information to government departments dealing with benefits, including the DWP agencies.[183] This includes information obtained by using CSA powers or disclosed to the CSA voluntarily. This can be used to inform the Jobcentre Plus of any change in child maintenance, but also applies to other details.

As the DWP has close links with the Home Office, disclosure may create problems for people from abroad, in particular possible illegal entrants and those subject to the public funds requirement. If there are any doubts about whether information ought to be disclosed to the CSA, you should get advice first from a law centre or independent advice centre dealing with immigration problems (see Appendix 5). You cannot be prosecuted for refusing to give information unless it was requested by the CSA or an inspector (see p112).

CSA staff can exchange information with their counterparts in Northern Ireland and *vice versa*. Once disclosed, the information is subject to local rules about unauthorised disclosure.[184]

Unauthorised disclosure

Unauthorised disclosure of information is a criminal offence. This offence applies to anyone who is or has been a child support officer (see p11), a CSA employee, a civil servant carrying out a function under the Child Support Acts (eg, a Jobcentre Plus officer helping the CSA make enquiries), staff of appeal tribunals, various ombudsmen and their staff, staff at the National Audit Office, and anyone who, whether or not a civil servant, is providing services to the DWP – eg, under contracted out work.[185] It does not apply to members of appeal tribunals or to child support commissioners.

It is not an offence to disclose information where:[186]
- the CSA can do so under the regulations for disclosure;
- the CSA has already done so under those regulations;
- it is in the form of a summary or statistics and it cannot be related to any particular person; *or*
- the person to whom the information relates gives consent, or if that person's affairs are being dealt with under a power of attorney, by a receiver under the Mental Health Act, a mental health appointee or a Scottish mental health custodian, and the attorney, receiver, custodian or appointee gives consent.

A person who has broken these rules would have a defence if s/he could prove that s/he believed s/he was making the disclosure under these rules, or believed that disclosure under these rules had already been made, and had no reason to think otherwise.[187]

On conviction, the maximum prison sentence is six months and the maximum fine is £5,000. On conviction on indictment, the maximum prison sentence is two years.[188] No prosecutions have been brought.

Disclosure of information about spent convictions, other than as part of an official duty, is also a criminal offence.[189]

7. Existing 'old rules' cases

When determining a maintenance assessment, revising or superseding an assessment decision or making a departure direction the law governing what information may be required is applied as if the changes introduced at 3 March 2003 do not apply to these cases.[190] This sounds convoluted but because more information is required to work out assessments under the 'old rules' formula or a departure all the old information gathering powers remain. This means that failure to supply such information in 'old rules' cases is also considered a criminal offence.

The majority of provisions already covered in this chapter apply equally to 'old rules' cases in relation to maintenance assessments. In this section we will outline the main differences to bear in mind when dealing with 'old rules' cases.

Information-seeking powers

In addition to the provisions covered in this chapter information can also be required about:[191]
- benefits and other income of the non-resident parent;
- the parent with care's income, including earnings, benefits and other income;
- housing cost of the parent with care and non-resident parent;
- persons living with the parent with care;
- the current or most recent employer of the parent with care;
- income of a qualifying child;
- income of anyone else living in the same household as the parent with care and non-resident parent;
- the employment, whether employed or self-employed, of anyone (other than a child) living in the same household with the parent with care or non-resident parent;
- benefits related to disability that the parent with care, non-resident parent or anyone living in the same household as them is entitled to or would be if certain conditions were satisfied;
- details and statements of any bank, building society account or similar account of the parent with care;
- information relating to any qualifying transfer.

Chapter 6: Information
7. Existing 'old rules' cases

This means that the parent with care's employer may also be required to provide information to allow maintenance to be assessed.[192]

Where the non-resident parent does not supply requested information, an interim maintenance assessment may be made (not a default maintenance decision). This is alongside any penalties for failure to provide requested information.

A section 6 parent who fails to provide information may have a reduced benefit decision made (see p75).

Contact with the non-resident parent

In 'old rules' cases a maintenance enquiry form was issued to non-resident parents to gather all the information need to make the assessment. The date of issue, unless the non-resident parent qualifies for the eight-week deferral, set the effective date of the assessment (see p400). A copy of this form may be issued with appeal papers.

From 3 March 2003 as much information as possible will be gathered by phone. Notifications will be issued to non-resident parents where further information is required.[193]

After 3 March 2003 an old style maintenance enquiry form will only be issued rarely – eg, where the non-resident parent claims they did not receive the original maintenance enquiry form. However, the effective date remains set by the issue of the original form.

Parentage investigations

These are carried out for pre- and post-assessment cases in the same way as for pre- and post-calculation investigations, apart from interviews with young non-resident parents.

When determining if a young non-resident parent between 16 and 19 is a child a series of three questions is asked:[194]
- Is he in full time non-advanced education?
- Has he been married?
- Does he satisfy the rule on registered for work or youth training?

The questions are asked in sequence and where no is answered to all the young person is no longer defined as a child.

Further investigation

Reflecting the need for more information, as outlined above, when using the 'old rules', verification (ie, written corroboration) is always sought for housing costs and the higher rate of child benefit.[195]

Chapter 6: Information
Notes

Notes

1. **Information-seeking powers**
   1. s14 CSA 1991; Sch 2 CSA 1991
   2. Positive client contact
   3. ss4(4), 7(5) and 6(9) CSA 1991
   4. Reg 3(1A) CS(IED) Regs as inserted by reg 2(3) CS(IED)A Regs 2003
   5. Contacting the NRP for the first time
   6. Reg 3(1) CS(IED) Regs
   7. Reg 3(1A) CS(IED) Regs as inserted by reg 2(3) CS(IED)A Regs 2003
   8. Reg 3(2) CS(IED) Regs
   9. s46(1)(c) CSA 1991
   10. Reg 2(1) CS(IED) Regs as amended by reg 2(2) CS(IED)A Regs 2003
   11. *Purdew v Seress-Smith, The Times,* 9 September 1992
   12. Regs 1(2) 'relevant person' and 2(2)(a) CS(IED) Regs
   13. Reg 2(2)(b) CS(IED) Regs
   14. Reg 2(2)(c) CS(IED) Regs
   15. Reg 2(2)(ba) CS(IED) Regs
   16. Reg 2(2)(cc) and (cd) CS(IED) Regs
   17. Reg 2(2)(g) CS(IED) Regs
   18. Reg 2(2)(f) CS(IED) Regs
   19. Reg 2(3) CS(IED) Regs
   20. Order 1 r3 CCR 1981
   21. Reg 2(2)(e) CS(IED) Regs
   22. Reg 2(2)(h) CS(IED) Regs
   23. See s3 SSA 1998
   24. Regs 2(2)(d) and 3(1)(a) CS(IED) Regs
   25. s122D SSAA 1992
   26. Sch 2 para 1 CSA 1991
   27. Reg 3(2)(h) CS(IED) Regs
   28. Sch 5 TCA 1999
   29. s6 and Sch 1 Taxes Management Act 1970; s182 Finance Act 1989
   30. Reg 3(4) CS(MCP) Regs
   31. Reg 5(1) CS(IED) Regs
   32. Evidence timescales
   33. s14A CSA 1991
   34. s14A(4) CSA 1991
   35. DSS letter to Lisson Grove Benefits Program, 16 January 2001
   36. s14A CSA 1991
   37. Reg 3A CS(IED) Regs
   38. CCS/16535/1996 to be reported as R(CS) 2/98; CCS/12686/1996 to be reported as R(CS) 8/98
   39. CCS/7966/1995

2. **Contacting the non-resident parent**
   40. Contacting the NRP for the first time
   41. Trace overview
   42. Basic trace; Additional Trace
   43. DCI
   44. Common enquiry screen
   45. Inland Revenue
   46. National Insurance Contributions Office
   47. Where the employer is the Ministry of Defence
   48. Prison Service; Prison Addresses in Northern Ireland
   49. Employers
   50. Local Authorities
   51. The driver and vehicle licensing agency (DVLA/DVLNI)
   52. DCI004 – General Trace
   53. Contacting a client
   54. App 3 IS GAP Circular 02/02 (revised)
   55. PWC in receipt of a prescribed benefit
   56. Suspending debt
   57. Regs 5(1) and 1(2) 'relevant person' CS(MCP) Regs
   58. Contacting NRP for the first time
   59. Contacting NRP for the first time
   60. NRP co-operation; Overview – Gather person evidence
   61. Collecting evidence
   62. NRP co-operation
   63. Prison service
   64. Reg 5(2) CS(MCP) Regs
   65. Reg 5(3) and (4) CS(MCP) Regs
   66. R(CS) 8/98
   67. NRP under 16; NRP between 16 & 19
   68. Definition of a child

3. **Parentage investigations**
   69. Disputed parentage post assessment/calculation
   70. s26 of the amended CSA 1991 – presumptions
   71. ANRP evidence for disputed parentage
   72. s26 of the amended CSA 1991 – presumptions
   73. Negative DNA test result
   74. Disputed parentage post maintenance assessment/calculation
   75. Section 26 of the amended CSA 1991-presumptions; Appeal to court under section 20 of the 1991 act

Chapter 6: Information Notes

76 Suspend debt
77 PWC evidence
78 PWC is under the age of 16; ANRP/NRP is under the age of 16
79 NRP under 16; NRP aged between 16 &19
80 ANRP child details dialog; NRP under 16
81 Ch3 paras 150-51 PG; Ch2 paras 175-204 TG
82 ANRP evidence
83 Gather ANRP statement
84 Gather ANRP statement
85 Part 5 para 232 FTFG; Ch3 para 175 PG
86 ANRP DNA Test information
87 Gather ANRP statement; Maintain parentage dispute information screen
88 Ch3 paras 182-83 PG
89 Part 5 para 292 FTFG
90 Part 5 para 293 FTFG
91 Ch3 paras 184-85 PG; Part 5 para 295 FTFG
92 Part 5 para 288 FTFG
93 Part 5 para 212 FTFG; Ch3 paras 162-63 PG
94 Part 1 para 110 FTFG
95 Part 5 para 161 FTFG
96 Contacting the PWC
97 Part 5 paras 180-81 FTFG
98 Ch2 paras 130-31 PG
99 Part 5 paras 182, 360, 370-379 and 380 FTFG; Ch2 para 141 and Apps 5 and 6 PG
100 Gathering PWC's statement; Parentage statement dialog
101 App 4 PG
102 App 5 PG
103 Consent for DNA testing
104 PWC refuses DNA test for herself
105 Action to be taken when the PWC refuses DNA test for herself (Prescribed benefits cases); PWC refuses DNA test for the QC
106 ANRP refuses to attend DNA test
107 ANRP refuses to attend DNA test
108 PWC not in receipt of prescribed benefits
109 ANRP DNA test info
110 DNA referral
111 Authorising the offer of a DNA test; ANRP/NRP unable to pay LGC Ltd invoice
112 Negative DNA test result
113 ANRP/NRP unable to pay LGC Ltd invoice
114 s27A CSA 1991
115 DNA testing
116 ANRP wants to arrange own DNA test
117 DNA test results
118 Positive DNA test result
119 Negative DNA test
120 Negative DNA test
121 s27 CSA 1991; Court action
122 Court action
123 Gathering evidence for court proceedings
124 Preparing the case for court proceedings
125 Obtaining birth certificates
126 Preparing the case for court proceedings (England and Wales)
127 Preparing the case for court proceedings (Scotland)
128 Authorising court proceedings; Authoirising court proceedings – Scotland
129 Lay representation (England and Wales)
130 Authorising court proceedings Scotland
131 Authorising court proceedings; Authorising court proceedings – Scotland
132 Directions hearing England and Wales
133 s20 FLRA 1969; *Re H (Paternity: Blood Test)* [1996] 2 FLR 65
134 *S v S; W v Official Solicitor* [1972] AC 24
135 s21 FLRA 1969
136 s23 FLRA 1969; *Re A (Paternity: Refusal of Blood Test)* [1994] 2 FLR 463; Court directed DNA test
137 *Regina v Secretary of State for Social Security ex parte 'G'* (Fam D) [1997] Current Law, October 1997, 448
138 s28(2) CSA 1991; s7 LR(PC)(S)A 1986; r152 AS(CSA) (AOCSCR)
139 Second directions hearing – (DNA cases only) England and Wales
140 ANRP declared to be the parent
141 ANRP declared not to be the parent
142 Court directed DNA testing
143 Suspending debt
144 s27 CSA 1991

4. Further investigations

145 Corroboration of evidence; Self-contradictory evidence: Inherently improbable evidence
146 Types of evidence
147 Hearsay evidence
148 Verification requirements; Evidence of earnings and income
149 Evidence and verification
150 Collecting evidence; Obtaining evidence by telephone; Obtaining further evidence
151 Collecting evidence; Employer income summary log
152 Collecting evidence
153 Self-employed earnings

Chapter 6: Information
Notes

154 Approaching Inland Revenue for self-employed income
155 s15(1) CSA 1991
156 Use of inspectors
157 HC Hansard, 2 February 1996, col 990
158 s15(2) CSA 1991
159 s15(8) CSA 1991
160 Part 6 paras 130-151 FTFG
161 Sch 1 para 8 CS(NIRA) Regs
162 s14(4A) CSA 1991
163 s15(4) CSA 1991
164 s15(11) CSA 1991
165 s15(4A) CSA 1991
166 s15(5) CSA 1991
167 s15(6) CSA 1991
168 s57 CSA 1991; reg 7 CS(IED) Regs
169 s15(7) CSA 1991
170 s15(9) CSA 1991
171 s15(9) CSA 1991
172 Collecting evidence
173 Referral reasons - fraud action; Referrals to the CSA criminal compliance team

5. Duty to disclose changes
174 Reg 6 CS(IED) Regs; s55 CSA 1991; s44 CSA 1991; Sch 1 para 16 CSA 1991

6. Disclosure of information by the CSA
175 Reg 9A(1) CS(IED) Regs; Disclosure
176 Reg 9A(2) CS(IED) Regs; Disclosure
177 Reg 9A(3) CS(IED) Regs; Disclosure
178 Reg 9A(4) CS(IED) Regs; Confidentiality
179 Reg 8(1) and (2) CS(IED) Regs; Disclosure
180 Reg 8(3) CS(IED) Regs; Disclosure
181 Disclosure
182 Disclosure
183 s3 SSA 1998
184 Sch 1 para 7 CS(NIRA) Regs
185 s50 CSA 1991; reg 11 CS(IED) Regs
186 s50 CSA 1991
187 s50(3) CSA 1991
188 s50(4) CSA 1991
189 s9 Rehabilitation of Offenders Act 1974

7. Existing 'old rules' cases
190 Reg 10(1) CS(IEDMAJ)(A) Regs
191 Reg 3(2) CS(IED) Regs prior to amendment by Reg 6 CS(IEDMAJ)(A) Regs
192 Reg 2(2)(c) CS(IED) Regs prior to amendment by Reg 5 CS(IEDMAJ)(A) Regs
193 Collecting evidence
194 ANRP child details
195 Verification requirements

Part 3
New rules maintenance

Chapter 7
The 'new rules' maintenance calculation

This chapter covers:
1. Maintenance calculation rates (below)
2. Net income (p132)
3. Shared care (p140)

> From 3 March 2003 all new cases of child support maintenance are worked out according to the new maintenance calculation.[1] For how to work out the child maintenance of an 'old rules' case see **Chapter 10**, or for an 'old rules' case which converts to the 'new rules', see **Chapter 9**.

1. Maintenance calculation rates

To carry out a child maintenance calculation the following information is needed:[2]
- the number of qualifying children;
- the number of relevant other children;
- the number of any relevant non-resident children (see p131);
- the number of persons with care;
- what (if any) benefits the non-resident parent receives;
- whether the non-resident parent meets the conditions for the nil rate (see p126);
- the income of the non-resident parent (see p132);
- the number of nights (if any) that the non-resident parent has care of a qualifying child (see p145);
- the number of nights (if any) that a local authority has care of a qualifying child (see p146).

Where a non-resident parent fails to provide sufficient information to calculate child support maintenance, a default maintenance decision may be made (see p384). A penalty for failing to provide information may also be imposed (see p94).

Chapter 7: The 'new rules' maintenance calculation
1. Maintenance calculation rates

There are four rates of child support maintenance that can be applied:
- nil rate (see below);
- flat rate (see p127);
- reduced rate (see p128);
- basic rate (see p130).

Child support maintenance will be calculated from each non-resident parent separately. This means a person with care may be receiving the flat rate of maintenance from one non-resident parent and an amount from the other non-resident parent worked out using the basic rate.

In all cases the amount of child maintenance calculated is a weekly amount.[3] Rounding rules apply to the different rates as follows:[4]
- in basic rate and reduced rate cases fractions of a pound will be disregarded if less than half or rounded up to the next pound if a half or over;
- in all other cases fractions of a penny will be disregarded if less than a half or rounded up to the next penny if a half or over – ie, where there is apportionment or shared care.

There is a maximum amount of income which can be taken into account for maintenance purposes (see p139).

Apportionment

Where there is more than one person with care in relation to a non-resident parent the amount of maintenance due may be apportioned between them in relation to the number of qualifying children of each person with care.[5]

Where apportionment occurs and rounding provisions would result in the total amount of maintenance being different from the total amount before any apportionment, the maintenance due will be adjusted.[6] This may mean that maintenance due to one of the persons with care has to be reduced by a penny, so that no one person with care is disadvantaged. This reduction will be reallocated between the persons with care from time to time.[7]

Apportionment occurs after the calculation of maintenance at the appropriate rate and before any decrease for shared care.[8]

In basic and reduced rate cases, where apportionment would result in a figure of less than £5 in maintenance in total to all persons with care, the amount payable will be the flat rate of £5 apportioned between the people with care.[9]

Where there is more than one person with care in relation to a qualifying child the maintenance due for this child may further be apportioned between the persons with care, but only where a request to apportion maintenance has been agreed to by the CSA (see p129).

Nil rate

This applies where the non-resident parent is:[10]

Chapter 7: The 'new rules' maintenance calculation
1. Maintenance calculation rates

- a student;
- a child;
- a prisoner;
- a 16/17-year-old (or his partner) receiving income support (IS)/income-based (JSA);
- receiving an allowance for Work-Based Training for Young People (Skillseekers in Scotland);
- a person who is resident in a care home, independent hospital or is being provided with a care home service or/and independent health care service who receives one of the prescribed benefits (as for the flat rate) or has the whole/part of the cost of his accommodation met by a local authority;
- a hospital inpatient on IS, who has been a patient for more than six weeks;
- a hospital inpatient in receipt of one of the prescribed benefits (except IS and income-based JSA) who has been in hospital for 52 weeks;
- a hospital inpatient in reciept of pension credit (PC) and who has been a patient for at least 13 weeks abut not exceeding 52;
- a person who would be liable to pay the flat rate because he or his partner are on IS/income based JSA but whose net income including that from any of the prescribed benefits (for the flat rate) is less than £5;
- a person with net income of less than £5 a week.

Example 7.1
Craig is a parent with care of two children, Mia and Lewis. His ex-partner Kerry is in prison. In this case the nil rate applies. However, even though Kerry is in prison she is still sent a child maintenance enquiry form to complete. When she comes out of prison Craig could ask for a supersession.

Flat rate

The flat rate of £5 applies where the non-resident parent does not qualify for the nil rate and:[11]
- his weekly income is £100 or less; *or*
- he receives one of the following:[12]
    - bereavement allowance;
    - retirement pension;
    - incapacity benefit;
    - carer's allowance;
    - maternity allowance;
    - severe disablement allowance;
    - industrial injuries benefit;
    - widowed parent's allowance;
    - widow's pension;

Chapter 7: The 'new rules' maintenance calculation
1. Maintenance calculation rates

- contribution-based JSA;
- a training allowance (other than Work-based Training for Young People or Skillseekers);
- war disablement pension;
- war widowers pension;
- a social security benefit paid by a country other than the UK; *or*
- IS or income-based JSA (or his partner does);[13]
- PC.

The flat rate can be halved for couples where the non-resident parent's partner is also a non-resident parent with a maintenance application in force, and either he or his partner receives IS or income-based JSA.[14] Where the non-resident parent is in a polygamous relationship and there is more than one partner, the flat-rate is apportioned between them.[15]

There are special rules about shared care in flat-rate cases (see p151).

Example 7.2
a) The situation is as in example 7.1. Kerry has now come out of prison and is claiming income-based JSA. Craig requests a supersession and Kerry has £5 a week flat rate maintenance deducted from her benefit.
b) If Kerry moved in with Jeff and they claimed income-based JSA as a couple, the flat rate of £5 would still apply and Craig would receive £5 a week. However, if Jeff was also a non-resident parent the flat rate would be halved. In this case Craig would receive £2.50 a week.
c) In the situation above if Jeff had two persons with care (Alison and Penny) each caring for one qualifying child, they would find their maintenance reduced as the flat rate applies at £2.50 and is then apportioned. Alison and Penny would each receive £1.25 each.

Reduced rate

This applies where neither the flat or nil rate applies and the non-resident parent has income of less than £200 but more than £100.[16] The flat rate of £5 is added to a percentage of the parent's income between £100 and £200.[17] This means that only the income above £100 but under £200 is used in the calculation – eg, if net income is £150 the percentage is applied to £50. The percentage depends on the number of qualifying children and the number of relevant children (see Table 7.1). (A relevant child is one for whom the non-resident parent or his partner receives child benefit.[18]) Rounding is to the nearest pound.

Chapter 7: The 'new rules' maintenance calculation
1. Maintenance calculation rates

Table 7.1: Reduced rate percentages depending on the number of qualifying and relevant children

Number of relevant other children	Number of qualifying children (including relevant non-resident children)		
	One	Two	Three or more
None	25%	35%	45%
One	20.5%	29%	37.5%
Two	19%	27%	35%
Three or more	17.5%	25%	32.5%

Step 1
Work out the net income that is over £100 but less than £200.

Step 2
Work out the relevant percentage depending on the number of relevant children and qualifying children. Apply this percentage to the income worked out at Step one and add this to £5, rounding to the nearest pound.

Step 3
Where there is more than one person with care, apportion this amount between them depending on the number of qualifying children each cares for, rounded to the nearest penny. (Where there is more than one person with care in relation to a qualifying child, maintenance may only be apportioned where a request to do so has been agreed to by the CSA.)

Example 7.3
a) Simon is due to pay maintenance to Fiona for two qualifying children, John and Margaret. Simon lives with a new partner, Julie, and their baby, Paul. Simon's net income is £180 a week. The reduced rate of maintenance would apply.

Step 1	Net income £180
	Income between £100 and £200 = £80
Step 2	Relevant percentage for one relevant child and two qualifying children is 29 per cent
	£5 + (29% of £80) = £5 + £23.20 = £28.20 (rounded to £28)

Simon is due to pay £28 maintenance to Fiona.

b) If the situation was as above except that Margaret was cared for by Fiona and John stayed with his grandmother, there would still be two qualifying children but now there would be two persons with care. The maintenance calculated would need to be apportioned between them.

Chapter 7: The 'new rules' maintenance calculation
1. Maintenance calculation rates

Step 3   Each person cares for one qualifying child; therefore the maintenance is divided by two
£28 ÷ 2 = £14
Simon now pays Fiona £14 and the grandmother £14.

Where the non-resident parent shares care for any of the qualifying child(ren) the reduced rate may be decreased further by applying the shared care rules (see p140).

Basic rate

The basic rate applies where none of the other rates (nil, flat or reduced) apply.[19] Thus where the non-resident parent has net weekly income of £200 or more maintenance will be calculated under the basic rate. The basic rate is a percentage of net income depending on the number of qualifying children and the number of relevant children. (A relevant child is one for whom the non-resident parent or his partner receives child benefit.[20]) There may be other relevant non-resident children who are taken into account (see p131). The percentages used are set out in Table 7.2 below.

Table 7.2: Basic rate percentages depending on the number of qualifying and relevant children

No. of qualifying children (including relevant non-resident children)	Percentage	No. of relevant children	Percentage
1	15%	1	15%
2	20%	2	20%
3 or more	25%	3 or more	25%

Where the non-resident parent has one or more relevant children his net income is reduced by an equivalent percentage (as above) before the basic rate is calculated. Therefore the basic rate may be worked out in two steps, depending on the circumstances.

Step 1
Work out the net income of the non-resident parent. Depending on the number of relevant children, reduce this by a percentage – ie, 15 per cent, 20 per cent or 25 per cent.

Step 2
Depending on the number of qualifying children, maintenance is a proportion of this remaining net income, rounded to the nearest pound.

Chapter 7: The 'new rules' maintenance calculation
1. Maintenance calculation rates

Step 3

Where there is more than one person with care, apportion this amount between them depending on the number of qualifying children each cares for, rounded to the nearest penny. (Where there is more than one person with care in relation to a qualifying child, maintenance may only be apportioned where a request to do so has been agreed to by the CSA.)

Example 7.4

a) The situation is as in example 7.3a except Simon now has a net income to £240 a week. Paul is a relevant child and John and Margaret are the qualifying children.

Step 1   Net income is £240. One relevant child means this is reduced by 15%
           15% of £240 = £36
           £240 – £36 = £204
Step 2   There are two qualifying children – ie, 20%
           20% of £204 = £40.80 (which is rounded to £41)
Simon therefore pays £41 in maintenance to Fiona.

b) If the situation was as in example 7.3b this £41 would be split equally between Fiona and the grandmother.
Step 3   £41 is apportioned between two persons with care. Each would receive £20.50 in maintenance from Simon.

Where the non-resident parent shares care for any of the qualifying children the maintenance calculated may be decreased further by applying the shared care rules (see p140).

Relevant non-resident children

A non-resident parent may have other children for whom child support maintenance cannot be applied because the non-resident parent is paying maintenance for them under a maintenance order (or in Scotland, registered maintenance agreement).[21] The CSA calls these children relevant non-resident children, although they are treated like qualifying children in relation to the calculation.[22]

Where child support is payable at either the basic rate or the reduced rate, or is calculated at one of these rates after applying a variation and would otherwise have been the flat or nil rate, the child is counted as a qualifying child.[23] The amount of maintenance calculated would then be apportioned between the persons with care in relation to the number of qualifying children they care for, including any adjustment for shared care.[24] Where the total amount payable by the non-residnet parent would be less than £5 the non-resident will instead pay £5, to be apportioned between the persons with care as appropriate.[25]

Chapter 7: The 'new rules' maintenance calculation
1. Maintenance calculation rates

No payment is actually made for the relevant non-resident child. There is also no adjustment of the notional amount worked out for the non-relevant child due to the non-resident parent sharing care or the child being in local authority care for part of the time.[26]

Example 7.5
James lives with his new partner, Amanda, and her son Liam. He has three other children; two (Emma and Joshua) are cared for by Elizabeth who has just claimed IS; one (Rachel) is cared for by Hilary. James has court orders for child maintenance for Emma, Joshua and Rachel. As Elizabeth is treated as applying for child maintenance on her claim for benefit and she does not opt out, a maintenance calculation will be done for her. Hilary cannot apply for child maintenance as the court order is in force (if it was made after 3 March 2003 she could apply for child maintenance had the order been in force for one year, otherwise the order must cease before she can apply). In this case:

Emma and Joshua are qualifying children.

Liam is a relevant child (even though he is not James's child, James's new partner Amanda gets child benefit for him).

Rachel is a relevant non-resident child.

If James had a net income of £275 a week his maintenance worked out using the basic rate would be:

Step 1   £275 − (15% of £275) = £275 − £41.25 = £233.75
Step 2   25% of £233.75 = £58.44 (rounded to £58)
Step 3   Apportionment applies between Elizabeth and Hilary. Elizabeth would receive two-thirds of the maintenance calculated − ie, £38.67 (when apportioning rounding apples to the nearest penny).

Hilary receives her normal court order maintenance.

Note: If Hilary could apply because her post − 3 March 2003 order had been in force for one year she would receive £19.33 in maintenance.

---

2. Net income

The non-resident parent's net weekly income includes earned income, self-employed earnings, tax credits and payments from a pension scheme, retirement annuity or other such scheme for provision of income in retirement,[27] less any relevant deductions. Only these forms of income will be included. All other income will be ignored.

Disregarded income

If a payment is made in a currency other than sterling, banking charges or commission for changing the payment into sterling are disregarded.[28] In addition,

Chapter 7: The 'new rules' maintenance calculation
2. Net income

a payment made in a country outside the UK with a prohibition against transfer into the UK is ignored.[29]

Earnings from employment

Earnings means 'any remuneration or profit from employment' and, as well as wages, includes:[30]
- any payments for overtime;
- any profit-related pay;
- any bonus or commission;
- any royalty or fees;
- any holiday pay (except that payable more than four weeks after ending employment);
- any retaining fee;
- statutory sick pay, statutory maternity pay, statutory adoption pay and statutory paternity pay;
- pay in lieu of notice.

Earnings do not include:[31]
- payments of expenses 'wholly, exclusively and necessarily' incurred in carrying out the duties of the job;
- any tax-exempt allowance paid by an employer to employee;
- any gratuities paid by customers of the employer (tips);
- payment in kind;
- any advance earnings or loan made by the employer to employee;
- payments made by an employer when the employee is on strike;
- payments for duties as an auxiliary coastguard, part-time fire fighter, or within the lifeboat services, territorial army or reserve forces;
- payments made by a local authority to local councillors in the performance of their duties;
- payments made after employment ends which relate to a specific period of time, provided that a period of equal length has elapsed between the job ending and the effective date;
- earnings from a previous job where they are paid in the same week or period that earnings from a second job are received.

A commissioner has held that payments made by the parent for expenses could be deducted from her/his earnings where the employer did not reimburse them.[32] It was emphasised that any such expenses had to be incurred 'in the performance of duties', and not just incurred in order to enable the parent's duties to be performed. It is possible that part of a payment (eg, towards a telephone rental or travel cost) could be 'wholly, exclusively and necessarily' incurred.[33]

133

Chapter 7: The 'new rules' maintenance calculation
2. Net income

Relevant week
The concept of the 'relevant week' is important in child support calculation, particularly when calculating income.[34] The relevant week is determined as follows:[35]
- on application by the non-resident parent, the seven days immediately before the application is made;
- on application in any other case, the seven days immediately before the date the non-resident parent was first given notice that an application for child support maintenance has been made, or treated as made;
- where the original decision is revised (or superseded because of ignorance, a mistake in material fact or error in law), the relevant week for the new decision is the same as the original decision;
- where the original decision is superseded due to a change in circumstances, the seven days immediately before the date on which the application to supersede was made;
- where the original decision is superseded by the Secretary of State on her/his own initiative (except for ignorance, mistake in fact or error as above), the seven days immediately before the date of notification of that intention.[36]

In some cases the Secretary of State may make separate maintenance calculations for different periods in a particular case.[37] Where this is due to changes of circumstances which occurred, the relevant week for each separate calculation made to take account of the changes is the seven days immediately before the date of notification of the change.[38]

Calculating normal weekly earnings
Averaged earnings are used in the child support calculation.[39] When calculating or estimating average earnings at the relevant week, the Secretary of State considers the evidence of the person's earnings over any appropriate period, beginning not more than eight weeks before the relevant week and ending not later than the date of the calculation. S/he may also consider cumulative earnings in the tax year in which the relevant week falls to the date of the calculation.

Where the Secretary of State believes that the amount of weekly earnings does not accurately reflect the person's normal amount of earnings, then another period can be used, taking into account earnings received and those due to be received (from past, present or future employment) and the duration and pattern (or expected duration and pattern) of any employment.[40]

The CSA must be satisfied first that the calculation of earnings at the relevant week produces a figure which is not normal,[41] and then that the period chosen reflects the parent's usual pattern of work – eg, the amount of overtime worked or sick leave.[42] A future period can be used to take into account – eg, earnings from a job which has not yet begun. The CSA must also consider the expected duration and pattern of any employment. A parent may want to suggest an alternative

Chapter 7: The 'new rules' maintenance calculation
2. Net income

period to the CSA, giving reasons as the CSA cannot be expected to consider this without substantial grounds and a prompt by one of the parents.[43] The CSA must use one continuous period.[44] Where a bonus, commission or profit-related pay is paid during a year ending with the relevant week separately from earnings, or in relation to a longer period than other earnings, those payments are totalled over the year and divided by 52.[45]

The Secretary of State has to take into account any change of circumstances s/he is aware of between the relevant week and the effective date (see p400).[46] However, s/he must first calculate earnings as above for the relevant week in order to determine whether there has been a material change of circumstances.[47] For changes after this date, see p383.

The calculation of earnings is one of the areas where errors are frequently made and therefore should be checked carefully. A commissioner has held that an appeal tribunal must enquire into whether the process used to determine income was correctly carried out and whether the period used for the averaging of earnings gave an accurate picture.[48]

Calculating net earnings

Net earnings from employment are counted as net income in full. Net earnings mean gross earnings less:[49]
- income tax;
- Class 1 national insurance contributions;
- all of the contributions made to an occupational/personal pension scheme (unless the scheme is intended partly to pay off a mortgage on the parent's home, in which case 75 per cent of contributions).

Income tax will be the actual amount deducted, including any tax in relation to payments not included as earnings.[50]

Pension contributions are only deducted if they are made to Inland Revenue-approved schemes.

Earnings from self-employment

Earnings from self-employment will in most cases be assessed on the basis of either:[51]
- total taxable profits from self-employment submitted to the Inland Revenue for income tax self-assessment; *or*
- the income from self-employment as set out in the tax calculation notice, or revised notice.

Where only one of these pieces of information is available the Secretary of State may request the other.[52] If s/he becomes aware that a revised tax calculation notice has been issued s/he may request this in preference to the other information.

Chapter 7: The 'new rules' maintenance calculation
2. Net income

Decision makers are instructed not to contact the Inland Revenue for earnings information until all other sources have been exhausted – eg, the parent, accountant, partnerships, inspectors.[53]

The net earnings taken into account will be the total taxable profit from self-employment less:[54]
- income tax (calculated using the personal allowances and tax rates applicable at the effective date[55]);
- national insurance (Class 2 and Class 4 contributions at the rates applicable at the effective date[56]);
- all of any pension premiums (75 per cent of the premium where the scheme is intended to pay off a mortgage) or on a retirement annuity contract.

The net weekly earnings can only be worked out based on a period not more than 24 months before the relevant week.[57]

Decision makers are reminded that if they find contradictions between information on the self-assessment form and evidence already held, this may be grounds for further investigation.[58] However, this does not mean that they have to use the alternative method of calculation based on gross receipts, merely that they may seek more information from accountants or the Inland Revenue.

It is likely to be rare for a case to be assessed under the alternative earnings rules based on gross receipts. The CSA would not consider revising or superseding a decision based simply on the fact that using the gross receipts method would produce a greater amount of maintenance due to the person with care than that calculated using the tax calculation notice. However, where a non-resident parent's earnings were assessed by the gross receipts method but they now have self-assessment details/tax calculation notice, the CSA may supersede the maintenance decision.

Earnings calculated using gross receipts less deductions

Earnings can be calculated by using gross receipts less deductions where:[59]
- the 24-month condition is not met; *or*
- the Secretary of State accepts is not reasonably practicable for the non-resident parent to provide the forms submitted to or issued by the Inland Revenue; *or*
- the Secretary of State believes that the earnings figure arrived at does not accurately reflect the normal weekly earnings of the earner.

Where this is the case the net earnings are the gross receipts less:[60]
- income tax;
- national insurance;
- all of any pension premiums (75 per cent of the premium where the scheme is intended to pay off a mortgage) or to a retirement annuity contract;
- any VAT paid in excess of VAT received in the same period as that over which the earnings are assessed; *and*

- any expenses which are reasonably incurred and wholly and exclusively defrayed for the purposes of the business. If the CSA is not satisfied that the full expense was appropriate or necessary to the business, it will allow that part considered reasonable.[61] Where an expense is part business and part private (eg, a car), the CSA has to decide on the breakdown between the two uses on the evidence available.[62] They may well follow the apportionment used by the Inland Revenue. CSA staff are given guidance on what may be allowable business expenses.[63]

Gross earnings includes all of any board or lodgings payments if this is the self-employed earner's only or main source of income.[64]

Income tax and national insurance is calculated in the same way as for taxable profit.[65]

Business expenses include:[66]
- repayments of capital on loans used for the replacement or repair of a business asset (but not for loans taken out for any other business purpose or where the costs are met by payments from an insurance policy);
- any income used for the repair of a business asset;
- any payment of interest on loans taken out for business purposes (this does not include loans taken out to acquire a share of a business, nor to pay business tax liabilities).[67]

Business expenses do *not* include:[68]
- capital expenditure;
- depreciation of capital assets;
- any sum employed in the setting up or expansion of the business;
- any loss incurred before the period of earnings being calculated;
- any expenses incurred in providing business entertainment;
- any loss incurred in any other self-employment.

The net weekly income for the self-employed earner will be averaged over the 52 weeks up to and including the relevant week, or if the person has been self-employed for less than a year, over the period during which the person has been self-employed (including the relevant week).[69]

The self-employed person is asked to provide other evidence of business receipts and expenses, such as business books, receipts of bills sent and paid, bank statements, records of wages paid, Inland Revenue forms and VAT bills.[70]

Where the Secretary of State believes that the above calculation would produce an amount which does not accurately represent the parent's true earnings, another period can be used.[71] This should not be used just because earnings fluctuate, receipts are irregular or come in a lump, trade is slow at times or work non-existent for a period, nor should a different period be used just because it is known that earnings will subsequently change.[72] In such cases the Secretary of

Chapter 7: The 'new rules' maintenance calculation
2. Net income

State will take into account earnings received or due to be received and the duration and pattern, or expected pattern, of any self-employment.[73]

Since most calculations will be based on the self-assessment form or tax calculation notice this alternative method may only be used where there has been a major change in trading which has resulted in higher or lower earnings or where a person has been trading for less than a year.[74]

Challenging earnings of the self-employed

There have often been delays in the self-employed parent producing all the information necessary to work out the maintenance due. The Secretary of State can impose penalties and a default maintenance decision (see p384) while awaiting the information. The person with care may want to request that this is done if there have been problems in the past; however, she cannot force the imposition of a penalty.

Under the old formula many self-employed non-resident parents received low assessments. Some persons with care alleged that the self-employed non-resident parent, sometimes with the help of an accountant, managed to disguise his true income. Once a calculation has been made, the person with care can seek a revision (see p416) and ask the Secretary of State to use an inspector (see p112) in order to obtain more detailed information. However, if the non-resident parent's accounts have been accepted by the Inland Revenue, it is very unlikely that the Secretary of State would consider it worthwhile to undertake further investigations. The Secretary of State may also refuse to revise the calculation if the person with care cannot substantiate her allegations. This can be challenged if the belief is reasonably held as it is very difficult for one party to obtain definitive details of the other's income. The Secretary of State is much better placed to do this.

If the person with care takes the case to an appeal tribunal (see Chapter 20), she will see details of the income in the appeal papers, and she may be able to argue that some of the expenses included are not reasonable or not wholly connected with the business. Tribunals may adjourn the hearing for further information to be collected. Alternatively, the tribunal can estimate net earnings based on the available evidence, including oral evidence from the person with care.[75]

The person with care can apply for variation from the calculation on the grounds that a person's lifestyle is inconsistent with his level of income or that assets which do not currently produce income are capable of doing so (see Chapter 8).

Tax credits

Working tax credit

Working tax credit (WTC) is counted as the income of the non-resident parent where WTC is solely based on his work and earnings.[76] If both members of a couple are working, then the WTC is treated as the income of the partner with the

Chapter 7: The 'new rules' maintenance calculation
2. Net income

higher earnings over the period used for assessing earnings for tax credit purposes, or halved if their earnings are equal.[77] The earnings taken into account for determining who is treated as having WTC treated as income is related to the earnings of each partner that was used for determining WTC.[78] This means that should the earnings change later the non-resident parent could be treated as having more income than he has. For example, when WTC is worked out he is earning more than his partner; WTC therefore counts in full as his income. Later his partner's income increases, but she does not notify the Inland Revenue but waits for an end of year adjustment. The non-resident parent will still have WTC counted as his income even though his partner currently earns more than he does. The rate of WTC used is that payable at the effective date.[79]

Employment credits

Employment credits paid to the non-resident parent (under New Deal 50-Plus) count in full as income, at the rate payable at the effective date.[80] Any employment credits paid to the non-resident parent's partner are ignored.

Child tax credit

Child tax credit paid to the non-resident parent or his partner counts in full as income, at the rate payable at the effective date.[81]

Other income

Periodic or other payments from an occupational or personal pension, retirement annuity or other scheme to provide income in retirement count in full as income.[82] Income is calculated or estimated on a weekly basis by considering the 26-week period ending in the relevant week (see p264).[83] If the income has been received during each week of the period, the total received over the 26 weeks is divided by 26. In other cases, the total received is divided by the number of complete weeks for which the payment was received. However, the Secretary of State can use a different period if the amount produced by the above calculation does not accurately reflect actual income.[84] Furthermore, a change occurring between the relevant week and the effective date (see p400) must be taken into account by the Secretary of State if s/he is aware of the change, in the same way as for earnings (see p266).

Maximum amount of net weekly income

The maximum amount of net weekly income that can be included in the calculation of child maintenance is £2,000.[85] This includes all income, whether from earnings, tax credits, self-employment or pension and other payments. Even where a variation is being applied the amount of net income cannot exceed this maximum figure.

In simple terms this means that the maximum amount of child maintenance that can ever be paid is £500 – ie, where the non-resident parent has three or more

Chapter 7: The 'new rules' maintenance calculation
2. Net income

children and no other relevant children. For other maximum amounts see, Table 7.3.

Table 7.3: Maximum maintenance payable

Number of relevant children	1 qualifying child	2 qualifying children	3 or more qualifying children
0	£300	£400	£500
1	£255	£340	£425
2	£240	£320	£400
3 or more	£225	£300	£375

3. Shared care

Shared care is the term used to describe a situation where there is more than one person looking after a particular qualifying child and those people live in different households. If the people providing care live in the same household (see p29), then this is not shared care.[86]

In real terms a number of individuals may be involved in caring for a qualifying child – eg, parents, grandparents, babysitters. For the shared care rules to apply there must be either:
- a non-resident parent who shares care (ie, looks after the qualifying child at least 52 nights a year on average) (see p145);
- a person with care (ie, with day-to-day care of a qualifying child because she cares for the child at least 104 nights a year on average) who is treated as a non-resident parent (see p142); *or*
- a qualifying child cared for by a local authority for part of the time (see p342).

One or all of these situations may apply in any individual case.

The CSA will make a decision on shared care by looking at all the evidence. As far as possible they will seek written evidence, although oral evidence will be accepted where the parents agree.[87] Normally this information will be gathered on application (ie, from relevant forms or phone contact with the person with care and non-resident parent). They will look at regular weekly patterns, exceptional weeks and other occasional nights. The amount of shared care is then calculated.[88] Where the evidence of the person with care and non-resident parent do not agree, further investigation will take place.[89]

Parents should keep a note of the nights the child(ren) spends with them and, in case of dispute, be willing to supply further evidence – eg, a diary. The CSA – and any subsequent appeal tribunal – must then determine the number of nights over the period spent in each person's care.[90]

Chapter 7: The 'new rules' maintenance calculation
3. Shared care

What is day-to-day care

For the purposes of the calculation and shared care regulations, a person will be treated as having day-to-day care of a child only if s/he cares for the child for at least 104 nights in the 12-month period ending with the relevant week.[91] See p264 for a definition of relevant week.

Another period, ending with the relevant week, may be used if that would be more representative of the current arrangement.[92] The number of nights of care in that period must be in the same ratio as 104 nights is to 12 months – ie, 52 nights in six months, 26 nights in three months, 13 nights in two months, nine nights in a month. Examples are given to decision makers of situations where it might be appropriate to use a period other than 12 months because the care arrangements have recently changed – due to a relationship breakdown, a court ruling on residence or contact, or the person now providing day-to-day care has been abroad, in prison, in hospital, away from home or otherwise unable to provide care.[93] If the arrangement has simply been renegotiated between the two parents, written acceptance of this should be provided so that the CSA knows that this is now the current arrangement and not a temporary change.

A period which does not end with the relevant week may only be used in specific circumstances if this gives a more accurate reflection of the care arrangements, for example where there is no established pattern before the relevant week or there is an intended change.[94]

Example 7.6
The relevant week for Joan's maintenance application is 14.02.04 to 20.02.04. The effective date of Serge's maintenance liability is 27.03.04 (the effective date is later than the relevant week because Joan is treated as applying and a court order is in force). Serge is going to begin caring for Chloe (the qualifying child) two nights a week from 15.03.04. Joan confirms this change.
The CSA decides that looking at the care ending in the relevant week would not give an accurate reflection of the current care arrangements, so an alternate period is used 15.03.04 to 27.03.04.

If a change occurs after the relevant week, the CSA should be informed as this may be grounds for supersession. If they refuse to use an alternate period an appeal can be sought.

Example 7.7
A father who only looks after the children for six weeks in the school holidays would not be accepted as a person with care. However, the father could request supersession during the summer holidays on the grounds that he is now a parent with care and a shorter period should then be used to calculate who has day-to-day care to reflect the current

arrangement. It is unlikely that this would be grounds for supersession if the six-week period had already been taken into account. However, if the arrangement for the holiday had not been known at the time, this may be successful. If day-to-day care were to be reassessed over the summer holidays, then the father would become the parent with care and the mother the non-resident parent. Indeed, the father may be able to apply for maintenance from the mother (in section 4 cases). (Note the relevant week in this case is the seven days preceding the request for supersession – see p420. Therefore the request should not be made right at the beginning of the summer holiday.)

If it is held that supersession cannot take place, such a father technically remains the non-resident parent over the holiday when he has the child(ren) full time. He would be liable to continue paying the mother the full level of maintenance even for those weeks the children spent with him. The parents may come to some voluntary arrangement whereby the mother would forgo the maintenance due, but this may not be financially possible, especially if she is in receipt of income support (IS).

The parent does not have to provide continuous care throughout a period of 24 hours, but during the night.[95] Where a child is a boarder at boarding school, a hospital inpatient, or temporarily in someone else's care, whoever would otherwise have day-to-day care is treated as providing care.[96] For example, if a babysitter or grandparent looks after the child one night a week, this would count as a night spent with the principal provider of day-to-day care. In the case of boarding school, the person who is treated as having day-to-day care for such periods need not be the person who pays the school fees.[97] However, a non-resident parent who pays school fees for a qualifying child may be able to apply for a variation (see p160).

Parent with care treated as non-resident

For the purposes of the calculation, where there are two or more persons with care (of a child for whom an application has been made or treated as made) and at least one of them is a parent special rules are applied.[98] In this case, a parent with care may be treated as a non-resident parent if they provide care:[99]
- to a lesser extent than the other parent or persons with care;
- to the same extent as the other parent but do not get child benefit; *or*
- to the same extent as the other parent and neither parent receives child benefit but the CSA decides she is not the principal provider of day-to-day care.

This means that even where there is a non-resident parent, the other parent, even though they have day-to-day care may be treated as a non-resident parent. Table 7.4 gives a quick guide to the range of situations which may occur.

A lesser extent could be interpreted as meaning either for fewer *nights* a week on average or fewer *hours* a week on average. The CSA will always consider the number of nights a determining factor.[100]

Chapter 7: The 'new rules' maintenance calculation
3. Shared care

Example 7.8
a) Robert looks after Geraldine from Friday afternoon to Monday morning. Nikki looks after Geraldine from Monday afternoon to Friday morning. Each is a parent with care but Robert cares for Geraldine for a lesser extent so he is treated as the non-resident parent.

b) A year later Robert has now moved onto shift work. One week he has Geraldine four nights, the second week three nights. Nikki cares for Geraldine the rest of the time. They now share care equally but as Nikki receives child benefit Robert is still treated as the non-resident parent.

As the right to receive child maintenance follows the receipt of child benefit, this may lead to competing claims for child benefit. Where more than one person who would otherwise be entitled makes a claim for child benefit, the following order of priority is used to determine who is to be awarded the benefit:[101]

- the person having the child living with her/him;
- the wife, where she is living with her husband (this continues for 13 weeks of a permanent separation);
- a parent, including a step-parent;
- the mother, if the parents are unmarried and living together;
- a person agreed by those entitled;
- failing all the above, the person selected by the Secretary of State.

Priority can be conceded by a higher priority claimant to someone else in writing. For more information on entitlement to child benefit, see CPAG's *Welfare Benefits and Tax Credits Handbook*.

In cases where a parent with care is treated as non-resident, a calculation is carried out to find out how much child maintenance s/he has to pay. This is worked out in the same way as for a non-resident parent who shares care.

Where the situation includes a remaining parent with care who does not have to discharge her/his responsibility under the Act by paying child maintenance, this assignment of non-resident parenthood can result in one parent paying child maintenance to another who has equal responsibility for the child. This can be particularly contentious where neither parent receives child benefit and the CSA must make a decision on principal provider of day-to-day care.[102]

Table 7.4: Quick guide to persons with care and parents treated as non-resident

Person listed first is principal provider of care unless otherwise stated	Who, if anyone, is treated as a non-resident parent
Parent, parent	Second parent
Parent, person with care	No one
Person with care, parent	Parent
Parent, parent, person	Second parent
Parent, person, parent	Second parent

143

Chapter 7: The 'new rules' maintenance calculation
3. Shared care

Parent, person, person	No one
Person, parent, parent	Second parent
Person, two parents sharing care equally	Parent who does not get child benefit, or where neither get child benefit, the one the Secretary of State decides
Person, person, parent	Parent
Person, parent, person	Parent

Who receives maintenance when there is more than one person with care

Where there are two or more people in different households who both have day-to-day care of a qualifying child either can make an application for child maintenance as long as both or neither of them has parental responsibility.[103] If only one of them has parental responsibility, then the person with parental responsibility must be the applicant. This means that if the person with parental responsibility decides not to apply, the other person with care could lose out on child maintenance, unless there is an application from the non-resident parent or a child in Scotland.

If both/all the persons with care can and do make an application, then only one will be accepted, depending on the order of priority (see p54). This may include a parent with care who is subsequently treated as a non-resident parent in relation to the calculation.

Where none of the persons with care is such a parent treated as a non-resident parent, the person whose application is accepted will receive all the maintenance calculated.[104] The applicant or other person with care may request that the payment is apportioned between them.[105] In making the decision, the Secretary of State will consider all the circumstances of the case and representations from the persons with care.[106] If agreed, the maintenance payable will be apportioned in relation to the amount of care provided. For a worked example, see example 7.9.

Where one of the persons with care is treated as a non-resident parent this split cannot take place. The entire amount of child maintenance from the non-resident parent is paid to the remaining person with care. In other words, a parent with care who shares care for the lesser time can never receive child maintenance from a non-resident parent, no matter the size of the bill being paid.

This may seem illogical, not to say unfair, particularly where the application has been made by the parent with care or where – although applications have been made by both persons with care – the application from the parent has been given priority (see p54). A parent with care who applies to the CSA for maintenance from the non-resident parent but ends up being deemed non-resident and paying maintenance can request withdrawal (see p392). However, they may find that the other person with care makes another new application.

When does a non-resident parent share care

A non-resident parent will share care where they look after a qualifying child at least one night a week on average.[107] The care must be provided overnight and the non-resident parent must stay at the same address as the child.[108] This means that the care could be provided away from the non-resident parent's normal home – eg, while on holiday or at other relatives' homes.

The number of nights is averaged over the 12 months ending with the relevant week.[109] A shorter period may be used – eg, because there is no pattern for the frequency or there is an intended change in frequency.[110] The number of nights of care in that period must be in the same ratio as 52 nights is to 12 months (52 weeks) – ie, 26 nights in six months (26 weeks), 13 nights in three months (13 weeks).[111]

Qualifying child spends time in hospital or at boarding school

Where a qualifying child goes into hospital or is at boarding school, any night spent there will count as a night with the person who would normally provide care at that time.[112] This includes nights normally spent with the:
- non-resident parent;[113]
- person with care;
- local authority.[114]

These nights count in determining whether the non-resident parent or local authority shares care. They are also counted when establishing who is a person with care or parent to be treated as non-resident.

Example 7.9
A child who has been living with his mother during the week and spends a Friday night with his father, goes to boarding school. The time as a boarder would continue to be treated as if he was living with his mother. Even where the care arrangement alters so that the child spends alternate weekends with the father the nights at school would still count as spent with the mother.

Where parents agree, or the periods involved are infrequent, the case may be straightforward. However, where the normal arrangements break down, a normal pattern cannot be established or the parents disagree, the CSA must make a decision on shared care.

145

Chapter 7: The 'new rules' maintenance calculation
3. Shared care

Example 7.10
Ella is a qualifying child cared for most of the time by her mother, Sarah, although her father, Stuart, looks after her on Wednesday and Saturday nights. Over the past year Ella has undergone treatment for cancer, which has resulted in her spending periods in hospital. Because of the periods in hospital Stuart has actually only looked after Ella for 42 nights in the year. On 16 of the remaining nights that Ella should have stayed with him she was in hospital. On the other nights that Ella should have stayed with Stuart she was unwell and wanted to stay with Sarah. The CSA would have to decide whether to consider Ella as staying with Stuart for 58 nights or accept that the intention was for her to stay with Stuart on 104 nights in the year.

Where, having counted these nights, that person is not a:
- person with care;
- non-resident parent who shares care;
- local authority who has part-time care,

the night is treated as if the child is in the care of the principal provider of day-to-day care.[115] For example, if a babysitter looks after a child one night a week, then the child goes into hospital, the babysitter is not a person with care, non-resident parent or local authority. Therefore that night is treated as one normally spent with the principal provider of day-to-day care.

Shared care and part-time local authority care

There are different rules depending on the calculation rate which applies:
- basic and reduced rate; *or*
- flat rate.

Basic and reduced rate where the non-resident parent shares care

A non-resident parent (or parent with care treated as non-resident) may share care in a number of situations:
- caring for different qualifying children at different times;
- caring for qualifying children with more than one person with care.

There may be any number of variations and permutations. Indeed, in any one family situation there may be a number of non-resident parents and children.

As a guide, here is a step-by-step process to follow in working out maintenance for a non-resident parent where they share care. (Where care is provided in part by a local authority there is an additional calculation at Step 3.)

Step 1
Work out the basic or reduced amount of maintenance due including any apportionment that may apply.

Chapter 7: The 'new rules' maintenance calculation
3. Shared care

Step 2

Work out any decrease fraction in relation to the qualifying children of the non-resident parent cared for by the same person with care. Where there are two or more qualifying children add the relevant fractions together and divide by the total number of qualifying children that the person cares for.

Where this includes elements to reflect the non-resident parent's shared care and a local authority with part-time care, work out each amount separately and add the two fractions together.

Apply the appropriate fraction to the amount worked out in Step 2.

Apply any abatement for equal shared care (see below).

Step 3

Add together the amounts of maintenance due to each person with care to get the total child maintenance due. Where this results in an amount that is less than £5, the flat rate of £5 is payable. Where the £5 flat rate is due this is apportioned between the persons with care based on the number of qualifying children. (Treat those persons who care for the same qualifying child(ren) as a single unit, and then apportion this amount between them, depending on the amount of care given.)

Note: apportioning and rounding may result in adjustments of a penny in some calculations done by the CSA, to ensure that over time each person with care receives the proper amount due (see p126).

The decrease when the non-resident parent shares care

Where a non-resident parent, or parent with care who is treated as a non-resident parent, shares care for a qualifying child for 52 or more nights a year the amount of maintenance they are due to pay is reduced by a suitable fraction depending on the number of nights of shared care.[116] The amount depends on the relevant band, as shown in Table 7.5 below.[117]

Table 7.5: The effect of shared care

Number of nights	Fraction to subtract
52 to 103	One-seventh
104 to 155	Two-sevenths
156 to 174	Three-sevenths
175 or more	One-half

Where the non-resident parent shares care of a qualifying child for a sufficient number of nights for the one-half fraction to apply, an additional £7 decrease in maintenance must also be applied.[118] The CSA refers to this situation as equal shared care, even though the amount of time spent with each may not be the same.[119] This extra allowance where there is equal shared care is known as

147

Chapter 7: The 'new rules' maintenance calculation
3. Shared care

abatement.[120] Abatement will be applied for each child to whom equal shared care applies.

Where the decreases applied because of shared care result in the non-resident parent being liable to pay the person with care less than £5, the non-resident parent will instead pay the flat rate of £5.[121] This includes the situation where the total amount of maintenance due to all persons with care is decreased to less than £5, in which case the £5 is apportioned between the persons with care in relation to the number of qualifying children. For more detail on situations involving more than one person with care, see p328.

When applying the decrease for shared care the rounding provisions apply to the nearest penny.[122]

Example 7.11 Shared care with one person with care
a) Alex shares care of Mark with the person with care, Diane. He looks after Mark on average two nights at the weekend and a couple of weeks in school holidays. Although Alex is a parent with care he is treated as a non-resident parent as he is not the principal provider of care. Alex's net income is £240.
Step 1   Basic rate (15% of £240 = £36)
Step 2   Apply decrease for shared care
         Alex shares care in the 104 – 155 band (two-sevenths)
         36 maintenance must be decreased by 2/7 (ie, £36 – £10.29 = £25.71)
Alex pays Diane £25.71 due to shared care.

b) Alex increases the amount of time he shares care of Mark to three nights one week and four nights the next. In this case Alex shares care for over 175 nights and the one-half fraction is applied. Alex's maintenance calculated under the basic rate remains £36.
Step 2   £36 decreased by half (and a further £7 subtracted, ie, £18 – 7 = £11)
Because of the increase in shared care Alex pays maintenance of £11 to Diane.

c) Alex's circumstances change and he now has income of £160.
Step 1   Reduced rate of maintenance – ie, £5 + (25% of £60) = £5 + £15 = £20
Step 2   The fraction to apply remains at one-half and there is an abatement of £7
         (£20 x ½) – £7 = £10 – £7 = £3
Step 3   **Maintenance due** is below £5 so Alex is due to pay maintenance of £5 a week to Diane

More than one qualifying child

Where the person with care and non-resident parent have more than one qualifying child, the fractions that apply due to shared care for each qualifying child are added together; then divided by the number of qualifying children.[123] This applies where care is shared for some but not all qualifying children or there are different shared care arrangements for each qualifying child.

Chapter 7: The 'new rules' maintenance calculation
3. Shared care

Example 7.12 Shared care where there is more than one qualifying child in relation to a person with care

a) Pat is the non-resident parent of Lea and Dylan. Both are cared for by their grandmother Jean. Lea doesn't really like staying with Pat and only does so occasionally. However, Dylan stays with him on a Friday night and on a Saturday night as they support their local football team at home and away matches. Both children stay with him for a few days at Christmas and during the school holidays. Pat has net income of £220.

Step 1 **Basic rate** for two children (20% of £220 = £44)
Step 2 **Apply decrease for shared care**
Lea doesn't stay with Pat enough for it to count as shared care.
Dylan is in the 104 to 155 band (two-sevenths).
The fractions which apply are added together and divided by two, as there are two qualifying children that Jean cares for.
2/7 divided by 2 = 2/14
Pat's maintenance is decreased by 2/14 (ie, £6.29)

Due to shared care Pat must pay £37.71 (£44 – £6.29) to Jean in maintenance.

(Note: where Pat has costs for keeping in contact with Lea he may be able to apply for a variation – see Chapter 8.)

b) Lea increases the amount of time she spends with her dad, and now this counts as shared care.

Step 2 Lea in the 52 to 103 band (one-seventh)
Dylan in the 104 to 155 band (two-sevenths)
The fraction are added together and divided by two – ie, three-sevenths (3/7) divided by two = 3/14
The maintenance due is therefore decreased by 3/14 because of shared care.
Pat's maintenance is decreased by 3/14 (ie, £9.43)

Due to shared care Pat must pay £34.57 (£44 – £9.43) to Jean in maintenance.

c) Dylan stays with his dad more often and increases the amount of care, so that:

Step 2 Lea is in the 52 to 103 band (one-seventh)
Dylan is in the 175 or more band (one-half)
The decrease will be (1/7 + 1/2) divided by 2 = 9/28 (ie, £44 decreased by 9/28 = £14.14).
£44 – £14.14 = £29.86. However, because care is shared equally for one qualifying child the abatement of £7 applies and maintenance due is decreased by a further £7.

Pat now pays Jean maintenance of £22.86 (£29.86 – £7).

More than one person with care

A non-resident parent may be due to pay maintenance to more than one person with care because there:

Chapter 7: The 'new rules' maintenance calculation
3. Shared care

- are several qualifying children with different persons with care (known as multiple maintenance units);
- is more than one person with care in relation to a qualifying child(ren).

One or both of these situations may apply in any one case, and the non-resident parent may share care with only one or all of the persons with care. In these cases there may be apportioning and shared care adjustments made throughout the calculation.

Example 7.13 Shared care in multiple maintenance units

a) Ivan is the non-resident parent for two children, Holly, whose parent with care is Ellen, and Jamie, whose parent with care is Laura. Ivan looks after Holly when Ellen is on night shifts, which is every other week apart from holidays, and takes her camping with him on the odd weekend. Jamie and Laura live further away so he only sees Jamie for a long weekend once a month when he visits his parents and two weeks in the summer holidays. Ivan's net income is £230.

Step 1   **Basic rate** applies for two qualifying children, there are no relevant children, net income is £230
20% of £230 = £46
There is apportionment between the persons with care. They each care for one qualifying child so halve the maintenance between them.
To Ellen for Holly = £23
To Laura for Jamie = £23

Step 2   **Apply decrease for shared care**
Maintenance paid to Ellen for Holly
Holly is in the 156 to 174 band (three-sevenths)
3/7 of £23 = £9.86
£23 − £9.86 = £13.14
Maintenance paid to Laura for Jamie
Jamie is in the 52 to 103 band (one-seventh)
1/7 of £23 = £3.29
£23 − £3.29 = £19.71

Step 3   Total maintenance due £13.14 (to Ellen) + £19.71 (to Laura) = £32.85

b) The situation is as above but now Laura has a new job which means she is away from home on average two nights a week and the occasional weekend. Her sister (Alice) looks after Jamie and Laura asks the CSA to split the maintenance between her and Alice.

Step 1   **Basic rate** = £46
Apportion between the persons with care, there are two qualifying children but three persons with care – Ellen in relation to Holly, Laura and Alice in relation to Jamie.
To Ellen for Holly = £23
Between Laura and Alice for Jamie = £23

Chapter 7: The 'new rules' maintenance calculation
3. Shared care

Alice looks after Jamie two nights a week on average (2/6 – ie, one-third)
To Alice for Jamie = £7.67 (one-third of £23)
Laura looks after Jamie for the remaining four nights (4/6 – ie, two-thirds)
To Laura for Jamie = £15.33 (two-thirds of £23)

Step 2 **Apply decrease for shared care**
Maintenance paid to Ellen for Holly
Ivan's care for Holly is in the 156 to 174 band (three-sevenths)
3/7 of £23 = £9.86 (ie, £23 – £9.86 = £13.14)
Maintenance paid to Alice for Jamie
Ivan's care for Jamie is in the 52 to 103 band (one-seventh)
1/7 of £7.67 = £1.10; £7.67 – £1.10 = £6.57
Maintenance paid to Laura for Jamie
Ivan's care for Jamie is in the 52 to 103 band (one-seventh)
1/7 of £15.33 = £2.19; £15.33 – £2.19 = £13.14

Step 3 **Total maintenance** due £13.14 (to Ellen) + £6.57 (to Alice) + £13.14 (to Laura) = £32.85

Overall, Ivan pays exactly the same amount of maintenance as in part (a) but this time it is split between three people.

Flat rate where there is shared care

As with basic or reduced rate maintenance the non-resident parent may have more than one person with care and share care with one or more of them. In these cases one point must be established:
- Is the non-resident parent liable for the flat rate because he has income of under £100?

Where the answer to this question is yes, there will be no adjustment of his maintenance liability regardless of how many nights of shared care there are.

If the flat rate applies because the non-resident parent:
- is in receipt of a relevant benefit, (eg, incapacity benefit, maternity allowance – for full list, see p127), or he or his partner receives IS or income-based JSA (including cases where a reduced flat rate of £2.50 applies); *and*
- carers for a qualifying child for at least 52 nights a year,

then the amount of child maintenance due to the person with care of that qualifying child is nil.[124]

Where there is more than one person with care the flat rate is apportioned in relation to the number of qualifying children before any adjustment for shared care. This may mean that the non-resident parent's liability reduces to nil for one person with care because of shared care. However, he is still liable for the

Chapter 7: The 'new rules' maintenance calculation
3. Shared care

remaining amounts to the other person(s) with care, in which case he will pay an amount which is less than £5.[125]

In simple terms the process is:
- Step 1 – check the reason why the flat rate applies;
- Step 2 – apportion the flat rate between the persons with care on the basis of the number of qualifying children. Where appropriate, apply any apportioning in relation to a qualifying child where there is more than one person with care;
- Step 3 – apply any reduction to nil due to shared care.

(Note: apportioning and rounding may result in adjustments of a penny in some calculations done by the CSA – see p125.)

Example 7.14

a) Alistair is the non-resident parent in relation to Keith, who stays with his older brother Neil, and Katie who stays with her mum, Rachel. Alistair looks after Katie one or two nights a week but Keith and he do not get on. Both Neil and Rachel apply for maintenance. Alistair receives incapacity benefit (IB) and IS.

Step 1   Alistair is due to pay maintenance at the flat rate of £5, as he receives IB and IS.
Step 2   Apportion the flat rate of £5 between the persons with care in relation to the qualifying children each cares for – ie, the amount is halved.
            To Neil for Keith £2.50
            To Rachel for Katie £2.50
Step 3   Alistair cares for Katie over 52 nights a year; therefore the amount due reduces to nil.
            Alistair remains liable to pay £2.50 in maintenance to Neil for Keith.

b) The situation is as above but now Keith goes to stay with his granddad two nights a week. Neil asks for maintenance to be split between them and the CSA agrees to do this.

Step 1   Remains the same
Step 2   Rachel is due £2.50 but now the £2.50 for Keith is to be split between Neil and his grandad.
            Neil looks after Keith five nights out of seven, granddad looks after him two out of seven therefore:
            5/7 of £2.50 is due to Neil = £1.79
            2/7 of £2.50 is due to granddad = £0.72

In total Alistair is due to pay £2.51. This is more than the amount before apportioning due to the rounding provisions. In this case the maintenance will be adjusted by one penny to one of the persons with care. In this case Neil has his adjusted to £1.78 for a period, after which the adjustment is made to grandad's and he will receive £0.71 and Neil will receive £1.79.

Chapter 7: The 'new rules' maintenance calculation
3. Shared care

Care provided in part by the local authority

This section only applies if:
- the non-resident parent is liable to pay maintenance at the basic or reduced rate, or after a variation has been made which results in the non-resident parent paying maintenance at either of these rates;[126] *and*
- the qualifying child is cared for at least one night a week on average but not more than five (see below).

The non-resident parent does not have to be sharing care for part-time local authority care to affect the amount of maintenance he pays.

Part-time local authority care does not affect how maintenance is worked out in flat rate cases.

A local authority cannot be a person with care.[127] Therefore, if a child is in the care of the local authority for more than five nights a week, no child maintenance is payable by the non-resident parent, because there will be no person with care.[128]

Where the local authority cares for the child for 52 nights or more in the 12-month period ending with the relevant week, the maintenance to be paid by the non-resident parent will be decreased.[129] As in deciding day-to-day care, the Secretary of State may use a period other than 12 months which she considers to be more representative of current arrangements, a future period may also be considered if the qualifying child is to go into local authority care at or after the effective date.[130] Where an alternative period is used, the number of nights of care must be in the same ration as 52 to 12 months.[131] (Nights spent in hospital or boarding school which normally would have been spent in care are included – see p145.)

Local authority care only affects the calculation of maintenance when it applies to a qualifying child. If a relevant other child is in local authority care (whether full- or part-time), this will not affect how s/he is treated so long as the non-resident parent or his partner receives child benefit for her/him.

The decrease for part-time local authority care

Where the local authority has part-time care of a qualifying child, the basic or reduced rate maintenance calculated from the non-resident parent is decreased in relation to the number of nights the qualifying child spends in local authority care, as shown in Table 7.6.

In relation to the steps set out in example 7.13(b), this calculation would be carried out at Step 2. It may be carried out either on its own, where the non-resident parent does not share care, or alongside one carried out because the non-resident parent shares care (see p145).

Chapter 7: The 'new rules' maintenance calculation
3. Shared care

Table 7.6: The effect of part-time local authority care

Number of nights	Fraction to subtract
52 to 103	One-seventh
104 to 155	Two-sevenths
156 to 207	Three-sevenths
208 to 259	Four-sevenths
260 -262	Five-sevenths

Where the person with care and non-resident parent have more than one qualifying child, the fractions that apply for each qualifying child in local authority care are added together and divided by the number of qualifying children for whom maintenance is calculated.[132] This applies where the local authority cares for one or all qualifying children or there are different care arrangements for each qualifying child.

Where the decrease due to part-time care by the local authority would reduce the amount of maintenance due to less than £5 in relation to the only or all persons with care, then the amount due will be £5.

Example 7.15 Local authority provides part-time care
a) Jake is the non-resident parent for Michael and Leanne. Michael has just been placed under local authority supervision, which means that over the next six months he is to spend four nights a week in a residential unit. The rest of the time he spends with his mum, Naomi. Jake has net income of £280 and currently pays maintenance of £56 (basic rate maintenance). This must be superseded because of local authority care. The CSA supersedes the decision, considering the ratio in the six-month period.

Step 1   Basic rate 20% of £280 = £56
Step 2   Local authority care for Michael is in the 208 – 259 band (four-sevenths)
          The fractions which apply are added together and divided by the number of qualifying children – ie, 4/7 divided by 2 = 4/14.
          Jake's maintenance is decreased by 4/14 (ie, £16).
Jake now pays Naomi £40 (£56 – £16) in maintenance.

b) If Leanne was also in care for two nights a week:
Step 1   Same as above
Step 2   Local authority care for Leanne 104 –155 band (two-sevenths).
          Local authority care for Michael 208 –256 band (four-sevenths).
          The fractions are added together and divided by two:
          (2/7 + 4/7) = 6/7 divided by 2 = 6/14.
          Jake's maintenance decreases by 6/14 = £24.
Jake now pays Naomi £32 (ie £56 – £24) in maintenance.

Chapter 7: The 'new rules' maintenance calculation
3. Shared care

The non-resident parent shares care and local authority has part-time care

Where the non-resident parent shares care for a qualifying child and the local authority has part-time care of a qualifying child, in relation to the same person with care, the appropriate fractions are worked out under each provision and are added together.[133] The amount of maintenance due from the non-resident is then decreased by this fraction.

Where this decrease would result in the non-resident parent being due to pay less than £5, in relation to the only or all persons with care, the non-resident parent will be due to pay £5.[134]

In relation to the five steps, this calculation is carried out at Step 3.

Example 7.16 Where there is both shared care and part-time local authority care

a) The situation is as in example 7.15a only this time Leanne spends one night a week with Jake but Michael doesn't.

Step 2   Jake cares for Leanne 52–103 band (one-seventh).
    The fractions which apply are added together and divided by the number of qualifying children.
    1/7 divided by 2 = 1/14.
    Jake's maintenance due to shared care should be reduced by 1/14.
    Because Michael is in local authority care the maintenance due should be reduced by 4/14. This is added to the amount due to shared care.
    1/14 + 4/14 = 5/14.
    Jakes maintenance is reduced by £20 (5/14 of £56).
Jake now pays Naomi £36 (£56 – 20) in maintenance.

b) If the situation is as in example 7.15b and Leanne still spends one night a week with Jake.

Step 2   Jake's maintenance due to shared care should reduce by 1/14 (as above).
    Local authority care for Michael and Leanne should reduce maintenance by 6/14 (as example 7.15b).
    These fractions are added together:
    1/14 + 6/14 = 7/14 = 1/2.
    Jake's maintenance to is reduced by £28 (1/2 of £56)
Jake now pays Naomi £28 (ie, £56 – £28) in maintenance.

Chapter 7: The 'new rules' maintenance calculation
3. Shared care

Fig 7.6: A summary guide to child support maintenance calculations, including where there is apportionment and shared care

Make sure you have the information needed – eg, care arrangements for qualifying children including where apportionment and shared care apply, details of relevant and other relevant non-resident children, net income, local authority part-time care.

For each non-resident parent work out if the nil rate or flat rate applies due to the person's circumstances or benefit claim.

Otherwise work out the net income and apply the appropriate rate.

	Basic rate (net income £200 or more)	Reduced rate (net income £100 – £200)	Flat rate (net income £100 or less)	Nil rate (net income £5 or less)
Work out the amount due	*Work out* the net income. *Work out* any percentage reduction for relevant children. *Apply* the appropriate percentage to this based on the number of qualifying children (including any relevant non-resident children). *Round* this amount to the nearest pound.	*Work out* the net income between £100 and £200 (rounded to the nearest pound). *Multiply* this by a percentage depending on the number of relevant and qualifying children (including any relevant non-resident children). *Add* this to £5. *Round* this amount to the nearest pound.	Maintenance due £5	
Apportionment	Where there is more than one person with care for each non-resident parent, apportion the amount due between them depending on the number of qualifying children for whom they care (rounded to the nearest penny). (Note: If there is more than one person with care for a qualifying child split the amount due between them depending on the amount of care given; this only applies where the CSA has agreed to a request for apportionment.)			

156

Chapter 7: The 'new rules' maintenance calculation
3. Shared care

Shared care	Where the non-resident parent shares care, work out any decrease fraction that applies for each qualifying child cared for by the person with care. *Add* these together and divide by the total number of qualifying children (of the non-resident parents) cared for by the same person with care. *Add* this fraction to any decrease fraction due to local authority care of a qualifying child. (To work out local authority decrease fraction, add together fractions that apply for local authority care for each qualifying child of the non-resident parents cared for by the same person with care and divide this by the total number of qualifying children of the non-resident parents cared for by the same person with care). *Multiply* the maintenance due by the total decrease fraction. *Apply* any abatement that is appropriate due to equal shared care.	Unless the flat rate is due because the non-resident parent has income of £100 or less, where the non-resident parent shares care reduce the amount due to the appropriate person with care to nil. *Ignore* any local authority part-time care.
Check the total amount due from the non-resident parent or to the parent with care	*Total* all the amounts due from the non-resident parent. Where this is less than £5 the maintenance due is £5 apportioned between the persons with care depending on the number of qualifying children. (Note: Where the care of a qualifying child is shared between two persons with care and the CSA has agreed the proportion due for this child may be further apportioned.)	*Total* all the amounts due from the non-resident parent. Where there is shared care with some but not all persons with care, the non-resident parent pays less than £5.

157

Chapter 7: The 'new rules' maintenance calculation
3. Shared care

Note: The amount due may be affected by a variation (see Chapter 8) or court order phasing-in.

In addition, where an 'old rules' case converts, the transitional phasing may apply for up to five years or until the new amount (as worked out above) is reached (see Chapter 9).

Notes

1   s11(6) and Sch 1 Part 1 CSA 1991

1. Maintenance calculation rates
2   Sch 1 CSA 1991; reg 2(5) CS(MCSC) Regs
3   Reg 2(1) CS(MCSC) Regs
4   Reg 2(2) and (3) CS(MCSC) Regs
5   Sch 1 Part 1 para 6 CSA 1991
6   Reg 6 CS(MCSC) Regs
7   Apportionment
8   Sch 1 Part 1 para 1(2) CSA 1991
9   Apportionment
10 Sch 1 Part 1 para 4 CSA 1991; reg 5 CS(MS&CS) Regs as amended by reg 6(4)CS(MA)(No2) Regs 2003
11 Sch 1 Part 4 CSA 1991
12 Reg 4 CS(MCSC) Regs as amended by reg 6(3) CS(MA(No2) Regs 2003
13 para 4(1)(c) CS(MCSC) Regs
14 Sch 1 part 1 para4(2) CSA 1991; reg 4(3)(a) CS(MCSC) Regs
15 Reg 4(3)(b) CS(MCSC) Regs
16 Sch 1 Part 1 para 3 CSA 1991
17 Reg 3 CS(MCSC) Regs
18 Sch 1 Part 1 para 10C CSA 1991
19 Sch 1 Part 1(1) CSA 1991
20 Sch 1 Part 1 para10C CSA 1991
21 Reg 11(1) CS(MCSC) Regs
22 Relevant children
23 Reg 11(2 and 3) CS(MCSC) Regs as amended by ref 6(5) CS(MA)(No2) Res 2003
24 Reg 11(3) CS(MCSC) Regs as amended by reg 6(5) CS(MA) No2) Regs 2003
25 Reg 11(5) CS(MCSC) Regs as inserted by reg 6(5) CS(MA)(No2) Regs 2003
26 Reg 11(4) CS(MCSC) Regs

2. Net income
27 Sch 1 para 1 CS(MCSC) Regs
28 Sch 1 para 2(a) CS(MCSC) Regs
29 Sch 1 para 2(b) CS(MCSC) Regs
30 Sch 1 para 4 (1) CS(MCSC) Regs
31 Sch 1 Para 4(2) CS(MCSC) Regs
32 CCS/4/1994; R(CS)2/96; Allowable expenses
33 CCS/12073/1996; Allowable expenses
34 Sch 1 paras 3(1)(a), 7(6) CS(MCSC) Regs
35 Reg 1(2) CS(MCSC) Regs
36 Reg 7C SS&CS(D&A) Regs
37 Sch 1 Part II para 15 CSA 1991
38 Reg 1(2) CS(MCSC) Regs
39 Sch 1 para 6(1) CS(MCSC) Regs
40 Sch 1 Part II para 6(4) CS(MCSC) Regs
41 CCS/16/1994; CCS/11873/1996
42 CCS/6810/1995
43 CCS/511/1995
44 CCS/7312/1995; CCS/556/1995; CSCS/1/1996; CSCS/6/1996
45 Sch 1 Part II para 6(3) CS(MCSC) Regs
46 Reg 2(4) CS(MCSC) Regs
47 CCS/2750/1995
48 CCS/556/1995
49 Sch 1 Part II para 5 CS(MCSC) Regs
50 Sch 1 Part II para 5(2) CS(MCSC) Regs
51 Sch 1 Part III para 7(1) CS(MCSC) Regs
52 Sch 1 part III para 7(2) CS(MCSC) Regs
53 Approaching the Inland Revenue for self-employed income
54 Sch 1 Part III para 7(3) CS(MCSC) Regs
55 Sch 1 Part III para 7(4) CS(MCSC) Regs
56 Sch 1 Part III para 7(5) CS(MCSC) Regs
57 Sch 1 part III para 7(6) CS(MCSC) Regs
58 Self-assessment returns
59 Sch 1 Part III para 8(1) CS(MCSC) Regs

Chapter 7: The 'new rules' maintenance calculation
Notes

60 Sch 1 Part III para 8(2) CS(MC&SC Regs
61 Reasonably incurred expense
62 Wholly and exclusively defrayed expense
63 Allowable expenses
64 Sch 1 Part III para 10 CS(MCSC) Regs
65 Sch 1 Part III para 8(4) CS(MCSC) Regs
66 Sch 1 Part III para 8(3)(a) CS(MCSC) Regs
67 CCS/15949/1996
68 Sch 1 Part III para 8(3)(b) CS(MCSC) Regs
69 Sch 1 Part III para 9(2) CS(MCSC) Regs
70 Business receipts; Business expenses
71 Sch 1 para 9(3) CS(MCSC) Regs
72 CCS/3182/1995; CCS/6145/1995
73 Sch 1 Part III para 9(3) CS(MCSC) Regs
74 Treatment of self-employed earnings
75 CCS/7966/1995
76 Sch 1 Part IV para 11(1) CS(MCSC) Regs
77 Sch 1 Part IV para 11(2) CS(MCSC) Regs
78 Sch 1 Part IV Para 11(2A) CS(MCSC) Regs
79 Sch 1 Part IV para 11(1) CS(MCSC) Regs
80 Sch 1 Part IV para 12 CS(MCSC) Regs
81 Sch 1 Part IV para 13A CS(MCSC) Regs
82 Sch 1 Part V para 15 CS(MCSC) Regs
83 Sch 1 Part V para 16 CS(MCSC) Regs
84 Sch 1 Part V para 16(2) CS(MCSC) Regs
85 Sch 1 para 10 CSA 1991

3. Shared care
86 Reg 8(1) CS(MCSC) Regs
87 PWC and NRP provide different information
88 Calculate shared care
89 PWC and NRP provide different information
90 CCS/11728/1996
91 Reg 1(2) 'day-to-day care' (a) CS(MCSC) Regs
92 Reg 1(2) 'day-to-day care' (b) CS(MCSC) Regs; CCS/6/1994
93 Alternative period for establishing day-to-day care
94 Reg 7(4) CS(MCSC) Regs
95 Regs 1(2) day-to-day care; CCS/449/1995
96 Reg 1(2)(b)(i) CS (MCSC) Regs
97 CCS/12686/1996
98 Reg 8 CS(MCSC) Regs
99 Reg 8(2) CS(MCSC) Regs
100 Deciding who should be treated as the NRP
101 s144(3) and Sch 10 SSCBA 1992
102 Deciding who should be treated as the NRP
103 s5(1) CSA 1991
104 Reg 14(2)(a) CS(MCSC) Regs
105 Reg 14(2)(b) CS(MCSC) Regs
106 Reg 14(2)(c) CS(MCSC) Regs
107 Sch 1 Part 1 paras 7 and 8 CSA 1991
108 Reg 7(1) CS(MCSC) Regs
109 Reg 7(3) CS(MCSC) Regs
110 Reg 7(4) CS(MCSC) Regs
111 Reg 7(5) CS(MCSC) Regs
112 Reg 12 CS(MCSC) Regs
113 Reg 7(6) CS(MCSC) Regs
114 Reg 9(10) CS(MCSC) Regs
115 Reg 1(2)(b)(i) CS(MCSC) Regs
116 Sch 1 part 1 para 7 CSA 1991
117 Sch 1 part 1 para 7(4) CSA 1991
118 Sch 1 part 1 para 7(6) CSA 1991
119 Equal shared care – new rules
120 Abatement
121 Sch 1 part 1 para 7(7) CSA 1991
122 Reg 2(2) CS(MCSC) Regs
123 Sh1 part 1 para 7(5) CSA 1991
124 Sch 1 part 1 para 8 CSA 1991
125 Shared care where flat rate liability applies
126 Reg 9(1) CS(MCSC) Regs
127 Reg 21(1)(a) CS(MCP) Regs
128 Care provided in part by the local authority
129 Reg 9(2) and (4) CS(MCSC) Regs
130 Reg 9(2)(c) CS(MCSC) Regs
131 Reg 9(5) CS(MCSC) Regs
132 Reg 9(7) CS(MCSC) Regs
133 Reg 9(8) CS(MCSC) Regs
134 Reg 9(9)(a) CS(MCSC) Regs

Chapter 8

Variations in 'new rules' cases

This chapter covers:
1. Grounds for a variation (below)
2. Applying for a variation (p173)
3. Procedure (p174)
4. The decision (p180)

This information only applies to 'new rules' or conversion cases. There are additional provisions which must be read with this information in conversion cases where there is an existing departure direction or application for a departure (see Chapter 9).

An application for a variation to the maintenance calculation may be made before a calculation is made or once a maintenance calculation is in force.[1]

A variation to the calculation can only be made under a ground laid out in the legislation and only if it would be just and equitable to do so (see p178).

An application may be rejected in specific circumstances, either at preliminary consideration or at a later stage (see p175). In certain cases the CSA may refer the application to an appeal tribunal for determination (see p180).

If an application is successful it may result in a maintenance calculation being made, or where a calculation already exists being revised or superseded, incorporating the variation (see p184).

There is no separate variation decision; the decision is whether to revise/ supersede the maintenance calculation or refuse to revise/supersede the maintenance calculation with or without a variation element. This simplifies appeal rights, as there is only one decision to appeal.

1. Grounds for a variation

The grounds for a variation fall into three groups:[2]
- special expenses (see p161);
- property or capital transfers made before 5 April 1993 (see p166);
- additional cases (see p168).

Special expenses

Variation can be considered on special expenses grounds where there are:[3]
- costs due to maintaining contact with the child(ren) for whom the calculation is, or will be, in force;
- costs due to the long-term illness or disability of a relevant child;
- prior debts, incurred before the couple separated;
- boarding school fees being paid for the child(ren) for whom the calculation is, or will be, in force;
- costs from paying a mortgage on the person with care's and child(ren)'s home.

Except for costs due to illness and disability of a relevant child, there is a threshold level, which must be exceeded.[4] Where the net income of the non-resident parent is:
- £200 or more, the threshold is £15;
- below £200, the threshold is £10.

The threshold applies to one ground or where there is more than one relevant ground, the sum of those costs. This also means that the first £10 or £15 of these special expenses will be disregarded when calculating the variation and any subsequent adjustment to the calculation.[5] The disregard, like the threshold, does not apply to the costs due to illness and disability of a relevant child.

The Secretary of State can also substitute a lower amount for any special expenses costs that s/he thinks are unreasonably high or have been unreasonably incurred.[6] This may be below the threshold amount or nil. In the case of contact costs, any reduced amount must not be so low that it makes it impossible for contact to occur at the level of frequency stated in any court order, so long as those visits are taking place.[7]

Contact costs

Only costs that relate to the non-resident parent maintaining contact with the qualifying child can be included.[8] They can be for the non-resident parent or the child. The cost of a travelling companion can also be included – eg, because of disability, long-term illness or the young age of the child.

Costs of contact cannot include those that arise where the non-resident parent shares care of the child and that are already taken into account under the shared care provisions.[9] For example, this excludes the cost of travel to pick the child up for an overnight stay that counts as a night of shared care that the non-resident parent already has taken into account in his maintenance calculation.

The costs of phone calls, day trips and upkeep of a car are not included.[10]

The following can count as contact costs:[11]
- tickets for public transport;
- fuel for a private car;

Chapter 8: Variations in 'new rules' cases
1. Grounds for a variation

- taxi fares – but only where the illness or disability of the non-resident parent or qualifying child makes it impractical to use another form of transport;
- car hire – where the cost of the journey would be less than by public transport or taxis or a combination of both;
- accommodation costs for the parent or the child for overnight stays – where a return journey on the same day is impractical, or the pattern of care includes contact over two or more days;
- minor incidental costs such as tolls or fees for roads/bridges. It may include parking fees and ticket reservation fees if it was necessary to incur these to maintain contact with the child.

The costs are based on an established pattern of visits if one exists.[12] If there is no current established pattern, a previous one may be referred to if contact is to begin again, or an intended pattern, agreed between the non-resident parent and person with care. The pattern set out in a court order may also be used, if the decision maker is satisfied that this level of contact is, or will be, taking place.[13]

The costs are calculated as an average weekly amount. This will be based on a 12 month, or shorter, period which ends just before the first day of the maintenance period in which the variation would take effect.[14] In other cases, it can be based on anticipated costs or, where it is based on a pattern which ends before the maintenance calculation, the CSA will consider the costs incurred between the effective date of the variation and the date on which it would cease (ie, the date on which the circumstances giving rise to the variation ended) and the date of the interim maintenance decision/maintenance calculation.[15]

When contact is set out in a court order, it may only specify an upper limit on visits. The CSA is advised to consider what is a reasonable balance between maintenance paid and visits made.[16] A non-resident parent who visits more often than the court order states may wish to change the order to reflect the true position.

To determine if the cost for fuel is reasonable the CSA will compare the amount claimed with an average figure.[17] This is 10.5p per mile assuming petrol costs 69.5p per litre. The CSA can adjust the figure to reflect changes in petrol prices or regional differences. The figure is used as a guide and need not be stuck to rigidly.

If the non-resident parent returns from abroad and contact is only one reason for the trip, the CSA may limit costs to those of travel from his home in the UK. The CSA will only allow those costs that are a necessary and integral consequence of maintaining contact with the child.

Overnight costs only include reasonable accommodation costs. It does not cover the cost of meals and sundries. The only exception is where breakfast is included as part of the accommodation cost – ie, its cost cannot be separately identified.[18]

Chapter 8: Variations in 'new rules' cases
1. Grounds for a variation

Changes in contact may mean changes to the variation element. If contact stops, even through no fault of the non-resident parent, the calculation may be superseded to reflect this change (see p184).

Example 8.1
Bronwen has a net income of £428 and pays basic rate maintenance of £86 to Ivan for Ursula and Gretchen. She claims special expenses cost for contact with her children, amounting to £450 over a six-month period since the girls went to boarding school. This includes travel from Northern Ireland by ferry, petrol and overnight stays in hotels, amounting to 18 nights over the six-month period.
The amounts included are deemed reasonable in the circumstances and the weekly amount is calculated:
£450 divided by 26 = £17.30 a week on average
This is above the threshold of £15; therefore a variation of £2.30 (£17.30 – £15) for contact costs may be considered.
If Bronwen and the children stayed together at the same hotel she would not be able to claim accommodation costs for both her and the children as part of her contact costs. Plus, as the number of nights that they stay together is 18 (ie, less than 26 nights in six months), the shared care rules would not result in an reduction of her maintenance.

Costs of the long-term illness or disability of a relevant child

The costs may only relate to a relevant child – ie, a child for whom the non-resident parent or his new partner receives child benefit.

A long-term illness is one current at the date of the variation application or from the date the variation would take effect. It must be likely to last for a further 52 weeks or to be terminal.[19] The child is considered disabled if:[20]
- disability living allowance (DLA) is paid for her/him;
- s/he would receive DLA but for the fact that s/he is in hospital; *or*
- s/he are blind or registered as blind.

Costs allowable are the reasonable additional costs of:[21]
- personal care, attendance and communication needs;
- mobility;
- domestic help;
- medical aids which cannot be provided under the NHS;[22]
- heating, clothing and laundry;
- food essential for a diet recommended by a medical practitioner;
- adaptations to the non-resident parent's home; *and*
- day care, respite care and rehabilitation.

Where an aid or appliance can be provided under the NHS (by health services or local authorities) a variation may not be agreed. This includes situations where

Chapter 8: Variations in 'new rules' cases
1. Grounds for a variation

the item cannot be supplied due to lack of funds. However, a variation may be agreed to prevent a serious deterioration of the child's condition which could result from any delay in accessing the aid.[23] The decision maker will also consider the cost of the aid and whether it can be obtained at a cheaper price.

Any financial help towards these costs from any source is deducted.[24] This includes DLA but only where it relates to the expense claimed – eg, where DLA is awarded for care and mobility, and the non-resident parent claims for the costs of travelling to and from hospital, only the amount of the mobility component will be offset against the costs.[25] Where DLA has been applied for but is not in payment it can be included if, when awarded, it will cover the date the variation starts. In other cases where no financial assistance is in payment, no amount will be offset against the costs.

Debts of the relationship

A non-resident parent may be repaying debts incurred *before* he became a non-resident parent (see p29) of the qualifying child (whether before or after April 1993). Repayment can count as special expenses, but only if the debt was incurred when the non-resident parent and person with care were a couple (see p32). The debts must be for the benefit of:[26]
- the non-resident parent and person with care, jointly;
- the person with care alone, if the non-resident parent is liable for the repayments;
- a person who is not a child but at the time the debt was incurred:
  – was a child;
  – lived with the non-resident parent and person with care; *and*
  – was the child of the non-resident parent or person with care or both of them;
- the qualifying child;
- any child other than the qualifying child who at the time the debt was incurred:
  – lived with the non-resident parent and person with care; *and*
  – is a child of the person with care.

Loans only count if they are from a qualified lender or from a current or former employer.[27] Qualified lender includes banks, building societies or other registered lenders (eg, hire purchase).[28]

The following do *not* count as debts:
- debts incurred to buy something which the non-resident parent kept after the relationship ended;[29]
- a loan other than one obtained from a qualified lender or the non-resident parent's current or former employer;[30]
- a debt for which the applicant took responsibility under a financial settlement with the ex-partner or a court order;[31]

Chapter 8: Variations in 'new rules' cases
1. Grounds for a variation

- a debt for which a variation has previously been agreed but which has not been repaid in the period for which the variation has been applied to the calculation;[32]
- secured mortgage repayments, except for amounts incurred to buy or repair/improve (see p243)[33] the home of the person with care and qualifying child; *and*
- endowment/insurance premiums, except for mortgage/insurance incurred to buy or repair/improve (see p243) the home of the person with care and qualifying child.[34]

Payments or a debt taken out to pay off any negative equity on the former marital home do not count as debts, as the person with care no longer lives there.[35]

The following also do *not* count as debts:[36]
- debts of a business or trade;
- gambling debts;
- legal costs of the separation or divorce;
- credit card repayments;
- overdrafts, unless it was taken out for a specified amount repayable over a specified period;
- fines imposed on the applicant;
- any debt incurred to pay off one of these; *or*
- any other debt the CSA considers it reasonable to exclude.

A debt incurred to partially pay a debt which would have counted may be included. However, only that part which could have counted is included as special expenses.[37]

A variation is normally based on the original debt repayment period; any rescheduling of the debt is usually ignored.[38] However, if the applicant has been unemployed or ill and the creditors have agreed to extend the repayment period, the CSA can take the extended period into account. There is discretion as to the length of time over which the debt may be taken as extended when setting the period for which the variation for prior debt applies to the calculation.

Boarding school fees

The maintenance element of boarding school fees incurred, or expected to be incurred, by the non-resident parent for the qualifying child attending the school may be considered.[39] Only term-time costs for non-advanced education at a recognised educational establishment can be included.[40]

If the maintenance element cannot be distinguished from other costs the Secretary of State can decide what to include, but this should not exceed 35 per cent of the total fees.[41]

Where the non-resident parent receives financial help to pay the fees or only pays part of the fees with someone else, a proportion of the costs are included. This is calculated in the same ratio as the maintenance element to overall fees.[42]

Chapter 8: Variations in 'new rules' cases
1. Grounds for a variation

In all cases, a variation for boarding school fees should not reduce the amount of income to be considered for calculating maintenance by more than 50 per cent.[43]

Example 8.2
Bronwen claims special expenses for her contribution to boarding school costs for Ursula and Gretchen. She pays the school £1,500 a term – ie, £4,500 a year. Ivan pays the rest of the fees – ie, £4,500 a year. Her net income is £428.
The fees for each child per term are £1,500 and the maintenance element is £500 a term. Bronwen's contribution to maintenance is worked out as £250 a child each term – ie, £500. Over the three terms this amounts to £1,500 which is converted into a weekly figure (£1,500 ÷ 365 x 7 = £28.77). This is above the threshold of £15 so a variation for a contribution to boarding school fees of £13.77 may be considered. (If this was accepted it would not reduce the net income by more than 50 per cent.)

Payments for certain mortgages, loans or insurance policies

This covers payments made to a mortgage lender, insurer or person with care for a mortgage or loan where:[44]
- it was taken out to facilitate the purchase of, or repairs/improvements to, the property by someone other than the non-resident parent;
- the payments are not made due to a debt or other legal liability of the non-resident parent for the period in which the variation is applied for;
- the property was the person with care's and non-resident parent's home when they were a couple, and it is still the home of the person with care and qualifying child; *and*
- the non-resident parent has no legal/financial rights in the property – eg, charge, equitable interest.

Payments may also be considered for an insurance/endowment policy taken out to discharge a mortgage or loan as above, except where the non-resident parent is entitled to any part of the proceeds when the policy matures.[45]

Property/capital transfers

Variation is only possible where a pre-5 April 1993 court order or written agreement was in force between the non-resident parent and the person with care and/or the child(ren) in the child maintenance application.[46] The court order must have been to transfer property/capital in lieu of maintenance for the child either wholly or in part.[47] If the court order specifies that it is in lieu of spousal maintenance only, the variation will be disallowed.[48]

The court order must be made under:[49]
- Part 2 of the Matrimonial Causes Act 1973;

Chapter 8: Variations in 'new rules' cases
1. Grounds for a variation

- the Domestic Proceedings and Magistrate's Court Act 1978;
- Part 3 of the Matrimonial and Family Proceedings Act 1984;
- the Family Law (Scotland) Act 1985;
- Schedule 1 to the Children Act; *or*
- any other prescribed enactment.

The transfer must mean that the non-resident parent has transferred any beneficial interest in the property/capital to:[50]
- the person with care;
- the qualifying child; *or*
- trustees where the trust is set up solely, or as one of its objects, to provide maintenance for the qualifying child.

Where the transfer does not satisfy any of these conditions but the Secretary of State is satisfied that some or all of the property subsequently transferred to the person with care, the transfer will be accepted.[51]

The CSA first works out the value of the transfer, ignoring any part which was not in lieu of child maintenance.[52] (Allowance is also made for any compensating transfer from the person with care to the non-resident parent.) Unless there is evidence to show otherwise, the CSA assumes that:[53]
- the property covered by the order/agreement was held in equal shares by the non-resident parent and person with care;
- if those parties had been married, half of the value of the transfer was for the person with care's benefit, and not for the child(ren);
- if those parties were *never* married, *none* of the value of the transfer was for the person with care's benefit.

The minimum value of the transfer must be £5,000.[54]

The equivalent weekly value is then worked out. The number of years of liability is deemed to begin on the date of the order/agreement and to end on the date it sets for maintenance to end (for the youngest child if there is more than one), or, if no date is given, when the youngest child reaches 18.[55] Using that figure and the interest rate at the date of the order/agreement, a multiplier is given by a table.[56] That gives an equivalent weekly value. If using that figure in the variation would lead to an amount of maintenance of less than the child maintenance payable under the order/agreement, a lower weekly value can be set.[57]

Example 8.3

Marcus and Helene divorced in 1990, when their youngest child, Robert, was two (he is now 14). Marcus transferred his share in the home to Helene, in lieu of maintenance for her and the children. Marcus applies for a variation on property transfer grounds.

Chapter 8: Variations in 'new rules' cases
1. Grounds for a variation

The value of the house at that time was £46,000 but there was a mortgage of £14,000. The CSA considers that of the £16,000 transferred (£46,000 – £14,000 divided by two as they each had equal shares) only £8,000 can be considered in lieu of child maintenance. This is above the threshold of £5,000.

The number of years of liability is worked out as 16 (ie, from the date of the order until Robert is 18). The interest rate for a judgement debt at the time of the order was 15 per cent. Based on the table of equivalent values this gives a multiplier of 0.00323.

The equivalent weekly value of the property transfer to be considered is £8,000 x 0.00323 = £25.84.

Additional cases

There are additional cases in which a variation may be applied for by a person with care or child in Scotland. These are where the non-resident parent has:[58]
- assets over £65,000;
- a lifestyle which is inconsistent with stated income;
- income which has not been taken into account in the calculation; *or*
- has diverted income.

The effect of a variation on additional cases grounds will be to increase the net weekly income of the non-resident parent to be taken into account in the calculation.[59] The maximum net weekly income, after adding any amount for additional cases variation(s) cannot exceed the capped amount of £2,000.

Where the non-resident parent is in receipt of a benefit (other than income support (IS) or income-based jobseeker's allowance (JSA)) that attracts the flat rate, even though they may not pay this because of shared care or because they qualify for the nil rate (but not on income grounds) there are special rules regarding the maximum amount payable when a variation is agreed on additional cases grounds.[60] This is known as the 'better buy' (see p182).

Assets over £65,000

The Secretary of State must be satisfied that the asset:[61]
- is under the non-resident parent's control, or is one which he has a beneficial interest in;
- has been transferred to trustees, but the non-resident parent is the beneficiary of the trust, and the transfer was made to reduce the amount of assets which could be considered under a variation application;
- is subject to a trust of which the non-resident parent is a beneficiary.

Assets include:[62]
- money – actual cash or deposits in banks, building society, post office accounts, premium bonds or savings certificates;
- legal estate, interest in or rights over land;

Chapter 8: Variations in 'new rules' cases
1. Grounds for a variation

- stocks and shares;
- claims it would be reasonable to enforce;
- in Scotland, monies due or an obligation owed which it would be reasonable to enforce; *and*
- any of the above located outside Great Britain.

The Secretary of State will not count assets where:[63]
- the total value of the assets after repaying any mortgage/charge on them is £65,000 or less;
- s/he is satisfied the non-resident parent is holding the asset for a reasonable purpose (eg, cash from the sale of a home that is intended to purchase a new home shortly);
- the asset is compensation for personal injury;
- the asset is used for a trade or business (except where it is a property which produces rental income);
- the asset is the home of the non-resident parent or his child; *or*
- the non-resident parent is a claimant and usually where the asset is a payment from certain trusts (eg, Macfarlane Trust or the variant CJD compensation trust).[64]

Where an asset is held in joint names the Secretary of State will assume that each person has equal shares unless there is evidence to suggest otherwise.[65]

The weekly value of the assets is worked out by multiplying the value of the assets by the statutory rate of interest and dividing the resulting figure by 52 to produce a weekly amount.[66] The statutory rate of interest is that which applies at the effective date in the non-resident parent's country of habitual residence (ie, England, Wales, Scotland or Northern Ireland); this is currently 8 per cent.[67] Where the non-resident parent works abroad for a UK-based employer the rate is based on the locality of the employer. The weekly value is added to other income, including benefits (ie, IS/JSA, those prescribed for the flat rate – less disregards) and bearing in mind the better buy rules for those on benefit (see p182).[68]

Example 8.4
Graham has a net income of £480 a week and pays maintenance to Andie of £96 a week. Andie applies for a variation on the grounds that Graham has substantial assets – ie, a holiday home in Spain and savings.
The property in Spain has a value of £52,000 and Graham has savings and investments of £17,000. The total value of his assets is £69,000, which is above the threshold of £65,000. A variation may be considered using a weekly value worked out as £106.15 (ie, £69,000 x 8% ÷ 52)

169

Chapter 8: Variations in 'new rules' cases
1. Grounds for a variation

If Graham had owned the property in Spain jointly with his new partner, Nadia, the total value of his assets would have been £26,000 + £17,000 = £43,000, which is below the threshold.

Income not taken into account and diversion of income

Income not taken into account covers situations where:[69]
- the non-resident parent is on the nil rate (except where this is due to income being below £5) or the flat rate due to receipt of a prescribed benefit (other than IS or income-based JSA), even though he may pay less due to shared care; *and*
- the Secretary of State is satisfied he has net income of over £100.

When working out the earnings of students when calculating a variation, the total income for the year, ending with the relevant week, is added together and divided by 52 to give a weekly amount. An alternative period may be used if the Secretary of State considers it more representative.

The weekly value of any additional income is added to other income from benefits, bearing in mind that the better buy (see p182) applies to those on benefit when calculating the maximum maintenance due.[70] Benefits include those prescribed for the flat rate, except IS/income-based JSA, less any disregards.[71]

> **Example 8.5**
> Joel is a mature student who works part time in a care home. He is on the nil rate for maintenance. Kaliani applies for a variation on income not taken into account grounds. Kaliani looks after one child, Selim.
> Joel's student grant and loan do not count as income, so only his part-time earnings are considered. Over the year Joel's net earnings are £9,367.80, which is converted into a weekly amount (ie, £9,367.80 ÷ 52 = £180.15). As this is over £100 a variation may be considered using a weekly value figure of £180.15. Therefore, if the variation to the calculation is agreed, instead of paying nothing Joel will now be due to pay a reduced rate of £25 (£5 + 25% of £80.15 = £25.04 rounded to the nearest pound).

Diversion of income is considered where the:[72]
- non-resident parent has the ability to control the income that he receives, including earnings from self-employment; *and*
- Secretary of State is satisfied that the non-resident parent has unreasonably reduced the amount of income he would have received by diverting it to someone else in order to reduce child support liability.

CSA guidance gives the following examples of diversion:[73]
- to a third party, such as a new partner or close family member;

Chapter 8: Variations in 'new rules' cases
1. Grounds for a variation

- to the business, such as where the non-resident parent takes a lower income, or to a pension scheme from which the non-resident parent will benefit later. It would, however, have to be reasonable to make a variation in such circumstances – eg, if the money is being used to develop the company, a variation should not be made;
- through the business, such as where the non-resident parent uses company assets for private use or business funds for day-to-day expenditure.

Example 8.6
Marcus runs his own import/export business, employing his new partner, Shamira, and his brother. Each has a company car, in his case a Jaguar. His brother is paid £600 a week and he and Shamira each receive £400. His ex-wife, Helene, gets basic rate maintenance of £80 for their two children. Helene applies for a variation because she thinks he is diverting income via the company, especially as Shamira doesn't seem to do any work.
Part of his day-to-day expenses are included in business expenses – eg, the car, business lunches. Shamira's salary could also be a token payment, as Marcus takes less from the business than he pays his brother. The CSA considers that on balance there could be diversion of income via the company and Shamira's wages. Given its contentious nature the case is referred to an appeal tribunal.

The full amount of any diverted income will be added to net weekly income when working out maintenance.[74]

Lifestyle inconsistent with declared income

The person with care or a section 7 applicant may apply for a variation on this ground where:[75]
- a maintenance calculation has been made based on net weekly income or not based on net weekly income (see Table 8.1 on p172); *and*
- the Secretary of State is satisfied that the income used in the calculation (or which would have been used) is substantially lower than that needed to support the non-resident parent's lifestyle.

However, a variation will not be allowed where it is clear that the lifestyle is paid for by:[76]
- income which is or would be disregarded under the maintenance calculation;
- income which could be considered under the diversion of income ground;
- assets, or income from assets; *or*
- a partner's income or assets, except if the non-resident parent is able to influence or control the amount of income or assets or income from the assets.

In addition to these situations, where the calculation is not based on net weekly income, a variation will not be allowed where the lifestyle is paid for from income

Chapter 8: Variations in 'new rules' cases
1. Grounds for a variation

of £100 or less, or which could be considered in the income not taken into account ground.[77]

Table 8.1: Situations where lifestyle inconsistent with declared income will be considered

Non-resident parent's child maintenance based on net weekly income is or would be:	Non-resident parent's child maintenance not based on net weekly income is or would be:
the basic rate;	the flat rate due to receipt of a benefit, other than IS or income based JSA (including where the amount paid is less than this due to shared care);
the reduced rate;	
the flat rate ie due to net weekly income of 100 or less;	
the nil rate (ie, due to net weekly income of less than £5);	the nil rate.
equivalent to the flat rate due to shared care;	
equivalent to the flat rate due to a property transfer variation, part-time care by a local authority or there is an 'old rules' case that has been converted with a property transfer departure.	

The amount of income which will be taken into account will be the difference between the income:[78]
- the non-resident parent needs to support his overall lifestyle; *and*
- taken into account (or which would have been taken into account) in the maintenance calculation.

This includes any income from benefits (ie, except for IS/income-based JSA, benefits prescribed for the flat rate less disregards), bearing in mind the better buy rules for those on benefit (see p182).

CSA guidance indicates that this ground is most likely to be used in situations where the non-resident parent is self-employed or where it is suspected that they are working in the black economy.[79] It would not be enough to show that the non-resident parent pursued one extravagant activity, as there may be good reasons for this (eg, economies in other areas). The non-resident parent must have an overall lifestyle which in most respects is inconsistent with declared income – eg, a large, expensively furnished home, expensive car, frequent foreign holidays and expensive leisure activities would all be considered.

Example 8.7
Marcus lives with his new partner, Shamira, in a townhouse in central London. He runs his own import/export business. His ex-wife, Helene, gets basic rate maintenance of £80 for

their two children. Helene applies for a variation because Marcus is able to afford to live in central London, drive a new Jaguar (changing cars every two or three years), he plays polo (keeping three ponies in stables), is a member of an exclusive golf club and he and Shamira frequently travel abroad.

Part of the expenses are included in business expenses – eg, the car and travel abroad on business trips, and the golf club membership is used for corporate entertaining. Shamira is also an employee of the company, meaning her income is under Marcus's control, though her wages are equivalent to that of other staff. The CSA considers that on balance his lifestyle does appear inconsistent with his income. However, it also considers that there could be diversion of income. Given its contentious nature, the case is referred to an appeal tribunal.

Had the situation been reversed, with Shamira independently wealthy, owning the business and paying for the lifestyle, including paying Marcus's wages, the case may have been refused. Helene may wish to appeal such a refusal. However, the CSA should also consider whether there has been diversion of income or assets which Marcus can control.

2. Applying for a variation

An application for a variation may be made before or after a maintenance calculation has been made.[80] Only a relevant person may apply – ie, a person with care, a non-resident parent or a section 7 applicant. An authorised representative may also make an application. However, the Secretary of State has discretion to reinstate a previous variation without any application in certain prescribed circumstances (see p186).

The application for a variation may be made either orally or in writing.[81] This means an applicant may give details over the phone, although the Secretary of State may ask for a written application. A form may be provided or the applicant may send a letter or fax.[82] Where a written application is required this should be provided within 14 days. Where the time limit is exceeded without good cause this can affect the effective date of the variation.

The application must state the grounds on which it is made.[83] Where the application does not state the grounds or at least give a reason it will not be accepted as properly made.

Example 8.8
(a) Joe applies for a variation because he believes his maintenance is too high. The CSA does not accept it as a properly made application.
(b) Joe applies for a variation because he believes his maintenance is too high and he cannot afford it due to the high cost of pet food. The CSA accepts the application as properly made but reject it on preliminary consideration, as it is not on a regulated ground.

Chapter 8: Variations in 'new rules' cases
2. Applying for a variation

(c) Joe applies for a variation because he believes his maintenance is too high because he cannot afford the kennel costs he incurs when he travels to have contact with his children. The CSA accepts the application is properly made and it is given preliminary consideration. It rejects it as kennel costs are not a recognised ground. However, had he made reference to other contact costs (eg, tickets or fuel) his application would probably have proceeded.

Where an application is made but there is insufficient information to decide whether to progress it, the Secretary of State may request further information.[84] The request may be made orally or in wiring.[85] The applicant is given one month, from the date of notification, in which to supply the information.[86] This time limit may be extended in special circumstances – eg, the applicant is in hospital. If the information is not provided, the Secretary of State may reject the application or proceed with it at their discretion.[87]

An application for a variation may be amended or withdrawn at any time before a decision is made on it.[88] This may be done orally or in writing. No amendment can be made where the change relates to a period after the effective date of the application.[89]

3. Procedure

Once an application has been made the procedure is as follows:
- preliminary consideration of the application;
- unless rejected, other parties may be notified and asked to make representations, known as contest (see p176);
- an interim maintenance decision may be made (see p177):
- a regular payment condition may be imposed (see p178);
- the decision will be considered (see p178).

In addition, the case may be passed to an appeal tribunal after preliminary consideration for a determination (see p180).

The application will proceed for determination unless it has already failed because:[90]
- one of the grounds for rejection is established;
- it is withdrawn; *or*
- the regular payment condition has not been met.

Two or more applications for a variation may be considered at the same time.[91] In addition, if appropriate, an application made on one ground may be treated as an application on a different ground.[92]

Preliminary consideration

Once an application is properly made there is a preliminary consideration of the case.[93] On this consideration the Secretary of State may reject the application and decide:
- to revise or supersede the maintenance calculation, or refuse to revise or supersede;[94] *or*
- make the maintenance calculation, or make a default maintenance decision.[95]

Any decision carries the normal appeal rights.

Grounds for rejecting or refusing a variation

An application for a variation may be rejected because:[96]
- the requirements of the stated ground are not met;
- in special expenses cases, the threshold is not exceeded;
- in property/capital transfer cases, the £5,000 minimum value is not exceeded;
- in additional assets cases, their value does not exceed £65,000;
- in income not taken into account cases, this is does not exceed £100;
- information requested by the Secretary of State has not been provided within the one-month time limit;
- a default maintenance decision is in force;
- the application is made by the person with care or qualifying child on additional cases grounds and the capped amount of income is already applied, or the non-resident parent or his partner are in receipt of working tax credit;
- the application is made by the non-resident parent on special expenses grounds and after deducting these, net income would exceed the capped amount;
- the non-resident parent is on the flat rate as he or his partner is on income support (IS) or income-based jobseeker's allowance (JSA) (including where the partner is also a non-resident parent) but is due to pay less than that or nil due to shared care or transitional rules on conversion;
- the non-resident parent is due to pay the flat rate (or the lower prescribed amount) due to the transitional rules on conversion, a property or capital transfer reducing maintenance below the flat rate or due to part-time care by a local authority;
- the application is made by the non-resident parent; *and*
  - he is on the nil rate; *or*
  - he is on the flat rate, because he receives a prescribed benefit (other than IS/income-based JSA) or has income of £100 or less; *or*
  - he pays the flat rate of £5 due to shared care, including care by a local authority (or less due to apportionment).

Chapter 8: Variations in 'new rules' cases
3. Procedure

In some cases, where a default maintenance decision applies, an application for a variation may contain sufficient information to revise the default decision and replace it with a maintenance calculation.

Contest

Where the application has not been rejected on preliminary consideration the other relevant parties will usually be notified. However, in some situations where the Secretary of State has discretion to reinstate a previous variation s/he does not need to notify or invite representations (see p186).

The notification may be done orally or in writing and in all cases it must:[97]
- state the grounds on which the application has been made and provide any information or evidence the applicant has given to support it;
- invite parties to make representations about the circumstances within 14 days; and
- not contain information that should not be disclosed.

In practice, non-applicants are informed in writing and supplied with the evidence. Where the application has been via a phone call the evidence may be a transcript of the telephone conversation.

In some cases, the applicant may be late in supplying further evidence or information (ie, outside the one-month time limit) but the Secretary of State may have decided to proceed with the application and notify the other parties. This information may be passed on to the other parties late and a further 14 days for representations may be allowed from the date of this later notification.[98]

However, if the Secretary of State is satisfied that it is reasonable, this time limit may be extended.[99] The other parties may respond orally or in writing, although the Secretary of State may require them to make a written submission. Where no contesting information is provided, the Secretary of State may make a determination on the application.[100]

Any information which the other party provides other than that which may not be disclosed, may be forwarded to the applicant if the Secretary of State considers this reasonable.[101] This will only happen where the other party has contradicted the statement of the applicant and the decision maker does not have sufficient evidence to decide the case, or they have provided supporting evidence to refute it.[102] The applicant will be given 14 days to comment on the evidence or information supplied by the other party.

Additional non-disclosure rules in variation notifications

There are additional rules on non-disclosure in variations cases. Supporting evidence or information from one party will not be part of disclosures or notification to the other on the following issues:[103]

- details of the illness or disability of a relevant other child if the non-resident parent has requested that this is not disclosed and the Secretary of State agrees;
- medical evidence which has not been disclosed to the applicant or a relevant person (person with care, non-resident parent or section 7 applicant) which would be harmful to that individual;
- the address of a relevant person or qualifying chid, or information which could lead to that individual or child being located, and there is a risk of harm or undue distress.

Where an applicant requests that information is not disclosed this will be discussed with them. It may be possible to make an amended application. Where the applicant refuses disclosure of information that is relevant for the other party to contest the application for a variation, the application will be rejected.[104]

Contest not required

Representations from the other relevant parties are not required where:[105]
- the Secretary of State is reinstating a variation at her/his own discretion (see p186);
- there is a property/capital transfer variation and a change of circumstances means that the CSA no longer has jurisdiction, but a subsequent change means it is acquired and an application for variation is made on a further application for a maintenance calculation;
- a variation is agreed and the non-resident parent has the maintenance calculation replaced by a default decision, but subsequently this is replaced with a maintenance calculation.

Interim maintenance decision

Where an application for a variation is made before the maintenance calculation, an interim maintenance decision may be made.[106] This means one can be made when the first calculation has not been made or where the process is complete but for the completion of an outstanding application for variation. The amount of the interim maintenance decision will be the maintenance calculated in the normal way, ignoring the variation. This is to allow the variation application to be considered. An interim maintenance decision may be replaced by a maintenance calculation, which is made whether or not a variation has been agreed. The effective date of the maintenance calculation will be the same as the interim maintenance decision.

The interim maintenance decision may be appealed in the normal way. However, when a maintenance calculation is made which replaces this any appeal may lapse.[107] Where the interim maintenance decision is superseded, the normal 5 per cent change in net income tolerance rule does not apply.

Chapter 8: Variations in 'new rules' cases
3. Procedure

Regular payment condition

A non-resident parent may have a regular payment condition imposed where he has applied for a variation.[108] This will be imposed after preliminary consideration. It is intended that this will be used where a non-resident parent has:
- a poor payment record or arrears or has never paid;
- failed to make payments while the variation application is being contested and considered; *or*
- special expenses which make it hard for him to meet the maintenance liability.

The amount due under a regular payment condition will be either the:[109]
- maintenance calculated, including that set under an interim maintenance decision; *or*
- amount of maintenance which would be due if the variation was agreed.

This means that where the CSA believes that the variation application will be successful it may set a regular payment condition that adjusts the maintenance calculated to reflect the variation, reducing the financial burden on the parent. However, where it believes that the application will be unsuccessful and a regular payment condition is imposed it will be set at the calculation rate.

A regular payment condition does not affect the amount of maintenance the non-resident parent is liable to pay.[110] Therefore, if the amount is set lower than the amount due there will be arrears if the variation application fails.

The condition is set independent of any other arrears arrangement the parent may have and ends either when the Secretary of State makes a final decision on the maintenance calculation, whether or not the variation is agreed to, or when the application is withdrawn.[111]

When a regular payment condition is imposed the non-resident parent, person with care and section 7 applicant will be sent written notification.[112] This will make it clear that if the condition is not met the application may lapse.[113]

Where a non-resident parent does not meet the regular payment condition within one month of this notification, the Secretary of State will refuse to consider the application for a variation.[114] Written notification of this refusal will be sent to the non-resident parent, person with care and section 7 applicant.[115] However, there are no appeal rights against a refusal to consider the application.

Considering the decision

The CSA may exercise some discretion in variations to the maintenance calculation. In addition to the normal rules the Secretary of State must be satisfied that:[116]
- the grounds are met; *and*
- it is just and equitable to agree to the variation.

Chapter 8: Variations in 'new rules' cases
3. Procedure

In considering the decision, the Secretary of State must bear in mind the general principles that:[117]
- a parent is responsible for maintaining her/his children when s/he can afford to do so;
- a parent is responsible for maintaining all her/his children equally;
- the welfare of any child affected by an application for a variation must be taken into account.

The decision may be made to agree to the variation in full or refuse it. This may result in a revision or supersession of the decision or replacement of the interim maintenance decision.[118] The revision/supersession decision will be dealt with under the normal rules (see p184).

Just and equitable

Even though the grounds are met, a variation decision will only be agreed if the Secretary of State agrees it is just and equitable considering all the circumstances of the case.[119] Certain factors must be taken into account in making the decision. These include:[120]
- whether agreeing to a variation would lead to the non-resident parent or parent with care giving up employment;
- where the applicant is the non-resident parent, whether there is any liability to pay child maintenance under a court order or agreement prior to the effective date of the maintenance calculation; *or*
- where the non-resident parent applies for a special expenses variation, whether he could make financial arrangements to cover those expenses or could pay for them from money currently spent on non-essentials.

The following must not be taken into account:[121]
- whether or not the child's conception was planned;
- who was responsible for the breakdown of the relationship between the non-resident parent and person with care;
- whether the non-resident parent or person with care is in a new relationship with someone who is not the qualifying child's parent;
- any contact arrangements;
- the income or assets of anyone other than the non-resident parent or his partner if an application is made on the ground of a lifestyle inconsistent with declared income;
- any failure of the non-resident parent to make child maintenance payments under CSA arrangements, court order or written agreement; *and*
- representations from individuals other than the person with care, non-resident parent or section 7 applicant.

This list is not exhaustive and other factors may be considered.

179

Chapter 8: Variations in 'new rules' cases
3. Procedure

Referral to an appeal tribunal

Once the application has passed the preliminary consideration and contest stage, the case may be passed to an appeal tribunal for a determination on whether or not to agree to the variation.[122] This will normally only occur where a novel or particularly contentious issue is being considered.[123]

A novel case is one that has not been encountered before within the CSA, while a particularly contentious is one that provokes a high degree of dispute. Guidance suggests that applications on additional cases grounds are ones where such a referral may be likely, particularly those on the lifestyle inconsistent with declared income ground.[124] The decision maker should also consider if only a tribunal would be able to obtain the necessary evidence to determine the application, in which case it should be referred.

An appeal tribunal considering a variation will apply the same rules as a CSA decision maker and will determine that the variation should be either agreed or refused.[125] The tribunal's determination will be passed back to the CSA to make the decision – eg, superseding the maintenance calculation with a variation element or refusing to supersede. This decision by the CSA (ie, to revise/supersede or refuse to revise/supersede the maintenance calculation) may then be appealed in the normal way (see p188).

At the time of writing it is not clear if, or how, the tribunal procedure may differ from the normal process when a variation application (referred by the CSA) is being dealt with by the tribunal. See CPAG's *Welfare Rights Bulletin* for further information as it becomes available.

4. The decision

A variation is an element of the maintenance calculation. The Secretary of State may agree or refuse the application for variation. In either case, it may result in a decision to:[126]

- revise or supersede the maintenance calculation/replace the interim maintenance decision or refuse to revise or supersede;
- make a maintenance calculation (this may replace an interim maintenance decision) or default maintenance decision.

The CSA's internal guidance indicates when to refuse to revise or supersede – eg, an application does not meet one of the grounds, refuse to revise or supersede; an application that could lead to a supersession fails after consideration, refuse to supersede.[127]

In some cases a variation may be agreed which makes no difference to the amount of maintenance calculated. A revision or supersession will still be carried out, as each decision gives further appeal rights.

Once a variation is made it will continue to be considered each time there is a revision or supersession of the maintenance calculation, under the normal revision/supersession rules (see Chapter 19). Due to some changes in circumstances the variation may cease to have effect, in which case the calculation may be suspended or cancelled in order to remove the variation element. When there is a further change in circumstances the variation may be reinstated by the Secretary of State without an application. In other cases a new request for a variation may need to be made.

Following variation to the maintenance calculation, as with other maintenance calculation decisions, the amount of maintenance paid may be affected by the special rules for court order phasing (see p387) or where there is a decision relating to an 'old rules' case converting to the 'new rules' (see Chapter 9).

The effect of the variation

The effect of the variation should not reduce the total amount of maintenance to less than £5,[128] and the maximum amount of net income that can be taken into account is the capped amount, £2,000.[129] The following examines the effect of variations where different grounds are agreed, including where there is more than one category – eg, both special expenses and additional cases grounds. The CSA calls these 'concurrent variations'.

Additional case element

Where a variation is made on additional cases grounds, the amount of any additional income is added to the net income of the non-resident parent.[130] Where this would result in a net income figure above the capped amount, the net income is restricted to the capped amount of £2,000.

Example 8.9
From example 8.6 the case is referred to an appeal tribunal and its determination is that there should be a variation for additional income with a weekly value of £360 for both diversion of income and a lifestyle inconsistent with declared income. This is added to Marcus's net income, as used in the maintenance calculation, of £400. His net income is now £760. The amount he is now due to pay Helene is £152.

Where the non-resident parent is in receipt of a benefit (other than income support (IS) or income-based jobseeker's allowance (JSA)) that attracts the flat rate, even though he may not pay this because of shared care or because he qualifies for the nil rate (but not on income grounds) there are special rules regarding the maximum amount payable when a variation is agreed on additional cases grounds.[131] This is known as the better buy (see p182).

181

Chapter 8: Variations in 'new rules' cases
4. The decision

Better buy

The maximum amount of maintenance a non-resident parent on benefit (other than IS or income-based JSA) will have to pay due to a variation on additional cases grounds is the lesser of:[132]
- the flat rate plus the amount calculated under the normal calculation rules on the additional income exclusive of the benefit income; *or*
- the amount calculated under the normal calculation rules on the total income (including any amount of benefit that attracts the flat rate liability less disregards).

The amounts disregarded in benefit income are:[133]
- industrial injuries benefit – constant attendance and exceptionally severe disablement allowances;
- war disablement pension – constant attendance, exceptionally severe disablement, severe occupational and mobility supplement allowance;
- service pensions – the unemployability allowances.

Example 8.10
Adam is on retirement pension of £75.50, and is due to pay Carol the flat rate of £5 for one child. He has a works pension of £97.50 a week and a personal pension providing a further £39 a week. Carol applies for a variation on income not taken into account grounds. As he has income over £100 the better buy calculation is carried out.
(a) £5 + (normal rules calculation on income of £136.50) = £5 + (reduced rate on £136.50)
£5 + (£5 + 25% of £36.50, rounded to nearest pound) = £5 + £14 (£5 + £9.13, rounded)
= £19
(b) normal rules calculation on total income (ie, £75.50 + £136.50 = £212)
Basic rate maintenance is 15% of £212 = £31.80 rounded to £32
Better buy will mean a variation may be considered which would result in maintenance of £19 (ie, the lesser of the two amounts).

Special expenses element

The total amount of any special expenses (less any threshold amounts) is deducted from the net weekly income of the non-resident parent and the calculation is carried out as normal using this amount.[134] Where there is more than one special expense included, the amounts are aggregated and only one threshold is applied (where applicable).[135]

Where the net income is the capped amount, the effect of the variation is worked out by subtracting the special expenses from the actual net weekly income.[136] Where this results in a figure above the capped amount of £2,000 the special expenses variation will be refused.

Chapter 8: Variations in 'new rules' cases
4. The decision

Example 8.11

Bronwen has a net income of £428 and pays basic rate maintenance of £86 to Ivan for Ursula and Gretchen. She claims special expenses cost for contact with her children, which amounts to £450 over a six-month period, and for the contribution that she makes to their boarding school costs, £1,500 a term (see example 8.2).

Her special expenses are worked out as £17.30 for contact and £28.77 for boarding school costs, totalling £46.07. The threshold of £15 applies and £15 is deducted from the total, leaving £31.07.

This is deducted from her weekly net income (£428 – £31.07 = £396.93)

Her maintenance is now worked out in the usual way, 20% of £396.93 = £79.39 rounded to £79.

Her variation for special expenses has reduced her maintenance from £86 a week to £79.

Property/capital transfer element

The transfer is treated as an advance payment of maintenance.[137] Therefore, the equivalent weekly value is subtracted form the maintenance calculated to produce the amount due after variation on property/capital transfer grounds.[138]

Example 8.12

From example 8.3 Marcus has a property transfer variation agreed with a weekly value of £25.84. His net weekly income is £400 and under the maintenance calculation he is due to pay Helene maintenance of £80 a week for Robert (14) and Heather (17). There is no reduction for shared care and so the weekly value of the property transfer is subtracted from the amount he is due to pay.

£80 – £25.84 = £54.16 is the amount he must pay following the variation.

Concurrent variations

Where there is more than one variation element (ie, special expenses, additional cases) to be applied, the calculation is carried out using the following steps.

Step 1

Work out the amounts of each element.

Step 2

Apply the additional cases element, capping the income at £2,000.

Step 3

Apply the special expenses element.

Step 4

Work out the maintenance due, applying any apportionment or reduction for shared care or part-time local authority care.

Chapter 8: Variations in 'new rules' cases
4. The decision

Step 5
Apply any property transfer element (only that which applies to the parent with care who benefited from the transfer).

Step 6
Check that the total amount of maintenance is not less than £5. If so, apportion this between the persons with care.

Example 8.13
The situation is as in examples 8.3 and 8.9. In this instance, both the property transfer and the additional cases variation are applied to work out how much Marcus must pay Helene for Robert and Heather. His net income before variation is £400, as before.
Step 1 The additional cases variation is that £360 additional income should be included. The property transfer variation has a weekly value of £25.84.
Step 2 £360 + £400 = £760, which is below the capped amount.
Step 3 Does not apply.
Step 4 Basic maintenance due is 20% of £760 = £152.
Step 5 Maintenance due is reduced by the property transfer (ie, £152 − £25.84 = £126.16). Therefore, due to variation, instead of receiving £80 from Marcus, Helene will now be due £126.16 a week.

Revisions and supersessions

A variation is not a separate decision to be challenged, it is a variation of the maintenance calculation. Where a variation is agreed and applied to the calculation this decision may be challenged through seeking a revision within one month, and any changes of circumstances, whether in relation to the variation or other factors, can result in a revision or supersession of the maintenance calculation under the normal rules, depending on the circumstances (see Chapter 19). This also applies to decisions made by an appeal tribunal following referral by the CSA for a decision – eg, in contentious cases.[139]

The variation will be taken into account in any reconsideration; however, there may be changes of circumstances which mean that the variation ceases to have effect. In certain circumstances a previous variation to the calculation may be reinstated, without an application, at the discretion of the Secretary of State.

Date the variation to the maintenance calculation takes effect

Where the ground existed at the effective date of the maintenance calculation (ie, when the non-resident parent was notified of the application or application treated as made), the date the variation takes effect will be the effective date of the maintenance calculation if either:
- the application is made before the calculation is made;[140] *or*

Chapter 8: Variations in 'new rules' cases
4. The decision

- the application is made within one month of the maintenance calculation, or meets the other normal rules applying to revision (eg, misrepresentation or failure to disclose information that meant the decision was to the person's advantage) or erroneous decisions.[141]

The exception to this rule is where the non-resident parent is applying for a variation on the grounds of prior debts or payments in respect of certain mortgages, loans or insurance policies and payments towards these are treated as voluntary payments in the initial payment period.[142] In this case the variation takes effect from the maintenance period following the date on which the non-resident parent was notified – ie, the start of the second week of liability.

Where the ground did not apply at the effective date of the maintenance calculation the variation is effective from:
- the first day of the maintenance period in which the ground arose, where this is after the effective date but before the maintenance calculation is made;[143]
- the first day of the maintenance period in which the relevant person requested the variation.[144] However, where the Secretary of State requests that the application is made in writing, and this is not supplied within 14 days, the date the request was made will be the date the application is received unless the Secretary of State accepts that the delay was unavoidable;[145]
- the first day of the maintenance period in which the ground will arise, where the application for variation is made in advance.[146]

A case may have a number of different grounds agreed over time, and each may have different dates from which they take effect.

Example 8.14
Tara claims maintenance. The effective date is 26 August 2003. She is notified of her maintenance calculation on 19 September 2003. She takes advice and applies for variation on the basis that an additional cases ground applied at 26 August 2003. She makes this application on 8 October 2003 (ie, within one month of her notification of the decision). The variation is agreed and the maintenance calculation is revised on 14 November 2003, with effect from 26 August 2003. Juan takes advice and on 3 December 2003 applies for a variation on the grounds that he has been paying off the car which they bought before splitting up and which Tara needs, as she lives in a secluded cottage. Also he is just about to start paying boarding school fees for the eldest child in late December. The variation is agreed and a revision is made on 3 January 2004 in which the elements for prior debt take effect from 2 December and the boarding school fees take effect from 16 December 2003. However, even though the variation for prior debts only applies from December, Juan could ask that the amounts he paid toward the car before the calculation was made be considered as voluntary payments to offset initial arrears. Had Juan taken advice at the same time as Tara and applied for a variation at the same time as she did on the grounds of prior debt and his repayments on the car were considered voluntary payments, then there

185

Chapter 8: Variations in 'new rules' cases
4. The decision

could have been a further variation to the calculation, with the decision taking effect from 2 September 2003.

When a variation to the maintenance calculation ceases to have effect

A variation will cease to have effect when the ground no longer applies or any other of the reasons for refusing a variation is met.[147] For example, in a property transfer the youngest child becomes 18. As a supersession, the date from which this takes effect is the first day in the maintenance period in which the change occurred.

Where there is a later change, unless the Secretary of State has discretion to reinstate the variation, a further application may need to be made. Table 8.2 illustrates where a further variation application would be required.

Table 8.2: Situations where a further application for variation is required

Ground	When variation ceases	When a further application could be made
Additional cases	- net income before any variation is greater than £2,000 - the non-resident parent or his partner receives WTC	- net income before variation would be less than £2,000 - when neither receives WTC
Special expenses	- net income after any variation is greater than £2,000	- net income after variation would be less than £2,000

Secretary of State's discretion to reinstate a previous variation

In some cases, the Secretary of State may revise or supersede a maintenance calculation to reinstate a variation that has previously been agreed. This discretion may be applied where there is:[148]

- a change of circumstances which means the non-resident parent's liability is reduced to nil or another rate where the variation cannot be taken into account; *then*
- a subsequent change of circumstances means his liability can now be adjusted to take the variation into account.

Examples of situations where this could apply could be where:

- the non-resident parent becomes a full-time student and so becomes liable for the nil rate, but subsequently returns to a basic or reduced rate;
- a variation is agreed and on a subsequent application for revision/supersession the non-resident parent fails to provide information. Therefore the maintenance calculation is replaced by a default decision, the information

required is provided and this default maintenance decision is replaced with a maintenance calculation. The variation may be reapplied without application.

Had the maintenance calculation ceased, this discretion would not apply. For example, if the parent had moved abroad and the CSA ceased to have jurisdiction, then s/he returns to the UK, a subsequent application would need to be made for a maintenance calculation including an application for variation. However, in some circumstances the CSA may be able to reinstate the variation without contest (see p177).

In exercising the discretion to reinstate, the Secretary of State must be satisfied that there has been no material change in circumstances which affects the earlier variation.[149] Where this is satisfied the previous variation can be reinstated without an application or any further contact with the relevant persons – ie, they are not invited to make representations. There is no obligation to investigate; therefore, decisions are made based on the information available to the decision maker. There is no time limit on the period between the variation ceasing to apply and being reinstated. However the Secretary of State must be satisfied that the circumstances that gave rise to the variation remain unchanged. This is most easily satisfied in pre-93 property/capital transfers.

Example 8.15
Joe applies for and obtains a variation from his basic rate maintenance on the grounds of contact costs with his children. He is convicted and sentenced to six months in prison. He becomes due to pay the nil rate. On his release three months later, he again becomes liable, this time at the reduced rate. The Secretary of State is not satisfied that the circumstances relating to eligibility are still the same and does not reinstate the variation. Joe will need to make a new application for a variation on the grounds of contact costs.
Had the variation been granted on the grounds of a pre-93 property/capital transfer the Secretary of State is likely to have reinstated the variation without Joe having to make a further application.

Revision and supersession of a previously agreed variation

Where a variation has been agreed it may be revised or superseded subsequently. When a request is received to revise or supersede such a decision the CSA may notify the other relevant parties and invite them to make representations.[150] This need not be done if the CSA thinks it would not agree to vary the calculation or that a revision/supersession would not be to the advantage of the applicant.

Where contest does take place, the procedure is the same as normal in considering a variation (see p176).[151]

The CSA may decide to revise/supersede or not to revise or supersede the decision and notify the applicant and any relevant parties as appropriate.

Chapter 8: Variations in 'new rules' cases
4. The decision

Appealing a decision

Decisions in relation to the maintenance calculation in response to a variation application, or where a variation element is reinstated to a maintenance calculation, may be appealed under the normal procedures. However, where an appeal is lodged and there is a revision or supersession of the appealed decision that is to the advantage of the appellant, the appeal will lapse.[152] For further details on appeals, see Chapter 20.

Notes

1 s28A(1) CSA 1991 (note the modifications, under the CS(V)(MSP) Regs, only apply in cases where the application is made after a maintenance calculation is in force)

1. Grounds for a variation
2 Sch 4B CSA 1991
3 Sch 4A para 2(3) CSA 1991 as substituted by s6 CSPSSA 2000 (and modified by reg 8(2) CS (V)(MSP) Regs)
4 Reg 15 CS(V) Regs
5 Reg 15(1) CS(V) Regs
6 Reg 15(2) CS(V) Regs
7 Reg 15(3) CS(V) Regs
8 Reg 10(1) CS(V) Regs
9 Reg 10(4) CS(V) Regs
10 Unacceptable expenses
11 Reg 10(1) CS(V) Regs
12 Reg 10(3)(a) CS(V) Regs
13 Frequency of visits
14 Reg 10(3)(b) CS(V) Regs
15 Frequency of visits
16 Frequency of visits
17 Travel costs
18 Accommodation costs
19 Reg 11(2)(c) CS(V) Regs
20 Reg 11(2)(a) CS(V) Regs
21 Reg 11(1) CS(V) Regs
22 Reg11(2)(b) CS(V) Regs
23 Illness or disability of a relevant child
24 Reg 11(3) CS(V) Regs
25 Illness or disability of a relevant child
26 Reg 12(2) CS(V) Regs
27 Reg 12(3)(k) and (6)(a) CS(V) Regs
28 Reg 12(6)(a) CS(V) Regs; s376(4) ICTA 1988; Prior debts
29 Reg 12(3)(a) CS(V) Regs
30 Reg 12(3)(k) CS(V) Regs
31 Reg 12(4) CS(V) Regs
32 Reg 12(3)(l) CS(V) Regs
33 Reg 12(3)(h) CS(V) Regs
34 Reg 12(3)(i) CS(V) Regs
35 Prior debts
36 Reg 12(3)(b)-(g), (j) and (m) CS(V) Regs
37 Reg 12(5) CS(V) Regs
38 Prior debts
39 Reg 13(1) CS(V) Regs
40 Reg 13(5) CS(V) Regs
41 Reg 13(2) CS(V) Regs
42 Reg 13(3) CS(V) Regs
43 Reg 13(4) CS(V) Regs
44 Reg 14(2)(a) CS(V) Regs
45 Reg 14(2)(b) CS(V) Regs
46 Sch 4B para 3(1) CSA 1991; regs 16(1) and (2) and 17(4) CS(V) Regs
47 Sch 4B para 3(2) CSA 1991
48 Property capital transfer overview
49 s8(11) CSA 1991; reg 16(1)(a) CS(V) Regs; Property capital transfer overview
50 Reg 16(2) CS(V) Regs
51 Reg 16(3) CS(V) Regs
52 Sch 4B para 3 CSA 1991; reg 17(1) CS(V) Regs
53 Reg 17(2) CS(V) Regs
54 Reg 16(4) CS(V) Regs
55 Sch para 1(3)(b) CS(V) Regs
56 Sch para 2 CS(V) Regs
57 Sch para 3 CS(V) Regs
58 Sch 4B para 4 CSA 1991
59 Reg 25 CS(V) Regs

Chapter 8: Variations in 'new rules' cases
Notes

60 Reg 26 CS(V) Regs
61 Reg 18(1) CS(V) Regs
62 Reg 18(2) CS(V) Regs
63 Reg 18(3) CS(V) Regs
64 Reg 18(3)(f) CS(V) Regs
65 Reg 18(4) CS(V) Regs
66 Reg 18(5) CS(V) Regs
67 Reg 18(6) CS(V) Regs; Determining the value of an asset
68 Reg 18(5) CS(V) Regs; reg 25 CS(V) Regs
69 Reg 19(1) and (2) CS(V) Regs
70 Regs 19(5)(a) CS(V) Regs; reg 25 CS(V) Regs
71 Reg 26(3) CS(V) Regs
72 Reg 19(4) CS(V) Regs
73 Diversion of income
74 Regs 19(5)(b) and 25 CS(V) Regs
75 Reg 20(1) and (2) CS(V) Regs
76 Reg 20(3) and 4(a) CS(V) Regs
77 Reg 20(4)(b) and (e) CS(V) Regs
78 Reg 20(5) CS(V) Regs
79 Lifestyle inconsistent with declared income

2. Applying for a variation

80 s28A CSA 1991 (note the modifications, under the CS(V)(MSP) Regs, take effect where the application is made when the maintenance calculation is in force); s28G CSA 1991; Applications – general
81 s28A(4) CSA 1991 (see previous note re modifications)
82 Reg 4(1) CS(V) Regs
83 s28A(4)(b) CSA 1991
84 Reg 8(1) CS(V) Regs
85 Insufficient information provided
86 Reg 8(1) CS(V) Regs
87 Regs 6(2)(c) and 8(2) CS(V) Regs
88 Reg 5(1) CS(V) Regs
89 Reg 5(2) CS(V) Regs

3. Procedure

90 s28D CSA 1991 (note the modifications, under the CS(V)(MSP) Regs, take effect where the application is made when the maintenance calculation is in force); Determination of applications
91 Sch 4B para 5(1) cSA 1991; reg 9(9) CS(V) Regs
92 Reg 9(8) CS(V) Regs
93 s28b(1) CSA 1991
94 Reg 6(1) CS(V) Regs
95 s28B CSA 1991 (note the modifications, under the CS(V)(MSP) Regs, take effect where the application is made when the maintenance calculation is in force); reg 7 CS(V) Regs
96 s28B CSA 1991 (see previous note re modification); regs 6&7 CS(V) Regs
97 Reg 9(1) CS(V) Regs
98 Contest – new information/evidence received
99 Reg 9(1) CS(V) Regs
100 Reg 9(5) CS(V) Regs
101 Reg 9(4) CS(V) Regs
102 Contest contradictory evidence
103 Reg 9(2) CS(V) Regs
104 Contest – information for non-disclosure
105 Reg 9(3) CS(V) Regs
106 s12 CSA1991
107 s28F(5) CSA 1991 (note the modifications, under the CS(V)(MSP) Regs, take effect where the application is made when the maintenance calculation is in force)
108 s28C CSA 1991 (see previous note re modification)
109 s28C(2) CSA 1991 (note the modifications, under the CS(V)(MSP) Regs, take effect where the application is made when the maintenance calculation is in force); reg 31(1) CS(V) Regs
110 Regular payments condition
111 s28C(4) CSA 1991 (note the modifications, under the CS(V)(MSP) Regs, take effect where the application is made when the maintenance calculation is in force)
112 s28C(3) CSA 1991 (note the modifications, under the CS(V)MSP) Regs, take effect where the application is made when the maintenance calculation is in force)
113 s28C(5) CSA 1991 (note the modifications, under the CS(V)(MSP) Regs, take effect where the application is made when the maintenance calculation is in force)
114 Reg 31(2) and (3) CS(V) Regs
115 s28C(7) CSA 1991 (note the modifications, under the CS(V)(MSP) Regs, take effect where the application is made when the maintenance calculation is in force)
116 s28F(1) CSA 1991 (note the modifications, under the CS(V)(MSP) Regs, take effect where the application is made when the maintenance calculation is in force)
117 s28E and s28F(2)(a) CSA 1991; Discretion

Chapter 8: Variations in 'new rules' cases
Notes

118 s28D(1) CSA 1991;s28F CSA 1991 (note the modifications on both sections, under the CS(V)(MSP) Regs, take effect where the application is made when the maintenance calculation is in force)
119 s28F(1) CSA 1991
120 Reg 21(1) CS(V) Regs
121 Reg 21(2) CS(V) Regs
122 s28D(1)(b) CSA 1991
123 Role of the Appeals Service
124 Novel or particularly contentious applications
125 s28D(3) CSA 1991 (note the modifications, under the CS(V)(MSP) Regs, take effect where the application is made when the maintenance calculation is in force)

4. The decision
126 s28B(2) CSA 1991; s28F(3) and (4) CSA 1991 (note the modifications to both sections, under the CS(V)(MSP) Regs, take effect where the application is made when the maintenance calculation is in force)
127 Revising/refusing to revise a maintenance calculation to take account of a variation application; Superseding/refusing to supersede a maintenance calculation to take account of a variation application
128 Reg 27(5) CS(V) Regs
129 Reg 25 CS(V) Regs
130 Reg 25 CS(V) Regs
131 Reg 26 CS(V) Regs
132 Reg 26(1) CS(V) Regs
133 Reg 26(3) CS(V) Regs
134 Reg 23(1) CS(V) Regs
135 Reg 15(1) CS(V) Regs
136 Reg 23(2) CS(V) Regs
137 Variation on the grounds of a property transfer
138 Reg 24 CS(V) Regs
139 s16(1A)(c) CSA 1991; s17(1)(d) CSA 1991
140 Reg 22 CS(V) Regs
141 s28G CSA 1991; reg 3A SSCS(D&A) Regs
142 Reg 22(2) CS(V) Regs
143 Reg 22(1)(b) CS(V) Regs
144 s28G CSA 1991; reg 6A(6) SSCS(D&A) Regs; reg 7B(6) SSCS(D&A) Regs
145 Reg 4 CS(V) Regs; Application properly made
146 Reg 6A(3) SSCS(D&A) Regs; reg 7B(5) SSCS(D&A) Regs
147 Suspension of variations
148 Reg 29 CS(V) Regs
149 Reg 9(3) CS(V) Regs
150 Reg 15B SSCS(D&A) Regs
151 Reg 15B SSCS(D&A) Regs
152 s16(6) CSA 1991

Chapter 9
Conversions

This chapter covers:
1. When do 'old rules' cases convert to the 'new rules' (below)
2. The conversion calculation and transitional phasing (p193)
3. The conversion decision (p199)
4. The linking rules (p202)
5. Revision, supersession and appeal (p207)
6. Conversion, benefits and collection (p212)

1. When do 'old rules' cases convert to the 'new rules'

The date that all 'old rules' cases convert to the 'new rules' is known as the **conversion date (C Day)**.[1] At the time of writing no date has been announced, and provisions in the regulations allow child allowances and premiums to be used in old rules calculations to April 2005. Some 'old rules' cases may convert earlier than this in certain circumstances; these are known as early conversions.

An 'old rules' case will continue to be assessed under the old legislation (eg, the Maintenance Assessment and Special Cases Regulations) until an early conversion or C Day. Where an 'old rules' assessment ceases to be in force a new application may be made. However, if this application is within 13 weeks of the old assessment being in force it will be treated as an application for an 'old rules' assessment under the linking rules (see p202). Where the application is after C Day, a conversion decision may be made (see p199).

Where an 'old rules' case converts there may be transitional phasing to increase or decrease the old amount to the new amount due (see p194).

Early conversions

An early conversion occurs where there is a maintenance assessment in force and a related decision is made.[2] The related decision may be that a maintenance calculation is made or there has been a change involving a new or existing partner who also has maintenance. An early conversion will occur where:[3]

Chapter 9: Conversions
1. When do 'old rules' cases convert to the 'new rules'

- a maintenance calculation is made in respect of a person who is a relevant person (person with care or non-resident parent) in the existing assessment whether or not in relation to a different qualifying child;
- an application is made or treated as made that would result in a maintenance calculation but there is an assessment in force, the non-resident parent in the new application is the non-resident parent in the existing case but the person with care in the new application is different from the one in the existing case;
- a maintenance calculation is made in relation to person A who is a partner to person B who has a maintenance assessment, either A or B are in receipt of income support (IS) or income-based jobseeker's allowance (JSA), and A and B are either both persons with care or both non-resident parents;
- a maintenance assessment is in force in relation to person C and a maintenance calculation is in force in relation to person D, either C or D are in receipt of IS or income-based JSA, C and D are either both persons with care or both non-resident parents, then C and D become partners; *or*
- a maintenance assessment is in force in relation to person E and a maintenance calculation is in force in relation to their partner F. E and F are either both persons with care or both non-resident parents and then they become entitled to IS or income-based JSA as partners.

The early conversion of one case may set of a chain of conversions of other cases where the relevant person in a conversion is also a relevant person in an existing maintenance assessment.[4] The CSA call these 'linked cases'. This may result in a lengthy sequence of interrelated decisions that need to be made. Where the 'old rules' case is converted, transitional phasing may apply (see p194).

Example 9.1
a) Celine is the parent with care of two children, Michelle and Francis. Franco is their non-resident parent in the 'old rules' assessment. After 3 March 2003 Francis goes to live with Franco and his new partner, Helen. Franco applies, as the parent with care of Francis, for maintenance from Celine as the non-resident parent. A maintenance calculation is made. As a relevant person in the old assessment is a relevant person in the new calculation (ie, Celine is a person with care in the old and a non-resident parent in the new), the old maintenance assessment converts early to the 'new rules' (transitional phasing may apply).
b) Celine is the parent with care of two children, Michelle and Francis. Franco is their non-resident parent, in the 'old rules' assessment. Celine is on IS. She forms a new relationship with Bill and they move in together. Bill is also a parent with care on IS with a maintenance calculation for his daughter Sophie. As they are both parents with care on a relevant benefit, Celine's 'old rules' case converts to the 'new rules' when Celine and Bill become partners (transitional phasing may apply). If Bill had been the non-resident parent instead of the person with care there would have been no case conversion.

c) If the situation in (a) had an effective date before 3 March 2003 then both Celine and Franco would have 'old rules' assessments – ie, Celine as the person with care of Michelle in one assessment and Franco as the person with care of Frances in the other 'old rules' assessment. Then if Celine moved in with Bill not only would her case convert but Franco's would as well due to the linking effect (see p202).

2. The conversion calculation and transitional phasing

The new amount is worked out applying the new calculation rates, using the information that the Secretary of State has at the calculation date (see p191).[5] Where there are decisions outstanding on the maintenance assessment at conversion, the calculation may be made and once the decision has been made the maintenance calculation may be revised or superseded (see p207). There are additional rules for calculating the new amount at conversion where a relevant departure direction or relevant property transfer was applied to the 'old rules' case (see p197).

Where there is an interim maintenance assessment (IMA) in force when the conversion decision is being made, this may be:
- used to make the conversion decision;[6] or
- replaced with a default maintenance decision, if there is insufficient information to make a maintenance assessment or conversion decision.[7]

At conversion the new rate will either be paid immediately or transitional phasing may be applied.[8] There are some situations where the new amount is always applied; in other cases the CSA checks if transitional phasing applies. If it does not then the new amount is paid.

Situations where the new amount is always applied

The new maintenance calculation amount will be applied immediately (ie, without checking whether transitional phasing applies) where the:[9]
- 'new rules' amount is nil;
- 'old rules' amount was nil and the 'new rules' amount is the flat rate reduced to nil rate due to shared care – for the only or all persons with care (where it reduces to nil for some but not all persons with care) – see p196;
- 'old rules' amount was more than nil but the 'new rules' amount is the flat rate (or halved flat rate where there is a partner who is a non-resident parent);
- 'old rules' amount was a category A or D IMA;
- 'new rules' amount is a default maintenance decision.

193

Chapter 9: Conversions
2. The conversion calculation and transitional phasing

Where none of the above apply, the CSA will check if transitional phasing should be applied; where it does not, the new amount will be payable.

Example 9.2
a) Sally is due to pay Mark maintenance at the minimum amount before conversion. After conversion she is liable at the flat rate. She pays the new amount from conversion.
b) Kieran pays Leah a maintenance assessment worked out under a category A IMA, at conversion, as there is insufficient information to make a maintenance calculation. A default decision replaces the IMA. This new amount applies from conversion.
c) If Kieran had been assessed under a category B IMA, sufficient information would have been available to make a maintenance calculation.

Transitional phasing

Transitional phasing will apply (unless the situation is one where the new amount is always applied) where the difference between the old amount and new amount is greater than the phasing amount.[10] Where there is more than one assessment in relation to the same non-resident parent, apportionment occurs, in which case the amounts referred to are those after the apportionment has been made.[11] Where there is an application from a new person with care while there is an existing assessment for a non-resident parent which triggers an early conversion (see p191), the apportionment in the new calculation will occur as normal, then the previous assessment amount is compared to the new amount due after apportionment.[12] There are special rules in some flat-rate cases (see p196).

The phasing amount depends on the net income of the non-resident parent. This is:[13]
- £2.50 where income is £100 or less;
- £5 where income is between £100 and £400; *or*
- £10 where income is £400 or more.

Net weekly income is as worked out under the 'new rules'. (This includes where a relevant departure direction is converted and treated as a variation.) Where the difference between old and new amounts is greater than the phasing amount, the old amount is increased or decreased by the phasing amount as appropriate.[14] This increase or decrease occurs on an annual basis during the transitional period. The transitional period lasts until the new amount is reached or for up to five years, unless there is a subsequent decision which affects this.[15]

Where transitional phasing applies, the **maximum transitional amount** that the non-resident parent may pay in maintenance (to all persons with care) is 30 per cent of his net income.[16] This is worked out under the normal rules, plus where there is a relevant additional cases departure the net income is taken to be the total of the additional income and the income from prescribed benefits

Chapter 9: Conversions
2. The conversion calculation and transitional phasing

(excluding those disregarded) and where there is an additional cases variation this means the total income after variation.[17]

In some situations (eg, early conversion), there may be a new case and an old case converting at the same time. If this happens, apportionment of the maintenance calculation is carried out as normal. Transitional phasing may be applied to the 'old rules' case, in which case the total amount of maintenance is checked against the 30 per cent maximum. This means adding together the apportioned amount due for the 'new rules' case and the phased amount due for the 'old rules' case converting. Where the 30 per cent maximum is breached the maintenance is capped at this amount. The amount for the person (or persons) with care in the new case is deducted from the maximum, and the remainder is the amount due to the person (or persons) with care in the 'old rules' case converting.[18] Rounding is to the nearest penny (amounts can be adjusted where rounding would result in inequalities over time).[19]

Example 9.3

a) Under her 'old rules' assessment Celine is due to get £68.40 in maintenance from Franco for Michelle and Francis. Franco lives with his new partner, Helen, and their son, Damien. Nothing changes and Celine's case converts at C Day. If Franco's net income is £360 a week at the conversion date, Celine's new amount is worked out under the basic rate:

Basic rate	Step 1	15 per cent reduction for relevant child (ie, £360 – 54 = £306)
	Step 2	Maintenance is 20 per cent of £306 = £61.20 (ie, £61 rounded to the nearest pound)

Does transitional phasing apply?
The phasing amount is £5, as Franco's income is between £100 and £400. Since there is more than £5 difference between the old and new amounts transitional phasing applies. Celine is paid a £63.40 (£68.40 – £5) in maintenance.

b) If Franco and Helen split up and Helen applied for maintenance for Damien after 3 March 2003 but before C Day, Celine's case would convert early. In this case there are now no relevant children living with Franco and three qualifying children.

Basic rate	Step 1	No reduction
	Step 2	25% of £360 = £90
	Step 3	Apportionment between two persons with care (£90 divided by three = £30)

Helen is due to receive £30.
Celine's new amount is £60.
Do transitional provisions apply?
As there is more than £5 difference between the old amount (£68.40) and the new amount (£60) phasing applies.

Year 1	£68.40 – £5 = £63.40
Year 2	£60

195

Chapter 9: Conversions
2. The conversion calculation and transitional phasing

Therefore the total amount of maintenance due is £93.40. This is less than the 30 per cent maximum (£108) so it does not affect maintenance.

c) If the situation was as in (b) but Celine's 'old rules' assessment was £100 a week, transitional phasing would mean:

Year 1	£100 – £5 = £95
Year 2	£95 – £5 = £90
Year 3	£90 – £5 = £85
Year 4	£85 – £5 = £80
Year 5	£60

This means Franco is due to pay £30 (Helen) + £95 (Celine) = £125

As this is greater than the 30 per cent maximum (£108) the calculation is adjusted. Helen still receives £30 but Celine receives £78 (ie, £108 – £30).

Transitional amount in certain flat-rate cases

Where the old amount was nil and the new amount is the flat rate (due to receipt of a prescribed benefit), transitional phasing is £2.50 in the first year and then the new amount £5 in the second.[20] In cases where the non-resident parent's partner is also a non-resident parent and is in receipt of income support (IS)/income-based jobseeker's allowance (JSA), transitional phasing is £1.25 in the first year and £2.50 in the second.[21]

Except where the old amount was nil, where the flat rate is due but reduces to nil due to shared care, the transitional amount due will be £2.50 in the first year and the new amount in the second.[22] (In cases where the flat rate is halved due to a partner being a non-resident parent, the phasing amount will be £1.25.[23]) This will occur where the non-resident parent shares care with the only or all persons with care.

If the amount due reduces to nil for some but not all of the persons with care, transitional phasing will only apply where:[24]
- the old amount is less than the new amount and the difference is more than £2.50; or
- the old amount is greater than the new amount but the new amount is less than £2.50.

Apportionment of the transitional amount takes place between those persons with care for whom the amount due does not reduce to nil due to shared care.[25]

Example 9.4
Andrew has four qualifying children. Claire and Hannah are each a person with care for one qualifying child, Millie is a person with care for two. Andrew has one child living with him and also shares care with Claire.

196

Under the 'old rules' he was exempt from paying the minimum amount. Under the 'new rules' he is liable for the flat rate of £5. This is apportioned between the persons with care: Hannah and Claire are due £1.25 each and Millie is due £2.50.

Due to shared care, Claire's maintenance is reduced to nil. This means £3.75 is now due in maintenance. As this is greater than the old amount, and there is more than a £2.50 difference between old and new amounts, phasing is applied. The £2.50 phased amount is apportioned between Hannah and Millie: Hannah receives 83p and Millie £1.67.

Where there is a relevant departure direction or a relevant property transfer

In 'old rules' cases where there is a departure direction or an allowance for property/capital transfer in the exempt income calculation these may be taken into consideration when working out the new amount used in the conversion calculation.[26] Only a relevant departure and relevant property/capital transfer affect the calculation.

Where a departure direction meets the rules to be considered as a variation, it is known as a **relevant departure direction**. A relevant departure direction is one for:[27]
- contact costs;
- prior debts;
- illness and disability costs, where the illness and disability is that of a relevant child – ie, the non-resident parent or his partner receives child benefit for the child;
- a property or capital transfer;
- diversion of income;
- lifestyle inconsistent with stated income; or
- assets, where the value of the assets is greater than £65,000.

In the case of contact costs and prior debts the £15 and £10 threshold that applies to special expenses variations must be met, for either amount or the sum of both where they apply.[28] Where the grounds are diversion of income or lifestyle inconsistent, the amount of income must exceed £100 in cases where the new amount would otherwise be:
- the flat rate due to receipt of a prescribed benefit (other than IS or income-based JSA);
- the flat rate as above but is reduced to nil due to shared care; or
- is the nil rate (other than on income grounds).[29]

Where there is a relevant departure direction an equivalent variation will be applied to the calculation of the new amount without any separate application for a variation.[30]

Chapter 9: Conversions
2. The conversion calculation and transitional phasing

Example 9.5
Joan has a maintenance assessment with a special expenses departure direction of £22 for contact costs and £18 for travel-to-work costs. When her case is converted her special expenses for contact costs counts as a relevant transfer but her travel-to-work costs do not.

A **relevant property transfer** is distinct from a property/capital departure in that this is where an allowance is included at the exempt income stage (see Chapter 12) of the 'old rules' assessment formula.[31] In these cases it means that the amount of the relevant property transfer is deducted from net income at conversion used to work out maintenance.[32] It may be advisable, where a relevant property transfer is applied, to seek a variation on property/capital transfer grounds.[33] Where this application is successful the conversion decision will be revised or superseded depending on when the application was made.

Adjustments to the conversion calculation where there is a relevant departure direction or relevant property transfer

Adjustments are made to the conversion calculation depending on the type of grounds under which the departure direction has been granted – ie, special expenses, additional cases or property/capital transfer. The effect of adjustments for departure directions and relevant property transfers (or the aggregate of those that apply) are as below, carried out in the following order:[34]

- **Additional cases departure direction** – the amount of the departure is added to the net income figure. Where this takes net income over the capped amount of net weekly income of £2,000, the net income figure used is £2,000.[35] Where the non-resident parent is on benefit there is a maximum amount payable – ie, a conversion better buy (see below).
- **Special expenses departure direction** – the amount of the departure is deducted from the net weekly income.[36] Where the net income is the capped amount of £2,000, deduct the expenses from the actual net income not the capped amount. If this reduces the net income figure to below £2,000 this is the net income figure to use in the calculation, otherwise it is the capped amount.
- **Relevant property transfer** – the amount of the transfer is deducted from the net income of the non-resident parent. Where the net income is the capped amount of £2,000 the transfer is deducted from this capped amount.[37]
- **Property/capital transfer departure direction** – the amount of the departure is deducted from the maintenance due to the person with care.[38] This deduction can only be completed after any reduction for shared care (or part-time local authority care) has been applied.[39]

Where these adjustments reduce the amount of maintenance due below the £5 flat rate, the amount due will be the £5 flat rate. This may be apportioned between the persons with care as appropriate.[40]

Conversion better buy

When the non-resident parent is on benefit, the maximum amount payable where there is a relevant departure on additional cases grounds is the lesser of:[41]
- the flat rate plus the appropriate rate (reduced or basic) applied to the additional income under the departure; *or*
- the amount calculated by applying the appropriate rate to the total of the additional income under the departure and the income payable under any prescribed benefits (excluding amounts that are disregarded).

The conversion calculation is carried out in the normal way. However, the conversion better buy is applied and may cap the amount to be paid.

3. The conversion decision

At conversion the CSA carries out a conversion calculation.[42] The new amount is worked out applying the new calculation rates, using the information that the Secretary of State has at the calculation date.[43] There are additional rules for calculating the new amount at conversion where a departure direction or relevant property transfer was applied to the 'old rules' case (see p197).

There is no requirement to seek more up-to-date information;[44] if the information used at the calculation date is incorrect a revision can be requested. This may be particularly important in cases where there have been significant changes, which could increase or decrease the 'old rules' maintenance assessment. The policy intention is not to routinely supersede maintenance assessment decisions before conversion.

Where there is an interim maintenance assessment in force when the conversion decision is being made, this may be:
- used to make the conversion decision;[45] *or*
- replaced with a default maintenance decision, if there is insufficient information to make a maintenance assessment or conversion decision.[46]

In either case, where information is subsequently provided by the non-resident parent to make a maintenance assessment the conversion decision or default maintenance decision may be superseded.[47]

The new rate worked out will either be paid immediately (ie, the maintenance calculation comes into force) or transitional phasing may be applied (see p194).[48] There are some situations where the new amount is always applied, in other cases the CSA checks if transitional phasing applies, if it does not then the new amount is paid.

Chapter 9: Conversions
3. The conversion decision

The effective date of the conversion decision

The effective date of the conversion decision is normally the beginning of the first maintenance period on or after the conversion date.[49] This is known as the **case conversion date**. Where there is an early conversion, the effective date may be the beginning of the first maintenance period on or after the effective date of the new calculation or another period depending on the circumstances, which are set out in Table 9.1.[50]

Table 9.1: Effective date of conversion decisions in certain circumstances

Situation	Effective date
A maintenance calculation is made in respect of a relevant person who is a relevant person in relation to the maintenance assessment, whether or not in respect of a different qualifying child.	The beginning of the first maintenance period on or after the effective date of the new calculation.
A maintenance calculation is made in relation to person A who is a partner to person B who has a maintenance assessment. Either A or B are in receipt of income support (IS)/income-based jobseeker's allowance (JSA), and A and B are either both persons with care or both non-resident parents.	The beginning of the first maintenance period on or after the effective date of the new calculation.
An application is made or treated as made that would result in a maintenance calculation but there is an assessment in force. The non-resident parent in the new application is the non-resident parent in the existing case but the person with care in the new application is a different one from the one in the existing case.	The beginning of the first maintenance period on or after the date of notification of the conversion decision.
A maintenance assessment is in force in relation to person C and a maintenance calculation is in force in relation to person D. Either C or D are in receipt of IS/income-based JSA. C and D are either both persons with care or both non-resident parents. C and D become partners and the benefit decision is superseded because of this.	The beginning of the first maintenance period on or after the date that the benefit supersession decision takes effect.

200

A maintenance assessment is in force in relation to person E and a maintenance calculation in force in relation to their partner F. E and F are either both persons with care or both non-resident parents and then they become entitled to IS/income-based JSA as partners.	The beginning of the first maintenance period on or after the date from which they become entitled to IS or income-based JSA.
All other circumstances.	The beginning of the first maintenance period on or after the conversion decision.

Notification

Once the conversion decision is made, the non-resident parent, person with care and Scottish child applicant are notified in writing.[51] Where the conversion is occurring at C Day the parties may be given advance notification of the case conversion.

This notification states the:
- new amount;
- any transitional amount appropriate;
- length of the transitional period;
- date the conversion decision was made and the date from which it is effective;
- non-resident parent's net weekly income;
- number of qualifying and relevant other children;
- adjustments for apportionment or shared care;
- details of departure directions or relevant property transfers taken into account;
- adjustments because of the maximum transitional amount rule.

The conversion decision is treated as a maintenance calculation decision so requests for revision, supersession, variation and appeal may be made.[52] However, when considering subsequent decisions there are additional rules to determine the amount of maintenance to be paid (see p209).

After notification of the conversion decision there may be an application for a departure direction or a variation (see p211). The conversion decision may be revised, superseded or appealed (see p207).

When does the conversion end

Transitional phasing may be applied for up to five years from the case conversion date or until the maintenance calculation amount is reached.[53] Where there are subsequent decisions that result in the new amount being paid immediately (ie, nil rate or default rate) these may be applied or where the calculation is cancelled conversion will end. However, in some cases where linking applies (see p202) a

Chapter 9: Conversions
3. The conversion decision

second subsequent decision or new application may be dealt with as if the conversion decision still applied. This may affect the amount to be paid under any subsequent decision (see p206).

4. The linking rules

The linking rules cover a range of situations where an 'old rules' assessment or a transitional amount has been in force and there are applications and subsequent decisions made after 3 March 2003. Whether or not linking is applied depends on the timescales and circumstances. In each instance there are two key factors:
- a 13-week linking period is used; *and*
- where there is another application in the interim that involves either the person with care or non-resident parent (but not both) there is no linking.

Where linking applies the rules on working out how much maintenance is paid are adjusted, the effect of linking is explained in Table 9.2.

Table 9.2: The linking rules and their effect

Scenario	Linking effect means maintenance is worked out as if:
After 3 March 2003 but before C Day there is an application but within 13 weeks there was a maintenance assessment in force for the same parent with care, non-resident parent and qualifying child.	it is a maintenance assessment. All the 'old rules', including the formula (see p203), are applied to the case.
After C Day there is an application but within the previous 13 weeks a maintenance assessment has been in force for the same parent with care, non-resident parent and qualifying child.	the maintenance assessment is still in force and the conversion calculation rules are applied (see p204).
£5 (£2.50) flat rate, flat rate reduced to nil for shared care, or nil rate is paid. After C Day another decision is made to which basic or reduced rate applies and within 13 weeks of this subsequent decision a maintenance assessment was in force of more than £5.40 for the same parent with care, non-resident parent and qualifying child.	the maintenance assessment is still in force and the conversion calculation rules are applied (see p204).

The conversion calculation ceases to have effect but within 13 weeks there is an application for the same parent with care, non-resident parent and qualifying child. A transitional amount is being paid. There is a first subsequent decision where the £5/£2.50 flat rate/reduced to nil for shared care/nil rate is paid. Within 13 weeks of the effective date of this, a second decision is made where none of these rates apply for the same parent with care, non-resident parent and qualifying child.

the conversion calculation is still in force and subsequent decision rules are applied (see p206).

the first subsequent decision had not been made (ie, the transitional amount is still in force) and the subsequent decision rules are applied (see p205).

Applications for a maintenance calculation after 3 March 2003 but before C Day

An application for a maintenance calculation after 3 March 2003 but before C Day can be treated as an application for a maintenance assessment if it is:[54]
- made within 13 weeks of a maintenance assessment being in force; *and*
- in relation to the same person with care, non-resident parent and qualifying child,

unless there is a new application which includes either the 'old rules' case person with care or non-resident parent (but not both) before the new application is made, in which case there is no linking and it is dealt with as a new case.[55]

Where linking applies, maintenance is worked out using the 'old rules' maintenance assessment (ie, the formula and departures regulations).

Where a new application is linked to an old assessment and there is then a new application which involves the person with care or non-resident parent, the old case will be treated as an early conversion and a conversion calculation will be done.

Example 9.6
a) Celine is the parent with care. Franco is the non-resident parent in an 'old rules' assessment. Celine asks the CSA to stop acting (ie, she opts out). After six week she applies for a 'new rules' maintenance calculation. Since her 'old rules' assessment was in force within the last 13 weeks her application is treated as an application for a maintenance assessment.
b) If Celine opts out and waits for 14 weeks and then applies, her case will be dealt with as a 'new rules' case.
c) Celine opts out but before she reapplies Franco and his partner, Helen, split up. Helen makes an application for a maintenance calculation as the parent with care with Franco the non-resident parent, three weeks after Celine opts out. Helen's is a 'new rules' case and

when Celine reapplies three weeks later her case is dealt with as a new case and no linking or conversion rules apply.

d) If Celine opts out but before she reapplies and Franco applies as the parent with care of Francis, Franco's case is a 'new rules' case. When Celine applies six weeks later the linking rules apply and a conversion calculation will be done. Transitional phasing may apply to her maintenance.

Applications for a maintenance calculation after C Day

An application for a maintenance calculation after C Day can be dealt with as a conversion of a maintenance assessment if it is:[56]

- made within 13 weeks of a maintenance assessment being in force; *and*
- in relation to the same person with care, non-resident parent and qualifying child,

unless there is a new application which includes either the 'old rules' case person with care or non-resident parent before the new application is made, in which case there is no linking and it is dealt with as a new case.[57]

Where linking applies the calculation is carried out as if it were a conversion calculation, including any transitional phasing. In this case the transitional period is treated as beginning on the date that would have been the case conversion date if the previous assessment had been in force. In practice, this means that any phasing cannot go on beyond the fifth anniversary of C Day.

Example 9.7
a) Sarah is the parent with care. Carl is the non-resident parent in an 'old rules' assessment. Sarah asks the CSA to stop acting (ie, she opts out) four weeks before C Day. After eight week she applies for a 'new rules' maintenance calculation. Since her 'old rules' assessment was in force within the last 13 weeks her application is calculated as if the maintenance assessment was in force, and unless the new amount is due to be paid immediately, a conversion calculation, including transitional provisions, may apply.
b) If Sarah opts out and waits for 14 weeks and then applies for maintenance from Carl there will be no linking and a conversion calculation will not apply.
c) Sarah opts-out but before she reapplies in relation to Carl, Carl makes an application for maintenance from his ex-partner Kerry. If Sarah subsequently applies there will be no linking and a conversion calculation will not be done.
d) Sarah opts-out and one of the qualifying children moves to live with Carl. Before she reapplies for maintenance from Carl for the two remaining qualifying children, Carl makes an application for maintenance from her. If Sarah subsequently applies there will be linking and a conversion calculation will be done (transitional phasing may apply).

A conversion decision ceases and there is a further application

An application for a maintenance calculation can be dealt with as if the conversion decision had not ceased to have effect if the application is made:[58]
- within 13 weeks of the conversion decision ceasing to have effect; *and*
- in relation to the same person with care, non-resident parent and qualifying child,

unless there is a new application which includes either the 'old rules' case person with care or non-resident parent before the new application is made, in which case there is no linking and it is dealt with as a new case.[59]

Where linking applies the maintenance calculation may be a transitional amount or it may be adjusted following the rules relating to subsequent decisions where there is a conversion decision (see p199).[60]

Example 9.8

a) Monica's 'old rules' assessment converted at C Day and transitional phasing applies. She and her ex-partner Lewis try to get back together and the conversion decision ceases. After two months Lewis discovers Monica is pregnant with someone else's child and leaves. Monica makes an application for child maintenance from Lewis; as this is within 13 weeks of the conversion decision ceasing, linking rules apply. Monica's new application is worked out as if the previous conversion calculation was in force and the rules on subsequent decisions apply (see below).

b) If Monica had the baby when she and Lewis got back together and she then applied for maintenance from the baby's father, if she and Lewis subsequently broke up, there would be no linking in the Monica/Lewis case.

A transitional amount is due and there are subsequent decisions

Where a transitional amount is being paid during the transitional period and there is a decision (first decision) which results in the non-resident parent paying the:[61]
- flat rate at £5 or £2.50 (except if this rate is due because income is less than £100);
- flat rate at £5 or £2.50 but is less or reduced to nil because of shared care; *or*
- nil rate.

Then if there is a further decision (second decision) which would mean that the non-resident parent is liable to pay at a rate other than one of those above there will be linking unless:
- there is an application which includes either the 'old rules' case person with care or non-resident parent before the second decision is made;[62] *or*
- the effective date of the second decision is not within 13 weeks of the first decision.[63]

Chapter 9: Conversions
4. The Linking rules

Where linking applies, the second decision will be worked out as if the first decision had not been made (ie, as if the transitional amount was still in force) and the rules on subsequent decisions where a transitional amount is in force are followed.[64]

Example 9.9
Amanda's 'old rules' case converted with transitional phasing. Her non-resident parent, Adam, is sentenced to two months in prison. There is a superseding decision and the nil rate now applies. After a month Adam is released and gets his old job back on a building site. She is now due maintenance at the reduced rate, since the effective date of the new calculation is within 13 weeks of the previous superseding decision. The amount due is worked out as if the superseding decision was not made – ie, as if the conversion decision still applies. As his income and circumstances are the same as before he went into prison, he pays the same as he did previously including transitional phasing.

If Adam had been in prison for six months, the linking rule would not have applied and he would have paid the new amount without any transitional phasing.

A conversion calculation/maintenance calculation is in force and there is a subsequent decision

Where there is a conversion calculation or a maintenance calculation (where the transitional period has ended or a relevant property transfer has ceased to have effect) that is paid at the:[65]
- flat rate of £5 or £2.50 (except if this rate is due because income is less than £100);
- flat rate of £5 or £2.50 but is less or reduced to nil because of shared care; *or*
- nil rate,

and after C Day a subsequent decision is made which would be paid at the basic or reduced rate, then if the effective date of that decision is within 13 weeks of a maintenance assessment being in force. The linking rules will apply **unless**:
- there is an application which includes either the 'old rules' case person with care or non-resident parent before the second decision is made, in which case there is no linking;[66] *or*
- the amount the non-resident parent paid under the maintenance assessment was the minimum amount, or he was exempt from paying the minimum.

Where linking applies the subsequent decision will be calculated as if the previous maintenance assessment was in force, including applying any transitional phasing.[67]

Example 9.10
a) Malcolm is on income-based JSA and paid the minimum amount of £5.60 under his 'old rules' maintenance assessment. When the case converts at C Day he is due to pay the flat

rate but this is reduced to nil because he has one night's shared care of the qualifying child (Lucy). He therefore pays a transitional amount of £2.50. Two months later Malcolm comes off benefit. The conversion decision should be superseded at the basic rate. However, even though there was a maintenance assessment in force within 13 weeks of the effective date of the superseding decision, because this was paid at the minimum amount, linking does not apply. Malcolm's new amount of maintenance will be not be phased.

b) If Malcolm had been working and paying a maintenance assessment of £57.80, then been on income-based JSA for two weeks before and at conversion but he started work within eight weeks of conversion, he has a basic rate of £69. However, since there was a maintenance assessment in force within 13 weeks of the decision, the linking rules apply. His new amount has transitional phasing applied and he is due to pay £62.80.

5. Revision, supersession and appeal

At conversion there may be decisions outstanding on a maintenance assessment or departure direction. In other cases decisions may have been made but the time limits for challenging them may not have expired (see below).

Once the conversion decision has been made it may be challenged in the normal ways (revision, supersession, appeal and application for variation) since it is treated as if it is a maintenance calculation.[68] However, there are some grounds on which conversion decisions may not be revised, superseded or appealed (see p208). There are also additional rules to be applied when working out how much maintenance should be paid on any subsequent decision (see p209).

Applications may also be made for a departure direction or variation that may result in decisions being revised or superseded (see p211).

Outstanding decisions and time limits at conversion

In some cases a decision may have been made on a maintenance assessment or departure direction where the time limit for seeking a revision or making an appeal has not expired at conversion.[69] In these cases, a revision or appeal may still be sought using the 'old rules'.

Alternatively, at the conversion date there may be outstanding decisions on:[70]
- the maintenance assessment;
- a departure direction;
- a revision or supersession;
- an appeal.[71]

Where this is the case a conversion decision may be made using the information held at the conversion date.[72] In the case of an outstanding maintenance assessment this may mean an interim maintenance assessment (IMA) is made

Chapter 9: Conversions
5. Revision, supersession and appeal

and at conversion a default maintenance decision becomes due. The outstanding decision may be determined using the 'old rules' as if they still applied.[73] Once the outstanding decision is made or appeal is decided, the conversion decision may be revised or superseded.[74]

Outstanding decisions on revision and supersession may themselves be appealed when they are made using the 'old rules'.[75] This means a decision not to make a departure direction may be appealed under the 'old rules'.[76] An appeal decision may be challenged on a point of law to the child support commissioners.

Conversion and subsequent decisions

Conversion and subsequent decisions can be revised, superseded and appealed in the same way as maintenance calculations,[77] except that:
- there are certain grounds on which a conversion decision may not be revised, superseded or appealed (see below);
- when appealing against a conversion decision, the time limit for making an appeal is extended. The time limit is either one month from notification or from the date of notification to one month after the case conversion date, whichever is later.[78] In practice, this means that where there is an early conversion the normal time limit applies. Other cases converting at C Day and getting advance notice have longer to appeal;
- the effective date of a revision or supersession of a conversion decision is either the conversion date or the date worked out under the normal rules, whichever is later;[79]
- notifications will contain details of any subsequent decision amount in place of the new amount and details of any variations taken into account;
- a conversion decision may be revised or superseded because of a revision/supersession/appeal of a maintenance assessment (including IMA) or departure direction after the calculation date;[80]
- when making further decisions the linking rules may be applied (see p202) and the rules on working out the amount of maintenance due on a subsequent decision are applied.

After notification of the conversion decision there may be an application for a departure direction or a variation. Where this is made after the calculation date but before the case conversion date this may result in a series of supersession decisions.

Grounds which are not allowed

A revision, supersession and appeal may not be allowed on the grounds:[81]
- that the CSA used the information they already had at the calculation date;
- that the CSA took into account a relevant departure direction (ie, one that counts as a variation under the 'new rules');

- that the CSA failed to take into account a departure direction (ie, where it does not count as a variation under the 'new rules');
- that the CSA applied a phasing amount;
- of the length of the transitional period;
- that the CSA took into account a relevant property transfer, except where the person with care or Scottish child applicant asks for it to be removed as it did not reflect the true value of the transfer or a relevant person applies for a variation.

How much is paid on a further decision after conversion

There are special rules on how to work out how much is paid when there are further decisions after conversion. These are applied to conversion cases where there is transitional phasing (or there has been in cases where the linking rules apply – see p202). These are in addition to the normal rules on revision and supersession.

When considering a revision of the conversion decision (ie, where the effective date is the case conversion date, not the revision of a later supersession) the rules for working out an initial conversion are used.[82]

Where there is a supersession of the conversion decision, or revision of such a decision, the additional rules, explained below are used to determine the amount of maintenance to be paid.[83]

These apply to such decisions on appeal.

The amount to be paid under a further decision could be:
- the nil rate, or £5 (£2.50) flat rate, or would be but is less than this or is reduced to nil due to shared care;
- the transitional amount, see rules below;
- a new transitional amount, see rules below; or
- the subsequent decision amount.

Where the decision is the nil rate, flat rate or flat rate reduced to nil due to shared care (including where the amount due is less than £5/£2.50), this is the amount that is paid and transitional phasing ceases.[84] However, if there is a subsequent decision after this and the linking rules may apply (see p202), the rules below may be applied and transitional phasing may be revived (see example 9.11(c)).

In all other cases the subsequent decision amount is compared to the former assessment and the new amount due under the maintenance calculation. Where there is more than one person with care the apportioning rules apply to the calculation (including any adjustments due to the maximum transitional amount).[85] The subsequent decision amount and new amount are the amounts worked out using the maintenance calculation, including adjustments for apportionment and shared care, before any transitional phasing is applied. If

Chapter 9: Conversions
5. Revision, supersession and appeal

linking applies (see p202), this may mean the new amount referred to is in a conversion calculation that has ceased to be in force or is in a previous decision.

Unless the conditions in the table below are met, the amount due will be the subsequent decision amount. If this applies, transitional phasing ceases and cannot be revived for any further decisions and only the normal supersession rules apply.

Where the original transitional phasing or a new transitional amount applies, transitional phasing then continues until the subsequent decision amount is reached or the five-year transitional period ends, whichever is earlier (see p194).

Any further decisions in the meantime will be worked out under these rules.[86] There are provisions to allow this where the subsequent decision (Decision B) replaces an earlier subsequent decision (Decision A) or one made with an incorrect effective date, so that in effect Decision A is ignored in applying the rules.[87]

Table 9.3: Other cases where the amount due will not be the subsequent decision amount

Condition one	Condition two	Amount due
The new amount is greater than the former assessment	Subsequent decision greater than new amount	A new transitional amount is worked out increasing the previous transitional amount by the difference between the new amount and the subsequent decision
The new amount is greater than the former assessment	Subsequent decision less than or equal to the new amount and greater than the previous transitional amount	Amount is previous transitional amount
The new amount is less than the former assessment amount	Subsequent decision is less than the new amount	A new transitional amount is worked out decreasing the previous transitional amount by the difference between the new amount and the subsequent decision
The new amount is less than the former assessment amount	Subsequent decision is greater than or equal to new amount and less than the previous transitional amount	Amount is the previous transitional amount

210

Chapter 9: Conversions
5. Revision, supersession and appeal

Example 9.11
a) Kevin is due to pay an assessment of £68. His net income is £248. When his case converts he is due to pay a basic rate of £50. This has transitional phasing applied, so he is due to pay £63. Four months later he gets a promotion and his ex-wife requests a supersession. As Kevin's net income has increased to £270, the 5 per cent tolerance level is breached and the CSA consider supersession. The amount he would now be due to pay is £54. The new amount of £50 was less than the assessment (condition one) and the subsequent decision amount £54 is greater than this and less than the previous transitional amount £63 (condition two). This means he continues to be due to pay the previous transitional amount of £63.

b) If Kevin's net income had increased to £325, the amount due would be £65. In this case he does not meet condition two as this is greater than the previous transitional amount (£63). This means he is due to pay £65. There is no more transitional phasing. If Kevin reduces his working hours and his income decreases to £270, his maintenance due would be £54 with no transitional phasing applied.

c) If the situation was different the linking rules may apply. If the case converts as in (a) but instead of a promotion Kevin is made redundant and claims contribution-based JSA, he is now due to pay at the flat rate of £5. Ten weeks later he gets a new job and has a net income of £210 a week. As this is within 13 weeks, the linking rules apply (see p202). The maintenance decision at the flat rate is ignored. The new amount in condition one is therefore £50 and the subsequent decision amount is £42. As this is lower than the new amount a new transitional amount is worked out. The difference between the two, £8 (£50 – £42), is subtracted from the first transitional amount (£63). Kevin now has to pay £55 (£63 – £8). Unless there are further decisions, a year later transitional phasing will mean he becomes due to pay £50 (£55 – £5).

Applications for a departure direction or variation

After notification of the conversion decision a relevant person may apply for a variation, in which case the conversion decision may be revised or superseded accordingly (see p207). Where the case is converting at C Day this may mean an application is made after the calculation date but before the case conversion date, in which case the application is treated as an advance application for a variation.[88]

Departure directions are slightly more complex. To be taken into account at conversion a departure direction must apply to the maintenance assessment used in the conversion calculation.

Where an application for a departure direction is made after the calculation date but before the case conversion date this may result in the maintenance assessment being superseded to take account of the departure direction and then the conversion decision would be revised to reflect the change.[89] Where it is a relevant departure direction this revision of the conversion decision will include a variation.[90] A departure direction application cannot be made after the case conversion date; however, it may be possible to seek revision or appeal a refusal to agree a departure direction if the relevant time limits have not expired.[91] For more information on decisions and time limits outstanding at conversion, see p207.

Conversion decision made in error

Where an early conversion decision, or subsequent decision on that early conversion, has been made and it is found that the early conversion grounds did not apply, the case will be treated as if those decisions had not been made.[92] This means the maintenance assessment will be reinstated, bearing in mind any revisions, supersessions or appeals made in the meantime which would have affected that assessment.

> **Example 9.12**
> Amy's maintenance assessment is converted early due to an administrative error, which is discovered two months later. When the error is discovered the maintenance assessment is reinstated. However, the non-resident parent notified changes in housing costs and travel-to-work costs that could not be taken into account under the 'new rules' but were relevant in the previous assessment. The assessment is superseded, the effective date being linked to the relevant date of notification of the changes by the non-resident parent, as there was a significant change under the 'old rules'.

6. **Conversion, benefits and collection**

All the provisions relating to 'new rules' maintenance calculations apply to old cases that convert, even though a transitional phasing may apply. This section clarifies how certain issues are dealt with at conversion.

Persons with care on benefit

Child maintenance bonus and child maintenance premium

Up to conversion of an existing maintenance assessment to the 'new rules', either as an early conversion or at C Day, a child maintenance bonus may be accrued.[93] The child maintenance bonus may also accrue up to C Day where the maintenance is paid under an agreement or order, unless maintenance is paid in relation to a different child or under a new agreement/order for the existing child(ren) in which case the child maintenance premium will apply from an earlier date.[94] Where the payment is made after 16 February 2004, and it is the first voluntary payment of maintenance since the person has been on IS/income-based JSA, then the child maintenance premium will apply.[95]

Chapter 9: Conversions
6. Conversion, benefits and collection

The rules on how to claim a child maintenance bonus before the case converts remain unchanged (see p405). When a child maintenance bonus is being replaced by a child maintenance premium at conversion, it may be possible to claim the bonus that has accrued.

When the case converts, either as an early conversion or at C Day, the bonus period will cease and a child maintenance premium will apply.[96] The bonus period will end the day before conversion.[97] The child maintenance premium will begin on the first day of the benefit week in which the conversion date falls.[98]

After conversion the bonus may be claimed where the conditions are met.[99] However:
- the normal time limit for the work condition to be met is extended from 14 days to one month;[100]
- the exceptional time limits for the work condition to be met (eg, where the non-resident parent or the only qualifying child die) apply if the change in circumstances occurs before conversion.

This means that if the work condition is not met within one month of conversion, the accrued bonus may be lost. Claims must be made within 28 days, though this may be extended by up to six months where there are good reasons for a late claim. For details of the other conditions on claiming a child maintenance bonus, see p405.

Non-resident parent on benefit

A non-resident parent on benefit may be due to pay the flat rate of maintenance or a transitional amount where under the 'old rules' he made a contribution to maintenance or was exempt. The new rules on deduction from benefit applying to conversion decisions and deductions may be made from benefit for maintenance and arrears. There may be no appeal against deductions from benefit for flat rate maintenance or to recover arrears (see p208).

Collection and enforcement

Maintenance worked out under a conversion decision is collected and enforced in the normal way, since it is treated as a maintenance calculation.[101]

Arrears built up under the 'old rules' may be recovered using the new deduction from earnings orders or the normal enforcement action. An existing deductions from earnings order may be cancelled and a new one issued, applying the new rules on protected earnings proportion.

A payment penalty may also be imposed but only on arrears or late payments that fall due after conversion.

Chapter 9: Conversions
Notes

1. **When do 'old rules' cases convert to the 'new rules'**
    1. Definition 'conversion date' reg 2 CS(TP) Regs
    2. Reg 15 CS(TP) Regs; reg 3 CSPSSA (Comm 12) Order 2003
    3. Reg 15 CS(TP) Regs
    4. Overview – CSR Case conversion

2. **The conversion calculation and transitional phasing**
    5. Reg 16(1) CS(TP) Regs
    6. Reg 3(1)(c) CS(TP) Regs
    7. Reg 3(4) CS(TP) Regs
    8. s29 CSPSSA 2000; reg 9 CS(TP) Regs
    9. Reg 14 CS(TP) Regs
    10. Reg 10 CS(TP) Regs
    11. Reg 11(2) CS(TP) Regs
    12. Reg 11(3) CS(TP) Regs
    13. Reg 24 CS(TP) Regs
    14. Reg 11(1) CS(TP) Regs
    15. Reg 2(1) CS(TP) Regs definition of transitional period
    16. Regs 2(1) CS(TP) Regs definition of maximum transitional amount; reg 25(1) CS(TP) Regs
    17. Reg 25 (5-7 CS(TP) Regs as inserted by reg 7(6) CS(MA)(No2) Regs 2003
    18. Reg 25(3) CS(TP) Regs
    19. Reg 25(4) CS(TP) Regs
    20. Reg 13(2) CS(TP) Regs
    21. Reg 13 (1) CS(TP) Regs
    22. Reg 12(1) CS(TP) Regs
    23. Reg 12(2) CS(TP) Regs
    24. Reg 12(3-5) CS(TP) Regs
    25. Reg 12(6) CS(TP) Regs
    26. s29(3)(b) CSPSSA 2000
    27. Reg 17 CS(TP) Regs as amended by reg 7(4)CS(MA)(No2) Regs 2003
    28. Reg 17(2) CS(TP) Regs
    29. Reg 17(6) CS(TP) Regs
    30. Reg 17(9) CS(TP) Regs
    31. Reg 17(8) CS(TP) Regs
    32. Reg 21 CS(TP) Regs
    33. Reg 17(10) CS(TP) Regs as inserted by reg 7(4) CS(MA)(No2) Regs
    34. Reg 23 and 23A CS(TP) Regs
    35. Reg 20 CS(TP) Regs
    36. Reg 18 CS(TP) Regs
    37. Reg 21 CS(TP) Regs
    38. Reg 19 CS(TP) Regs
    39. Reg 23(4) CS(TP) Regs
    40. Reg 23(5) CS(TP) Regs
    41. Reg 22 CS(TP) Regs

3. **The conversion decision**
    42. Reg 3 CS(TP) Regs
    43. Reg 16(1) CS(TP) Regs
    44. Reg 16(1) CS(TP) Regs
    45. Reg 3(1)(c) CS(TP) Regs
    46. Reg 3(4) CS(TP) Regs
    47. Reg 3(5) CS(TP) Regs
    48. s29 CSPSSA 2000
    49. Reg 15(1) CS(TP) Regs
    50. Reg 15 (2-3G) CS(TP) Regs
    51. Reg 3(3) CS(TP) Regs
    52. Reg 16(2) CS(TP) Regs
    53. Reg 2 CS(TP) Regs definition of transitional period

4. **The linking rules**
    54. Reg 28(2) CS(TP) Regs
    55. Reg 28(2A) CS(TP) Regs
    56. Reg 28(2) CS(TP) Regs
    57. Reg 28(2A) CS(TP) Regs
    58. Reg 28 (6-7) CS(TP) Regs
    59. Reg 28(7A) CS(TP) Regs
    60. Reg 28(7) CS(TP) Regs
    61. Reg 28(4) CS(TP) Regs
    62. Reg 28(5A) CS(TP) Regs
    63. Reg 28 (4)(b) CS(TP) Regs
    64. Reg 28(5) CS(TP) Regs
    65. Reg 28(8) CS(TP) Regs
    66. Reg 28(9) CS(TP) Regs
    67. Reg 28(8) CS(TP) Regs

5. **Revision, supersession and appeal**
    68. Reg 16(2) CS(TP) Regs
    69. Regs 14(2)(b&c) and 15(b) CS(D&A)(A) Regs
    70. Reg 5 CS(TP) Regs
    71. Reg 8 CS(TP) Regs
    72. Regs 5(b) and 8(1) CS(TP) Regs
    73. Reg 14(2) and 15(1)CS(D&A)(A) Regs
    74. Regs 4(3) and 8(2) CS(TP) Regs
    75. Regs 14 and 15 CS(D&A)(A) Regs
    76. Reg 15(1) CS(D&A)(A) Regs
    77. Reg 4(1) CS(TP) Regs
    78. Reg 4(5)(b) CS(TP) Regs
    79. Reg 4(4)(a) CS(TP) Regs

Chapter 9: Conversions
Notes

80   Reg 4(3) CS(TP) Regs
81   Reg 7 CS(TP) Regs as amended by reg 7(3) CS(MA)(No2) Regs 2003
82   Reg 26 CS(TP) Regs
83   Reg 27 CS(TP) as amended by reg 7(7) CS(MA)(No2) Regs 2003
84   Reg 27(6) CS(TP) Regs
85   Reg 27 (7-8) CS(TP) Regs
86   Reg 27(9) CS(TP) Regs
87   Reg 27(10) CS(TP) Regs
88   Reg 6(10)(c) and (2)(c) CS(TP) Regs
89   Reg 6(1)(a) and (2)(a) CS(TP) Regs
90   Reg 6(1)(b) and (2)(b) CS(TP) Regs
91   Reg 15 SSCS(D&A)(A) Regs
92   Reg 33 CS(TP) Regs

6. **Conversion, benefits and collection**
93   Art 6 CSPSSA (Comm12)
94   Art 6 CSPSSA (Comm 12)
95   Reg 1(3) SS(CMP) A Regs 2004
96   s23 CSPSSA 2000; reg 4(1) SS(CMPMA) Regs
97   Reg 4(7) SS(CMB) Regs
98   para 104 IS/GAP Circular 02/02 (revised)
99   Reg 4(2-5) SS(CMPMA) Regs 2002
100 Reg 3 (1)(f)(iii) SS(CMB) Regs
101 Reg 16(2A) CS(TP) Regs

Part 4
Old rules formula

Chapter 10
The 'old rules' formula in outline

This chapter covers:
1. A rigid formula (below)
2. The five steps of the 'old rules' formula (p221)
3. Minimum child maintenance (p223)
4. 'Old rules' non-resident parents on certain benefits (p224)
5. Special cases (p227)

> *This chapter contains information relevant to existing cases under the 'old rules'. For calculations under the 'new rules', see Chapter 7.*

1. A rigid formula

The Child Support Act 1991 introduced a statutory, non-discretionary formula for the calculation of child maintenance. This applies to 'old rules' cases. The 'old rules' formula is contained in algebraic form in Schedule 1 to the 1991 Act prior to its amendment by the Child Support, Pensions and Social Security Act 2000 and, in detail, in the Child Support (Maintenance Assessment and Special Cases) Regulations. Both these and the Child Support (Maintenance Assessment Procedure) Regulations now only apply to 'old rules' cases. The amount of the child maintenance assessment is not open for negotiation. There is a right of appeal against the assessment, but the appeal tribunal which hears the case is bound by the same law as the CSA (see p434).

The amount of child maintenance payable depends largely on the circumstances and the income of the parents, particularly the income of the non-resident parent. Often parents, and therefore advisers, will not have access to all the information needed from the other parent in order to carry out an exact calculation. This will particularly affect parents with care who may find they have very little of the information required to predict or check the maintenance assessment.

Chapter 10: The 'old rules' formula in outline
1. A rigid formula

However, understanding the way in which the formula works is important for explaining the result of an assessment as well as forecasting the effect of any change of circumstances and deciding whether to seek a revision or supersession (see p413). It may be used to estimate the amount of child maintenance due before the CSA notification is sent in order to prevent a build-up of unmanageable initial arrears (see p468).

Deviation from the 'old rules' formula

A number of people have a duty to provide information to the CSA. If the CSA does not have enough information to carry out a full assessment, an interim maintenance assessment can be imposed (see p399) in 'old rules' cases. These are usually penalty assessments, and therefore higher than the formula assessment would be, in order to encourage non-resident parents to co-operate with the CSA.

The formula is not used to calculate the contribution towards child maintenance if the non-resident parent is on income support (IS) or income-based jobseeker's allowance (see p224).

Non-resident parents with second families have the assessment phased in where there would be an increase in the payments of over £20 a week, as compared with a pre-April 1993 maintenance agreement (see p387).

Departure

There is a system of departing from the standard 'old rules' formula in certain circumstances. Departure is a way of taking into account a financial factor particular to that family – eg, the costs of the non-resident parent travelling to visit the children, or a partner's contribution towards housing costs. Although the decision is discretionary as to whether or not to take into account the factor and to what extent, an adjusted formula is then used to obtain the final assessment. See Chapter 17 for details of departure.

The calculation

The child maintenance payable under the 'old rules' formula is given as a weekly rate and all stages of the calculation use weekly figures.[1] Fractions of a penny will be disregarded if less than one-half or rounded up to the next penny if equal to or more than one half-penny (except when calculating 70 per cent net income for the protected level, see p310, when any fraction of a penny is ignored).[2]

Income support rates

The formula for assessing child maintenance is based on IS components – both the personal allowances and the premiums. The 2004/05 rates are given at the front of this *Handbook*. It is important to note that although the allowances and premiums have ceased to have effect for many claimants they still apply for the

Chapter 10: The 'old rules' formula in outline
2. The five steps of the 'old rules' formula

purpose of working out 'old rules' assessments. For the conditions of entitlement for the IS premiums, see Appendix 2.

The IS rates used in the calculation are those which apply on the date that the maintenance assessment comes into effect, known as the effective date (see p400).[3] As the effective date is usually some time before the date on which the assessment is being made, assessments may be made in 2004/05 using a previous year's rates. The benefit rates increased on 12 April 2004. The maintenance assessment is not automatically altered at the annual April uprating of IS rates, but if a re-assessment is requested after a change of circumstances, the new rates would then be relevant. The CSA intends to carry out periodic re-assessments of maintenance payable (case checks) at various intervals but there is no legal requirement for them to do so (see p423).

Changes to the formula

Since the 'old rules' formula for setting assessment was introduced in April 1993, there have been two major sets of changes to it – the first on 7 February 1994 and the second on 18 April 1995. There have also been numerous other smaller changes. Unless there is a specific provision, the general rule is that the calculation must be done using the regulations which applied on the effective date (see p400) of the assessment.[4] This edition of the *Handbook* covers the formula in effect during 2004/05; make sure you refer to the appropriate earlier edition for assessments with earlier effective dates.

2. The five steps of the 'old rules' formula

It might appear that some of the formula's steps are not always needed. However, as a note of caution, we would warn advisers not to skip steps unless they are very familiar with the formula. See Appendix 3 for the calculation sheets for each stage.

Although only a non-resident parent is liable to pay child maintenance, the calculation involves the income of both parents. The term 'parent' applies to both the non-resident parent and the parent with care.

As elsewhere in this *Handbook*, for the sake of simplicity the parent with care is referred to as 'she' and the non-resident parent as 'he'. However, all aspects of the formula apply if the parent with care is in fact the father and the non-resident parent the mother. If the person with care is *not* the parent of the child, then the income of that person with care does not affect the amount of child maintenance payable.

Step 1: The maintenance requirement

The maintenance requirement represents the minimum day-to-day expenses of maintaining children. However, the maintenance requirement is neither the

221

Chapter 10: The 'old rules' formula in outline
2. The five steps of the 'old rules' formula

minimum nor the maximum amount of child maintenance payable. A non-resident parent might not be able to afford to pay the maintenance requirement in full or, alternatively, he may have sufficient income to pay over and above the maintenance requirement.

The main significance of this step is that a non-resident parent pays 50 per cent of his assessable income (see Chapter 13) in child maintenance until the maintenance requirement figure has been met. At this point he pays a lower percentage of any remaining assessable income.

For full details of the maintenance requirement, see Chapter 11.

Step 2: Exempt income

Exempt income represents the minimum day-to-day living expenses of the parent and covers the housing costs of the family s/he lives with. However, it includes only amounts for the living expenses of any of the parent's *own* children who are living with the parent, but does *not* include any such amount for a new partner or step children. An allowance in recognition of property/capital settlements pre-dating April 1993 may also be included in exempt income.

Each parent is allowed to keep income equal to the exempt income before being expected to pay any child maintenance.

For full details of exempt income, see Chapter 12.

Step 3: Assessable income

Assessable income is income which is available to pay child maintenance. It is the amount of the parent's income which remains after the exempt income has been taken into account. If a non-resident parent has no assessable income, he may have to pay the minimum payment.

For full details of assessable income, see Chapter 13.

Step 4: Proposed maintenance

Proposed maintenance is the amount of child maintenance the non-resident parent is expected to pay as long as it does not bring his income below the protected income level (see step 5).

A non-resident parent pays 50 per cent of his assessable income in child maintenance until he has met the maintenance requirement figure of step 1. Once the maintenance requirement is met, he pays 15, 20 or 25 per cent of any further assessable income, depending on the number of children he is being assessed to pay maintenance.

The assessable income of the parent with care can reduce the proposed maintenance.

222

There is an upper limit to the amount of child maintenance payable under the formula. It is still possible for the parties to go to court to seek additional child maintenance (see p37).

For full details of proposed maintenance, see Chapter 14.

Step 5: Protected income

The protected income step ensures that a non-resident parent's disposable income does not fall below a certain level as a result of paying the proposed maintenance. At this stage the whole family's expenses and income are taken into account, including those related to a new partner and stepchildren.

In addition, a non-resident parent is not expected to pay more than 30 per cent of his own net income.

For full details of protected income, see Chapter 15.

3. Minimum child maintenance

There is a standard minimum payment of child maintenance that applies to non-resident parents where the formula results in an amount less than this minimum.[5] (The formula is not applied to non-resident parents on income support (IS), pension credit (PC) or income-based jobseeker's allowance (JSA); however, deductions from IS/PC/income-based JSA may be made as a contribution towards child maintenance – see p281.)

The amount of the minimum payment is currently £5.60. This is calculated by rounding 5 per cent of the IS personal allowance for someone aged 25 or over (£55.65) up to the next 5 pence and doubling it.[6]

The minimum payment must be made unless the non-resident parent falls into a category which is specifically excluded (see p223). In other words, a non-resident parent who has been assessed under the formula as liable to pay less than £5.60 will have to pay child maintenance of £5.60 a week unless he falls into one of the exempt categories.

Only one minimum payment will be due where a person is the non-resident parent for the purposes of more than one application.[7] For example, where a non-resident parent has children with two or more women with whom he does not live, or where the children of his first family are being cared for by different people in different households, the minimum payment will be divided between the persons with care in proportion to the relative maintenance requirements (see Chapter 11).

Exempt non-resident parents

A few non-resident parents will not have to pay any child maintenance at all. If a non-resident parent has been assessed under the formula as having to pay £5.60 or less, he is exempt from paying any child maintenance if he:[8]

Chapter 10: The 'old rules' formula in outline
3. Minimum child maintenance

- has the family premium (see Appendix 2) included in the calculation or estimation of his protected income level – ie, a child is a member of his family for at least two days a week;
- is a prisoner;
- receives (or would receive but for failure to satisfy the national insurance contribution conditions or for receipt of an overlapping benefit) one of the following:
    - incapacity benefit (IB) or statutory sick pay;
    - maternity allowance or statutory maternity pay;
    - severe disablement allowance;
    - disability living allowance or attendance allowance;
    - an industrial disablement benefit;
    - a war disablement benefit;
    - carer's allowance; or
    - payments from the Independent Living (1993) Fund or the Independent Living (Extension) Fund;
- is under 16 years old, or under 19 and receiving full-time non-advanced education (ie, a child within the meaning of the Acts – see p26);
- has a net income of less than £5.60 (for full details of what is net income, see Chapter 13). Trainees on the Work-Based Training for Young People scheme (Skillseekers in Scotland) whose income consists solely of a training allowance under the scheme, or students whose only income is a grant, grant contribution or student loan, have these incomes ignored when calculating net income purposes. Most, therefore, are exempt from paying child maintenance.[9]

These exempt categories do not mean, for example, that all non-resident parents on IB automatically pay no child maintenance. In order to be exempt from paying maintenance, they must first have been assessed according to the formula as only being able to afford to pay an amount of £5.60 a week or less.

4. 'Old rules' non-resident parents on certain benefits

If the non-resident parent is in receipt of income support (IS), pension credit (PC) or income-based jobseeker's allowance (JSA), the formula is not used to assess the child maintenance payable. Instead, the Secretary of State can make a deduction from the IS/income-based JSA of a non-resident parent as a contribution towards child maintenance.[10] The deduction can be made from a partner's IS/PC/income-based JSA if the partner of a non-resident parent is claiming for the couple.[11]

The parties will first receive notification of a nil assessment and then be contacted with a decision about deductions from IS/income-based JSA.

Who can have the deduction made

Deductions cannot be made if the non-resident parent:[12]
- is aged under 18; *or*
- qualifies for the family premium (see Appendix 2) and/or has day-to-day care (see p28) of any child; *or*
- receives any of the following benefits, or would receive one except for contribution requirements or overlapping benefit rules:
  – statutory sick pay;
  – incapacity benefit (IB);
  – severe disablement allowance;
  – attendance allowance or disability living allowance;
  – carer's allowance;
  – maternity allowance;
  – statutory maternity pay;
  – an industrial disablement benefit;
  – a war disablement benefit; *or*
  – payments from the Independent Living (1993) Fund or the Independent Living (Extension) Fund.

(Thus, someone who is incapable of work but has insufficient national insurance contributions to receive IB cannot have deductions made.)

Amount of the deduction

A non-resident parent on IS/income-based JSA or PC who is not exempt may have an amount equal to the minimum payment (see p223) deducted from his benefit by the DWP, irrespective of the age of the non-resident parent.[13] This is currently £5.60 a week. In some cases, half of this amount may be deducted. Whether the deduction is actually made by the DWP depends upon the number of other deductions of higher priority (see below).

There will not be more than one deduction made if there is more than one person with care looking after the non-resident parent's qualifying children. Instead, the payment is apportioned between the persons with care in the same ratio as their respective maintenance requirements.[14]

What the deduction is for

Technically this deduction is not a payment of child support maintenance, but a payment in lieu of child maintenance.[15] It is not a maintenance assessment and therefore the rules which apply to assessments do not apply to these contributions. In particular, liability for the contributions will not be backdated to the effective date, and arrears will not accrue, if the DWP is unable to make the deduction because there are other deductions with higher priority.

In theory, deductions can also be made to recoup arrears of child maintenance which arose before the non-resident parent claimed IS/PC/income-based JSA. No

Chapter 10: The 'old rules' formula in outline
4. 'Old rules' non-resident parents on certain benefits (JACQUI – IS THIS OK?)

more than one deduction of £5.60 can be made from an IS/PC/income-based JSA claim at any one time.[16] In other words, the CSA will not be seeking any deductions for arrears at the same time as the current contribution in lieu of child maintenance. However, as deductions can only be made from IS/PC/income-based JSA while there is a non-resident parent with a current liability, no deduction for arrears can be made in practice. Arrears of child maintenance could still be collected by other methods (see Chapter 21). Usually the arrears will just be held in abeyance until the non-resident parent leaves IS/PC/income-based JSA. If a non-resident parent is in receipt of contribution-based JSA, and not income-based JSA, an amount can be deducted from his benefit towards arrears (see p421).

Deductions made by the DWP

When an application is received by the CSA and it is found that the non-resident parent is on IS/PC/income-based JSA, both parties will be notified as to whether or not deductions from benefit are a possibility. If the non-resident parent is not exempt from deductions, the DWP will then be sent notification requesting that a deduction is made. This is binding on the DWP, unless there are other deductions being made from the benefit which take precedence.[17]

Direct deductions for contributions of child maintenance cannot be made from any benefit other than IS/PC/income-based JSA, unless contribution-based JSA, IB, severe disablement allowance or retirement pension are paid in the same girocheque or order book as the IS/PC/income-based JSA.[18] After the deductions are made, 10 pence a week must be left of benefit.[19]

There is a maximum amount which can be deducted from IS/PC/income-based JSA.[20] The total deducted for arrears of housing costs, rent arrears, fuel arrears, arrears of water charges, council tax arrears, fines and contribution towards child maintenance cannot be greater than £8.40 a week. The contribution for child maintenance has a lower priority than any of the other mentioned deductions.[21] Therefore, in some cases where non-resident parents have other deductions, it will not be possible to deduct the full £5.60 for the contribution to child maintenance. The DWP can deduct half of the £5.60 contribution.[22] Non-resident parents who are having difficulties meeting basic bills should consider requesting direct payments – eg, £2.80 for gas arrears and £2.80 for electricity arrears would ensure that only £2.80 for child maintenance is payable. If full deductions from IS/PC/income-based JSA are not possible, arrears of child maintenance contributions do *not* accrue.

The DWP will tell the CSA whether deductions are possible. The CSA, in turn, notifies the non-resident parent and the person with care that the deductions will begin on a date in the near future. The £5.60 (or £2.80) is paid over to the person with care via the CSA.[23] The CSA notifies her of the way in which the payments will be made. If the person with care is on IS/PC/income-based JSA, the contribution is generally paid with the benefit (see pp394 and 461). Otherwise, the person with care usually receives payments on a quarterly basis.

Challenging decisions

CSA decisions about direct contributions from benefit can be challenged in the same way as other CSA decisions[24] – ie, by seeking a review[25] or supersession[26] (see Chapter 19) or by appealing to a tribunal[27] (see Chapter 20). If it is the DWP decision which is being contested (ie, the question being disputed is whether the non-resident parent can have £5.60 deducted from his IS given his other, higher priority debts) then that decision can be challenged in a similar way (see CPAG's *Welfare Benefits and Tax Credits Handbook*).

5. Special cases

The legislation uses the phrase 'special cases' to cover situations which are not as straightforward as where one non-resident parent has left one family and there is one person with care looking after all the children from that family.[28] However, in order to enable people to carry out calculations for all family situations, we have integrated these situations into the relevant steps of the formula – eg, where:
- both parents are non-resident (see pp232 and 298);
- more than one person with care applies for child maintenance from the same non-resident parent (see p300);
- a person cares for children of more than one non-resident parent (see pp233 and 306).

Where care of a child is being shared between different people, several modifications of the formula are necessary. Shared care under the 'old rules' is, therefore, treated separately (see Chapter 16).

Shared care does not cover the situation where different children of the same family have different homes. Where the children of a family are divided between two households (eg, where one child lives with one parent and another child with the other parent), this involves two maintenance assessments. In one assessment, the first parent is the parent with care and the second parent is the non-resident parent. In the second assessment the roles are reversed. We have called this situation 'divided families' (see p305).

Chapter 10: The 'old rules' formula in outline
Notes

Notes

1. A rigid formula
1 Reg 33(1) CS(MAP) Regs; reg 2(1) CS(MASC) Regs
2 Reg 2(2) CS(MASC) Regs
3 Regs 3(2), 9(5) and 11(5) CS(MASC) Regs
4 Reg 2(3) CS(MASC) Regs; CCS/7312/1995

3. Minimum child maintenance
5 Sch 1 para 7 CSA 1991
6 Reg 13 CS(MASC) Regs
7 Reg 22(4) CS(MASC) Regs
8 Reg 26 and Sch 4 CS(MASC) Regs
9 Reg 7(3) CS(MASC) Regs

4. 'Old rules' non-resident parents on certain benefits
10 s43 and Sch 1 para 5(4) CSA 1991
11 Sch 9 para 7A(1) SS(C&P) Regs
12 Reg 28 CS(MASC) Regs
13 Reg 28(2) CS(MASC) Regs; Sch 9 para 7A(3) SS(C&P) Regs
14 Reg 28(3) and (4) CS(MASC) Regs
15 s43(2)(a) CSA 1991
16 Sch 9 para 7A(2) SS(C&P) Regs
17 Sch 9 para 7A(1) SS(C&P) Regs
18 Sch 9 paras 1 and 2(1)(f) SS(C&P) Regs
19 Sch 9 para 2(2) SS(C&P) Regs
20 Sch 9 para 8 SS(C&P) Regs
21 Sch 9 para 9 SS(C&P) Regs
22 Sch 9 para 7A(4) SS(C&P) Regs
23 Sch 5 para 9 CS(MASC) Regs
24 s43(3) CSA 1991
25 Sch 4C para 1(a) CSA 1991
26 Sch 4C para 2(1)(a) CSA 1991
27 Sch 4C para 3(1)(a) CSA 1991

5. Special cases
28 Part III CS(MASC) Regs

Chapter 11

The maintenance requirement: Step 1 of the 'old rules' formula

This chapter covers:
1. What is the maintenance requirement (see below)
2. How much is the maintenance requirement (p230)
3. Both parents are non-resident (p232)
4. More than one non-resident parent (p233)

> This chapter contains information relevant to existing cases under the 'old rules'. For calculation under the 'new rules', Chapter 7.

This chapter should be read in conjunction with calculation sheet 1 in Appendix 3.

1. What is the maintenance requirement

The maintenance requirement is intended to represent the minimum weekly cost of caring for the child(ren) for whom child maintenance is being assessed.[1] The maintenance requirement is based on income support (IS) rates. For information on the conditions of entitlement for the IS premiums, see Appendix 2.

Both parents will contribute towards meeting the maintenance requirement if they can afford to do so. In the case of the parent with care, it is a notional contribution which may reduce the amount of child maintenance that a non-resident parent has to pay.

The parents may not have sufficient income to be able to pay the full maintenance requirement. If this is the case, the non-resident parent pays 50 per cent of his available income, known in the formula as 'assessable income'. Equally, the maintenance requirement is not the total amount of child maintenance that may be expected from a non-resident parent. However, once the maintenance requirement is met, the non-resident parent then pays a lower

Chapter 11: The maintenance requirement: Step 1 of the 'old rules' formula
1. What is the maintenance requirement

percentage of any further income. In other words, the maintenance requirement is the point at which the non-resident parent stops paying 50 per cent of his assessable income and instead pays 15, 20 or 25 per cent of any remaining assessable income (see Chapters 13 and 14).

The maintenance requirement is also used where child maintenance has to be apportioned between two persons with care. This occurs where a parent is a non-resident parent for two different maintenance assessments (see p305).

Interim maintenance assessments in 'old rules' cases

When the CSA does not have adequate information from the non-resident parent to carry out an assessment, it can make an interim maintenance assessment. This assessment is usually set at 1.5 times the maintenance requirement where the information about the non-resident parent's income is being withheld (see p399).[2]

2. How much is the maintenance requirement

The maintenance requirement includes an allowance for each qualifying child (see p26) being looked after by that person with care. The person who is being assessed to pay child maintenance *must* be the parent (see p23) of that qualifying child. If a person with care is looking after children of different non-resident parents, a different maintenance requirement is calculated for each of the assessments (see p233).

The maintenance requirement calculation

The maintenance requirement is calculated as follows:[3]
- for each qualifying child, the amount of the income support (IS) personal allowance for a child of that age (see below); *plus*
- the amount of the couple rate of IS family premium (£15.95); *plus*
- a 'parent as carer' element (see also p231):
  – where at least one qualifying child is under 11 years of age, the amount of the adult IS personal allowance, at the rate for a person aged 25 years or over, irrespective of the age of the person with care (£55.65); *or*
  – where none of the qualifying children are under 11 but at least one is under 14 years of age, 75 per cent of this adult allowance (£41.74); *or*
  – where none of the children is under 14 but at least one is under 16 years of age, 50 per cent of the adult allowance (£27.83); *less*
- an amount of child benefit for the qualifying child(ren) (see p231).

This is the basic maintenance requirement calculation, which is adapted in situations where more than one non-resident parent is involved (see p233).

The rates used in the calculation are the IS and child benefit rates applicable at the date on which the maintenance assessment takes effect, known as the effective date (see p400).[4] The figures given above are those for 2004/05 and all the examples in this edition have effective dates after 6 April 2004. The (transitional) lone parent rate of family premium is not used in child support assessments.[5]

Children's personal allowances

The calculation uses the IS personal allowances for children:[6]
- £42.27 from birth until September following 16th birthday; *and*
- £42.27 from September following 16th birthday to the day before 19th birthday.

Deduction of child benefit

The amount of child benefit deducted is:[7]
- £16.50 for the only, elder or eldest child for whom child benefit is payable; *and*
- £11.05 for all other children.

The lone parent rate of child benefit does not apply here. For other reasons, the amount of child benefit deducted from the maintenance requirement may be different from that actually being paid to the person with care – eg, where no claim has been made by the person with care or where the rate being paid is not correct under the child benefit legislation. There may be cases where someone other than the person with care is receiving child benefit – eg, a non-resident parent. In such cases the person with care should consider claiming child benefit or asking the non-resident parent to make the payment of child benefit in addition to the maintenance payment (see example 11.4).

If child benefit is not payable for a child because s/he is in the care of an institution, an amount of child benefit is still deducted.[8] However, in other situations where no one is entitled to child benefit for that child (eg, because of the residence rules) no deduction is made.

The parent as carer element

The inclusion of the adult personal allowance is intended to represent the care costs of the child, and the reduction of the allowance for children over 11 years of age is recognition of the reduction of the care needs as children grow up.[9] This means that the maintenance requirement as a whole can reduce after a child's birthday. This reduction is not delayed until September (as with the child's personal allowance – see above).

The parent as carer element is not spousal maintenance – ie, maintenance for a former spouse.[10] Spousal maintenance continues to exist and is completely separate from child maintenance calculated by the CSA. Any application for maintenance for the parent with care must be made to the court (see p34).

231

Chapter 11: The maintenance requirement: Step 1 of the 'old rules' formula
2. How much is the maintenance requirement

Couples
The personal allowance for couples is never included in the maintenance requirement. This is because the non-resident parent is not responsible for maintaining a partner of the person with care.

Children with disabilities
The disabled child premium is not included in the calculation of the maintenance requirement and neither is any related carer premium. Instead, the courts can consider a top-up maintenance award in respect of a child with disabilities (see p37).[11]

Example 11.1: Calculation of the maintenance requirement

(a) Anita and Bob have two children. They split up, and Anita remains in the family home with Carol (13) and David (8).

		£
Personal allowances	Anita	55.65
	Carol (13)	42.27
	David (8)	42.27
Family premium		15.95
Sub-total		156.14
Less child benefit		27.55
Maintenance requirement		128.59

(b) Five years later, Anita has remarried. David is 13 and Carol is 18 but still at school.

		£
Personal allowances	Anita	41.74 (75% of 55.65)
	Carol (18)	42.27
	David (13)	42.27
Family premium		15.95
Sub-total		142.23
Less child benefit		27.55
Maintenance requirement		114.68

---

3. Both parents are non-resident

An application for maintenance can be made by a person with care who is not a parent – eg, if a child lives with her/his grandparents or another relative (see p44). Both parents of that child are then non-resident parents and liable to pay maintenance. An assessment can be carried out for each non-resident parent if an application is made in respect of her/him, and each contributes to the

Chapter 11: The maintenance requirement: Step 1 of the 'old rules' formula
4. More than one non-resident parent

maintenance requirement (see p298 for the calculation of the proposed maintenance).

An application may be made for maintenance from only one of the non-resident parents; in this case the maintenance requirement for the one non-resident parent is halved.[12] However, it is not halved when an application is made for maintenance from both non-resident parents even if an assessment cannot be made for both – eg, one parent cannot be traced or is habitually resident outside the UK.

Example 11.2: Maintenance requirement where both parents are non-resident
Beverley (15) lives with her grandmother, who is a widow.

		£
Personal allowances	Grandmother	27.83 (50% of 55.65)
	Beverley	42.27
Family premium		15.95
Sub-total		86.05
Less child benefit		16.50
Maintenance requirement		69.55

This maintenance requirement will be halved to £34.78 if the grandmother applies for child maintenance only from her son-in-law and not her daughter.

4. More than one non-resident parent

A person with care may look after qualifying children who have different parents – eg, a mother is looking after her children who have different fathers, a grandmother is looking after children of two of her sons, or a lone parent is also looking after a friend's child. In these cases, if applications are made for child maintenance from each non-resident parent, a number of different assessments must be carried out, one for each non-resident parent. This does not occur where one of the non-resident parents is dead.[13]

The maintenance requirement for each non-resident parent includes only the child(ren) who are his own responsibility. However, the adult personal allowance and the family premium are divided among the non-resident parents,[14] in proportion to the number of non-resident parents and not in proportion to the number of the children who are their responsibility.[15] This apportionment should occur whether or not child maintenance is being pursued from all the non-resident parents.[16] For example, a person with care may apply for child maintenance from one father and not another, or one of the parents may be resident abroad and hence outside the CSA's jurisdiction.

233

Chapter 11: The maintenance requirement: Step 1 of the 'old rules' formula
4. More than one non-resident parent

The apportioned 'parent as carer' element is then further reduced if the children in the individual assessment are aged 11 or over – ie, 75 per cent of the apportioned amount is used if the youngest child is aged 11-13 and 50 per cent of the apportioned amount if s/he is 14 or 15 years old.[17] (This can mean that less than the full adult personal allowance is included across all assessments, even though it would have been included in full had the children had the same non-resident parent – see example 11.3b.)

See p306 for the calculation of proposed maintenance where a parent with care is looking after the child(ren) of more than one non-resident parent.

Example 11.3: Maintenance requirement where the children have different fathers

(a) Zoe is a single parent and has three children, all of whom live with her. Wayne is the father of Yvonne (12) and Veronica (10). Terence is the father of Scott (3).

Wayne's assessment (maintenance requirement):

		£	
Personal allowances	Zoe	27.83	(half of 55.65)
	Yvonne (12)	42.27	
	Veronica (10)	42.27	
Family premium		7.98	(half of 15.95)
Sub-total		120.35	
Less child benefit		27.55	
Maintenance requirement		92.80	

Terence's assessment (maintenance requirement):

		£	
Personal allowances	Zoe	27.83	(half of 55.65)
	Scott	42.27	
Family premium		7.98	(half of 15.95)
Sub-total		78.08	
Less child benefit		11.05	
Maintenance requirement		67.03	

(b) Two years later, Zoe is living with Bob and her four children. Wayne is the father of Yvonne (14) and Veronica (12). Terence is the father of Scott (5). Bob is the father of Ricky (1). However, as Bob is not a non-resident parent, the apportionment occurs between Wayne and Terence only. Terence's assessment remains as above.

Wayne's assessment (maintenance requirement):

		£	
Personal allowances	Zoe	20.87	(75% of half of 55.65)
	Yvonne (14)	42.27	
	Veronica (12)	542.27	
Family premium		7.98	(half of 15.95)
Sub-total		113.39	

Chapter 11: The maintenance requirement: Step 1 of the 'old rules' formula
4. More than one non-resident parent

Less child benefit	27.55
Maintenance requirement	**85.84**

If a person with care is looking after children of different parents, but two of the non-resident parents are parents of the same child (ie, the person with care is *not* a parent of that child), those two non-resident parents will be treated as one person for the purposes of apportioning the relevant elements of the maintenance requirement.[18]

Example 11.4: Maintenance requirement with more than one non-resident parent, and both parents of one child are non-resident

Zoe's niece, Rebecca, who is aged 17 and still at school, comes to live with Zoe and Bob when her parents split up. Rebecca joining the household alters the maintenance requirement for the other children (see example 11.3b). For the four qualifying children Zoe is now looking after, there are four non-resident parents (Wayne, Terence, and both of Rebecca's parents). However, Rebecca's parents count as one unit for this purpose and therefore the amounts are divided by three.

Wayne's assessment (maintenance requirement):

		£	
Personal allowances	Zoe	13.91	(75% of a third of 55.65)
	Yvonne (14)	42.27	
	Veronica (12)	42.27	
Family premium		5.32	(third of 15.95)
Sub-total		103.77	
Less child benefit		22.10	
Maintenance requirement		**81.67**	

Terence's assessment (maintenance requirement):

		£	
Personal allowances	Zoe	18.55	(third of 55.65)
	Scott (5)	42.27	
Family premium		5.32	(third of 15.95)
Sub total		66.14	
Less child benefit		11.05	
Maintenance requirement		**55.09**	

Rebecca's parents (maintenance requirement):

		£	
Personal allowance	Rebecca (17)	42.27	
Family premium		5.32	(third of 15.95)
Sub-total		47.59	
Less child benefit		16.50	
Maintenance requirement		**31.09**	

Chapter 11: The maintenance requirement: Step 1 of the 'old rules' formula
4. More than one non-resident parent

An assessment is carried out separately for both of Rebecca's parents, each using the maintenance requirement of £31.09 (see example 11.7). If Zoe chose to apply for child maintenance only from one of Rebecca's parents, the maintenance requirement would be halved to £15.55.

Note: Bob is unemployed and claiming jobseeker's allowance. Although Zoe was required to apply for maintenance for Scott, Yvonne and Veronica under the 'old rules' (see Chapter 5), she could choose whether or not to make an application for maintenance from Rebecca's parents. However, even if she chose not to make an application for child maintenance for Rebecca, the apportionment between three should still take place for the other two assessments.

As Rebecca is 17, no adult personal allowance is included in her maintenance requirement. Yet, only one-third of the allowance is included in each of the other two maintenance requirement calculations and this is further reduced in Wayne's assessment where the children are over 11 years old.

We have assumed that Zoe has claimed child benefit for Rebecca, which means that under the child benefit regulations the higher rate is applicable to Rebecca and the lower rate now applies to Yvonne. As the person with whom Rebecca is living, Zoe takes priority over the mother for child benefit purposes (see p331).[19]

If Rebecca's mother had continued to claim child benefit instead, then the higher rate would be payable for Rebecca as the only child for whom her mother is claiming. At the same time the higher rate will still be payable for Yvonne as she is the eldest child for whom Zoe is claiming child benefit.[20] If this were the case, the child benefit of £16.50 should be deducted for both children in calculating the maintenance requirements, even though Zoe is not actually receiving the £16.50 child benefit for Rebecca.

If Rebecca's mother did not hand over at least £16.50 each week to Zoe, whether as child maintenance or on top of the maintenance assessment, she would no longer be entitled to child benefit.[21] In this case, the maintenance requirements should be as shown above, as child benefit is not legally payable to Rebecca's mother, even though in practice it is still being paid. It would be to Zoe's advantage to claim the child benefit for Rebecca.

Chapter 11: The maintenance requirement: Step 1 of the 'old rules' formula
Notes

Notes

1. What is the maintenance requirement
1. Sch 1 para 1(1) CSA 1991
2. Reg 8(3)(a) and 8A(1) CS(MAP) Regs

2. How much is the maintenance requirement
3. Sch 1 para 1 CSA 1991; reg 3 CS(MASC) Regs
4. Regs 3(2) and 4 CS(MASC) Regs
5. Reg 3(1) CS(MASC) Regs
6. Sch 2 para 2 IS Regs
7. Reg 4 CS(MASC) Regs
8. Sch 1 para 1(2) CSA 1991
9. Children Come First, Vol 1/8 White Paper, October 1990; DSS Press Release, 22 December 1993
10. CCS/11729/1996
11. s8(8) and (9) CSA 1991

3. Both parents are non-resident
12. Reg 19(2)(d) CS(MASC) Regs

4. More than one non-resident parent
13. CS/7436/1999
14. Reg 23 CS(MASC) Regs
15. Reg 23(3) CS(MASC) Regs
16. Reg 23(1) CS(MASC) Regs
17. Reg 23(2A) CS(MASC) Regs
18. Reg 23(3) CS(MASC) Regs
19. Sch 10 para 2 SSCBA 1992
20. Reg 2 CB&SS(FAR) Regs
21. s143(1)(b) SSCBA 1992

Chapter 12

Exempt income: Step 2 of the 'old rules' formula

This chapter covers:
1. What is exempt income (below)
2. How much is exempt income (p239)
3. Housing costs (p241)
4. Pre-April 1993 property settlements (p249)
5. Travel-to-work costs (p253)
6. Second families (p255)

> *This chapter contains information relevant to existing cases under the 'old rules'. For calculation under the 'new rules', see Chapter 7.*

This chapter should be read in conjunction with calculation sheet 2 in Appendix 3.

1. What is exempt income

Exempt income is income a parent can keep for her/his own essential expenses before any child maintenance is expected. The expenses are based on income support (IS) rates but also include housing costs.

Exempt income was intended to represent the minimum day-to-day living expenses of parents and their *own* children who are living with them.[1] If the parent has a partner, the partner's personal expenses are *not* included in exempt income. However, the housing costs for the whole family – including any heterosexual partner and stepchildren – are covered in exempt income.

'Own child' means a child for whom the parent is, in law, a parent – ie, biological or adoptive parent (see p23). Exempt income does *not* include amounts for any other children in the family – eg, stepchildren. Allowances for other children are not even initially included if the child is the primary responsibility of the parent – eg, where the stepchild's other parent is dead or cannot afford to pay any child maintenance. In some cases departure from the 'old rules' assessment could be sought on these grounds (see p349).

Chapter 12: Exempt income: Step 2 of the 'old rules' formula
2. How much is exempt income

Exempt income applies to *both* the non-resident parent and the parent with care as both are liable to maintain their children. If the parent with care has any income available to maintain the children, this might reduce the non-resident parent's contribution (see Chapter 14). However, if the parent with care is on IS, pension credit (PC), income-based jobseeker's allowance (JSA), working tax credit (WTC), it is assumed that she has no income available for child maintenance,[2] and therefore the exempt income step is carried out for the non-resident parent only. This applies even where the parent with care's partner is the benefit claimant. If the non-resident parent is on IS/PC/income-based JSA, there is no need to calculate exempt income for either parent, as the formula is not used at all in this case. Instead, the non-resident parent may have deductions made from his IS/income-based JSA as a contribution towards child maintenance (see p224). If the non-resident parent is on WTC, the child support calculation is still carried out unless there is also an assessment being considered or in force for a child for whom he is the parent with care (see p28).[3] If he is a parent with care in this position, he is not liable to pay any child maintenance as a non-resident parent.

If the person with care is not a parent, this step does *not* apply to them as only parents have a liability to maintain their children. If the person with care is not a parent, there will usually be two non-resident parents and a maintenance assessment can be carried out for both parents (see pp232 and 298).

2. How much is exempt income

Exempt income is generally calculated in the same way for parents with care as for non-resident parents.[4] Any reference to 'parent' below applies equally to the parent with care and the non-resident parent.

The rates used in the calculation are the income support (IS) rates applicable on the date at which the maintenance assessment takes effect, known as the effective date (see p400).[5] The rates given below are for 2004/05.

For the qualifying conditions of the IS premiums, see Appendix 2.

The exempt income calculation

Exempt income is calculated as follows for each parent:[6]
- the amount of the IS personal allowance for a single person aged 25 or over, irrespective of the age of the parent (£55.65); *plus*
- if there is a child – ie, the parent's own child (see above) – living with the parent, the amount of the IS personal allowance for a child of that age (42.27);*†*plus*
- if an allowance for a child is included, the amount of the IS family premium (15.95).*† The lone parent rate of family premium is not used in the calculation; *plus*

239

Chapter 12: Exempt income: Step 2 of the 'old rules' formula
2. How much is exempt income

- if any of the children included would qualify for the IS disabled child premium, the amount of that premium for each child entitled (£42.49);*†*plus*
- if any of the children included would qualify for the IS enhanced disability premium, the amount of that premium for each child entitled (£17.08);*†*plus*
- if the parent would qualify for the IS disability premium if s/he was under 60 years old, the amount of the premium for a single person (£23.70); the disability conditions must be satisfied by the parent her/himself; *plus*
- if the parent would qualify for the IS carer premium, the amount of that premium (£25.55); *plus*
- if the parent would qualify for the IS severe disability premium, the amount of that premium (£44.18); *plus*
- if the parent would qualify for the IS enhanced disability premium, the amount of that premium (£11.60); *plus*
- housing costs (see p243); *plus*
- where applicable, an allowance for a pre-April 1993 property settlement (see p249); *plus*
- where an employee travels more than 150 miles a week to and from work, an amount towards travel costs (see p254).

* Where the child's other parent also lives in the family and has sufficient income to help support the child, these amounts may be halved (see p256).
† These amounts will be included at a proportionate rate if the parent looks after the child(ren) for less than seven days but at least two nights on average per week (see Chapter 16). For parents with care, this apportionment will only take place where another person has day-to-day care of the child.[7] Special expenses can be added to exempt income after a departure direction (see p364).

Example 12.1
Bob and Anita have split up. Anita is looking after Carol and David, and remains in the family home. There is no need to calculate Anita's exempt income as she is in receipt of IS.
(a) Bob is living on his own in a bedsit, paying rent of £48 a week. He is not entitled to any housing benefit. He does not qualify for any premiums. He travels less than 150 miles a week to work.

Bob's exempt income is therefore:	£
Personal allowance	55.65
Housing costs	48.00
Total exempt income	**103.65**

(b) If Bob had moved in with his parents, his exempt income would be £55.65 If Bob was in receipt of severe disablement allowance, his exempt income would then be:

Chapter 12: Exempt income: Step 2 of the 'old rules' formula
3. Housing costs

	£
Personal allowance	55.65
Disability premium	23.70
Total exempt income	**79.35**

3. Housing costs

Housing costs for the parent and any of her/his family (see p32) living with her/him are included in exempt income. Where the other party believes that the parent's partner can afford to contribute to the housing costs, s/he may be able to apply for a departure direction (see p357).

To be included in exempt income, housing costs must be eligible (see p243) and payable in respect of the parent's home (see p244). Housing costs which are excessive may not be included in full (see p247).

Responsibility for housing costs

Eligible housing costs relating to the parent's home are included where the parent or partner is responsible for the costs and the payment is made to a person who is not a member of the same household.[8] Therefore, where a parent lives with a new partner, the housing costs are accepted, even where they are the responsibility of the partner. (This does not apply to homosexual couples as the definition of partner does not include gay and lesbian partners.) The amount of the housing costs included in exempt income can be reduced if it is reasonable to expect the partner to contribute (see p357).[9] Otherwise the full eligible costs are covered, and not the amount paid by the parent towards the housing costs.[10]

As well as where s/he is actually liable for the costs, a parent will be treated as responsible for housing costs if:[11]
- s/he has to meet the costs in order to live in the home; *and*
- the person liable to make the payments is not doing so; *and*
- either the parent is the former partner of the liable person or is someone else whom it is reasonable to treat as liable.

Where costs are shared with another person who is not a partner, then only her/his actual share of the costs is used (except where the parent is treated as liable because the other person or persons are not paying their share).[12] This means that where the non-resident parent continues to pay his liability of the housing costs on the matrimonial home in which the parent with care remains, this amount cannot be included as the parent with care's housing costs.[13] If the non-resident parent stops paying his liability, the full amount is treated as the parent with care's housing costs.[14] If three friends are joint tenants and share the rent equally, one-third of the rent will be considered to be the responsibility of the parent, unless the CSA believes that such a division would not be reasonable – eg, one of the joint occupiers is not paying their share (in which case the amount the parent actually pays may be used), or they have unequal shares of the accommodation so a different amount can be used.[15]

The parent may be treated as responsible for housing costs that s/he shares with other members of the household (see p29), some of whom are not close relatives (see p314), even where s/he makes those payments via another member of the household.[16] This applies where:
- it is reasonable for a parent to be treated as responsible for a share of the costs; *and*
- the person with responsibility is not a close relative; *and*
- either s/he has an equivalent responsibility for those costs as the parent or s/he is meeting the costs because the liable person is not.

However, where a parent is a non-dependent member of a household (see p314), no housing costs will be included in exempt income, even if s/he is paying a contribution for housing costs to another member of the household.[17] This appears partly to contradict the last statement that a parent can be treated as responsible for costs s/he shares with another member of the household, as long as they are not close relatives, even where it is the other person who is commercially liable for the payments. Remember that in order for a parent to be a non-dependant, not only can there be no commercial arrangement, but s/he has to be a member of the same *household* as the person liable to make the payments, and this will not always be the case where a parent moves into a friend's house. However, where a parent moves in with a gay partner there can be no argument over household.

In practice it may be that no housing costs are included if payment is to a close relative, whereas the other rule is used where costs are shared with members of the household who are not close relatives. So far the interpretation has only been tested in the first situation where a parent was living with her/his parents as a non-dependant and therefore clearly not entitled to have her/his contribution to the housing costs included in exempt income.[18] However, in the second situation, if it is found that housing costs are not included in the parent's exempt income when s/he is paying half of the costs on a voluntary basis it might, depending on the circumstances of the case, be arguable that it is reasonable to treat the parent as responsible for a share of the costs. This is most likely to succeed in cases where the costs have previously been shared with someone else and the parent has taken over that person's share. However, if the parent becomes a co-owner or joint tenant, half of the housing costs will be treated as the parent's responsibility. On the other hand, if the parent became a sub-tenant, s/he would be responsible for the costs specified in the tenancy agreement.

Chapter 12: Exempt income: Step 2 of the 'old rules' formula
3. Housing costs

Eligible housing costs

Eligible housing costs are costs which have to be incurred in order to buy, rent or otherwise secure possession of the parent's home or to carry out repairs and improvements as defined below.[19] Eligible costs are:[20]
- rent (net of housing benefit[21] – see p244);
- mortgage interest payments;
- capital repayments under a mortgage
- premiums paid under an endowment or other insurance policy, a personal equity plan (PEP) or personal pension plan to the extent that the policy was taken out to cover the cost of the mortgage (see p245);
- interest payments on any loans for repairs and improvements to the home taken out before the maintenance application or enquiry form is sent to the parent;
- interest payments on loans for major repairs necessary to maintain the fabric of the home and for measures which improve its fitness for occupation, such as the installation of a bath, shower, wash basin or lavatory; the provision of heating, electric lighting and sockets, drainage facilities, or storage facilities for fuel and refuse; improvements to ventilation, natural lighting, insulation or structural condition; or any other improvements considered reasonable by the CSA (the previous 'unfitness' which necessitated the improvement needs to be demonstrated[22]);
- interest payments under a hire purchase agreement to buy a home;
- payments in respect of a licence or permission to occupy the home;
- payments in respect of or as a result of the occupation of the home (this is intended to cover payments made by a former licensee who occupies premises unlawfully – eg, after a notice to quit has expired.[23] However, the extent of this provision is unclear but it does not include property and contents insurance,[24] payments in respect of the purchase of a home,[25] nor council tax[26]);
- payments of ground rent or feu duty;
- payments under co-ownership schemes;
- payments of service charges if such payments are a condition for occupying the home (but see p246);
- mooring charges for a houseboat;
- site rent for a caravan or mobile home;
- payments for a tent and its site;
- payments under a rental purchase scheme;
- payments in respect of croft land;
- payments in respect of a home made to an employer who provides the home;
- payments for Crown tenancy or licence;
- payments in respect of a loan taken out to pay off (in full or in part[27]) another loan that covered eligible housing costs;

243

Chapter 12: Exempt income: Step 2 of the 'old rules' formula
3. Housing costs

- the fees (net of any housing benefit), where a parent or a partner lives in a care home or an indedpendent hospital, or is being provide with a care home service or indpendent health care service.[28]

Repayments of an advance of salary (see also p263) used to purchase a home cannot be housing costs.[29]

Home

For the purposes of housing costs, the parent's home is either the dwelling in which the parent normally lives or, if s/he normally lives in more than one home, her/his principal home.[30] Therefore, if a non-resident parent is paying the costs of the family home in which the parent with care remains with the child(ren), these costs cannot be included as this is not the non-resident parent's own home.[31] Before deciding which dwelling is the principal home, the facts must show that the parent does actually live in more than one home.[32]

The test of a principal home is not simply the parent's own view nor a calculation of the time spent at each home;[33] it has been held that an army officer's own home where he spent his leave can be his principal home over and above army married quarters. (However, the argument that expenditure on army accommodation should be taken into account as expenses was rejected by this child support commissioner – see p264.) Somewhat unexpectedly, another commissioner decided that army officers serving abroad could have the costs of both a home in the UK and quarters overseas included in exempt income.[34]

The only other exception to the rule about just including one set of housing costs is where the parent is in a residential care or nursing home. The residential fees can be included as well as the costs of the parent's own home if the parent has been in the residential accommodation for less than a year or if the CSA believes that the parent intends to return home.[35]

Where the payments for the property cover accommodation used for other purposes (eg, business use) the CSA has to identify the proportion of the cost attributable to housing.[36]

Housing benefit

Housing benefit (HB) is subtracted from housing costs if the parent has claimed and been awarded HB.[37] In fact, the CSA will use as housing costs the weekly amount treated as rent under the HB regulations minus the amount of HB calculated by the local authority.

If a parent delays claiming HB until after completing the maintenance enquiry form or maintenance application form, full housing costs will be included as exempt income (unless they are excessive – see p247). If a parent is awaiting a decision on an HB claim, the excessive housing costs rule does not apply, but the CSA may later seek further information about the claim.

Chapter 12: Exempt income: Step 2 of the 'old rules' formula
3. Housing costs

Mortgage and other loan payments

Unlike for IS, payments made towards mortgage repayment – whether directly as capital repayments or through certain policies – are eligible housing costs for exempt income purposes.[38] Such payments are not eligible at the protected income stage (see p314).

As well as endowment policies, other insurance policies taken out to pay off a mortgage on the home are considered to be eligible housing costs. These include premiums paid towards a mortgage protection policy to cover the mortgage in the event of unemployment, sickness or disability.[39] Life assurance policies taken out with the mortgage in order to discharge the debt on death are also included.[40] However, neither building nor contents insurance is included.[41] The mortgage on which any such policy is intended to discharge need not exist at the time of the assessment.[42]

Only loans for the provision of a home are eligible. A loan used to buy out a former partner's interest in a property will only be eligible if it can be shown that the loan is necessary to protect the right of occupancy.[43]

If a loan is partly for the provision of a home (see p244), only that part is an eligible housing cost.[44] If only part of the mortgage is eligible, the nature of any insurance policies should be investigated; it cannot be assumed that the proportions of the premiums allowed should follow the proportion of the mortgage interest allowed.[45]

PEPs and personal pension plans taken out, at least in part, to discharge a mortgage on the parent's home are eligible housing costs.[46] Where a personal pension plan has been obtained both to discharge the mortgage and to pay a pension, 25 per cent of the contributions made are included as housing costs in exempt income.[47]

Where the mortgage is under £60,000, all the premiums paid to an endowment policy or PEP will be eligible housing costs.[48] Where the policy was also taken out to produce a lump sum and the mortgage is over £60,000, 0.0277 per cent of the mortgage is taken to be weekly housing costs if the CSA is unable to ascertain what proportion of the premium is to cover the mortgage. Where the parent's endowment/PEP premium is larger than this 0.0277 per cent figure, it is worth pursuing the issue of how much capital is likely to be produced, especially as many endowment policies may not produce any capital in excess of the mortgage. Any payments made in excess of those required by the mortgage agreement are not eligible housing costs.[49]

There is nothing to prevent repayments to a member of the family or friend for a loan to purchase a home being considered as housing costs where a mortgage or charge has been created by depositing the title deeds or a land certificate to prevent the borrower disposing of the property without the lender's consent.[50]

Repayments made under an agreement for a loan taken out for eligible repairs and improvements (see p243) or a service charge to cover these items are included in exempt income as housing costs.[51] So are insurance policies associated with

Chapter 12: Exempt income: Step 2 of the 'old rules' formula
3. Housing costs

such a loan or which are taken out to pay off another loan for an eligible housing cost.[52]

Ineligible charges

Charges made for food, fuel, water or sewerage services do not count as eligible housing costs.[53] If the housing costs payments include an ineligible charge, an amount attributable to the service must be deducted.

If meals are provided, a standard weekly deduction is made:

	Aged 16 or over	For each child under 16
Full board	£19.85	£10.05
Half board	£13.20	£6.65
Breakfast only	£2.45	£2.45

If the parent provides information about the level of the fuel charge inclusive in the housing payment, this actual or estimated amount can be deducted. Otherwise a standard weekly deduction is made: heating £9.80; hot water £1.20; cooking £1.20; and lighting 80 pence. If the parent has exclusive use of only one room, the deduction for heating, hot water and/or lighting is £5.90 a week.

Where the amount for water and sewerage charges is not separately identifiable, an amount will be attributed.

Where other service charges are included in the rent payments, they are taken into account as housing costs provided they are no more than 25 per cent of total eligible housing costs.[54] If the amount of the charge is not identifiable, the CSA can attribute a reasonable amount. Where service charges other than food, fuel and water/sewerage do account for more than 25 per cent of housing costs, either the excess is taken into account or, if this would be less, only those which are ineligible for the purposes of housing benefit are deducted. Ineligible services include:
- personal laundry service;
- sports and other leisure facilities, including TV rental and licence fees, but excluding children's play areas;
- cleaning, other than communal areas or where no one in the accommodation is able to do it;
- transport;
- medical or nursing services; *and*
- any other charge not connected with the provision of adequate accommodation.

Weekly amount of housing costs

The amount allowed for housing costs is usually the amount payable at the effective date (see p400), converted into a weekly amount.[55] If the costs are

monthly, the amount at the effective date must be multiplied by 12 and divided by 52. Where the housing costs are paid on any basis other than weekly or calendar monthly, the CSA considers the amount and payment period of the housing costs payable on the effective date:
- divide 365 by the number of days in the payment period, rounding to the nearest whole number;
- multiply this figure by the amount of the costs due in the payment period; *and then*
- divide this figure by 52 to give the weekly costs.

Where rent is payable to a local authority or housing association on a free-week basis, the rent payable in the relevant week (see p264) is used unless that was a free week, in which case the last week which was not a free week is used.

Where the housing costs are a repayment mortgage and the parent has failed to provide information on repayments and interest on the effective date but has provided a mortgage statement from the lender for a period ending less than a year before the relevant date, this statement can be used to calculate the capital repayments and, where possible, the interest payments.[56]

The calculation of housing costs should be carefully checked as this is an area where the CSA often makes mistakes.

Excessive housing costs

Excessive housing costs of a non-resident parent are not generally allowed in full. Parents are exempt from restrictions on housing costs if they:[57]
- have day-to-day care of any child;
- have claimed or been awarded housing benefit;
- would qualify for an income support disability premium (see Appendix 2);
- remain in a home previously occupied with a former partner;[58]
- have high housing costs because money which would otherwise be available is tied up in the former family home which is still occupied by an ex-partner;
- have been meeting those costs for over 52 weeks and the only increase in costs has been due to an increase in the rate of mortgage interest or rent;
- the costs only exceed the limit because of an increase in mortgage interest payments or rent.

Departure can be sought by the other parent if the exemption applies and the housing costs are unreasonable (see p357).

Unless exempt, eligible housing costs are otherwise only allowed up to the greater of £80 or half of the parent's net income.[59] (See p262 for the calculation of net income.) Therefore, parents who have a net income of less than £160 are allowed to include housing costs of up to £80, while those with higher net incomes can include housing costs of up to half their net income (see example 12.5).

Chapter 12: Exempt income: Step 2 of the 'old rules' formula
3. Housing costs

The excessive housing costs rule does not apply to parents with care and it is unlikely that the notional income or capital rules could be used where a parent with care takes on excessive housing costs (see p278).[60]

Example 12.2
Bob goes to live with Zoe who has three children – Yvonne (12), Veronica (10) and Scott (3). Zoe's rent on a three-bedroomed council house is £45 a week. They do not receive housing benefit. Even though it is Zoe who is legally liable for the rent, it is still an eligible cost.

Bob's exempt income is now:	£
Personal allowance	55.65
Housing costs	45.00
Total exempt income	**100.65**

Example 12.3
(a) Anita is now in paid employment. As long as she is not in receipt of working tax credit, her exempt income must be calculated. She lives with her two children, Carol (13) and David (8). Her mortgage is under £60,000 and the payments, including the capital repayments, are £75 a week.

		£
Personal allowance	Anita	55.65
	Carol (13)	42.27
	David (8)	42.27
Family premium		15.95
Mortgage payment (total)		75.00
Total exempt income		**231.14**

(b) Anita marries Joe and together they buy a house, taking out a mortgage of £85,000. The interest payments are £495 a month and the endowment premium £108 a month – ie, £114.23 and £24.92 a week. However, as the CSA does not have information about how much of the premium is to cover the mortgage, the endowment premium is restricted to £23.55 (0.0277% of £85,000) (see p245).

		£
Personal allowance	Anita	55.65
	Carol (now 15)	42.27
	David (now 10)	42.27
Family premium		15.95
Mortgage payment	(114.23 + 23.55)	137.78
Total exempt income		**293.92**

The excessive housing costs rule does not apply because there are children in the family. Bob should consider seeking a departure (see p357) on the grounds that Joe can afford to contribute towards the mortgage.

4. Pre-April 1993 property settlements

In order for an allowance to be included in 'old rules' exempt income, the property or capital transfer must satisfy certain qualifying criteria (see below).[61] Departure can be sought where the allowance in exempt income does not properly reflect the effect of the settlement (see p357).

Unlike other elements of exempt income, this allowance applies only to a parent with care if she was the non-resident parent at the time the property was transferred.[62] However, where a parent with care also transferred capital to the non-resident parent or the child(ren), this 'compensating transfer' may be offset against that of the non-resident parent's 'qualifying transfer'.[63]

Qualifying transfer

A qualifying transfer is one which was made:[64]
- as part of a court order or written maintenance agreement which itself was made before 5 April 1993;
- when the non-resident parent and parent with care were living separately;
- between the non-resident parent and either the parent with care or a child for whom maintenance is being assessed;
- with the effect that the recipient was given the whole of the value of the transferred property (this condition can be met where whole value of a part share in a property or asset is transferred);[65] *and*
- without the only purpose of the transfer being to replace maintenance payments (either periodic or a lump sum) for the parent with care – ie, for herself as opposed to the child(ren) and to compensate the parent with care for the loss of any right to apply for or receive such payments, or to compensate her for a reduction in such payments. 'Loss of any right' in this context should be taken to mean 'loss of any one right' rather than 'loss of all rights';[66] this means that where a maintenance agreement for a low or nominal sum exists, it may still be the case that the only purpose of the transfer is to compensate the parent with care for this reduced maintenance and hence the transfer will not qualify.[67]

For a transfer to be excluded by this final condition guidance to decision makers states that there need not be an express statement in the agreement that the transfer is only to compensate the parent with care. If there is no specific written intention in the court order or agreement or the transfer refers to another purpose in addition to the replacement of spousal maintenance, CSA staff are instructed to decide applications on the balance of probabilities, taking an open-minded view of all the relevant evidence.[68] The CSA will want to see the actual transfer document but, where this is not available or does not exist (eg, there was a transfer of cash between the parties), CSA staff may make their decision on the basis of

Chapter 12: Exempt income: Step 2 of the 'old rules' formula
4. Pre-April 1993 property settlements

other available written evidence. The guidance mentions information from building societies, banks, solicitors, accountants, estate agents and insurance companies; written evidence from other sources may also be considered.[69] This guidance conflicts with a commissioner's view that although decision makers may consider other evidence beyond the transfer agreement in order to determine the purpose of the transfer, the purpose must be 'clearly and explicitly' shown by the evidence and not inferred on the balance of probabilities.[70]

A transfer made under a court order applying the Family Law Act (Scotland) 1985 can only be for the purpose of compensating the parent with care and therefore cannot be a qualifying transfer; transfers made under a written maintenance agreement rather than a court order may still qualify.[71]

It is possible for the non-resident parent to transfer the whole of the asset to the parent with care, but the building society insists that the non-resident parent's name is retained on the mortgage – eg, where the amount of the mortgage is more than the parent with care can borrow. This does not negate the fact that the whole of the asset has been transferred to the parent with care. Even where the non-resident parent retains a partial beneficial interest in the property it may still be considered a relevant transfer.[72] If a charge is placed on the property to benefit the non-resident parent, this will be deducted when calculating the allowance.[73]

Property is defined as:[74]
- cash and savings in a bank, building society or equivalent account;
- a legal estate or an equitable interest in land (or in Scotland, an interest in land);
- an endowment or other insurance policy obtained in order to discharge the mortgage or charge on a property which was also being transferred;
- a business asset, whether in the form of money, land or otherwise, which before it was transferred was being used in the course of a business in which the non-resident parent was a sole trader, a partner or a participator in a 'close' company.

It does not include other assets – eg, a car or contents of the home. The value of a trust fund established for the parent with care or the child can be considered.[75]

Providing evidence

Once a non-resident parent has notified the CSA that he wants a property/capital settlement taken into account, he has to supply evidence within a reasonable time.[76] The non-resident parent is asked to supply the evidence within 28 days. If this does not happen, he will be sent a reminder giving a further 14 days, and this is only extended if the parent contacts the CSA and his grounds for needing the time are reasonable.[77] An interview at the field office is used only as a last resort. If the evidence is not produced within this time, the application will be decided on the information available including refusing an allowance.

The non-resident parent must send written evidence to the CSA of:[78]

- a court order or maintenance agreement which required the transfer of property (this evidence must be contemporaneous);
- the fact of the transfer (this would be, for example, solicitors' or building society correspondence, or a copy of a Land Registry extract);
- the value of the property transferred at the date that the court order/written agreement was made (confirmed by a building society, insurance company or firm of property valuers); *and*
- the amount of any mortgage or charge outstanding at the date that the court order/written agreement was made (confirmed by a building society, bank, solicitors or accountants).

If the parent does not have this documentary evidence, it could be contained in solicitors' files if still available. The most difficult information to obtain may be the historical value of the asset and a charge will usually be made for such a valuation.

When the non-resident parent applies, the person with care is notified and asked for any relevant information.[79] The allowance is not calculated until 14 days after the person with care has been contacted.

Calculating the allowance

The qualifying value of a transfer of property, land or a business asset is calculated using the following formula.[80]

Qualifying Value = (VP-MCP) / 2 – (VAP-MCR) – (VCR)

Where:
- VP is the value of the property or business asset which is (wholly or in part) transferred.
- MCP is amount of any mortgage or charge outstanding on the property immediately prior to the date of the agreement.
- VAP is the value of any interest in the property which continues to be beneficially owned by the non-resident parent (eg, where the non-resident parent transfers three-quarters of the interest in a house to the parent with care, VAP would be one-quarter of the total value).
- MCR is the amount of any mortgage or charge on the property for which the non-resident parent remains liable immediately following the transfer (this will be the same proportion of MCP as VAP is of VP).
- VCR is the value of any charge in favour of the non-resident parent on the property immediately following the transfer.

Any change in house prices since that time is irrelevant – the above figures are based on values at the agreement date. The home is valued on the basis that the parent with care and the child(ren) were not to remain there.[81] The total net value

Chapter 12: Exempt income: Step 2 of the 'old rules' formula
4. Pre-April 1993 property settlements

is used irrespective of whether or not the property was previously in joint ownership.

The qualifying value in the case of a bank or building society account is half of the balance on the date of the order/agreement, and for an endowment policy, half of the surrender value at that date.[82]

Where the evidence produced shows that the whole of the transfer was made in lieu of ongoing child maintenance, the qualifying value is twice that arrived at by the above formula (in the case of property, land or business assets)[83] or (in the case of money or endowment policies) the full value transferred.[84] Where there has been more than one qualifying transfer, the qualifying values of the transfers are totalled.[85]

Transfers made by the parent with care to the non-resident parent or child(ren) which satisfy the qualifying criteria (see p249), except that they are made in the reverse direction, are called compensating transfers.[86] In addition, there is provision for the whole amount of money raised by a parent with care (eg, by taking out a loan) after the date of the court order or written agreement in order that she or her child(ren) is entitled to the whole of the property to be taken into account as a compensating transfer;[87] this applies where a non-resident parent transfers the matrimonial home to the parent with care on the condition that she buys out his interest in the property. Otherwise, compensating transfers are valued in the same way as qualifying transfers.[88]

The value of any compensatory transfer is deducted from that of the qualifying transfer to give the relevant value.[89] The allowance included in the exempt income relates to this relevant value:[90]

Relevant value	Weekly allowance
less than £5,000	Nil
£5,000 – £9,999	£20
£10,000 – £24,999	£40
not less than £25,000	£60

Remember that this is an allowance in the exempt income, and therefore its inclusion does not mean that the assessment itself will be reduced by a corresponding amount.

Example 12.4: Pre-April 1993 property settlement allowance
Debbie and Steve were divorced in 1991. The family home was transferred to Debbie; at the time of the court settlement, the property was worth £58,000 and the outstanding mortgage was £22,000. Almost all the contents of the house were left with Debbie, as was the car. Instead of Steve paying maintenance for Debbie, as part of the settlement, their joint savings account of £14,200 was transferred into Debbie's name. In addition, Steve gave each of the two children £3,000.

Chapter 12: Exempt income: Step 2 of the 'old rules' formula
5. Travel-to-work costs

(a) The house contents and the car do not come within the definition of property. The savings account is not a qualifying transfer as it was payment in lieu of maintenance for Debbie.
In this case, VP = £58,000 and MCP = £22,000 (see p251). VAP, MCR and VCR are nil. The qualifying value of the transfer of the house is therefore (£58,000 – £22,000) ÷ 2 = £18,000
The qualifying value of the cash to the children is the whole actual value – ie, 2 x £3,000 = £6,000.
Total qualifying value = £24,000.
There is no compensating value to offset.
Therefore, as the relevant value is over £10,000 but less than £25,000, the allowance included in exempt income is £40.

(b) If the savings transferred to Debbie were only £10,000 of the £14,200 and this was not for any specified purpose, this would have been another qualifying transfer valued at £5,000. Total qualifying value = £29,000.
There is a compensating transfer with a value of £4,200 ÷ 2 = £2,100.
Relevant value = £29,000 – £2,100 = £26,900;
therefore the allowance is £60.

(c) If Steve had transferred only three-quarters of the property to Debbie (retaining a quarter interest himself), the qualifying value of the transfer of the home would be lower.
VP = £58,000, MCP = £22,000, VAP = £14,500 (25% of VP) and MCR = £5,500 (25% of MCP). VCR is nil.
QV = (£58,000 – £22,000) ÷ 2 – (£14,500-£5,500) =
£18,000 – £9,000 = £9,000
In this case, if the house was the only asset transferred, the allowance included in exempt income would be £20.

5. Travel-to-work costs

An allowance towards travel costs can be included in 'old rules' exempt income for parents in employment who travel long distances.[91] It does not apply to self-employed parents.

As well as buying petrol or a ticket, travel-to-work costs include contributing to someone else's travel costs and paying someone else to provide the transport.[92] The allowance does not apply where the employer either provides transport (including a company car) for any part of the journey between home and the workplace, or pays for any part of the travel-to-work cost.[93] Where the employer has made a loan to the parent, increases the amount of pay, or makes a payment which would be taken into account as part of net income (see p263), this will not be classed as an employer paying for the transport.

Chapter 12: Exempt income: Step 2 of the 'old rules' formula
5. Travel-to-work costs

Calculating the allowance

The parent must supply the required information.[94] Then the CSA calculates or, where this is not possible, estimates:[95]
- the straight-line distance (ie, as the crow flies), rounded to the nearest mile, between the parent's home and workplace (usually by means of a computer program using UK postcodes and Ordnance Survey grid references);
- the number of journeys made between home and the workplace over a period of whole weeks which s/he thinks is representative of the parent's normal pattern of work (disregarding any two journeys made between the home and workplace within a period of two hours); *and*
- the number of journeys multiplied by the distance and divided by the number of weeks in the period used.

No allowance is included where this figure comes to less than or equal to 150 miles. However, where it is over 150 miles, 10 pence is included for each mile over 150.[96]

If the allowance does not reflect the real travel costs, either party can apply for a departure direction (see pp352 and 357).

> *Example 12.5: Exempt income including travel costs*
> Steve has remarried and has a net income for child support purposes of £380 a week. He and his wife Lisa have a mortgage of just under £60,000 and make monthly interest and endowment premium payments totalling £416 a month. They have no children.
> Steve commutes five days a week to London with a straight-line distance from home to work of 80 miles. 10 journeys x 80 miles = 800 miles a week.
> Days of annual leave or sickness are ignored.
> This gives 650 miles over 150 and thus an allowance of 650 x 10 pence = £65 a week.
>
> | Steve's exempt income: | £ | |
> |---|---|---|
> | Personal allowance | 55.65 | |
> | Mortgage in full* | 96.00 | |
> | Property settlement allowance | 40.00 | (see example 12.4a) |
> | Travel-to-work costs | 65.00 | |
> | **Total exempt income** | **256.65** | |
>
> *Although the housing costs are over £80, they are not considered excessive as half of Steve's net income is £190 a week (see p247).

More than one workplace

There are special rules to deal with the situation where the parent works at more than one workplace, whether for one employer or in more than one job.[97] If the pattern of work is irregular in a job, the CSA can select one of the workplaces or another location connected with the employment and assume that each day the parent travels to and from this deemed workplace.[98]

Otherwise the CSA must calculate the straight-line distances between any of the workplaces between which the parent travels, as well as between the home and each of the workplaces.[99] The pattern of journeys is obtained over a representative period as above, except that the two-hour rule only applies where the second journey is to return home. Each distance is multiplied by the number of times that journey is made over the period, and the total number of miles is divided by the number of weeks in the period.

6. Second families

We use the term 'second family' loosely to describe the situation where the parent is now living with a partner and children. The children may be her/his own children and/or the partner's. We recognise that the word 'second' is not precise, as the family could be a parent's third or fourth family, or indeed a first family – eg, in the case of a married man who, despite having a child with another woman, is still living with his wife.

We have already looked at the general position of second families as regards the 'old rules' exempt income calculation. Partners and children who are not the parent's children are not considered when including personal allowances and premiums at this stage. However, a child of the parent is included and that child may have another parent who is liable to maintain her/him. If the other parent is non-resident, then the child is a qualifying child and there is the possibility of receiving child maintenance.

Alternatively, if the other parent is also living in the family, then the 'old rules' exempt income calculation can be adjusted to recognise the other parent's liability to maintain the joint child. In other words, if a parent is living with her/his own child and the child's other parent, then the partner may be able to help support the child. This will reduce the parent's responsibility for their joint child included in exempt income. If the partner has sufficient income, this will halve the amounts for the joint child in the exempt income calculation.

The partner can refuse to disclose her income, in which case it is assumed that she can afford to help support her children and their allowances are halved. Except for families on low incomes needing the benefit of protected income, or where the partner has little income of her own, there is in effect no penalty for non-disclosure.

This assessment will need to be done not only where the non-resident parent has a second family, but also where a parent with care has had a child with a current partner. This is the only time in the formula that the income of the parent with care's partner is involved.

Chapter 12: Exempt income: Step 2 of the 'old rules' formula
6. Second families

Can the partner afford to maintain the joint child

Before including the full allowance and premiums for a joint child in the parent's exempt income, the net income of the partner must be assessed. The partner's net income is calculated in the same way as the parent's net income when working out her/his assessable income (see Chapter 13), with just one difference.[100] The income of any of the partner's own children is *not* included. This means that maintenance for any of her own qualifying children from their non-resident parent (ie, stepchildren in the second family) is ignored.

To assess whether the partner can help support a joint child or children, compare the amount of her/his net income with the total of:[101]
- the income support (IS) personal allowance for a person aged 25 or over (£55.65); *plus*
- half the amount of the IS personal allowance for the child(ren) of that age; *plus*
- if the child(ren) would qualify for the IS disabled child premium (see Appendix 2), half the amount of that premium for that child(ren); *plus*
- half the amount of the IS family premium (ie, £7.98 – half of £15.95) (except where the family premium would be payable in respect of another child who is included in exempt income – see p231 and Appendix 2); *plus*
- any contribution the partner is expected to make towards housing costs after a departure direction (see p357).

No personal allowances are included for any other children of the partner.

If the partner's net income is higher than the figure above, s/he can afford to contribute to their joint child's support. Therefore, the parent's exempt income will include only half the child's personal allowance, and half of any disabled child premium and (if there is no other child included the exempt income), only half the family premium.[102]

Example 12.6: Exempt income with a joint child
Bob and Zoe have a baby, Ricky. They are still living in the same house with a rent of £45 a week and Zoe's other three children (see example 12.2).
(a) Zoe stays at home full time. Her only income is child benefit and maintenance for Yvonne and Veronica, both of which are ignored. Therefore, Zoe cannot afford to contribute to Ricky's upkeep and Bob's exempt income will include the full allowances for Ricky.
Bob is not the father of Yvonne, Veronica and Scott, and therefore they are not included in the exempt income calculation.

Bob's exempt income:		£
Personal allowances	Bob	55.65
	Ricky	42.27

256

Chapter 12: Exempt income: Step 2 of the 'old rules' formula
6. Second families

Family premium	15.95
Housing costs	45.00
Total exempt income	**158.87**

(b) Zoe begins paid work and brings home £90 a week.
Her earnings are compared with:

		£
Personal allowances	Zoe	55.65
	Ricky (half)	21.14
Family premium (half)		7.98
Total		**84.77**

Note: Half the family premium is allowed in Zoe's means test as the family premium is only included in Bob's exempt income in respect of Ricky. There is no other child included in exempt income.

Zoe's other three children are not taken into account.

No departure application has been made concerning Zoe's contribution towards housing costs.

As her earnings are higher than £84.77, Zoe is seen as being able to contribute to the maintenance of Ricky. Therefore, Bob's exempt income is adjusted:

		£
Personal allowance	Bob	55.65
	Ricky (half)	21.14
Family premium (half)		7.98
Housing costs		45.00
Total exempt income		**129.77**

Family premium

If the only children who are included in the parent's exempt income are joint children with the current partner, then the question arises of whether the family premium should be included in full or halved in the exempt income. This depends solely on the net income of the partner. When calculating whether the partner can afford to help support the children, half the family premium is included in the amount with which the partner's net income is compared, as in example 12.6.

However, if there is another child in the family who is the parent's, but not the partner's child, s/he will be included in the exempt income calculation of her/his parent. Therefore, the family premium is payable in full for this other child and the question of halving the family premium does not arise. The family premium is therefore excluded from the amount with which the partner's net income is compared when calculating whether she can support half the joint child.[103]

Example 12.7: Exempt income with a joint child and a qualifying child
The situation is the same as in example 12.6b except that Bob's daughter, Carol (15), has come to live with Bob and Zoe.

Chapter 12: Exempt income: Step 2 of the 'old rules' formula
6. Second families

Zoe's earnings would now be compared with:

		£
Personal allowances	Zoe	55.65
	Ricky (half)	21.14
Total		**76.79**

Half of the family premium is not included as Bob is entitled to the full family premium in his exempt income for Carol, and between the two partners there cannot be more than one family premium.

As her earnings are higher than £76.79, Zoe is seen as being able to contribute to half the maintenance of Ricky. Therefore, Bob's exempt income is adjusted:

		£
Personal allowances	Bob	55.65
	Carol	42.27
	Ricky (half)	21.14
Family premium (in full)		15.95
Housing costs		45.00
Total		**180.01**

If Carol only comes to stay some of the time, her personal allowance may be included in Bob's exempt income, but at reduced rate, depending on how often she stays with him (see Chapter 16). For a detailed explanation of the family premium in exempt income where there is a joint child and a shared care child, see p332 and example 16.4.

Notes

1. What is exempt income
1 Children Come First, Vol 1/10, White Paper, October 1990
2 Sch 1 para 5(4) CSA 1991; reg10A and reg 10B(CS(MASC) Regs as inserted by reg 4(5) CS(MA)(no2) Regs 2003
3 Sch 1 para 5(4) CSA 1991; reg 10A CS(MASC) Regs

2. How much is exempt income
4 Reg 10 CS(MASC) Regs
5 Reg 9(5) CS(MASC) Regs

6 Sch 1 para 5 CSA 1991; reg 9(1)CS(MASC) Regs as amended by reg 4(3)CS(MA)(No2) Regs 2003
7 Reg 10(b) CS(MASC) Regs

3. Housing costs
8 Reg 14 and Sch 3 para 4(1)(b) and (c) CS(MASC) Regs
9 Reg 40(7) CSDDCA Regs
10 CCS/6741/1995; CCS/2852/1995; Eligible housing costs for protected and exempt income
11 Sch 3 para 4(2)(a) CS(MASC) Regs
12 Reg 15(3) CS(MASC) Regs

Chapter 12: Exempt income: Step 2 of the 'old rules' formula
Notes

13 CSCS/8/1995; CCS/8189/1995
14 CCS/13698/1996
15 Joint liability for housing costs
16 Sch 3 para 4(2)(b) CS(MASC) Regs
17 Reg 15(4) CS(MASC) Regs
18 CSCS/2/1994; CSCS/5/1995
19 Sch 3 para 4(1)(a) CS(MASC) Regs
20 Sch 3 paras 1, 2, 2A and 3 CS(MASC) Regs; CCS/12/1994 and CCS/2750/1995
21 Reg 15(2) CS(MASC) Regs
22 CSCS/3/1996
23 Payments in respect of or as a consequence of the use and occupation of the home
24 CSCS/1/1994; R(CS) 3/96
25 CCS/11252/1995
26 CSCS/13/1995
27 CCS/12897/1996
28 Regs 9(1)(h) as amended by reg 4(3) CS(MA)(No2)Regs 2003 and 11(1)(i) CS(MASC) Regs as amended by reg 4(5) CS(MA)(No2) Regs 2003
29 CCS/11252/1995
30 Reg 1(2) CS(MASC) Regs
31 CSCS/8/1995; CCS/8189/1995
32 CCS/19/1994
33 CCS/4/1994; R(CS) 2/96
34 CCS/4305/1995
35 Regs 1(2), 9(1)(h) and 11(1)(i) CS(MASC) Regs
36 Sch 3 para 5 CS(MASC) Regs; Accommodation used for one or more purpose
37 Reg 15(2) CS(MASC) Regs
38 Sch 3 para 3 CS(MASC) Regs
39 Sch 3 para 3(4) CS(MASC) Regs; CCS/12598/1996
40 Life insurance premiums (endowment); Sch 3 para 3 CS(MASC) Regs
41 CSCS/1/1994; Property buildings and contents insurance
42 CCS/1321/1997
43 CCS/11591/1995
44 Sch 3 para 4 CS(MASC) Regs
45 CCS/2750/1995
46 Sch 3 para 3(5A) and (5B) CS(MASC) Regs
47 Sch 3 para 3(5B) CS(MASC) Regs
48 Sch 3 para 3(5) and (5A) CS(MASC) Regs
49 Sch 3 para 3(6) CS(MASC) Regs
50 CCS/9/1995
51 Sch 3 para 3(2A) CS(MASC) Regs
52 Sch 3 para 4A CS(MASC) Regs
53 Sch 3 para 6 CS(MASC) Regs
54 Sch 3 para 6(d) CS(MASC) Regs
55 Reg 16(1) CS(MASC) Regs
56 Reg 16(2) CS(MASC) Regs
57 Reg 18(2) CS(MASC) Regs
58 CCS/12769/1996
59 Reg 18(1) CS(MASC) Regs
60 CCS/6/1995

4. Pre-April 1993 property settlements
61 Reg 9(1)(bb) and Sch 3A CS(MASC) Regs
62 Reg 10(a) CS(MASC) Regs
63 Sch 3A paras 1, 8 and 9 CS(MASC) Regs
64 Sch 3A para 1(1) CS(MASC) Regs
65 Sch 3A para 1(1)(d) CS(MASC) Regs; CCS/14368/1997; CCS/97/1997
66 CCS/97/1997
67 Sch 3A para 1(1)(d) CS(MASC) Regs
68 Formula POCSA's
69 Formula POCSA's
70 CCS/97/1997
71 CSCS/1/1998; CSCS/2/1998
72 Formula POCSA's
73 Calculating the value of the property transfer
74 Sch 3A paras 1(1) and 11 CS(MASC) Regs
75 Trust funds
76 Sch 3A para 2(2) CS(MASC) Regs
77 Further information not provided
78 Sch 3A para 2(1) CS(MASC) Regs
79 Contest overview
80 Sch 3A para 4(1) CS(MASC) Regs; Calculating the value of the property transfer
81 Sch 3A para 4(2) CS(MASC) Regs
82 Sch 3A para 5 CS(MASC) Regs
83 Sch 3A para 6(a) CS(MASC) Regs
84 Sch 3A para 6(b) CS(MASC) Regs
85 Sch 3A para 7 CS(MASC) Regs
86 Sch 3A para 1 CS(MASC) Regs
87 Sch 3A para 8A CS(MASC) Regs
88 Sch 3A para 8 CS(MASC) Regs
89 Sch 3A para 9 CS(MASC) Regs
90 Sch 3A para 10 CS(MASC) Regs

5. Travel-to-work costs
91 Reg 9(1)(i) and Sch 3B CS(MASC) Regs
92 Sch 3B para 1 CS(MASC) Regs
93 Sch 3B paras 21-23 CS(MASC) Regs
94 Sch 3B para 2 CS(MASC) Regs
95 Sch 3B paras 3-6 CS(MASC) Regs
96 Sch 3B paras 7, 14 and 20 CS(MASC) Regs
97 Sch 3B paras 8-20 CS(MASC) Regs
98 Sch 3B paras 8(2) and 15(2) CS(MASC) Regs
99 Sch 3B paras 9-13 and 16-19 CS(MASC) Regs

Chapter 12: Exempt income: Step 2 of the 'old rules' formula
Notes

6. **Second families**
   100 Reg 9(2) CS(MASC) Regs
   101 Reg 9(2)(c) CS(MASC) Regs
   102 Reg 9(1)(f) and (g) CS(MASC) Regs
   103 Reg 9(2)(c)(iv) CS(MASC) Regs

Chapter 13

Assessable income: Step 3 of the 'old rules' formula

This chapter covers:
1. What is assessable income (below)
2. What is net income (p262)
3. Calculating assessable income (p281)

> This chapter contains information relevant to existing cases under the 'old rules'. For calculations under the 'new rules', see Chapter 7.

This chapter should be read in conjunction with calculation sheet 3 in Appendix 3.

1. What is assessable income

Assessable income is the parent's income remaining after basic living expenses (as represented by exempt income, see Chapter 12) have been accounted for. A proportion of this remaining income is used to contribute towards child maintenance payments (see Chapter 14). In the case of the parent with care this is a notional contribution which can have the effect of reducing the maintenance payable by the non-resident parent.

Assessable income is the parent's net income minus exempt income.[1]

This step of the formula is carried out in the same way for non-resident parents and parents with care,[2] and therefore any reference to parent in this chapter applies to both. It does not apply to a person with care who is not the parent of the qualifying child.

It is useful to calculate the non-resident parent's assessable income first because if he has no assessable income there is no need to calculate that of the parent with care (see p281).

A parent who is in receipt of income support (IS) or income-based jobseeker's allowance (JSA) is treated as having *no* assessable income.[3] If only the parent with care is on IS/income-based JSA, then this step must be done for the non-resident

Chapter 13: Assessable income: Step 3 of the 'old rules' formula
1. What is assessable income

parent alone. If the non-resident parent is on IS/income-based JSA, then the formula calculation is not carried out at all and instead the non-resident parent may have a deduction from his benefit (see p226). If the benefit claim of one party is thought to be fraudulent, this can be challenged by the other party (see p415).

Parents who are on pension credit (PC) are treated as having no assessable income.[4] As with income-based JSA a non-resident parent may have a deduction made from this towards maintenance.

Parents with care who are on working tax credit (WTC) are treated as having no assessable income.[5] This, as for IS/income-based JSA, applies whether the benefit is being paid to the parent herself or to her partner. A non-resident parent on WTC is only treated as having no assessable income where he is also a parent with care and either there is a maintenance assessment in force for his qualifying child(ren) or an application for an assessment is being considered.[6]

2. What is net income

Net income under the 'old rules' is the total income of the parent taken into account when assessing how much child maintenance the parent can afford to pay.

Net income includes earnings, benefits and other income.[7] The types of income that come within each of these categories are clearly defined in the regulations.[8] Certain types of income are ignored in full or in part.[9] The rules about income are similar, but not identical, to those for income support (IS) – eg, there are no earnings disregards when calculating net income.

The net income of a parent's partner is calculated using these rules when assessing whether s/he can afford to contribute to the support of any joint child in the exempt income calculation (see p306).[10]

These rules for calculating net income are also used when working out the family's total income at the protected income stage of the formula (see Chapter 15). However, there are a few exceptions which are highlighted in this chapter.[11]

If any income which is normally received at regular intervals is not received, it can be treated as though it were received if there are reasonable grounds for believing that the payment will actually be made.[12]

Capital itself is not taken into account, although any income generated from the capital does count as income (see p275).

In certain cases, a parent can be treated as having income (or capital which is a source of income) which s/he does not possess if the CSA believes the parent deprived her/himself of it with the intention of reducing her/his assessable income (see p278).

Verification of income details is expected (see p111).

Chapter 13: Assessable income: Step 3 of the 'old rules' formula
2. What is net income

Whose income is included

A partner's income is *not* included in the net income when calculating assessable income. This is commonly misunderstood (see pp83 and 311 for the way in which a partner's income may affect the assessment). Where a source of income is held jointly and the proportions are not known or defined, then the income available will be divided equally between the people who are entitled to receive it.[13]

The income of the parent's own child living in the household can be treated as though it was the income of the parent (see p277).[14]

Earnings from employment

Earnings mean 'any remuneration or profit derived from employment' and, as well as wages, include:[15]
- any payments for overtime;
- any profit-related pay;
- any bonus or commission (including tips);
- any holiday pay (except any payable more than four weeks after the job ends);
- payment in lieu of notice;
- statutory sick pay and statutory maternity pay;
- any payment for expenses not 'wholly, exclusively and necessarily incurred' in actually carrying out the job (these include payments made to cover travelling expenses from home to work and the care costs of any other member of the family);
- allowances paid to local councillors for local authority duties, as opposed to expenses 'wholly, exclusively and necessarily incurred';
- payment for duties as an auxiliary coastguard, part-time firefighter, or with the lifeboat services, territorial army or reserve forces relating to a period of less than one year (such payments for a period of one year or more are disregarded);[16]
- awards of compensation for unfair dismissal;
- certain employment protection payments;
- any retaining fee;
- remuneration, but not share dividend or debenture interest (which is other income), paid to a director of a limited or unlimited registered and incorporated company (as opposed to a sole trader or partner who is self-employed – see p266).[17]

The CSA should not simply adopt the Inland Revenue's estimate (eg, of expenses) and should carry out an independent examination of the facts; however, CSA staff would have to consider carefully taking a different position.[18] Several commissioners have held that non-taxable allowances are not automatically excluded as earnings for child support purposes.[19]

Earnings do *not* include:[20]

263

Chapter 13: Assessable income: Step 3 of the 'old rules' formula
2. What is net income

- payments received of occupational pension (these count as other income – see p272; for payments made into pension scheme, see p266);
- payments for expenses 'wholly, exclusively and necessarily' incurred in carrying out the duties of the job (see below);
- payments in kind;
- any advance of earnings or loan made by an employer to an employee (such a payment is also disregarded as other income,[21] and any repayments made will be included as earnings, not deducted from them[22]);
- payments made after employment ends which relate to a specific period of time, provided that a period of equal length has elapsed since the payment was received;
- earnings from a previous job where they are paid in a week or a period that earnings from a second job are received;
- payments made by an employer when an employee is on strike;
- any tax-exempt allowance paid by an employer to an employee;
- a compensation payment negotiated and made on the termination of employment[23] (with the exception of any payment in lieu of notice – see above);
- the value of free accommodation provided by an employer (although the CSA may consider the issue of notional earnings – see p278 – if the actual earnings are low in relation to the job performed).[24]

Staturoty adoption pay and statutorty paternity pay are not expressly listed in the legislation, however, the policy intention is that they are treated as earnings.

A commissioner has held that payments made by the parent for expenses could be deducted from her/his earnings where the employer did not reimburse them.[25]

It was emphasised that any such expenses had to be incurred 'in the performance of duties', and not just incurred in order to enable the parent's duties to be performed. It is possible that part of a payment (eg, towards a telephone rental or travel costs) could be 'wholly, exclusively and necessarily' incurred.[26]

Local overseas allowance paid to members of the armed forces abroad is disregarded,[27] whereas a rent or mortgage allowance paid by an employer (eg, to a police officer,[28] an army major in the UK,[29] a civil servant[30]) would normally be taken into account as earnings except where the housing expenses are necessarily incurred in the performance of their duties.[31] For the same reason, meals allowances are to be treated as earnings.[32]

Relevant week

The concept of the 'relevant week'[33] is important in child support assessments, particularly when calculating income.

For the parent who is not the applicant, the relevant week is the seven days immediately before the date that the maintenance enquiry form (see p97) is sent

Chapter 13: Assessable income: Step 3 of the 'old rules' formula
2. What is net income

to him. For the applicant, the relevant week is the seven days immediately before the maintenance application form (see p48) is submitted to the CSA. For the purpose of calculating earnings only, where the CSA has not been able to make an assessment (except perhaps an interim maintenance assessment – see p399), but is later supplied with the information required, the relevant week is the seven days immediately before the date on which the required information or evidence was received.[34]

Where a decision is revised (or where it is superseded because of ignorance or a mistake as to a material fact), the relevant week of the new decision is the same as that for the original decision. Where a decision is superseded on other grounds, the relevant week is the seven days immediately prior to the application for supersession (or the seven days prior to the date of notification where the Secretary of State supersedes on her/his own initiative).[35]

Calculating normal weekly earnings

Averaged earnings are used in the child support calculation.[36] When calculating or estimating average earnings at the relevant week (see p264), the CSA considers the evidence of the parent's earnings over any appropriate period, beginning no more than eight weeks before the relevant week and ending by the date of the assessment. S/he may also consider cumulative earnings to date in the tax year covering the relevant week.

Where a parent has claimed or been paid working tax credit (WTC)/child tax credit (CTC) on any day during the eight weeks before the relevant week or up to the date the assessment is made, the CSA may use the amount of earnings taken into account in the WTC/CTC calculation even though those earnings may relate to a period outside that normally used for a child support assessment.

CSA staff are advised to give reasons for the assessment period chosen for calculating earnings.[37]

Where the parent is a student (see p273 for definition of a student), earnings are averaged over 52 weeks ending with the relevant week, or as many weeks as the parent has been a student if this is shorter.[38]

Where the CSA believes that the amount of weekly earnings arrived at does not accurately represent the parent's normal earnings, then any other period can be used, taking into account earnings received and those due to be received.[39] The CSA must be satisfied first that the calculation of earnings at the relevant week produces a figure which is not normal,[40] and then that the period chosen reflects the parent's usual pattern of work – eg, the amount of overtime worked or sick leave.[41] A future period can be used to take into account – eg, earnings from a job which has not yet begun. The CSA must also consider the expected duration and pattern of any employment. A parent may want to suggest an alternative period to the CSA, giving reasons as the CSA cannot be expected to consider this without substantial grounds and a prompt by one of the parents.[42] The CSA must use one continuous period.[43]

Chapter 13: Assessable income: Step 3 of the 'old rules' formula
2. What is net income

Where a bonus, commission or profit-related pay is paid during a year ending with the relevant week separately from earnings or in relation to a longer period than other earnings, those payments are totalled over the year and divided by 52 weeks.[44] Such a payment cannot be disregarded on the grounds that it distorts normal earnings.[45]

The CSA has to take into account any change of circumstances it is aware of between the relevant week and the effective date (see p400).[46] However, it must first calculate earnings as above for the relevant week in order to determine whether there has been a material change of circumstances.[47] For changes after this date, see p383.

The calculation of earnings is one of the areas where errors are frequently made and therefore should be checked carefully. A commissioner has held that an appeal tribunal must enquire into whether the process used to determine income was correctly carried out and whether the period used for the averaging of earnings gave an accurate picture.[48]

Calculating net earnings

Net earnings from employment are counted as net income in full. Net earnings mean gross earnings *less*:[49]
- income tax;
- Class 1 national insurance contributions;
- one-half of any contributions made to an occupational pension scheme; *and*
- one-half of any contributions made towards a personal pension scheme (unless that scheme is intended partly to pay off a mortgage on the parent's home, in which case 37.5 per cent of such contributions). Certain retirement savings plans do not come within this provision,[50] but regular contributions under a retirement annuity contract may be deducted.[51]

The amount of tax and national insurance actually paid is usually deducted.[52] However, where earnings are being estimated, the amount to be deducted as income tax is calculated using the personal allowances and the tax rates applicable at the relevant week (see p264).[53] Similarly, the amount to be deducted as Class 1 national insurance contributions has to be calculated by using the appropriate percentage rate applicable in the relevant week.

Earnings from self-employment

Earnings from self-employment will in most cases be assessed on the basis of total taxable profits from self-employment submitted to the Inland Revenue for income tax self-assessment.[54] This includes earnings which fall under the self-employment, partnerships and land and property sections of the self-assessment form. Where the parent cannot provide the submission to the Inland Revenue but can provide a tax calculation notice, the total taxable profit from self-employment will be taken from the tax calculation notice instead.[55] If the CSA

Chapter 13: Assessable income: Step 3 of the 'old rules' formula
2. What is net income

becomes aware of a revision by the Inland Revenue of the total taxable profit from self-employment, the revised figure will be used.[56]

The intention is that self-employed parents will send the CSA copies of their self-assessment forms or tax calculation notices voluntarily. Where the CSA is satisfied that it is not reasonably practicable for a parent to provide the taxable profit figure, the earnings will be calculated under the rules applying before 4 October 1999 (see below).[57]

The earnings taken into account will be the total taxable profit from self-employment less tax, national insurance and half of pension premiums (37.5 per cent of the premium where the scheme is intended to pay off a mortgage).[58] The tax, national insurance and pension premium deductions from self-employed earnings are calculated using the rates applicable at the effective date.

Where self-employed earnings are assessed by reference to taxable profits submitted to the Inland Revenue, those profits must relate to a period of not less than six months and not more than 15 months ending within two years of the relevant week.[59] Where there is more than one such period, the figure used will be the taxable profits relating to the latest period.[60] Where the CSA believes that the earnings figure arrived at in this way does not accurately reflect the normal weekly earnings of the earner (eg, because there are no periods to which a taxable profit relates which meet the criteria), then self-employed earnings will be assessed in the same way as they were prior to 4 October 1999.[61]

The use of self-assessment details is intended to simplify the assessment of self-employed earnings; however, if a decision maker finds contradictions between information on the self-assessment form and evidence already held, this may be grounds for further investigation.[62]

Decision makers are advised only to contact the Inland Revenue for earnings details where it has been impossible to obtain the self-assessment details and all other options have been exhausted – ie, contact with the non-resident parent (by phone, letter and face-to-face), accountant, other companies and partnerships.[63]

Some parents with care who were previously assessed on the basis of their non-resident parent's taxable profit may find that their non-resident parent may now provide self-assessment information. This may result in a lower assessment as the allowances against profit are more generous under income tax rules than the CSA rules for calculating taxable profit. Where a parent has had their maintenance reduced because of this they should raise the issue with their MP or complain to the CSA and ask for compensation.

Earnings from self-employment not calculated from taxable profit

Where the CSA is satisfied that it is not reasonably practical for a self-employed parent to provide a taxable profit figure (see above) or where the taxable profit figure does not reflect their normal weekly earnings, earnings will be assessed on the following basis (these are the rules which applied to all self-employed assessments prior to 4 October 1999).

Chapter 13: Assessable income: Step 3 of the 'old rules' formula
2. What is net income

In these cases, earnings mean the gross receipts of the business. They include any business start-up grant which is paid for in the same period as the receipts, unless it was ended by the relevant week, in which case it is disregarded.[64] Earnings do not include any payments received for providing board and lodging accommodation unless this is the largest part of the parent's income.[65] Where a parent is a childminder, only one third of her gross receipts count as earnings.[66]

Net earnings to be included as net income are the gross receipts of the business *less*:[67]
- income tax (calculated for the chargeable earnings using the personal allowance and the tax rates applicable on the effective date – see p400);
- national insurance contributions (Class 2 and Class 4 contributions at the rates applicable on the effective date[68]);
- half of any premium on a personal pension scheme (unless that scheme is intended partly to pay off a mortgage on the parent's home, in which case 37.5 per cent of the contributions are deducted) or on a retirement annuity contract;
- any VAT paid in excess of VAT received in the same period as that over which the earnings are assessed;
- any expenses which are reasonably incurred and wholly and exclusively defrayed for the purposes of the business. If the CSA is not satisfied that the full expense was appropriate or necessary to the business, it will allow that part considered reasonable.[69] Where an expense is part business and part private (eg, a car), the CSA has to decide on the breakdown between the two uses on the evidence available. CSA staff are given examples of how to deal with apportionment.[70] They may well follow the apportionment used by the Inland Revenue. CSA staff are also given guidance on what may be allowable business expenses.[71]

Business expenses include:[72]
- repayments of capital on loans used for the replacement or repair of a business asset (but not for loans taken out for any other business purpose);
- any income used for the repair of a business asset;
- any payment of interest on loans taken out for business purposes (this does not include loans taken out to acquire a share of a business, nor to pay business tax liabilities).[73]

Business expenses do *not* include:[74]
- capital expenditure;
- depreciation of capital assets;
- any sum employed in the setting up or expansion of the business;
- any loss incurred before the period of earnings being calculated;
- any expenses incurred in providing business entertainment;
- any loss incurred in any other self-employment.

Chapter 13: Assessable income: Step 3 of the 'old rules' formula
2. What is net income

There is a separate rule for share fishermen.[75]

If a profit and loss account is provided for a period of at least six months (but no longer than 15 months) which ended within the last two years, it can be used to calculate average weekly earnings.[76] The two years end on the date on which the assessment takes effect – ie, the effective date (see p400). The CSA may decide to wait if accounts will shortly be available and impose a Category C interim maintenance assessment in the meantime.

If there is more than one such profit and loss account covering different periods, the account covering the latest period will be used unless the CSA is satisfied that this latest account is not available for reasons beyond the parent's control.[77] Not being available includes an accountant or another government department (eg, the Inland Revenue) holding them without a date set for their return, the Official Receiver has the accounts, or they have been destroyed, lost or stolen.

A trading account or balance sheet might be requested in addition to the profit and loss account.[78] The accounts do not need to be prepared by accountants or even typed. However, if they do not contain the required information, the CSA may request other evidence of gross receipts.

Where no appropriate profit and loss account is available, earnings for the self-employed will be averaged over the previous 52 weeks or, if the person has been self-employed for less than a year, over the period during which the person has been self-employed.[79] In this case, the last week of the 52-week period is the relevant week (see p264). The self-employed person is asked to provide other evidence of business receipts and expenses, such as business books, receipts of bills sent and paid, bank statements, records of wages paid, Inland Revenue forms and VAT bills.[80]

Whatever period is used for assessing earnings, only those receipts and expenses *relevant* to that period should be used.[81] This is not necessarily the same as the payments made and received during the period.

Where the CSA believes that either or both of the above calculations produce an amount which does not accurately represent the parent's true earnings, another period can be used.[82] This may happen where there has been a major change in trading which has resulted in higher or lower earnings or where a person who has been trading for less than a year has not established a regular pattern of trading.[83] This should not be used just because earnings fluctuate, receipts are irregular or come in a lump, trade is slow at times or work non-existent for a period, nor should a different period be used just because it is known that earnings will subsequently change.[84]

Self-employed parents on tax credits

If a self-employed parent has claimed or been paid WTC/CTC on any day during the eight weeks before the relevant week or up to the date the assessment is made, the CSA may use the amount of earnings taken into account in the WTC/CTC

Chapter 13: Assessable income: Step 3 of the 'old rules' formula
2. What is net income

calculation even though those earnings may relate to a period different from those described above.[85]

Challenging earnings of the self-employed

There have often been delays in the self-employed parent producing all the information necessary to carry out the assessment. The CSA can impose a Category C interim maintenance assessment while awaiting the information, but this is rare. The person with care may want to request that this is done.

Many self-employed non-resident parents receive low assessments. Some persons with care allege that the self-employed non-resident parent, sometimes with the help of an accountant, has managed to disguise his true income. Once an assessment has been made, the person with care can seek a revision of the assessment (see p416) and ask the CSA to use an inspector (see p112) in order to obtain more detailed information. However, if the non-resident parent's accounts have been accepted by the Inland Revenue, it is very unlikely that the CSA would consider it worthwhile to undertake further investigations. The CSA may also refuse to revise the assessment if the person with care cannot substantiate her allegations. This can be challenged if the belief is reasonably held as it is very difficult for one party to obtain definitive details of the other's income. The CSA is much better placed to do this.

If the person with care takes the case to an appeal tribunal (see p434), she will see details of the income in the appeal papers, and she may be able to argue that some of the expenses included are not reasonable or not wholly connected with the business (see above). She should also consider the notional earnings rules (see p278) and, if relevant, suggest the tribunal makes a finding on this issue. Tribunals may adjourn the hearing and instruct the CSA to collect further information. Alternatively, the tribunal can estimate net earnings based on the available evidence, including oral evidence from the person with care.[86]

The person with care can apply for departure from the assessment on the grounds that a person's lifestyle is inconsistent with his level of income or that assets which do not currently produce income are capable of doing so (see p356).

Benefits

Benefits paid by the DWP count as income for the purposes of net income, although some of these are disregarded in full or in part.[87] Remember that where IS/income-based jobseeker's allowance (JSA) or pension credit is received by the parent or her/his partner, the parent is treated as having no assessable income (see p262). The same applies to a parent with care in receipt of WTC.

The amount of the benefit to be taken into account is the rate applying on the effective date (see p400).[88]

Whose benefit it is

The income of a partner is not included when working out a parent's net income. Some non-means-tested benefits contain an extra amount for a partner, called an adult dependency increase. The amount paid in respect of that dependant is treated as the dependant's income, not the claimant's[89] – ie, if the parent is the claimant, s/he is treated as not receiving the adult dependency addition and, if the partner is the claimant, the parent is assumed to have income equal to the addition paid to the partner in respect of her/him. If a parent receives a non-means-tested benefit which includes a dependency addition for a child, this addition is treated as the income of the child (see p277). These rules also apply to adult and child dependency increases to war disablement, war widows' and war widower's pensions.[90]

Child benefit

Child benefit is ignored when working out net income, but only up to the basic rate.[91] Parents receiving the lone parent rate of child benefit have the difference between the higher rate for the first child and the basic rate taken into account – this is currently £1.05. When calculating total family income for protected income purposes, child benefit is counted in full.[92]

Benefits ignored in full

The following benefits are ignored in full:
- housing benefit;[93]
- council tax benefit;[94]
- disability living allowance (or a mobility supplement);[95]
- attendance allowance (or constant attendance allowance or exceptionally severe disablement allowance paid because of industrial injury or war injury);[96]
- social fund payments;[97]
- guardian's allowance;[98] *and*
- Christmas bonus.[99]

Payments made to compensate for the loss of benefits are also disregarded.[100] Special war widows' payments granted in 1990 are likewise disregarded in full.[101]

Benefits ignored in part

A total of £10 of a war disablement pension, war widow's or war widower's pension is disregarded.[102] However, only £20 in total can be disregarded from a combination of war pensions, charitable payments and student income.

Other income

Unless specified below, all other income is taken into account on a weekly basis by considering the 26-week period ending in the 'relevant week' (see p264).[103] If

Chapter 13: Assessable income: Step 3 of the 'old rules' formula
2. What is net income

the income has been received during each week of the period, the total received over the 26 weeks is divided by 26. In other cases, the total received is divided by the number of complete weeks for which the payment was received. However, the CSA does have discretion to use a different period if the amount produced by the above calculation does not accurately reflect actual income. Furthermore, a change occurring between the relevant week and the effective date (see p400) must be taken into account by the CSA if it is aware of the change in the same way as for earnings (see p266).

Other income includes any payments received on a periodic basis which are not covered as earnings, benefits, or a child's income, as well as the following types of payment. It does not include a non-resident parent's payments towards his share of a parent with care's housing costs.[104] Some payments are taken into account in full or in part, while others are ignored completely. Payments which are ignored as earnings cannot be taken into account as other income.

Working tax credit

WTC is usually treated as the income of the parent who had qualified for the payment through their normal engagement in remunerative work.[105] Where WTC is based on the earnings of the non-resident parent and another person it is treated as the income of the non-resident parent if their income is higher than the other person's during the period used to calculate earnings for the assessment. If the earnings are equal, half the amount of the WTC counts as the earnings of the non-resident parent. If the non-resident parent's earnings are less than the other person's then it is not counted as their income.

Child tax credit

All payments of CTC are to be ignored in full.[106]

Payments from occupational or personal pension schemes

These and any analogous payments are taken into account in full.[107]

Income from rent

Different provisions apply, depending on the type of income from the property:
- payments made towards household expenses by a non-dependant (see p314 for a definition) are completely ignored;[108]
- the first £20 a week of a payment from a boarder is disregarded, as is 50 per cent of any amount over £20 (as long as this is not the largest part of a parent's income when it would be treated as earnings from self-employment).[109] A boarder is someone who is liable to pay for board and lodging which includes at least one meal a day;
- payments from a person who is liable to pay for accommodation in the parent's home (but who is not a lodger or a non-dependant) are treated as

Chapter 13: Assessable income: Step 3 of the 'old rules' formula
2. What is net income

income. However, there is a disregard of £13.70 (or £4 if the payment is not inclusive of heating);[110]
- payments for the use of a property which is not the parent's home are taken into account as other income, unless the parent is self-employed. In this case, the income is treated as part of the gross receipts of the business. If the parent is not self-employed, the amounts to cover income tax,[111] mortgage interest, interest on loans for repairs and improvements, council tax and water rates can be deducted from the amount received as rent.[112] Commissioners differ on whether other expenses necessary to obtain the rental income (eg, servicing gas fires) may also be deducted; guidance for decision makers suggests that they cannot.[113]

Students' income

A student is defined as someone following a full-time course of study at an educational establishment and, if under 19 years old, the course must be advanced education – ie, above A-level or Scottish Higher.[114] This can include sandwich courses. There is no definition of full time and it does not relate to the number of hours of attendance. The CSA attaches great weight to evidence from the educational establishment.[115] Once a course has begun, a person continues to be treated as a student until either the course ends or s/he leaves the course.

Unless they have income in addition to an educational grant (including any contribution due) or student loan, students are treated as having no net income and hence are exempt from having to pay child maintenance.[116]

In other cases, income paid to a student as a grant, grant contribution, covenant income or student loan, is taken into account except to the extent that it is:[117]
- intended to meet tuition fees or examination fees;
- intended to meet additional expenditure as a result of a disability;
- intended to meet expenditure connected with residential study away from the educational establishment;
- made on account of the student maintaining a home away from the educational establishment;
- intended to meet the cost of books and equipment, or, if not specified, £335 (this goes up each September);
- intended to meet travel expenses;
- a payment from the access fund.[118]

The amount of a student's grant, covenant income and loan are apportioned equally between the weeks for which they are payable.[119] The amount of the weekly covenant income that is disregarded is £5 and £10 of any loan, although not more than £10 a week can be deducted in total.[120] Any amount disregarded under this provision counts towards the £20 disregard for charitable/voluntary payments (see p276).[121]

Chapter 13: Assessable income: Step 3 of the 'old rules' formula
2. What is net income

Educational maintenance awards for courses of further education are disregarded.[122]

New Deal for 18- to 24-year-olds

Payments from an employer under the New Deal Employment option are treated as earnings (see p263). This also applies to payments from employment under the Voluntary Sector and Environmental Task Force options.[123] Participants in other New Deal options may receive a training allowance; most of them will receive income-based JSA and will therefore not be assessed under the formula (see p223).

Training allowances

Training allowances are taken into account (but see below), except for the training premium, travelling expenses or any living away from home allowance.[124]

Work-Based Training for Young People

These training schemes for young people aged under 18 include modern apprenticeships, national traineeships, other work-based training and (in Scotland) Skillseekers training. Trainees under these schemes who have no income other than their training allowance are taken to have no net income and hence are exempt from paying any child maintenance (see p223).[125] Trainees who are employees have their earnings taken into account in the usual way (see p263).

Maintenance in respect of a parent

This income is taken into account in full. There is a specific rule which applies for calculating the amount of maintenance to take into account. It is calculated by averaging the payments received in the 13 weeks preceding the assessment over the number of weeks for which a payment was due.[126] A commissioner has held that payments of maintenance to a parent with care by a non-resident parent cannot be counted as the parent with care's income.[127] This approach is not reflected in guidance to CSA staff[128] and the CSA continues to regard such payments as income.

Child maintenance

Child maintenance from a non-resident parent for the qualifying child for whom the assessment is being carried out is ignored when calculating the income of the parent with care.[129]

Except at the protected income stage (see p312), the CSA treats maintenance paid to a parent for any other child as the child's income. This may still be included in net income, but there are separate rules covering when and how much of the child's income can be taken into account as the parent's income (see p277).

In the calculation of protected income, any maintenance being paid for other children under a court order is deducted from the liable person's income, as long as an application cannot be made to the CSA (see p43).[130] See p312 for further details.

Lump sum maintenance

There is provision to disregard other maintenance payments in full, whether child support maintenance or other forms, if they are not income.[131] However, as all payments received on a periodic basis are income, this disregard appears only to apply to irregular maintenance payments. It does not apply to maintenance payments made periodically.[132]

Payments made by a local authority under the Children Act 1989 or Social Work (Scotland) Act 1968

Payments made where the local authority is looking after a child and has placed the child with a family, relative or other suitable person, including a foster parent, are ignored completely.[133] Payments made by local authorities to promote the welfare of children being looked after, or who were formerly in their care, are also ignored.[134]

Payments made as a contribution towards the maintenance of a child living with the family as a result of a residence order under the Children Act are ignored where they exceed the personal allowances and any disabled child premium included for the child in the exempt income calculation (see p239).[135]

Adoption allowances

A payment for an adopted child is disregarded:[136]
- to the extent that it exceeds the personal allowance and any disabled child premium for the child, if child maintenance is *not* being assessed for that particular child;
- only up to the amount of any income of the child which is included as income of the parent, if child maintenance is being assessed for that child.

Income from capital

A payment of capital is not income in that it is not paid for a period and is not intended to form part of a series of payments.[137] Such capital payments are not taken into account. However, the interest, dividend or any other income produced by capital is taken into account as income and is calculated by dividing the total received over 52 weeks by 52.[138] If this gives a figure which the CSA decides is not representative of the income produced, it can use another period.

Where capital is jointly held and the shares are unknown, any income from the capital is divided equally between the joint owners.[139] Where capital is divided on divorce or separation and it is intended for the purchase of a new home or furnishings, then income from that capital will be ignored for one year.[140]

Although CSA staff are given examples of what may constitute capital and ownership, there is no guidance on the calculation of income from different types of capital.[141]

Chapter 13: Assessable income: Step 3 of the 'old rules' formula
2. What is net income

Prisoners' pay

Unless they have another source of income, prisoners receiving only prisoners' pay will be assumed to have no net income and will be exempt from paying child support.[142]

Regular charitable or voluntary payments

These are disregarded in full if they are intended and used for any items *other than* food, ordinary clothing, household fuel, housing costs or council tax.[143] There has to be a mutual understanding between the donor and the recipient as to the purpose of the payment, but this does not need to be a formal agreement.[144] If the payment is in respect of school fees, then it is not counted as income at all even if part of the school fees relates to one of the specified items – eg, school meals.[145]

If the payment is for one of these specified items, then the first £20 will be disregarded, although no more than £20 in total can be disregarded from a student's income, a war pension and such voluntary payments.[146] See p312 for the position if the voluntary or charitable payment is made direct to a third party.

This provision does not apply to payments made by non-resident parents which are treated as maintenance (see p274).

Other disregarded income

The following will also not be taken into account as income:
- any income tax payments;[147]
- payments in kind (except for self-employed earners);[148]
- payments made instead of milk tokens or free vitamins;[149]
- all NHS health benefits such as fares to hospital;[150]
- payments for prison visiting;[151]
- resettlement benefit paid to long-term hospital patients on their discharge from hospital;[152]
- payments made by a local education authority to help a child take advantage of a course of study or educational facilities, including a scholarship, or an assisted place;[153]
- payments under a mortgage protection insurance policy to the extent that they exceed the interest, capital payments and any further mortgage protection premiums;[154]
- payments of expenses to unpaid voluntary workers (as long as the expenses cannot be treated as notional earnings);[155]
- payments made to assist a person with a disability to obtain or keep employment;[156]
- payments made to a person under the relevant community care provision to enable her/him to obtain community care services;[157]
- payments made by a local authority for welfare services under section 93(1 and 2) Local Government Act 2000, and in Scotland under section 91(1) Housing (Scotland) Act 2001 for housing services;[158]

- payments made by a health authority, local authority or voluntary organisation for a person who is temporarily a member of the household in order to receive care;[159]
- compensation for personal injury and any payments made from a trust fund set up for that purpose[160] (a firefighter's injury pension and analogous payments are not compensation);[161]
- payments from the Macfarlane Trust, Independent Living (1993) Fund or Independent Living (Extension) Fund;[162]
- payments from the Family Fund;[163]
- payments (other than those for lost earnings and benefits) made to jurors and witnesses for court attendance;[164]
- certain home income annuities purchased when aged 65 or over;[165]
- charges for converting payments in another currency to sterling;[166]
- amounts payable outside the UK where transfer to the UK is prohibited;[167] *and*
- payments to a person as a result of holding the Victoria or George Cross.[168]

Children's income

Where the parent has a child of her/his own living with her/him for at least 104 nights a year, the income of that child may be included in the parent's net income.[169] This does not have effect where the child is *not* a child (as defined by the 1991 Act) of the parent whose income is being assessed. If a parent of the qualifying child has, for example, stepchildren or grandchildren living with her/him, the income of these children does not count in calculating net income at assessable income stage, but is taken into account at protected income stage.

The child's income is taken to be her/his own parent's income when calculating both net income for assessable income purposes and total family income for protected income purposes. However, the child's income is *not* included when calculating the net income of her/his parent's partner in order to find out whether the partner can help support a joint child included in the exempt income (see p306).[170]

What counts as the child's income

Child maintenance received for a child is the child's income, even if it is paid to the parent.[171] Child maintenance already being received for a qualifying child who is the subject of the assessment being undertaken is ignored in full.[172] The child dependency additions of any benefit received by an adult is taken to be income of the child.[173]

The following are *not* included when calculating the child's income:[174]
- a child's earnings;
- interest payable on arrears of child maintenance;
- payments from a discretionary fund which benefit the child, as long as they do not cover food, ordinary clothing/footwear, household fuel or housing costs.

Chapter 13: Assessable income: Step 3 of the 'old rules' formula
2. What is net income

How much of the child's income counts as the parent's

The first £10 a week of any income of a child is ignored.[175] In addition, once the child's income is treated as that of her/his parent, the same disregards apply as for the parent's own income.[176]

How much of the child's net income is taken into account as her/his parent's income depends on whether the child is the subject of the maintenance assessment. Where the child is *not* the subject of the maintenance assessment, her/his income up to the amount of the personal allowance (and any disabled child premium) included in the exempt income calculation in respect of that child is counted as the parent's income.[177] Income above that amount is disregarded.

Where the child is the subject of the maintenance assessment, the child's income counts in full if s/he is the only child for whom an assessment is being made.[178] Where there is more than one child, each child's income is counted up to the level of child's proportion of the maximum child maintenance payment (see p296) – ie, a share of the maintenance requirement plus 1.5 times the basic rate of the family premium and the personal allowance.[179]

At the protected income stage of the formula, the rules about how much of the child's income is taken into account are different (see p312).

Notional income

Parents can be assumed to have income which they do not possess.[180] Such notional income is treated in the same way as if it were actual income.[181] It appears that, in practice, this provision is not used often, and parents who are contesting the other party's income may want to remind the CSA that notional income should be considered.

Notional earnings

The issue of notional earnings arises where a person has done some work, without being paid at all or not at a sufficient rate for the job, for an employer who could afford to pay full wages.[182] This cannot apply if the employer is a charity or voluntary organisation or a member of the parent's family. The estimated forgone income is treated as earnings if the CSA decides that the principal purpose of the person doing the work without pay or for reduced pay was to reduce her/his assessable income. To estimate an appropriate level of forgone earnings the decision maker has to consider:[183]

- what is the nature of the service from which the employer benefits?
- what is a comparable rate of pay?
- if the employer is paying less than this rate, could s/he afford to pay more for the service?

If the question of notional earnings is raised, the parent should let the CSA know her/his motives for doing the work. Notional earnings will be an issue where a parent is paid via a personal service company at less than the market rate.[184]

Deprivation of income or capital

If the CSA decides that a parent intentionally deprived her/himself of income in order to reduce her/his assessable income, then an amount equal to that income will be included as her/his net income.[185]

This rule applies equally to capital which would have been a source of income – eg, it would apply where shares are given away or sold at less than their market value.[186] Lump sum voluntary contributions towards a retirement annuity contract may count as deprivation of capital.[187] The CSA has to estimate a notional income from the notional capital, and guidance to CSA staff suggests that it may be reasonable to use rates of interest paid by high street banks and building societies.[188] When the CSA has decided that a certain sum is notional capital, that capital is reduced after 52 weeks by an amount equal to the income which would have been generated from that capital over the year.[189]

Deprivation refers both to income or capital that a person has disposed of and that which a person has failed to obtain – eg, by failing to apply for a benefit. However, it does not apply to the lone parent rate of child benefit, contribution-based JSA if IS is payable, nor to a payment from a discretionary trust or a trust set up with personal injury compensation.[190] Apart from social security benefits, the other examples given to CSA staff of payments which could be acquired are unclaimed councillors' attendance allowances, occupational pensions or Premium Bond wins.[191] Where income would have been available to a parent on application, an estimated amount is included as her/his net income from the date on which it could be expected to have been paid.[192]

The CSA is most likely to identify a potential deprivation of income or capital when considering supersession, where it finds that a source of income previously declared is no longer included.[193] The first question to be considered is whether the parent has actually disposed of the income or capital, and the onus is on the parent to prove s/he no longer has the resource.[194] CSA staff are given examples of deprivation of capital – making a lump-sum payment, putting money into a trust which cannot be revoked, gambling, using capital to fund an extravagant lifestyle or purchase personal possessions.[195] Although not mentioned in the guidance, deprivation can apply to a parent who has transferred assets to a new partner or possibly to a self-employed parent who is paying his partner a reasonable salary but not drawing much himself. Once it is shown s/he no longer possesses it, then the intention behind the deprivation has to be examined and decided on the balance of probabilities whether the aim was to reduce assessable income for child support purposes.[196]

This rule is similar, but not identical, to those for means-tested benefits (see CPAG's *Welfare Benefits and Tax Credits Handbook*) and an adviser should therefore consider whether any social security commissioners' decisions could be cited as persuasive. Although it may be argued that the reduction of assessable income need not be the only or even principal motive, the CSA has to be able to show that it is satisfied that such an intention existed. The onus of proof remains with the CSA.[197]

When deciding whether reducing assessable income was a significant factor in the disposal of the resource, CSA staff are advised to consider all the parent's reasons and the timing of the action.[198] If deprivation of capital is an issue, the CSA will consider whether the parent was aware that reducing capital would reduce the maintenance assessment.

This deprivation rule cannot be used against a parent who refuses an offer of employment,[199] and similarly it is unlikely to apply to a non-resident parent who gives up his job on finding out the amount of child maintenance expected from him. Also, it is most probably not applicable to a case where a parent has taken out a higher mortgage which reduces her/his assessable income.[200] A non-resident parent in this situation needs to consider the excessive housing costs rule (see p348). On the other hand, the use of capital as a deposit to buy a property could possibly be considered to be deprivation and motives would need to be examined.

Payments to third parties

If a payment is made on behalf of a parent or a child to a third party, it will only be treated as the parent's income if it is a payment for food, ordinary clothing or footwear, household fuel, housing costs or council tax.[201] For example, if a grandparent paid the parent's fuel bill direct to the fuel company, this would be notional income, whereas paying the telephone bill would not. Some of this notional income can be disregarded as a voluntary payment if made regularly (see p276).

A payment made by a partner to meet her/his own liability (eg, for a mortgage to a building society) is not made on behalf of the parent or child.[202] The same applies to payments made by an ex-partner for his own liability towards the matrimonial home in which the parent with care remains, whereas payments made by him towards her part of the mortgage count as the parent with care's income.[203] A commissioner has held that no payments from a non-resident parent to a parent with care can count as the parent with care's income even where these are made to meet her share of housing costs.[204] This approach conflicts with earlier decisions and guidance to CSA staff.[205] It is understood that the CSA will continue to regard such payments as income.

Chapter 13: Assessable income: Step 3 of the 'old rules' formula
3. Calculating assessable income

3. Calculating assessable income

Assessable income is the parent's total net income less her/his exempt income. For details of exempt income, see Chapter 12.

If the parent's exempt income is higher than her/his net income, assessable income is taken to be nil.[206] Where his assessable income is nil, the non-resident parent may still have to make the minimum payment of child maintenance. There is, however, no need to continue with the steps of the formula in this case as the maintenance due will either be the minimum payment of £5.60 or nil (see p223). If a non-resident parent's net income is itself less than £5.60, he is exempt from paying child maintenance.[207]

Where the parent with care's assessable income is nil, the proposed maintenance step is carried out with just the non-resident parent's assessable income.

Example 13.1: Assessable income of an non-resident parent
(a) Bob is living in a bedsit on his own. His exempt income is £103.65 (see example 12.1a). His income is £154 a week in earnings after tax, national insurance and £12 weekly superannuation contribution. Only half his superannuation is taken into account when calculating Bob's net earnings for child support purposes, which are therefore £154 + £6 = £160.
Bob's net income is, therefore, his net earnings: £16.

	£
Net income	160.00
Less exempt income	103.65
Assessable income	**56.35**

(b) Bob moves in with Zoe and her three children (see example 12.2).

	£
Net income*	160.00
Less exempt income	100.65
Assessable income	**60.35**

*A claim for working tax credit (WTC) has not yet been determined but an award would increase Bob's assessable income (see example 13.3 below).

(c) Bob is in receipt of severe disablement allowance (SDA) of £60.35 and lives with his parents (see example 12.1b):

	£
Net income	60.35
Less exempt income	79.35
Assessable income	**Nil**

281

Chapter 13: Assessable income: Step 3 of the 'old rules' formula
3. Calculating assessable income

As he receives SDA Bob is exempt from the minimum payment (see p223) and would receive a nil assessment; no further calculation is required.

Example 13.2: Assessable income of a parent with care

While Anita is on income support (IS) or WTC, she is automatically treated as having no assessable income.

(a) Anita receives child benefit of £28.60. Bob has been paying £30.50 a week in maintenance for Carol (13) and David (8). This is not taken into account as income because it is maintenance for the qualifying children – ie, the children for whom the re-assessment is being carried out.

Anita is now bringing home £265 a week (after tax, NI and a £15 superannuation contribution). She is entitled to child tax credit (CTC) (which is ignored as income) but not to any WTC. Only half of the superannuation payment can be taken into account (ie, £7.50) and therefore her net earnings for exempt income purposes are now £272.50 a week. The extra amount of child benefit which Anita, as a lone parent, receives for Carol is taken into account.

	£
Earnings	272.50
Child benefit (£17.55 – £16.50)	1.05
Total net income	273.55
Less exempt income (from example 12.3a)	231.14
Assessable income	**42.41**

(b) Anita remarries. She brings home £195 a week after tax, national insurance and a £15 superannuation contribution. Her husband, Joe, earns £205 a week.

Net income is now £202.50 (she no longer gets child benefit at the lone parent rate). Joe's income is not taken into account.

	£
Net income	202.50
Less exempt income (from example 12.3b)	293.92
Assessable income	**Nil**

Example 13.3: Bob and Zoe have a baby

(a) Bob is now living with Zoe, their son Ricky and three stepchildren (aged 13, 11 and 4 years old). The exempt income is £158.87 (see example 12.6a). Bob's net earnings are £260 a week. Any income of Zoe's is not taken into account, including the maintenance of £20 a week for her daughters. The couple receive £104.53 a week of CTC that is ignored.

	£
Earnings (Bob)	260.00
Total net income	260.00
Less exempt income	158.87
Bob's assessable income	**101.13**

(b) Zoe begins paid work, bringing home £90 a week. The total net income remains at

£260, as Zoe's earnings are not taken into account at this stage. However, her earnings have affected the exempt income (see example 12.6b) as she is now helping to support Ricky.

	£
Total net income	260.00
Less exempt income	129.77
Bob's assessable income	**130.23**

As it is the start of the tax year and Zoe's income will increase their annual income by more than £2,500, they inform the Inland Revenue rather than wait for an adjustment. Due to Zoe's income their CTC is reduced to £49.03 a week, while this does not affect assessable income it may affect the calculation at protected income stage.

Notes

1. What is assessable income
1. Sch 1 para 5(1) and (2) CSA 1991
2. Regs 8 and 10 CS(MASC) Regs
3. Sch 1 para 5(4) CSA 1991
4. Reg 10B CS(MASC) Regs as inserted by reg 4(4) CS(MA)(No2) Regs 2003
5. Reg 10A CS(MASC) Regs
6. Reg 10A(2) CS(MASC) Regs

2. What is net income
7. Reg 7(1) CS(MASC) Regs
8. Sch 1 CS(MASC) Regs as amended by Reg 5 CS(MA)(No2) Regs 2003
9. Sch 2 CS(MASC) Regs as amended by reg 5 CS(MA)(No2) Regs 2003
10. Reg 9(2)(c) CS(MASC) Regs
11. Reg 11(2) CS(MASC) Regs
12. Reg 7(5) CS(MASC) Regs
13. Reg 7(4) CS(MASC) Regs
14. Sch 1 para 9(a) CSA 1991; reg 7(1)(d) CS(MASC) Regs
15. Sch 1 para 1(1) CS(MASC) Regs
16. Sch 2 para 48B CS(MASC) Regs
17. Directors of limited or unlimited liability companies; Other Directors
18. CCS/2750/1995; CCS/318/1995
19. CCS/11364/1995; see also notes 25, 28 and 29
20. Sch 1 para 1(2) CS(MASC) Regs
21. Sch 2 para 6 CS(MASC) Regs
22. CCS/11252/1995; CCS/5352/1995
23. CCS/3182/1995
24. Accommodation provided by the employer
25. CCS/4/1994; R(CS) 2/96
26. CCS/12073/1996
27. CCS/318/1995
28. CCS/10/1994; CCS/12598/1996; CCS/1321/1997; CCS/2320/1997; CCS/2561/1998
29. CCS/5352/1995
30. CCS/11242/1995
31. CCS/12769/1996
32. CCS/6807/1995
33. Reg 1(2) CS(MASC) Regs
34. Sch 1 para 2(3A) CS(MASC) Regs
35. Reg 1(2) CS(MASC) Regs
36. Sch 1 para 2(1) CS(MASC) Regs
37. The Assessment Period; Recording decisions
38. Sch 1 para 2(3) CS(MASC) Regs
39. Sch 1 para 2(4) CS(MASC) Regs
40. CCS/16/1994; CCS/11873/1996
41. Earnings in the assessment period are not normal; CCS/6810/1995
42. CCS/511/1995
43. CCS/7312/1995; CCS/556/1995; CSCS/1/1996; CSCS/6/1996

Chapter 13: Assessable income: Step 3 of the 'old rules' formula
Notes

44 Sch 1 para 2(2) CS(MASC) Regs
45 CCS/5079/1995
46 Reg 2(3) CS(MASC) Regs
47 CCS/2750/1995
48 CCS/556/1995
49 Sch 1 para 1(3) CS(MASC) Regs
50 CSCS/5/1994
51 CCS/3542/1998
52 Sch 1 para 1(3) CS(MASC) Regs
53 Reg 1(2A) CS(MASC) Regs
54 Sch 1 para 2A(1) CS(MASC) Regs
55 Sch 1 para 2B(1)(a) CS(MASC) Regs
56 Sch 1 para 2B(1)(b) CS(MASC) Regs
57 Sch 1 para 2C CS(MASC) Regs
58 Sch 1 para 2A(2) CS(MASC) Regs
59 Sch 1 para 5A(1) CS(MASC) Regs
60 Sch 1 para 5A(2) CS(MASC) Regs
61 Sch 1 para 5A(3) CS(MASC) Regs
62 Self-assessment returns
63 Approaching Inland Revenue for self-employed income
64 Sch 1 para 3(1) and (2)(a) CS(MASC) Regs
65 Sch 1 para 3(2)(b) CS(MASC) Regs; People providing board and lodging
66 Sch 1 para 4 CS(MASC) Regs
67 Sch 1 para 3(3) CS(MASC) Regs
68 Sch 1 para 3(6) and (8) CS(MASC) Regs
69 Reasonably incurred
70 Wholly and exclusively defrayed expenses
71 Allowable Expenses
72 Sch 1 para 3(4)(a) CS(MASC) Regs
73 CCS/15949/1996
74 Sch 1 para 3(4)(b) CS(MASC) Regs
75 Sch 1 para 3(7) CS(MASC) Regs; Share fisherman
76 Sch 1 para 5(2) CS(MASC) Regs
77 Sch 1 para 5(2A) CS(MASC) Regs
78 Appropriate accounts
79 Sch 1 para 5(1) CS(MASC) Regs
80 Business Receipts; Business expenses
81 Sch 1 para 5(2) CS(MASC) Regs; Assessment period (self-employed)
82 Sch 1 para 5(3) CS(MASC) Regs
83 Assessment period – not an accurate reflection
84 CCS/3182/1995; CCS/6145/1995; Assessment period – not an accurate reflection
85 Sch 1 Para 5(5)CS(MASC) Regs
86 CCS/7966/1995
87 Sch 1 para 6 CS(MASC) Regs; reg 10B CS(MASC) Regs as inserted by reg 4(4) CS9MA) (No2) Regs 2003
88 Sch 1 para 6(3) CS(MASC) Regs
89 Sch 1 para 7(1) CS(MASC) Regs
90 Sch 1 para 9A and 22(1B) CS(MASC) Regs as amended by reg 4(6) CS(MA)(No2) Regs 2003
91 Sch 2 para 16 CS(MASC) Regs
92 Reg 11(2)(a)(i) CS(MASC) Regs
93 Sch 2 para 7 CS(MASC) Regs
94 Sch 2 para 7 CS(MASC) Regs
95 Sch 2 para 8 CS(MASC) Regs
96 Sch 2 para 9 CS(MASC) Regs
97 Sch 2 para 11 CS(MASC) Regs
98 Sch 2 para 48A CS(MASC) Regs
99 Sch 2 para 10 CS(MASC) Regs
100 Sch 2 paras 8 and 12-15 CS(MASC) Regs the latter as amended by reg 4(6) CS9MA)(no2) Regs 2003
101 Sch 2 para 40 CS(MASC) Regs
102 Sch 2 para 18 CS(MASC) Regs as amemnded by reg 4(7) CS(MA)(No2) Regs 2003
103 Sch 1 Para 16 CS(MASC) Regs
104 Sch 1 para 15 CS(MASC) Regs
105 Sch 1 Para 14B CS(MASC) Regs
106 Sch 2 para 48D CS(MASC) Regs
107 Sch 1 para 9 CS(MASC) Regs
108 Sch 2 para 35 CS(MASC) Regs
109 Sch 2 para 24 CS(MASC) Regs
110 Sch 2 para 22 CS(MASC) Regs
111 Sch 2 para 2 CS(MASC) Regs
112 Sch 2 para 23 CS(MASC) Regs
113 CCS/5310/1995; CCS/3542/1998; Income from rented or leased property; Costs in connection with rented out property
114 Reg 1(2) CS(MASC) Regs; Courses or advanced education
115 Full-time course
116 Regs 7(3)(b) and 26(1)(b)(v) CS(MASC) Regs
117 Sch 1 paras 11 and 12 CS(MACS) Regs; Calculation of student income
118 Reg 1(2) CS(MASC) Regs; Access Fund
119 Sch 1 para 16(3) CS(MASC) Regs
120 Sch 1 para 16(4) CS(MASC) Regs
121 Sch 2 para 20 CS(MASC) Regs
122 Sch 2 para 36 CS(MASC) Regs
123 Voluntary Sector and Environmental Task Force Options
124 Sch 2 para 21 CS(MASC) Regs
125 Regs 7(3)(a) and 26(1)(b)(v) CS(MASC) Regs; Net income when calculating assessable income; Youth Training
126 Sch 1 paras 14 and 16(2) CS(MASC) Regs
127 CCS/13698/1996; CCS/13923/1996
128 Spousal maintenance payment paid to person
129 Sch 2 para 28 CS(MASC) Regs
130 Reg 11(2) CS(MASC) Regs

Chapter 13: Assessable income: Step 3 of the 'old rules' formula
Notes

131 Sch 1 para 15 and Sch 2 para 44 CS(MASC) Regs
132 CCS/4514/1995
133 Sch 2 para 29 CS(MASC) Regs
134 Sch 2 para 31 CS(MASC) Regs
135 Sch 2 para 26 CS(MASC) Regs
136 Sch 2 para 25 CS(MASC) Regs
137 Interest, dividends and capital
138 Sch 1 para 16(5) and (6) CS(MASC) Regs; Interest, dividends and capital
139 Reg 7(4) CS(MASC) Regs
140 Sch 2 para 45 CS(MASC) Regs; CCS/4923/1995
141 Interest, dividends and capital
142 Regs 7(3) and 26(1)(b) CS(MASC) Regs
143 Sch 2 para 19 CS(MASC) Regs; Regular charitable payments
144 R(SB) 53/83; CCS/15/1994
145 Sch 1 para 31 CS(MASC) Regs
146 Sch 2 paras 19 and 20 CS(MASC) Regs
147 Sch 2 para 2 CS(MASC) Regs
148 Sch 2 para 46 CS(MASC) Regs
149 Sch 2 para 17 CS(MASC) Regs
150 Sch 2 para 33 CS(MASC) Regs
151 Sch 2 para 42 CS(MASC) Regs
152 Sch 2 para 32 CS(MASC) Regs
153 Sch 2 para 36 CS(MASC) Regs
154 Sch 2 para 27 CS(MASC) Regs
155 Sch 2 para 48 CS(MASC) Regs
156 Sch 2 para 34 CS(MASC) Regs
157 Sch 2 para 48C CS(MASC) Regs
158 Sch 2 para 48D CS(MASC) Regs
159 Sch 2 para 30 CS(MASC) Regs
160 Sch 2 para 5 CS(MASC) Regs
161 CCS/3510/1997; Police and firefighters disablement pension
162 Sch 2 para 38 CS(MASC) Regs
163 Sch 2 para 47 CS(MASC) Regs
164 Sch 2 para 39 CS(MASC) Regs
165 Sch 2 para 37 CS(MASC) Regs
166 Sch 2 para 3 CS(MASC) Regs
167 Sch 2 para 4 CS(MASC) Regs
168 Sch 2 para 41 CS(MASC) Regs
169 Sch 1 Part IV CS(MASC) Regs
170 Reg 9(2)(c) CS(MASC) Regs
171 Child Income
172 Sch 2 para 28 CS(MASC) Regs
173 Sch 1 paras 7 and 22 CS(MASC) Regs
174 Sch 1 para 23 CS(MASC) Regs
175 Sch 1 para 23 CS(MASC) Regs
176 Sch 1 para 24 CS(MASC) Regs
177 Sch 1 para 21 CS(MASC) Regs
178 Sch 1 para 19 CS(MASC) Regs
179 Sch 1 para 20 CS(MASC) Regs
180 Reg 7(1)(e) and Sch 1 Part V CS(MASC) Regs
181 Sch 1 para 32 CS(MASC) Regs
182 Sch 1 para 26 CS(MASC) Regs; Notional earnings: definition
183 Earnings that are assumed
184 CCS/4912/1998
185 Sch 1 para 27 CS(MASC) Regs
186 CCS/4912/1998; Deprivation of capital: definition
187 CCS/3542/1998
188 Capital which could be acquired
189 Sch 1 para 30 CS(MASC) Regs; Notional capital reduction
190 Sch 1 para 28 CS(MASC) Regs
191 Capital which could be acquired
192 Sch 1 para 29 CS(MASC) Regs
193 Identifying Deprivation
194 R(SB) 38/85; Occurrence of deprivation
195 Occurrence of deprivation
196 CCS/8172/1995; Deprivation of capital definition
197 R(SB) 38/85
198 Timing of the parent disposing of the capital; Reason for the parent disposing of the capital
199 CCS/7967/1995
200 CCS/6/1995
201 Sch 1 para 31 CS(MASC) Regs; Payments to third parties
202 CCS/6/1995
203 CSCS/8/1995; CSCS/1/1996; CCS/8189/1995
204 CCS/13698/1996; CCS/13923/1996
205 Calculating the amount of the income

3. **Calculating assessable income**
206 Sch 1 para 5(3) CSA 1991
207 Reg 26(1)(b)(v) CS(MASC) Regs

Chapter 14

Proposed maintenance: Step 4 of the 'old rules' formula

This chapter covers:
1. What is proposed maintenance (see below)
2. How much is proposed maintenance (p287)
3. The 50 per cent calculation (p289)
4. The additional element calculation (p291)
5. Maximum child maintenance (p296)
6. Both parents are non-resident (p298)
7. More than one person with care (p300)
8. Divided family (p305)
9. More than one non-resident parent (p306)

This chapter contains information relevant to existing cases under the 'old rules'. For calculations under the 'new rules', see Chapter 7.

This chapter should be read in conjunction with calculation sheet 4 in Appendix 3.

1. What is proposed maintenance

'Proposed maintenance' is not a term which is used in the legislation. We use it to describe the amount of child maintenance that, given the maintenance requirement and the assessable income of the parents, the non-resident parent would be expected to pay. There is no specific legal term for this amount; it is already referred to in the legislation as 'the amount of the assessment'. However, the proposed maintenance step is not the end of the maintenance assessment. The protected income calculation still has to be done and this may reduce the amount of child maintenance payable. Therefore a term is needed for this intermediate stage. The CSA uses the phrase 'the non-resident parent's notional assessment'.

Although the proposed maintenance figure may be reduced by the protected income calculation, it will never be increased. No non-resident parent ever pays more than the proposed maintenance figure.

There is a lot of misunderstanding about the way in which the income of a partner of the non-resident parent affects the maintenance assessment. At the protected income stage (see Chapter 15) the partner's income *is* taken into account in order to assess whether the family as a whole can afford the proposed maintenance. However, the partner's income *cannot* increase the assessment above the proposed maintenance which is arrived at using the non-resident parent's net income (see p262). The income of the partner is also used to decide whether s/he can help support their own children (see p255). If the partner objects to providing income details, s/he should consider the option of withholding the information and taking a Category B interim maintenance assessment.

2. How much is proposed maintenance

Proposed maintenance is based on the assessable incomes of both parents. In some situations a deduction rate of 50 per cent assessable income is used and in others a more complex calculation must be carried out. The 50 per cent calculation gives an amount of proposed maintenance which is smaller than the maintenance requirement figure (from step 1). The additional element calculation applies where the parents have higher incomes and the maintenance requirement figure is met. The calculation for proposed maintenance becomes increasingly complex with more complex family situations.

To illustrate the principles of proposed maintenance, we first give an overview of the calculation in Figure 14.1 (see below). To help readers through this step of the formula, we then identify the four situations, beginning with the most straightforward, in which the calculation of proposed maintenance varies. These are set out in the following figures:
- the 50 per cent calculation of proposed maintenance where the parent with care has no assessable income – see Figure 14.2;
- the 50 per cent calculation of proposed maintenance where both parents have assessable income – see Figure 14.3;
- the additional element calculation of proposed maintenance where the parent with care has no assessable income – see Figure 14.4;
- the additional element calculation of proposed maintenance where both parents have assessable income – see Figure 14.5.

These calculations are adapted if both parents are non-resident, or where there is more than one non-resident parent or more than one parent with care.

Chapter 14: Proposed maintenance: Step 4 of the 'old rules' formula
2. How much is proposed maintenance

> Figure 14.1: **Overview of proposed maintenance step**
> There are two alternative calculations:
> - the 50 per cent calculation if the maintenance requirement is not met;
> - the additional element calculation if the maintenance requirement is met.
>
> To decide which to use, first try the 50 per cent calculation:[1]
> - add together both parents' assessable incomes (if the parent with care is on income support or working tax credit, her assessable income is nil);
> - take 50 per cent of the joint assessable income;
> - compare the figure obtained with the maintenance requirement (from step 1 as calculated in Chapter 11).
>
> If 50 per cent of the joint assessable income is less than or equal to the maintenance requirement, then the proposed maintenance is 50 per cent of the non-resident parent's assessable income.[2]
>
> If 50 per cent of joint assessable income is higher than the maintenance requirement, the additional element calculation must be done. This involves two components of proposed maintenance: a basic element and an additional element (see p291).[3] The end result is that the non-resident parent pays less than 50 per cent of his assessable income.

The general rule is that 50 per cent of the parents' assessable income goes towards child maintenance until the maintenance requirement is met.[4] Once the maintenance requirement is met, the non-resident parent continues to pay maintenance. However, only 15, 20 or 25 per cent of his remaining assessable income is paid as maintenance and up to a maximum amount.[5]

Both parents are liable to maintain their child(ren) and, therefore, both their assessable incomes must be taken into account when calculating whether the maintenance requirement has been met. Although the assessable income of the parent with care may reduce the proposed maintenance, she will never end up paying child maintenance herself.

If the assessable income of the non-resident parent is nil, then the proposed maintenance is nil and the minimum payment rules must be considered (see p223). The non-resident parent either pays £5.60 or is exempt. Similarly, if the proposed maintenance is less than £5.60, the non-resident parent pays the minimum payment of £5.60 unless he is exempt. In these cases there is no need to calculate the protected income level as the proposed maintenance cannot be further reduced.

3. The 50 per cent calculation

Once assessable income has been calculated for both parents, the next step is to check whether the 50 per cent calcilation is applicable. If the parent with care has assessable income, see p290.

The parent with care has no assessable income

In most cases the parent with care will have no assessable income – eg, if she is on income support (IS) or working tax credit (WTC).

Figure 14.2: **50 per cent calculation for proposed maintenance where the parent with care has no assessable income**
- Take 50 per cent of the non-resident parent's assessable income;
- compare the figure obtained with the maintenance requirement (from step 1 as calculated in Chapter 11).

If 50 per cent of the non-resident parent's assessable income is less than or equal to the maintenance requirement, then the proposed maintenance is this figure – ie, 50 per cent of his assessable income.[6]

If 50 per cent of the non-resident parent's assessable income is higher than the maintenance requirement, then the additional element calculation is used to obtain proposed maintenance (see Figure 14.4).

It is estimated that four-fifths of all non-resident parents do not meet the maintenance requirement, and in these cases the proposed maintenance calculation ends at this point, with non-resident parents charged 50 per cent of their assessable income.

The protected income calculation must now be done (see Chapter 15).

Example 14.1: The 50 per cent calculation where the parent with care has no assessable income
Anita is on IS and therefore has no assessable income.
The maintenance requirement is £128.59 (see example 11.1).
(a) Bob is living on his own and has assessable income of £56.35 (see example 13.1a). As Anita has no assessable income, the first stage is to take 50 per cent of Bob's assessable income.
50 per cent of Bob's assessable income = 50% x £56.35 = £28.18
This is less than £128.59 (the maintenance requirement) and therefore £28.18 is the proposed maintenance for Carol and David.

(b) Bob is living with Zoe, three stepchildren and his baby son. His assessable income is £101.13 (see example 13.3a).

Chapter 14: Proposed maintenance: Step 4 of the 'old rules' formula
3. The 50 per cent calculation

50 per cent of Bob's assessable income = 50% x £101.13 = £50.57
This is less than £128.59 (the maintenance requirement) and therefore £50.57 is the proposed maintenance.
Note: The maintenance payable may be reduced by the protected income step.

Where the parent with care has assessable income

Even when the parent with care has assessable income, this income does not necessarily affect the proposed maintenance. If, together, the parents do not have enough joint assessable income to meet the maintenance requirement, then the non-resident parent pays half of his own assessable income. This is exactly what he would have paid anyway had the parent with care had no assessable income.

> Figure 14.3: **50 per cent calculation for proposed maintenance where the parent with care has assessable income**
> - Add both parents' assessable incomes to give joint assessable income;
> - take 50 per cent of the joint assessable income;
> - compare the 50 per cent figure with the maintenance requirement (from step 1 as calculated in Chapter 11).
>
> If 50 per cent of the joint assessable income is less than or equal to the maintenance requirement:
> - take 50 per cent of the non-resident parent's own assessable income to give proposed maintenance.
>
> If 50 per cent of joint assessable income is higher than the maintenance requirement, the additional element calculation must be done (see Figure 14.5).

A parent with care's income will not reduce the maintenance she receives unless her notional contribution towards the maintenance requirement *plus* the non-resident parent's proposed maintenance is over the maintenance requirement. The level of the joint assessable income is the deciding factor. The higher the assessable income of a non-resident parent, the sooner the assessable income of the parent with care will reduce the maintenance payable (see p294).

> Example 14.2: **50 per cent calculation where both parents have assessable income**
> Anita is now working full time and has assessable income of £42.41 (see example 13.2a).
> (a) Bob's assessable income is £56.35 (see example 13.1a).
> Anita's assessable income = £42.41
> Joint assessable income = £56.35 + £42.41 = £98.76
> 50 per cent of joint assessable income = 50% x £98.76 = £49.38

Chapter 14: Proposed maintenance: Step 4 of the 'old rules' formula
4. The additional element calculation

This is well below the maintenance requirement of £128.59 (see example 11.1a) and so Bob pays 50 per cent of his own assessable income (assuming the protected income calculation allows it).
Proposed maintenance = 50% x £56.35 = £28.18 a week.
This is the same amount of proposed maintenance as when Anita had no assessable income (see example 14.1a). In this case Anita is earning too much to qualify for WTC, taking home £265 a week. Although this is more than Bob, who takes home £154, her income still does not affect the level of proposed maintenance for David and Carol.
(b) If Bob had net earnings of £360 a week (rather than £160 as in example 13.1a), his assessable income would be £256.35.
Anita's assessable income = £42.41
Bob's assessable income = £256.35
Joint assessable income = £42.41 + £256.35 = £298.76
50 per cent of joint assessable income = 50% x £298.76 = £149.38.
This is above the maintenance requirement of £128.59 and so the additional element calculation would have to be done to calculate the proposed maintenance (see figure 14.5). Anita's assessable income, although still £42.41, would now reduce the proposed maintenance. This is because Bob's assessable income is higher and together they meet the maintenance requirement.

4. The additional element calculation

If the maintenance requirement is met in full by the assessable incomes of the parents, then the non-resident parent is expected to pay an additional amount over and above his contribution to the maintenance requirement. Where the 50 per cent calculation has shown that assessable income more than meets the maintenance requirement, an alternative calculation is used to obtain the proposed maintenance.

Proposed maintenance is composed of a basic element and an additional element. Likewise, the non-resident parent's total assessable income is composed of basic assessable income and additional assessable income.

The basic assessable income contributes towards the basic element at the rate of 50 per cent. The additional assessable income contributes towards the additional element at a lower rate, up to a maximum amount. The deduction rate is 15 per cent if there is one qualifying child, 20 per cent if there are two, and 25 per cent if there are three or more qualifying children in the assessment.[7]

The assessable incomes of both parents are taken into account in calculating the basic proposed maintenance. However, to illustrate the principle of what is a complex calculation, we first address the situation where only the non-resident parent has assessable income.

Chapter 14: Proposed maintenance: Step 4 of the 'old rules' formula
4. The additional element calculation

The parent with care has no assessable income

If 50 per cent of the non-resident parent's assessable income is higher than the maintenance requirement, ignore the 50 per cent figure and continue as in figure 14.4 below.

Where the parent with care has no assessable income, the basic element equals the maintenance requirement.[8] As basic assessable income contributes towards the basic element at the rate of 50 per cent, the non-resident parent must (in order to meet the maintenance requirement) use up assessable income equal to twice the maintenance requirement. Additional assessable income which is not used up in meeting the maintenance requirement contributes towards the additional element at the rate of 15, 20 or 25 per cent.

The non-resident parent thus pays more than the maintenance requirement, but overall less than 50 per cent of his assessable income.

When proposed maintenance has been obtained using the additional element calculation, this figure must be compared with the maximum amount (see p296).

Chapter 14: Proposed maintenance: Step 4 of the 'old rules' formula
4. The additional element calculation

Figure 14.4: **Additional element calculation of proposed maintenance where the parent with care has no assessable income**

To calculate the proposed maintenance where only the non-resident parent has assessable income and the 50 per cent calculation has shown that it more than meets the maintenance requirement:

- multiply the maintenance requirement (the basic element) by two to give the basic assessable income;
- deduct the basic assessable income from the total assessable income to give the additional assessable income;
- take: 15 per cent if there is one qualifying child; or
  20 per cent if there are two qualifying children; or
  25 per cent if there are three or more qualifying children,
  of the additional assessable income to give the additional element;
- add the basic element (the maintenance requirement) to the additional element to give the proposed maintenance.

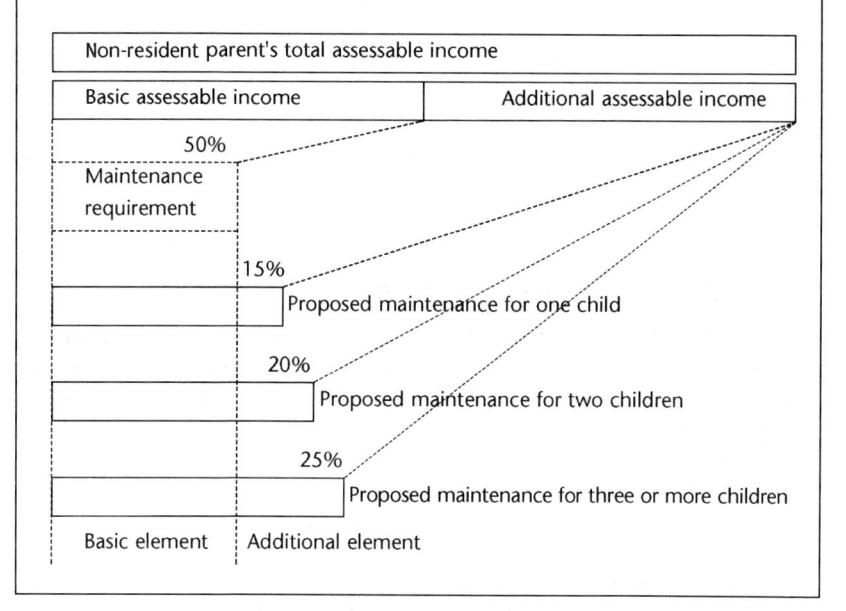

```
| Non-resident parent's total assessable income            |
| Basic assessable income    | Additional assessable income |
       50%
   Maintenance
   requirement
              15%
                  Proposed maintenance for one child
              20%
                  Proposed maintenance for two children
              25%
                  Proposed maintenance for three or more children
   Basic element | Additional element
```

Example 14.3: Additional element calculation where the parent with care has no assessable income

Jeremy has just left his wife, Evie, who has no income of her own other than child benefit. They have four children, Francis (14), Georgina (12), Henry (8) and Isobel (4), who are all living with Evie.

Chapter 14: Proposed maintenance: Step 4 of the 'old rules' formula
4. The additional element calculation

		£
The maintenance requirement is therefore:		
Personal allowances	Evie	55.65
	Francis (14)	42.27
	Georgina (12)	42.27
	Henry (8)	42.47
	Isobel (4)	42.47
Family premium		15.95
Sub-total		240.68
Less child benefit (see p231)		49.65
Maintenance requirement		**191.03**

Jeremy has an assessable income of £600 a week.
  50% x £600 = £300
This is well above the maintenance requirement of £191.03. Therefore, to calculate proposed maintenance, do the additional element calculation:
Basic element = £191.03 (the maintenance requirement)
Basic assessable income = 2 x £191.0 3= £382.06
Additional assessable income = £600 – £382.03 = £217.94
Additional element = £217.94 x 25% = £54.49 (the 25 per cent deduction rate is applicable as there are four qualifying children)
Proposed maintenance = £191.03 + £54.49 = £245.52
Check whether this figure is above the maximum child maintenance payable (see example 14.5).

Where the parent with care has assessable income

Both parents contribute towards the maintenance requirement if they can afford to do so, although in the case of a parent with care this is a notional transaction. We have seen that if the parents together cannot meet the maintenance requirement, the income of the parent with care does not affect the maintenance assessment (see p290).

However, if 50 per cent of the parents' joint assessable income more than meets the maintenance requirement, the parent with care's assessable income reduces the non-resident parent's proposed maintenance. Each parent contributes towards the maintenance requirement in proportion to her/his assessable income. The parent with care's notional contribution towards the maintenance requirement reduces the amount of the non-resident parent's assessable income required to meet that maintenance requirement. Therefore, the non-resident parent begins paying at the lower deduction rate earlier than he otherwise would have done.

The additional element calculation is used to work out the proposed maintenance; the basic element does not now equal the full maintenance requirement, but only the proportion of the maintenance requirement that the

Chapter 14: Proposed maintenance: Step 4 of the 'old rules' formula
4. The additional element calculation

non-resident parent has to contribute.[9] Once the basic element has been calculated, the rest of the calculation is the same as before.

The parent with care's assessable income can reduce the proposed maintenance below the maintenance requirement, but cannot reduce the non-resident parent's proposed maintenance to zero. The non-resident parent still pays at least some contribution towards the maintenance requirement and then a percentage of his additional assessable income.

> Figure 14.5: **Additional element calculation of proposed maintenance where parent with care has assessable income**
>
> To calculate proposed maintenance where both parents have assessable incomes which jointly more than meet the maintenance requirement:
> - add together both parents' assessable incomes to give their joint assessable income;
> - multiply the maintenance requirement by the non-resident parent's assessable income divided by the joint assessable income (ie, the non-resident parent's proportion of the joint assessable income) to give the basic element (ie, the non-resident parent's contribution to the maintenance requirement);
> - multiply the basic element by two to give the basic assessable income;
> - deduct the basic assessable income from the non-resident parent's total assessable income to give his additional assessable income;
> - take: 15 per cent if there is one qualifying child; *or*
>   20 per cent if there are two qualifying children; *or*
>   25 per cent if there are three or more qualifying children,
>   of the additional assessable income to give the additional element;
> - add the basic element to the additional element to give the proposed maintenance.

Example 14.4: Additional element calculation where both parents have assessable incomes

Evie has now taken a paid job. Her exempt income is high as it includes allowances for the four children and a significant mortgage. Although she is earning £26,000 pa, her assessable income is only £70 a week (she is not entitled to any WTC). Jeremy's assessable income is still £600 a week.

The maintenance requirement is still £191.03 (see example 14.3)

Joint assessable income = £70 + £600 = £670

50 per cent of the joint assessable income is £335, which more than meets the maintenance requirement. Therefore, the additional element calculation of proposed maintenance has to be done:

Basic element (the proportion of the maintenance requirement that Jeremy has to pay) =

$£191.03 \times \dfrac{£600}{£670} = £171.07$

Basic assessable income = £171.07 × 2 = £342.14

Chapter 14: Proposed maintenance: Step 4 of the 'old rules' formula
4. The additional element calculation

Additional assessable income = £600 – £342.14 = £257.86
Additional element = £257.86 x 25% = £64.47
Proposed maintenance = £171.07 + £64.47 = £235.54
Check whether this figure is above the maximum child maintenance payable (see example 14.6).

5. Maximum child maintenance

There is an upper limit on the amount of child maintenance payable for a child under the child support formula.[10] No further child maintenance is deducted from assessable income once the maximum is being paid.

When the maximum is being paid under the formula, it is open to the parties to go to court to seek any further maintenance. The courts can consider the issue of further weekly child maintenance in the context of any other arrangements which have been made for the children (see p34).

Like proposed maintenance, maximum child maintenance is composed of a basic element and an additional element. The basic element is the same as the basic element of proposed maintenance, whereas the additional element relates to the number and age of the qualifying children.[11]

Again, like proposed maintenance, the calculation varies slightly if the parent with care has assessable income.

The parent with care has no assessable income

When the parent with care has no assessable income, the basic element of maximum child maintenance equals the maintenance requirement. The maximum amount of child maintenance equals the maintenance requirement plus the additional element.

The additional element equals 1.5 times the total of the income support (IS) personal allowance for each child and the amount of the IS family premium at the basic rate for each child.[12]

Example 14.5: Maximum child maintenance where the person with care has no assessable income

Assuming Evie has no assessable income of her own, the maximum Jeremy would have to pay for the four children, Francis (14), Georgina (12), Henry (8) and Isobel (4), is as follows:
The maintenance requirement is £191.03 (see example 14.3)
The additional element = 1.5 x [(4 x 42.27) + (4 x 15.95)]
= 1.5 x 232.88 = £349.32

Chapter 14: Proposed maintenance: Step 4 of the 'old rules' formula
5. Maximum child maintenance

	£
The basic element	191.03
The additional element	349.32
Maximum child maintenance	540.35

Therefore, in example 14.3, the proposed maintenance of £245.52 is less than the maximum.

In order to pay the maximum amount, Jeremy would have to have an assessable income of (£191.03 x 2) + (£349.32 x 4) = £1779.34 a week. This represents a net income for a single man of between £95,419.48 with no housing costs, and £141,682.32 with maximum housing costs, a year (assuming a journey to work of under 150 miles).

The parent with care has assessable income

The non-resident parent is responsible only for paying the proportion of the maximum child maintenance which corresponds to his proportion of joint assessable income.

The basic element of the maximum child maintenance is the proportion of the maintenance requirement which the non-resident parent must contribute. It is calculated as for the additional element calculation for proposed maintenance – ie:
- *add* together both parents' assessable incomes to give their joint assessable income;
- *multiply* the maintenance requirement by the non-resident parent's assessable income divided by joint assessable income.

To calculate the additional element:
- multiply the total of the IS personal allowance for each child and the family premium for each child by 1.5; *then*
- multiply this figure by the non-resident parent's assessable income divided by the joint assessable income.

The maximum child maintenance equals the basic element plus the additional element.

Alternatively, there is a short cut for this calculation. Multiply the maximum amount as calculated where the parent has no assessable income by the non-resident parent's proportion of the joint assessable income.

Example 14.6: Maximum child maintenance where the parent with care has assessable income

To check whether the proposed maintenance calculated in example 14.4 (£235.54) is above the maximum:

Evie's assessable income = £70

Chapter 14: Proposed maintenance: Step 4 of the 'old rules' formula
5. Maximum child maintenance

Jeremy's assessable income = £600
Joint assessable income = £670
The maintenance requirement = £191.03

Basic element = £191.03 x $\frac{£600}{£670}$ = £171.07 (as in example 14.4)

Additional element = 1.5 ([4 x 42.27] + [4 x15.95]) x $\frac{£600}{£670}$

= £349.32 x $\frac{£600}{£670}$ = £312.82

Maximum child maintenance = basic element plus the additional element = £171.07+ £312.82 = £483.89

(Alternatively, multiply the maximum figure from example 14.5 by Jeremy's proportion of joint assessable income: £540.35 x $\frac{£600}{£670}$ also gives £483.89)

Jeremy therefore pays the proposed maintenance of £235.54.
Evie's income has reduced the assessment by just £9.98.

6. Both parents are non-resident

Where the person with care is not a parent, this usually means that there are two non-resident parents. If an application is made for maintenance from both parents, an assessment is carried out for each non-resident parent. The same maintenance requirement is used in both assessments (see p233).

When calculating the proposed maintenance of each parent, the other non-resident parent's assessable income is used where the parent with care's income would normally be taken into account – ie, to give joint assessable income.[13] In other words, the parents will together contribute towards the maintenance requirement at the rate of 50 per cent of assessable income and, once the maintenance requirement is met, each will pay a lower percentage of their own additional assessable income.

Example 14.7: Proposed maintenance where both parents are non-resident
Zoe is looking after her 17-year-old niece, Rebecca, whose parents have separated. Zoe's income is not taken into account as she is not Rebecca's mother.
The maintenance requirement = £31.09 (see example 11.4)
(a) 50 per cent calculation
Her mother's assessable income = £14.50
Her father's assessable income = £23.90
Joint assessable income = £38.40
50 per cent of joint assessable income = £19.20

Chapter 14: Proposed maintenance: Step 4 of the 'old rules' formula
6. Both parents are non-resident

This is less than the maintenance requirement.
Proposed maintenance from her mother = 50% x £14.50 = £7.25
Proposed maintenance from her father = 50% x £23.90 = £11.95
(b) The additional element calculation
Her mother's assessable income = £52
Her father's assessable income = £84
Joint assessable income = £136
50 per cent of joint assessable income = £68
This is more than the maintenance requirement of £31.09.
Therefore the additional element calculation has to be done as in Figure 14.5. The 15 per cent deduction rate is used as Rebecca is the only qualifying child in the assessment.

Mother's proposed maintenance is:

Basic element = £31.09 x $\dfrac{£52}{£136}$ = £11.89

Basic assessable income = £11.89 x 2 = £23.78
Additional assessable income = £52 − £23.78 = £28.22
Additional element = £28.22 x 15% = £4.23
Proposed maintenance from mother = £11.89 + £4.23 = £16.12

Father's proposed maintenance is:

Basic element = £31.09 x $\dfrac{£84}{£136}$ = £19.20

Basic assessable income = £19.20 x 2 = £38.40
Additional assessable income = £84 − £38.40 = £45.60
Additional element = £45.60 x 15% = £6.84
Proposed maintenance from father = £19.20 + £6.84 = £26.04

Note that the basic proposed maintenance from both parents is the maintenance requirement – ie, £11.89 + £19.20 = £31.09

(c) An application is made for maintenance from the mother only. The maintenance requirement is therefore halved (see p232) to £15.55.

With assessable income of £14.50, the mother still cannot meet the maintenance requirement and therefore she pays 50% x £14.50 = £7.25. This is the same as in (a).

With assessable income of £52, the mother can now meet the maintenance requirement on her own (50% x £52 = £26). The basic element is the maintenance requirement of £15.55.

Basic assessable income = £15.55 x 2 = £31.10
Additional assessable income = £52 − £31.10 = £20.90
Additional element = £20.90 x 15% = £3.14
Proposed maintenance = £15.55 + £3.14 = £18.69

The total proposed maintenance for a child with two non-resident parents is the same as if there were one non-resident parent (with assessable income equal to the joint assessable income of the two non-resident parents) and a parent with care with no assessable income. However, with two non-resident parents the total liability is split between the parents in proportion to their assessable incomes.

If an application is made for maintenance from both parents and the CSA does not have the information about the other parent's income within the fortnight given to provide it (see p92), it is assumed that this second non-resident parent has no assessable income when calculating the first non-resident parent's proposed maintenance.[14] When this information is available, a fresh assessment will be carried out.[15]

The regulations do not distinguish between non-resident parents who live separately from one another and those who, although they are no longer living with their child, still live together as a couple. Therefore, in the case of a couple being assessed, two separate assessments would be carried out following the same basic rules up to this stage (ie, net income and exempt income would be calculated separately for each parent), even though between the two assessments the same housing costs would be included twice. If Rebecca's parents were still living together, the calculation of proposed maintenance would still follow that in example 14.7.

The person with care who is not a parent of the qualifying children may be looking after children who have different parents. For example, a grandmother may be looking after two grandchildren, one the child of her son and the other the child of her daughter. This involves two maintenance requirements. The proposed maintenance steps for the two children are completely separate and each can be carried out for both the non-resident parents of each child (see above). In theory, the grandmother could receive child maintenance from four non-resident parents.

7. More than one person with care

'More than one person with care' does not refer to the situation where a child is looked after for part of the time by one person and the rest of the time by another; we call that 'shared care' (see Chapter 16).

Here we cover the situation where different children of an non-resident parent are being looked after by different people. This includes both where the non-resident parent has two or more families by different women with whom he does not live and where the children of one family are split between two carers, perhaps with one child living with the mother and the other with grandparents. The non-resident parent is equally liable to maintain all the qualifying children and must therefore pay child maintenance to each of the persons with care who makes an application.[16]

The regulations describe this as 'multiple applications relating to a non-resident parent'. We have not used this phrase, as 'multiple applications' is also used to describe the situation when more than one application is made for child

Chapter 14: Proposed maintenance: Step 4 of the 'old rules' formula
7. More than one person with care

maintenance for the same child. More than one person with care involves applications for maintenance for *different* children from the *same* non-resident parent.

Sharing out the proposed maintenance

If the children of a non-resident parent are in the care of two or more people and a maintenance application has been made by more than one of those persons with care, the proposed maintenance has to be shared between the persons with care.[17] This is achieved by dividing the non-resident parent's assessable income between the maintenance assessments in the same proportions as their maintenance requirements.[18] Where an allowance for a pre-April 1993 property settlement has been included in exempt income (see p249), an adjustment is made when apportioning the assessable income (see below). The proposed maintenance step is then carried out separately for each application using the relevant portion of assessable income.

Only one protected income calculation (see Chapter 15) is carried out for the non-resident parent, using the total amount of proposed maintenance for all the assessments.[19] Where the total maintenance payable to all the persons with care is less than £5.60 (see p223), the minimum payment is divided between the persons with care in proportion to the maintenance requirements.[20]

Example 14.8: 50 per cent calculation where there is more than one parent with care

Wayne is the father of Yvonne (12) and Veronica (10) who live with Zoe. Zoe has no assessable income. She has been receiving £20 a week child maintenance from Wayne. Zoe's maintenance requirement for Yvonne and Veronica is £92.80 (see example 11.3a). Wayne's girlfriend Lauren has recently had his baby, Keith. Wayne is not living with Lauren who is claiming income support (IS) as a single parent.

Lauren's maintenance requirement is:

		£
Personal allowances	Lauren	55.65
	Keith	42.27
Family premium		15.95
Sub-total		113.87
Less child benefit		16.50
Total maintenance requirement		**97.37**

Joint maintenance requirement is £92.80 + 97.37 = £190.17

Wayne's total assessable income is £40 a week.
For calculating Zoe's child maintenance, Wayne's assessable income =

$£40 \times \dfrac{£92.80}{£190.17} = £19.52$

Chapter 14: Proposed maintenance: Step 4 of the 'old rules' formula
7. More than one person with care

For calculating Lauren's child maintenance, Wayne's assessable income =

$£40 \times \dfrac{£97.37}{£190.17} = £20.48$ (or $£40 - £19.52 = £20.48$)

Proposed maintenance: 50 per cent assessable income
For Zoe: 50% x £19.5 2= £9.76
For Lauren: 50% x £20.48 = £10.24

Subject to the protected income calculation, Wayne is still paying £20 in total, but divided between the two parents with care.

When Lauren makes an application for child maintenance, Zoe's assessment will be reduced from £20 to £9.76 a week. Zoe receives less than half the maintenance paid by Wayne, although she has two of his children and Lauren has only one younger child (see below).

By dividing the non-resident parent's assessable income in proportion to the different maintenance requirements, persons with care responsible for a larger number of children will usually receive a greater amount of child maintenance. However, in example 14.8 (see above), Zoe's maintenance requirement is smaller than would usually be expected for two children. She is receiving only half of certain allowances in the maintenance requirement, as her other child, Scott, has a different non-resident father (see example 11.3).

The division in the proposed maintenance occurs only if both of the persons with care involved actually make an application for child maintenance from the same non-resident parent.[21]

Where one assessment is already in force when the second application involving the same non-resident parent is made (eg, when his second marriage breaks down) the first assessment is reduced from the date the assessment to the second person with care takes effect (see p388).[22]

Where there is a pre-April 1993 property settlement

Before dividing the non-resident parent's assessable income between the persons with care, any allowance for a pre-April 1993 property settlement (see p249) is added on to the assessable income.[23] Once this has been apportioned, the property settlement allowance (if any) relevant to that person with care is deducted from her portion of assessable income.

Example 14.9: More than one parent with care and a property settlement allowance

The situation is as in example 14.8 except that Wayne has an allowance of £20 included in his exempt income in recognition of the capital settlement he made to Zoe at the time of their divorce in 1987.

Assessable income to be apportioned = £40 + £20 = £60

For Lauren's child maintenance, Wayne's assessable income =

$£60 \times \dfrac{£97.37}{£190.17} = £30.72$

Proposed maintenance for Lauren = 50% x £30.72 = £15.36

For Zoe's child maintenance, Wayne's assessable income =

$(£60 \times \dfrac{£92.80}{£190.17}) - £20 = £9.28$

Proposed maintenance for Zoe = 50% x £9.28 = £4.64

(The minimum payment of £5.60 applies only where the total payments due from an non-resident parent to all persons with care are less than £5.60.)

Again, Wayne continues to pay £20 a week in total, although Zoe sees her maintenance reduced from £20 to £4.64 when Lauren applies to the CSA.

The additional element calculation

The additional element calculation of proposed maintenance when there is more than one person with care is done in the same way as when there is only one person with care, except that a proportion of the non-resident parent's assessable income is substituted for his total assessable income.

Example 14.10: Additional element calculation where there is more than one person with care

Jeremy has left his wife, Evie, who has no income of her own. Of their four children, Francis (14), Georgina (12), Henry (8) and Isobel (4), the three youngest are living with Evie, but Francis is living with Jeremy's brother and sister-in-law. Jeremy has an assessable income of £600 a week.

The income of Jeremy's brother is irrelevant as he is not Francis' parent. Francis now has two non-resident parents who are liable to maintain him. Evie is now a non-resident parent in respect of Francis, but as she is on IS, she has no assessable income. Because she has children living with her, she is exempt from the deductions from IS.

Jeremy must pay his brother child maintenance for Francis as well as paying Evie child maintenance for Georgina, Henry and Isobel. Both the brother and Evie have made applications for child maintenance.

Evie: the maintenance requirement:

		£
Personal allowances	Evie	55.65
	Georgina (12)	42.27
	Henry (8)	42.27
	Isobel (4)	42.27
Family premium		15.95
Sub-total		198.41
Less child benefit		38.60
Total maintenance requirement		159.81

Chapter 14: Proposed maintenance: Step 4 of the 'old rules' formula
7. More than one person with care

Francis: the maintenance requirement:		£
Personal allowance	Adult (half)	27.83
	Francis (14)	42.27
Family premium		15.95
Sub-total		86.05
Less child benefit		16.50
Total maintenance requirement		**69.55**

(The adult personal allowance is halved since Francis, the only qualifying child in the assessment, is 14 years old – see p230.)

Joint maintenance requirement = £159.81 + £69.55 = £229.36

Jeremy's £600 of assessable income has to be split between the two assessments in proportion to their maintenance requirements.

Evie's child maintenance

Jeremy's assessable income = £159.81 x $\dfrac{£600}{£229.36}$ = £418.06

Proposed maintenance = 50% x £418.06 = £209.03

This is above the maintenance requirement of £159.81; therefore the additional element calculation must be done (as in Figure 14.4):

Basic assessable income = £159.81 x 2 = £319.62
Additional assessable income = £418.06 – £319.62 = £98.44
Additional element = £98.44 x 25% = £24.61
Proposed maintenance = £159.81 + £24.61 = £184.42

When Francis leaves home, Evie's maintenance falls from £245.52 a week (see example 14.3) to £184.42.

Note that if Evie had assessable income, then the additional element calculation would follow Figure 14.5, using £418.06 as Jeremy's assessable income.

Child maintenance for Francis

Jeremy's assessable income = £69.55 x $\dfrac{£600}{£229.36}$ = £181.94

Proposed maintenance = 50% x £181.94 = £90.97

This is above the maintenance requirement of £69.55; therefore:

Basic assessable income = £69.55 x 2 = £139.10
Additional assessable income = £181.94 – £139.10 = £42.84
Additional element = £42.84 x 15% = £6.43
Proposed maintenance = £69.55 + £6.43 = £75.98

Jeremy is paying £75.98 to his brother and £184.42 to Evie, a total of £260.40. This is £14.88 more than he paid to Evie when the four children were living together. The non-resident parent usually ends up paying more in total when there are two or more applications. This is because he is paying a larger amount of his assessable income at the 50 per cent rate, as he now has two or more maintenance requirements to meet.

Chapter 14: Proposed maintenance: Step 4 of the 'old rules' formula
8. Divided family

8. Divided family

We use the term 'divided family' to cover the situation where some children of a family are in the care of the mother and the others in the care of the father. This could involve two separate maintenance applications and assessments. If only one of the parents applies for maintenance, then only that application will be assessed. The calculations do not involve any variation from the basic formula.

This is not the same situation as where the care of the same child(ren) is shared between the parents (see Chapter 16).

Example 14.11: Two proposed maintenance calculations for a divided family
Carol (now 15) does not like her stepfather, Joe, and decides that she wants to live with Bob and Zoe's family – Yvonne (14), Veronica (12), Scott (5) and Ricky (1). David (10) is still living with Anita and Joe.
Therefore, Anita is the non-resident parent for Carol and Bob is the non-resident parent for David.
Maintenance requirement for Carol (15) = £69.55
Maintenance requirement for David (10) = £97.37
Although Carol is older, her maintenance requirement is lower as the carer element is halved because she is over 14.
Anita's exempt income (housing costs as in example 12.3b) = £251.65
(Anita's exempt income is as in example 9.3b but without the £42.27 for Carol)
Anita's assessable income = £270 (net income) – £251.65 = £18.35
Bob's exempt income (see example 12.7) = £180.01
Bob's assessable income = £260 (net income) – £180.01 = £79.99
Joint assessable income = £18.35 + £79.99 = £98.34
50 per cent of joint assessable income = £98.34 x 50% = £49.17
The 50 per cent joint assessable income figure (£49.17) is lower than the maintenance requirement for David (£97.37) and that for Carol (£69.55).
Proposed maintenance from Bob = 50% x £79.99 = £40.00
Proposed maintenance from Anita = 50% x £18.35 = £9.18
The protected income calculation (see example 15.8) shows that both Anita and Bob can afford these amounts. Therefore Bob in effect pays Anita: £40.00 – £9.18 = £30.82 a week.
If either or both of the maintenance requirements had been lower than 50 per cent joint assessable income, then the proposed maintenance would have been obtained using the additional element calculation (see Figure 14.5).

Chapter 14: Proposed maintenance: Step 4 of the 'old rules' formula
9. More than one non-resident parent

9. More than one non-resident parent

A person with care may be looking after children of different non-resident parents. Here we look at the situation where the person with care is a parent of all the qualifying children. The situation where the person with care is not the parent of the qualifying child(ren) is dealt with on p298 – ie, both parents are non-resident.

If a parent with care is looking after children of different non-resident parents and applies for maintenance from more than one non-resident parent, then more than one maintenance assessment has to be done. If the parent with care has no assessable income, the two (or more) assessments will not alter from the basic formula.

Example 14.12: Proposed maintenance from more than one non-resident parent where the parent with care has no assessable income

Zoe has applied for maintenance from her ex-husband, Wayne, for Yvonne (14) and Veronica (12), and from Terence for Scott (5). She is living with Bob, and has no income of her own other than child benefit. This means that her net income is nil and therefore her assessable income is nil.

Child maintenance from Wayne:

Step 1: Maintenance requirement = £85.84 (see example 11.3b)

Step 2: Exempt income:

Wayne, Zoe's ex-husband, lives on his own in a rented flat. His rent is £65 a week, but he receives £2.77 a week in housing benefit.

	£
Personal allowance	55.65
Housing costs	65.00
Total exempt income	**120.65**

Step 3: Assessable income:

Total net income	160.00	(net earnings)
Less exempt income	120.65	
Assessable income	**39.35**	

Step 4: Proposed maintenance: 50% x £39.35 = £19.68

This is below the maintenance requirement of £85.84.

Therefore the proposed maintenance is £19.68.

(You may remember that Wayne had a son with Lauren. However, she has now married Sean and moved to Eire where the CSA has no jurisdiction.)

Child maintenance from Terence:

Step 1: Maintenance requirement = £67.03 (see example 11.3a)

Step 2: Exempt income:

Terence is married to Dipa and, although they have three children, only Rana, 17 and still at school, counts as dependent. They have a mortgage of £34.18 a week. Dipa receives

Chapter 14: Proposed maintenance: Step 4 of the 'old rules' formula
9. More than one non-resident parent

carer's allowance for looking after her mother, but this is not enough income to support half of Rana. They get working tax credit of £19.42 and £52.21 child tax credit.

		£	
Personal allowance	Terence	55.65	
	Rana (17)	42.27	
Family premium		15.95	
Housing costs		34.18	
Total exempt income		148.05	
Step 3: Assessable income:		190.21	(net earnings)
		19.42	WTC
Total net income		209.63	
Less exempt income		148.05	
Assessable income		*61.58*	

Step 4: Proposed maintenance: 50% x £61.58 = £30.79
This is below the maintenance requirement of £67.03.
Therefore the proposed maintenance for Scott is £30.79
The protected income calculations now have to be done to see whether Wayne and Terence can afford these amounts (see example 15.5).

Where the parent with care has assessable income

If the parent with care has assessable income and makes an application for child maintenance from more than one non-resident father, then a proportion of her assessable income is taken into account for each of the assessments. Her assessable income is divided between the maintenance assessments in proportion to the maintenance requirements.[24] This apportioning will only happen if an application is made for maintenance from more than one non-resident parent.

Example 14.13: More than one non-resident parent where parent with care has assessable income

Jeremy left his wife, Evie, when he discovered that her youngest child, Isobel (4) was not his daughter. Evie is also looking after his three children, Francis (14), Georgina (12) and Henry (8). Evie decided to apply for child maintenance from Isobel's father, Max, as well as from Jeremy.

Maintenance requirement for three eldest:		£	
Personal allowances	Evie	27.83	(half of 55.65)
	Francis (14)	42.27	
	Georgina (12)	42.27	
	Henry (8)	42.27	
Family premium		7.98	(half of 15.95)
Sub-total		162.62	
Less child benefit		38.60	

307

Chapter 14: Proposed maintenance: Step 4 of the 'old rules' formula
9. More than one non-resident parent

Total maintenance requirement		124.02
Maintenance requirement for Isobel:		£
Personal allowances	Evie	27.83 (half of 55.65)
	Isobel (4)	42.27
Family premium		7.98 (half of 15.95)
Sub-total		78.08
Less child benefit		11.05
Total maintenance requirement		67.03

Joint maintenance requirements = £124.02 + £67.03 = £191.05

Evie's total assessable income is £70. This has to be shared between the two assessments in proportion to the maintenance requirements.

Proposed maintenance from Max: 50 per cent calculation

Evie's assessable income used in this assessment = £70 x $\dfrac{£67.03}{£191.05}$ = £24.56

Max's assessable income is £42.50

Max and Evie's joint assessable income = £24.56 + £42.50 = £67.06

50% x £67.06 = £33.53

This is less than the maintenance requirement of £67.03

Therefore, proposed maintenance is 50 per cent of Max's own assessable income: 50% x £42.50 = £21.25

Proposed maintenance from Jeremy: additional element calculation

Evie's total assessable income is £70

Her assessable income used in this assessment = £70 x $\dfrac{£124.02}{£191.05}$ = £45.44

Jeremy's assessable income is now £235

Jeremy and Evie's joint assessable income = £45.44 + £235 = £280.44

50% x £280.44 = £140.22

This is larger than the maintenance requirement of £124.02 and therefore an additional element calculation has to be done:

Basic element = £124.02 x $\dfrac{£235}{£280.44}$ = £103.92

Basic assessable income = £103.92 x 2 = £207.84

Additional assessable income = £235 − £207.84 = £27.16

Additional element = £27.16 x 25% = £6.79

Proposed maintenance = £103.92 + £6.79 = £110.71

Subject to the protected income stage, Evie will receive £21.25 from Max and £110.71 from Jeremy.

Chapter 14: Proposed maintenance: Step 4 of the 'old rules' formula
Notes

Notes

2. How much is proposed maintenance
1 Sch 1 para 2(1) CSA 1991
2 Sch 1 para 2(2) CSA 1991
3 Sch 1 para 2(3) CSA 1991
4 Sch 1 para 2 CSA 1991; reg 5 CS(MASC) Regs
5 Sch 1 para 4 CSA 1991; reg 6 CS(MASC) Regs

3. The 50 per cent calculation
6 Sch 1 para 2(2) CSA 1991

4. The additional element calculation
7 Sch 1 para 4(1) CSA 1991; reg 6(1) CS(MASC) Regs
8 Sch 1 para 3 CSA 1991
9 Sch 1 para 3 CSA 1991

5. Maximum child maintenance
10 Sch 1 para 4(2) CSA 1991
11 Sch 1 para 4(3) CSA 1991
12 Reg 6(2) CS(MASC) Regs

6. Both parents are non-resident
13 Reg 19(2) CS(MASC) Regs
14 Reg 19(3) CS(MASC) Regs
15 Reg 19(4) CS(MASC) Regs

7. More than one person with care
16 Reg 22(5) CS(MASC) Regs
17 Reg 22(1) CS(MASC) Regs
18 Reg 22(2) CS(MASC) Regs
19 Reg 22(3) CS(MASC) Regs
20 Reg 22(4) CS(MASC) Regs
21 Reg 22(1)(a) CS(MASC) Regs
22 Reg 22(1)(b) and (2A) CS(MASC) Regs
23 Reg 22(2) CS(MASC) Regs

9. More than one non-resident parent
24 Reg 23(4) CS(MASC) Regs

Chapter 15

Protected income: Step 5 of the 'old rules' formula

This chapter covers:
1. What is protected income (below)
2. Basic protected income (p313)
3. Total protected income (p315)
4. What is the maintenance payable (p317)
5. Change of circumstances (p321)

> This chapter contains information relevant to existing cases under the 'old rules'. For calculation under the 'new rules', see Chapter 7.

This chapter should be read in conjunction with calculation sheet 5 in Appendix 3.

1. What is protected income

Protected income is income which cannot be used for paying child maintenance;[1] to this extent, the non-resident parent's needs take first priority. At the end of the protected income calculation, the amount of maintenance payable will be known. It will either be the proposed maintenance figure or a reduced amount. The non-resident parent never ends up paying more than the proposed maintenance. This step should be carried out for all non-resident parents. The only time is does not apply is where the proposed maintenance is £5.60 or less (see p223).

There are two forms of protection for non-resident parents; one prevents them having to pay an excessive proportion of their own income as child maintenance, and the other considers the needs of the whole family.

Thirty per cent cap

No non-resident parent has to pay more than 30 per cent of his net income (see p262).[2] His partner's income is ignored. If the proposed maintenance is greater

Chapter 15: Protected income: Step 5 of the 'old rules' formula
1. What is protected income

than this, it will be reduced to 30 per cent of net income. In other words, 70 per cent net income is a protected level of income; all non-resident parents (except a few of those making the minimum payment) are left with at least 70 per cent of their own net income. This applies even where a non-resident parent is paying more than one CSA assessment (see p320). Also, if a non-resident parent is paying maintenance for other children under a court order, whether inside or outside the UK, this can be deducted from net income at this point (see p312).[3]

> *Example 15.1*
> (a) Bob is living with his parents, and is liable to pay maintenance for Carol and David. His net earnings are £160 a week.
> Step 1 maintenance requirement: £128.59 (see example 11.1a)
> Step 2 exempt income (personal allowance): £55.65
> Step 3 assessable income: £160 – £55.65 = £104.35
> Step 4 proposed maintenance: 50 per cent of £104.35 = £52.18 (less than the maintenance requirement)
> Step 5 protected income: 30 per cent of £160 = £48.00
> The maintenance is therefore reduced to £48.00, before proceeding with the rest of the protected income step.
> (b) Two years later, Bob is living with Zoe and her four children. His net income is £260 (see example 13.3a) and the proposed maintenance is £50.57 (see example 14.1b).
> 30% x £260 = £78
> The proposed maintenance is less than 30 per cent net income and therefore remains at £50.57.

Even where the proposed maintenance has been capped at 30 per cent net income, the second protected income calculation is carried out, as the maintenance payable may be further reduced. When carrying out this second calculation, substitute the capped maintenance for proposed maintenance where the latter is more than 30 per cent net income.

Total protected income

This second part of the protected income calculation is intended to prevent the non-resident parent and his family being left below the income support (IS) level as a result of paying child maintenance.[4] The 'family' is the same as that used for means-tested benefits – ie, the non-resident parent, his heterosexual partner and any children living in the same household (see p32 for a detailed definition).

What is total family income

'Total family income' includes the incomes of all members of the non-resident parent's family (see above).[5] The regulations and the assessment notification call

311

Chapter 15: Protected income: Step 5 of the 'old rules' formula
1. What is protected income

total family income 'disposable income'. We do not use this term at this stage as disposable income is also used to specify the income remaining after proposed maintenance has been paid.

Income for total family income purposes is calculated in the same way as net income (see Chapter 13) except that:[6]
- child benefit is included in full as income;
- child tax credit is included in full as income, whether it is payable to the non-resident parent or his partner;
- part of payments under a mortgage protection insurance policy which exceed the mortgage interest repayments are disregarded; *and*
- with the exception of child maintenance, which is counted in full as the parent's income, the income of any child is included as income up to the amount of the personal allowance for that child and any disabled child premium included in the protected income calculation. As at exempt income stage, children's earnings and the first £10 a week of other income are disregarded.

Child maintenance paid

Where a non-resident parent or his partner is paying maintenance for a child under a court order where an application to the CSA cannot be made (see p44), the amount of that payment is deducted from total family income.[7] The effect is to protect the payments under the court order at the possible expense of the proposed maintenance resulting from the CSA application. This certainly applies where the person with care receiving the maintenance under the court order is not the parent of the child or where she is not receiving one of the specified benefits (see p43). Arguably, it also applies where a parent with care on benefit has refused to make an application to the CSA (eg, to preserve the court order) and the non-resident parent is now being assessed for his liability to maintain other children. It also applies where the non-resident parent or his partner is paying any child maintenance due under a court order made outside Great Britain.[8] However, no account is taken of voluntary payments, whether made in this country or abroad. In the former situation, the non-resident parent should consider making an application to the CSA as he may be better off with two CSA assessments.

Example 15.2: Total family income

The proposed maintenance from Bob to Anita for Carol and David is £50.57 (see example 14.1b). Can he afford it?

Bob is living with Zoe and four children – Yvonne (14), Veronica (12), Scott (4) and Ricky (baby). Bob has net earnings of £260 (see example 13.3a). Zoe receives weekly maintenance of £20 for Yvonne and Veronica, child tax credit (CTC) £104.53 and child benefit of £49.65.

	£
Earnings (net)	260.00
Maintenance for Yvonne and Veronica	20.00
Child tax credit	104.53
Child benefit	49.65
Total family income	*434.18*

What is total protected income

Total protected income is the level below which the non-resident parent's or second family's income must not fall. To make the calculation more manageable, we have separated the total protected income level into basic protected income (see below) and additional protected income (see p315).

The basic protected income is based on IS rates, and it includes personal allowances, premiums, an amount towards high travel-to-work costs, housing costs for all members of the non-resident parent's family, and £30 as a margin above IS. The family is allowed additional protected income of 15 per cent of any family income over and above the basic protected level.

Maintenance payable

The total protected income level is compared with the family's income remaining were the proposed maintenance, or capped maintenance if it is lower, to be paid. If the family's income would be brought below the total protected income level by paying the proposed maintenance, the maintenance due is reduced. The child maintenance is then payable at an amount which would leave the family with disposable income equal to the protected income level.[9] However, the maintenance due cannot be reduced to less than the minimum payment[10] unless the non-resident parent is exempt (see p223).

If the family would have income remaining over the protected income level after paying the proposed maintenance, then the non-resident parent is due to pay the proposed maintenance, or the capped maintenance if that is lower. In other words, the non-resident parent pays the *lowest* of:
- 30 per cent of his net income; *or*
- the amount which would leave his family with disposable income equal to the total protected level; *or*
- the proposed maintenance from step 4.

2. Basic protected income

Basic protected income includes income support (IS) personal allowances and any relevant premiums for all the members of the family. See Appendix 2 for the qualifying conditions and 2004/05 rates of the premiums.

Chapter 15: Protected income: Step 5 of the 'old rules' formula
2. Basic protected income

Basic protected income is calculated as follows:[11]
- the amount of the IS personal allowance for someone aged 25 or more (£55.65) *or* if the non-resident parent has a partner, the IS personal allowance for a couple both aged 18 or over (£); *plus*
- for each child in the family, the amount of the IS personal allowance for a child (£42.27);* *plus*
- the amount of any IS premiums for which the conditions are satisfied* (note that, unlike at exempt income stage, pensioner premiums are included); *plus*
- housing costs for the whole family (see below); *plus*
- council tax liability less any council tax benefit (CTB – see p315); *plus*
- an allowance towards high travel-to-work costs of a non-resident parent (see p315); *plus*
- a standard margin of £30.

*A proportion of the full rate of the personal allowances and any related premiums will be used if a child lives in the household for between two and six nights a week (see Chapter 15). The lone parent rate of family premium is not used in the calculation.[12] The enhanced disability premium (adult and child) and bereavement premium are also not included.

Housing costs

The rules for assessing housing costs are the same as those used at the exempt income stage (see p243),[13] except that:
- if there is a mortgage, only interest payments are allowed;[14]
- if the non-resident parent is living as a non-dependant in someone else's house, an amount is included as housing costs (see below);[15]
- excessive housing costs are now the higher of £80 or half the total family income.[16] Housing costs will be restricted to this figure unless the non-resident parent is exempt from that rule – eg, because the family includes a child (see p247).

The non-resident parent is a non-dependant

A non-resident parent may be a non-dependant where he lives in a household with people who are not 'family' (see p32). He is *not* a non-dependant if he, or a partner, is:[17]
- a co-owner or joint tenant of the home;
- employed by a charitable or voluntary body as a resident carer;
- liable to make a commercial payment in order to live in the home – it will not be considered a commercial arrangement if payments are made to a close relative in the household; a close relative is a parent, son, daughter (including step-relatives and in-laws), brother and sister, and any of their partners.

The weekly amount to be included in protected income is:[18]

Circumstances of the non-resident parent
Working 16 hours or more a week and with a gross income* of:

	£
£308 or more	47.75
£247-307.99	43.50
£186-246.99	38.20
£144-185.99	23.35
£97-143.99	17.00
Under £97	7.40
All those not working 16 hours a week	7.40

* When calculating gross income, disability living allowance/attendance allowance is ignored.[19]

Council tax

Where the non-resident parent is the only person, other than a partner, who is liable to pay council tax in respect of the home for which housing costs are included, the weekly council tax (less any CTB) is included in basic protected income. However, if there are other people resident in the home, the amount of council tax included is either:[20]
- the weekly liability divided by the number of liable people; *or*
- the weekly amount actually paid by the non-resident parent where he is required to pay more than his share because another liable person has defaulted.

Where the non-resident parent lives in Northern Ireland, liability for rates replaces council tax. Likewise, if the person with care has applied to the CSA (Northern Ireland) but the non-resident parent lives in Great Britain, council tax is used.[21]

High travel-to-work costs

This allowance applies for non-resident parents who travel more than 150 miles a week to and from work.[22] The allowance is calculated in exactly the same way as at exempt income stage (see p253). It does not apply to partners.

3. Total protected income

In order to obtain total protected income, additional protected income has to be calculated. To do this, basic protected income must be compared with total family income.

Chapter 15: Protected income: Step 5 of the 'old rules' formula
3. Total protected income

Where the total family income *exceeds* the basic protected income, an addition is made to the basic protected income.

Deduct the basic protected income from the total family income to give the excess family income. The additional protected income equals 15 per cent of this excess family income.[23] This figure is added to basic protected income to give total protected income.

Where the total family income is *below* the basic protected income, there is no additional protected income. Any payment of child maintenance will bring the family's disposable income below the protected income level. Therefore, the non-resident parent will either pay the minimum amount (£5.50) or be exempt from paying altogether (see p223).

Example 15.3: Total protected income

(a) The situation is as for example 15.1(a), with Bob living with his parents. He is contributing towards the household but is not a co-owner of the home, nor liable to pay council tax. He travels less than 150 miles a week to and from work.

	£
Basic protected income:	
Personal allowance	55.65
Housing costs (as a non-dependant)	23.35
Margin	30.00
Basic protected income	**109.00**
Additional protected income:	
Total family income	160.00
Less basic protected income	109.00
Excess family income	51.00

Additional protected income 15% x $\dfrac{£51.00}{£7.65}$

Total protected income:	
Basic protected income	109.00
Plus additional protected income	7.65
Total protected income	**116.65**

(b) Two years later, Bob lives with Zoe and the situation is the same as for example 15.2. Their rent is £45 a week and the council tax liability is £1,050.92 a year. Bob and Zoe are not entitled to housing benefit or CTB.

		£
Basic protected income:		
Personal allowances	Couple	87.30
	Yvonne (14)	42.47
	Veronica (12)	42.27
	Scott (4)	42.27
	Ricky (baby)	42.27
Family premium		15.95
Housing costs		45.00

Chapter 15: Protected income: Step 5 of the 'old rules' formula
4. What is the maintenance payable

Council tax liability		20.21
Margin		30.00
Basic protected income		**367.54**
Total family income (from example 15.2)		**434.18**
Additional protected income:		
Total family income		434.18
Less basic protected income		367.54
Excess family income		66.64
Additional protected income	15% x £66.64	**10.00**
Total protected income:		
Basic protected income		367.54
Plus additional protected income		10.00
Total protected income		**377.54**

4. What is the maintenance payable

There are two methods of calculating the maintenance payable. We cover first the full logic of the step and then a short cut.

The family's disposable income which would remain after paying child maintenance, is obtained by subtracting the proposed maintenance (Step 4) from the total family income. If the proposed maintenance has been capped at 30 per cent net income (see p310), this capped amount is used instead of the proposed maintenance.

If the disposable income is *higher* than the total protected income, the parent can afford to pay the full proposed/capped maintenance. Maintenance payable is the proposed/capped maintenance figure. Where the proposed maintenance has been capped, it cannot be increased back to the originally proposed level.

If the disposable income is initially *below* the total protected income, the maintenance payable is reduced until the disposable income equals the total protected income.[24] Therefore, the maintenance payable is the total family income minus the total protected income.

The minimum payment rule still applies (see p223).[25]

The alternative way of arriving at the maintenance payable is to cut out the disposable income step and in all cases to deduct total protected income from total family income to give an alternative proposed maintenance. This is compared with proposed maintenance from Step 4 and also 30 per cent of net income; the non-resident parent pays whichever figure is smallest.

317

Chapter 15: Protected income: Step 5 of the 'old rules' formula
4. What is the maintenance payable

Example 15.4: Maintenance payable

(a) The proposed maintenance from Bob to Anita for Carol and David has been capped at £48.00 (see example 15.1a) and Bob's total protected income is £116.65 (see example 15.3a).

	£
Total family income	160.00
Less capped maintenance	48.00
Disposable income would be	**112.00**

As this is below the total protected income level, the capped maintenance is reduced. Bob can only afford to pay:

Total family income	160.00
Less total protected income	116.65
Maintenance payable	**43.35**

(b) Two years later, when Bob is living with Zoe, the proposed maintenance is £50.57 (see example 15.1b)

Total family income (from example 15.2)	434.18
Less proposed maintenance	50.57
Disposable income would be	**383.61**

This is more than the total protected income of £377.54 (see example 15.3b) and therefore the proposed maintenance is paid.

Example 15.5: Protected income step from start to finish

A few months later child maintenance from Zoe's ex-husband Wayne for Yvonne and Veronica and from Terence for Scott is being assessed (see example 14.12). The proposed maintenance from Wayne is £19.68 and from Terence £30.79. Can each of them afford it?

(a) Wayne lives on his own in a rented flat. He earns on average £160 net a week and only travels a few miles to work. His rent is £65 a week and his council tax is £6 a week. He is not entitled to any council tax benefit (CTB) or housing benefit (HB). The 30 per cent cap does not reduce the proposed maintenance as: 30% x £160 = £48.00. Therefore, the proposed maintenance remains at £19.68.

	£
Basic protected income:	
Personal allowance	55.65
Housing costs	65.00
Council tax	6.00
Margin	30.00
Basic protected income	**156.65**
Total family income	**160.00**
Less basic protected income	156.65
Excess family income	3.35
Additional protected income (15% x £3.35)	**0.50**
Total protected income	**157.15**

Chapter 15: Protected income: Step 5 of the 'old rules' formula
4. What is the maintenance payable

Payment of the proposed maintenance of £19.68 would leave Wayne with a disposable income of £140.32, below his total protected income.

Total family income	160.00
Less total protected income	157.15
	2.85

However, Wayne is not exempt from the minimum maintenance payment and therefore he is liable to pay £5.60 a week.

(b) Terence is married to Dipa and they have one dependent daughter, Rana (17), who lives with them. Their mortgage is £34.18 a week, half of which is capital repayments. Their council tax is £9.32 a week. Terence is self-employed and his net earnings average £190.21 a week. Dipa receives carer's allowance of £44.35 and child benefit of £16.50 a week. They get £19.42 working tax credit and child tax credit of £52.21 per week.

The 30 per cent cap does not reduce the proposed maintenance as: 30% x £209.63 (earnings plus working tax credit = £62.89. Therefore the proposed maintenance remains at £23.57.

		£
Basic protected income:		
Personal allowances	Couple	87.30
	Rana (17)	42.27
Family premium		15.95
Carer premium		25.55
Housing costs (mortgage interest)		17.09
Council tax		9.32
Margin		30.00
Basic protected income		**227.48**
Total family income:		
Net earnings		190.21
Carer's allowance		44.35
Child benefit		16.50
Working tax credit		19.42
Child tax credit		52.21
Total family income		322.69
Less basic protected income		227.48
Excess family income		**95.21**
Additional protected income	15% x 95.21	14.28
Total protected income		241.76
Total family income		322.69
Less proposed maintenance		30.79
Disposable income		***291.90***

As disposable income is above the total protected income, the maintenance payable is the proposed maintenance of £30.79.

Chapter 15: Protected income: Step 5 of the 'old rules' formula
4. What is the maintenance payable

More than one person with care

Where a non-resident parent is being assessed to pay child maintenance to two or more persons with care for different qualifying children, only one protected income step is carried out on the total proposed maintenance. Both the 30 per cent cap and the total protected income check are carried out for this total.[26] If the non-resident parent cannot afford the total proposed maintenance, the amount he can afford is divided between the persons with care in proportion to their proposed maintenance.

Example 15.6: Protected income step for more than one person with care
Lauren has returned to the UK. She claims income support (IS) and applies for child maintenance for Wayne's son, Keith. Wayne is also the father of Zoe's daughters. His net wages are now £174, his rent remains £65 (see example 15.5). He lives 17 miles as the crow flies from his new workplace.

Step 1 maintenance requirement:

	£	
Zoe's	85.84	(see example 11.3b)
Lauren's	97.37	(see example 14.8)
Total	183.21	

Step 2 Wayne's exempt income: £122.65
Step 3 Wayne's assessable income: £51.35
(Neither parent with care has any assessable income.)
Step 4 proposed maintenance:

Zoe: $£85.84 \times \dfrac{£51.35}{£183.21} \times 50\% = £12.03$

Lauren: $£97.37 \times \dfrac{£51.35}{£183.21} \times 50\% = £13.65$

Total proposed maintenance = £12.03 + £13.65 = £25.68
Step 5 protected income:
Check whether the total proposed maintenance is more than 30 per cent net income:
30% x £174 = £52.20
The total proposed maintenance of £25.68 is less than this and therefore does not need to be capped. Now carry out the second protected income calculation.

	£
Personal allowance	55.65
Housing costs	65.00
Council tax	6.00
Travel-to-work costs	2.00
Margin	30.00
Basic protected income	**158.65**
Total family income	**174.00**
Less basic protected income	158.65

Chapter 15: Protected income: Step 5 of the 'old rules' formula
5. Change of circumstances

Excess family income	15.35
Additional protected income = 15% x £15.35	2.30
Total protected income = £158.65 + £2.30	160.95
Total family income	174.00
Less total proposed maintenance	25.68
Disposable income	**148.32**

This is below the toal protected income (£160.95), so Wayne cannot afford to pay the proposed maintenance.

Total family income	174.00
Less total protected income	160.95
Maintenance payable	13.05

The maintenance is split between Zoe and Lauren in proportion to their proposed maintenance:

Zoe's £12.03 x $\frac{£13.05}{£25.68}$ = £6.11

Lauren's £13.65 x $\frac{£13.05}{£25.68}$ = £6.94

Note that Lauren ends up with a greater proportion of the maintenance, even though she has one young child and Zoe has two older children. In this case, as neither of them has assessable income, the difference is entirely due to the maintenance requirement rules.

5. Change of circumstances

An increase in the total family income of a second family on the protected income level can result in an increase in the maintenance payable to the first family. This arises because the total protected income level only increases by 15 per cent of any increase in family income. The net effect of a £1 a week increase in total family income is an 85 pence increase in the child maintenance payable to the first family. This begins as soon as the maintenance payable is £5.60 a week and only ceases once the maintenance due reaches the capped or proposed maintenance level.

This recycling effect is the same irrespective of whether the income is the non-resident parent's or a partner's. There is no exception for income specifically meant for stepchildren in the second family – eg, child maintenance paid for them. The theory is that an increase in the income of the non-resident parent's partner means that she is better able to support herself and her own children. This in turn releases more of the non-resident parent's income away from supporting his partner and his stepchildren and into paying maintenance to his own children. However, this distinction has certainly not been obvious to second families.

Chapter 15: Protected income: Step 5 of the 'old rules' formula
5. Change of circumstances

Once the proposed maintenance level is due, a £1 increase in the non-resident parent's income results in an increase of between 50 pence and 15 pence in the maintenance assessment. The partner's income then no longer increases the assessment at all (except to a limited extent in some instances where there is a joint child – see p256).

If the proposed maintenance has been capped, then increases in the partner's income do *not* increase the maintenance payable. While the maintenance remains capped, a £1 increase in the non-resident parent's own net income produces a 30 pence increase in the assessment.

Example 15.7: Change in total family income
Zoe decides to take a job, earning £90 net a week. Bob is still taking home £260 a week. When their child tax credit (CTC) award is reassessed, they are now entitled to £49.03 a week (see example 13.3b). Zoe now receives child maintenance as assessed in example 15.5.

Step 1 Maintenance requirement: £128.59 (see example 11.1a)
Step 2 Bob's exempt income: £129.77 (see example 12.6b)
Step 3 Bob's assessable income: £130.23 (see example 13.3b)
Step 4 Proposed maintenance: 50% of £130.23 = £65.12
(Anita has no assessable income)
Step 5 Protected income:
To check whether the proposed maintenance is less than 30 per cent net income (see example 13.3): 30% x £260 = £78
Therefore the proposed maintenance remains at £65.12.

	£
Bob's earnings	260.00
Zoe's earnings	90.00
Maintenance from Wayne	5.60
Maintenance from Terence	30.79
Child benefit	49.65
Child tax credit	49.03
Total family income	485.07
Less basic protected income (see example 15.3b)	367.54
Excess family income	117.53
Additional protected income = 15% x 120.06	17.63
Total protected income = £367.54 + £17.63	385.17
If the proposed maintenance were paid, disposable income would be: Total family income	485.07
Less proposed maintenance	65.12
Disposable income	**419.95**

This is higher than the total protected income (£385.17) and therefore the proposed maintenance is the maintenance payable. Bob is now paying Anita £65.12 instead of £50.57 (see example 15.4b). Although Bob and Zoe's total family income has increased by

Chapter 15: Protected income: Step 5 of the 'old rules' formula
5. Change of circumstances

£50.89, their disposable income after maintenance has been paid has increased by £36.34 which does not quite cover Zoe's childminding and travel-to-work costs. Since the proposed maintenance is being paid, any wage increase of Zoe's will not increase Bob's maintenance assessment any further.

It would not be to Bob's advantage to ask for a supersession of the assessment on the grounds of change of circumstances (see p420).

For two reasons, not every change of circumstances will immediately affect the amount of child maintenance payable. First, the person concerned does not have to request a supersession if there is a change in their circumstances. It is optional. Second, if a supersession is requested and undertaken, the general rule is that the maintenance in payment will only be altered if the new assessment is at least £10 more or less than the assessment in force. However, a new assessment which is reduced by only £1 or more or increased by £5 or more from the previous assessment will always take effect if it leaves the non-resident parent's family on protected income level (see p422). Therefore, cases which involve a non-resident parent on the protected income level will be more frequently changing than cases where the full amount of the proposed maintenance is being paid.

Example 15.8: Change in family composition

Bob's daughter Carol (now 15) moves, leaving Anita, to live with Bob and Zoe. Child benefit increases to £60.70, as it is near the end of the tax year child tax credit will be adjusted at the end of the year to reflect Carol becomes part of the family, so remains the same currently. Otherwise the situation is as in example 15.7 (see above).

David (10), Bob's son, still lives with Anita and her husband, Joe. Anita has net earnings of £270 and Joe has net earnings of £295. Anita's child benefit entitlement is now £16.50. Their mortgage interest payments are £114.23 a week, the endowment policy premium is £24.92 a week, and council tax £14.50 a week.

See example 14.11:
Proposed maintenance from Anita for Carol: £9.18
Proposed maintenance from Bob for David: £40.00

Protected income calculation for Bob
The 30 per cent cap does not reduce the proposed maintenance as:
30% x £260 = £78.

Basic protected income:		£
Personal allowances	couple	87.30
	Carol (15)	42.27
	Yvonne (14)	42.27
	Veronica (12)	42.27
	Scott (5)	42.27
	Ricky (1)	42.27

323

Chapter 15: Protected income: Step 5 of the 'old rules' formula
5. Change of circumstances

Family premium	15.95
Housing costs	45.00
Council tax liability	20.21
Margin	30.00
Basic protected income	**409.81**

Total family income:
£434.18 (see example 15.2 above) + £11.05 (child benefit) = £445.23
Excess family income = £445.23 – £409.81 = £35.42
Additional protected income = 15% x £35.42 = £5.31
Total protected income = £409.81 + £5.31 = £415.12

Total family income	445.23
Less proposed maintenance	40.00
Disposable income	**405.23**

This is below the total protected income of £415.12 and therefore Bob cannot afford to pay the proposed maintenance. Bob's maintenace will be adjusted.

Total family income	445.23
less total protected income	415.12
Maintenance payable	30.11

Protected income for Anita

Basic protected income: £

Personal allowances	couple	87.30
	David (10)	42.27
Family premium		15.95
Housing costs (mortgage interest only)		114.23
Council tax liability		14.50
Margin		30.00
Basic protected income		**304.25**

Total family income:

Anita's earnings	270.00
Joe's earnings	295.00
Child benefit	16.50
Total family income	581.50
Less basic protected income	304.25
Excess family income*	**277.25**

*At this point it is already clear that Anita will pay the proposed maintenance, but we continue with the calculation for completeness.

Additional protected income = 15% x £277.25 = 41.59
Total protected income = £304.25 + £41.59 = 345.84

Total family income	581.50
Less proposed maintenance	9.18
Disposable income	**572.32**

Chapter 15: Protected income: Step 5 of the 'old rules' formula
Notes

This is well above the total protected income of £354.84 and therefore Anita can afford to pay the proposed maintenance.

Note that the formula works in such a way as to leave Anita and Joe with disposable income of £572.32 when they have the care of one child, whereas Bob and Zoe are left with £415.12 when they are looking after five children and this takes no account of Zoe's childminding expenses.

Notes

1. **What is protected income**
    1 Sch 1 para 6 CSA 1991
    2 Regs 11(6)-(6A) and 12 CS(MASC) Regs
    3 Reg 12(1)(c) CS(MASC) Regs
    4 Reg 11(1)-(5) CS(MASC) Regs
    5 Regs 11(1)(l) and 12(1)(a) CS(MASC) Regs
    6 Reg 11(2) CS(MASC) Regs as amended by reg 6(4) CS(MA) Regs 2003
    7 Reg 11(2)(a)(ii) CS(MASC) Regs
    8 Reg 11(2)(a)(v) CS(MASC) Regs
    9 Reg 12(2) CS(MASC) Regs
    10 Reg 12(3) CS(MASC) Regs

2. **Basic protected income**
    11 Reg 11(1)(a-kk) CS(MASC) Regs as amended by reg 4(5) CS(MA(No2) Regs 2003
    12 Reg 11(1)(f) CS(MASC) Regs
    13 Reg 11(1)(b) CS(MASC) Regs
    14 Sch 3 para 3(1) CS(MASC) Regs
    15 Reg 11(1)(b) CS(MASC) Regs
    16 Reg 18(1)(b) CS(MASC) Regs
    17 Reg 1 CS(MASC) Regs; reg 3 HB Regs
    18 Reg 63(1) and (2) HB Regs
    19 Reg 63(9) HB Regs
    20 Reg 11(1)(j) CS(MASC) Regs
    21 Sch 1 para 5(4) CS(NIRA) Regs
    22 Reg 11(1)(kk) CS(MASC) Regs

3. **Total protected income**
    23 Reg 11(1)(l) CS(MASC) Regs

4. **What is the maintenance payable**
    24 Reg 12(2) CS(MASC) Regs
    25 Reg 12(3) CS(MASC) Regs
    26 Reg 22(3) CS(MASC) Regs

Chapter 16

Shared care under the 'old rules'

This chapter covers:
1. What is shared care (below)
2. Care shared by separated parents (p328)
3. Care shared between a parent and another person (p337)
4. Care shared between two people who are not parents (p341)
5. Three persons with care (p341)
6. Care provided in part by the local authority (p342)
7. The maintenance requirement is met in full (p342)

> This chapter contains information relevant to existing cases under the 'old rules'. For calculations under the 'new rules', see Chapter 7.

1. What is shared care

We use the term 'shared care' to describe a situation where there is more than one person looking after a particular child and those people live in different households. If the people providing care live in the same household (see p29), then this is not shared care.[1] The legislation only acknowledges shared care where more than one person has day-to-day care of a child.

What is day-to-day care

When deciding whether someone is a person with care under section 3 of the 1991 Act, there is no definition of day-to-day care. Therefore an everyday definition can be used (see p28). A person who is not a parent can apply to receive child maintenance only if s/he has day-to-day care of a child. Parents with care and non-resident parents can both apply for a maintenance assessment, although there are some exceptions (see p43) as well as rules governing which application takes precedence (see p54). There can be more than one person with care of a child.

Chapter 16: Shared care under the 'old rules'
1. What is shared care

For the purposes of the formula and shared care regulations, a person will be treated as having day-to-day care of a child only if s/he cares for the child for at least 104 nights in the 12-month period ending with the relevant week.[2] See p264 for a definition of relevant week.

Another period, ending with the relevant week, may be used if that would be more representative of the current arrangement.[3] The number of nights of care in that period must be in the same ratio as 104 nights is to 12 months – ie, 52 nights in six months, 26 nights in three months, 13 nights in two months, nine nights in a month. Examples are given to decision makers of situations where it might be appropriate to use a period other than 12 months because the care arrangements have recently changed – due to a relationship breakdown, a court ruling on residence or contact, or the person now providing day-to-day care has been abroad, in prison, in hospital, away from home or otherwise unable to provide care.[4] If the arrangement has simply been renegotiated between the two parents, written acceptance of this should be provided so that the CSA knows that this is now the current arrangement and not a temporary change. A future period cannot be used; the period should generally end with the relevant week, but does not have to.[5] Therefore, if a change occurs after the relevant week, supersession can be sought (see p420).

The parent does not have to provide continuous care throughout a period of 24 hours, but during the night.[6] Where a child is a boarder at boarding school or a hospital inpatient, whoever would otherwise have day-to-care is treated as providing care. The person who is treated as having day-to-day care for such periods need not be the person who pays the school fees.[7] Parents should keep a note of the nights the child(ren) spends with them and, in case of dispute, be willing to supply further evidence – eg, a diary. The CSA – and any subsequent appeal tribunal – must then determine the number of nights over the period spent in each person's care.[8]

Fewer than 104 nights in the year

If a non-resident parent is providing some care but to an extent less than that described as day-to-day care, he is not only still liable to pay child maintenance but also the level of care he provides is not acknowledged by the child support formula. Therefore, such a non-resident parent is expected to contribute the same amount of child maintenance as if he were not looking after the child at all. This means, for example, that fathers who have the children to stay every other weekend will pay the same level of maintenance as those who do not.

A father who looks after the child(ren) for all of the school holidays would not be accepted as a person with care if the time spent with the children was assessed over 12 months. However, the father could request supersession during the summer holidays on the grounds that he is now a parent with care and a shorter period should then be used to calculate who has day-to-day care in order to reflect

Chapter 16: Shared care under the 'old rules'
1. What is shared care

the current arrangement. It is unlikely that this would be grounds for supersession if the six-week period had already been taken into account when averaging over the year for the current assessment. However, if the arrangement for the holiday had not been known at the time, this may be successful. If not, an appeal should be considered (see p434).

If day-to-day care were to be re-assessed over this shorter period, then the father would become the parent with care and the mother the non-resident parent. Indeed, the father could then apply for maintenance from the mother. (Note that the period used to assess day-to-day care ends with the relevant week which precedes the request for supersession – see p420. Therefore the request should not be made right at the beginning of the summer holiday.)

On the other hand, if it is held that supersession cannot take place, such a father technically remains the non-resident parent over the holiday when he has the child(ren) full time. He would be liable to continue paying the mother the full level of maintenance even for those weeks the children spent with him. The parents may come to some voluntary arrangement whereby the mother would forgo the maintenance due, but this may not be financially possible, especially if she is in receipt of income support.

More than one person with care

Where there are two people in different households who both have day-to-day care of a qualifying child, either can make an application for child maintenance as long as both or neither has parental responsibility (see p23) for the child.[9] If only one of them has parental responsibility, then the person with that responsibility must be the applicant. This means that if the person with parental responsibility decides not to apply, the other person with care could lose out on child maintenance.

If both persons with care can and do make an application, then only one will be accepted (see p54).[10] Which application is accepted is largely a technicality, however, as this does not change the status of the people involved nor the way in which the assessment is carried out. It does, though, affect who can cancel the assessment (see p392).

The basic formula is varied to take into account the fact that there is more than one person with care. The way in which the formula is adjusted depends on which people share the care.

2. Care shared by separated parents

Under the 1991 Act, where both the parents are accepted as having day-to-day care, there is initially no one who can be assessed as having to make child maintenance payments in order to discharge liability to maintain the child.

Therefore, in order to make an assessment, one of the parents with care has to be treated as a non-resident parent. The regulations provide that one of the parents with care is deemed a non-resident parent and is assessed to pay child maintenance.[11] CPAG took a case to the child support commissioners (see p450) to argue that the Act did not allow for this to happen, but the commissioner decided that, although the regulation was ambiguous and produced some fairly anomalous results, it was consistent with the purpose of the Act.[12]

Only a parent who provides day-to-day care as defined by the regulations – ie, care of at least 104 nights out of 12 months (see p326) – can be deemed non-resident (see below). In almost all cases the parents with care will both be providing care for at least 104 nights out of 12 months and therefore one will be deemed non-resident. (In less usual situations, a different definition of day-to-day care could have been used under the 1991 Act – see p28. For example, if the mother provides care during the day but the children sleep at their father's home, each cares for the children an equal number of hours a week and, although there are two parents with care, the shared care rules cannot be used to deem one of them non-resident. No maintenance assessment could be carried out. The CSA may refuse to use a broader interpretation of day-to-day care possible under the Act in order to avoid this problem; an appeal could be considered by the parent who has not been seen as a parent with care.)

In cases where a parent with care is treated as non-resident, an assessment is carried out to find out how much child maintenance s/he has to pay to the other parent. As the remaining parent with care does not have to discharge her/his responsibility under the Act by paying child maintenance, this assignment of non-resident parenthood can result in one parent paying child maintenance to another who has equal responsibility for the child.

Who is treated as the non-resident parent

The parent who provides day-to-day care to a **lesser extent** is treated as the non-resident parent.[13] A lesser extent could be interpreted as meaning either for fewer *nights* per week on average or fewer *hours* per week on average. The number of nights will be considered first by the CSA, but it should be argued on the basis of hours if this would give a fairer result. Indeed, it could be said that nights involve less care than days. For example, if one parent had a school-age child from 4pm Friday to 8.30am Monday (three nights), this could be argued to be as much care as the other parent who is with the child from 4pm Monday to 8.30am Friday (four nights). It might be possible to argue that the degree of responsibility, as well as the amount of time, is relevant to determining the extent of the care – eg, who buys the child's clothes, who attends school functions or arranges visits to the dentist. These issues need not be raised if both parents agree that the number of nights of care fairly determines the question.

Chapter 16: Shared care under the 'old rules'
2. Care shared by separated parents

It is helpful if parents keep a record of the time the children spend in each household, especially if there are changes to the usual pattern of care. The extent of care is measured over the period explained on p326, usually the last year or since a change in the arrangements.

If the parents provide care for an equal amount of time, the parent who does *not* receive child benefit is treated as the non-resident parent.[14] As the right to receive child maintenance follows the receipt of child benefit, this may lead to competing claims for child benefit. Where more than one person who would otherwise be entitled makes a claim for child benefit, the following order of priority is used to determine who is to be awarded the benefit:[15]

- the person having the child living with her/him;
- the wife, where she is living with her husband (this continues for 13 weeks of a permanent separation);
- a parent, including a step-parent;
- the mother, if the parents are unmarried and living together;
- a person agreed by those entitled;
- failing all the above, the person selected by the Secretary of State.

Priority can be conceded by a higher priority claimant to someone else in writing. For more information on entitlement to child benefit, see CPAG's *Welfare Benefits and Tax Credits Handbook*.

If care is shared equally and neither parent receives child benefit, the CSA decides who is the principal carer.[16]

> **Example 16.1: Shared care and a deemed non-resident parent**
> Marcia and Nathan are divorced. They have two children, Oscar (7) and Patrick (5). Every fortnight the children spend five nights with Nathan. The rest of the time they live with Marcia.
> Marcia has the children 9 out of every 14 nights = 234 nights a year.
> Nathan has the children 5 out of every 14 nights = 130 nights a year.
> Do both parents have day-to-day care? Yes.
> But Nathan looks after the boys to a lesser extent. Therefore, Nathan is deemed a non-resident parent and an assessment is carried out to decide how much child maintenance he should pay to Marcia.
> Marcia remains a parent with care and has no liability to pay child maintenance.

For the purposes of simplicity in this chapter, it is assumed that the parent who remains the person with care is the mother and the deemed non-resident parent is the father. There may be cases where each child of a family spends a different amount of time with the two parents – ie, the mother may be deemed the non-resident parent for one child and the father for the other. If this is the case, the situation is similar to that of a divided family in which different children live full

Chapter 16: Shared care under the 'old rules'
2. Care shared by separated parents

time with different parents (see p305). Two completely separate assessments are carried out: if the mother cares for the daughter for the greater amount of time, the daughter's child maintenance will be assessed with the father as the deemed non-resident parent; child maintenance for the son, who spends more time with the father, will be assessed with the mother as the deemed non-resident parent.

Calculating child maintenance

When two parents share care, there is a remaining parent with care and a deemed non-resident parent (see p329). The five steps of the formula as described in Chapters 10 to 15 are still applicable in calculating how much maintenance the deemed non-resident parent must pay. However, the standard formula is adjusted to take into account the time that the so-called non-resident parent looks after the child(ren).

Step 1: Maintenance requirement

Only one maintenance requirement is calculated (see Chapter 11). (Although it may appear from the legislation that a maintenance requirement is needed for each parent in order to calculate the deemed non-resident parent's proposed maintenance – 'X' in the regulations – and the parent with care's notional maintenance – 'Y' – in practice, the same maintenance requirement is used for both calculations.[17])

Example 16.2: Maintenance requirement
The situation is as described in example 16.1. Marcia has remarried and looks after Oscar (7) and Patrick (5) for nine nights every fortnight.
Maintenance requirement with Marcia as parent with care:

		£
Personal allowance	Marcia	55.65
	Oscar (7)	42.27
	Patrick (5)	42.27
Family premium		15.95
Sub-total		156.14
Less child benefit		27.55
Maintenance requirement		128.59

Step 2: Exempt income

When calculating the exempt income of the parents, a proportion of the personal allowance for the child (plus any disabled child premium) is included to reflect the average number of nights a week the parent does have care of the child.[18] Similarly, only a proportion of the family premium is allowed unless another of the parent's children lives in the household all week (see p332 for the situation

Chapter 16: Shared care under the 'old rules'
2. Care shared by separated parents

where there is another child).[19] See example 16.10, where the care of more than one child is shared but the children spend a different number of nights with the parent.

For full details of exempt income, see Chapter 12.

Example 16.3: Exempt income for shared care when no child lives in the household for seven nights a week

Marcia looks after Oscar and Patrick for an average of 4.5 nights a week.
Nathan looks after Oscar and Patrick for an average of 2.5 nights a week.
Marcia married Gareth recently. Their mortgage payments are £120 a week.

Marcia's exempt income: £
Personal allowance	Marcia	55.65	
	Oscar (7)	27.17	(for 4.5 days)
	Patrick (5)	27.17	(for 4.5 days)
Family premium		10.25	(for 4.5 days)
Housing costs		120.00	
Total exempt income		**240.24**	

Nathan lives on his own when the children are not with him. His privately rented flat costs £75 a week. He lives within a few miles of his work.

Nathan's exempt income: £
Personal allowance	Nathan	55.65	
	Oscar (7)	15.10	(for 2.5 days)
	Patrick (5)	15.10	(for 2.5 days)
Family premium		5.70	(for 2.5 days)
Housing costs		75.00	
Total exempt income		**166.55**	

See example 16.10 for the apportionment of premiums where the children spend a different number of nights with each parent.

Premiums where there is a shared-care child and another child

Only read this section if there is a child who lives in the household all week, as well as the child(ren) there part time. If the household includes only the children whose care is shared and stepchildren, the premiums are apportioned as above; go to step 3.

Where another child of the parent lives in the household for seven nights a week, this child can be either another qualifying child or a joint child with a new partner. The family premium is either included in full or halved.[20] It will be included in full if:
- the parent qualifies for the family premium for the shared child(ren) (ie, receives child benefit for her/him, or where no one receives child benefit, or has claimed child benefit or is the person with whom the child usually lives) hereafter referred to as 'with child benefit'; *or*

Chapter 16: Shared care under the 'old rules'
2. Care shared by separated parents

- there is another qualifying child (of that parent) in the household; *or*
- a new partner cannot support the joint child (see p256).

The following outlines the various permutations:
- a lone parent with shared-care children (with or without child benefit) and another qualifying child – full family premium;
- a parent with shared-care children (with child benefit) and a joint child with a new partner – full family premium at the basic rate. Note that the personal allowance for the joint child is halved if the new partner can contribute to her/his support;
- a parent with shared-care children (no child benefit) and a joint child with a new partner – the family premium is halved if the new partner can contribute to the support of the joint child, but is included in full if the partner cannot (see p256).

Example 16.4: Exempt income where there is shared care and a joint child
Marcia still has the qualifying children, Oscar and Patrick, 9 out of 14 nights (an average of 4.5 nights a week) and receives child benefit for them. Marcia and her husband, Gareth, now have a baby daughter, Megan. Gareth earns £450 a week. Their mortgage payments are £120 per week.

Marcia's exempt income:

		£	
Personal allowance	Marcia	55.65	
	Oscar	27.17	(4.5 days)
	Patrick	27.17	(4.5 days)
	Megan (half*)	21.14	
Family premium (in full**)		15.95	
Housing costs		120.00	
Total exempt income		**267.08**	

* As Gareth earns £450 a week, he can afford to contribute to his daughter's maintenance and therefore only half of Megan's personal allowance is included (see p256 for details of the means test).

** Because Megan lives in the household all week, the family premium is not apportioned according to how many nights Oscar and Patrick stay. Instead, consideration has to be given to whether Marcia is entitled to the family premium as a result of looking after Oscar and Patrick. As she receives child benefit for them, she is entitled to the full rate of the premium. (If her ex-husband received the child benefit, Marcia would not be due the full family premium for them. Consideration would then be given to Megan and, since Gareth can afford to maintain half of Megan, the family premium would be halved.)

Step 3: Assessable income
This step is exactly the same as for other situations (see Chapter 13).

Chapter 16: Shared care under the 'old rules'
2. Care shared by separated parents

Example 16.5: Assessable income
Before the birth of her daughter, Marcia's income is net earnings of £145 a week. Her husband's earnings are not taken into account in the net income calculation and neither is any child benefit.

Marcia's assessable income:	£
Net income	145.00 (net earnings)
Less exempt income	240.24 (from example 16.3)
Assessable income	**Nil**

Nathan takes home £220 a week, after £40 superannuation is deducted. Only half of the superannuation is taken into account (see p266).

Nathan's assessable income:	£
Net income	240.00 (net earnings)
Less exempt income	166.55 (from example 16.3)
Assessable income	**73.45**

Step 4: Proposed maintenance[21]

The proposed maintenance step is carried out in full for each parent in order to obtain both the proposed maintenance from the deemed non-resident parent and a notional proposed maintenance from the remaining parent with care. When calculating the proposed maintenance from each parent, the assessable income of the other parent is taken into account in the same way as if both were non-resident parents (see example 14.7).

The amount of the deemed non-resident parent's proposed maintenance and the notional amount of proposed maintenance from the remaining parent with care are then added together to give the joint proposed maintenance. The deemed non-resident parent is taken to have already contributed a proportion of the maintenance in kind. His assumed contribution is the proportion of the joint proposed maintenance that is equivalent to the proportion of time the children spend with him. The proportion of time the parent spends with his children is given in terms of the average number of nights per week divided by seven. The average number of nights per week does not have to be a round figure; it is calculated to two decimal figures – eg, if a deemed non-resident parent has the child one week in three, the average number of nights per week is 2.33. If there is more than one child, the total average number of nights per week is divided by the number of children – eg, if a father has one child two nights a week and another child four nights a week, the average number of nights per week is three.

This contribution in kind is then subtracted from the non-resident parent's proposed maintenance to give an adjusted proposed maintenance figure. If this produces a figure less than zero, no child maintenance is payable.[22] The non-resident parent has more than contributed his proportion of the total proposed maintenance in kind by providing a certain amount of care.

Chapter 16: Shared care under the 'old rules'
2. Care shared by separated parents

The minimum payment rule (see p223) applies to an adjusted proposed maintenance figure of between £0 and £5.50.[23] Therefore all deemed non-resident parents calculated to pay child maintenance of up to £5.50 are exempted from the payment (as they have at least part of the family premium included in their protected income calculation).

Example 16.6: Proposed maintenance

As Marcia has no assessable income, the proposed maintenance is 50 per cent of Nathan's assessable income (see example 16.5):

50% x £73.45 = £36.73

This is less than the maintenance requirement of £128.59 (see example 16.2), so £36.73 is the proposed maintenance.

As there is no proposed maintenance from Marcia, the joint proposed maintenance is also £36.73.

Nathan contributes a proportion of the care:

$$\frac{2.5 + 2.5}{7 \times 2} \text{ nights in the average week} = 35.71\%$$

(2 represents the number of children for whom care is shared.)

As he contributes 35.71% of the care, he is taken as contributing 35.71% of the joint proposed maintenance in kind:

35.71% x £36.73 = £13.11

Nathan is deemed to have contributed £13.11 and is therefore due to pay the remainder of his proposed maintenance (if protected income allows).

Adjusted proposed maintenance = £36.73 – £13.11 = £23.62

(If the caring roles had been reversed and Nathan had the children for 4.5 nights a week, then the proposed maintenance from Marcia, as a deemed non-resident parent, to Nathan would have been nil, as Marcia has no assessable income.)

Example 16.6 gives the most straightforward shared-care situation where only the deemed non-resident parent has assessable income and even then not enough to meet the maintenance requirement. See example 16.10 for an example of the additional element calculation where both parents have assessable income.

However, any of the situations explained in Chapter 14 can apply to the assessments carried out for parents sharing care. In effect, two separate assessments are being carried out up to step 4 to give a proposed maintenance from the deemed non-resident parent and a notional proposed maintenance from the parent with care. First, arrive at the proposed maintenance for each parent in the same way as for non-resident parents before adding together the two amounts of proposed maintenance to give the joint proposed maintenance. Only at this stage is the non-resident parent's proposed maintenance reduced in recognition of his payment in kind.

Chapter 16: Shared care under the 'old rules'
2. Care shared by separated parents

The shared care calculation is complicated, but there is a certain amount of logic to it. Both parents have a liability to maintain and therefore, in theory, maintenance is due from each of them for the nights that the child spends with the other parent. For the child there is a notional amount of maintenance available per week. Imagine the joint proposed maintenance divided by seven to give a daily rate of maintenance. Each night of care provided is equivalent to having paid this amount of maintenance. A deemed non-resident parent has to make payments of child maintenance if the amount equivalent to the number of nights' care he contributes does not exceed his portion of the proposed maintenance.

However, the calculation can mean that the parent with a lower income who has the child for less time can end up paying maintenance to a parent with a higher income. Although this is equally true in standard cases, in cases of shared care the deemed non-resident parent may find that he does not have what he considers to be sufficient income left for those days when he is responsible for the child. The deemed non-resident parent on a low income will never receive any maintenance from a remaining parent with care with a higher income. This may appear particularly galling when the care is shared equally, and it may lead to competing claims for child benefit (see p329).

It is also bizarre that a parent with care on income support (IS) or income-based jobseeker's allowance (JSA) who is required to apply for maintenance can be deemed a non-resident parent and thus not entitled to any child maintenance at all. A parent with care who is deemed to be non-resident does not, however, have deductions for contributions to child maintenance from IS/JSA.

Step 5: Protected income

Protected income is still the final stage of the calculation (see Chapter 15).[24] The deemed non-resident parent may not be able to afford the proposed adjusted maintenance. When assessing the basic protected income, the allowances for the child are adjusted as for exempt income (see p331) to represent the proportion of the average week that a child spends with the non-resident parent.[25] If there is more than one shared-care child and they spend different nights with the family, the family premium is included in proportion to the average number of nights per week that a child is in the household.[26] If another child lives in the household full-time, the premium is included in full.

Example 16.7: Shared care and protected income
Nathan lives on his own, when the children are not with him. His rent is £75 a week and his council tax is £342 a year. He earns £240 net a week. He has Oscar and Patrick for five nights per fortnight. Can Nathan afford to pay the proposed maintenance of £23.62 (see example 16.6)?
The 30% cap does not reduce the proposed maintenance as:
30% x £240 = £72

Chapter 16: Shared care under the 'old rules'
3. Care shared between a parent and another person

Therefore the proposed maintenance remains at £23.62

Basic protected income:		£	
Personal allowance	Nathan	55.65	
	Oscar (7)	15.10	(for 2.5 days)
	Patrick (5)	15.10	(for 2.5 days)
Family premium		5.70	(for 2.5 days)
Housing costs		75.00	
Council tax		6.58	
Margin		30.00	
Basic protected income		**203.13**	
Additional protected income:			
Total family income	240.00		
Less basic protected income	203.13		(net earnings)
Excess total family income	36.87		
15% x £36.87 = £5.53			
Total protected income = £203.13			
+ £5.53 = £208.66			
Total family income	240.00		
Less proposed maintenance	23.62		
Disposable income	*216.38*		

This disposable income is above the total protected income level of £208.66. Nathan can pay the proposed maintenance of £23.62 a week.

---

3. Care shared between a parent and another person

Once again, both the parent and the other person involved must provide day-to-day care (see p326) and live in different households. The way in which this situation is treated depends upon which of the persons with care provides day-to-day care to the lesser extent (see p329).

The parent provides care for less time

Although there are two persons with care as defined by the 1991 Act, the parent with care, for the purposes of the formula, is again deemed by the regulations to be non-resident, as she provides day-to-day care for less time.[27] Therefore, there is no longer a parent with care, but a person with care and a deemed non-resident parent.

In most cases, the second parent will also be involved as a non-resident parent. For example, the grandmother has the child Monday night to Thursday night (the person with care), the mother has the child Friday to Sunday nights (deemed

337

non-resident parent) and the father has the child for only two weeks in the summer (non-resident parent).

Both non-resident parents are liable to pay maintenance to the person with care. Therefore, two separate assessments are carried out, one for each of the liable parents as long as an effective application has been made in each case. The person with care who is actually going to receive the child maintenance cannot apply if she (the grandmother) does not have parental responsibility while the deemed non-resident parent (the mother) does have that responsibility (see p23).

How child maintenance is calculated

In the case of the non-resident parent who does not participate in the caring of the child, the assessment is the same as it would be if there were no shared care arrangement. The fact that the care of the child is shared between two people does not affect the amount that the non-resident parent can afford to pay. However, where an application is only made against the non-resident parent, and not the parent with care, the maintenance requirement is not halved as it would be when an application is made against one of two truly non-resident parents (see p232).[28]

At the proposed maintenance step of the calculation, the assessable income of the deemed non-resident parent is added to the non-resident parent's assessable income to give the parents' joint assessable income, in the same way as if both parents were truly non-resident (see p298).

The deemed non-resident parent's calculation follows that described above for a deemed non-resident parent sharing care with the other parent. The only difference is that instead of adding a notional proposed maintenance for the parent with care, the actual proposed maintenance of the non-resident parent is used to obtain joint proposed maintenance.[29] Where there is no non-resident parent (eg, he has gone abroad or is deceased) or where the non-resident parent's assessable income is unknown (eg, he has not been traced) the deemed non-resident parent just pays child maintenance for those days for which she is not caring for the child(ren).[30]

> **Example 16.8: Care shared between a parent to a lesser extent and another person to a greater extent**
> Gran, who is a widow, has Beverley (15) for four nights a week and her mother has her for the remaining three nights. As the mother looks after Beverley for less time than Gran, the mother is deemed to be non-resident. The mother has parental responsibility and receives child benefit.
> The maintenance requirement is £69.55 (see example 11.2).
> The mother's assessable income is £42 a week. (When working out her exempt income, 3/7ths of the personal allowance for Beverley and 3/7ths family premium would have been included.)
> (a) The non-resident father's assessable income is £57.

Chapter 16: Shared care under the 'old rules'
3. Care shared between a parent and another person

> Parents' joint assessable income = £42 + £57 = £99
> 50% of joint assessable income = £49.50
> This is below the maintenance requirement and therefore the 50 per cent calculation applies to each parent.
> Father's proposed maintenance = 50% x £57 = £28.50
> Mother's proposed maintenance = 50% x £42 = £21
> Joint proposed maintenance = £28.50 + £21 = £49.50
> The mother provides three out of seven nights' care = 42.86%
> This is equivalent to paying 42.86% x £49.50 = £21.22 a week maintenance.
> The mother's adjusted proposed maintenance: £21 – £21.22 = nil
> As she is exempt from the minimum payment, she is not liable to pay any child maintenance as her contribution in kind outweighs the financial contribution.
> Assuming the protected income calculation allows it, the father pays £28.50 a week to the grandmother, but nothing to the mother.
> See example 16.11 for the assessment where the parents have higher assessable incomes.
> (b)If the father emigrated or no application was made against him, the mother would pay 4/7ths of her proposed maintenance to the grandmother, assuming that the protected income calculation did not reduce this.
> The mother's proposed maintenance would still be £21. She is still providing care three nights a week or 42.86% of the proposed maintenance in kind: 42.86% x £21 = £9.
> This leaves her with adjusted proposed maintenance of £21 less £9 = £12 a week to the grandmother. The protected income calculation has to be carried out and would include 3/7ths of Beverley's personal allowance and 3/7ths family premium.

The regulations do not allow for the maintenance paid by the non-resident parent to be split between two persons with care where one is a deemed non-resident parent. The entire amount of child maintenance from the non-resident parent is paid to the remaining person with care. In other words, a parent with care who shares care for the lesser time can never receive child maintenance from a non-resident parent, no matter the size of the bill being paid.

This may seem illogical, not to say unfair, particularly where the application has been made by the parent with care or where – although applications have been made by both persons with care – the application from the parent has been given priority (see p54). A parent with care who applies to the CSA for maintenance from the non-resident parent but ends up being deemed non-resident and paying maintenance can have the assessment cancelled (see p392).

Parent provides care for greater amount of time

If a parent does a greater proportion of the caring than another person with care, then she remains a parent with care for the purposes of the maintenance assessment.[31] This also applies where the parent provides care to the same extent as someone else, but the parent receives the child benefit. There is no deemed

339

Chapter 16: Shared care under the 'old rules'
3. Care shared between a parent and another person

non-resident parent. Instead there is usually a parent with care, another person with care and a non-resident parent. It can also cover the rare situation where a person is not technically a person with care under the 1991 Act (see p28) even though s/he is providing care of at least two nights a week on average.

If only one of the persons with care has applied for a maintenance assessment, that person will receive all the child maintenance payable by the non-resident parent.[32] This also applies where both persons with care have made an application, but only one has been accepted. There is an order of priority as to which application will be accepted (see p55). It also covers cases where the second carer cannot make an application – eg, s/he does not have parental responsibility or s/he does not share a home with the child.

However, if a request is made to the CSA by *either* of the people looking after the child(ren), the child maintenance may be divided between the two of them in proportion to the day-to-day care provided.[33] The ratio of care provided does not have to be calculated on the basis of the number of nights a child spends with the carer. An alternative method could be argued for if this gives a fairer division of the maintenance (see p328).

It is not specified in the regulations what form such a request needs to take. It is arguable that the request could be verbal, but we suggest that it should be put in writing on the maintenance application form or in a letter that part of the maintenance should go to another person. There is no time limit for making the request.

The decision to share the child maintenance assessment between the persons with care is a discretionary decision made by the Secretary of State who must consider the interests of the child, the current care arrangements and all representations received about the payment proposals.[34]

The alternative is for the persons with care to come to a voluntary arrangement, but this may not be feasible where the person who is the applicant for the CSA purposes is in receipt of a means-tested benefit.

Example 16.9: Care shared between a parent to a greater extent and another person to a lesser extent

If the caring responsibilities of the grandmother and mother in example 16.8 are swapped, so that the mother has Beverley for four nights a week, the calculation is as follows:

The mother now remains the parent with care and the grandmother is still a person with care. (This also applies where care is shared equally but the mother is in receipt of child benefit.)

The father's proposed maintenance remains £28.50 a week.

However, this time the mother will receive the full amount if she makes the application for maintenance and there is no request to split the payment. If there is such a request and it is granted, then the mother will receive 4/7ths – ie, £16.29 – and the grandmother the remainder – ie, £12.21 a week.

4. Care shared between two people who are not parents

The situation may arise where two people living in different households each have day-to-day care (as defined in the regulations – see p326) of a child of whom neither is the parent. The same rules apply here as where care is shared between a parent for the greater part and another (see p339)[35] – ie, if a request is made by either person, the maintenance payable by each non-resident parent may be divided between the carers in proportion to the amount of care being provided. If no request is made, then the full amount goes to the applicant.

In this situation it is likely that there are two non-resident parents and therefore maintenance could be paid by both non-resident parents. If one of the persons with care chooses to apply for maintenance from only one of the non-resident parents, there is no reason why the second person with care cannot apply for child maintenance from the other non-resident parent.

5. Three persons with care

As a person with care has to look after the child for a minimum of two nights a week on average, there can be no more than three persons with care for any child. However, there may be a combination of parents and others providing the care as follows (in each case the first person provides the greatest amount of care and the third, the least):

- parent, parent, other person – this situation is not covered specifically, although the intention must be to deem the second parent non-resident and for maintenance to be paid by him to the applicant;
- parent, other person, parent – second parent is deemed non-resident and maintenance is paid by him to the applicant;
- other person, parent, parent – second parent is deemed non-resident and maintenance is paid by him to the applicant;
- parent, other person, other person – applicant receives maintenance from the non-resident parent or it may be apportioned on request;
- other person, parent, other person – this does not appear to be explicitly covered by the regulations, but we presume that the intention is that the parent would be deemed non-resident; there would, of course, be a second parent who is non-resident;
- other person, other person, parent – parent with care deemed non-resident and other parent non-resident are both liable;
- three other people – maintenance from both non-resident parents may be apportioned on request.

Chapter 16: Shared care under the 'old rules'
6. Care provided in part by the local authority

6. Care provided in part by the local authority

A local authority cannot be a person with care.[36] Therefore, if a child is in the care of the local authority for seven nights a week, no child maintenance is payable by the non-resident parents. There may be cases where a child is not being provided with care by the local authority all the time, but only for part of the time. If the local authority care is less than day-to-day care (see p326), such a level of care can be ignored.

However, if the element of care provided by the local authority amounts to day-to-day care, child maintenance is not payable for any night that the child is in that local authority care.[37] Instead, the person with care who looks after the child for the remainder of the time receives reduced child maintenance from the non-resident parent. The maintenance payment is reduced to correspond to the number of nights per week that the child is in that person's care – eg, if the child is in local authority care for five nights a week, the person with care will receive two-sevenths of the amount of the maintenance assessment from the non-resident parent.

Where there is more than one qualifying child and the local authority provides some day-to-day care for at least one of the children, again the maintenance payable is reduced.[38] For example, a person with care looks after two children: one spends the whole week with the person with care, the other child spends four nights in local authority care and three nights with the person with care. To work out the maintenance payable in this circumstance, calculate the total number of nights spent with the person with care per week, and divide this by seven times the number of qualifying children. In this case 10 (7+3) out of 14 (7x2) nights are spent with the parent with care. The maintenance payable is ten-fourteenths (or 71.43 per cent) of the maintenance assessed.

7. The maintenance requirement is met in full

The calculations described earlier in this chapter hold true when the maintenance requirement is met in full. If 50 per cent of the parents' joint assessable income is greater than the maintenance requirement, the additional element calculation has to be used for proposed maintenance. For a full explanation of the additional element calculation, see Chapter 14.

Example 16.10: Care shared by parents
This is the same family as in examples 16.1 to 16.7.
Oscar (now aged 9) now spends every other week with Nathan, while Patrick (6) still spends five days a fortnight with him. Marcia still receives child benefit for both boys and therefore Nathan is still deemed to be a non-resident parent in respect of Oscar as well as

Chapter 16: Shared care under the 'old rules'
7. The maintenance requirement is met in full

Patrick. A calculation, therefore, has to be done to assess how much Nathan pays Marcia. However, in assessing Nathan's actual contribution, a notional contribution from Marcia has to be calculated.

Nathan's take-home earnings have risen to £362 a week, and his superannuation contribution is now £50 a week.

Marcia has increased her hours and now earns £340 net a week. Her husband, Gareth, earns £450 net a week. Their mortgage payments are £120 a week. Their daughter Megan is two years old.

Step 1: The maintenance requirement £128.59 (see example 16.2)

Step 2: Exempt income

Marcia's exempt income is as in example 16.4, except that Oscar's personal allowance is now included for 3.5 days (£21.14) instead of 4.5 days: therefore exempt income = £261.05.

Nathan's exempt income:		£	
Personal allowance	Nathan	55.65	
	Oscar	21.14	(for 3.5 days)
	Patrick	15.10	(for 2.5 days)
Family premium *		7.98	(for 3.5 days)
Housing costs		75.00	
Total exempt income		**174.87**	

* The family premium is included in proportion to the average number of nights a week that care is provided for a child. In this case Patrick stays with Nathan on nights that Oscar is there – ie, care is provided for at least one child for an average of 3.5 nights a week and for the other 3.5 nights Nathan is a single man. However, if the children stayed different nights, 6/7ths of the premiums would be included.[39]

Step 3: Assessable income

Marcia's assessable income:		£
Net income	Earnings	340.00
Less exempt income		261.05
Assessable income		**78.95**
Nathan's assessable income:		£
Net income	Earnings*	387.00
Less exempt income		174.87
Assessable income		**212.13**

* Only half of the superannuation is taken into account.

Step 4: Proposed maintenance

Joint assessable income: £78.95 + £212.13 = £291.08

50% x £291.08 = £140.54

This is above the maintenance requirement of £128.59 and therefore an additional element calculation must be done (see Figure 14.5).

Chapter 16: Shared care under the 'old rules'
7. The maintenance requirement is met in full

Marcia's notional proposed maintenance:

Basic element = $\dfrac{£128.59 \times £78.95}{£291.08} = £34.88$

Basic assessable income = £34.88 × 2 = £69.76
Additional assessable income = £78.95 − £69.76 = £9.19
Additional element = 20% × £9.19 = £1.84
Notional proposed maintenance = £34.88 + £1.84 = £36.72

Nathan's proposed maintenance to Marcia:

Basic element = $\dfrac{£128.59 \times £212.13}{£291.08} = £93.71$

Basic assessable income = £93.71 × 2 = £187.42
Additional assessable income = £212.13 − £187.42 = £24.71
Additional element = 20% × £24.71 = £4.94
Proposed maintenance = £93.71 + £4.94 = £98.65
Joint proposed maintenance = £36.72 + £98.65 = £135.37

Nathan contributes in kind = $\dfrac{3.5 + 2.5}{7 \times 2} = 42.86\%$ of the care

This is equivalent to £58.14 (42.86% × £135.65)

Nathan's proposed maintenance after taking into account his portion of the care = £97.65 − £58.14 = £39.51 a week.

This is below the maximum payment (see p296).

Step 5: Protected income
This follows example 16.7, except that now half Oscar's personal allowance and half the family premium are included (see p336). The protected income calculation shows that Nathan can afford the proposed maintenance of £39.51. He may not be very happy about this as he has the children for almost as much time as Marcia, Marcia has the child benefit, her take-home pay is almost the same as his, and her husband has a significant salary.

There could be times when there is more then one child and because the care is shared in different ways for the different children, each parent would be the person with care for one child and the deemed non-resident parent for the other. In this case, two shared care calculations would have to be carried out. This would happen in the situation described in example 16.10 (see above) if Nathan was in receipt of the child benefit for Oscar.

Example 16.11: Care shared between a parent and another person
Gran has Beverley (15) for four nights a week and her mother has her for the remaining three nights. The mother is therefore deemed to be a non-resident parent. When the mother's assessable income was £42 and the father's was £57, the mother's child maintenance liability was nil while the father's proposed maintenance was £28.50 (see example 16.8).
(a) The mother's assessable income has increased to £100

Chapter 16: Shared care under the 'old rules'
7. The maintenance requirement is met in full

Joint assessable income = £100 + £57 = £157
50 per cent of joint assessable income = 50% x £157 = £78.50
This is above the maintenance requirement of £69.55 (see example 11.2) and so an additional element calculation has to be done.

Father's proposed maintenance:

Basic element = $\dfrac{£69.55 \times £57}{£157}$ = £25.25

Basic assessable income = £25.25 x 2 = £50.50
Additional assessable income = £57 – £50.50 = £6.50
Additional element = £6.50 x 15% = £0.98
Proposed maintenance = £25.25 + £0.98 = £26.23

Mother's proposed maintenance:

Basic element = $\dfrac{£69.55 \times £100}{£157}$ = £44.30

Basic assessable income = £44.30 x 2 = £88.60
Additional assessable income = £100 – £88.60 = £11.40
Additional element = £11.40 x 15% = £1.71
Proposed maintenance = £44.30 + £1.71 = £46.01
Joint proposed maintenance = £26.23 + £46.01 = £72.24

The mother provides care three out of seven nights = 42.86% of the care. This is equivalent to paying 42.86% of £72.24 – ie, £30.96 a week maintenance. The mother's adjusted proposed maintenance = £46.01 – £30.96 = £15.05

Assuming the protected calculations allow these figures, Gran now receives £15.05 from the mother and £26.23 from the father, a total of £41.28 (instead of the £28.50 from the non-resident father).

(b) If the non-resident father's assessable income had been £157 and the mother's £100 a week, again an additional element calculation would have been done.
Father's proposed maintenance would be £53.29.
Mother's proposed maintenance would be £33.94.
Joint proposed maintenance = £53.29 + £33.94 = £87.23.
The mother provides care three out of seven nights = 42.86% of the care.
This is equivalent to paying 42.86% x £87.23 = £37.39 a week maintenance.
The mother therefore does not have to pay any maintenance as her contribution in kind (£37.39) just outweighs her financial liability (£33.94). Despite the fact that her assessable income is the same as in (a), her liability has been reduced to nil as a result of the increased liability of the father.
The father still has to pay his proposed maintenance, assuming this does not bring his disposable income below the protected income level. The maintenance of £53.29 is paid to the grandmother.

Chapter 16: Shared care under the 'old rules'
Notes

Notes

1. What is shared care
1. Regs 20(1)(a) and 24(1)(a) CS(MASC) Regs
2. Reg 1(2) CS(MASC) Regs
3. Reg 1(2) CS(MASC) Regs; CCS/6/1994
4. Alternative period for establishing day-to-day care
5. CCS/128/2001
6. Regs 1(2) and 20(1) CS(MASC) Regs; CCS/449/1995
7. CCS/12686/1996
8. CCS/11728/1996; Deciding principal provider of day-to-day care
9. s5(1) CSA 1991
10. s5(2) CSA 1991

2. Care shared by separated parents
11. Reg 20(2) and (3) CS(MASC) Regs
12. CCS/13455/1996
13. Reg 20(2)(a) CS(MASC) Regs
14. Reg 20(2)(b)(i) CS(MASC) Regs
15. s144(3) and Sch 10 SSCBA 1992
16. Reg 20(2)(b)(ii) CS(MASC) Regs
17. Reg 20(4) CS(MASC) Regs
18. Reg 9(4) CS(MASC) Regs
19. Reg 9(3) CS(MASC) Regs
20. Reg 9(1)(f) and (2)(c)(iv) CS(MASC) Regs
21. Reg 20(3) and (4) CS(MASC) Regs
22. Reg 20(5) CS(MASC) Regs
23. Reg 20(6) CS(MASC) Regs
24. Reg 20(6) CS(MASC) Regs
25. Reg 11(3) and (4) CS(MASC) Regs
26. NRP has shared care of more than one QC on different nights of the week

3. Care shared between a parent and another person
27. Reg 20 CS(MASC) Regs
28. Reg 19(1) CS(MASC) Regs
29. Reg 20(4)(i) CS(MASC) Regs
30. Reg 20(4)(ii) CS(MASC) Regs
31. Reg 24(1) CS(MASC) Regs
32. Reg 24(2)(a) CS(MASC) Regs
33. Reg 24(2)(b) CS(MASC) Regs
34. Reg 24(2)(c) CS(MASC) Regs

4. Care shared between two people who are not parents
35. Reg 24 CS(MASC) Regs

6. Care provided in part by the local authority
36. Reg 51 CS(MAP) Regs
37. Reg 25 CS(MASC) Regs
38. Reg 25(3) CS(MASC) Regs; para 6762 DMG

7. The maintenance requirement is met in full
39. Reg 9(3) and (4) CS(MASC) Regs

Chapter 17
Departures under the 'old rules'

This chapter covers:
1. Grounds for departure (p348)
2. Applying for departure (p358)
3. Procedure (p359)
4. Considering departure (p362)
5. The departure direction (p364)

> For information on 'old rules' cases with departures converting to the 'new rules', see Chapter 9.

The CSA can 'depart' from the standard formula (see Chapters 10-15) in special cases, but only once a maintenance assessment has been made (see Chapter 18). There can be no departure from a Category A or C interim maintenance assessment (IMA) (see p399).[1] A non-resident parent cannot request departure from a Category D IMA.[2] Not all types of departure can be used with a Category D IMA where the person with care applies or with a Category B IMA.[3]

There can be no departure if, on the date from which any departure direction would have effect (see p370):[4]
- the non-resident parent was being paid income support (IS), income-based jobseeker's allowance (JSA) or pension credit (PC) or one of those benefits was being paid for him; or
- the person with care was being paid IS, income-based JSA, PC or working tax credit (WTC) or one of those benefits was being paid for her. This only applies to a departure application by:
  – the person with care for special expenses (see p348); or
  – the non-resident parent on additional cases grounds (see p355).

A departure direction can only be made for a reason given in the legislation and only if it would be just and equitable to do so (see p362). Departure can mean changes to the amounts used in the standard formula to work out the assessment.

Chapter 17: Departures under the 'old rules'
1. Grounds for departure

1. Grounds for departure

Grounds for departure fall into three groups:
- **special expenses** (see below) which the standard formula does not take into account – this is mostly used by non-resident parents;
- **additional cases** (see p355) because of under-use of available income/assets or unreasonably high outgoings – this is mostly used by persons with care;
- **property/capital transfers** made before April 1993 (see p357).

Special expenses

Departure is possible where the applicant has:[5]
- travel costs of contact with the child(ren) named in the assessment (see below);
- costs of supporting a stepchild and other children in the family (see p349);
- travel-to-work costs not taken into account in the assessment (see p352);
- costs of a long-term illness or disability of the applicant or a dependant (see p353);
- debts incurred before the couple separated (see p353); *or*
- pre-April 1993 financial commitments from which it would be impossible or unreasonable to withdraw (see p354).

With contact costs, travel-to-work costs, debts and pre-1993 financial commitments, the first £15 of the total of all these costs is disregarded.[6] There can be no departure for special expenses if the non-resident parent is on income support (IS), income-based jobseeker's allowance (JSA) or pension credit (PC) or the person with care is on IS or income-based JSA, PC or working tax credit (WTC).

Contact costs

The only costs which count are the non-resident parent's costs of his contact with the children named in the assessment.[7] A parent with shared care who is treated as a non-resident parent (see p329) does not count as a non-resident parent for contact costs.[8]

Only travel costs count, not the cost of treats or overnight stays. Travel costs can be for the non-resident parent travelling to see the children, or the children travelling to see him.[9] We are advised by the DWP child support policy department that if a travelling companion is necessary, say because the children are young or the parent is disabled, that person's travel costs may not count. We would urge individuals to appeal any refusal to consider such costs on the grounds that the regulations refer to travel costs 'incurred for the purpose of maintaining contact' and it would be unreasonable to exclude such costs. CSA guidance states that travel for day trips does not count.[10] Costs incurred for the purpose of maintaining contact may include costs of some travel once the non-resident parent and

Chapter 17: Departures under the 'old rules'
1. Grounds for departure

child(ren) are together – eg, taking the child from the person with care's home to the non-resident parent's home; however, the cost of travel to the cinema from the person with care's home will not normally be considered.

Only the following count as travel costs:[11]
- by public transport (eg, train, coach, boat or plane) – the cost of the ticket(s);
- by private vehicle – fuel only, there is no allowance for repairs, etc;
- by taxi – fares, but only for a non-resident parent whose disability or illness makes it impracticable for him to use another form of available transport.[12] Any financial assistance he receives towards contact costs is offset from the fare.[13]

Minor incidental costs also count. These may include bridge tolls, parking and ticket reservation fees.[14]

The costs are based on an established pattern of visits if one exists.[15] If there is no established pattern, the non-resident parent and person with care must have agreed a pattern of future contact. This will be used.[16]

The CSA can decide that contact costs are unreasonably high or unreasonably incurred – eg, because the method of travel is too expensive. For rail, as there are different rates of fares, the CSA is likely to consider the full cost of first class tickets unreasonable and will substitute a lower amount.[17] Petrol costs may be based on the shortest route, or a smaller car.[18] If the non-resident parent returns from abroad and contact is only one reason for the trip, the CSA may limit costs to those of travel from his home in the UK.[19]

Where visits are frequent, the CSA may only allow travel costs of some visits. The CSA must allow enough costs for visits specified in a court order, as long as those visits are being made.[20] Non-resident parents who visit more often than the court order states may wish to change the order to reflect the true position.

Changes in contact may mean changes in any departure direction. If contact stops, even through no fault of the non-resident parent, the departure direction will be cancelled.[21]

The first £15 is disregarded (but see p348).

Costs of supporting a stepchild

Where a non-resident parent or person with care supports a child who is part of her/his household (see p29), but of whom s/he is not the parent (see p23), an amount for those costs may be allowed.[22] This amount is set by a formula (see below). This ground cannot be used by a departure applicant subject to a Category B interim maintenance assessment (IMA).[23]

We use 'stepchild' here because the CSA does. A stepchild is one who:[24]
- counts as a member of the applicant's family. This is limited to children of:
  – the applicant's current partner; *and*
  – the applicant's former partner and they live in the applicant's household every night of the week; *and*

Chapter 17: Departures under the 'old rules'
1. Grounds for departure

- was part of the applicant's family and household before 5 April 1993; *and*
- remained part of that family and household from 5 April 1993 continuously to the effective date the proposed direction would have (see p370).[25]

The expenses allowed depend upon the support for the stepchild from her/his non-resident parent and, where the applicant's partner is the child's parent, from that partner. The **cost** of the stepchild is based on the amount excluded from exempt income and is:[26]
- IS personal allowance for a child of that age; *plus*
- IS family premium where the family contains no children of whom the applicant is the parent. Where special expenses are sought for more than one stepchild, the family premium is divided equally between them;[27] *plus*
- IS disabled child premium if the stepchild would qualify.

Where the care of the stepchild is shared between the applicant's current partner and the stepchild's other parent, the cost is reduced by the proportion of time the child spends away from the applicant's household.[28]

No expenses are allowed if maintenance payable to or for the stepchild by her/his non-resident parent is more than the cost, where it is a deduction from his IS/income-based JSA (see p224) *or* is under an order or written agreement for maintenance or a maintenance assessment.[29] The CSA can ignore maintenance payable (but not deductions due) if, for example, the stepchild's non-resident parent cannot be found.[30]

If maintenance is less than the cost, the **allowable amount** is the cost less any maintenance payable (unless ignored) or deductions.[31]

If the applicant's partner is *not* the stepchild's parent, the maximum special expenses allowed is the allowable amount.[32]

Where special expenses are sought for stepchildren of different parents, a separate allowable amount is worked out for each child (or group of children who have the same parents), and the allowable amount is the total of those amounts.[33]

If the applicant's partner is the stepchild's parent, her ability to support the child is taken into account, in a similar way to the joint child calculation for exempt income (see p256). Her **net income** is worked out as if it were a non-resident parent's assessable income (see Chapter 13) plus child benefit for the stepchildren and any income of her children (except earnings) above £10.[34] Her **outgoings** are:[35]
- the IS personal allowance for a person aged 25 or over (regardless of the partner's actual age); *plus*
- any partner's contribution for joint child(ren) assumed under the standard formula (see p256); *plus*
- the allowable amount (see above); *plus*
- any partner's contribution to housing costs assumed under an existing departure direction (see p357).

Chapter 17: Departures under the 'old rules'
1. Grounds for departure

If the partner's net income is more than her outgoings, no costs are allowed.[36] If it is less, maximum special expenses are the allowable amount.[37]

Example 17.1

(a) Bob has been assessed to pay £50.57 for Carol and David (example 15.4b). He lives with his partner, Zoe, their child, Ricky, and three stepchildren so departure is possible if the step-family was formed before April 1993. Zoe receives maintenance of £20 a week for Yvonne (14) and Veronica (12), but nothing for Scott (5). The **allowable amount** is worked out for each non-resident parent:

		£
Wayne's children		
Personal allowances:	Yvonne (14)	42.27
	Veronica (12)	42.27
Total *		84.54
Less maintenance due		20.00
Allowable amount		64.54
Terence's child		
Personal allowance:	Scott (5)	42.27
Allowable amount* (no maintenance due)		
Total allowable amount		**106.81**

* no family premium applies as there is a joint child, Ricky. It is included in Bob's exempt income (see example 12.6).

Zoe's **net income** is child benefit £49.65

Personal allowance		55.65
Total allowable amount		106.81
Outgoings		**162.46**

Zoe's income is less than her outgoings so the maximum special expenses is the total allowable amount of £106.81. (Working tax credit counts as Bob's income and not Zoe's because he is the partner in employment.) A departure direction for a special expense of £106.81 can therefore be made (but see example 17.6). However, if Zoe had refused to accept maintenance for Scott, the departure decision maker may decide that departure would not be fair.

Zoe had recently applied for a CSA assessment: the departure decision maker may not make a decision until that application is decided.

(b) Some months later the CSA issues assessments of £5.60 from Wayne and £30.79 from Terence. Also, Zoe is now working and when Bob's liability is reassessed it rises to £65.12. The new allowable amount is:

Wayne's children (total personal allowances)		84.54
Less child support due		5.60
Allowable amount		78.94
Terence's child (personal allowance)		**42.27**
Less child support due		30.79

351

Chapter 17: Departures under the 'old rules'
1. Grounds for departure

Allowable amount		11.48
Total allowable amount		**90.42**

Zoe's maintenance has increased from £20 to £36.39, and the total allowable amount has gone down by £16.39. Zoe's **net income** is now:

Child benefit	49.65
Earnings	90.00
Net income	**139.65**

Because Zoe is now treated as able to support the joint child (see example 12.6b) her **outgoings** are considered to be higher:

Personal allowances	Zoe	55.65
	Ricky (half)	21.14
Family premium (half)		7.98
Allowable amount		90.42
Partner's contribution to housing costs		Nil
Total		**175.19**

Zoe's net income is lower than this, so Bob's departure application would include the reduced allowable expenses of £90.42; however, had Zoe's income been higher it would have failed.

Travel-to-work costs

If the travel-to-work costs of a non-resident parent or person with care are not adequately covered by the broad-brush allowance in the formula (see p253), a departure can be made. As the formula allowance works on straight-line distances, those who travel around estuaries or mountains or are in rural areas may benefit. Those whose reasonable public transport costs are more than 10 pence per straight line mile may also benefit. Self-employed people can benefit for travel costs which are not tax-deductible.[38]

Travel costs allowable are the same as for contact costs (see p348), except that taxi fares are allowable regardless of disability, but only where the journey is unavoidably taken at a time when no other reasonable type of transport is available.[39] Minor incidental costs count. Costs can be reduced or refused where they are considered high or unreasonably incurred.[40] CSA staff are advised to treat disabled people's parking costs as costs of a long-term disability (see p353) because there is no £15 disregard.[41]

The travel cost special expenses allowance replaces the formula allowance (see p253). There is a £15 disregard (but see p348).

Example 17.2
Steve (see example 12.5) has an allowance of £65 included in his exempt income for travel to work. However, Steve's season ticket to London is £5,100 a year or £98 a week. Even with the first £15 disregarded this is greater than the allowance. The departure decision

Chapter 17: Departures under the 'old rules'
1. Grounds for departure

maker has decided that a direction is reasonable because Steve lives in Leicestershire in order to be near his two children, and he has not been able to find an equivalent job nearer to home. The special expense of £83 replaces the broad-brush allowance of £65. See example 17.4 for the recalculated assessment.

Costs of a long-term illness or disability

Special expenses include costs due to a long-term illness or disability of the non-resident parent or person with care and/or his/her dependant(s).[42] Long-term illness is one that is current at the date of the departure application and which is likely to last for a further 52 weeks or to be terminal.[43] Dependant means:[44]
- the departure applicant's partner (see p32);
- a child (see p26) of the applicant or partner, living with the applicant, except a child named in the assessment to which the departure application applies (see also p37 for additional maintenance).

Costs allowable are the reasonable costs of:[45]
- personal care, attendance and communication needs;
- mobility;
- domestic help;
- medical aids which cannot be provided under the NHS;[46]
- heating, clothing and laundry;
- food essential for a diet recommended by a medical practitioner;
- adaptations to the applicant's home; *and*
- day care, respite care and rehabilitation.

Any financial help towards these costs from any source is deducted.[47] This includes disability living allowance (DLA) and attendance allowance (AA). If a DLA/AA claim has been made, the CSA will wait for that decision before deciding on departure.[48] If no claim has been made, but the CSA considers that the disabled person may be entitled, the CSA will notify the applicant, who has six weeks in which to claim. If no claim is made, the CSA will deduct the highest rate of the appropriate component(s) of DLA (or AA if appropriate) from the costs.[49] The CSA has a discretion to ignore DLA/AA awarded to a dependant.[50]

Debts of the relationship

A non-resident parent or person with care may be repaying debts incurred *before* the non-resident parent became a non-resident parent (see p29) of the child named in the assessment (whether before or after April 1993). Repayment can count as special expenses, but only if the debt was incurred when the departure applicant and ex-partner were a couple (see p32) and was for the benefit of:[51]
- the departure applicant and an ex-partner, jointly;
- the ex-partner alone, if the applicant is liable for the repayments;

353

Chapter 17: Departures under the 'old rules'
1. Grounds for departure

- a child (see p26) of the applicant and/or ex-partner, who lived with the applicant and ex-partner at the time the debt arose; *and/or*
- a child named in the assessment to which the departure application applies.

Ex-partner includes any ex-partner of the non-resident parent (not just the parent with care), but, if the person with care applies for departure only the non-resident parent counts as an ex-partner.[52]

Loans only count if they are from a bank, building society or other registered lender or the departure applicant's current or former employer.[53] The following do *not* count as debts:
- debts incurred to buy something which the applicant kept after the relationship ended;[54]
- a debt for which the applicant took responsibility under a financial settlement with the ex-partner or a court order;[55]
- secured mortgage repayments; *and*
- endowment/insurance premiums,[56] except for mortgage/insurance incurred to buy or repair/improve (see p243)[57] the home of the parent with care and child named in the assessment.

The following also do *not* count as debts:[58]
- debts of a business or trade;
- gambling debts;
- legal costs of the separation or divorce;
- credit card repayments;
- overdrafts, unless it was taken out for a specified amount repayable over a specified period;
- fines imposed on the applicant;
- any debt incurred to pay off one of these (except for business/trade debts); *or*
- any other debt the CSA considers it reasonable to exclude.

A debt counts if it was incurred to pay a debt which would have counted.[59] However, any direction is based upon the repayment period and rate of the original debt.[60]

The first £15 is disregarded (but see p348).

Any departure direction is for the debt repayment period.[61] If the applicant cannot meet the repayments, the direction can be extended, but only if the creditor agreed to extend time for repayment because of:[62]
- the applicant's unemployment or incapacity for work; *or*
- a substantial fall in the applicant's income.

Pre-April 1993 financial commitments

Special expenses can include other financial commitments of the non-resident parent – eg, hire purchase, school fees. Commitments like those in the listed

Chapter 17: Departures under the 'old rules'
1. Grounds for departure

on p353 (under 'Debts of the relationship') do not count. The only commitments which count are those:[63]
- made before 5 April 1993;
- from which it would be impossible or unreasonable to expect him to withdraw; *and*
- where an order or written agreement for maintenance was made before 5 April 1993 for all the non-resident parent's children (see p26) (including at least one child named in the assessment) *and* that order/agreement was in force on both the date the commitment was made and on 5 April 1993.[64] There can be more than one order/agreement for different children.

Additional cases

This can be used by a person with care who is not a parent. However, for convenience, we refer to 'parent'.

Grounds for departure are:[65]
- a parent's lifestyle is inconsistent with the level of her/his income;
- a parent's assets could produce some or more income;
- a parent has diverted her/his income so it is not taken into account for the formula;
- housing costs used in the formula are unreasonably high;
- it is reasonable for a parent's partner to contribute towards the couple's housing costs;
- travel-to-work costs used in the formula are unreasonably high; *or*
- travel-to-work costs should be disregarded completely

There can be no departure on additional cases grounds if the non-resident parent is on IS or income-based JSA *or* if he is the departure applicant and the person with care is on IS, income-based JSA or WTC (see p347). However, any reliable information about undeclared income will be passed to the Jobcentre Plus (see p116)[66] and/or the case can be referred to CSA to consider whether there is notional income (see p278).[67]

> *Example 17.3*
> A non-resident parent has a large well-furnished house in a stockbroker belt, with several cars in the drive and a lifestyle which suggests wealth. He is a director of his own company and pays a modest salary to himself and to his new partner. His declared income is only a few pounds above the mortgage so the assessment is nil. He is not subject to the excessive housing cost rule (see p247) nor to the minimum payment (see p223) as the couple have a child. The person with care could seek a departure on three grounds:
> • the non-resident parent's lifestyle is incompatible with his declared income;
> • the non-resident parent's partner should contribute to housing costs; *and*
> • the housing costs are unreasonably high.

Chapter 17: Departures under the 'old rules'
1. Grounds for departure

If the new partner does not do much work for the business, his income may have been unreasonably diverted to her.

Lifestyle inconsistent with income

Departure is possible where a parent's overall lifestyle requires substantially higher income than the amount of her/his income on which the maintenance assessment is based.[68] This cannot be done if the lifestyle is paid for:[69]
- from the parent's capital; *or*
- by her/his partner, unless the parent can influence the amount of the partner's income (eg, as employer). If s/he cannot, the CSA can consider whether the partner could contribute to housing costs (see p357).[70]

The CSA is unlikely to investigate a parent's lifestyle. If there are grounds for investigation, the CSA might refer the case to an appeal tribunal, which may direct the parties to provide evidence (see p440).[71]

If departure is directed, notional extra income will be set (see p369).

Under-use of assets

A parent may be under-using her/his money or property. Departure can only happen if the total value of the assets found to be under-used (less any mortgage or charge) is £10,000 or more.[72] This can apply if s/he is the beneficiary of (for details see CPAG's *Welfare Benefits and Tax Credits Handbook*, 'Trusts') or can control:[73]
- an asset which does not produce income but could do;
- an investment producing less income than is reasonable;
- a claim to money (eg, a debt or legal action)[74] which it is reasonable to enforce; *and/or*
- an asset which it would be reasonable to sell.

This also applies to any trust funds of which the parent is a beneficiary.[75]

The CSA can ignore assets which are to be used for a reasonable purpose.[76] The parent's home would not normally be treated as an asset for the purpose of this ground; however, any second or holiday homes could be considered.

If an under-used asset exists, any departure direction will set the notional extra income which the asset could produce. The asset is assumed to produce income at the judgement rate: currently 8 per cent.[77] Any actual income from the asset is deducted from that notional income.

Diversion of income

Departure is possible where a parent can control his income *and* has unreasonably reduced his income (as worked out for the standard formula) by diverting it to other people or other purposes.[78] For example, a non-resident parent's company pays him no salary but pays his partner an inflated one.

Unreasonable housing costs

Where a parent's housing costs are more than the amount normally allowed under the formula but s/he is exempt from that restriction (see p247), departure is possible if those costs are unreasonably high.[79] Departure only removes the exemption, so weekly housing costs still cannot be set at less than the greater of £80 or half the parent's net income.[80]

Partner's contribution towards housing costs

Departure is possible where a parent has a partner who occupies the home and it is reasonable for that partner to contribute towards housing costs.[81] The CSA will decide what proportion the partner should pay, considering the parent's income and the partner's income.[82] This can be 100 per cent, especially if a Category B IMA is in force and/or the parent is withholding information about her/his partner's income.[83]

Unreasonable travel to work costs/allowance

Departure is possible where travel costs allowed under the formula (see p254):
- are unreasonably high – eg, the parent shares a car;[84] *or*
- ought not to be allowed because the parent can pay maintenance assessed without an allowance for part or all of those costs.[85]

Property/capital transfers

The broad-brush formula allowance for pre-1993 property transfers (see p249) may not result in a proper reflection of the effect of that transfer in the amount of child support maintenance. Also, some parents cannot use that allowance – eg, because of lack of evidence. Departure allows for a more flexible approach. Property is not defined (as it is for the broad-brush allowance – see p249) so it includes things such as household items and shares.[86] This is not a ground for departure from a Category D IMA.[87]

Departure is possible where:[88]
- before 5 April 1993 a court order or written agreement was in force between the non-resident parent and the person with care and/or the child(ren) named in the assessment; *and*
- in connection with that order/agreement, property which the non-resident parent owned (or had the benefit of) was transferred to that person with care or that child, or to a trust for payment of the normal day-to-day living expenses of that child; *and either:*
  - that transfer reduced the non-resident parent's maintenance liability (not child support) *and* the effect of that transfer is not properly reflected in the current maintenance assessment; *or*
  - that transfer did *not* reduce the non-resident parent's maintenance liability (not child support) *but* the current maintenance assessment is reduced

357

because of that transfer *and* that reduction is inappropriate because of the purpose of the transfer – eg, it was for spousal maintenance.

No departure can be made if:
- the change in maintenance would be less than £1;[89] *or*
- the transfer is temporary and ends before the effective date which any direction would have.[90]

To see if the broad-brush property allowance fairly reflects the child maintenance forgone, the CSA first works out the value of the transfer ignoring any part which was not in lieu of child maintenance. Unless there is evidence to show otherwise, the CSA assumes that:[91]
- the property covered by the order/agreement was held in equal shares by the non-resident parent and person with care;
- if those parties had been married, half of the value of the transfer was for the person with care's benefit, and not for the child(ren);
- if those parties were *never* married, *none* of the value of the transfer was for the person with care's benefit.

The equivalent weekly value is then worked out. The number of years of liability is deemed to begin on the date of the order/agreement and to end on the date it sets for maintenance to end (for the youngest child if there is more than one), or, if no date is given, when the youngest child reaches 18.[92] Using that figure and the interest rate on judgment debt at the date of the order/agreement, a multiplier is given by a table.[93] That gives an equivalent weekly value which replaces the broad-brush allowance (see p249). If that would lead to a departed assessment of less than the child maintenance payable under the order/agreement, a lower weekly value can be set. The weekly value of a transfer of less than £5,000 is nil.[94]

The result is difficult to predict (see example 17.7). The assessment may be increased or reduced, irrespective of who applied for departure.

2. Applying for departure

Once an assessment has been made, a person with care, non-resident parent or child applicant in Scotland may apply for a departure direction.[95] This applies to any assessment – whether made on initial application or after a revision or supersession – but not to all categories of interim maintenance assessment (see p347). Information about departure will be provided with an assessment.

The application should be made on Form 580D, but the CSA may accept a letter which has all the information that form requires.[96] The applicant should fill in the form as fully as possible. The date of the application is the date it is received by the CSA, unless there was unavoidable delay in the CSA receiving it.[97] The date of the application affects the effective date of any direction (see p370).

If the application is not accepted because it is not properly made, the CSA can send it back (or send a form) to the applicant. If it is properly made within 14 days of the day the CSA sends it back, it counts as made when the defective application was made.[98]

An application cannot be made before the assessment is made.[99] Even if the reason for departure is in the maintenance application form or maintenance enquiry form, a separate application must still be made.

A departure applicant can be represented by any other person.[100]

A departure application can be withdrawn or amended by the applicant at any time up to a decision on it.[101] S/he may want to do this after seeing the other party's information. However, a person considering applying may want to try to work out what any departure would be *before* applying. This is because a departure may work against the applicant.

3. Procedure

Departure applications on several grounds or by both parties will be considered together to ensure that the outcome is just and equitable (see p363). Each party may have a departure direction granted (on multiple grounds) and applied to the assessment.[102]

Preliminary consideration

The decision maker will carry out a check (or 'sift') of each application before asking the other party for information.[103] If the application has no chance of success, it will be refused.

The CSA may ask the applicant for further information which must be provided within one month (longer may be allowed if the CSA is satisfied that this is reasonable).[104] If it is not, and the decision maker is satisfied on the available evidence that a departure direction should not be given, the application may be refused without the other party being asked for information.[105]

Because the decision maker wants the assessment to be correct *before* departure is considered, s/he may pass the case to other CSA staff for revision or supersession before completing the sift (see p371).

There is a right of appeal against refusal on preliminary consideration (see p374).

If the case passes the sift but the decision maker considers that a direction is unlikely to be given, s/he can decide the application without asking the other party for information.[106] However, if the decision maker then considers a direction should be made, s/he must ask for that information before making a decision (see below).[107]

Information

If the application passes preliminary consideration, the CSA must (unless a direction is unlikely to be made – see above) write to the other party (or parties if the maintenance application was by a Scottish child):[108]
- notifying her/him that the departure application has been made;
- sending details of the grounds for the application and any relevant information the applicant has given (but see below); *and*
- asking for representations about the application, which must be made within 14 days.[109]

If representations are sent, the CSA may send them to the applicant asking for comments.[110] However, this is only likely to happen where the evidence provided by the parent contradicts that supplied by the applicant, and the CSA cannot make a decision based on the evidence available. The contradictory evidence may then be copied to the other party asking for comments.[111] Any party can send further information to the CSA at any time. If a response cannot be made within 14 days, the information available should be sent with a request for more time to provide the rest. The CSA is unlikely to make its own enquiries so each party must make their own case. On appeal/reference the appeal tribunal can require information to be provided (see p436).

Where one party does not know the whereabouts of another party or a child named in the maintenance assessment and that party has not agreed to disclosure, then that address and any information which could reasonably be expected to lead to them being located will not be disclosed unless:[112]
- that address/information is necessary to decide the departure application; *and*
- there is no risk of harm or undue distress to that party/child if disclosure were made.

Undisclosed medical evidence will not be sent to a person if it would harm her/his health.[113]

Regular payments condition

If a non-resident parent applies for departure, the CSA can impose a regular payments condition (RPC).[114] This will only normally be done where the non-resident parent persistently fails to pay maintenance due and only once the application has passed preliminary consideration (see p359).[115] A person with care who knows a departure application has been made can ask the CSA to make an RPC.

Decisions about an RPC may be initiated by the CSA debt management section but the decision maker decides whether to impose the RPC and the rate at which it should be paid. An RPC will usually be set at the rate of the current assessment.[116] The exception is where the departure application is for special expenses for travel costs, contact costs or illness/disability.[117] If this applies, the RPC will be set for a lower amount on the assumption that a departure direction has been made for those expenses, unless the non-resident parent has exaggerated or claimed unreasonable expenses.[118]

The CSA notifies the non-resident parent and person with care of any RPC and the effect of failing to comply.[119] If the non-resident parent fails to comply, the decision maker may suspend consideration of the application.[120] The non-resident parent will then usually be contacted and the RPC may be re-negotiated.[121]

If this does not work, the CSA can decide that the non-resident parent has failed to comply with the RPC. Written notice of this is sent to the non-resident parent and person with care.[122] If the CSA decides that the non-resident parent has failed to comply with the RPC within 28 days of the notice, the departure application lapses.[123]

An RPC does not affect the amount of maintenance the non-resident parent is *liable* to pay. Even if he complies with the RPC, if this is less than the amount of the current assessment, there will be arrears if the departure application fails (see p467).

The RPC will end once the departure decision has been made.

Revision or supersession of the assessment

A departure application can be made even if a revision or supersession of the existing assessment has been applied for.[124] An assessment can also be revised or superseded while a departure application is being considered. In a case where a fresh assessment is made on such a revision or supersession the decision maker may direct that the departure application lapse unless the applicant asks for it to stand.[125] See Chapter 19 for revisions and supersessions.

A departure will not be made until the assessment is correct and up to date.[126] If the application shows a ground for changing the assessment (eg, a mistake or a change of circumstances), the case will be considered for revision or supersession.[127]

Normally, decision makers will wait for the outcome of the revision or supersession before considering departure. However, where a non-resident parent is failing to co-operate with a 'case check' the decision maker may proceed with departure without waiting for the outcome.[128]

Where an assessment is revised or superseded (see p371) the departure decision maker treats that fresh assessment as the current assessment when considering departure.[129]

Chapter 17: Departures under the 'old rules'
3. Procedure

Decision on the application

If the decision maker decides the application (rather than referring it to a tribunal) s/he must notify the parties of that decision and the reasons for it.[130] If the decision is to make a direction, the notification must state the way in which maintenance is to be worked out as a result of the direction. The CSA will then make a new assessment taking account of the instructions in the departure direction (see p364). The departure will produce two appealable decisions:
- the departure direction; *and*
- the maintenance assessment after taking the departure into account.

It is therefore important to be clear which decision is being appealed to the tribunal. For more information on appeals, see Chapter 20.

Referral to an appeal tribunal

Once a departure application has passed preliminary consideration and the parties' representations have been sought, a decision maker can refer it to an appeal tribunal instead of deciding it her/himself.[131] Many departure cases will be complex or difficult, but these should normally be decided by a decision maker. Current CSA guidance states that referral may be made if:[132]
- the case raises new points – ie, ones which have never arisen in a departure case before; *or*
- the case is very contentious – eg, both parties have solicitors and the evidence is completely contradictory; *or*
- only an appeal tribunal will be able to obtain the necessary evidence.

An appeal tribunal considering a referral is subject to the rules which apply to a decision maker and will either give a direction or refuse to give one.[133] However, the procedure will be similar to an appeal and the tribunal's decision can be appealed on a point of law (see p450).

4. Considering departure

A departure direction can only be made if it would change the amount of the assessment by £1 or more.[134] The possible effect of 'old rules' phasing-in (see p387) is ignored.[135]

Discretion to make a direction

When considering whether and how to make a direction, the departure decision maker must:[136]
- treat parents as responsible for maintaining their children when they can afford to do so;

- treat parents as responsible for maintaining all their children equally;
- ignore the fact that all or part of the income of the person with care (or her partner) includes (or would on departure include) income support, income-based jobseeker's allowance, working tax credit, housing benefit or council tax benefit, or that child maintenance might be taken into account for benefit entitlement.

Just and equitable

Even though the grounds for departure are met and the assessment would change by £1 or more, a direction will only be made if it would be just and equitable to do so, that is, fair to all concerned.[137] The decision maker will first work out what direction would be appropriate and how it would affect the assessment.[138] When considering whether it would be fair to make that direction, the decision maker must consider:[139]

- the financial circumstances of the non-resident parent, including any liability to pay maintenance before the assessment's effective date;
- the financial circumstances of the person with care (but ignore her receipt of certain benefits – see above);
- whether a direction would lead to the non-resident parent or person with care giving up employment;[140]
- where the application is for special expenses, whether the applicant could have made financial arrangements to cover those expenses, or could pay for them from money s/he is spending on non-essentials.

The decision maker must *not* take into account:
- the circumstances of the child's conception;
- the reasons for the breakdown of the relationship;
- the fact that either party is now involved in a new relationship;
- any contact arrangements;
- the failure of the non-resident parent to pay maintenance under the CSA assessment or any previous arrangement; *nor*
- any representations made by a person other than the person with care, the non-resident parent or a Scottish child applicant.

CSA guidance states that discretion will only rarely be used to refuse a departure direction outright.[141] However, it may well be used to reduce the amount of the direction.[142] This guidance emphasises the parties' responsibilities for organising their lives so as to support their children. Where parties have unreasonably taken on new responsibilities (eg, a second family), failed to reduce outgoings (eg, re-schedule debts) or failed to increase their income (person with care who could take work), the guidance suggests that in fairness no direction should be made.

5. The departure direction

A direction is not a new assessment. It is a direction to reassess child maintenance on a different basis.[143] The CSA must comply as soon as reasonably practicable.[144]

The direction cannot take maintenance above the formula maximum (see p296) or below the £5.60 weekly minimum (see p223).[145] A non-resident parent cannot fall below the protected income level (see Chapter 15), though the direction may change that level (see p364).[146]

Phased assessments

If the assessment is being phased in (see p387), special rules apply. If the effective date of the departure direction (see p370) is the *same* as that of the assessment, the direction is applied to the formula assessment.[147] The CSA then applies any phasing to that departed assessment.

If the effective date of the departure direction is *later* than that of the assessment, the direction is applied to the formula assessment. This proposed departed assessment is then compared with both the formula assessment and the phased assessment – ie, the formula assessment with phasing. If the proposed departed assessment is:[148]
- higher than the formula assessment, then the difference between them is added to the phased assessment to give the actual departed assessment;
- less than the formula assessment but more than the phased assessment, then departure has no effect and the phased assessment is used; *or*
- less than the phased assessment, then the proposed departed assessment is used.

Special expenses directions

The direction states an amount for special expenses. The CSA includes this in the applicant's exempt income and any protected income.[149] Expenses for a stepchild do not change protected income, because they are already included (see example 15.6).[150] If the direction is for travel-to-work costs (see p352), any amount for those already included in exempt income or protected income is replaced by the amount stated in the direction.[151]

If the direction reduces the non-resident parent's assessable income, the departed assessment is *the lowest of*:[152]
- the assessment current on the direction's effective date (see p370);
- 50 per cent of his assessable income after departure (see Chapter 13); *and*
- protected income level (see Chapter 15). This applies regardless of the maintenance requirement or the number of children.

If the direction would also change the figures to be used because of over-generous provision (see p355), the same calculation is done assuming those changes have taken effect.[153] For the rules where a direction for property/capital transfer is also made, see p367.

If a non-resident parent is liable to more than one person with care (see p300), his total liability is set by these rules.[154] The amount of each departed assessment will be the same proportion of total liability as it would be if liability were based on the maintenance requirements.[155]

Example 17.4: Special expenses – debts and travel costs
Steve has been assessed to pay £62.18 a week to Debbie as maintenance for Paul (17), Grace (15) and Lewis (10). In July 2003, Steve applies for departure on the grounds of travel-to-work costs, debts of the relationship and pre-April 1993 commitments. He does not apply on the ground of the property settlement (see example 12.4) as he wants first to ask his solicitor whether it would be to his advantage.

Steve is awarded special expenses of £83 travel-to-work costs (see example 17.2). He divorced in 1991 and has already cleared some debts, but there remains one debt of the relationship and another commitment pre-dating the divorce. The total repayments amount to £34.60 a week: there is no £15 disregard as this has already been applied to the travel costs.

Debbie has net earnings of £210 and assessable income of £28.60. These were taken into account under the formula but, on departure, Steve simply pays 50 per cent of his own assessable income (as long as this is below the current assessment).

Steve's exempt income:	£
Personal allowance	55.65
Mortgage (in full – see example 12.5)	96.00
Property settlement allowance	40.00
Travel-to-work costs	83.00
Debt repayments	34.60
Total	*309.25*

Steve's net income for child support purposes: £380 a week earnings
Steve's assessable income = £380 – £309.25 = £70.75
Proposed maintenance = 50% x £70.75 = **£35.38**

Protected income:		£
Personal allowance	Couple	87.30
Mortgage (interest only)		78.46
Council tax		15.00
Travel-to-work costs		83.00
Debt repayments		34.60
Standard margin		30.00
Basic protected income		*328.36*

Total family income: Steve's new wife Lisa has net earnings of £280, so total family income = £380 + £280 = £660. This is far above protected income so Steve can afford the proposed maintenance of **£35.38**.

The departure direction has therefore reduced the assessment from £62.18 to £35.38.

Chapter 17: Departures under the 'old rules'
5. The departure direction

Because the 50 per cent taper applies right up the income range, there comes a point where a non-resident parent's income is too high to benefit from departure (see example 17.5 below).

Example 17.5: The well off and special expenses
a) Jeremy has been assessed to pay £245.52 a week for his four children (see example 14.3). He applies for departure on two grounds – contact costs and the commitment of school fees for the children. The children stay with Jeremy every other weekend. He collects and returns them in his car. This is cheaper than four return train fares: the petrol used is £38 a weekend. As this is £19 a week, the £15 disregard leaves a special expense of £4.

All four children are in private education, but the commitments for Henry (8) and Isobel (4) were made after 1993. The decision maker could decide that it would not be unreasonable to move Georgina (12) to another school whereas Francis (14) has already begun his GCSE courses.

The decision maker decides that in principle special expenses of £80 a week should be allowed for the next 18 months. Jeremy's exempt income would be increased by £4 + £80 = £84.

His assessable income would be now £516 (instead of £600).

The proposed maintenance after the departure would be: 50% x £516 = £258. As this is higher than the current maintenance assessment of £245.52, no departure direction is given.

b) If instead Jeremy had net income of £600 a week and assessable income of £392.25 a week, the current assessment would be:
Basic element = maintenance requirement = £191.03 (see example 14.3)
Basic assessable income = 2 x £191.03 = £382.06
Additional assessable income = £392.25 – £382.06 = £10.19
Additional element = £10.19 x 25% = £2.55
Proposed maintenance = £191.03 + £2.55 = £193.58
The 30% protected income affects, so the assessment is capped at = £180 (total protected income does not affect the assessment)
If Jeremy were awarded special expenses of £84, his assessable income would be £392.25 – £84 = £308.25
Proposed maintenance = 50% x 308.25 = **£154.13**, which is less than the previous assessment of £180.
The protected income needs checking again as special expenses are now included:

	£
Personal allowance	55.65
Mortgage (interest only)	123.08
Council tax	21.00
Travel-to-contact costs allowed	4.00
Pre-1993 commitments allowed	80.00
Standard margin	30.00

Basic protected income	313.73

His total family income = £600 net earnings
Excess income = £600 − 313.73 = £286.27; 15% x £286.27 = £42.94
Total protected income = £313.73 + £42.94 = £356.67

Jeremy can therefore afford to pay the £154.13 assessment without his disposable income falling below £356.67 a week.

Jeremy's housing costs in exempt income are £152.10 a week. Even if Evie applies for departure for excessive housing costs, none can be made because these are less than half Jeremy's net income.

Example 17.6: Special expenses – stepchildren

Bob has been awarded a departure on the grounds of costs of stepchildren: a special expense of £106.81 (see example 17.1(a)).

The £106.81 is therefore included in Bob's exempt income, increasing it from £158.87 (see example 12.6(a)) to £265.68. His net income is £260 (see example 13.3(a)).

Bob has only £5.68 assessable income, he is due to pay the minimum amount but is exempt as he has the family premium in the calculaiton of protected income.

This is less than the previous proposed maintenance of £50.57 (see example 14.1(b)), which was not reduced by the protected income step (see example 15.4(b)). The departure direction reduces Bob's maintenance to nil. However, should Zoe's income increase, the allowance for the stepchildren in exempt income would be reduced (perhaps to nil – see example 17.1(b)).

Property/capital transfer directions

The direction states the weekly value of the transfer (see p357). Any property settlement allowance in exempt income (see p249) is removed, even if the weekly value is nil.[156] Proposed maintenance (see Chapter 14) is then reduced by the amount of any transfer value and the protected income level worked out again.[157] Maintenance payable cannot be below the £5.60 minimum (see p223).[158]

If a special expenses direction is also made, any property settlement allowance is removed from assessable income and the special expenses calculation is then carried out (see p364).[159] The result is then reduced by the transfer value (if any).[160]

If a non-resident parent is liable to more than one person with care (see p300) the transfer value is deducted from the assessment for the person with care or for the child for whom the transfer was made.[161]

The removal of the allowance from exempt income continues after the direction ends because it has compensated for the transfer.[162]

Where the transfer was to trustees and the weekly value is more than nil, any child maintenance from that trust is disregarded from the parent with care's assessable income.[163]

Chapter 17: Departures under the 'old rules'
5. The departure direction

Example 17.7: Property transfer direction

Hamish and Kirsty divorced in 1989, when their only child Angus was two years old (now 16 at April 2004). The house, then worth £31,000, was transferred to Kirsty with a mortgage of about £9,000. From April 1995, Kirsty's assessment was reduced when Hamish was given an allowance of £40 in his exempt income. Kirsty has remarried, has a baby and has no net income of her own. Hamish is single.

a) The current assessment is:

	£
Maintenance requirement:	69.55
Hamish's exempt income:	
Personal allowance	55.65
Housing costs	45.00
Property settlement allowance	40.00
Total	**140.65**

Hamish's net income = £205 a week net earnings.
Assessable income = £205 − £140.65 = £64.35
Proposed maintenance = £64.35 x 50% = **£32.18** (less than the maintenance requirement).
Protected income shows that Hamish can afford this.

The purpose of the capital transfer was unspecified. Kirsty believes it was in lieu of spousal maintenance forgone and to provide a home for Angus. Hamish also had to pay £15 a week under a court order as maintenance for Angus. The departure decision maker decides that the property transfer in lieu of child maintenance was £6,000. Given that Angus was to be dependent for at least another 12 years from the date of the order, a transfer of £6,000 does not amount to £20 a week child maintenance in advance as implied by the £40 allowance.

No date was set in the order for maintenance payment to end, so it is deemed to end when Hamish turns 18. The number of years of liability is therefore 16. The interest rate for judgment debt was 14 per cent at the time of the order so the table gives a multiplier of 0.00320. £6,000 x 0.00320 = **£19.20**. This is therefore the equivalent weekly value.
Hamish's exempt income = £55.65 + £45 = £100.65.
Hamish's net income = £205 a week net earnings.
Assessable income = £205 − £100.65 = £104.35
Proposed maintenance = (£104.35 x 50%) = £52.18.
The amount under the departure direction is then deducted:
£52.18 − £19.20 = £32.98.
Protected income shows that Hamish can afford this.
Departure makes a difference of less than £1 a week (£32.98 − £32.18 = £0.80) and is therefore refused.

(b) If Hamish's net income is instead £315, but exempt income the same (£140.65), the current assessment would be:
Assessable income = £315 − £140.65 = £174.35
£174.35 x 50% = £87.18 (more than maintenance requirement of £69.55).

Chapter 17: Departures under the 'old rules'
5. The departure direction

Therefore proposed maintenance =
£69.55 + 15% (£174.35 – (£69.55 x 2)) = **£74.84**
Protected income shows that he can afford this.
With a property transfer direction of £19.20 (where the £40 allowance in exempt income does not apply):
Assessable income = £315 – £100.65 = £214.35
Proposed maintenance = £69.55 + 15% (£214.35 – (£69.55 x 2)) = £80.84
The amount under the departure direction is deducted:
£80.84 – £19.20 = **£61.64**
The departure has in fact ended up reducing the assessment by £13.20

Additional cases directions

If departure is on the grounds of *lifestyle inconsistent with income, under-use of assets, or diversion of income*, the direction states a figure of notional income to be added to net income (see p238) and so also included in protected income (see p313).[164]

If *housing costs are unreasonably high*, the direction states the costs considered reasonable, and this replaces actual housing costs for exempt income (see p241) and protected income (see p314).[165] The limit of half income/£80 still applies.

If the *partner is to contribute to housing costs*, the direction states the proportion of costs by which housing costs are to be reduced (which may be 100 per cent).[166] Housing costs are reduced by that proportion for exempt income, but not for protected income (see p314). If the direction also states that housing costs are unreasonably high (see above), housing costs used in exempt income are reasonable costs reduced by the stated proportion.[167] The limit of half income/£80 still applies.

If *travel-to-work costs are unreasonably high or should be disregarded*, the direction states the amount of costs allowed (which may be nil). This replaces any travel costs included in exempt income or protected income.[168]

If a direction for special expenses has been given and one for over-generous provision is then sought (or vice versa), the case is reconsidered as if a single application were made on both grounds (see p355).[169]

Example 17.8: Housing costs relating to the partner
A departure direction (see example 17.4) reduced Steve's assessment from £62.18 to £35.38 a week. Debbie, his ex-wife, then applies for departure on the ground that Steve's second wife, Lisa, can contribute towards the couple's housing costs.
Lisa has net earnings of £280 compared with Steve's net earnings of £380. However, once Steve's travelling expenses of £83 a week are taken from his earnings, both partners have roughly the same amount to contribute towards the joint mortgage. Therefore, the departure decision maker decides Lisa can afford to contribute half the mortgage payments.

369

Chapter 17: Departures under the 'old rules'
5. The departure direction

	£
Therefore, Steve's exempt income is now:	
Personal allowance	55.65
Mortgage (half of £96)	48.00
Property settlement allowance	40.00
Travel-to-work costs	83.00
Debt repayments	34.60
Total	**261.25**

Steve's assessable income = £380 – £261.25 = £118.75
Proposed maintenance = 50% x £118.75 = £59.38.
The protected income calculation remains as in example 17.4 and therefore Steve can afford **£59.38** (which is still slightly below the original assessment).
Note: the 50 per cent calculation is used because of the special expenses departure; if only the housing costs departure had been made, proposed maintenance would have been calculated in the usual way (see Chapter 14).

Effective date of the direction

Normally, the effective date of a departure direction is:[170]
- the maintenance assessment's effective date, if the departure application is made within one month of the notification of the current assessment (see p386). If there was unavoidable delay the CSA can treat the application as received in time;[171] *otherwise*
- the first day of the maintenance period in which the departure application was received.

However, if the reason for departure is a change of circumstances after the assessment's effective date, the effective date of the direction is:
- the first day of the maintenance period after the change of circumstances, if the departure application is made within one month of the notification of the assessment (see p386);[172] *otherwise*
- the first day of the maintenance period in which the departure application was received.[173]

Where the direction is for contact costs and there was no established pattern of visits at the date of the application (see p358), the effective date is the first day of the first maintenance period after *either* the date the parents have agreed that pattern is to start *or*, if there is no agreed date, the date of the direction.[174]

Normally, a direction can only be made for the assessment current when the departure application was made. However, in some cases an application cannot be made while the assessment is current, because notification was not sent until after the period covered by the assessment – eg, because it is made for a past period. The departure decision maker can still make a direction for that assessment, as if it were the current one, if:[175]

- a departure direction is given for the current maintenance assessment; *and*
- s/he considers that a direction would have been made for the assessment for the earlier period if an application had been made.

Duration of the direction

The direction may last for a specified period (eg, a 30-week repayment period) or until a specified event – eg, a child leaves school.[176] A direction may require the CSA to make a fresh assessment on a later change of circumstances and specify how that assessment is to be made.[177]

Changing the direction

The rules on changing a decision on departure are similar to those on changing a decision on the assessment itself and follow the same revisions/supersessions framework (see Chapter 19). Any decision of the CSA (or one referred to an appeal tribunal – see p434) regarding departure can be revised[178] or superseded.[179] This would appear to include a decision that regular payments conditions have not been complied with. Where it is considered that an application for departure is defective, there is no formal notified decision and this may only be challenged by judicial review. Refusal and rejection of applications may be revised. The 'test-case' rules (see p427) also apply to revision and supersession of departure decisions.[180]

The rules on who can initiate a revision/supersession, on what grounds and when are summarised below:

Change of decision	Grounds	Initiated by	Time limit
Revision	Any	CSA/Any party*	1 month
Revision	Official error	CSA	No limit
Revision	Misrepresentation	CSA	No limit
Supersession	Change of circumstances	CSA/Any party*	No limit
Supersession	Erroneous in point of law	CSA/Any party*	No limit
Supersession	Ignorance/Mistake as to fact	CSA/Any party*	No limit

*'Any party' includes any parent with care, non-resident parent or Scottish child applicant of the assessment to which the departure relates.

Revision of a decision on departure (disputing decisions)

Any party to an assessment can apply to have a decision relating to a departure direction revised. This includes decisions made on referral to an appeal tribunal (see p362). The CSA can also act (without an application by any party) to revise a decision on any grounds within one month of notification of the original decision.[181] In addition, the CSA can also act to revise a decision at any time where that decision was made as a result of official error (see p418)[182] or where the original decision was wrong because a person misrepresented or failed to disclose a material fact (see p418) and the decision was therefore more advantageous to that person.[183] Revision cannot occur if a material change of circumstances has occurred (or is expected to occur) since the original decision;[184] in this case supersession may be possible. Revision is not possible where the original decision is being appealed to an appeal tribunal and the revised decision (if made) would be less advantageous to the person making the appeal.[185]

An application for revision must normally be made within one month of notification of the decision.[186] Where an application for revision is made and the CSA informs the applicant that the revision will not be made because there is insufficient evidence or information, the applicant has one month from the date of this notification to reapply with the required information.[187] The one-month time limit may be extended where the CSA accepts that it is reasonable to grant an extension. The application for the decision to be revised must have merit and there must have been special circumstances which meant that it was not practicable for the application for revision to be made within the one-month limit.[188] The longer the extension requested, the more compelling the relevant special circumstances would need to be;[189] any application for an extension, must be made within 13 months of notification of the original decision.[190] When deciding whether to grant an extension the CSA will take no account of an applicant's ignorance of or misunderstanding of the law relating to her/his case, nor will account be taken of a commissioner's or court's new interpretation of the relevant law (see p417).[191] Applications for extension which are refused cannot be renewed.[192]

The revised decision normally takes effect on the same date as the original decision;[193] where the effective date from which the original decision takes effect is wrong, the revised decision takes effect from the correct date.[194] If, on revision of the decision, the CSA decides that a departure direction should not have been given, the direction will be cancelled.[195]

Supersession of a decision on departure

A decision relating to departure may be superseded if there has been a material change of circumstances since the original decision was made. Any party to the assessment can apply for a supersession on this ground or, where the CSA becomes aware of a relevant change of circumstances, it can act on its own initiative.[196] A party to the assessment can also apply for supersession where s/he expects that a material change of circumstances is going to occur.[197] No supersession on a change of circumstances will be made where the amount of child maintenance payable would be changed by less than £1.[198] Decisions may also be superseded (either on application by a party or on the initiative of the CSA) where the original decision was made in ignorance of (or based on a mistake as to) a material fact[199] or (apart from decisions given on appeal) where the original decision was wrong in point of law.[200] Decisions to refuse or reject an application for departure and decisions to cancel a departure direction cannot be superseded,[201] nor can any decision which can be revised (see p371).[202]

A superseding decision normally takes effect on the first day of the maintenance period (see p391) in which the application for supersession is made;[203] this also applies where the CSA supersedes a decision on its own initiative on the basis of information or evidence contained in an unsuccessful application for revision or supersession.[204] Where an application is made because of an anticipated change of circumstances, the new decision takes effect from the first day of the maintenance period immediately after the maintenance period in which the change of circumstances is expected to occur.[205] Where the CSA supersedes a decision on its own initiative because it becomes aware of a change of circumstances following a revision or supersession of a social security decision, the superseding decision takes effect from the first day of the maintenance period in which the DWP officer making the social security decision became aware of the change of circumstances.[206]

If, on supersession, the CSA decides that a departure direction should no longer have effect, the direction will be cancelled.[207]

Correction of accidental errors

A minor accidental error can be corrected by the departure decision maker at any time, without making a fresh direction. The parties must be notified and the normal time for appealing starts to run again (see Chapter 20).[208]

Change to assessment

If the assessment is changed on revision or supersession, the direction normally applies to any fresh assessment. This may not mean there is a decision on departure that may be appealed at this stage. A recent commissioner's decision recommended that the Secretary of State should always give a departure decision when making a new assessment to allow the party appeal rights.[209] Where this does not occur and an appeal relates in part to the continuation of the departure direction, the tribunal does not have jurisdiction to deal with the departure issue and should refer the case to the CSA as a request for supersession of the departure, which would lead to a decision that carried appeal rights.

In some cases, the CSA may replace the existing assessment with an interim maintenance assessment (IMA) (see p399). If the direction could not have been made for that IMA (see p347), the direction is suspended.[210] The suspension continues until the IMA is replaced by an assessment for which the direction could have been made.

If an assessment is cancelled or ceases to have effect (see p403), the direction normally ceases to have effect and does not apply to any later assessment.[211] However, if the cancellation is due to the CSA ceasing to have jurisdiction, and the CSA later gets jurisdiction again for the same parties and at least one of the

Chapter 17: Departures under the 'old rules'
5. The departure direction

same children, a property transfer direction has effect again from the effective date of any new assessment.[212] This only applies where a party moves away from the UK and then returns or where the parents reconcile but later split up again.

Appealing the decision

Decisions on departure can be appealed to a tribunal.[213] Any party to the assessment can appeal. The time limit and procedures for appealing are the same as for other appeals (see p434).[214] Any decision with respect to a departure application can be appealed.[215] This includes a decision to refuse an application and one to make a direction. Arguably, this also extends to decisions that an application is defective or that a regular payments condition has not been complied with. However, guidance from the DWP child support policy department indicates that a defective application may only be challenged via judicial review. Where more than one departure direction is appealed and those departure directions relate to the same maintenance assessment, a tribunal can consider both appeals at the same time.[216]

When making an appeal it is important to distinguish whether the appeal is against the direction and/or any fresh maintenance assessment. See Chapter 20 for further details of appeals.

Notes

1 Reg 10(1)(a) CSDDCA Regs
2 Reg 10(1)(c) CSDDCA Regs
3 Reg 10(1)(b) and (c) CSDDCA Regs
4 Reg 9 CSDDCA Regs as amended by reg 2 CS(MA)(No2) Regs 2003

1. Grounds for departure
5 Sch 4B para 2 CSA 1991
6 Reg 19 CSDDCA Regs
7 Reg 14(1) CSDDCA Regs
8 Reg 14(4) CSDDCA Regs
9 para 5.4.29 DDMG
10 para 5.4.4 DDMG
11 Reg 14(1) CSDDCA Regs
12 Reg 14(1)(c) and (6) CSDDCA Regs
13 Reg 14(5) CSDDCA Regs
14 Reg 14(1) CSDDCA Regs
15 Reg 14(1) CSDDCA Regs
16 Reg 14(7) CSDDCA Regs
17 para 5.4.11 DDMG

18 paras 5.4.14-15 DDMG
19 para 5.4.7 DDMG
20 Reg 14(3) CSDDCA Regs
21 Reg 32F(b) CSDDCA Regs; paras 5.4.27-28 DDMG
22 Reg 18 CSDDCA Regs
23 Reg 10(1)(b) CSDDCA Regs
24 Sch 4B para 2(6) CSA 1991; reg 18(8)(a) CSDDCA Regs
25 Reg 18(1) 'relevant child' and (2)(a) CSDDCA Regs
26 Reg 18(4) CSDDCA Regs
27 Reg 18(4B) CSDDCA Regs
28 Reg 18(4A) CSDDCA Regs
29 Reg 18(2)(b) CSDDCA Regs
30 Reg 18(7) CSDDCA Regs
31 Reg 18(3) CSDDCA Regs
32 Reg 18(3) CSDDCA Regs
33 Reg 18(7A) CSDDCA Regs
34 Reg 18(5) CSDDCA Regs

Chapter 17: Departures under the 'old rules'
Notes

35 Reg 18(6) CSDDCA Regs
36 Reg 18(2)(c) CSDDCA Regs
37 Reg 18(3) CSDDCA Regs
38 Reg 13(3) CSDDCA Regs
39 Reg 13(1) CSDDCA Regs
40 Reg 13(2) CSDDCA Regs; paras 5.3.13-18 DDMG
41 para 5.3.19 DDMG
42 Reg 15(1) and (6)(a) and (b) CSDDCA Regs
43 Reg 15(6)(b) CSDDCA Regs
44 Reg 15(5) CSDDCA Regs
45 Reg 15(1) and (2) CSDDCA Regs
46 Reg 15(6)(c) CSDDCA Regs
47 Reg 15(3) CSDDCA Regs
48 Reg 15(4)(a) CSDDCA Regs
49 Reg 15(3)(b) and (4)(b) CSDDCA Regs; see also reg 32(6) CSDDCA Regs
50 Reg 15(4A) CSDDCA Regs
51 Reg 16(1) CSDDCA Regs
52 Reg 16(5)(b) CSDDCA Regs
53 Reg 16(2)(k) and (5)(c) CSDDCA Regs; s376(4) ICTA 1988
54 Reg 16(2)(a) CSDDCA Regs
55 Reg 16(3) CSDDCA Regs
56 Reg 16(2)(h) and (i) CSDDCA Regs
57 Reg 16(5)(d) CSDDCA Regs
58 Reg 16(2)(a)-(g), (j) and (m) CSDDCA Regs
59 Reg 16(4) CSDDCA Regs
60 Reg 37(4) CSDDCA Regs
61 Regs 37(3) and 16(2)(l) CSDDCA Regs
62 Reg 37(3) CSDDCA Regs
63 Reg 17 CSDDCA Regs
64 Reg 17(1)(a) CSDDCA Regs
65 Sch 4B para 5 CSA 1991; regs 23-29 CSDDCA Regs
66 para 3.5.4 DDMG
67 para 7.2.1 DDMG
68 Reg 25 CSDDCA Regs
69 Reg 25(2) CSDDCA Regs
70 Reg 25(3) CSDDCA Regs
71 para 7.4.1 DDMG
72 Reg 23(2)(a) CSDDCA Regs
73 Reg 23(1)(a) CSDDCA Regs
74 paras 7.2.3 and 7.2.30-32 DDMG
75 Reg 23(1)(b) and (c) CSDDCA Regs
76 Reg 23(2)(b) CSDDCA Regs
77 Reg 40(2) and (3) CSDDCA Regs
78 Reg 24 CSDDCA Regs
79 Reg 26 CSDDCA Regs
80 Reg 40(6) CSDDCA Regs
81 Reg 27 CSDDCA Regs
82 Reg 40(7) CSDDCA Regs
83 Reg 40(9) CSDDCA Regs; paras 7.7.14 DDMG
84 Reg 28 CSDDCA Regs
85 Reg 29 CSDDCA Regs
86 para 6.3.3 DDMG
87 Reg 10(1)(c) CSDDCA Regs
88 Sch 4B paras 3(1) and 4(1) CSA 1991; regs 21(1) and (2) and 22(4) CSDDCA Regs
89 Reg 21(5)(a) CSDDCA Regs
90 Reg 21(5)(b) CSDDCA Regs
91 Reg 22(2) CSDDCA Regs
92 Sch para 1(3)(b) CSDDCA Regs
93 Reg 22(3) and Sch CSDDCA Regs
94 Sch para 3 CSDDCA Regs

2. **Applying for departure**
95 s28A(1) CSA 1991
96 s28A(2) and (3) CSA 1991; reg 4(1) CSDDCA Regs; para 2.3.2 DDMG Application form request and How to issue an application form
97 Reg 2 CSDDCA Regs
98 Reg 4(4)-(8) CSDDCA Regs
99 s28A(1) CSA 1991
100 Reg 4(9) and (10) CSDDCA Regs
101 Reg 5 CSDDCA Regs

3. **Procedure**
102 paras 11.1.5-6, 11.2.1 and 11.3.1 DDMG
103 s28B(2) CSA 1991; reg 7 CSDDCA Regs; Ch 3 DDMG Conduct sift overview and Notification to direct parties
104 Reg 6 CSDDCA Regs
105 Reg 8(4) CSDDCA Regs
106 Reg 8(1) CSDDCA Regs
107 Reg 8(4A) CSDDCA Regs
108 Reg 8(1) and (3) CSDDCA Regs
109 Reg 8(5) CSDDCA Regs
110 Reg 8(6) CSDDCA Regs
111 Reg 8(7) CSDDCA Regs
112 Reg 8(2)(b) CSDDCA Regs
113 Reg 8(2)(a) CSDDCA Regs
114 s28C(1) CSA 1991
115 paras 4.1.2 and 4.3.1 DDMG
116 s28C(2)(a) CSA 1991
117 Reg 45 CSDDCA Regs
118 Reg 45(1)-(3) CSDDCA Regs
119 s28C(3) CSA 1991
120 para 4.5.2 DDMG
121 para 4.5.3 DDMG
122 s28C(8) CSA 1991
123 s28C(6)(b) CSA 1991; reg 45(4) CSDDCA Regs
124 s28A(4) CSA 1991
125 s28B(6) CSA 1991
126 paras 3.7.2 DDMG
127 para 3.7.3 DDMG
128 para 3.7.4 DDMG
129 Regs 11A and 46A CSDDCA Regs

375

Chapter 17: Departures under the 'old rules'
Notes

130 s28F(8) CSA 1991; reg 8(9)(a) and (10)(a) CSDDCA Regs
131 s28D(1)(b) CSA 1991 as amended by Sch 7 para 36 SSA 1998; para 13.2.5 DDMG
132 paras 13.2.6-8 DDMG
133 s28D(3) CSA 1991 as amended by Sch 7 para 36 SSA 1998

4. Considering departure
134 s28F(4)-(5) CSA 1991; reg 7 CSDDCA Regs; para 3.6.1 DDMG
135 Reg 44(4) CSDDCA Regs
136 s28E(2) and (4) CSA 1991; reg 12 CSDDCA Regs as amended by reg 4(3) CS(MA) Regs 2003 as amended by reg 2(1)-(2) SS&CS(TC)CA Regs
137 s28F(1)(b) CSA 1991; Ch 8 DDMG
138 para 8.4.2 DDMG
139 s28F(2) and (3) CSA 1991; reg 30 CSDDCA Regs
140 Reg 1 CSDDCA Regs 'relevant person'
141 para 8.4.6 DDMG
142 para 8.4.7 DDMG

5. The departure direction
143 s28F(6) CSA 1991 as amended by Sch 7 para 37 SSA 1998
144 s28G(1) CSA 1991
145 Sch 1 paras 4(2) and (3) and 7 CSA 1991. A direction does not change the way these work.
146 Sch 4B para 6(6) CSA 1991
147 Reg 44(1) and (2) CSDDCA Regs
148 Reg 44(1) and (3) CSDDCA Regs
149 Regs 37(1) CSDDCA Regs
150 Reg 38(2) CSDDCA Regs
151 Regs 37(2) and 38(3) CSDDCA Regs
152 Reg 41(1)-(5) CSDDCA Regs
153 Reg 42A(1)-(6) CSDDCA Regs
154 Reg 43(1) CSDDCA Regs
155 Reg 43(2) CSDDCA Regs
156 Reg 39(1)(a) and (c) and (6) CSDDCA Regs
157 Reg 39(1)(b) CSDDCA Regs
158 Reg 39(2) CSDDCA Regs
159 Reg 42(1) and (2) CSDDCA Regs
160 Reg 42(3) CSDDCA Regs
161 Reg 43(3) CSDDCA Regs
162 Reg 39(5) CSDDCA Regs
163 Reg 39(3) CSDDCA Regs
164 Reg 40(2)-(5) CSDDCA Regs
165 Reg 40(6) CSDDCA Regs
166 Reg 40(7) CSDDCA Regs
167 para 7.7.18 DDMG
168 Reg 40(10) CSDDCA Regs
169 Reg 42A(7) and (8) CSDDCA Regs
170 Reg 32(1)(a) and (2)(a) CSDDCA Regs. Different rules apply for assessments in force on 2 December 1996 where the application was made before 2 December 1997: see 1997/98 edition of this *Handbook*.
171 Reg 32(2)(b) CSDDCA Regs
172 Reg 32(1)(b) CSDDCA Regs
173 Reg 32(4) CSDDCA Regs
174 Reg 32(3A) CSDDCA Regs
175 Reg 46 CSDDCA Regs
176 s28G(2) CSA 1991
177 Sch 4A para 5 CSA 1991
178 Reg 32A CSDDCA Regs
179 Reg 32D CSDDCA Regs
180 s28ZA CSA 1991; Sch 4C para 1(a)(i) CSA 1991
181 Reg 32A(1)(f) CSDDCA Regs
182 Reg 32A(1)(c) CSDDCA Regs
183 Reg 32A(1)(d) CSDDCA Regs
184 Reg 32A(2)(a) CSDDCA Regs
185 Reg 32A(2)(b) CSDDCA Regs
186 Reg 32A(1)(a) CSDDCA Regs
187 Reg 32A(1)(b) CSDDCA Regs
188 Reg 32B(4) CSDDCA Regs
189 Reg 32B(5) CSDDCA Regs
190 Reg 32B(3)(a) CSDDCA Regs
191 Reg 32B(6) CSDDCA Regs
192 Reg 32B(7) CSDDCA Regs
193 s16(3) CSA 1991
194 Reg 32C CSDDCA Regs
195 Reg 32F(a) CSDDCA Regs
196 Regs 32D(3)(a)(i) and (2)(a) CSDDCA Regs
197 Reg 32D(3)(a)(ii) CSDDCA Regs
198 Reg 32D(6) CSDDCA Regs
199 Regs 32D(4) and (2)(b) CSDDCA Regs
200 Reg 32D(5) CSDDCA Regs
201 Reg 32D(10) CSDDCA Regs
202 Reg 32D(9) CSDDCA Regs
203 s17(4) CSA 1991; reg 32E(2) CSDDCA Regs
204 Reg 32E(5) CSDDCA Regs
205 Reg 32E(4) CSDDCA Regs
206 Reg 32E(3) CSDDCA Regs
207 Reg 32F(b) CSDDCA Regs
208 Reg 34A CSDDCA Regs. This does not say the error must be minor, but its terms suggest it does not cover major errors.
209 CCS/1641/01
210 Reg 35(4) CSDDCA Regs; see also para 12.8.3 DDMG
211 Reg 35(1) CSDDCA Regs
212 Reg 35(2) CSDDCA Regs

Chapter 17: Departures under the 'old rules'
Notes

213 Sch 4C para 3(4) CSA 1991
214 Regs 31, 32 and 33 SS&CS(DA) Regs
215 Sch 4C para 3(1)(a) CSA 1991
216 Reg 45 SS&CS(DA) Regs

Part 5
Decisions and beyond

Chapter 18
Maintenance decisions

This chapter covers:
1. Making the initial maintenance decision (see below)
2. Default maintenance decisions (p384)
3. Notification of decisions (p386)
4. Court order phasing of calculations (p387)
5. When the first maintenance calculation begins (p388)
6. When a maintenance calculation ends (p391)
7. How a maintenance calculation affects benefit (p394)
8. Taxation of child maintenance (p398)
9. Existing 'old rules' cases (p398)

> This chapter does not contain information on the conversion of 'old rules' maintenance assessments to the new rules. For information on conversion decisions, see Chapter 9. For information on revision and supersession decisions, see Chapter 19.
>
> Where there are multiple applications under the old and new rules, the CSA decides which application to proceed with and then proceeds with the maintenance decision. For more information on how the CSA decides applications, see Chapter 4.

1. Making the initial maintenance decision

Once an effective maintenance application has been made and the CSA has obtained or tried to obtain the necessary information, the CSA decides whether to:[1]
- make a maintenance calculation (see Chapters 10–15);
- make a default maintenance decision (see p399); *or*
- refuse to make a maintenance calculation (p384).

Details of the case are entered onto the CSA computer and maintenance is calculated automatically.

Chapter 18: Maintenance decisions
1. Making the initial maintenance decision

Relationship with CSA Northern Ireland

For child support cases, there are two territories: Great Britain and Northern Ireland (see p12). If the person with care, non-resident parent and qualifying child do not all reside in the same territory, the application is dealt with by the CSA of the territory where the person with care lives.[2] If more than one application names the same non-resident parent, those applications are dealt with by the CSA of the territory where the person with care named in the first application received by the CSA lives.[3] Where a case has been allocated to a CSA by these rules and the person with care applies again, naming a further non-resident parent, that application is dealt with by the CSA already dealing with the earlier case(s).[4]

These rules do not apply where an application is made by a child in Scotland (see p44). Instead, that application and any others naming the same non-resident parent are dealt with by the CSA for the territory where the person with care of the child applicant lives.[5]

Any calculation made under these rules must take into account the rules of the other territory.[6] Because the rules for the two territories are very similar, this should not make any difference.

Waiting for the calculation decision

The CSA aims to have payments begin within 90 working days of application (see p17).[7]

Delays in dealing with applications

Even though it is intended that much of the contact with parents to gather and check information needed to make a maintenance calculation and collect payments is done by phone there may still be a delay between the application and a decision.

Applicants are contacted at certain stages during the progress of the case – eg, to let them know about negotiations with the non-resident parent about collection or where the applicant has made a complaint. However, this does not include calling applicants when there are delays in processing. Applicants should, therefore, contact the CSA regularly for a progress report.

Delay after the non-resident parent is contacted about the application does not normally put off the starting date of any calculation (see p388), but the date of the decision on maintenance may be delayed. Liability under an order or agreement continues and these remain enforceable. Other non-resident parents should consider starting to put money aside or make voluntary payments (see p468). Parents who are already contributing voluntarily should check if such payments might be used to offset initial arrears (see p465).

If the non-resident parent is not co-operating, the CSA should make a default maintenance decision (see p384) and may impose a criminal sanction. If the person with care is told by the CSA that the non-resident parent is causing the delay by failing to provide information and the CSA has not made a default maintenance decision, the person with care should write to the CSA requesting that one be made. If this does not happen, a complaint should be made (see p18).

Withdrawing the application

Where an application is withdrawn or treated as withdrawn (or the section 6 parent opts-out) before the CSA makes a decision on it, the CSA cannot make a calculation. If a calculation *is* made after withdrawal, it can be challenged (see Chapter19).

The application cannot be withdrawn after a decision on it has been made, but the applicant can ask the CSA to cease acting, in which case the calculation can be cancelled (see p392). In other cases, the decision may be revised or superseded (see Chapter 19).

Change of circumstances

Unlike with social security, there is no general requirement to notify the CSA of changes. However, the person with care is required to notify some changes (see p113), and the non-resident parent must inform changes when a deduction from earnings order is in force (see p478).

However, any party may want to tell the CSA of changes or new information about the case – eg, the parent with care may have discovered that the non-resident parent has a second job which she believes has not been disclosed to the CSA.

Where the CSA is told about a change or given new information that relates to *before* the effective date (see p400), the CSA has discretion as to whether to take this information into account. This can be done in the initial calculation or by making two or more calculations for the different periods.[8]

Where the date or period normally used under child support regulations is before the effective date (eg, for earnings) and the CSA knows about a relevant change which happened after that date or period but before the effective date, the CSA must take that change into account.[9] If the change is after the normal 'relevant week' (see p264) then the relevant week for each later calculation is the week before the date the CSA was notified of the relevant change.[10]

Any information about a change *after* the effective date but before the maintenance calculation can lead to a series of calculations.[11] The effective date of each such maintenance calculation will be the beginning of the maintenance period in which the change occurred or is expected to occur.[12]

Once a calculation is made, the person with care has a duty to notify the CSA of certain changes that happen after that (see p113). These may result in a revision or supersession depending on when the change is notified and its significance (see Chapter 19).

Chapter 18: Maintenance decisions
1. Making the initial maintenance decision

Refusal to make a calculation

The CSA *must* refuse to make an calculation where:
- the application was made by a person who is *not* a non-resident parent, a person with care or, in Scotland, a qualifying child aged 12 or over (see p43);
- the application is under section 4 or 7 and there is a pre-3 March 2003 court order (registered agreement in Scotland) or written agreement (see p44);
- the application is under section 4 or 7 and there is a post-3 March 2003 court order (registered maintenance agreement in Scotland) that has been in force for less than one year (see p44);
- the application is under section 4 (made by the non-resident parent or the person with care) and the parent with care is on income support (IS) or income-based jobseeker's allowance (JSA);
- not all the parties are habitually resident in the UK (see p33);
- there is no non-resident parent, either because both parents live in the same household as the child (see p29), or because the CSA does not accept that the person named is a parent of the child (see p23); *or*
- there is no qualifying child (see p26).

The CSA *may* refuse to make a calculation, for the time being, where the test case rules apply (see p427).

Otherwise, the CSA must make a calculation.

Where there is a change of circumstances so that one of these situations applies but only for a period beginning after the effective date (see p400), the CSA makes a calculation that ends on the date of the change.

Where the only child (or all the children) dies before the calculation is made, the CSA can treat the application as if it had not been made.[13] The CSA cannot refuse to make a calculation just because it has insufficient information or because it may affect the welfare of a child.[14] The CSA may make a default maintenance decision (see p384). If the CSA refuses to make a calculation, the applicant (and, if the applicant was a child in Scotland, any person with care or non-resident parent who had been notified of the application) must be notified in writing of the decision, the right of appeal (see Chapter 20) and how to seek revision and supersession (see Chapter 19).[15]

A fresh application may be made after the refusal – eg, if there is a change of circumstances such as the non-resident parent returning to live in the UK.

2. Default maintenance decisions

Where the CSA does not have enough information to make a maintenance calculation, or revise or supersede a decision, it may make a default maintenance decision.[16] A default maintenance decision may also be made at conversion (see p193).

The amount of the default maintenance decision is based on the number of qualifying children applied for:[17]
- £30 where there is one qualifying child;
- £40 where there are two qualifying children; *or*
- £50 where there are three or more qualifying children.

This amount may be apportioned where there is more than one person with care. (Any relevant non-resident children are ignored.[18])

Court order phasing may be applied to a default maintenance decision (see p387).

The effective date of a default maintenance decision is the same as it would have been for a maintenance calculation decision (see p400).

Notification of a default maintenance decision must state the effective date, the default rate, number of qualifying children, details of any apportionment, revison/supersession/appeal rights and the information needed to make a maintenance calculation.[19]

When a default maintenance decision ends

A default maintenance decision may be revised at any time – eg, when it is replaced by a maintenance calculation.[20] Where the default decision is replaced with a maintenance calculation, the date from which this revision takes effect depends on the circumstances:[21]
- where the total amount of maintenance for the relevant period is greater than the default maintenance decision, the date the revision takes effect is the date of the default maintenance decision; *or*
- where the total amount of maintenance for the relevant period is less than the default maintenance decision, the date the revision takes effect is the first day of the maintenance period in which the information needed to make the calculation was provided.

Example 18.1
Paul was contacted on 7 April 2004 about Cassandra's application for maintenance for his two daughters Hannah and Ella. He refused to provide information to calculate maintenance.
A default maintenance decision was made for £40 with an effective date of 7 April 2004. Paul took advice from an advice agency and he provided information on 29 April 2003 which enabled the CSA to calculate maintenance.
a) If Paul's maintenance is based on net income of £190, he is due to pay £37 a week at the reduced rate. As this is less than the default maintenance decision, he is due to pay £40 a week for the period 7 April to 27 April and £37 a week from 28 April when the default maintenance decision is revised by the maintenance calculation.

Chapter 18: Maintenance decisions
2. Default maintenance decisions

b) If Paul's maintenance is based on net income of £220, he is due to pay £44 a week at the basic rate. As this is greater than the default maintenance decision, it is revised and the maintenance calculation of £44 takes effect from 7 April 2004.

Example 18.2
If the situation is as in example 18.1 but Paul was in hospital and did not return a child maintenance enquiry form that had been sent on 7 April 2004 then a default maintenance decision of £40 would have been applied with effect from 7 April 2004. On coming out of hospital on 16 May 2004 Paul contacts the CSA and tells them what has happened and they accept the failure to provide information was not Paul's fault. In this case, if his net income is £190, the maintenance calculation of £37 would revise the default decision with effect from 7 April 2004.

If the Secretary of State is satisfied that the failure to provide information was not the parent's fault and that they tried their best to provide it, the date the revision takes effect is the date of the default maintenance decision.[22]

'Relevant period' means the period for which the default maintenance decision applied.[23]

In other circumstances, for example, the person with care stops being the person with care, normal revision and supersession rules apply (see Chapter 19).

3. Notification of decisions

The CSA must notify the person with care, non-resident parent and Scottish child applicant once a maintenance calculation or interim maintenance decision has been made.[24] This also includes default maintenance decisions (but see below). There are similar rules regarding notification of revision and supersession decisions (see Chapter 19).

The notification of the maintenance calculation or interim maintenance decision *must* include information on:[25]
- the effective date (see p400);
- the net weekly income of the non-resident parent;
- the number of qualifying children;
- the number of relevant other children;
- the weekly rate;
- any variations;
- any adjustments for apportionment, shared care by the non-resident parent or part-time local authority care, or maintenance to another relevant non-resident child; *and*
- revision, supersession and appeal.

Notification of a default maintenance decision must state the effective date, the default date, the number of qualifying children, details of any apportionment, revison/supersession/appeal rights and the information needed to make a maintenance calculation.[26]

Unless there is written permission, the notification should not contain:[27]
- the address of anyone else other than the recipient or information that could lead to them being located; *or*
- information that could lead to anyone other than persons with care, non-resident parents or qualifying children.

Where there are errors or the person disagrees with the decision, the person may seek a revision (see p416) or appeal (see Chapter 20).

Where there is a court order for maintenance, the court is notified of the calculation (see p37). In addition, where court order phasing applies the amount due may be replaced by a transitional amount (see p388).

4. Court order phasing of calculations

Where weekly liability under the calculation is higher than under an existing court order or agreement, the calculation can be introduced in up to three stages.

A calculation may *only* be phased in if:[28]
- a court order or maintenance agreement (see below), in relation to one or more qualifying children, was in force on 4 April 1993 and remained in force until the date the calculation was made;
- the calculation exceeds that due under the old order/agreement; *and*
- either the non-resident parent is a member of a family or there is a reduction for shared care to the basic or reduced rate of the maintenance calculation.

Any payments in kind or to third parties are ignored when determining the old amount. Arrears are also ignored – it is the weekly liability that counts.[29]

Maintenance agreements, which count for phasing, are those that are:[30]
- made in writing (see p44); *or*
- evidenced in writing,

and which meet all the other requirements of a maintenance agreement (see p44).

Court orders, which count for phasing, are those made under:[31]
- one of the provisions listed in Appendix 4 for court maintenance orders;
- section 151 of the Army Act 1955;
- section 151A of the Air Force Act 1955;
- Articles 1(b) or 3 of the Naval and Marine Pay and Pension (Deductions for Maintenance) Order 1959.

Chapter 18: Maintenance decisions
4. Court order phasing of calculations

The CSA will seek verification of the order or written maintenance agreement, which could be an original document or a copy.[32] In some instances confirmation may be obtained via the Jobcentre Plus.[33]

Where court order phasing applies, instead of the calculation amount a transitional amount is paid.[34] The transitional amount is:[35]
- for the first 26 weeks, the old amount *plus* the greater of £20 and a quarter of the difference between the calculation and the old amount;
- for the next 26 weeks, the old amount *plus* the greater of £40 and half of the difference between the calculation and the old amount; *and*
- for the last 26 weeks of the phasing-in period, the old amount *plus* the greater of £60 and three-quarters of the difference between the calculation and the old amount.

The maintenance payable becomes the calculation amount if the transitional amount would be larger than that.[36] Therefore, it is only where the difference between the old amount and the calculation amount is more than £60 a week that the phasing-in period lasts the full 18 months.

Revision and supersession where there is court order phasing

Where phasing applies and there is a subsequent decision, then the following amount is payable:[37]
- where the subsequent decision is less than the calculation amount and less than or equal to the transitional amount, the subsequent decision;
- where the subsequent decision is less than the previous calculation but more than the transitional amount, the transitional amount;
- where the subsequent decision is higher than the previous calculation, the transitional amount is increased by the same amount as the increase between the calculation and the subsequent decision.

5. When the first maintenance calculation begins

The date a maintenance calculation takes effect is called the **effective date** (see below).[38] There are different rules for effective dates after supersession (see Chapter 19), for calculations replacing default maintenance decisions (see p384), and where there is conversion of an 'old rules' case (see p391).

The effective date

Unless there is a maintenance order in force in relation to all the qualifying children (see p416), the effective date of the calculation depends on who made the

388

application. However, where there is, or has been, a maintenance calculation (or 'old rules' maintenance assessment) in force special rules may apply (see p390).

Where the application is made before 3 March 2003 but the effective date worked out under the 'old rules' is after 3 March 2003 the case is dealt with as a 'new rules' case (unless the linking rules apply). However, the effective date remains that worked out under the 'old rules'.[39]

Where the application was made by the **person with care, a Scottish child applicant or treated as made by a parent with care on benefit**, the effective date is:[40]
- the date the non-resident parent is notified of the application; *or*
- where the non-resident parent has intentionally avoided notification, the date on which notification would have been given but for the avoidance.

The non-resident parent is normally notified of the application by phone. In some cases a maintenance enquiry form may be issued (see p87). In this case notification is treated as given or sent on the day it is given or posted.[41]

The non-resident parent cannot delay the effective date of a calculation by disputing paternity. The CSA does not make a calculation until the issue of paternity is resolved (see p25), but, if the CSA later decides that the alleged non-resident parent is the father, the calculation is then backdated to the effective date. However, disputing paternity does delay the *payment* of maintenance as recovery action is suspended during investigations.[42]

Where the **non-resident parent** made the application, the effective date of the first calculation is the date of the effective application (see p400).[43]

If there are multiple applications for child maintenance and these are treated as a single application (see p54), the effective date is set by the earlier or earliest application.[44]

Court orders

The following rules apply where there is, or has been, a maintenance order in force for all of the qualifying children named in the calculation.[45] This means that where the order covers one but not all of the qualifying children the normal rules regarding the effective date applies to those qualifying children.

The following rules apply in relation to court orders regardless of whether a maintenance calculation or default maintenance decision is being made.[46]

Where the application is treated as made by a parent with care on benefit and the order is in force on the date the calculation is made, the effective date is two days after that.[47]

If the decision is in response to a voluntary application where an order made on or after 3 March 2003 has been in force for one year, the effective date is two months and two days after the application is made.[48]

In either case if the order ceases to have effect after the application is made, the effective date is the day after the order ceased to have affect.[49]

389

Chapter 18: Maintenance decisions
5. When the first maintenance calculation begins

Liability for maintenance continues until the order stops being in force, so the non-resident parent should continue making payments while awaiting the calculation. For collection and enforcement of arrears, see Chapter 21.

Effective dates in special cases

The effective date may be set earlier or later than under the normal rules in certain circumstances where there is or has been a maintenance calculation in force.

Condition	Effective date
A maintenance calculation is in force; the non-resident parent in the new application is the non-resident parent in the current calculation; *and* the application is in respect of a different person with care and qualifying child.	The beginning of the maintenance period in the existing case which is not more than 7 days after the non-resident parent is notified of the new application.[50]
A maintenance calculation is in force; *and* the person with care in the new application is the non-resident parent in the current calculation.	The beginning of the maintenance period in the existing case which is not more than 7 days after the non-resident parent in the new application is notified.[51]
A maintenance calculation was in force within 8 weeks of the application in relation to the same non-resident parent and qualifying child(ren) but a different person with care.* (This does not apply if the parent with care on benefit opts out.)	The date on which the previous maintenance calculation ceased to have effect.[52]
A maintenance calculation was in force within 8 weeks of the application and the parent with care and non-resident parent have swapped roles in relation to the same qualifying child(ren) – ie, the person with care in the old calculation is the non-resident parent in the new application.* (This does not apply if the parent with care on benefit opts out.)	The date on which the previous maintenance calculation ceased to have effect.[53]

* In cases where it is a section 6 application that is treated as made, the date that the application is made means whichever is the later of the following:[54]
- the date of the claim for income support (IS) or income-based jobseeker's allowance (JSA) made by or on behalf of the parent with care; *or*
- the date that the parent with care or their partner report a change in circumstances to the Secretary of State or the Inland Revenue that relates to an existing claim for IS/income-based JSA and it has the effect that the parent with care is treated as applying for maintenance.

Effective date of a maintenance calculation when there is or has been an existing 'old rules' maintenance assessment in force

Where an 'old rules' maintenance assessment is or has been in force, the case may be dealt with under the 'old rules' or 'new rules' depending on who is involved and when the application is made.

Applications for a maintenance calculation after 3 March 2003 but within 13 weeks of an assessment being in force, involving the same person with care, non-resident parent and qualifying child(ren), may be treated as an application for a maintenance assessment.[55] In these circumstances the effective date is set in relation to the 'old rules'. Where the application is after C Day but within 13 weeks of an assessment being in force a conversion decision may be applied (see p199).

Otherwise the effective date of the new maintenance calculation is dealt with under the:
- normal effective date rules; *or*
- special cases rules explained above, as if references to calculation were to assessment.[56]

However, where there is a maintenance assessment in force that converts to the 'new rules' early (eg, due to an application for a new calculation by another person with care) there are special rules for working out the effective date of the conversion decision for that existing assessment (see Chapter 9).

Maintenance periods

Child maintenance is calculated on a weekly basis, although it is not always paid weekly (see p461). It is payable in respect of successive seven-day periods with the first period beginning on the effective date.[57]

The only exception is where, when the calculation is made, there is already a calculation in force for the same non-resident parent but for a different child and person with care. In that case, the maintenance periods of the new calculation begin on the same day of the week as the existing calculation.[58]

After supersession, any fresh calculation comes into effect on the first day of the maintenance period (see p425).

6. When a calculation ends

A calculation continues until the CSA:
- cancels it following a request (see p392);
- revises it (see p416);
- supersedes it because it has ceased to have effect (see p392); *or*
- supersedes it for another reason (see p420).

Chapter 18: Maintenance decisions
6. When a calculation ends

In some cases the calculation is replaced by another, while in others no further calculation is made. Any arrears remaining after a calculation ends may still be collected (see Chapter 21). Also, if an application is made for children of the non-resident parent who are not named in the existing calculation, the new calculation replaces the old one.

Requests to cancel calculations

A maintenance calculation must be cancelled when the applicant (under section 4) or parent treated as applying (under section 6) requests the CSA to cease acting.[59] Such a request by a parent with care on benefit is known as opting-out and a reduced benefit decision made and imposed (see p75).

The request may be made verbally or in writing. Where the request is made the CSA must stop all action, including collection and enforcement of arrears, though the person may specifically ask that this continues.

Living together

When the request is made reasons need not be given. However, if the reason is because the parent with care and non-resident parent are living together the CSA should be told. This is because once the parties all share a household, the non-resident parent is no longer non-resident (see p29), so the child is no longer a qualifying child and the calculation ceases to have effect anyway (see below).[60] Both parents should inform the CSA, though the CSA will seek other verification.[61] Where there is a suspicion of fraud the Jobcentre Plus may be informed.[62]

Where the calculation ceases to have effect

Some changes of circumstances lead to a cancellation whether or not a request is made. The CSA may be aware of a change from, for example, a request, a notification by the parent with care under her duty to do so (see p113) or from the DWP computer. The CSA *must* supersede the decision and cancel a calculation (including a default decision) where the calculation ceases to have effect. The calculation will cease to have effect if:[63]
- the non-resident parent or person with care dies;
- the only or all qualifying children is no longer is a qualifying child; *or*
- the non-resident parent ceases to be a parent of the only or all the qualifying child(ren).

This means cancellation occurs, for example, when:
- the child leaves school or becomes too old to count as a child;
- the qualifying child, non-resident parent and parent with care start living together;
- the qualifying child goes to live with someone else and as a result the person with care no longer counts as a person with care;

- the qualifying child is adopted, in which case the non-resident parent is no longer a parent; *or*
- the non-resident parent is no longer considered a parent because of the results of a DNA test or a declaration of parentage.

Where the maintenance calculation has been made due to an application by a child in Scotland and that child is no longer a child, the CSA must notify the person with care, non-resident parent and other children over 12.[64]

Other cancellations

The CSA must cancel the calculation where the person with care, non-resident parent or qualifying child is no longer habitually resident in the UK (see p33).[65]

A non-resident parent who has successfully contested paternity will have any maintenance calculation cancelled, and where they have paid maintenance may obtain a refund.

If a section 4 applicant (or a section 6 applicant who would now count as a section 4 applicant) fails to provide the CSA with enough information to make a revision or supersession decision, the CSA *may* cancel the calculation (see pp431 and 424).

Date cancellation has effect

Where the calculation is cancelled because the calculation ceases to have effect or another relevant change, the cancellation takes effect from the first day in the maintenance period in which the change occurred. This includes where:
- the person with care is no longer the person with care for the child(ren) named in the calculation;[66] *or*
- a party is no longer habitually resident in the UK;[67] *or*
- the person with care, non-resident parent or qualifying child died;[68]
- the non-resident parent ceased to be a parent;[69]
- the section 4 applicant stopped co-operating by providing information.[70]

Where the cancellation is because the non-resident parent is not considered to be the parent because of a DNA test or declarator of parentage, the effective date is the date of the original maintenance calculation.[71]

Cancellation due to a request

A calculation is cancelled with effect from the first day of the maintenance period in which the request was received *or* a different date depending on the reason for the cancellation.[72] A later date may be appropriate where an applicant has requested that the calculation ends on a later date.[73]

Where a parent who was on income support/income-based jobseeker's allowance, stops claiming and requests the CSA to stop acting the effective date is

Chapter 18: Maintenance decisions
6. When a calculation ends

the first day of the maintenance period after the request is made.[74] Ironically, this means that had the parent made the request to opt out while on benefit the maintenance calculation would have been cancelled from the first day of the maintenance period in which the request was made. Where a calculation is cancelled because the non-resident parent and parent with care are living together, and both request the cancellation, it takes effect from the first day of the maintenance period in which the later request to cancel the calculation is made.[75]

Notification of cancellation decision

When the CSA cancels a calculation or refuses to cancel one, it must notify the non-resident parent, person with care and Scottish child applicant of that decision, and must also provide information on the right of appeal and on revision and supersession.[76]

Where the maintenance calculation has been made due to an application by a child in Scotland, and that child is no longer a qualifying child, the CSA must notify the person with care, non-resident parent and other children over 12 who are potential section 7 applicants.[77]

7. How a calculation affects benefit

In this section, we cover the effect of *receiving* child support maintenance on means-tested benefits: income support (IS), income-based jobseeker's allowance (JSA), housing benefit (HB) and council tax benefit (CTB). Other social security benefits are not affected.

Child maintenance *paid* by a non-resident parent is not taken into account when calculating his, or his partner's, means-tested benefits. However, deductions for flat-rate maintenance or arrears may be taken from a non-resident parent's benefits when the CSA requests this to be done.[78] For full details of how means-tested benefits are calculated, including the effect of maintenance other than child support, see CPAG's *Welfare Benefits and Tax Credits Handbook*. For the benefit penalty, see p84.

Income support/income-based jobseeker's allowance

The following covers special provisions within these benefits in relation to child maintenance. Payments of child maintenance may be made direct to the person with care or via the CSA.

Housing costs protection

Full mortgage interest is not usually included in the calculation for the first 26 or 39 weeks of any IS/income-based JSA award. Nevertheless, the benefit calculation includes 100 per cent of eligible mortgage interest where:[79]

394

Chapter 18: Maintenance decisions
7. How a calculation affects benefit

- a person with care stops being entitled to IS/income-based JSA as a result of receiving child maintenance; *and*
- when that happened, she was receiving IS/income-based JSA including 100 per cent eligible mortgage interest; *and*
- her maintenance calculation is later reduced or ended because:
  - the child support regulations are changed; *or*
  - the calculation is an interim maintenance assessment (IMA) under the 'old rules' and it is ended and not replaced or is replaced by another IMA/default decision or by a full assessment/calculation; *and*
- she then claims IS/income-based JSA within 26 weeks of the date she stopped being entitled to either benefit.[80]

Child maintenance premium

From 3 March 2003 a person with care on IS/income-based JSA who is paid child maintenance under the 'new rules' will have a child maintenance premium applied when working out their benefit.[81] Where an 'old rules' case converts to the 'new rules' the child maintenance premium may replace a child maintenance bonus (see p405). The premium also applies if maintenance is paid under an agreement or court order, if the maintenance is first paid on or after 3 March 2003.[82] Just because the parent was paid, or due to be paid, maintenance for a different child or under an earlier agreement/order, it does not preclude the premium from being applied. In some circumstance this may mean a parent ceases to accrue a bonus and instead will have a premium applied. She may claim the bonus if she meets the relevant conditions (see p405).

A person with care on IS/income-based JSA who is paid child maintenance will have up to £10 a week ignored when working out benefit entitlement.[83] This means that where maintenance paid is £6 only £6 will be ignored. The maintenance may be made in respect of one child or more but the amounts are aggregated and only up to £10 will be ignored. The child maintenance premium applies whether maintenance is paid direct to the parent with care or via the CSA. Payments can be made under a CSA calculation, maintenance order, written maintenance agreement or voluntary payments.[84] This includes where the Secretary of State makes a payment in lieu of maintenance where the non-resident parent is on the flat rate of maintenance.[85]

Payment direct to the person with care

The parent with care may ask that payments of maintenance are not made via the CSA but direct from the non-resident parent. For how to request a change to the collection service, see p460. Payments of child maintenance, including lump sums, are treated as income and are taken into account for assessing entitlement to IS/income-based JSA on a weekly basis.[86] Payments are treated as income in the week they are received by the parent with care, except that child maintenance

395

Chapter 18: Maintenance decisions
7. How a calculation affects benefit

due before the benefit award is always treated as paid in the week it was due – ie, before the award began.[87]

Payments made regularly are converted into a weekly amount to work out IS/income-based JSA – eg, where payments are made monthly, multiply by 12 and divide by 52.[88] Where payments are made at irregular intervals, each payment is divided over the weeks since the previous payment.[89]

Where the child maintenance premium applies, up to £10 of the maintenance is ignored. The remainder counts in full as income and benefit is therefore reduced by this amount.

The Jobcentre Plus should not assume that child maintenance is paid as soon as the CSA sends notification of the calculation. If the Jobcentre Plus asks for a person with care's order book before payments begin, she should contact the Jobcentre Plus and explain the situation. Her benefit should not be reduced until payments begin.

Once a person with care's benefit has been reduced because of maintenance payments, if a payment due direct from the non-resident parent is missed, she should ask the Jobcentre Plus for extra benefit to be paid for that period. The Jobcentre Plus should do this without waiting for the CSA to enforce payment of maintenance. The person with care can contact the CSA to chase missing payments and to have payments made to the CSA (see Chapter 21).

Payment to the Child Support Agency

The CSA usually arranges to collect maintenance so that the non-resident parent does not have to pay direct to the person with care. The CSA normally keeps any payments made to them by the non-resident parent for a person with care on IS/income-based JSA.[90] When the CSA does this, the Jobcentre Plus does not take that payment into account.[91]

Payment of arrears

Non-resident parents are encouraged by the CSA to pay arrears direct to the CSA, which then keeps the arrears up to the amount of IS/income-based JSA that was paid because the maintenance was not paid on the due date.[92] Any balance is passed to the person with care. If child maintenance is paid late, but the person with care has not had her IS/income-based JSA made up, there is no need for any adjustment to her benefit. If the arrears are collected by the CSA, they should be passed on in full to the person with care.

If the non-resident parent pays arrears direct to the person with care, the full amount of overpaid benefit for the period when that maintenance was due can be recovered from her by the Jobcentre Plus.[93]

Loss of income support/income-based JSA

Persons with care lose IS/income-based JSA when the child maintenance paid increases their income over the benefit applicable amount. If the person with care

Chapter 18: Maintenance decisions
7. How a calculation affects benefit

is only a few pounds over the benefit level, she may find herself worse off because of the loss of passported benefits – eg, free school meals, full health service benefits (see below) and access to the social fund.

A person with care who is not a parent of the qualifying child is a section 4 applicant (see p45) and can therefore ask for the calculation to be cancelled (see p392). When she re-claims IS/income-based JSA, notional income may be an issue (see CPAG's *Welfare Benefits and Tax Credits Handbook*).

For a section 6 applicant, particularly one with school-age children, the loss of passported benefits could have a greater effect than a reduced benefit decision (see p84). Where benefit entitlement is low and a reduced benefit decision is imposed the amount of the reduction may be modified to retain the minimum amount of benefit. Where the claim ends and maintenance is not paid on time, a new IS/income-based JSA claim can be made. If the Jobcentre Plus delays a decision on the claim for the CSA to enforce maintenance, make a complaint (see p18). The Jobcentre Plus cannot take into account child maintenance that has not yet been paid (see p394).

Housing benefit and council tax benefit

There are no special rules for child maintenance when calculating HB/CTB, except that £15 weekly is disregarded as income for persons with care who are not in receipt of IS/income-based JSA.[94] The disregard applies to all forms of maintenance paid by a former partner or a parent of a child, but only if there is a child in the HB/CTB claimant's family. Only £15 is disregarded from total maintenance paid.

If there is a change in the amount of child maintenance received, the person with care should tell the local authority benefits section. Persons with care claiming HB/CTB who are not on IS/income-based JSA cannot be treated as applying to the CSA. However, a local authority might use the notional income rules and decide that a claimant who does not apply to the CSA has deprived herself of child maintenance.[95] This would be extremely difficult for the authority to do, as it would not have enough information to work out the maintenance calculation that would be made.

For the notional income rules, see CPAG's *Welfare Benefits and Tax Credits Handbook*.

Health service benefits

People on IS/income-based JSA are automatically exempt from all NHS charges. Others may be entitled to full or partial reductions of charges on low-income grounds. This covers prescriptions, dental treatment, sight tests, glasses, wigs, fabric support and fares to hospital.

For these purposes, where child maintenance payments are made:
- regularly, income is the weekly equivalent of payments; *or*

- not regularly, income is total payments in the 13 weeks before the claim, divided by 13.

There is no disregard. For full details see CPAG's *Welfare Benefits and Tax Credits Handbook*.

8. Taxation of child maintenance

Person with care

Child support maintenance is not taxable income. It does not affect entitlement to or the amount of working tax credit or child tax credit.[96]

Non-resident parent

From 6 April 2000 maintenance, including child support maintenance, no longer qualifies for tax relief. Payments up to 5 April 2000 may qualify for tax relief in the 1999/2000 tax year.

9. Existing 'old rules' cases

Existing cases will continue to be dealt with under the legislation prior to reform, except for some provision for parents with care on benefit – eg, to ask the CSA to cease acting. This means the Child Support (Maintenance Assessment Procedure) Regulations are the principal regulations. For full details of the 'old rules', see Chapter 14 in the 2002/03 edition of this *Handbook*.

This section outlines the areas where there are minor and major differences between the 'new rules' and 'old rules' and provides an overview of the relevant provisions.

Areas where there are minor differences between the old and new rules:
- Notifications under the 'old rules' are treated as given or sent by the CSA two days after posting apart from issue of a maintenance enquiry form, which is treated as given or sent on the day that it is posted.
- Cancellations are now possible by 'old rules' section 6 parents – ie, they can opt out (see p68). There are several other differences for parents with care on benefit (see p394).

Provisions that are completely different:
- Interim maintenance decisions (IMA – see p399) are made under the 'old rules' where there is insufficient information to make an assessment. Default maintenance decisions apply to 'new rules' cases only. At conversion an IMA

Chapter 18: Maintenance decisions
9. Existing 'old rules' cases

may convert to a maintenance calculation or default maintenance decision (see p384).
- The effective dates of a maintenance assessment or IMA are set following different rules (see p400).
- A person with care on benefit may accrue up to £5 a week child maintenance bonus (see p405). The child maintenance premium does not apply to 'old rules' cases. When a case converts, the premium may apply, but any bonus may be claimed if the conditions are met.

For full details on these see Chapter 14 of the 2002/03 edition of this *Handbook*. The following is a brief guide to the main issues.

Interim maintenance assessments

Where the CSA does not have enough information to make a full assessment using the formula, or to decide whether to revise or supersede a decision, it may make an IMA rather than a full assessment.[97] The decision to make an IMA is discretionary, so the CSA must take into account the welfare of any child(ren) the decision may affect (see p31).

There are four types of IMA: Categories A, B, C and D, see table 18.1.[98] For IMA commencement see p402, for cancellation see p403, and for revision and supersession see Chapter 19.

Table 18.1: Quick guide to interim maintenance assessments

Type of IMA	When it is applied	How it is worked out
A	A non-resident parent has failed to provide information about his own circumstances (not any new partner).	One-and-a-half times the maintenance requirement.
B	Either the person with care or non-resident parent has failed to provide information about their new partner or other members of their family.	Calculated as a full assessment except: • in exempt income it is assumed a new partner can help maintain a joint child; • there is no protected income calculation although the 30 per cent cap may apply.

399

Chapter 18: Maintenance decisions
9. Existing 'old rules' cases

C	Where the non-resident parent is self-employed and is unable to provide information about earnings.	Normally £30 but may be less.
D	Where a Category A IMA is in force but on the information available it appears that a full assessment would be higher.	Calculated as a full assessment, except: • there is no protected income, nor a 30 per cent cap; • no housing costs are allowed; • exempt income is the adult personal allowance only; *and* • when working out income, there is no disregard of payments to personal or occupational pension schemes or to pension schemes intended to provide capital sums to discharge a mortgage.

For full information on interim maintenance assessments see the 2002/03 edition of this *Handbook*.

The effective date of an assessment

Under the 'old rules' there are different rules on setting the effective date of assessments, IMAs and maintenance assessments replacing IMAs. In some cases the CSA may set an interim effective date.

Effective date of assessments

Circumstances	*Effective date is*
Application by section 4, 7 or 6 applicant.[99]	Eight weeks from the date on which the maintenance enquiry form (MEF) is given or sent to an non-resident parent as long as, within four weeks of being sent the MEF, he returns it with his name, address and written confirmation that he is the parent of the child(ren) named in the maintenance application form (MAF); *otherwise* the date the non-resident parent was actually given or sent the MEF.

Chapter 18: Maintenance decisions
9. Existing 'old rules' cases

Application by non-resident parent.[100]	Eight weeks from the date on which the application was received by the CSA as long as the non-resident parent provides his name, address and written confirmation that he is the parent of the child(ren) named in the MAF as part of the MAF or provides these details within four weeks of the date of the application; *otherwise* the date an effective MAF (see p51) is received.
In either case where there is a court order in force for at least one of the qualifying children on the date the assessment is made.[101]	Two days after the date the assessment is made. The order for maintenance ceases to have effect from the effective date (see p36).[102]
Where the court order ceases (not because of an IMA) before the assessment is made and after the MEF/MAF is received depending on the applicant.[103]	The day after the order ceased to be in force.
Another assessment is already in force and an application by a different person with care is then made.[104]	The CSA may treat the new application as received up to eight weeks earlier than the date it was actually received, but no earlier than the date on which the previous assessment ended.[105]
A section 7 assessment has been cancelled at the request of the Scottish child applicant or because s/he is no longer a child, and an application for children who were qualifying children under the previous assessment has been made.[106]	The CSA may treat the new application as received up to eight weeks earlier than the date it was actually received, but no earlier than the date on which the previous assessment ended.[107]
An assessment is in force for an non-resident parent and a different person with care then applies for child maintenance.	The first day of the first maintenance period (see p391) after the parties are notified of the second assessment.[108] If this would make the effective date fall within the eight-week period and the non-resident parent meets the rules for that period (see p400), the effective date is the first day of the first maintenance period after the eight-week period.[109]

If there are multiple applications for child maintenance and these are treated as a single application, the effective date is set by the earlier or earliest application.[110]

401

Chapter 18: Maintenance decisions
9. Existing 'old rules' cases

Effective dates of interim maintenance assessments

Circumstances	Effective date is
Category A or C unless there is a court order in force.	The first day after it is made which falls on the same day of the week as the day the MEF was actually given or sent to the non-resident parent or, where the non-resident parent is the applicant, the day the MAF was received by the CSA (but see the exception below).[111]
Category B unless there is a court order in force.	The date the MEF was actually given or sent to the non-resident parent or, where the non-resident parent is the applicant, the day the MAF was received by the CSA (but see exception below).[112]
Where there is a court order in force.	See normal effective date rules.
Superseding IMA with another category A, C or D IMA.	The first day of the maintenance period in which the CSA decides to make the new IMA.[113]
Superseding IMA is a Category B IMA.	Where the cancelled IMA (or the first cancelled IMA, if there is more than one) had caused a court order to cease to have effect, the effective date of that (or that first) IMA;[114] *otherwise* the day the MEF was actually given or sent to the non-resident parent or, where the non-resident parent is the applicant, the day the MAF was received by the CSA.[115]

The exception to these rules is that, if the effective date set by them would fall within the eight-week period and the non-resident parent meets the rules for that period for a full assessment (see p388), the effective date is set by those rules.[116]

Effective date of a maintenance assessment replacing an IMA

Where the CSA:
- has enough information to make a full assessment for the *whole of the period* beginning with the usual effective date (see p400), then the IMA ceases to have effect on the first day of the maintenance period (see p391) in which the CSA received the information.[117] The CSA revises (see p416) the IMA decision.[118] The amount payable under the IMA becomes that of the full assessment;[119] *or*

Chapter 18: Maintenance decisions
9. Existing 'old rules' cases

- has enough information to make a full assessment for *only part of that period*, then the IMA ceases to have effect on the first day of the maintenance period in which the CSA received the information.[120] The CSA supersedes the IMA decision.[121] The effective date of the full assessment is also that date.[122] The amount payable under the IMA remains that of the IMA.[123]

Where the information which enables the CSA to make a full assessment is that income support (IS) or income-based jobseeker's allowance (JSA) has been awarded, the CSA is treated as receiving that information on the day benefit became payable.[124]

Interim effective date

If the CSA does not have enough information to make a full assessment from the usual effective date (see p400), but has enough to make one running from a later date, it can make a full assessment from that later date.[125] The interim effective date is the first day of the maintenance period (see p402) in which the CSA received the information.[126]

If the CSA later receives enough information to make a full assessment from the usual effective date, the assessment already made for the later period then has effect from the usual effective date instead.[127]

Cancelling assessments

The information on ending assessments is the same as that under the 'new rules' except for the following:
- From 3 March 2003 any applicant or section 6 parent under the 'old rules' may ask the CSA to stop acting. The calculation will be cancelled although a section 6 parent may have a reduced benefit decision made and imposed (see p75).
- Under the 'old rules', where a Scottish child applicant is no longer habitually resident in Scotland the assessment is cancelled.[128] This takes effect from the first day in the maintenance period in which the change occurred.
- Under the 'old rules', the CSA has discretion, in some cases, on when to set the effective date of the cancellation – eg, where the person with care and non-resident parent are living together.[129] Guidance indicates that effective dates are set in the same way for cancellation under both old and new rules, though under different legislative authority.
- The full amount of the assessment is due for the maintenance period in which the cancellation date falls,[130] except where a Category A or D IMA is cancelled, when it is only due to the cancellation date.[131]
- An IMA must be cancelled when the CSA has enough information to make a full assessment. Otherwise the only provision for cancellation is when the CSA accepts that the non-resident was unavoidably delayed in providing the information. The effective date of the maintenance assessment is as under the

normal rules. However, where the new decision is another category of IMA, the date is:[132]
- for category A or D IMA, the first day of the maintenance period in which the CSA decides to make the new IMA; *or*
- for category B, the day the MEF was given or sent to the non-resident parent or where the non-resident parent is the applicant the day the MAF was received by the CSA.

Court order phasing of assessments

The definition of maintenance agreement and court order are the same as in court order phasing, but the legislative references are slightly different.[133] Evidence of the order must be provided.

In the regulations there are two similar types of phasing, which we call 'original phasing' and '1994 phasing'. CSA guidance refers to one type of phasing, our 1994 phasing.[134]

For full information on court order phasing and supersession of decisions where court order phasing applies, see the 2002/03 edition of this *Handbook*.

Original phasing

This has existed since April 1993 and the reduced amount payable is known as the **modified amount**.[135] It does not apply to a Category A IMA.[136] It applies where:[137]
- the old maintenance order/agreement covered all the children named in the assessment; *and*
- the non-resident parent is responsible for maintaining a child (see p26) living with him who is not named in the assessment; *and*
- the assessment is £60 or less.

The weekly modified amount is the weekly amount due under the old order/agreement *plus* £20.[138] This continues for a year, but ends before that if one of the above conditions is no longer met.

1994 phasing

This was introduced on 7 February 1994 and the reduced amount payable is known as the **transitional amount**.[139] It does not apply to a Category A or D IMA.[140] It applies where:[141]
- the old maintenance order/agreement covered at least one child named in the assessment; *and*
- the non-resident parent was a member of a family (see p32) which included at least one child on the effective date (see p400) and is still a member of a family with a child; *and*
- original phasing does not apply;[142] *and*

- the assessment does not replace a Category A or D IMA made after 22 January 1996.[143]

Where the assessment is £60 or less, the transitional amount is the amount under the old order/agreement *plus* £20.[144] This lasts for 52 weeks.

Where the assessment is more than £60 a week, the transitional amount is:[145]
- for the first 26 weeks, the old amount *plus* the greater of £20 and a quarter of the difference between the assessment and the old amount;
- for the next 26 weeks, the old amount *plus* the greater of £40 and half of the difference between the assessment and the old amount; *and*
- for the last 26 weeks of the phasing-in period, the old amount *plus* the greater of £60 and three-quarters of the difference between the assessment and the old amount.

The maintenance payable becomes the assessment amount if the transitional amount would be larger than that. Therefore, it is only where the difference between the old amount and the assessment amount is more than £60 a week that the phasing-in period lasts the full 18 months.

Which type of phasing applies

CSA guidance covers only 1994 phasing, implying that original phasing cannot be applied. However, the provisions remain in force.[146] This is only likely to matter if a Category D IMA is made or replaced, because only original and not 1994 phasing can apply to a Category D IMA. If the wrong (or no) phasing is applied, an appeal can be made (see Chapter 20).

Supersession where court order phasing-in applies

Where original phasing applies and the assessment decision is revised (see p416) or superseded (see p420) and the conditions for phasing are still met, phasing continues until the 52-week period ends.[147]

Where 1994 phasing applies (or where original phasing applies and there is a change of circumstances), then the following amount is payable:[148]
- where the fresh assessment is less than the modified/transitional amount, the fresh assessment;
- where the fresh assessment is less than the previous assessment but more than the modified/transitional amount, the modified/transitional amount;
- where the fresh assessment is higher than the previous assessment, the modified/transitional amount is increased by the same amount as the increase between the two formula assessments.

Child maintenance bonus

The child maintenance bonus is not available to cases under the 'new rules', or where maintenance is first paid under an agreement or court order after 3 March

Chapter 18: Maintenance decisions
9. Existing 'old rules' cases

2003.[149] Persons with care who were entitled to a child maintenance bonus at 3 March 2003 will continue to be entitled to a bonus until C Day, unless:[150]
- in 'old rules' cases, the case converts early to the new rules (see p191);
- in cases where maintenance is paid under a voluntary agreement or court order (in Scotland registered agreement), either maintenance is paid for a different child or there is a new agreement or order for the existing child(ren).

Where the child maintenance bonus is replaced by a child maintenance premium, see p395.

A person caring for a child(ren) builds up a child maintenance bonus for weeks in which maintenance for the child (not just child support maintenance) is paid or payable to her and in which she or her partner is entitled to IS or income-based JSA.[151] This does not include where the urgent cases rate is being paid because she is treated as if she were receiving income due to her.[152]

This bonus normally builds up at a rate of £5 a week. It can be claimed as IS or income-based JSA when the person with care (or partner) finds work (or more work/pay) and so comes off IS/income-based JSA. There are special rules for retired people (see p409).

As the bonus is IS/income-based JSA, decisions about the bonus are made by the Jobcentre Plus. The usual IS/income-based JSA rules apply to revision/supersession and appeals about bonus decisions; the overpayments rules also apply (see CPAG's *Welfare Benefits and Tax Credits Handbook*).

The table below explains the main provisions. For more detail and worked examples see the 2002/03 edition of this *Handbook*.

	Conditions
To build up the bonus, the person with care must:[153]	live with a qualifying child for whom she gets child maintenance (note the child may be temporarily absent for up to 12 weeks[154]); be entitled (or their partner is) to IS/income-based JSA (even if it isn't paid); *and* have not yet reached the day before her 60th birthday (or, for a man on income-based JSA, his 65th birthday).[155] This is known as a bonus period.
The child maintenance paid by the non-resident parent must be either:[156]	child support; under a court order or an agreement, including an informal agreement; *or* a deduction from IS/income-based JSA as a contribution to child maintenance (see p224).

406

Chapter 18: Maintenance decisions
9. Existing 'old rules' cases

Where there is break (eg, due to loss of entitlement) two bonus periods may be linked,[157] if the break is either:[158]	a period of 12 weeks or less; a period throughout which maternity allowance is payable to the person claiming the bonus; or any period of two years or less throughout which incapacity benefit, severe disablement allowance or carer's allowance is payable to the person claiming the bonus.
The bonus is payable if the person:	meets the **work condition** within the **time limits** and because of that ceases to be entitled to IS/income-based JSA[159] (the bonus must also be **claimed**); or has reached or is approaching **retirement age** (see special rules below). There are **special rules if the person with care dies** which allow someone else to acquire the bonus, see below.
The work condition:	the person or their partner must take up or go back to work, earn more from employment, or increase their hours sufficiently to bring their benefit entitlement to an end.[160] (Note: A person involved in a trade dispute who then returns to work does not count under these rules as 'going back to work'.[161])
The time limit:	the time limit for meeting the work condition is 14 days from the end of the bonus period,[162] but it can be extended if: the non-resident parent dies, ceases to be habitually resident and/or is found not to be the parent of the qualifying child (ren), to 12 weeks from the date of that event (or where there is more than one – the first);[163] the person cares for only one child and that child dies, to 12 months from the date of death.[164] (Note: Where the child maintenance bonus is replaced by a child maintenance premium the time limit is amended.)

Chapter 18: Maintenance decisions
9. Existing 'old rules' cases

Claims must be made:	by sending or delivering a claim form to the Jobcentre Plus;[165] *and*
	within 28 days of the day after IS/income-based JSA ends.[166] (This can be extended to up to six months, if there are good reasons.[167])
	There are special rules for:
	a person approaching retirement age who does not meet the work condition. The 28 days begin on the day after her 60th birthday (or, for a man on income-based JSA, his 65th birthday);[168]
	a person who dies after a bonus becomes payable but without having claimed it. Another person can apply to the Jobcentre Plus to be appointed to claim the bonus, but must do so within six months of the death; this is extendable to up to 12 months in exceptional circumstances.[169]

How much is the child maintenance bonus

The total child maintenance bonus is the *lowest* of the following:
- £5 for each week in which at least £5 maintenance was due,[170] *plus* for any other week in which less than £5 maintenance was due, the amount due in that week;[171]
- the total maintenance paid during the bonus period.[172] This includes any maintenance retained by the CSA.[173] Any maintenance paid but not declared to the Jobcentre Plus and so not taken into account for benefit purposes does not count towards the bonus;[174]
- £1,000.[175]

This means that if you qualify for a bonus at the end of an unbroken bonus period (including any linked periods), the bonus is the whole amount built up, with the maximum bonus payable £1,000. The minimum is £5.[176]

The bonus is paid as IS or income-based JSA: whichever benefit the person was entitled to when the bonus stopped being built up.[177]

Where the person with care dies

Where a person with care dies, the bonus built up passes to the new person with care if:[178]
- the deceased person with care was entitled (or her partner was entitled) to IS/income-based JSA in the 12 weeks before the death;
- the new person with care was not a person with care before the death;

- the new person with care is a close relative of the deceased person with care – ie, a parent, step-parent, parent-in-law, son, stepson, son-in-law, daughter, stepdaughter, daughter-in-law, brother or sister, or the partner of any of those people; *and*
- the new person with care (or her partner) becomes entitled to IS/income-based JSA within 12 weeks of the day the deceased person with care (or her partner) was last entitled to IS/income-based JSA.

Only the current bonus period passes to the new person with care, not any linked period.[179]

Retired people

Special rules apply to a person who is entitled to IS/income-based JSA on the day before her 60th birthday (or, for a man on income-based JSA, his 65th birthday) and to some people approaching that age.

The bonus stops building up on the day before a person's 60th birthday (or, for a man on income-based JSA, his 65th birthday).[180] The bonus is then payable without a claim being needed.

If IS/income-based JSA entitlement stops in the 12 weeks before that date, and the person does not meet the work condition, the bonus is payable but a claim must be made.[181]

If a man's entitlement to income-based JSA stops after the age of 60, but he then becomes entitled to IS, the bonus is payable without a claim being needed.[182] This only applies if entitlement to IS begins within 12 weeks (plus any linked period) of income-based JSA entitlement ending, or longer if other conditions (not set out here) are met.

The bonus and other benefits/tax credits/tax

The bonus does not count as income for IS, income-based JSA, working tax credit, child tax credit, HB and CTB.[183] It is disregarded as capital for IS, income-based JSA, HB and CTB for 52 weeks from the date it is received.[184] None of the deductions which can be made from IS/income-based JSA (eg, mortgage or fuel direct) can be made from a bonus.[185]

The bonus is not subject to income tax.[186]

Chapter 18: Maintenance decisions
Notes

1. **Making the initial maintenance decision**
    1. s11 CSA 1991
    2. Sch 1 Art 5(5) CS(NIRA) Regs
    3. Sch 1 Art 5(1) CS(NIRA) Regs
    4. Sch 1 Art 5(3) CS(NIRA) Regs
    5. Sch 1 Art 5(2) and (6) CS(NIRA) Regs
    6. Sch 1 Art 5(4) and (7) CS(NIRA) Regs
    7. CSA Standards
    8. Sch 1 para 15 CSA 1991
    9. Reg 2(4) CS(MCSC) Regs; CCS/2750/1995
    10. Reg 1(2) definition of relevant week para (c) CS(MCSC) Regs
    11. Sch 1 para 15 decisions; Taking accout of changes that happen at different times
    12. Reg 25(5) CS(MCP) Regs
    13. Reg 6 CS(MCP) Regs
    14. R(CS) 2/98 paras 17-20
    15. Reg 10(1) and (4) CS(MAP) Regs

2. **Default maintenance decisions**
    16. s12(1) CSA 1991
    17. Reg 7 CS(MCP) Regs
    18. Calculation of a DMD
    19. Reg 23(2) CS(MCP) Regs
    20. s16(1B)CSA 1991; reg 3A(5) CS(D&A) Regs
    21. Reg 5A(2) CS(D&A) Regs
    22. Reg 8A(2)(a) SSCS(D&A) Regs
    23. Reg 5A (3) CS(D&A) Regs

3. **Notification of decisions**
    24. Reg 23 CS(MCP) Regs
    25. Reg 23(1) CS(MCP) Regs
    26. Reg 23(2) CS(MCP) Regs
    27. Reg 23(3) CS(MCP) Regs

4. **Court order phasing of calculations**
    28. Reg 30 CS(TP) Reg
    29. Reg 30 CS(TP) Regs; Court order phasing
    30. Reg 30(a)(iii) CS(TP) Regs
    31. Reg 30(a)(i) and (ii) CS(TP) Regs
    32. Court order details dialog box: Court order and WMA verification levels
    33. Court order details dialog box
    34. Reg 31 CS(TP) Regs
    35. Reg 31(2) CS(TP) Regs
    36. Reg 31(3) CS(TP) Regs
    37. Reg 32 CS(TP) Regs

5. **When the first maintenance calculation begins**
    38. Reg 1(2) CS(MCP) Regs
    39. Reg 31(2) CS(MCP) Regs
    40. Reg 26(3&4) CS(MCP) Regs
    41. Reg 2 CS(MCP) Regs
    42. Suspend debt
    43. Reg 26(2) CS(MCP) Regs
    44. Reg 4(3) CS(MCP) Regs
    45. Regs 26 and 27 CS(MCP) Regs
    46. Effective date of a new rules calculation
    47. Reg 27 CS(MCP) Regs
    48. Reg 26 CS(MCP) Regs
    49. Reg 28 CS(MCP) Regs
    50. Reg 7B(21) SS&CS(D&A) Regs as inserted by reg 9 CS(D&A)(A) Regs
    51. Reg 29(1)(b) CS(MCP) Regs as amended by reg 7(5) CS(MA) Regs 2003
    52. Reg 29(1)(a) CS(MCP) Regs as amended by reg 6(7) CS(MA) Regs and reg 7(5) CS(MA) Regs
    53. Reg 29(1)(c) CS(MCP) Regs as inserted by reg 7(7) CS(MA) Regs
    54. Reg 29(2&3) CS(MCP) Regs
    55. Reg 28(1) CS(TP) Regs
    56. Reg 31(1) CS(MCP) Regs
    57. s4A CSA 1991
    58. Reg 7B(21) CS(D&A) Regs

6. **When a calculation ends**
    59. ss4(5), 7(6) and 6(5) CSA 1991
    60. User initiated – reason and effective date for withdrawl/cancellation
    61. NRP and PWC living together verificaiton levels
    62. Referral reason fraud action
    63. Sch 1 para 16 CSA 1991
    64. Reg 24 CS(MCP) Regs
    65. s44(1) CSA 1991; reg 7 CS(MAJ) Regs (technically this is not ceasing to have effect as stated in s16, however, as there may be no relevant parties in the UK)
    66. Reg 7B(17A) SSCS(D&A) Regs; Person not a PWC
    67. Reg 7B (18) SSCS(D&A) Regs; PWC not within jurisdiction

Chapter 18: Maintenance decisions
Notes

68 Reg 7B(17) SSCS(D&A) Regs; Death of the PWC/NRP/QC
69 NRP ceased to be a parent of the only qualifying child
70 PeWC or private PaWC failing to co-operate
71 s16(3) CSA 1991; Paternity disproved for only or all qualifying children
72 s17(4) CSA 1991
73 Customer does not want to continue with claim
74 Reg 7B(19) SCS(D&A) Regs
75 Reg 7B(20) SSCS(D&A) Regs; NRP and PWC living together (PWC address)
76 Reg 15C(5) SSCS(D&A) Regs
77 Reg 24 CS(MCP) Regs; reg 15C(5)(b) SSCS(D&A) Regs

7. How a calculation affects benefit
78 s43 CSA 1991; Sch 9B SS(C&P) Regs
79 Sch 3 para 14(2) IS Regs; Sch 2 para 13(2) JSA Regs
80 Reg 32 IS Regs; Sch 2 para 18(1)(c) JSA Regs
81 Art 6 CSPSSA (Comm 12)O
82 Art 6(3-5) CSPSSA (Comm 12)O (note the SS(CMP)A Regs make provision to clarify that this applies, from 16 Feb 2004, however the provisions were in place prior to this date under the preceeding order)
83 Sch 9 para 73 IS Regs and as substituted by reg 2 SS(CMP)A Regs (see note above); Sch 7 para 70 JSA Regs and as substituted by reg 3 SS(CMP)A Regs
84 Sch 9 para 73(4) IS Regs and as substituted by reg 2 SS(CMP)A Regs; Sch7 para 70 JSA Regs and as substituted by reg 3 SS(CMP)A Regs
85 Reg 60A IS Regs; reg 125 JSA Regs
86 Reg 60B IS Regs; reg 126 JSA Regs
87 Reg 60D IS Regs; reg 129 JSA Regs
88 Reg 60C(2) and (3) IS Regs; reg 128(2) and (3) JSA Regs
89 Reg 60C(4) IS Regs; reg 128(4) JSA Regs
90 s74A SSAA 1992
91 Reg 60E IS Regs; reg 127 JSA Regs
92 Reg 8 CS(AIAMA) Regs
93 s74(1) SSAA 1992; reg 7(1)(b) SS(PAOR) Regs
94 Sch 4 para 47 HB Regs; Sch 4 para 46 CTB Regs
95 Reg 35(2) HB Regs; reg 26(2) CTB Regs

8. Taxation of child maintenance
96 Reg 19 and Table 6 para 10 TC(DCI) Regs

9. Existing 'old rules' cases
97 s12(1) CSA 1991
98 Reg 8 CS(MAP) Regs
99 Reg 30(2)(a) CS(MAP) Regs
100 Reg 30(2)(b) CS(MAP) Regs
101 Reg 3(5) CS(MAJ) Regs
102 Reg 3(6) CS(MAJ) Regs
103 Reg 3(8) CS(MAJ) Regs
104 Reg 3(1) CS(MAP) Regs
105 Reg 3(3) CS(MAP) Regs
106 Reg 3(2) CS(MAP) Regs
107 Reg 3(3) CS(MAP) Regs
108 Reg 33(7) CS(MAP) Regs
109 Reg 33(9) CS(MAP) Regs
110 Reg 4(3) CS(MAP) Regs
111 Reg 8C(1)(a) CS(MAP) Regs
112 Reg 8C(1)(b) CS(MAP) Regs
113 Regs 23(13) and 9(4) CS(MAP) Regs
114 Reg 9(5) and (6) CS(MAP) Regs
115 Reg 9(3) CS(MAP) Regs
116 Reg 8C(1)(d) CS(MAP) Regs
117 Reg 8D(5) CS(MAP) Regs
118 Reg 17(3)(a) CS(MAP) Regs
119 Reg 30A(2) CS(MAP) Regs
120 Reg 8D(6) CS(MAP) Regs
121 Reg 20(6) CS(MAP) Regs
122 Reg 30A(1) CS(MAP) Regs
123 Reg 8D(2) CS(MAP) Regs
124 Reg 8D(8) CS(MAP) Regs
125 Reg 30A(4) CS(MAP) Regs
126 Reg 30A(3) CS(MAP) Regs
127 Reg 30A(6) CS(MAP) Regs
128 Sch 1 para 16(5) CSA 1991; reg 7(1) CS(MAJ) Regs; reg 32A(1) CS(MAP) Regs
129 Sch 1 para 16(7) CSA 1991
130 Reg 33(5) CS(MAP) Regs
131 Reg 8D(4) CS(MAP) Regs
132 Reg 9(1) CS(MAP) Regs
133 Sch para 7(1)(a)(iii) CSA(Comm3)O; reg 7(1)(a) CS(MATP) Regs
134 Court order phasing
135 Sch para 6 CSA(Comm3)O
136 Sch para 7(2) CSA(Comm3)O
137 Sch para 7(1) CSA(Comm3)O
138 Sch paras 6 'modified amount' and 8 CSA(Comm3)O
139 Reg 6(1) CS(MATP) Regs
140 Reg 7(2)(a) CS(MATP) Regs
141 Reg 7(1) CS(MATP) Regs
142 Reg 7(2)(b) CS(MATP) Regs
143 Reg 7(2)(c) CS(MATP) Regs
144 Reg 8(2)(a) CS(MATP) Regs
145 Reg 8(2) CS(MATP) Regs
146 Reg 7(2)(b) CS(MATP) Regs
147 Sch para 8 CSA(Comm3)O
148 Sch para 12 CSA(Comm 3)O; reg 11 CS(MATP) Regs

Chapter 18: Maintenance decisions
Notes

149 Article 6 CSPSSA (Comm 12)O as substituted by Art 2 CSPSSA (Comm 13)O
150 Article 6 CSPSSA (Comm 12)O as substituted by Art 2 CSPSSA (Comm 13)O
151 s10 CSA 1995; reg 4(1) SS(CMB) Regs
152 Reg 4(1) and (9) SS(CMB) Regs
153 Reg 4(1) SS(CMB) Regs
154 Reg 4(6) SS(CMB) Regs
155 Reg 8(1) and (3) SS(CMB) Regs
156 Reg 1(2) SS(CMB) Regs
157 Reg 4(2) SS(CMB) Regs
158 Reg 4(3) SS(CMB) Regs
159 Reg 3(1)(d) SS(CMB) Regs
160 Reg 3(1)(c) SS(CMB) Regs
161 Reg 3(2) and (3) SS(CMB) Regs
162 Reg 3(1)(iii) SS(CMB) Regs
163 Reg 3(1)(f)(ii) SS(CMB) Regs
164 Reg 3(1)(i) SS(CMB) Regs
165 Regs 10(1) and (2) and (92) SS(CMB) Regs
166 Reg 10(1)(b) SS(CMB) Regs
167 Reg 11(4) SS(CMB) Regs
168 Reg 10(1)(d) SS(CMB) Regs
169 Reg 13 SS(CMB) Regs
170 Reg 5(1)(a)(i) SS(CMB) Regs
171 Reg 5(1)(a)(ii) SS(CMB) Regs
172 Reg 5(1)(b) SS(CMB) Regs
173 Reg 4(1)(c)(ii) SS(CMB) Regs
174 Reg 5(3) SS(CMB) Regs
175 Reg 5(1)(c) SS(CMB) Regs
176 Reg 5(5) SS(CMB) Regs
177 Reg 12 SS(CMB) Regs
178 Reg 7 SS(CMB) Regs
179 Reg 7(1) SS(CMB) Regs
180 Reg 8(1) SS(CMB) Regs
181 Reg 8(4) and (5) SS(CMB) Regs
182 Reg 8(2) SS(CMB) Regs
183 Reg 14 SS(CMB) Regs
184 Sch 10 para 7 IS Regs; Sch 8 para 12 JSA Regs; Sch 5 para 52 HB Regs; Sch 5 para 52 CTB Regs
185 Schs 9 para 1 'specified benefit' and 9A para 1 'relevant benefits' SS(C&P) Regs; reg 16(8) SS(PAOR) Regs 'specified benefit'; reg 4 Social Fund (Recovery by Deductions from Benefits) Regs 1988 SI No.35
186 s617(2)(ad) ICTA 1988

Chapter 19
Revision and supersession

This chapter covers:
1. Changing decisions (see below)
2. Revision (p416)
3. Supersession (p420)
4. Test case rules (p427)
5. Existing 'old rules' cases (p430)

> This chapter does not include information on revisions and supersessions outstanding at conversion, which are covered in Chapter 9. Conversion decisions themselves may be revised or superseded as described in this chapter.[1] However, the amount of any maintenance to be paid (eg, transitional amount) will be worked out using the rules described in Chapter 9.

1. Changing decisions

Most decisions may be changed or challenged by revision or supersession. However, there are some decisions that cannot (see p415).

A revision or supersession normally happens because the CSA is told that something is wrong or has changed since the decision was made. The CSA may also initiate a revision or supersession itself.

Table 19.1 is a quick guide to when decisions are revised and superseded. Put simply the main difference between revision and supersession is that:
- a revision means the decision that is wrong or has been challenged is itself changed;
- a supersession means that a new decision is made with effect from a later date.

Where a decision is challenged within one month it may be revised, but outside this time period a decision will only be revised in special circumstances – eg, there has been official error (see p418). If these special circumstances are not met it may mean that the decision is not revised, instead it may be superseded.

413

Chapter 19: Revision and supersession
1. Changing decisions

Table 19.1: Quick guide to revision and supersession

Why is the decision being challenged?	When	What can be done
The decision is wrong for any reason.	Within a month of being told the decision.	The decision can be revised.
The CSA made a mistake ('official error'), were misled or did not know about something that would have affected the decision.	At any time.	The decision can be revised.
The decision is wrong for any reason.	Later than one month after being told the decision.	The decision may be superseded but the person can ask for a late application for revision to be considered (see p417).
Something that affects the decision has changed.	At any time.	The decision can be superseded.
The CSA has not dealt with the case properly.	At any time.	The person may make a complaint (see p415).

Variations are an element of the calculation and not a separate decision. This means that any change relating to a variation element can give rise to a revision or supersession of the maintenance calculation.

For when calculations can be cancelled or superseded when they cease to have effect, see pp000-403. For changing reduced benefit decisions, see p80. For changing deductions of maintenance from income support (IS)/income-based jobseeker's allowance (JSA), see p226.

All decisions made by CSA/Jobcentre Plus staff are made on behalf of the Secretary of State for Work and Pensions. However, only certain decisions are subject to revision, supersession and appeal. Decisions of appeal tribunals and child support commissioners (see Chapter 20) can also be superseded or revised but only in certain circumstances (see pp417, 421 and 429).

Under the closer working initiative, the Jobcentre Plus now makes some child support decisions — eg, reduced benefit decisions. Applications to change these should be made to the Jobcentre Plus who will apply child support legislation when making a determination. This chapter will refer to applications to change a CSA decision. However, where the decision is made by the Jobcentre Plus, information should be read as such. For more information on Jobcentre Plus decision making see CPAG's *Welfare Benefits and Tax Credits Handbook*. If a non-resident parent thinks the revision/supersession may reduce the amount of his

414

calculation, he may try to negotiate lower payments pending the decision, although this is usually difficult (see p470).

For the CSA approach to parentage disputes, see p25.

Challenging CSA decisions which cannot be revised or superseded

Most of these are in the areas of information gathering, collection and enforcement. Deduction from earnings orders can be appealed to a court (see p477). Complaints can be made, including to the Independent Case Examiner (see p19). Judicial review may also be possible (see below).

Further information can be given to the CSA and the officer asked to reconsider. If the officer refuses to change the decision, a complaint can be made. There may be other occasions that do not involve a decision, but where the behaviour of CSA staff is unsatisfactory – eg, intimidating or unnecessarily intrusive questioning, or unwarranted demands for evidence and documentation. In these cases also a complaint can be made.

Judicial review

A person affected by a decision or action of a public body or one of its officers can ask the High Court to carry out a judicial review of the decision or action. The court can set aside the decision and also order the decision maker to consider it again in a lawful way. Judicial review cannot usually be brought where there is a right to raise the issue on an appeal to a tribunal, commissioner or court. Apart from that though, judicial review may be sought of a decision of the CSA (eg, on enforcement) or of an appeal tribunal or child support commissioner (eg, to refuse to grant leave to appeal) that cannot be appealed. Legal advice *must* be taken as soon as possible after the decision is made. Legal aid may be available.

Judicial review can succeed if there is:[2]
- illegality – where the decision maker does something s/he has no power to do; *or*
- irrationality – where a decision maker fails to have regard to a relevant matter or has regard to an irrelevant matter, or where a decision is 'so outrageous in its defiance of logic or of accepted moral standards that no sensible person who had applied his mind to the question could have arrived at it'; *or*
- procedural unfairness.

Challenging decisions about benefit entitlement

Some CSA decisions depend upon a decision of the Jobcentre Plus. In particular, a person in receipt of IS or income-based JSA is due to pay the flat rate or £5 (see p223). As long as the Jobcentre Plus pays one of these benefits, even if the non-resident parent has other income there can be no application for a variation on additional income grounds. A parent who believes that the other parent should

Chapter 19: Revision and supersession
1. Changing decisions

not be allowed to claim IS/income-based JSA (eg, because s/he is working full time) must therefore challenge the Jobcentre Plus decision to award that benefit. This can be done by raising it with the CSA. The CSA reports it to the Jobcentre Plus, which investigates. However, an appeal tribunal should not adjourn a child support appeal for this to be done. The Jobcentre Plus reports the result to the CSA but not to the person who made the allegation. The other parent cannot appeal to an appeal tribunal against the Jobcentre Plus decision,[3] although judicial review could be sought.[4]

2. Revision

The CSA can revise a decision if a person applies within the 'dispute period' of one month (or longer if special circumstances exist – see p417), applies for a variation within one month or if the CSA initiates revision. A revised decision normally has effect from the date the decision under revision had effect.

Information on revision of child support decisions made by the Jobcentre Plus is the same as that for CSA decisions, except that applications are made to the Jobcentre Plus.

Decisions which can be revised

Most child maintenance decisions can be revised. The following are some examples of such decisions:[5]
- a decision to make or refuse to make a maintenance calculation, including an interim maintenance decision and default maintenance decision (see p399);
- a decision to make a reduced benefit decision. This is a Jobcentre Plus decision;
- a decision of an appeal tribunal to make or refuse to agree a variation to a maintenance calculation;
- a decision to adjust maintenance payable or to cancel an adjustment (see p465);[6]
- any of those decisions made on supersession (see p420).[7]

It may also be possible to revise other sorts of CSA decisions, depending upon how the CSA (and, eventually, appeal tribunals and commissioners) interpret the rules. A person who disputes a CSA interpretation of these rules should seek advice. Decisions that it may be possible to revise include:
- a decision to treat a maintenance application as withdrawn when a section 6 applicant becomes a section 4 applicant (see p53);[8]
- a decision to refuse to cancel or to suspend a reduced benefit decision (see p80);[9]
- a decision to impose a regular payments condition on a variation applicant (see p360).[10]

When a decision can be revised

The CSA can revise a decision if within **a month** of notification of the decision:[11]
- the CSA starts action leading to revision;
- a person (person with care, non-resident parent or Scottish child applicant) applies for revision;
- a person applies for a variation; *or*
- the revision is refused because of insufficient information or evidence, the person reapplies (or a longer period if there are sufficient reasons) and provides sufficient information or evidence to revise.

Outside this one-month time period the CSA can revise a decision if:[12]
- the decision arose from 'official error' (see p418);
- the decision was wrong because of a misrepresentation or failure to disclose a material fact (see p418) *and,* because of that, the decision was more advantageous to the person who misrepresented or failed to disclose;
- a late application is accepted;[13] *or*
- the decision was made under the rules about a pending test case decision which has now been given (see p427).

Where an appeal is lodged, the CSA checks to see whether the decision should be revised (see p416).

A decision *cannot* be revised because of any change of circumstances after the date the decision was made, or because of an expected change.[14] Instead, the decision may be superseded (see p420).

For revision of default maintenance decisions, see p385.

Under the test case rules (see p427), the CSA may refuse to follow the law as decided by the commissioners or courts, or even suspend a decision on revision while an appeal is being brought in another case.

Late applications

Because supersession (see p420) cannot usually lead to a decision being backdated to the original effective date, a late application for revision (which can) may need to be made. However, in case it should not be accepted, an application for supersession can be made at the same time, if appropriate. For example, a decision may be based on the wrong mortgage payment details. If the person concerned missed the deadline for applying for revision, s/he can make a late application (giving special reasons – see below) and also apply for supersession on the grounds of mistake of fact (see p421).

The CSA can extend the one-month period for applying for revision if the CSA considers that:[15]
- it was not practicable to apply within one month because of 'special circumstances' (see p418);
- the application for revision has merit; *and*

Chapter 19: Revision and supersession
2. Revision

- it is reasonable to grant the application.

'**Special circumstances**' are not defined, but they are *not* the same as the special circumstances needed for bringing a late appeal (see p438). However, ignorance of or a mistake about the law, including time limits, or a new interpretation of the law by a commissioner or court are *not* special circumstances and must be ignored when considering the application.[16] The person applying for revision must apply for an extension at the latest within 13 months of the notification.[17] The longer the delay, the more compelling the special circumstances must be.[18]

An application for an extension must identify the decision that it is sought to revise and explain why an extension should be granted.[19] An application that is refused may not be renewed,[20] though the CSA may have power to reconsider a refusal to extend.[21] Judicial review of a refusal to extend time may be possible (see p415).

Official error

'Official error' is a mistake made by an officer of the CSA, Jobcentre Plus or designated authority, which was not caused or contributed to by anyone outside the Jobcentre Plus or designated authority.[22] This includes mistakes of law (see p422), except those only shown as an error by a child support commissioner or court, as well as mistakes of fact, such as:
- a mistake of arithmetic;
- a wrong assumption about a person's circumstances, where there was no evidence for it;
- a mistake made because CSA staff did not pass information or evidence to the officer who made the decision, when they should have done.

Misrepresentation and failure to disclose

A 'misrepresentation' is a written or spoken statement of fact which is untrue.[23] This applies to untrue statements, even if the person making it believes it to be true – ie, 'innocent misrepresentation'.[24]

There is only a 'failure to disclose' a fact if there is a legal duty to report that fact to the CSA.[25] Therefore, a person who is asked to give information but leaves that out, has failed to disclose that information. However, if the person is not asked for the information, there can be no failure to disclose it, unless it is one of the facts a parent with care must always report (see p113). There is no general duty to report changes of circumstances to the CSA (see p113).

The decision that the CSA wishes to revise must have been wrong due to the fact misrepresented or failed to be disclosed and the decision was more advantageous to the person who misrepresented or failed to disclose.[26] Therefore, if the CSA ignored that fact or if that fact made no difference, the CSA cannot base revision on misrepresentation or failure to disclose.

Chapter 19: Revision and supersession
2. Revision

Example 19.1
When Amy applied for maintenance she also applied for a variation on the ground that Shaun had assets over £65,000. However, the variation was not agreed and her maintenance calculation was made without this element, based on the information Shaun provided. A few months later Amy discovers that Shaun inherited a property from his aunt a few weeks before her application for maintenance. She informs the CSA, it investigates and confirms that he failed to disclose this when he was asked to provide information for the variation element. Because he failed to disclose the inheritance his maintenance calculation is less than it would have been with the variation element. Since there was failure to disclose that resulted in a decision that was more advantageous to him the CSA revise the original maintenance calculation.

However, had Shaun only inherited the property some time after he was asked for information in relation to the variation application the CSA could not decide he had failed to disclose information. In this case the maintenance calculation could not be revised but it may be superseded if Amy asks for a variation to be considered.

Procedure for revising

Notification of a decision sets out how to ask the CSA to revise that decision.[27] The revision request may be made by telephone. However, unless the issue is straightforward, it is still best to follow up any telephone call with a letter to the CSA confirming the reason for the request.

There is no general requirement for the CSA to notify the parties that it is considering revision or to inform one party that the other has applied for revision. However, where an application for variation has passed preliminary consideration[28] or there is a request for revision of a calculation with a previously agreed variation,[29] the other parties may be contacted and asked for their representations.

The rules about disclosure apply to the information given in any notification (see p114).

Where a revision has been requested the burden of proof is upon the applicant.[30] In cases where the applicant fails to provide sufficient information to make a decision, the CSA may contact the applicant and ask her/him to provide further information within an agreed time limit. In this situation the CSA may decide to:[31]
- close the case, where a section 4 person with care is not co-operating; *or*
- make a default maintenance decision, where the non-resident parent is failing to co-operate; *or*
- refuse to revise.

Where a default decision would be less than the current maintenance calculation the CSA may refuse to revise rather than make a default maintenance decision. For further information on default maintenance decisions, see p384.

Chapter 19: Revision and supersession
2. Revision

Where a parent with care on benefit comes off benefit before the application is determined there are special provisions regarding notifications and treating the application as never made.

Where a revision is considered due to an appeal that has been lodged, unless the revised decision would be worse for the appellant, the revision goes ahead and the appeal lapses.[32] Where a person thinks a revision may make them worse off, it may be in their interests to lodge an appeal to stop such a revision. However, unless they win that appeal, they will then have to deal with the unfavourable decision and pay any arrears.

The revised decision

A revised decision is where the CSA makes the decision it should have made instead of the decision under revision.

The revised decision normally has the same effective date as the decision it replaces.[33] However, if the effective date of that decision was wrong, the revised decision has the effective date that the replaced decision should have had.[34]

Notification

If the decision is revised, whether or not this results in a fresh or new maintenance calculation (including a default maintenance decision), the parties must be notified of the decision and given the usual details (see p386).[35] Where there is more than one person with care in relation to a non-resident parent this means all must be notified. The normal rules on information disclosure apply.[36]

Where the request for revision is refused only the applicant may be informed, unless the other parties have been contacted – eg, where there has been a request for a variation. Notification of the decision includes reasons for refusal and details of appeal rights.[37]

The time limit for appeal runs from the date of the notice of the revised decision or refusal to revise.[38]

3. Supersession

The CSA can supersede a decision at any time if certain rules are met, with or without an application. Usually a supersession decision is made due to a change of circumstances. A superseded decision normally has effect from the date of the application for supersession or, if there was none, the date the decision under revision has effect. Unlike in social security cases, there is no duty to tell the CSA of all changes of circumstances (see p113 for changes which must be notified). An application for a variation to the maintenance calculation may be treated as a request for supersession (see p362).

Chapter 19: Revision and supersession
3. Supersession

Information on supersession of child support decisions made by the Jobcentre Plus is the same as that for CSA decisions, except that applications are made to the Jobcentre Plus.

Decisions which can be superseded

Most child support decisions (whether made by the CSA, Jobcentre Plus, appeal tribunal or commissioner) may be superseded. The following are examples of such decisions:[39]
- a decision to make a maintenance calculation, including a default maintenance decision and interim maintenance decision (see p386);
- a decision to make a reduced benefit decision (see p75). This is a Jobcentre Plus decision;
- a decision of an appeal tribunal which was made on a CSA referral of a variation application (see p362);
- a decision to adjust maintenance payable or to cancel an adjustment for overpayments of maintenance or voluntary payments (see p465);[40]
- any of those decisions made on revision (see p416).

It may also be possible to supersede other sorts of CSA decisions, depending upon how the CSA (and, eventually, appeal tribunals and commissioners) interpret the rules. For those decisions which we suggest it may be possible to revise, see p416.

When a decision can be superseded

The CSA can *normally* supersede a decision if:[41]
- a material change of circumstances has taken place (or is expected to take place) since the effective date of the decision and there would be a significant change in the amount of the calculation;
- the decision was made in ignorance of or was based on a mistake as to some material fact;
- there is an application for a variation to the calculation; *or*
- the decision was made by the CSA (*not* by an appeal tribunal or commissioner) and it is wrong in law (see p422).

However, the CSA cannot supersede a decision:
- which can be revised instead (see p416);[42]
- refusing to make or cancelling a maintenance calculation.[43] A further application for a maintenance calculation should be made instead.

The CSA can initiate supersession even though a party has already applied for supersession[44] – eg, where the CSA is aware of a change of circumstances which has not been raised in the supersession application. The CSA may supersede to reinstate a previously applied variation.

421

Chapter 19: Revision and supersession
3. Supersession

The CSA also carries out periodic case checks. In some cases a notified change of circumstances can be treated as a periodic case check instead of a request for supersession (see p424).

Under the test case rules, the CSA may refuse to follow the law as decided by the commissioners or courts, or even suspend a decision on supersession while an appeal is being brought in another case. See p427 for details.

When may a decision not be superseded

A decision cannot be superseded unless there is a change in the non-resident parent's net income used in the calculation of 5 per cent or more.[45] The CSA refers to this as the tolerance level. In some cases, this net income tolerance rule does not apply. The net income tolerance rule does not apply where the superseding decision:[46]
- is on the outcome of a variation application;
- affects a variation ground in a maintenance calculation, or revised/superseded such a decision;
- is made on an interim maintenance decision, or revised/superseded such a decision;
- is made on a decision to adjust or cease to adjust amounts due to take account of overpayments of maintenance or voluntary payments, or revised/superseded such a decision;
- is due to the non-resident parent or his partner going on or off benefit – ie, benefits that count for the flat rate (other than income support (IS)/income based jobseeker's allowance (JSA)) or child benefit.[47]

The tolerance rule is not applied to other changes of circumstances, for example:[48]
- relevant children joining or leaving the household;
- applications for other qualifying children;
- changes in shared care arrangements;
- changes notified by a third party (eg, Jobcentre Plus);
- a qualifying child dies or ceases to be a child;[49]
- either the person with care, non-resident parent or qualifying child are no longer habitually resident in the UK;[50] *or*
- the person with care and non-resident parent start living together.[51]

Where there is more than one reason for the request for supersession, the tolerance rule may only apply to that ground relating to the net income of the non-resident parent, bearing in mind the exceptions above.[52]

Wrong in law

A decision is 'erroneous in point of law' if:[53]
- when making the decision, the CSA misinterpreted or overlooked part or all of an Act of Parliament, a regulation or relevant caselaw;

- there is no evidence to support the decision;
- the facts are such that no reasonable person applying the law could have come to such a conclusion;
- there is a breach of natural justice – ie, the procedure used led to unfairness or the CSA officer who took the decision appeared to be biased;[54]
- the CSA has not given enough reasons for the decision;
- when exercising a discretion, the CSA took into account something irrelevant or ignored something relevant – eg, welfare of the child.[55]

A decision is wrong in law if it breaches European Community law. Commissioners have decided that Article 119 of the European Community Treaty and Council Directives 75/117 and 79/7 on equal treatment of men and women do not apply to child support.[56]

European Community law does not include the European Convention on Human Rights (ECHR), which cannot overrule British law in the British courts.[57] However, British courts and the commissioners can use the ECHR to over rule British regulations (but not Acts of Parliament) via the Human Rights Act 1998 which came into force on 1 October 2000.[58] This Act requires the courts and commissioners to interpret Acts of Parliament consistently with the ECHR if at all possible.[59]

A decision is also wrong in law if the regulation it is made under is not made lawfully. Such a regulation is said to be *ultra vires* (outside the powers). The courts, appeal tribunals and commissioners can decide that a regulation is *ultra vires*,[60] and appeal tribunals and commissioners have done so in benefit cases.

Otherwise, the CSA, Jobcentre Plus, tribunals and commissioners cannot override or ignore the Acts or regulations.

Procedure for superseding

A party to the calculation can apply for supersession at any time. There are no time limits, but any superseding decision usually runs from the date of the application (see p425). If an application is made, the CSA must consider it and supersede if the conditions set out above are met.

The CSA has a discretion whether to initiate supersession itself, so it must take into account the welfare of the child (see p31) when considering whether to do so. The CSA learns of some changes automatically from the Jobcentre Plus computer or may do so from a third party.

If the CSA is considering supersession on its own initiative, it must give 28 days' notice to the relevant parties – ie, person with care, non-resident parent and/or Scottish child applicant.[61] The CSA can give notice of its intention to supersede orally (eg, by telephone) or in writing.[62] Where more than one method of notification is used the earliest date is treated as the date of notification. Where the parties are notified on different dates the latest is counted as the date of notification.[63]

Chapter 19: Revision and supersession
3. Supersession

Where the supersession is in relation to an application for a variation that has passed preliminary consideration,[64] or a supersession of a previously agreed variation,[65] the other relevant parties may be contacted. Otherwise the other party may not be notified of the application for supersession. The normal rules about disclosure apply to the information given in any notification (see p114).[66]

The CSA does not have to check all the facts again so can (and usually will) limit its consideration to the issues raised in any application and/or on its own initiative.[67] Information that is provided may need to be verified in the normal way (see Chapter 6). Where the tolerance rule is breached or there are other relevant changes a decision to supersede will be made.

Periodic case checks

The CSA carries out a **periodic case check** on each calculation on average every two years, though this can occur every one to four years at the CSA's discretion.[68] The tolerance rule does not apply to periodic case checks.[69]

A periodic case check may be requested by any party but the CSA may decide not to conduct one – eg, because the non-resident parent remains on IS/income-based JSA.[70] A case check is not a supersession, but if the information gathered shows there are grounds for supersession the CSA does so.

Where there is a change of circumstances within 26 weeks of a periodic case check it may be treated as a case check rather than supersession.[71]

When a periodic case check is due or the CSA decides to conduct one, each party should be given 28 days' notice.[72] This notification may be orally or in writing, with the date of notification being the earliest where more than one method is used. Where the parties are notified at different dates the notification is counted from the latest. The parties are invited to tell the CSA about any changes within 14 days. Where the parties do not respond or no relevant changes are notified no further action is taken. Where changes are reported these may need to be verified.

If the information does not show there are grounds for supersession, the CSA does not make a new decision, so no notification need be issued. However, where there is a supersession decision notification continues in the normal way (see p426).

The effective date of any supersession depends on how the periodic case check was initiated:
- initiated by the CSA – the first day of the maintenance period that contains the 28th day from the date of notification of the periodic check;[73]
- change of circumstances treated as periodic case check – the first day of the week in the maintenance period on or prior to the date the change of circumstances was notified.[74]

The superseding decision

The CSA may decide that:

Chapter 19: Revision and supersession
3. Supersession

- there are no grounds for supersession and refuse to supersede;
- there are grounds for supersession but the maintenance calculation remains unchanged;
- there are grounds for supersession and the maintenance calculation is changed; *or*
- the maintenance calculation should be cancelled (see p431).

Effective date of supersession decision

The general rule is that a supersession takes effect from the first day in the maintenance period in which the decision is made, or the application for supersession/variation was made.[75] However, the effective date may be from a different date in certain circumstances as shown in Table 19.2. There are special rules for supersession decisions relating to reduced benefit decisions (see p75), periodic case checks (see p424) and cancellations.

Table 19.2: Effective dates of supersession decisions in certain circumstances

Circumstances	Effective date
An application for an anticipated change in circumstances.	The first day in the maintenance period that the change is expected to occur.[76]
The relevant circumstance is a variation ground expected to occur.	The first day in the maintenance period in which the ground is expected to occur.[77]
There is a further qualifying child in relation to the same non-resident parent and person with care.	Where the:[78] application for supersession is made by the non-resident parent, the date of the request; application for supersession is made by the person with care, or a maintenance calculation is made in response to a section 7 application, the date of notification to the non-resident parent. However, where either or these dates falls on the first day of the maintenance period in relation to the existing calculation, this will be the effective date.
The non-resident parent (or his partner) claims benefit and notifies the CSA within a month of the award.	If benefit commences on or before notification, the first day in the maintenance period the parent notified the CSA.[79] If benefit commences after notification, the first day in the maintenance period entitlement begins.[80]

Chapter 19: Revision and supersession
3. Supersession

Ignorance or mistake where the non-resident parent (or his partner) had claimed benefit before notice of the maintenance calculation and where benefit is payable, the CSA is notified within one month of the award.	If benefit commences on or before notification – the first day in the maintenance period the parent notified the CSA.[81] If benefit commences after notification – the first day in the maintenance period entitlement begins.[82]
The decision being superseded was made by an appeal tribunal or commissioner; *and* the supersession is because of a misrepresentation or failure to disclose a material fact; *and* that misrepresentation/failure meant the decision was more favourable to the person who misrepresented/failed to disclose.	The date the tribunal/commissioner decision took or was to take effect.[83]
The CSA is superseding on its own initiative.	The first day of the maintenance period that is 28 days after the date of notification of this intention to the parties involved.[84] However, where the decision is superseded on the basis of information or evidence in relation to decisions about the relationship between the CSA and maintenance orders/agreements, the first day of the maintenance period in which the information or evidence was brought to the attention of the CSA.[85]
The supersession is due to a change in circumstances brought to the attention of another agency with authority to act under the Child Support Act – ie, Jobcentre Plus.	The first day in the maintenance period in which information or evidence was first brought to the relevant officer.[86]

For the general rule, see p425.

Notification

If the decision results in a supersession, whether or not a new maintenance calculation is made (including interim maintenance decision or default maintenance decision), the parties must be notified of the decision and given the usual details (see p386).[87] The notice must also state how to seek revision, supersession and appeal.[88]

If the decision is to refuse to supersede, notification will be given including the reasons for refusal and appeal rights.[89]

Where the CSA intends to cancel the case it may notify each party and, where the reason for cancellation is a section 7 applicant ceasing to be a qualifying child, inform other potential section 7 applicants.[90]

Whether to request supersession

Before requesting supersession because of a change, you should try to work out whether a fresh calculation would be higher or lower. You only need tell the CSA about the changes in your favour. If the change only relates to one party, the CSA may not tell the other person but if it does, that party might tell the CSA about other changes. These may cancel out the effect of the changes which led you to ask for supersession.

If you believe the other person's circumstances have changed (eg, a non-resident parent no longer has children living with him) you can ask for supersession and for the CSA to investigate (see Chapter 6). The CSA does not have to, but any changes it is aware of must be taken into account when it decides whether to supersede.

4. Test case rules

Since 1 June 1999, special rules apply if a court decision on a 'test case' is pending or a commissioner's or court decision on a test case has been made. By 'test case' we mean a case where a person is challenging the CSA's interpretation of the law, even if it is now the CSA's appeal from a tribunal, commissioner or court decision and even if the person never considered the case to be a test case.

These rules apply to maintenance calculation decisions, reduced benefit decisions, revision and supersession decisions and an appeal in relation to a different matter by a child support commissioner or court. Even though they are not limited to revision and supersession cases, they are dealt with here because that is when they will most often arise. Similar rules apply to appeals (see p430).

Test case pending

If a test case is decided against the CSA, then normally the CSA would have to follow the law as decided in that case in all other cases (see p453). However, if an appeal is pending before a child support commissioner or court, then, in any case which might be affected by the decision to be given in that appeal, the CSA can:[91]
- suspend a decision on the application, revision or supersession until the test case appeal has been decided; *or*
- make a decision on the assumption that the test case appeal has already been decided and has been decided against the person who applied for the decision (ie, the calculation, revision or supersession), but *only if*:[92]

Chapter 19: Revision and supersession
4. Test case rules

- the CSA would otherwise have to make a calculation (including one on revision or supersession) leading to the parent with care becoming entitled to income support (IS) or a higher rate of IS; *or*
- the non-resident parent is employed or self-employed.[93]

An appeal is pending before a court if:[94]
- an appeal (including a judicial review) about child support has been made to the High Court, Court of Session, Court of Appeal or House of Lords, but has not been determined;
- an application for permission to make such an appeal (or judicial review) has been made, but has not been determined;
- the CSA has certified in writing that it is considering making such an appeal or application *and* the time for appealing/applying has not expired *and* the CSA considers that the appeal might result in the non-resident parent having no, or less, liability for child maintenance.[95]

An appeal also counts as pending if a court (but not a commissioner) has referred a question to the European Court of Justice for a preliminary ruling. This does not apply to an application to the European Court of Human Rights, because that is made by an individual and is not referred by a British court.

Where the CSA does not make an application/appeal in time, it can no longer suspend making a decision. The time limits for making applications/appeals are as follows:
- applying to a commissioner for permission to appeal to the Court of Appeal/Court of Session: three months from the date the commissioner's decision is issued (for details, see p453);[96]
- applying to the Court of Session/Court of Appeal for permission to appeal from a commissioner to it (or appealing to one of those courts with permission of the commissioner): four weeks from the date the commissioner's decision is issued;[97]
- applying to the Court of Session/Court of Appeal for permission to appeal to the House of Lords: this is usually done at the end of the hearing in which the court gives its judgment;
- applying to the House of Lords for permission to appeal to it: one month from the date the order of the Court of Session/Court of Appeal is sealed;[98]
- appealing to the House of Lords with permission of the Court of Session/Court of Appeal: three months from the date it is sealed;[99]
- applying to the High Court/Court of Session for permission to apply for judicial review: promptly, and in any event three months from the date of the decision.[100] Because an application must be made promptly (ie, normally before three months has expired) the time limit is not clear.

Chapter 19: Revision and supersession
4. Test case rules

A decision to suspend or make a decision on the assumption that the CSA will win the test case is a discretionary one. The CSA must therefore have regard to the welfare of the child when making it.

Test case decisions

Where a commissioner or court interprets child support law, the CSA would normally have to apply the commissioner's/court's interpretation of the law to the period before that decision was given. This would usually require the CSA to supersede all decisions which are affected.

However, where the commissioner/court rejected the CSA interpretation of the law, that test case decision only has effect from the date it is given by the commissioner/court.[101] For the period before that date, the CSA (and any appeal tribunal or commissioner) assumes that it was right in its (or the child support officer's) interpretation of the law when making the original decision which led to the appeal.[102] This includes cases where the test case appeal began with an appeal tribunal's decision on a *referral* of an application for a variation to the maintenance calculation (see p362). This rule applies:

- to decisions on maintenance calculations, or reduced benefit decisions referral;[103]
- even where the application for revision or supersession was made before the test case decision was given and regardless of whether the person applying raised that issue of law;[104]
- even where the commissioner/court decides that a regulation is *ultravires* (see p422).[105] Where this decision is made because the regulation is inconsistent with the European Convention on Human Rights (see p422), this rule may also breach that Convention;[106]
- even to decisions of the European Court of Justice (ECJ).[107] This rule is unlawful under European Community law, except in a case where the ECJ has itself decided that its decision only has effect from the date it is given.[108]

This rule does *not* apply to:

- an application for maintenance made before 1 June 1999 or a reduced benefit decision;[109]
- revision of any decision made before 1 June 1999;[110]
- supersession of any decision made before 1 June 1999;[111]
- a decision in a case where the CSA had suspended a decision under the test case pending rules (see p427);[112]
- a revision or supersession decision in a case where the CSA had required the tribunal or commissioner to refer the case to the CSA or deal with it on the assumption that the test case had already been decided against the appellant (see p430).[113]

429

Chapter 19: Revision and supersession
4. Test case rules

The CSA can make regulations for treating a decision of a court upholding a decision of a lower court or commissioner as if it had been made on the date of the lower court/commissioner's decision and/or the other way around.[114] The CSA can also make regulations for deciding the date of a test case decision.[115] No regulations of either sort have been made at the time of writing.

Test case rules affecting appeals

If a test case pending before a court may affect a similar case pending before an appeal tribunal or commissioner, the CSA may:[116]
- direct the tribunal/commissioner to refer the similar case to the CSA. The CSA makes no decision until the test case is decided. It then revises the CSA decision under appeal or supersedes the tribunal decision under appeal; *or*
- direct the tribunal/commissioner to deal with the case itself. The tribunal/commissioner *must* then either:
  - stay the appeal (ie, postpone its decision) until the test case is decided; *or*
  - decide the appeal on the assumption that the test case appeal has already been decided and has been decided against the person who appealed to the tribunal in the similar case. If the test case is later decided in that person's favour, the CSA supersedes the tribunal/commissioner decision in the similar case.

The definition of pending appeal is the same as for 'test case pending' (see p427), except that, where the CSA is considering appealing/applying, the CSA only has to consider that the test case decision would affect the similar appeal.[117]

5. Existing 'old rules' cases

The rules on revisions and supersessions of 'old rules' maintenance assessments are broadly the same as under 'new rules' maintenance calculations; however, legislative referencing is different. In addition, given the scope of the different schemes, there are slightly different decisions that can be revised or superseded, including:
- a decision to make or refuse to make a departure direction (see Chapter 17);[118]
- a decision to make or refuse to make a deduction of maintenance from the non-resident parent's income support/income-based jobseeker's allowance (see p224).[119]

Provisions on the procedure of revisions/supersessions under the 'old rules' and the relevant timescales are identical. However, notifications contain information relevant to maintenance assessments and notification is treated as being given or sent two days after posting.

Chapter 19: Revision and supersession
Notes

For full details of legislative referencing in 'old rules' cases see the 2002/03 edition of this *Handbook*.

For information on conversion of 'old rules' cases and revision/supersession of conversion decisions, see Chapter 9.

Cancellation

The CSA can cancel a calculation where the usual rules for cancellation apply (see p392). It can also cancel if a section 4 or section 7 applicant fails to provide enough information for revision to be carried out, (see p62).

Before cancelling a calculation, the CSA must, if possible, give written notice to the person with care, non-resident parent and any Scottish child applicant of intention to cancel the calculation, and allow 14 days from the date the notice is sent before cancelling.[120]

Notes

1 Reg 4(1)(a) CS(TP) Regs

1. Changing decisions
2 *Council of Civil Service Unions v Minister for the Civil Service* [1984] 1 WLR 1174; [1984] 3 All ER 935
3 s23(3) SSAA 1992; s12(2)(b) SSA 1998; reg 25 SS&CS(DA) Regs
4 See comments at CCS/5021/1995 para 11

2. Revision
5 s16 CSA 1991
6 Reg 3A(6) SS&CS(DA) Regs
7 s16 1A(1) CSA 1991
8 s11(3) CSA 1991
9 Regs 16, 17 and 18 CS(MCP) Regs
10 s28C CSA 1991
11 Reg 3A(1)(a, b & d) SS&CS(DA) Regs
12 Reg 3A(1)(c & e) SS&CS(DA) Regs
13 Reg 4 SS&CS(DA) Regs
14 Reg 3A(2) SS&CS(DA) Regs
15 Reg 4(4) SS&CS(DA) Regs
16 Reg 4(6) SS&CS(DA) Regs
17 Reg 4(5) SS&CS(DA) Regs
18 Reg 4(7) SS&CS(DA) Regs
19 Reg 4(3) SS&CS(DA) Regs
20 Reg 4(7) SS&CS(DA) Regs

21 See CIS/93/1992
22 Reg 1(2) SSCS(D&A) Regs
23 R(SB) 9/85
24 *Page and Davis v Chief Adjudication Officer*, CA, appendix to R(SB) 2/92, Times, 4 July 1991; Misrepresentation or failure to disclose information
25 CCS/15846/1996
26 Reg 3A(c) SS&CS(DA) Regs
27 Reg 23(4) CS(MCP) Regs
28 Reg 9 CS(V) Regs
29 Reg 15B SS&CS(DA) Regs
30 Burden of proof
31 Failure to provide information; Default maintenance decisions
32 s16(6) CSA 1991; reg 30(1) and (2)(f) SS&CS(DA) Regs
33 s16(3) CSA 1991
34 Reg 5A SS&CS(DA) Regs
35 Reg 15C SS&CS(DA) Regs
36 Reg 15C(3) SS&CS(DA) Regs
37 Reg 15C(9-11) SS&CS(DA) Regs
38 s16(5) CSA 1991; reg 31(2) SS&CS(DA) Regs

3. Supersession
39 s17(1) CSA 1991
40 Reg 6A(9) SS&CS(DA) Regs

Chapter 19: Revision and supersession
Notes

41 Reg 6A(2-6) SSCA(D&A) Regs
42 Reg 6A(7) SSCA(D&A) Regs
43 Reg 6A(8) SSCA(D&A) Regs
44 Reg 6A(2&5) SSCA(D&A) Regs
45 Reg 6B(1) SS&CS(DA) Regs
46 Reg 6B(4) SS&CS(DA) Regs
47 Regs 6B(4)(e) and 7B(2-3) SS&CS(DA) Regs
48 When tolerance is applied – new rules cases
49 Regs 6B(4)(e) and 7B(17) SS&CS(DA) Regs
50 Regs 6B(4)(e) and 7B(18) SS&CS(DA) Regs
51 Regs 6B(4)(e) and 7B(20) SS&CS(DA) Regs
52 Reg 6B(3) SS&CS(DA) Regs
53 R(A) 1/72; R(SB) 11/83
54 *R v Gough* [1993] AC 646; [1993] 2 WLR 883; [1993] 2 All ER 724
55 *Wednesbury Corporation v Ministry of Housing and Local Government (No.2)* [1965] 3 WLR 956; [1965] 3 All ER 571
56 R(CS) 3/96; R(CS) 2/95; CCS/17/1994. The Sex Discrimination Act 1975 also has no effect: CCS/6/1995
57 CCS/4741/1995 para 18 applying *Brind v Secretary of State for the Home Department* [1991] 1 All ER 720. The non-resident parent appealed to the Court of Appeal, but did not apparently appeal that part of the Commissioner's decision: *AM-S v CSO* [1998] 1 FLR 955
58 s6 HRA 1998
59 s3 HRA 1998
60 *CAO v Foster* [1993] AC 754; [1993] 2 WLR 292; [1993] 1 All ER 705
61 Reg 7B(7) SS&CS(DA) Regs
62 Reg 7B(8)(b) SS&CS(DA) Regs
63 Reg 7B(8)(a) SS&CS(DA) Regs
64 Reg 9 CS(V) Regs
65 Reg 15B SS&CS(DA) Regs
66 Reg 15B SS&CS(DA) Regs
67 s17(2) CSA 1991
68 Periodic case checks
69 Periodic case checks
70 Deciding if a periodic case check is appropriate
71 Treating a notified change as a case check
72 Reg 7B(7-8) and 7C SS&CS(DA) Regs
73 Reg 7B(7) SS&CS(DA) Regs
74 Effective date of a periodic case check
75 s17(4) CSA 1991
76 Reg 7B(5) SS&CS(DA) Regs as inserted by reg 9 CS(D&A)(A) Regs
77 Reg 7B(6) SS&CS(DA) Regs as inserted by reg 9 CS(D&A)(A) Regs
78 Reg 7B(17B) SS&CS(DA) Regs as inserted by reg 3(2) CS(MA) Regs 2003
79 Reg 7B(3)(a) SS&CS(DA) Regs as inserted by reg 9 CS(D&A)(A) Regs
80 Reg 7B(3)(b) SS&CS(DA) Regs as inserted by reg 9 CS(D&A)(A) Regs
81 Reg 7B(2)(a) SS&CS(DA) Regs as inserted by reg 9 CS(D&A)(A) Regs
82 Reg 7B(2)(b) SS&CS(DA) Regs as inserted by reg 9 CS(D&A)(A) Regs
83 Reg 7B(9) SS&CS(DA) Regs as inserted by reg 9 CS(D&A)(A) Regs
84 Reg 7B(7) SS&CS(DA) Regs as inserted by reg 9 CS(D&A)(A) Regs
85 Reg 7B(1) SS&CS(DA) Regs as inserted by reg 9 CS(D&A)(A) Regs
86 Reg 7B(1) SS&CS(DA) Regs as inserted by reg 9 CS(D&A)(A) Regs
87 Reg 15C SS&CS(DA) Regs
88 Reg 15C(4) SS&CS(DA) Regs
89 Reg 15C (9-11) SS&CS(DA) Regs
90 Reg 15C(5) SS&CS(DA) Regs; Sending notification of the decision

4. Test case rules
91 s28ZA(1) and (2) CSA 1991
92 Reg 23(3) and (5) SS&CS(DA) Regs; Staying
93 As defined in s2(1) SSCBA 1992
94 s28ZA(4) and (5) CSA 1991
95 s28ZA(4)(c) CSA 1991; reg 23(4) SS&CS(DA) Regs
96 Reg 30(1) CSC(P) Regs
97 Order 59 r4(1)
98 para 2.1 House of Lords Practice Directions on Civil Appeals
99 Direction 2.1 House of Lords Practice Directions on Civil Appeals
100 Order 53 r4(1)
101 s28ZC(1) and (3) CSA 1991; reg 7B(10) SS&CS(DA) Regs
102 s28ZC(1) and (6) CSA 1991
103 s28ZC(3) CSA 1991
104 s28ZC(5) CSA 1991
105 s28ZC(4) CSA 1991
106 Art 13 European Convention on Human Rights requires an effective remedy for violations
107 s28ZC(6) CSA 1991
108 Case C-35/97 *Commission v France* [1998] ECR I-5325 para 49
109 s28ZC(1)(b)(i) CSA 1991
110 s28ZC(1)(b)(ii) CSa 1991
111 s28ZC(1)(b)(iii) CSA 1991
112 s28ZC(2)(a) CSA 1991
113 s28ZC(2)(b) CSA 1991
114 s28ZC(8)(a) CSA 1991
115 s28ZC(8)(b) CSA 1991

Chapter 19: Revision and supersession
Notes

116 s28ZB CSA 1991
117 Reg 24 SS&CS(DA) Regs

5. **Existing 'old rules' cases**
118 s28H and Sch 4C para 1(a) CSA 1991;
    reg 17(8)(a) CS(MAP) Regs
119 s43(3) and Sch 4C para 1(a) CSA 1991;
    reg 17(8)(a) CS(MAP) Regs
120 Reg 32B CS(MAP) Regs

Chapter 20
Appeals

This chapter covers:
1. Appeal tribunals (see below)
2. Procedure (p437)
3. Oral hearings (p444)
4. Decisions (p447)
5. Child support commissioners (p450)
6. Existing 'old rules' cases (p454)

> This chapter does not include information on appeals outstanding at conversion (see Chapter 9). However, conversion decisions themselves may be appealed as described in this chapter.[1]

Most important child maintenance decisions, whether they are made by the CSA or Jobcentre Plus, can be appealed to an independent appeal tribunal run by the Appeals Service. Also, an application for a variation can be referred to the tribunal by the CSA.[2] A tribunal decision can be appealed on a question of law to a child support commissioner.

In this chapter we refer to CSA decisions. Appeals against Jobcentre Plus decisions are progressed in the same way under child support legislation. However, the appeal is made to the Jobcentre Plus and the case will be prepared and presented by Jobcentre Plus staff (see CPAG's *Welfare Benefits and Tax Credits Handbook*).

1. Appeal tribunals

An appeal tribunal usually consists of a legal member of the panel for appeal tribunals, sitting alone.[3] This is a person qualified as a lawyer.[4] If the appeal raises difficult issues about financial accounts, the tribunal includes a financially qualified member – ie, a chartered or certified accountant.[5] A medically qualified member may also be included, where required.[6] This may not be a person who has advised, prepared a report or treated anyone whose medical treatment is relevant to the appeal.[7] The President of appeals tribunals decides who is on the

Chapter 20: Appeals
1. Appeal tribunals

panel and who hears each sort of appeal.[8] The President can also appoint one extra member to sit on any appeal,[9] but this is expected to happen only rarely. If there is more than one member, the legal member is the chairperson.

Table 17.1 lists the types of decisions which can be appealed and who the appeal may be made by.

Table 17.1: Quick guide to who can make appeals

An appeal can only be made from the following decisions:[10]	The appeal may be made by:[11]
A decision to make a maintenance calculation (including default and interim maintenance decisions) or supersede one; a refusal to make a maintenance calculation (including default and interim maintenance decisions), or supersede, but only by the qualifying person.	The person who made the application or supersession request to whom the decision applies. Where the application is made by a Scottish child, either the person with care, non-resident parent or child are considered the qualifying person.
A reduced benefit decision (this is a Jobcentre Plus decision).	The parent with care, but once benefit has started to be reduced.[12]
A decision to impose penalty payments or payment of fees.	The parent required to pay the penalty or person required to pay the fees.
An adjustment, or cancellation of an adjustment, to the amount paid due to overpayment of maintenance or voluntary payments;[13] a supersession decision, whether as originally made or as revised;[14] one of those decisions made on revision/supersession or a refusal to revise one of those decisions.[15]	Any relevant person – ie, person with care, non-resident parent or Scottish child applicant.

Conversion decisions are therefore open to appeal, since these are supersession decisions.

The CSA may decide that some reported changes are ones which it needs to act on but do not constitute an application for supersession – eg, a change of address which does not affect the assessment.[16] Where there is no new decision to appeal the person may instead seek a late appeal from the original decision (see p438) or may even consider judicial review (see p415).

The CSA may also refer a variation application to an appeal tribunal in certain cases (see p362).

Chapter 20: Appeals
1. Appeal tribunals

Parties to the appeal

Except for appeals from a refusal to make a calculation and reduced benefit decision, each party to the calculation has the right of appeal. Only the CSA and a person who has a right of appeal can take part in the appeal.[17]

This means in the case of reduced benefit decision appeals the non-resident parent is **not** contacted and takes no part in it.

Otherwise, regardless of who appealed, all parties have the same rights, except that only the appellant can ask to withdraw the appeal. Because an appeal can be withdrawn without the consent of any other party (see p443), it is best for each party who wishes to challenge the decision to bring their own appeal. The appeals can be heard together.

A party is not obliged to take part in the appeal, except if directed to provide evidence (see p441) or to attend as a witness (see p445).

What the tribunal can do

The tribunal looks afresh at the issues raised in the appeal as the situation stood up to the date of the CSA decision under appeal.[18] It can consider any evidence and arguments, including those rejected or overlooked by the CSA and those which have not been used before.[19] The tribunal has no duty to consider any issue not raised on the appeal.[20] However, the tribunal is 'inquisitorial', which means it can raise legal arguments and factual questions on its own initiative, if appropriate.[21] It is, however, bound by the Acts and regulations, unless these are themselves unlawful (see p422). The tribunal cannot use discretion to override the regulations. It is also bound by case law (see p453), unless the test case rules apply (see p430). If the tribunal reaches a different conclusion from that of the CSA, it allows the appeal (see p447).

Where the appeal is against a refusal to revise/supersede, the tribunal must decide whether revision/supersession can be carried out. When considering this, the tribunal looks at the facts as they were when the CSA refused to revise/supersede, even if the CSA did not know those facts.[22] Unless there was a basis for revision/supersession at that time, a later change of circumstances is irrelevant.[23] A request for supersession on the basis of the later change (see p420) should be made instead.

On a reduced benefit decision appeal, the tribunal itself exercises discretion considering the welfare of the child, and decides whether a decision *should* be imposed on all the evidence now available, not simply whether the Jobcentre Plus was *entitled* to impose a decision.[24]

Change of circumstances

When deciding the appeal, the tribunal cannot take into account any change of circumstances occurring after the date of the decision under appeal.[25] (This does not apply to an appeal made before 21 May 1998.[26]) If the tribunal decides to

436

allow the appeal because the decision was wrong on the facts at the time it was made, it cannot go on to direct how the CSA should deal with a later change of circumstances. Supersession could be sought instead.

Parentage disputes

If the appellant disputes parentage of a child named in the maintenance application, that appeal must be made to a court, not the tribunal (see p25).[27] If there are other grounds of appeal apart from parentage, a separate appeal should be made on those grounds to the tribunal.[28] If both sorts of grounds are raised on an appeal to a tribunal, it can only deal with the non-parentage grounds.[29] Likewise, a court considering an appeal appears to be limited to parentage issues. If a person raises parentage grounds for the first time at the tribunal hearing, s/he must make a separate appeal to a court on those grounds, or apply for revision or supersession (see Chapter 19).[30] For parentage disputes before the appeal stage is reached, see pp25 and 99.

2. Procedure

When the CSA makes a decision which can be appealed, each person must get a notice of that decision and information on the right of appeal.[31] If no reasons are given for the decision, the person can request written reasons within one month of the notice,[32] and the CSA must issue them within 14 days of receiving the request.[33]

If a person is informed of a CSA decision, but the CSA does not accept there is any right of appeal, s/he can make an appeal so that the tribunal can decide whether there is a right of appeal (see p442).

How to appeal

An appeal must be made within one month of notice of the decision, *unless* a request for a written statement of reasons for the decision is made, when the time limit is one month plus 14 days.[34] Where the statement is not provided within the one-month period, the time limit is extended to within 14 days of the statement being provided.[35] See below for extensions of time.

Notification is deemed to happen on the day the notice is issued by the CSA.[36] If the decision is a revision, supersession or refusal to revise, time runs from the date the notice of that decision is issued.[37]

Where an accidental error in a decision has been corrected, written notification must be given of that correction.[38] If this occurs, any days before this notice is given are ignored when calculating the time limit for appealing.[39]

An appeal must be received by a CSA office within the time limit.[40]

Appeals must:[41]

Chapter 20: Appeals
2. Procedure

- be made on a CSA appeal form (or be accepted as sufficient by the CSA);
- be signed either by the appellant or a person whom s/he has authorised in writing to represent her/him;
- identify the decision being appealed; *and*
- give the grounds of appeal.

The appeal form is passed to the CSA Appeals Unit (CAU). If the CAU considers that the form/letter meets these rules, it prepares a submission on the appeal (see p439). The appeal is only sent to the Appeals Service when this submission has been prepared. The appeal is handled by the appropriate Appeals Service regional office (see Appendix 1).

Appeal form/letter has insufficient information

The CSA can forward to the tribunal a written appeal which is not on the appeal form (or which is, but is not fully completed) if it contains sufficient information for the appeal to proceed.[42] However, if the form is not used or is not properly completed, the CSA may return it to the appellant for completion or ask for further information.[43] If the appellant returns the completed form/information within 14 days of the CSA request (or a longer period if the CSA accepts) the appeal is treated as made on time.[44] If the appellant does not do this, the CSA refers the appeal form/letter (with any relevant documents or evidence) to a legal member to decide if it meets the rules for appeals above.[45] The decision must be notified to the appellant and the CSA.[46] The member can hold an oral hearing to consider this (but is very unlikely to do so).[47] Any information received by the CSA after the referral is made but before the member's decision is given must be referred to the member, who must take it into account.[48]

Appeal is out of time

A CSA decision maker may allow a late appeal, but only if s/he is satisfied it is in the interest of justice (see below).[49] Where s/he is not satisfied, the application for late appeal is passed to the appeals service, for a legally qualified tribunal member to make a decision.

A legal member may extend the time for appealing so that the appeal can be considered, if s/he is satisfied that:[50]
- the appeal has reasonable chances of success; *or*
- it is in the interest of natural justice.

A written application seeking an extension must be made, which meets the rules for appeal forms/letters.[51] The rules for insufficient information apply to applications for an extension of time.[52] No appeal may be made more than one year after the date the time for appealing ran out.[53]

The interests of justice may be served if it was not practicable to make the application in time because of special circumstances – ie:[54]

Chapter 20: Appeals
2. Procedure

- the applicant, her/his partner or dependent died or suffered serious illness;
- the applicant is not resident in the UK;
- normal postal services were disrupted; *or*
- other wholly exceptional special circumstances.

The later the appeal, the more compelling the special circumstances must be.[55] When considering this, the member (or CSA) must *not* take into account any mistake made by the applicant (or her/his representative) about the law or a time limit *or* an interpretation of the law by a commissioner or court which is different from the way the CSA had understood and applied the law.[56]

The rules are the same as those for late appeals to an appeal tribunal in a social security case. The rules for late appeals to a social security commissioner are different (see p450).

When appealing late, give as many details of special reasons as possible, but do not delay appealing to do this.

If the legal member refuses to extend time, there is no right to have this decision reconsidered.[57] There is no appeal against a refusal to extend time: it is not clear if such a refusal can be set aside (see p449).[58]

Preparing a case

The tribunal may be the first chance for an independent evaluation of the decision under appeal. It may also be the last chance, because there can only be an appeal to a commissioner on a point of law. Therefore, each party should make sure that the tribunal knows the facts and arguments about the case.

Papers provided by the CSA

The CSA prepares a 'submission': a written statement of the facts and law involved in the decision under appeal.[59] If the CSA considers the appeal is misconceived (see p442), only a short submission is prepared. The CSA should attach copies of all relevant evidence, including correspondence and documents.[60] If a document is difficult to read, for example the appeal letter, a retyped version can be provided.[61]

The CSA asks the parties whether they consent to waive the confidentiality rules (see p114).[62] This does not apply to an appeal against a Jobcentre Plus reduced benefit decision, where there is only one party. A refusal to consent must be received within 14 days or disclosure may follow. If one (or both) parties refuses to consent, parts of the papers (ie, addresses) are blacked out. The tribunal and all the parties should see the same copies.[63]

A party can remind the CSA not to include papers on its file which are irrelevant to the appeal – eg, an earlier dispute about parentage when the current appeal is about a variation. Also, the legal member can be asked to direct the CSA not to include them.

439

Chapter 20: Appeals
2. Procedure

The submission is prepared by the CAU, which gathers information from the computer system and copies of relevant documentation.[64] The CSA prepares almost all submissions within three months of receiving the appeal.[65]

If the CSA officer preparing the submission accepts that the decision is wrong, s/he revises it (see p416). The appeal either lapses or continues (see p441).

Considering the facts and law

Each party should:
- read the CSA submission to see whether the CSA now accepts some of the arguments previously rejected or ignored. However, just because the CSA accepts part of a person's case does not mean that the tribunal will, especially if the other party disputes it;
- check the law using this book and/or *Child Support: The Legislation* (see Appendix 6). If the CSA quotes a commissioner's decision, consider getting a copy from the CSA or commissioner (see p453). The Appeals Service does not have copies of unreported decisions. A party can quote the CSA's internal procedural guidance but it is not legally binding;
- check the documents attached to the submission. If anything relevant is missing, ask the CSA to send it to the Appeals Service.

If the CSA delays producing a submission, the legal member can be asked to direct that the appeal be heard. This may mean that the tribunal will not have all the evidence the CSA has. However, a party can ask the legal member to direct the CSA (see p441) to provide copies of all the papers, explaining why those papers are needed.

Further evidence

Each party should consider:
- whether s/he has (or can get) any further relevant written evidence. This can be sent to the tribunal at any stage, but it is best to do this soon after the submission is sent out so papers can be copied to the other parties. If evidence or unreported commissioners' decisions are produced at the hearing or sent in shortly before, this may cause a postponement (see p444) or an adjournment (see p447);
- how to tell the tribunal about the facts and law at the hearing. A party can 'give evidence' – ie, say what s/he has seen and heard. For example: 'I look after the child from Friday night to Monday night' may be the best evidence of those facts;
- whether to call any witnesses at the hearing (see p445);
- whether to send a letter setting out what s/he thinks is in dispute and what the correct answers are. This is important if those points are not in the grounds of appeal or if the party has changed her/his mind about something.

Obtaining information and evidence

A party may want another person to provide further information or documents and the legal member can make a direction for the other person to provide this.[66] If so, it is best to send a prepared list to the Appeals Service which is as precise as possible. For example, the parent with care may believe the non-resident parent has received a pay increase; she decides to ask for 'pay-slips from February to May 2003 (inclusive)'.

To get a direction, the party concerned writes to the Appeals Service (see Appendix 1) asking the legal member to direct the person to 'produce the documents' in the list and to 'provide further particulars' – ie, the answers to the questions in the list. The letter to the Appeals Service should explain the steps taken to get this information and why it is relevant.

The legal member can direct any *party* (see p436) to provide evidence or information. A person who is not a party (eg, an employer) cannot be directed to provide evidence, but can be ordered to attend as a witness and produce documents (see p445). This should be done before the full hearing, so the parties can consider that evidence. It may be possible to direct a non-party to provide further particulars.

The legal member usually decides about directions without a hearing, but one may be held.[67] The chairperson may also make a direction when no one has requested it. A copy of any direction is sent to all the parties.

There is no legal requirement to comply with the direction. However, if a person fails to comply without a good explanation, the tribunal hearing the appeal may decide that s/he has something to hide and so may disbelieve that person's evidence. If the person is the appellant, the appeal can be struck out (see p442). A party can ask the High Court in England and Wales to order a person to comply with a direction.[68] Such an order has been made against a bank in a child support appeal. A person who fails to comply with an order can be fined and/or sent to prison by the court. The Court of Session in Scotland cannot do this.

There is no appeal from a direction or a refusal to make one, but the legal member can be asked to reconsider her/his decision.

Ending an appeal without a right to a full hearing

There are three ways an appeal can end without the parties having a right to a full hearing. If a party dies, the appeal does not end. The CSA can appoint a person to continue an appeal in the place of the person who has died.[69]

Lapsing appeals

If an appeal is made, the CSA reconsiders the decision under appeal. If the CSA decides to revise (see Chapter 19) that decision, the appeal lapses unless the revised decision is no more favourable to the appellant.[70] A decision is favourable which results in the appellant having any financial gain (including one which accrues in the future).[71] A decision which results in no actual change does not cause the appeal to lapse.

If the appeal lapses the appellant can appeal again from the revised decision. The usual time limits apply (see p437).

If the appeal does not lapse, it is treated as an appeal from the revised decision.[72] The appellant is asked whether s/he wishes the appeal to go ahead and, if so, for further representations.[73] Unless s/he withdraws the appeal, the tribunal hears the appeal unless the CSA again revises the decision, this time more favourably to the appellant (when the appeal lapses).[74]

If there is a dispute whether the revised decision is more favourable (eg, the appellant is worse off in the short run, but the CSA says s/he will be better off in the long run), a party can ask for a tribunal hearing to decide whether the appeal has lapsed.

Striking out appeals

An appeal can be struck out (ie, dismissed without consideration) if:
- the appeal is misconceived;[75]
- the appellant fails to 'prosecute' the appeal – ie, pursue it properly.[76] This includes making a late appeal where an extension of time is not made (see p438);
- the appellant fails to comply with a direction of the tribunal or clerk, but only if s/he has been notified that striking out may result.[77]

A failure of a party other than the appellant cannot lead to striking out.

A **misconceived appeal** is one which is frivolous, vexatious or obviously hopeless.[78] This includes one which the tribunal obviously has no jurisdiction to hear – eg, an 'appeal' from a response to a complaint (see p18). Where this is the reason for striking out, only a legal member can strike out the appeal. If the CSA considers the appeal is misconceived, it only prepares a short submission to this effect. The appellant must first be given notice of intention to do this and of her/his right to an oral hearing of the issue if s/he asks for one within 14 days of that notice.[79] If the appeal is struck out, written notification is given to the appellant.[80] If it is not, the tribunal clerk sends a written statement of the tribunal's reasons to the CSA and the appellant.[81] Unless the appeal lapses because the decision under appeal is revised or superseded in favour of the appellant, the CSA must refer the appeal back to the tribunal.[82]

A tribunal clerk can strike out on the grounds of **want of prosecution** and/or **failure to comply**.[83] The clerk can always decide to refer the matter to a legal member instead.[84] Written notice of the decision to strike out and how to seek reinstatement is sent to the appellant.[85]

A struck out appeal can be **reinstated** by the clerk if the appellant provides written reasons why s/he thinks the appeal should not have been struck out and the clerk is satisfied that there are reasonable grounds for reinstating the appeal.[86]

If the clerk is not satisfied that there are reasonable grounds the appeal is passed to a legally qualified member to make a decision.

A legal member may reinstate if:[87]
- the appellant makes representations within one month of the decision to strike out being issued and the member considers there are reasonable grounds for reinstating the appeal;
- the appellant did not receive notice of intention to strike out as a misconceived appeal;
- the conditions for striking out for want of prosecution or failure to comply are not met; *or*
- even though those conditions are met, it is not in the interests of justice to strike out on those grounds.

A recent commissioner's decision held that a decision to strike out can be appealed to the social security commissioner.[88] This held that the use of the word 'determination' describes the process but where a decision is made, that may be appealed. Where the chairperson denied the right of appeal this constituted a rejection of leave to appeal from which the appellant was able to apply to the commissioner for leave to appeal.

In social security cases 'out of jurisdiction', appeals may be struck out by the tribunal clerk.[89] However, at the time of writing this does not apply to child support appeals.[90]

Withdrawing appeals

The appellant has the right to withdraw an appeal at any time, and the CSA can withdraw a variation referral at any time.[91] If the appellant gives written notice that s/he does not want the appeal to continue before the appeal is forwarded to the Appeals Service, all action ceases on the appeal.[92] An appeal/referral is withdrawn by oral notice at the hearing or, at any time before a decision is given on the appeal, by written notice to the tribunal clerk.[93] The other parties are notified of the withdrawal in writing if it was not withdrawn at a hearing at which they were present.[94]

There is no need for the chairperson/other parties to consent to a withdrawal. This may cause injustice where another party is relying on the appeal to decide a point in her/his favour. Such a person should make a late appeal if s/he is a party to the proceedings (see p438).

A withdrawn appeal cannot be reinstated, but any of the parties can appeal the same CSA decision again, though an extension of time is likely to be needed (see p438).[95]

3. Oral hearings

The tribunal *can* hold an oral hearing of any appeal, application or referral. A hearing *must* be arranged if any party requests one.[96] In the case of an appeal or referral (but not an application), the tribunal clerk writes to each party directing them to state in writing if a hearing is wanted.[97] This notice warns an appellant (not all parties) that the appeal can be struck out if s/he does not reply (see p442).[98] The time limit for the reply is 14 days.[99] The clerk can extend this, but it is important to reply in time if possible. However, a party who wants a hearing should always ask for one, no matter how late. If no party requests a hearing in time, the chairperson can still direct a hearing if s/he considers one is needed to decide the appeal.[100] If not, the appeal is decided on the papers and a decision notice is issued (see p446).

It is usually best to ask for a hearing.

If both parties have appealed the same decision, those appeals must be heard together.[101] Two variation applications about the same maintenance application or calculation can also be heard together.[102]

The tribunal clerk must give the parties notice of the time and place of the hearing of at least 14 days, ending the day before the hearing (unless that party has waived her/his right to this).[103] A party can ask for the hearing to be postponed.[104] This is done by writing to the Appeals Service, explaining in detail why a postponement is needed. The clerk can decide the request or pass it to a legal member to decide.[105] If a postponement is refused, the clerk notifies the person who applied in writing and the papers about the request and refusal are put before the tribunal.[106] The clerk or tribunal member can postpone a hearing at any time with or without a request.[107]

Good reasons for a postponement include that the appellant needs, but cannot get, representation. However, if there have been previous postponements or the request is made very late, a refusal is likely. If this happens, the tribunal hearing the case can be asked to adjourn (see p446).

Members of the tribunal

The tribunal hearing the appeal is usually made up of one legal member, but can also have one or two other members (see p434). If there is more than one member, the legal member acts as the chairperson. A commissioner has recommended that where an appeal involves the accounts of the self-employed or company directors that an accountant should be included as a panel member.[108]

The tribunal clerk is not a member and cannot take part in the hearing, but can be present during the tribunal's consideration and make some directions – eg, striking out (see p442) and postponing.

Chapter 20: Appeals
3. Oral hearings

Where there is a panel, a member, other than the chairperson, may attend the hearing via live television link.[109] This can only occur where the chairperson gives permission and the appellant consents.

Attending the hearing

Every party has the right to be present.[110] This includes attendance via a live television link, if the tribunal member (where they sit alone) or chairperson gives permission and the appellant consents.[111]

The CSA usually sends a member of staff from a local office, called a **presenting officer**. A commissioner has decided it is bad practice for that to be a CSA official who has been involved in the case.[112] A party may be represented by a lawyer or lay person, whether the party attends the hearing in person or not.[113]

The hearing can go ahead in the absence of one, several or all of the parties.[114] However, a commissioner has said that the tribunal should only exceptionally go ahead without the presenting officer.[115] CSA guidance indicates that in each case a presenting officer is identified in advance and provided with papers to prepare for the hearing.[116] The CSA Appeals Unit (CAU) receives notice of a schedule of hearings 15 working days in advance; other parties to the appeal receive similar notice.

The Appeals Service intends every hearing venue to have separate waiting rooms for the non-resident parent, parent with care and presenting officer. Where another party or witness may be violent, the tribunal clerk should be told as soon as possible and asked what steps will be taken.

The hearing is usually held in the appellant's area. Expenses, including travel expenses, subsistence and some compensation for loss of earnings, are paid to those who attend a tribunal as a party, witness or unpaid representative.[117] The clerk pays travel and subsistence on the day unless these are high. Travel expenses can be paid in advance.

A party whose disabilities make it difficult to attend the hearing venue can request a 'domiciliary hearing' – ie, one at her/his home. This would have to be open to the other parties as well as the tribunal.[118]

Witnesses

Any person can come voluntarily to a hearing to give evidence if the tribunal member (if they sit alone) or the chairperson allows them to be present.[119] However, sometimes a person may not want to come. The chairperson (or single member) can summon or, in Scotland, cite, witnesses to the hearing and require them to answer any relevant questions or produce documents.[120] The witnesses must be in Great Britain, be given 14 days' notice and be paid their necessary expenses for attending.[121] Before issuing a summons, the chairperson must take into account the need to protect intimate personal and financial circumstances, commercial sensitivity, confidential information and national security.[122]

However, since almost all child support cases involve intimate circumstances and confidentiality, those alone ought not to prevent a summons being issued.

A witness cannot be required to give evidence which a court could not compel her/him to give at a civil trial.[123] This means that:
- neither diplomats nor the Queen can be summoned as witnesses;[124]
- if a person claims public interest immunity, the tribunal has to decide whether the public interest in the secrecy of the evidence outweighs the importance of disclosure.[125] This means that Inland Revenue documents *may* be disclosed.[126]

These rules do not seem to prevent questions to a witness about criminal offences which s/he or her/his spouse may have committed or about their convictions, because those rules apply only to criminal trials.[127]

CSA staff may be witnesses – eg, about what was said at an interview.

If a party wants information or documents from a person and the chairperson will not issue a direction, or that person is wanted at the hearing to be asked questions, a summons can be applied for. A written application should be sent to the Appeals Service, stating the information or documents wanted, why this will help the tribunal decide the case and why this is the only way of getting the information or documents. This is particularly important where the witness is a CSA staff member, because the chairperson may be reluctant to summon her/him. If only documents are wanted, the person can be summoned to produce them at a hearing arranged only for that purpose, so they can then be copied to the parties.

There is no legal requirement to comply with a summons or citation, but the tribunal may treat a failure to comply in the same way as it would a failure to comply with a direction (see p441). The High Court in England and Wales has the same powers as for a direction (see p441).

A person named in a summons or citation can write to the chairperson asking her/him to vary it or set it aside.[128] There is no appeal against a summons or citation or a refusal to issue one, but judicial review can be used (see p415).

Conduct of the hearing

The hearing is usually in public, unless the tribunal member or chairperson decides that it should be held in private:[129]
- to protect the privacy or family life of one of the parties;
- in the interest of national security, morals, public order or children; *or*
- because publicity would not be in the interest of justice.

Even when held in private, the following can attend but not take part: the clerk, the President of the appeal tribunals or anyone acting on her/his behalf in training, supervising or monitoring tribunal members, any member of the Council on Tribunals or Scottish Committee of the Council of Tribunals and anyone training to be a tribunal member or clerk.[130] If all the parties present and the chairperson (or single member) agree, any other person can attend a private hearing. Usually, only the tribunal, clerk and the parties are there.

Where one of the parties to the appeal or a panel member are attending via a live television link, that link should of a suitable standard to allow the person not present to see and hear the proceedings and be seen and heard themselves.[131]

Tribunals hearing child support appeals use the same members and staff as other appeal tribunals. The tribunal tries to be informal. Its member(s) usually sit on one side of a table. The clerk shows the parties into the room and they usually sit on the other side of the table, with the presenting officer between them. The chairperson/single member introduces everyone and explains the tribunal's role. If anyone's role is unclear (eg, is the non-resident parent's wife a witness, representing him or just observing?) the chairperson/single member should be asked to clarify.

Every party has the right to address the tribunal, give evidence, call witnesses and put questions to any other party, the presenting officer or witnesses.[132] The order in which the parties present their cases is up to the chairperson/single member.[133]

The CSA is there to explain the decision, not to argue for the CSA. The presenting officer has a role, for example, in informing the tribunal about CSA procedures. It is rare for the presenting officer to call any witnesses. The tribunal may require any witness, including a party, to take an oath or affirm.[134] It is Appeals Service policy to arrange an interpreter, if requested, in good time.

The tribunal can appoint an expert if a very difficult question arises.[135] The expert gives evidence at the hearing like a witness and/or writes a report which is sent to the tribunal and all the parties.[136] The expert is drawn from the panel of tribunal members,[137] but does not take part in making the decision in the case in which s/he acts as an expert.

The chairperson/single member must keep a record of the proceedings.[138]

The tribunal is not allowed to carry out a physical examination of any person.[139]

The tribunal can adjourn a hearing at any point, whether or not one of the parties asks them to.[140] If the hearing is adjourned to another day and the same tribunal cannot continue with the case, the hearing starts again before a tribunal made up of different people/person.[141]

Hearings can take one hour or longer. Smoking is not allowed in the hearing.[142]

4. Decisions

After all the evidence and submissions, the tribunal member(s) consider(s) the case. They normally do this with only the clerk present.[143] However, in rare cases they may be observed by the President, someone acting on her/his behalf, a member of the Council on Tribunals or Scottish Committee of the Council of

Chapter 20: Appeals
4. Decisions

Tribunals and, if all the parties present and the chairperson (or single member) agree, any other person.[144] An observer cannot take part in the tribunal's discussion or decision.

The decision is taken unanimously or by a majority.[145] If there are two members, the chairperson has a casting vote.[146] It is almost always announced to the parties at the hearing and a decision notice given.[147] If it is not, the decision notice is sent to the parties later.[148]

If the tribunal decides the decision appealed was wrong, it allows the appeal. When it allows an appeal, the tribunal can send the case back to the CSA to be implemented.[149] Where there are problems the CSA may go back to the tribunal for clarification of directions.[150] These directions ought to resolve all the issues on the appeal, but the tribunal does not usually work out any fresh maintenance calculation.[151] For example, in a case where income was disputed, the tribunal could direct the CSA to make a fresh calculation on the same basis as the one appealed, except that the non-resident parent's net income is £234 a week.

A tribunal considering a variation referral (see p362) deals with the application as if the tribunal were the CSA.[152] This means the tribunal decision is to agree or refuse a variation to the maintenance calculation, either revising/superseding the decision or refusing to do so.

The decision notice does not give full reasons. It must tell the parties of their right to apply for a statement of reasons and how to appeal to a commissioner. A party has one month from the giving or sending of the decision notice to ask the clerk for a full statement of reasons.[153] This must be done in writing and received by the clerk within the time limit. **A party considering an appeal to a commissioner should always ask for a full decision.** The one-month period can be extended by a legal member for the same reasons as extending time for a late appeal (see p438), except that the maximum period is three months from the date the decision notice was issued.[154] When working out the time limit, days are ignored that are before a notification of a correction or refusal not to set aside (except if the determination not to set aside the decision was because of a refusal to extend the time for applying).[155] If a dispute may arise about the evidence given at the hearing, a party should ask for the chairperson's/member's record of proceedings. This only needs to be kept for six months from the date of the decision.[156]

If the CSA considers that a tribunal decision is given in ignorance or mistake of fact there may be grounds to set aside the decision (see p449).[157]

Accidental errors in a decision or on an appeal (but not on a referral) can be corrected by the clerk or legal member.[158] Written notice of the correction must be given to the parties.[159] The CSA must follow the tribunal's directions, including any fresh calculation required, and only then supersede that decision (see Chapter 19).[160] Each party should check that the CSA follows the tribunal's decision (including any directions). If the CSA does not, judicial review (see p415) can force the CSA to implement the decision. If the decision is not clear, correction or appeal to a commissioner should be considered.

If any party is dissatisfied with the tribunal decision, s/he can appeal on a point of law to a child support commissioner (see p450).

Setting aside decisions

A tribunal decision can be set aside by a legal member on application to set aside, if it appears just to do so because:[161]
- a document relating to the proceedings in which the decision was made was not:
  - sent to or received at an appropriate time by one of the parties or their representative; *or*
  - was sent to but was not received at an appropriate time by the tribunal which made the decision; *or*
- a party or a representative was not present at the hearing. This does not apply to a party who did not ask for a hearing, unless setting aside is manifestly required by the interests of justice[162] – eg, if the tribunal decided the appeal on a point raised for the first time at the hearing.

Following an application for leave to appeal to the commissioners where:[163]
- the chairperson considers that the decision was erroneous in law; *or*
- each of the principal parties (Secretary of State, parent with care and non-resident parent)[164] expresses the view that the decision is erroneous in law,

the chairperson may set aside the decision.

An application to set aside a tribunal decision must be made in writing to the clerk to the tribunal within one month of the decision being given or sent to the parties or a full statement of reasons being given or sent, whichever is the later.[165] This time limit may be extended to one year in certain circumstances – eg, due to serious illness or residence abroad.[166] Each of the parties is asked to comment in writing on the application before a determination is made on the application to set aside.[167] The determination, and reasons for it, is sent to the parties.[168] If a decision is set aside, then another tribunal hearing is arranged and the case re-heard in full. This can be by the original tribunal or a different one. Where the application to set aside is refused there is no right of appeal against the determination. A dissatisfied applicant may apply for judicial review or leave to appeal against the decision of the tribunal.[169]

It is not clear if a refusal to extend time for appealing to a tribunal or for applying to set aside a tribunal decision can itself also be set aside.

Chapter 20: Appeals
5. Child support commissioners

5. Child support commissioners

Any party can appeal against a decision of an appeal tribunal to a child support commissioner on the ground of an error of law (see p422).[170] The decision is erroneous in law if the CSA failed to put a relevant document in the case papers before the tribunal, even though the tribunal is not at fault.[171] An appeal can be made by the CSA. Only a final decision can be appealed, but this includes a decision made without a hearing (see p444). A tribunal determination to set aside its decision (or a refusal to set aside) cannot be appealed; judicial review (p415) may be possible.[172]

An appeal *cannot* be made only on the grounds that further evidence shows that the tribunal was wrong or that circumstances have changed. These should be dealt with by supersession (see Chapter 19).

A commissioner is a very experienced lawyer. Almost all commissioners are full time, dealing also with social security appeals. In very difficult cases, a tribunal of three commissioners decides the case.

If there is an error of law, the commissioner sets aside the tribunal's decision. S/he will then:[173]
- if appropriate, make further findings of fact (this is unusual where relevant facts are disputed) *and* give the appropriate decision (eg, make a maintenance assessment);[174] *or*
- give the decision the tribunal should have given, which may be to the same effect as the decision appealed; *or*
- refer the case to the CSA or a tribunal giving directions for its determination. Where the CSA appealed the tribunal decision, the commissioner cannot refer the case to the CSA.[175]

Northern Ireland has its own child support commissioners and a chief child support commissioner.[176]

How to appeal

Obtaining leave (permission) to appeal is the first stage of appealing to a commissioner. An application for leave to appeal must be made in writing to the tribunal chairperson at the Appeals Service (see Appendix 1) within one month of the date the tribunal's statement of reasons was issued.[177] The time limit for requesting a statement of reasons is one month after the tribunal's decision notice was issued (see p447). When working out the time limit for appeal to the commissioner, days are ignored that are before notification of correction of a decision or a determination not to set aside a decision (except where the decision was not to set aside because of a refusal to extend the time for applying).[178] There is no right of appeal against a correction.

Chapter 20: Appeals
5. Child support commissioners

If the CSA applies for leave, a copy of its application is sent to the other parties, who have one month to send written comments to the chairperson, who must take them into account.[179]

The application for leave to appeal may be determined by the chairperson or by:[180]
- a salaried, legally qualified tribunal member, if the chairperson of the tribunal was a fee-paid, legally qualified tribunal member; *or*
- another legally qualified member if this is impractical or it would cause undue delay for the application to be determined by the person who was the chair.

The chairperson/legally qualified member may decide to grant leave, set aside the tribunal decision as erroneous in law or refuse leave. The decision on the application is sent to all the parties.[181] If s/he gives leave to appeal, the appellant must send a notice of appeal to the commissioner's office within one month of the notification of leave to appeal.[182] If s/he sets aside the decision the case will be referred to the original tribunal for a redetermination or to a different tribunal.[183] If the chairperson refuses leave to appeal, an application for leave to appeal can be made to the commissioner within one month of the notification refusing leave.[184]

If no application is made to the chairperson within time, the chairperson can admit a late application up to one year after the month ran out, but only if there are special reasons.[185] If the chairperson then refuses to give leave or if the notice of appeal or application for leave is not sent in time to the commissioner, the commissioner can admit a late application up to one year after the month ran out (or, within one month of the claimant's refusal, if later) but only if there are special reasons.

Special reasons are not defined and so are wider than the reasons needed for a late appeal *to* the tribunal (see p438). Special reasons for late commissioner applications/appeals can be much wider. For full details on special reasons see CPAG's *Welfare Benefits and Tax Credits Handbook*. When appealing late, give as many details of the reasons as possible, but do not delay appealing to do this.

An application for leave or notice of appeal must state the grounds of appeal and have the tribunal's decision and, if separate, the statement of reasons (see p448), attached.[186] The Appeals Service can provide a form for applications and appeals, but this does not have to be used. A copy of any application for leave made to the commissioner is sent to the other parties.[187]

For the addresses of the commissioners' offices see Appendix 1.

The commissioner usually considers applications for leave without a hearing. If leave is refused, no reasons have to be given, and a short written decision is sent to the parties. A refusal of leave can be judicially reviewed (see p415).

An application for leave can be withdrawn at any time before a decision on it is made, by writing to the office it was sent to.[188] An appeal may be withdrawn by the appellant, but only with the commissioner's permission.[189] A commissioner

Chapter 20: Appeals
5. Child support commissioners

is unlikely to allow an appeal to be withdrawn if another party supports the appeal. An application for leave made to a commissioner or an appeal which has been withdrawn can be reinstated with the commissioner's permission.[190]

The written procedure

Unlike the tribunal, on a commissioner's appeal the parties are expected to explain their cases mostly in writing. If leave is granted, the papers which were before the tribunal are sent to all the parties. These are in a particular order and are numbered, and should be checked to see that all the documents are included and whether there are any new ones.

If it is not the CSA's appeal, the CSA is asked to comment in writing within one month of the papers being issued. The CSA may support the appeal, but it is the reasons for doing so which matter. For example, the CSA may support an appeal because the tribunal did not make all necessary findings of fact and give adequate reasons, but propose that the commissioner give a decision to the same effect, or even to worse effect, as far as one or both of the other parties are concerned.

The other parties are then given one month to comment. The appellant is then given one month to comment on everyone else's observations.

Before commenting, consider whether it would be best to have the case go back to another tribunal or the CSA, or instead be decided by the commissioner. However, where there is a dispute of relevant fact, the commissioner is likely to send the case back to a tribunal.

Oral hearings

If one party's case is not fully supported by the CSA or there is a point of law which the commissioner might decide against that party, that party should request an oral hearing.[191] The CSA or another party can also request a hearing. The commissioner usually grants a request for an oral hearing. The CSA is almost always legally represented and other parties should consider getting expert representation (see Appendix 5).

Oral hearings are usually heard in London or Edinburgh, but are also heard in some other large cities. Plenty of notice is given and travel expenses are paid.[192] The hearings are usually in public but, unless the other party brings observers, it is very unlikely that anyone else will be there.[193] The hearing is more formal than a tribunal. While oral evidence can be given, it is uncommon. The commissioner can postpone or adjourn a hearing and usually does so if it would help a parent get representation. The commissioner may summon witnesses; the rules are the same as for the tribunal (see p445).[194]

Decisions

A written decision is sent to all the parties.[195] The decision must not contain the surname of the child concerned in the appeal or any other information which may lead to the child being identified.[196] An accidental error in a decision can be corrected at any time. Written notice of any correction must be sent to the parties.[197]

A commissioner's decision can be set aside if:[198]
- a document was not received at an appropriate time by one of the parties, a representative or the commissioner;
- a party or a representative was not present at the hearing;
- there was some other procedural irregularity or mishap.

An application for setting aside must be made within one month of notification of the decision.[199]

Jurisdictional issues may result in the commissioner's decision being void and of no effect, as occurred in a previous joined decision, under the 'old rules'.[200] This situation arose where the CSA implemented the appeal tribunal decision (ie, the one under appeal to the commissioner), then this was replaced by a number of fresh assessments on review. As the subsequent assessments had the same effective date as the original decision they completely replaced it and so the commissioner had no jurisdiction. This could also apply in 'new rules' cases.

Caselaw

Commissioners' decisions are legally binding on tribunals and the CSA. Decisions have a reference number which shows the country they were made in and the year the application or appeal was brought (not the year the decision was made in). CCS 3/1997 is from England or Wales, CSCS 3/1997 is from Scotland and CSC 3/1997 is from Northern Ireland. Each of those appeals was the third appeal to be brought in that country in that year.

The commissioner who gives a decision may 'star' it if s/he thinks it would be useful for other cases. The decision is marked with a star and given a 'starred' number. Some starred decisions are reported and are then given a new number – eg, R(CS) 1/95. Use the original number (not the starred one) for an unreported decision. Use the 'R number' for a reported decision.

British decisions are binding on the CSA and tribunals throughout Great Britain. Where there are conflicting decisions, a reported decision carries more weight,[201] but starring does not matter. Where there is no British decision on the point, a Northern Irish decision is very persuasive. Where there is no child support commissioner's decision, a social security commissioner's decision on the point (eg, a similar regulation) is persuasive.

Social security decisions follow the same numbering system as child support – eg, IS decisions are numbered CIS 3/1997 or R(IS) 4/96.

Commissioners, tribunals and the CSA are bound by judgments of the House of Lords and, in England and Wales, the High Court and Court of Appeal, and, in Scotland, the Court of Session. A commissioner is not bound by her/his own previous decisions or those of other commissioners, though they usually follow long-standing decisions. A commissioner will follow a decision of a tribunal of commissioners unless there are good reasons for not doing so. The exception is where the test case rules apply (see p427).

Unreported decisions are available from the appropriate commissioners' office, price £1, or £2–£3 for Scottish decisions. Reported decisions are published by Central Adjudication Services.

Further appeal

Appeals on a point of law can be made from a commissioner's decision to the Court of Appeal or, in Scotland, the Court of Session.[202] Applications for leave to appeal must be made first to the commissioner within three months of notification of her/his decision.[203] Legal advice should be sought if possible. See CPAG's *Welfare Benefits and Tax Credits Handbook* for appeals in person.

6. Existing 'old rules' cases

The legislation that applies to 'old rules' cases is the same as prior to amendment by the Child Support, Pensions and Social Security Act and associated legislation. For full legislative references see the 2001/02 edition of this *Handbook*.

Essentially, the provisions in relation to appeals are the same as appeals under the 'new rules' except that the decisions that may be appealed are different. These are:
- a refusal to make a maintenance assessment or interim maintenance assessment (IMA) but only by the person who applied for the assessment;[204]
- a decision to make a maintenance assessment or IMA;[205]
- a decision to cancel or a refusal to cancel a maintenance assessment or IMA;[206]
- a reduced benefit direction, but only once benefit has started to be reduced (this is a Jobcentre Plus decision);[207]
- a decision on deductions from the non-resident parent's income support/income-based jobseeker's allowance;[208]
- a decision to make or refuse to make a departure direction (see Chapter 17);[209]
- one of those decisions made on revision/supersession or a refusal to revise one of those decisions (but not to supersede).[210]

Appeal tribunals have the same powers to consider departures as described in relation to variations within this chapter. In addition, references to reduced benefit decisions are equivalent to 'old rules' reduced benefit directions. The main difference is therefore that there is no general provision under the 'old rules' for appeals against supersessions and refusal to supersede.

Chapter 20: Appeals
Notes

1 Reg 4(1)(b) CS(TP) Regs
2 s28D(1)(b) CSA 1991

1. Appeal tribunals
3 Reg 36(1) SS&CS(DA) Regs
4 Sch 3 para 1 SS&CS(DA) Regs; s7(2) SSA 1998
5 Reg 36(3) and Sch 3 para 4 SS&CS(DA) Regs
6 Reg 36(2) SS&CS(DA) Regs
7 Reg 36(8) SS&CS(DA) Regs
8 s5 SSA 1998; reg 36(3) SS&CS(DA) Regs
9 s7(1) SSA 1998; reg 36(5) SS&CS(DA) Regs
10 s20(1) CSA 1991
11 s20(2)CSA 1991
12 s20(6) CSA 1991
13 Reg 30A SS&CS(DA) Regs
14 Reg 30A SS&CS(DA) Regs
15 Reg 31(2) SS&CS(DA) Regs
16 Change of circumstances – overview
17 Reg 1(3)(b) SS&CS(DA) Regs 'party to the proceedings' is limited to the CSA and those who have a right of appeal under CSA 1991
18 s20(7)CSA 1991
19 CCS/16351/1996 para 26
20 s20(7)(a) CSA 1991
21 CSCS/2/1994 para 20; CCS/12/1994 para 46
22 CSCS/2/1994 paras 10, 20 and 23; CSCS/3/1994 paras 14-15 (considering old s18 review)
23 CCS/511/1995 paras 19 and 26 (considering old s18 review)
24 CCS/15109/1996 paras 12-13. CCS/6096/1995 was wrong to decide otherwise (the point was not argued)
25 s20(7)(b) CSA 1991
26 On 21 May 1998 Sch 6 para 9 SSA 1998 came into effect, inserting s20(5) CSA 1991, later replaced on 1 June 1999
27 Arts 3 and 4 CSA(JC)O
28 CCS/16351/1996 para 26
29 CCS/16351/1996 para 23
30 We consider that the Northern Ireland commissioner in CSC/1/1994 and CSC/3/1994 was wrong to say it was too late to appeal to a court once an appeal was sent to the tribunal. That commissioner assumed that there could only be one notice of appeal, and not two, as CCS/16351/1996 paras 23 and 26 decides: one to the tribunal and one to the court raising the issues not raised before.

2. Procedure
31 Reg 28(1) SS&CS(DA) Regs
32 Reg 28(1)(b) SS&CS(DA) Regs
33 Reg 28(2) SS&CS(DA) Regs
34 Reg 31(1) SS&CS(DA) Regs
35 Reg 33(1)(c) SS&CS(DA) Regs
36 Reg 2(b) SS&CS(DA) Regs
37 Reg 31(2) SS&CS(DA) Regs
38 Reg 9A SS&CS(DA) Regs
39 Reg 9A(3) SS&CS(DA) Regs
40 Reg 33(1)(b) and (2)(d) SS&CS(DA) Regs
41 Reg 33(1) SS&CS(DA) Regs
42 Reg 33(4) and (5) SS&CS(DA) Regs
43 Reg 33(3) SS&CS(DA) Regs
44 Reg 33(7) SS&CS(DA) Regs
45 Reg 33(8)(a) SS&CS(DA) Regs
46 Reg 33(8)(b) SS&CS(DA) Regs
47 There is no duty to hold an oral hearing (under reg 39 SS&CS(DA) Regs) but we consider that one can be directed under reg 38(2) SS&CS(DA) Regs
48 Reg 33(9) SS&CS(DA) Regs
49 Reg 32(2) SS&CS(DA) Regs
50 Reg 32(4)(b) SS&CS(DA) Regs
51 Reg 32(2) and (3) SS&CS(DA) Regs
52 Reg 33 SS&CS(DA) Regs
53 Reg 32(1) SS&CS(DA) Regs
54 Reg 32(5) and (6) SS&CS(DA) Regs
55 Reg 32(7) SS&CS(DA) Regs
56 Reg 32(8) SS&CS(DA) Regs
57 Reg 32(9) SS&CS(DA) Regs; CIS/93/1992
58 Regs 57(1) or 38(1) SS&CS(DA) Regs might apply
59 Writing the appeal against a child support decision

Chapter 20: Appeals
Notes

60 CCS/12682/1996 para 8; Submission completed
61 Part 9 para 9606 DMG
62 Reg 44 SS&CS(DA) Regs; Editing
63 President's Circular No.11, September 1996
64 Writing the appeal against a child support decision
65 Vol 8 Referrals to CAU Ch 1 para 151 CSG
66 Reg 38(2) SS&CS(DA) Regs
67 Reg 38(2) SS&CS(DA) Regs
68 Order 38 r19, Supreme Court Rules
69 Reg 34 SS&CS(DA) Regs
70 s16(6) CSA 1991
71 Reg 30(2)(f) SS&CS(DA) Regs
72 Reg 30(3) SS&CS(DA) Regs
73 Reg 30(4) SS&CS(DA) Regs
74 Reg 30(5) SS&CS(DA) Regs
75 Reg 46(4) SS&CS(DA) Regs
76 Reg 46(1)(b) SS&CS(DA) Regs
77 Reg 46(1)(c) SS&CS(DA) Regs
78 Reg 1(3) SS&CS(DA) Regs; Misconceived appeals
79 Regs 46(4) and 48(1)-(3) SS&CS(DA) Regs
80 Reg 48(4) SS&CS(DA) Regs
81 Reg 48(5)(a) and (b) SS&CS(DA) Regs
82 Reg 48(5)(c) and (d) SS&CS(DA) Regs
83 Reg 46(1) SS&CS(DA) Regs
84 Reg 46(3) SS&CS(DA) Regs
85 Reg 46(2) SS&CS(DA) Regs
86 Reg 47(1) SS&CS(DA) Regs
87 Reg 47(2) SS&CS(DA) Regs
88 CCS/292/2000
89 Regs 1(3) and 46(1)(a) SS&CS(DA) Regs
90 Because the definition in reg 1(3) SS&CS(DA) Regs only applies to appeals from decisions listed in reg 27 and Sch 2 SS&CS(DA) Regs, and no child support appeals are listed there.
91 Reg 40(1) SS&CS(DA) Regs
92 Reg 33(10) SS&CS(DA) Regs
93 Reg 40(2) SS&CS(DA) Regs
94 Reg 40(2) and (3) SS&CS(DA) Regs
95 R(IS) 5/94

3. Oral hearings
96 Reg 39(4) SS&CS(DA) Regs
97 Reg 39(1) SS&CS(DA) Regs
98 Reg 39(2) SS&CS(DA) Regs
99 Reg 39(3) SS&CS(DA) Regs
100 Reg 39(5) SS&CS(DA) Regs
101 CCS/13450/1996
102 Reg 45 SS&CS(DA) Regs
103 Reg 49(2) and (3) SS&CS(DA) Regs
104 Reg 51(1) SS&CS(DA) Regs
105 Reg 51(1) SS&CS(DA) Regs
106 Reg 51(2) SS&CS(DA) Regs
107 Reg 51(3) SS&CS(DA) Regs
108 CCS/872/2000
109 Reg 49(7)(b) SS&CS(DA) Regs
110 Reg 49(7) SS&CS(DA) Regs
111 Reg 49(7)(b) SS&CS(DA) Regs
112 CCS/1037/1995 para 16
113 Reg 49(8) SS&CS(DA) Regs
114 Reg 49(4) and (5) SS&CS(DA) Regs; CSCS/7/1995 para 9
115 CCS/2618/1995 para 11
116 Schedule of hearings
117 Sch 1 para 4 SSA 1998
118 President's Circular No.4, October 1995
119 Reg 49(11) and (10) SS&CS(DA) Regs the latter as amended by reg 14(d) SS&CS(DA)(MA) Regs 2002
120 Part 43 SSCS&CS(D&A) Regs
121 Reg 43(1) SS&CS(DA) Regs
122 Reg 43(3) SS&CS(DA) Regs
123 Reg 43(2) SS&CS(DA) Regs. This refers to 'action', which means a civil, not criminal, trial. Scottish law applies if the hearing is in Scotland.
124 Sch 1 Arts 31(2) and 37(1)-(3) Diplomatic Privileges Act 1964; Sch 1 Art 44(1) Consular Relations Act 1968; Sch 1 paras 9, 14 and 20-23 International Organisations Act 1968
125 See Keane, The Modern Law of Evidence, Butterworths, and Cross on Evidence
126 *Lonrho plc v Fayed* (No.4) [1994] QB 749; [1994] 2 WLR 209; [1994] 1 All ER 870
127 see s80 Police and Criminal Evidence Act 1984; s1 Criminal Evidence Act 1898
128 Reg 43 SS&CS(DA) Regs
129 Reg 49(6) SS&CS(DA) Regs
130 Reg 49(9) SS&CS(DA) Regs
131 Reg 49(13) SS&CS(DA) Regs
132 Reg 49(7) and (11) SS&CS(DA) Regs
133 Reg 49(1) SS&CS(DA) Regs
134 Reg 43(5) SS&CS(DA) Regs
135 s7(4) SSA 1998
136 Reg 50 SS&CS(DA) Regs
137 s7(5) SSA 1998
138 Reg 55(1) SS&CS(DA) Regs
139 Reg 52 SS&CS(DA) Regs
140 Reg 51(4) SS&CS(DA) Regs; President's Circular No.1, July 1996
141 Reg 51(5) SS&CS(DA) Regs
142 President's Circular No.4, October 1995

4. Decisions
143 Reg 49(12) SS&CS(DA) Regs
144 Reg 49(12) SS&CS(DA) Regs
145 s7(3)(b) SSA 1998

Chapter 20: Appeals
Notes

146 s7(3)(c) SSA 1998
147 Reg 53(2) SS&CS(DA) Regs
148 Reg 53(3) SS&CS(DA) Regs
149 Tribunal decision received from AS
150 Consideration of the AS decision
151 CCS/5310/1995 paras 14-15. See also CCS/4741/1995 paras 20-21
152 s28D (3) CSA 1991
153 Reg 53(4) SS&CS(DA) Regs
154 Reg 54 SS&CS(DA) Regs
155 Reg 54(13) SS&CS(DA) Regs
156 Reg 55(2) SS&CS(DA) Regs
157 Application for setting aside
158 Reg 56(1) SS&CS(DA) Regs
159 Reg 56(2) SS&CS(DA) Regs
160 CCS/11260/1995 para 15
161 Reg 57(1) SS&CS(DA) Regs
162 Reg 57(2) SS&CS(DA) Regs
163 s23A CSA 1991
164 s23A CSA 1991
165 Reg 57(3) SS&CS(DA) Regs
166 Reg 57(6)-(11) SS&CS(DA) Regs
167 Reg 57(4) SS&CS(DA) Regs
168 Reg 57(5) SS&CS(DA) Regs
169 R(SB) 55/83

5. Child support commissioners
170 s24(1) CSA 1991
171 CCS/12682/1996 para 8 applying *R v Leyland Justices ex parte Hawthorne* [1979] QB 283 and following R(SB) 18/83 para 11
172 Only decisions, and not determinations, can be appealed: *Bland v Supplementary Benefit Officer* [1983] 1 All ER 537, R(SB) 12/83.
173 s24(3) CSA 1991
174 As in CCS/5310/1995
175 s24(3)(c) and (d) CSA 1991
176 s23 CSA 1991
177 Regs 10(1) and 12 CSC(P) Regs
178 Reg 57A SS&CS(DA) Regs
179 Reg 10(2)-(4) CSC(P) Regs
180 Reg 58(6) SS&CS(DA) Regs
181 Reg 10(4) CSC(P) Regs; reg 58(4) SS&CS(DA) Regs
182 Reg 15(1) CSC(P) Regs
183 s23A CSA 1991
184 Reg 11(2) CSC(P) Regs
185 Reg 10(5) CSC(P) Regs
186 Regs 12(2) and 14(2) CSC(P) Regs
187 Reg 12(3) CSC(P) Regs
188 Reg 24(1) CSC(P) Regs
189 Reg 24(2) CSC(P) Regs
190 Reg 24(3) CSC(P) Regs
191 Reg 21(2) CSC(P) Regs
192 Sch 4 para 3 SSA 1998
193 Reg 22(5) CSC(P) Regs
194 Reg 23 CSC(P) Regs
195 Reg 26 CSC(P) Regs
196 Reg 9 CSC(P) Regs
197 Reg 27 CSC(P) Regs
198 Reg 28(1) CSC(P) Regs
199 Reg 28(2) CSC(P) Regs
200 CCS/2731/1997; CCS/3753/1997
201 R(I) 12/75
202 s25 CSA 1991
203 Reg 30 CSC(P) Regs

6. Existing 'old rules' cases
204 s20(1) CSA 1991
205 s20(2) CSA 1991
206 s20(3) CSA 1991
207 Sch 4C para 3(1) and (3) CSA 1991
208 Sch 5 para 8 CS(MASC) Regs
209 Sch 4C para 3(1) and (4) CSA 1991
210 Reg 31(2) SS&CS(DA) Regs

21

Chapter 21
Collection and enforcement

This chapter covers:
1. Payment of child maintenance (p459)
2. Collection of other payments (p466)
3. Arrears (p467)
4. Deduction from earnings orders (p477)
5. Enforcement (p483)
6. Existing 'old rules' and conversion cases (p489)

The CSA can arrange the collection and enforcement of child support maintenance[1] and certain other maintenance payments (see p466).[2] This service has been free to all CSA clients since April 1995 and continues to be so as the fees regulations have been revoked.[3] However, fees may be introduced at some time in the future.

Once the calculation has been made, a collection schedule will be set up by the case worker in the new client team dealing with the case. When payments are established the case will be passed to the maintain compliance team (see p12) to deal with ongoing collection and other issues. Where the payments schedule breaks down and arrears accrue the case may be passed to the enforcement team.

Most of the decisions covered by this chapter are made by CSA staff working in these teams (see p14). Within the limits of the regulations, these decisions are discretionary, so there is scope for negotiation between CSA staff and the individuals involved. Where there are instructions or practices for dealing with a type of case in a certain way, the CSA should be told about these if they are helpful. If they are not, the CSA can be reminded that they are not binding, and the individual officer dealing with the case may apply discretion. As the decisions are discretionary, the welfare of any child likely to be affected must be taken into account by the CSA (see p31).

The amount of maintenance calculated cannot be altered except by revision, supersession, appeal or variation ('old rules' – departure). The CSA does not suspend current collection just because the non-resident parent states that he cannot afford to pay. However, the CSA may agree to lower payments if a revision, supersession, appeal or variation ('old rules' – departure) is pending (see p470).

There is no appeal to an appeal tribunal from a decision on collection and enforcement (see p434 for CSA decisions which can be appealed). A deduction

Chapter 21: Collection and enforcement
1. Payment of child maintenance

from earnings order can, in limited circumstances, be appealed to a magistrates' court (see p477) and judicial review may be possible for other decisions (see p415). The Independent Case Examiner (see p19) considers complaints about the CSA's exercise of discretion – eg, the amount of maintenance due which includes payment towards arrears. For regular payment conditions imposed because a departure application has been made, see p360. For internal CSA complaints, see p18.

1. Payment of child maintenance

Where a maintenance calculation has been made and the CSA is arranging for the collection and enforcement of the maintenance, it has discretion to decide:
- the method by which the non-resident parent pays child maintenance;[4]
- the person to whom it is paid;[5]
- where payment is made through the CSA or someone else, the method by which payment is made to the person with care;[6]
- the timing of payments;[7] *and*
- the amount of payments towards arrears.[8]

Before making these decisions about payments, the CSA must, as far as is possible, give the non-resident parent and the person with care an opportunity to make representations, and must take any representations into account.[9] In every case, the CSA must notify the non-resident parent in writing of the amounts and timing of payments due, to whom he must make payment, how he must pay and details of any amount that is overdue and remains outstanding.[10] This notice is sent as soon as possible after the calculation is made and again after any change in the details in the notice.[11] A copy is sent to the person with care. Where the payments are to be made directly between the two parties, the CSA takes no further action regarding collection unless the person with care notifies the CSA that the non-resident parent has failed to comply as directed. Therefore, the parties can agree between them to use another method or frequency of payment.

Where there are arrears and the CSA has imposed a penalty payment, see p473.

Who is paid

The CSA can require the non-resident parent to pay child maintenance:[12]
- direct to the person with care;
- direct to a Scottish child applicant;
- to or through the CSA (this cannot be required in all cases); *or*
- to or through another person.

The CSA prefers the non-resident parent to make payments direct to the person with care, except where the parent with care is on income support (IS)/income-

459

Chapter 21: Collection and enforcement
1. Payment of child maintenance

based jobseeker's allowance (JSA).[13] These direct payments are not monitored by the CSA. Although some non-resident parents and, indeed, some persons with care, may want to have payments made to a third party (eg, their mortgage lender) the CSA does not usually accept those to be child maintenance payments. However, any such payments made in between the effective date and the date of calculation may be considered as voluntary payments to offset initial arrears.

The collection service

When child maintenance payments are to be made to or via the CSA, this is referred to as the collection service. Any party to a case can request that payment be via the CSA.[14] The CSA normally provides the collection service if an applicant requests it, even where the other party does not.

In the case of section 6 applicants (see p44), the collection service is applied automatically.[15] In practice, this means that the parent is not asked if they wish to use the collection service when they complete the child maintenance administration form. They may request to change to direct payments from the non-resident parent but this is not encouraged due to the possibility of fraud.[16] In the case of section 4 and 7 applicants (see pp44 and 43), the CSA can only provide the collection service on the request of one of the parties to the calculation.[17] This can be done when the application is made, when each party is asked if they wish to use the CSA to collect maintenance or arrange payments direct.

The collection service can be requested at a later date – eg, if payments become irregular. The request can be made verbally or in writing.[18] The CSA can collect arrears already due when the request is made.[19]

Where payments are made to the CSA, only payments actually received by the CSA can be passed on. About half of total maintenance collected by the CSA, from all non-resident parents, is passed on to persons with care, while the other half is kept to offset payment of IS/income-based JSA (see p461).[20]

The collection service has a number of advantages:
- it removes the need for direct contact between the non-resident parent and person with care;
- where the person with care is on IS/income-based JSA, her benefit payments will not be affected if the non-resident parent does not pay the CSA (see p461); *and*
- where the person with care is not on IS/income-based JSA, the collection service is supposed to ensure regular payments by starting enforcement action (see p483) as soon as payments are missed, though this does not always happen.

Disadvantages of the collection service are:
- that a payment statement is only issued periodically or on request (see p464) and that such statements are often considered to be inaccurate. The parties should therefore always keep their own records and evidence of payments.

Chapter 21: Collection and enforcement
1. Payment of child maintenance

The majority of accounts are in arrears and many persons with care and some non-resident parents are unhappy with the level of service from the CSA; *and*
- the CSA negotiates collection and arrears schedules with the parents and may agree to an arrears arrangement, notwithstanding objections from the person with care.

Persons with care on benefits

Where the parent with care is on IS/income-based JSA, the CSA may require payments for ongoing liability via the CSA from when the calculation is made, especially if there is evidence that the non-resident parent will not be a reliable payer. Where the person with care is not a *parent* with care, this is only usually done if she requests the collection service or the non-resident parent requests it. Arrears are always collected and retained by the CSA where the person with care or her partner is (or was during the relevant period) in receipt of IS/income-based JSA (see p396).[21]

Where payments are made via the CSA, the claimant receives one order book, girocheque or credit transfer from the Jobcentre Plus that includes both IS/income-based JSA and child maintenance. If the non-resident parent does not make a payment to the CSA, the person with care's order is still cashable, but it now represents only benefit.[22] In this way, benefit claimants are guaranteed a weekly income regardless of whether child maintenance is actually paid by the non-resident parent. For when arrears of child maintenance are paid later, see p396.

For the effect of child maintenance on IS/income-based JSA, see p394.

In some cases the calculation may be cancelled because the parent with care opts out (see p68). At this point arrears may remain due to the Secretary of State in lieu of benefit already paid that the CSA may collect; however, in practice the CSA is unlikely to do so. CSA policy guidance states that all action, including collection of arrears should cease when the parent with care opts out. If collection does continue, this should be challenged and advice sought.

Method of payment

Payment by the non-resident parent can be made by standing order, direct debit, automated credit transfer, cheque, postal order, debit card or cash.[23] (A debit card means one that can be used as a substitute for a cheque – ie, where the non-resident parent's bank account is debited instantly, such as a Switch card.[24] While this facility is provided for in the legislation the CSA does not have the facility to be able to accept such payment at the time of writing.) Where payment is via the CSA, a deduction from earnings order (DEO) can also be used (see p477). Unless the non-resident parent asks to pay by DEO from the outset or a default maintenance decision is in force, the CSA prefers payment by direct debit.[25] The CSA can direct a non-resident parent to take all reasonable steps to open a bank or building society account.[26] However, there is no penalty if he fails to do so. Some non-resident parents pay by deductions from benefit (see p224).

Chapter 21: Collection and enforcement
1. Payment of child maintenance

When deciding the method of payment, the CSA must take into account any representations of the parties,[27] and staff are reminded to record these as well as considerations about the welfare of any children and the reason for the decision.[28]

The CSA can accept payment by cheque, bankers draft, postal order, cash and foreign currency, but they do not encourage the use of these methods.[29] Non-resident parents who wish to pay by these methods should insist on doing so. So long as payments are made when due, no DEO should be made.

Where payment is made via the CSA, the person with care is paid by automated credit transfer wherever possible, and if not, by girocheque (although in theory all of the above methods of payment are possible).[30]

Non-resident parents on benefit

Where a non-resident parent on benefit is required to pay child maintenance at the flat rate, the CSA may request the Jobcentre Plus to make a deduction from benefit for maintenance.[31] Deductions can be made from the following benefits:[32]

- IS;
- income-based JSA;
- contribution-based JSA;
- maternity allowance;
- bereavement benefit;
- widow's benefit;
- retirement pension;
- incapacity benefit;
- carer's allowance;
- severe disability allowance;
- industrial injuries schemes benefits;
- incapacity benefit in youth;
- war disablement pension;
- pension credit.

Where an individual should pay at the flat rate but a variation has been made which results in the reduced or basic rate being payable, deductions may be made towards the new amount of maintenance calculated.

Where both the non-resident parent and their partner are:[33]

- on IS or income-based JSA; *and*
- each is a non-resident parent,

the £5 flat rate deduction will be split between them so that each contributes £2.50 to their respective persons with care.[34] (In polygamous relationships where there is more than one new partner who is also a non-resident parent the £5 is apportioned between all the non-resident parents.[35])

The CSA requests the deduction and the Jobcentre Plus must make the full deduction wherever possible. When making the deduction the parent must be left with at least 10p a week benefit entitlement.[36] Partial deductions will not be

Chapter 21: Collection and enforcement
1. Payment of child maintenance

made. In addition, priority debt rules do not apply to deductions for child support maintenance. Therefore a deduction will be made after any deduction for mortgage interest.

Both the person with care and non-resident parent are notified that deductions are to be made.

Where there are arrears of maintenance, a £1 deduction towards arrears may be made from most benefits except for IS/income-based JSA.

Timing of payments

The CSA decides the day and frequency of payments.[37] The CSA asks for the person's preference as to weekly, monthly or other intervals. When deciding the day and the interval for payment by the non-resident parent, the CSA must take into account:[38]

- the day on which and the interval at which the non-resident parent receives his income;
- any other relevant circumstances of the non-resident parent;
- time for cheques to clear and for payments to be transferred to the person with care; *and*
- any representations of the parties, in particular the preference of the non-resident parent.[39]

Unless undue hardship would be caused to the non-resident parent or the person with care, the frequency of payments to the person with care will be the same as the frequency set for the non-resident parent's payments (but see p478 for DEOs).[40]

Unless payments are to be by direct debit or standing order, the non-resident parent is advised to make each payment three to four days before the due date in order to ensure that payments are received on time and avoid issue of an arrears notice. However, as the due date is usually set as the non-resident parent's payday,[41] this may not be easy for the non-resident parent to manage. In any case, the CSA allows a clearance time from the due date when setting dates for payments to persons with care:[42]

Payment method	Clearance time
Direct debit	five banking days
Standing order	two banking days
Cheque	five banking days
Bank head office collection account	five banking days
Transcash	immediate
Cash/postal orders	immediate
Deductions from benefit	immediate
Debit card	facility not available at time of writing

Chapter 21: Collection and enforcement
1. Payment of child maintenance

Almost all payments are passed to the person with care within 10 working days of receipt from the non-resident parent. If a payment is not passed on within 28 days of receipt by the CSA, the CSA pays interest on that payment to the person with care if the interest is £5 or more.[43] The interest rate is 1 per cent above the base rate (the same as any interest charged to a non-resident parent, see p476).

The CSA cannot pay the person with care before the non-resident parent makes his payment.

Payment statements

Payment statements should be automatically sent to CSA clients using the collection service every six months. Otherwise statements of the CSA account are supplied when a request is made, by a person with care, non-resident parent or child in Scotland.[44] These statements usually cover the previous 12 months. They can be important when contesting the level of arrears. However, both parties should keep records and evidence of payments made and received, given the high level of errors on CSA accounts.

Overpayments

An overpayment can arise either because the amount of the maintenance due for a past period has been reduced, there has been a CSA error or the non-resident parent has paid more than the regular payment due. The CSA has a discretion about allocating the overpayment,[45] including setting it against any arrears of child maintenance resulting from a previous calculation.[46] In practice the CSA allocates payments in the following order of priority:[47]
- current collections of regular maintenance;
- arrears to the person with care;
- arrears to the Secretary of State; *and*
- other liability with the oldest debt dealt with first.

Where there is a surplus remaining after current maintenance, arrears and other liabilities have been met the non-resident parent may have the amount he pays adjusted or a refund made.[48] An adjustment is the preferred option.

Where the CSA receives an unexpected payment from the non-resident parent, it will check to determine the reason for this – eg, it could be for an overdue collection to offset arrears or an amount towards a future collection date.[49] Following this investigation the amount may be allocated to one of the following options:[50]
- current and overdue collections – plus any other arrears;
- arrears scheduled in the future;
- as an advance collection;
- refund;

- voluntary payment, if received in the initial payment period; *or*
- early payment – ie, where the intention is that the person with care gets a maintenance payment early.

The CSA cannot pass on financial gifts from the non-resident parent to the person with care.[51] Any such payments may be refunded.

Refunds can only be made if there are no overdue collections or arrears on the case.[52]

The CSA refunds overpayments made because of CSA error – eg, where a person was told to pay more than the calculation required.[53]

Adjustments

If an overpayment remains after offsetting against regular maintenance, arrears and other liability, the CSA can reduce the amount payable to compensate the non-resident parent for the overpayment.[54] Adjustments may also be made where there are overpayments of voluntary payments in the initial payment period.[55] When making this discretionary decision, the CSA must consider, in particular:

- the circumstances of the non-resident parent and person with care;
- the welfare of any children (see p31);
- the amount of the overpayment in relation to the amount of the current calculation; *and*
- the period over which it would be reasonable to recoup it.

The amount payable cannot be reduced below the flat rate (see p223).[56]

Where the amount of an adjusted calculation changes because of revision, supersession or variation, the adjustment applies to the fresh calculation, unless the CSA considers that this would be inappropriate, in which case it can either change the amount of the adjustment or cancel it.[57]

The non-resident parent, person with care and any Scottish child applicant must be notified of an adjustment or cancellation of an adjustment.[58] The decision to make or cancel an adjustment can be revised or superseded by the CSA (see Chapter 19) or appealed to an appeal tribunal (see Chapter 20).[59]

Recovery of overpayments from the person with care

Where the CSA reimburses an overpayment to a non-resident parent, the CSA can recover from the person with care any maintenance overpaid to her.[60] This includes where the overpayment is from voluntary payments.[61] The CSA cannot enforce recovery of overpayments due to CSA administrative error; however, in practice the person with care will be asked if they are prepared to repay the overpayment.[62]

Recovery of overpayments is a discretionary decision, so the welfare of any children likely to be affected by reimbursement must be taken into account (see p31). The CSA cannot recover the overpayment where:[63]

Chapter 21: Collection and enforcement
1. Payment of child maintenance

- the person with care was on IS or income-based JSA at any time during the period she was overpaid; *or*
- the person with care was on IS/income-based JSA on any of the dates reimbursement to the non-resident parent was made; *or*
- either of the above apply, where the non-resident parent made voluntary payments.

The overpayment is therefore collected from any current maintenance and where there is no ongoing maintenance other collection arrangements can be made.[64]

2. Collection of other payments

The CSA can collect and enforce other forms of maintenance where child support maintenance is being collected.[65] The power in the 1991 Act to collect maintenance where no child support maintenance is payable is not in force.[66] No date has been set for its introduction.

The power to collect other maintenance is discretionary. However, the CSA may agree to requests to collect other types of maintenance for section 6 applicants and, where the court order was made after April 1993, for section 4 and 7 applicants. The CSA can only collect other maintenance that falls due after the CSA gives the non-resident parent written notice that the other maintenance will be collected.[67]

The following payments under a court order (see p37) can be collected by the CSA:[68]
- additional child maintenance in excess of the CSA maximum;
- maintenance for a child's education or training;
- maintenance paid to meet the expenses of a child with disabilities;
- maintenance paid for a stepchild – ie, a child living with the person with care who used to live with the non-resident parent and was accepted by him as a member of his family;
- spousal maintenance for a person with care of a child for whom child support maintenance is being collected.

The methods used by the CSA for collecting and enforcing other types of maintenance are the same as those for child support maintenance.[69] Where a non-resident parent is paying more than one type of maintenance, and pays less than the total amount required, he should stipulate how the amounts are to be allocated. The CSA will allocate as requested, except that where arrears of child support maintenance are specified, current child support maintenance will be paid before arrears. If the non-resident parent does not stipulate, the CSA will allocate according to the following order of priority:[70]
- current child support maintenance liability;

- regular child maintenance;
- arrears of child support maintenance to the person with care;
- arrears of other child maintenance to the Secretary of State; *and*
- other liabilities with the oldest first.

Where arrears of child support maintenance are due to the CSA and others are due to the person with care, the priorities are the same as for overpayments caused by a change in the amount of the calculation (see p464).

Where there is more than one person with care the CSA will apportion the payment between cases.[71] This means that the non-resident parent cannot choose to pay one parent but not the other.

Collection of CSA fees, court costs and penalty payments

Although fees are not being charged for CSA services from April 1995 (see p458), any outstanding fees from previous years are still collected.[72] For liability to pay fees from 1993 to 1995 and their collection and enforcement, see p369 of the 1995/96 edition of this *Handbook*.

Court costs, DNA test fees, and penalty payments

Where the CSA applies to court for a decision that a person is a parent and the court decides that he is, the court can order him to pay the CSA's costs in bringing the case, including the cost of any DNA tests which have been carried out (see p109). Also, a non-resident parent may have agreed to pay DNA test fees to the CSA without a court order (see p105).

The CSA may also have imposed a penalty payment on the non-resident parent for failure to pay.

The CSA will negotiate with the liable person about payment of these other liabilities.[73] They will initially request the full amount but payment may be agreed.

Enforcement of fees and costs

Fees and costs can only be enforced through court action for debt. The rules for enforcement of maintenance (see p483) do not apply. The court is the sheriff court in Scotland and the county court in England and Wales. If the case is contested, a hearing is arranged in the court with jurisdiction for the area in which the parent lives. A money judgment can be enforced by the usual debt enforcement procedures – eg, distress, diligence, attachment of earnings.

3. Arrears

The CSA acts on arrears only if the collection service (see p460) is being used. If a person with care has not requested the collection service, she should consider

Chapter 21: Collection and enforcement
3. Arrears

doing so if a payment is missed. The CSA should then pursue all outstanding arrears.

Initial arrears

As the first calculation is made after its effective date, there are always initial arrears. The exception is where a court order has been in force, since the effective date is two days after the calculation (see p389). (In some cases where the effective date has been deferred under the 'old rules' this may also be the case.)

The CSA prefers to notify the non-resident parent about the collection schedule, including initial arrears, by telephone.[74] The parent can request and negotiate changes to the schedule. Written confirmation of the collection schedule is issued once the non-resident parent has agreed to it. Where telephone contact is not possible they will write to the non-resident parent.

The written notification states:[75]
- the amount due and to whom it is to be paid;
- how it is to be paid – ie, method, day and interval between payments;
- any amounts that are overdue and outstanding.

The CSA requests payment of the initial arrears as a lump sum.[76] If a non-resident parent cannot pay this all at once he may negotiate an agreement to pay in instalments or a collection schedule to cover both the initial payment and ongoing liability (see p469).

A parent who fails to make payment of the outstanding arrears within seven days of written notification of the amount due may face financial penalties and further enforcement action.

A parent who thinks the calculation is wrong may be able to seek a revision or make an appeal. Where he objects to the way the CSA is dealing with collections he may make a complaint.

Voluntary payments made in the initial period

Voluntary payments made by the non-resident parent through the CSA (or, where the CSA agrees, to the person with care or a third party), after the effective date but before the calculation is made and notified, may be offset against arrears of child maintenance.[77]

Only the following types of payment can be offset:[78]
- in lieu of child support maintenance;
- in respect of a mortgage or loan on the child's home, or for repairs or improvements to the property;
- rent on the child's home;
- mains gas, water or electricity at the child's home;
- council tax payable at the child's home;
- repairs to the heating system at the child's home; *or*
- repairs to the child's home.

Payments can be made in cash, standing order, cheque, postal order, debit card or other method/arrangement for payments to be made from an account of the non-resident parent.[79] (At the time of writing the CSA does not have the facility to take payments via debit card.)

Where the payments are made to the CSA they will be passed on to the person with care (in section 4 and 7 cases) or held by the CSA in section 6 cases.[80] Once the calculation has been made the voluntary payments will be offset against the initial arrears.

Where the payments are made direct to the person with care or a third party the CSA will check with the person with care if payments have been made.[81] This is normally done by phone. If the person with care confirms the payments were made this is usually accepted without any further need for proof. If there is a dispute over whether a payment has been made the CSA will ask the non-resident parent to provide proof. Evidence of a payment may include bank statements, duplicate of cashed cheques, receipts or paid bills/invoices.[82] Once the non-resident parent provides proof of payment the person with care must be able to show that this has not been received for it not to be considered as a voluntary payment.[83] It is in the interest of both parties to ensure payments are recorded.

If either party disagrees with a decision about offsetting, a complaint can be made to the CSA and then to the independent case examiner (see p19).

If offsetting means that there is an overpayment, the calculation may be adjusted to compensate the non-resident parent or a refund may be made (see p465).

Negotiating an arrears agreement

Where the non-resident parent is in arrears, the CSA will seek an arrears agreement.[84]

Negotiations with the CSA may begin on notification of the collection schedule or at a later date if the non-resident parent has difficulty making ongoing payments. However, the CSA does not normally agree to defer payment of current liability, though it may do so if a revision, supersession or appeal is pending.

There are no regulations limiting the amounts of payments or how quickly the arrears must be cleared. Although CSA staff always begin by requesting full payment of the outstanding arrears, an arrears agreement may be reached to pay the amount off in instalments. The maximum amount that the CSA can enforce for arrears collection is 5 per cent of net income.[85] There is no minimum amount and the parent may arrange to pay more than 5 per cent to reduce the arrears more quickly. In making this discretionary decision the CSA should consider the:[86]

- needs of the non-resident parent or any new family;
- representations of the non-resident parent about hardship; *or*
- needs of the person with care and the qualifying child.

If a non-resident parent has other priorities (eg, fuel) or other large debts, he should seek independent money advice. Existing agreements with other creditors may have to be renegotiated to take into account the CSA calculation. However, it is important to keep the CSA informed so that it does not assume that the non-resident parent is refusing to come to an agreement. Where there is a change of circumstances the non-resident parent may find it hard to pay the current liability and an arrears agreement in full while the change is processed. The CSA may accept a reduced payment but this does not alter the parent's liability and enforcement action may be taken on the arrears that accrue. The CSA may suspend the debt temporarily pending investigations.[87] The arrears agreement may also be adjusted to include missed payments.

The CSA can use other methods of recovery, such as a deduction from earnings order (see p477). Therefore, CSA staff are unlikely to agree to a non-resident parent making low payments over a very long period. It is in his interests to come to an agreement if he wishes to avoid further payment penalties and enforcement action. If he has children living with him, the welfare of those children must be taken into account.

Repayments may be spread over several years. Although this may help non-resident parents who are in financial hardship, it is very late payment to the person with care. She may want to make representations to the CSA. Staff are reminded to balance the needs of the non-resident parent with that of the person with care or the CSA.[88]

Revision, supersession or appeal pending.

The CSA can suspend collection of arrears if revision, supersession, variation or appeal is pending. Where the calculation is likely to be reduced, the CSA may agree to suspend collection of some of the ongoing payments. However, this does not often happen: the CSA prefers to speed up its consideration of the case.

A non-resident parent who requests a revision, supersession or appeal and is having problems paying the current maintenance or any arrears agreement should make representations to the CSA for lower regular payments.

Payment of arrears

Arrears do not have to be paid by the same method as continuing child maintenance payments. For example, arrears could be collected via the CSA, while ongoing payments are made to the person with care. However, in practice the CSA prefers to use the same method of payment for both, and non-resident parents are particularly encouraged to pay by direct debit.[89]

The CSA collects arrears if income support (IS)/income-based jobseeker's allowance (JSA) is paid to or for the person with care. The CSA keeps that part of the arrears payments that would not have been passed to the parent with care had it been made when due.[90] Payments of arrears are allocated between the CSA and person with care in the same way as overpayments (see p464).

Chapter 21: Collection and enforcement
3. Arrears

Collection of arrears from a non-resident parent on benefit

If the non-resident parent is in receipt of one of the following contribution-based benefits a deduction of £1 may be made towards arrears. This is in addition to a deduction for flat rate maintenance. The £1 deduction can be made from the following benefits:[91]
- contribution-based JSA;
- maternity allowance;
- bereavement allowance;
- widowed parent's allowance;
- war widow's pension;
- widow's pension;
- widowed mother's allowance;
- reduced earnings allowance;
- industrial death benefit and retirement allowance;
- retirement pension;
- incapacity benefit;
- carer's allowance;
- severe disability allowance;
- industrial injuries schemes benefits;
- incapacity benefit in youth;
- war disablement pension.

This means that arrears action will be suspended against non-resident parents on IS/income-based JSA. Where a person with care believes that the arrears action should be pursued, she should contact the CSA and explain her reasons. Where the CSA is unwilling to take action, a complaint may be made.

Starting recovery action

The CSA begins to consider recovery action when:[92]
- a payment from the non-resident parent to the CSA is not received;
- the person with care notifies the CSA that a payment due direct to her has not been received; *or*
- the person with care requests an increase in IS/income-based JSA because child maintenance has not been paid.

The CSA will contact the non-resident parent to investigate the situation.[93] Contact is normally by telephone, though the non-resident parent may have been issued an arrears notice already.[94] The non-resident parent may request an appointment through the local service base (see p12) if he wishes to discuss payment face to face with CSA staff.

If the non-resident parent intends to pay the amount, the CSA may:[95]
- accept a delayed payment, setting two further days for receipt (normally only two delayed payments are allowed in any 12-month period); *or*

471

- reschedule the amount to include it within arrears.

Where the non-resident parent indicates that they are having difficulty in making the payments due, this may be because of a change of circumstances.[96] The CSA will collect information to check whether or not there should be a supersession. Occasionally they may also take a decision to suspend collection.[97]

Where the non-resident parent refuses to make payment the CSA will inform them of the powers to collect and enforce maintenance. The CSA may discuss imposing a payment penalty to encourage the non-resident parent to pay the maintenance due.

To avoid payment penalties and other methods of recovery, the non-resident parent should come to an agreement (see p469) as soon as possible and comply with that agreement. The CSA has discretion over the agreements reached with non-resident parents about debt recovery. However, where a parent fails to come to a voluntary agreement or breaks it, the CSA may then impose payment penalties. The CSA may enforce a deductions from earnings order (DEO) at up to 40 per cent of net income and/or take further enforcement action.

Arrears notice

Where the non-resident parent has missed one or more child maintenance payments, the CSA must send him an arrears notice itemising the amounts owed. The notice also explains the regulations about arrears and requests payment of all outstanding arrears.[98] The notice may be issued automatically by the system unless a previous notice has been issued in the last 12 weeks.[99] The CSA will then contact the non-resident parent to discuss the issue.

The non-resident parent should check that the amount owed is correct, and tell the CSA of any mistakes. There have been high levels of mistakes on accounts in the past. Therefore, if there is a concern that the balance is incorrect, the non-resident parent should ask for a payment statement (see p464) and compare this with his own record of payments. While doing this, it is important that he keeps the CSA informed so that a penalty payment and a DEO are not imposed in the meantime.

The non-resident parent can contact the CSA to negotiate payment by instalments (see p469). Once an arrears notice has been served, another does not have to be sent if arrears remain uncleared, *unless* the non-resident parent has paid all arranged payments for a 12-week period.[100]

When the non-resident parent defaults

If the non-resident parent fails to keep to an arrears agreement then:
- a penalty payment may be imposed; *and*
- a DEO (see p477) or other method of enforcement may be considered (see p483).

In all cases a non-resident parent who wants to co-operate should try to renegotiate an agreement in good time before a change in his circumstances – eg, redundancy. Where the non-resident parent has paid regularly and the change would produce a reduction in the amount due, the CSA may accept a lower amount. Arrears may be temporarily suspended where personal circumstances make it difficult or insensitive to enforce recovery – eg, he is unemployed, sick or in prison.[101]

Penalty payments

A penalty payment may be may be imposed on a non-resident parent who is in arrears with his maintenance payments.[102] These are intended to encourage late/non-payers to make payments on time; it is not passed to the person with care.

The amount of the penalty cannot be more than 25 per cent of the maintenance owed for the appropriate week.[103] The CSA has discretion to decide when to impose the penalty and the percentage to use. This means a non-payer may have a 5 per cent penalty imposed for one missed maintenance payment; this may increase to 10 per cent on a further occasion.[104] Only one penalty payment per maintenance period may be imposed. This means where there are several weeks' maintenance upon which penalties apply they may be at different rates. The penalty may be imposed where:[105]

- an unpaid payment remains overdue at the date the next payment is due;
- the amount is not paid within seven days of notification of the amount outstanding;
- the non-resident parent fails to keep to an agreement to pay the arrears.

Guidance indicates that the CSA should consider if the imposition or threat of a penalty could be an effective way to encourage the non-resident parent to pay.[106] The CSA should also consider not imposing a penalty if:[107]

- there was a genuine lack of awareness that the payment was due;
- an agreement to pay arrears by instalments is being kept;
- there are good reasons for late/non-payment – eg, hospitalisation, imprisonment, death in the family; *or*
- the non-resident parent's bank failed to operate a standing order.

The CSA may consider a payment penalty when contacting a non-resident parent over late or missed payments. In some cases the threat of a penalty may be enough to improve the payment record – eg, the payment is made within a reasonable period or an agreement is reached to pay the missed amount. However, the penalty may be imposed if a payment agreement is made and the non-resident parent fails to keep to it.[108] Where there have been penalties imposed in the past that have been ineffective, the CSA should not consider further penalties, but should take enforcement action against the non-resident parent instead.[109]

Chapter 21: Collection and enforcement
3. Arrears

Example 21.1
A non-resident parent is due to pay child maintenance of £48 a week. By the time the calculation is made and he is notified, there is initial arrears of six weeks – ie, arrears of £288. The non-resident parent makes no payment and does not respond positively to attempts to negotiate an agreement. He is notified of the arrears and the risk of penalty payments. The next payment is missed and no arrears have been paid, a penalty payment is imposed, of 5 per cent for each missed week – ie, £2.40 a week for six weeks = £14.40. The non-resident continues to resist attempts to negotiate about regular maintenance and arrears. No payments are made so the CSA decides to impose a 25 per cent penalty on a further weeks arrears – ie, £12. By the next payment date no payments have been made and there has been no contact from the non-resident parent. The CSA should now consider other collection and enforcement action – eg, through a DEO or obtaining a liability order. There are now arrears of nine weeks maintenance (ie, £432) and penalty payments of £26.40 to be recovered.

When a penalty payment is imposed the non-resident parent will be sent notification as soon as possible.[110] This will state the:
- amount of maintenance payable and arrears;
- amount of the penalty payment (interest or fees where they apply);
- method of payment and day of payment; *and*
- information about challenging decisions – ie, seeking a revision.

The decision to impose a penalty payment may also be appealed. Where the CSA revises the penalty payment decision the non-resident parent must be sent notification that sets out the amounts now due.[111]

The non-resident parent is required to make payment within 14 days.[112] The CSA normally seeks payment of the penalty in a lump sum. Where payment of the full amount of the penalty and arrears or an agreement to pay is not made, a DEO or further enforcement action may be taken.

When making an agreement the CSA usually seeks to recover the maintenance arrears first and, after these have been cleared, collect the payment penalty.[113] This is to ensure the collection of penalties or other amounts does not affect the collection of maintenance owed to the person with care. If the non-resident parent's circumstances change, any agreement may be re-negotiated.

The person with care will not be notified of any late payment penalties imposed, though they may provide information to the CSA on the non-resident parent's circumstances and may ask for a penalty to be imposed. If the CSA does not impose a penalty the person with care may make a complaint and ask to be informed of the reasons.

Guidance from the CSA policy department suggests that penalty payments are unlikely to be a common feature. The provisions may be rarely used to encourage non-resident parents who are reluctant to make arrangements but likely to

Chapter 21: Collection and enforcement
3. Arrears

respond to this type of incentive. These judgements may be extremely difficult for the CSA to make in individual cases.

Delays in collection and enforcement

Despite CSA steps to avoid debts building up, many cases may accumulate arrears. The new scheme is intended to take action more quickly to respond to failure to pay and impose financial penalties to encourage payment or establish arrears agreements.

Persons with care who are concerned at the speed of pursuit and who want quicker action should contact the CSA by phone, letter or in person. A person with care may want to explain any effect the lack of arrears action has on the welfare of the child(ren). In particular, a person with care may want to request that a DEO be issued, and if there is undue delay she can make a complaint (see p18). If a DEO or other form of enforcement sought is refused, the person with care should be given the reasons for this. She can ask for the decision to be reconsidered by the CSA and then the Independent Case Examiner (see p19). Judicial review (see p415) should also be considered.

Where there are arrears of over £100 that have built up because of CSA maladministration the person with care may be eligible for an advance payment (see below). This may be in addition to any payment of compensation (see p491).

There are persons with care who, as a result of the payment of child maintenance, are no longer on IS/income-based JSA because their income, including child maintenance, is now too high. If child maintenance is not paid, a fresh benefit claim should be made.

Advance payments

An advance payment of maintenance is not compensation. The payment is to ensure the person with care is not worse off due to maladministration by the CSA.[114] Essentially, it is advance payment of arrears that the CSA is collecting from the non-resident parent. The decision on whether or not to make an advance payment is discretionary. It may only be considered where the:

- arrears of maintenance due to CSA maladministration are £100 or more;
- non-resident parent is making regular maintenance payments;
- non-resident parent has made, and is paying, an arrears agreement and it would take more than 26 weeks to pay these arrears;
- CSA is satisfied that the non-resident parent would have complied with the calculation but for the maladministration; *and*
- person with care has shown an interest in progressing the case during the period of delay.

There must be clear evidence that there has been maladministration by the CSA for an advance payment to be considered. Maladministration may include:[115]
- rudeness;

475

Chapter 21: Collection and enforcement
3. Arrears

- delay;
- refusal to answer reasonable questions;
- knowingly giving advice which is misleading or inadequate;
- incompetence;
- bias because of sex, ethnicity, etc; *or*
- disregard of guidance that is intended to be followed.

The CSA may consider payment on its own initiative or at the request of the person with care. Where an advance payment is to be made the amount is worked out as the arrears of maintenance that are due to the CSA's maladministration plus interest, but only where interest is £10 or more. Allowances are made for normal processing time so only that time over and above the normal processing time is considered. Payment is usually in the form of a lump sum, paid either directly into the person's bank account or by girocheque.[116] The person with care must sign a declaration agreeing that the CSA retains payments made for the period and to refund any relevant direct payments.

Where a decision is made not to make a payment there is no right of appeal. The person with care may provide further information to support her case, use the internal complaints procedure, complain to the Independent Case Examiner, contact her MP or seek judicial review (see p415).

Enforcement by the person with care

While there is no provision in child support legislation for the parent with care to bring her own court action against the non-resident parent for the child support maintenance due, it may be possible for the parent to raise an action to recover the amount owed to her. However, such action may be difficult in practice. Where the person with care has lost out because of CSA delay or maladministration, it may be possible to sue the CSA for negligence. Anyone considering doing either of the above should seek legal advice.

Interest

Interest can only be charged on arrears of child maintenance accrued before 17 April 1995.[117] Interest can continue to accrue on arrears outstanding at 17 April 1995 at one per cent over base rate and new demands for interest may still be issued – eg, where a non-resident parent defaults on an arrears agreement concerning amounts due before 17 April 1995. However, in practice the collection of interest takes a lower priority than current liability for and arrears of maintenance. For details of the charging and enforcement of interest, see the 1997/98 edition of this *Handbook*, p390.

4. Deduction from earnings orders

The CSA may make a deduction from earnings order (DEO): that is, an order to the non-resident parent's employer to make deductions from earnings and pay them to the CSA.[118]

CSA staff are instructed to make a DEO if the non-resident parent chooses it (see p461).[119] If possible, a DEO is also made if the account is in arrears and the non-resident parent does not respond to enquiries, refuses to make an arrears agreement or persistently defaults on an agreement.[120] Persons with care complain that the CSA is slow to make DEOs.

The best way for a non-resident parent to avoid a DEO is to negotiate an arrears agreement (see p469) and keep to it wherever possible. However, making ongoing liability payments in full may be enough to prevent a DEO being made. A non-resident parent's objection to a DEO is likely to be outweighed if it is unlikely that regular payments would be made using a different method.

The decision to make a DEO is discretionary and the welfare of any children must be considered (see p31).[121] If warned of a DEO, the non-resident parent should tell the CSA, preferably in writing, how any child(ren) would be affected by a DEO. Any challenge should be by judicial review (see p415) and/or to the Independent Case Examiner (ICE – see p19), rather than by appeal to a court (see p482).

A DEO can be made while the non-resident parent is awaiting a revision, supersession or appeal. Staff should consider the grounds of revision, supersession or appeal before making a DEO. They may check the likelihood and timing of any change in the calculation, and arrange for that consideration to be 'fast-tracked'. A non-resident parent can also make representations about the amount and method of payments (see pp470 and 461). The CSA may accept lower payments but this will not remove their right to impose a DEO.[122]

A DEO cannot be made where the employer is based outside the UK and has no place of business in the UK,[123] but a DEO can be made in Great Britain against an employer in Northern Ireland and *vice versa*.[124]

A DEO cannot be made if the non-resident parent is in the armed forces. Instead, the CSA can request the armed forces to make deductions for child maintenance under armed forces law, known as a DER, which sets limits to the amounts which can be deducted.[125]

If the full amount requested by the CSA cannot be deducted from earnings, the CSA uses other methods to collect and enforce the remainder.

How does a DEO work

A DEO is an instruction to the employer of a non-resident parent to make deductions from his earnings.[126] A copy of the DEO must be served on the employer and the non-resident parent.[127] The employer has to comply with the

DEO within seven days of receiving it.[128] Failure to take all reasonable steps to comply with a DEO is an offence punishable by a fine of up to £500.[129]

The DEO must state:[130]
- the name and address of the non-resident parent;
- the name of the employer;
- the non-resident parent's place of work, the nature of his work, works number and national insurance number (where known by the CSA);
- the normal deduction rate(s) (see p490) and the date on which each takes effect;
- the protected earnings proportion;
- the address to which the deductions are to be sent.

The CSA helpline (see Appendix 1) provides further information for employers. The CSA leaflet *Advice for Employers* and the *Lord Chancellor's Handbook* also provide guidance to employers on deductions. If an employer is implementing a DEO incorrectly and the non-resident parent is disputing this, the non-resident parent should ask the CSA to intervene.

Date of payment

The employer must pay the CSA monthly by the 19th of the month following the month in which the deduction is made.[131] This means that there is always a delay before the person with care receives the first payment from the CSA. Because the employer makes monthly payments, the person with care receives monthly payments, even if the non-resident parent is having weekly deductions. These monthly payments may not always be for the same amount (see p490 and example 21.1).

The payment by the employer may be made by credit transfer, cheque or any other method to which the CSA agrees.[132] The DEO reference number must be given so that the CSA can identify the person with care.

The employer commits a criminal offence punishable by a fine of up to £500, if s/he fails to take all reasonable steps to pay the CSA on time.[133]

Providing information

In each of the following cases, any notice that is sent from the CSA will be treated as though it was given or sent on the day that it was posted.[134]

Failure to take all reasonable steps to comply with any of the following requirements to provide information to the CSA is an offence punishable by a fine of up to £500.[135]

The non-resident parent

The non-resident parent must provide the name and address of his employer, the amount of earnings and anticipated earnings, place of work, nature of work and any works number, within seven days of being asked to do so in writing by the

CSA.[136] Once a DEO is in force, a non-resident parent must inform the CSA within seven days of leaving employment or becoming employed or re-employed.[137]

The employer

An employer must inform the CSA in writing within 10 days of being served with a DEO if s/he does not, in fact, employ the non-resident parent.[138] If a non-resident parent who is subject to a DEO leaves his job, the employer must notify the CSA within 10 days of his leaving.[139] If an employer finds out that a DEO is in force against an employee (eg, on becoming a non-resident parent's employer), s/he must notify the CSA within seven days of becoming aware of this information.[140]

The employer must inform the non-resident parent in writing of the amount of each deduction no later than the date of the deduction or, if not practicable, by the following payday.[141] Although child support law imposes no penalty on an employer who fails to do this, employment protection law requires the employer to give the non-resident parent a written statement of deductions on or before the payday.[142] Where the deduction will always be the same amount, this can be done by a standing statement given at least annually.[143] If the employer does not give notice of the deduction, the non-resident parent may complain to an employment tribunal, which can order the employer to pay the non-resident parent a fine up to the total amount of the unnotified deductions, even if paid on to the CSA.[144] This fine would not affect deductions already paid to the CSA.

For other duties about the provision of information, see p89.

Earnings

Earnings include wages, salary, fees, bonus, commission, overtime pay, occupational pension or statutory sick pay, any other payment made under an employment contract and a regular payment made in compensation for loss of wages.[145] Earnings do not include a payment by a foreign government or the government of Northern Ireland,[146] or a payment to a special member of a British reserved armed force.[147] Payments of working tax credit also do not count as earnings for a DEO.[148] Net earnings means, in this context, the amount remaining after tax, national insurance and contributions towards a pension scheme have been deducted.[149]

How much is deducted

The DEO states a **normal deduction rate** and a **protected earnings proportion**.[150] These rates should usually correspond to the pay periods of the non-resident parent – ie, at a weekly rate if paid weekly and a monthly rate if paid monthly.[151] More than one normal deduction rate can be set, each applying to a different period.[152]

Chapter 21: Collection and enforcement
4. Deduction from earnings orders

Normal deduction rate

The normal deduction rate is the amount that will be deducted each payday as long as net earnings are not brought below the protected earnings proportion. The normal deduction rate can include not only current maintenance liability but also an amount for any arrears, penalty payments (interest in rare cases – see p476) and fees due. There are no special rules for DEOs as to how quickly the CSA should seek to clear the liability. This is normally negotiated and CSA guidance sets limits for payments towards arrears (see p469).

Protected earnings proportion

The protected earnings proportion is the level below which earnings must not be reduced by the deductions. The protected earnings proportion is 60 per cent of net earnings.[153]

Administering a DEO

The employer can deduct a charge for administrative costs each time a deduction is made under the DEO.[154] This means that employees paid weekly can be charged more for administrative costs. The additional amount must not exceed £1 per deduction and can be made even where this would bring earnings below the protected earnings proportion.

Each payday the employer should make a deduction from net earnings at the normal deduction rate plus any administration charge, unless deducting the normal deduction rate would reduce net earnings below the protected earnings proportion. If this would be the case, the amount of the deduction is the excess of net earnings over the protected earnings proportion, with any administration charge deducted in addition.[155]

Where the employer fails to make a deduction or the deduction is less than the normal deduction rate, arrears build up and are deducted at the next payday in addition to the normal deduction, applying the same rules for protected earnings.[156]

If on a payday the non-resident parent is paid for a period longer than that for which the normal deduction rate is set, the deduction is increased in proportion to the length of the pay period.[157]

Such fluctuations in deductions mean that the person with care receives irregular payments. This should not affect persons with care on income support (IS)/income-based jobseeker's allowance (JSA) paid via the CSA as their benefit is paid gross (see p461).

> **Example 21.2**
> Following on from Example 21.1, the non-resident parent is due to pay child maintenance of £48 a week and his net earnings are £240 a week. When a DEO is considered there are arrears of £432 and penalty payments of £24.40. The DEO shows a normal deduction rate

Chapter 21: Collection and enforcement
4. Deduction from earnings orders

of £60 (maintenance due + 5 per cent net income) and a protected earnings proportion of £144. His employer can deduct £1 administrative costs in weeks that a deduction is made.

Payday	Net pay (£)	Child support due (£)	Deduction (£)	Pay (£)	DEO unpaid (£)
5/7	240	60	61	179	
12/7	250	60	61	189	
19/7	160	60	17	143	44
26/7	160	104	17	143	88
2/8	240	148	97	143	52
9/8	250	112	107	143	6
16/8	250	66	67	183	
23/8	240	60	61	179	
30/8	120	60	Nil	120	60
6/9	240	120	97	143	24
13/9	240	84	85	155	
20/9	250	60	61	189	
27/9	240	60	61	179	

In the week 19/7 the full deduction cannot be made, as this would take income below the protected earnings proportion. A deduction is made of £16 plus a £1 administration fee. The amount of the DEO outstanding is added to the next amount due on 26/7. As earnings are again low the full deduction cannot be taken and is carried forward.

In the week 30/8 earnings are too low for a deduction to be made, therefore there is no deduction and no administrative charge.

Payment to the person with care
The employer has to pass the month's payments to the CSA by the 19th of the following month. When this has reached the CSA's account, the payment should be passed on to the person with care within 10 days – unless it is retained because the person with care is on IS (see p461). Where the person with care has come off IS, the current liability will be due to her, but some or all of the arrears may be retained in lieu of IS paid for an earlier period.

Month	Payment to CSA by the 19th of the month (£)	Current liability paid (£48 a week due) (£)	Arrears paid (assigned to oldest debt) (£)
July		Nil	Nil
August	156	156	Nil
September	328	192	136
October	300	192	108

By the time the parent gets her first payment from the DEO in August she is owed £624 (£432 + £192 (July)), but because of the fluctuating earnings of the non-resident parent she will receive less than the maintenance due. It is only in September she begins to obtain arrears of maintenance, even though the DEO was put into place in July.

Priority of orders

A DEO takes priority over an attachment of earnings order for a judgment or administration debt (non-priority debts), and any arrestment of earnings under Scottish law.[158] In England and Wales, when a DEO is served on an employee who is already subject to an attachment of earnings order for a priority debt (eg, council tax or fine), the earliest has priority.[159]

Any deductions under a lower priority order are taken from the net earnings left after deductions under the first order have been made.[160]

Review, cancellation and lapsing of DEOs

The CSA must **review** a DEO if there is a change in the amount of the calculation or if any arrears, penalty payments (interest in some cases – see p476) and fees included have been paid off.[161] This does not apply where a normal deduction rate that takes into account the change has already been specified (see p490). A DEO can be changed on this review.[162] The employer must comply with the change within seven days of a copy of the new DEO being served on her/him.[163] The usual penalties for failure to comply apply.

The CSA can **cancel** the DEO if:[164]
- no further payments are due under it;
- the DEO is ineffective or there appears to be a more effective way of collecting the payments;
- the DEO is defective (see *Appeals* below) or does not comply with some other procedural provision in the legislation;
- the CSA did not have, or has ceased to have, jurisdiction to make a DEO; *or*
- a DEO being used to enforce a default maintenance decision or interim maintenance decision is no longer appropriate given the compliance or attempted compliance of the non-resident parent.

The CSA must send written notice of cancellation to the non-resident parent and employer.[165]

A DEO lapses when a non-resident parent leaves the employment.[166] The CSA can revive it if he finds a new job with the same or a different employer.[167] If it is revived, copies of the notice must be served on the non-resident parent and new employer.[168] Any shortfall under the DEO prior to the revival cannot be carried over to the revived DEO.[169]

Appeals

A non-resident parent can appeal against a DEO to the magistrates' court in England and Wales or sheriffs' court in Scotland.[170] The appeal must be made within 28 days.[171] An appeal can only be made on the grounds that the order is defective (see below) or that the payments made to the non-resident parent are not earnings (see p479).[172] Where the complaint is that the CSA has not exercised its discretion to make a DEO properly, judicial review can be used (see p415) and/or a complaint made first to the CSA and then to the ICE (see pp18 and 19).

A DEO is defective if it is impracticable for the employer to comply with it because it does not include the correct information required.[173] Many DEOs have included incorrect information (such as errors in names, addresses and dates) but an appeal will not succeed on this basis if the employer can still comply with the DEO. Although some early appeals were upheld because the DEO was unsigned, there is no requirement in the regulations for a signature.

In Scotland, the form of the application is laid out in the child support rules.[174] In England and Wales, a complaint is made against the Secretary of State for Work and Pensions (who acts through the CSA). As there is no specific form given, we suggest that the Scottish wording is followed as an example, but including, 'This complaint is made under section 32(5) of the Child Support Act 1991 and regulation 22 of the Child Support (Collection and Enforcement) Regulations 1992'.

Once the complaint or application is made, the court notifies the CSA. The CSA checks the DEO and contacts the employer to check the earnings. If the DEO is based on the wrong amounts, the CSA varies and reissues it. If the case does get as far as a court hearing, the magistrate/sheriff may quash the DEO or specify which payments, if any, constitute earnings.[175] The court cannot question the maintenance calculation itself.[176]

Even if the court quashes the DEO, it cannot order the CSA to repay deductions to the non-resident parent.[177] Because of this, where deductions are being made from payments that are not earnings or on the basis of the wrong normal deduction rate or protected earnings proportion, it may be better to challenge the DEO by judicial review.

Either party can be represented by a lawyer. The CSA can (and does) instead appoint its own staff to conduct DEO appeals and appear at related hearings before magistrates in England and Wales or a sheriff in Scotland.[178] The non-resident parent can also be represented by a lay person, if the sheriff accepts s/he is suitable. An authorised lay representative does not have the full rights of a legal representative, but may be entitled to expenses.

5. Enforcement

A case is considered for enforcement action if:[179]
- the non-resident parent has missed payments and there is no acceptable explaination of this; *or*

Chapter 21: Collection and enforcement
5. Enforcement

- a deduction from earnings order (DEO) cannot be implemented or has proved ineffective.

Previous guidance indicated that only debts over £250 would be pursued, this is no longer stated, however it is unlikely that enforcement action would be taken for an amount under £250. There must be no outstanding revisions, supersessions or appeals if enforcement action is to be taken.[180] To take enforcement action, the CSA must obtain a **liability order**.[181] The CSA cannot get an injunction (inhibition in Scotland) to prevent the non-resident parent from disposing of assets or removing them out of the jurisdiction before a liability order is made.[182] When making any discretionary decision about enforcement, the CSA must consider the welfare of any children likely to be affected.[183]

The CSA does not enforce if the non-resident parent is under 18 years old, ie considered a child.[184] A liability order cannot be sought if the debt is already more than six years old.[185] Debts that become due more than six years after the day the payment was charged cannot be enforced and will be recovered by other methods, such as a DEO.

Obtaining a liability order

If a DEO is inappropriate (eg, because the non-resident parent is not employed) or one has been made but proved ineffective, the CSA may apply to the magistrates' court in England and Wales, or sheriff's court in Scotland, for a liability order.[186] A liability order provides the CSA with legal recognition of the debt, and allows the CSA to take further enforcement measures.

If the court decides that the payments are due but have not been made, it must make the order.[187] The court cannot question the maintenance calculation itself.[188] The great majority of liability orders have been against self-employed non-resident parents.[189]

An order (including one made in Northern Ireland) can be enforced anywhere in the UK.[190]

Either party can be represented by a lawyer. The CSA can (and does) instead appoint its own staff to apply for liability orders and appear at related hearings before magistrates in England and Wales or a sheriff in Scotland.[191] The non-resident parent can also be represented by a lay person, if the sheriff accepts s/he is suitable. An authorised lay representative does not have the full rights of a legal representative, but may be entitled to expenses.

If the court makes the order, it can (and usually will) order the non-resident parent to pay the CSA's legal expenses.

England and Wales

The CSA must give the non-resident parent seven days' notice of its intention to seek a liability order.[192] The notice must state the amount of maintenance outstanding, including any penalty payments. If the non-resident parent makes an arrangement to pay, the action may be stopped but where there is a history of broken agreements the CSA may pursue a liability order.[193] The application must be made to the court having jurisdiction for the area in which the non-resident parent lives and within six years of the date the amount became due.[194] The non-resident parent will be sent a summons giving 14 days' notice of the hearing. The magistrate decides whether or not to issue the liability order. The magistrate may decide not to issue an order if the non-resident parent appears to be co-operating. However, the CSA will still ask for the order to be granted but on the understanding that it will not be enforced if the non-resident parent continues to co-operate.[195] If the non-resident parent does not attend, the CSA may still obtain the order unless it is defective. If the non-resident parent attends, the magistrate may adjourn to allow more time.

The form of the court order in England and Wales is set out in the regulations. The order must specify the outstanding amounts of child support maintenance, penalty payments, fees (interest in some cases – see p476) and other forms of maintenance.[196]

Scotland

A CSA litigation officer can sign the liability order application instead of a solicitor.[197] Court officials serve notice of the application on the non-resident parent.[198] The non-resident parent has 21 days to object to the liability order being made. This should be done in writing by returning the notice stating the grounds of the objection and enclosing evidence. If objections are received, a hearing is held. Even if the non-resident parent does not attend, the sheriff must still consider his objections.[199] An extract of the liability order may be issued 14 days after the order is actually made. All the forms used in this procedure are included in the child support rules.[200]

Enforcing a liability order in England and Wales

The CSA can decide to levy by distress or take action in the county court.

Levying of distress

Where a liability order has been made, the amount specified on the order can be enforced in England and Wales by distress and sale of goods.[201] The bailiff levying distress must either carry written authority to hand to the non-resident parent, or leave at the address where distress is to be levied a copy of the relevant regulations and a memorandum setting out the amount to be levied.[202] If payment is made in full, the levy of the goods or the subsequent sale will not take place.[203]

Certain items cannot be seized. These are:[204]
- tools, books, vehicles and other items necessary for work; *and*
- clothing, bedding, furniture, household equipment and provisions necessary to meet the basic domestic needs of the non-resident parent and any member of his family who lives with him; *and*

- any money, promissory notes, bond or other securities for money belonging to the non-resident parent.

Charges can be made at each of the stages involved in distress proceedings[205] – eg, a £10 charge for sending a letter, a charge for making a visit to the property (the maximum for this charge is £12.50 if the amount owed is less than £100, or if the amount is more than £100, £12.50 plus 4 per cent of the next £400 due, 2.5 per cent of the next £1,500, 1 per cent of the next £8,000 and 0.25 per cent of anything more).

Any person aggrieved by the levy, or by an attempt to levy distress, can appeal to the magistrates' court by making a complaint to the court.[206] If the court is satisfied that the levy was irregular, it may order the goods to be returned if they have been seized, and order compensation in respect of any goods sold.

County court action

Once a liability order has been made, the CSA can arrange for the county court to record the order as if it were a judgment debt.[207] This record is publicly available and damages the non-resident parent's credit rating. The CSA can also use the county court to recover any amount that remains unpaid.[208] This means applying for a charging order or using third party debt proceedings.

A **charging order** allows a debt to be registered against certain assets such as land, stocks, shares and any interest the non-resident parent may have in a trust. Where a charge is registered and the assets are sold, the debt due under the liability order can be recovered from the proceeds of the sale. In some cases it may not be possible to register a charge, in which case a caution against dealings may be obtained to prevent the property from being sold without the CSA's knowledge. Once a charge or caution has been registered the CSA can consider applying to the courts for an order of sale.

A **third party debt order** can be obtained by the CSA if it is aware that the non-resident parent has a bank account or is owed money by a third party. The order freezes funds in the account and requires that person to release funds to the CSA up to the amount of the liability order.

Enforcing a liability order in Scotland

In Scotland, a liability order can be enforced by diligence.[209] The form of the demand for payment sent by the sheriff's court is given in the child support rules.[210] It states the sum owed, including court charges, and specifies that further action will be taken if payment is not made within 14 days (28 days if the non-resident parent is outside the UK). Otherwise, there are no procedures specific to child maintenance. The procedures are the same as for any other debt enforced under Part II of the Debtors (Scotland) Act 1987.

The liability order may be enforced by inhibition of sale of property and arrestment of bank accounts.[211] Enforcement via poinding and warrant sale was abolished on 31 December 2002.[212]

Disqualification from driving or imprisonment

The CSA may take action for disqualification from driving or imprisonment where all other methods of recovery have failed.[213]

Before taking action every attempt must be made to contact the non-resident parent. Where no phone contact has been successful during the enforcement action, a face-to-face visit may be appropriate.

When considering whether to take committal or disqualification action the CSA should consider:[214]
- the welfare of any child(ren) affected;
- ill health or disability of the non-resident parent or a member of his family;
- whether the action could affect future regular maintenance;
- whether the CSA could be considered insensitive in pursuing action; or
- whether the non-resident parent is on benefit.

Where any of these is an issue no committal or disqualification action should be taken. Where the decision is made not to pursue the action the person with care should be informed.[215] In these circumstances enforcement action may be suspended for six months.

Action for committal or disqualification from driving

In England and Wales, if distress and/or county court proceedings have been tried, or in Scotland diligence via arrestments or inhibitions on sale (poinding and warrant sale were abolished on 31 December 2002), but an amount is still due under the liability order, the CSA can apply to the court to issue either a warrant committing the non-resident parent to prison or an order disqualifying them from driving.[216] The hearing must take place in the presence of the non-resident parent.[217] The court can summon the non-resident parent to appear in court and produce any driving licence held by him.[218] If the parent does not appear the court may issue a warrant (citation in Scotland) for his arrest.[219] The Secretary of State can make representations to the court on whether to issue a warrant or order disqualification.[220] The non-resident parent may reply to these.

The court must enquire into the non-resident parent's means, whether he needs a driving licence to make a living and whether there has been 'wilful refusal or culpable neglect' on his part.[221] Only if there has been, can the court commit the non-resident parent to prison or disqualify him from driving,[222] and the decision whether to do so is at the discretion of the court. A non-resident parent should seek advice in preparing a statement of his income and outgoings.[223] A written statement from an employer will be accepted as proof of earnings.[224] The

CSA can appoint its own staff to apply for committal and appear at related hearings before magistrates in England and Wales or a sheriff in Scotland.[225]

Imprisonment

If the court decides that there has been wilful refusal or culpable neglect and committal is appropriate a warrant for imprisonment will be issued.[226] A warrant for imprisonment cannot be issued against a non-resident parent who is under 18.[227]

Instead of immediate committal, the court usually fixes a term of imprisonment and postpones it on conditions, usually of regular payments.[228] A warrant of commitment is issued stating the total amount outstanding, including child maintenance, penalty payments, fees (interest in some cases – see p476), court costs and any other charges.[229] If the amount is paid in full, the non-resident parent will not be imprisoned.

The maximum period of imprisonment is six weeks.[230] If, after the warrant has been issued, part-payment is made, then the period of imprisonment is reduced by the same proportion as that by which the debt has been reduced.[231]

The court cannot write off the arrears, but the CSA will not apply for further imprisonment for the same debt. However, it can consider enforcement through other methods should the non-resident parent's circumstances change, including disqualification.[232]

Disqualification from driving

If the court decides that there has been wilful refusal or culpable neglect and disqualification is appropriate an order will be issued.[233] The order may be issued but its implementation suspended on conditions – eg, regular payments. The order will state the amount outstanding, including child maintenance, interest, court costs and any other charges.[234] If the amount is paid in full the order is revoked.

The maximum period of disqualification is two years.[235] If, after the order has been issued, part payment is made, then the period of disqualification is reduced.[236] Where the amount is paid in full the order is revoked. If at the end of the period of disqualification the arrears have not been paid in full the Secretary of State may apply again for imprisonment or disqualification.[237]

Bankruptcy/sequestration in Scotland

The CSA does not pursue bankruptcy/sequestration, but a non-resident parent may have child support maintenance arrears when they are made bankrupt.[238]

In England and Wales, the CSA can take action to obtain a liability order including amounts due before the date of the bankruptcy.

In Scotland, a liability order can only recover amounts due after the date of the sequestration.

In either case, the CSA may decide not to enforce the order because it may not be practical – eg, a charging order/inhibition on sale may not be effective, as any property may already have been sold to pay off creditors. The CSA may secure a liability order to remind the non-resident parent that they cannot avoid their maintenance responsibility.

Bankruptcy/sequestration may not prevent the CSA considering action for committal to prison or disqualification from driving – eg, the non-resident parent may have a steady income and it would be up to him to show in court that he cannot afford to meet his child support liability.[239]

6. Existing 'old rules' and conversion cases

Existing 'old rules' maintenance assessments are collected and enforced in much the same way as 'new rules' maintenance calculations – involving negotiations, deduction from earnings orders (DEOs), liability orders and action for committal or disqualification from driving. However, there are some differences to bear in mind.

The **legislation** applied to existing 'old rules' is that prior to reform by the Child Support, Pensions and Social Security Act 2000 and associated regulations. On **conversion** the case comes under the reformed legislation.

Penalty payments do not apply to 'old rules' cases; once the case converts the 'new rules' penalty payments may be applied. This means that penalty payments can only be made on missed or late payments after the date of conversion.

Voluntary payments under the 'new rules' are governed by statue. Under the 'old rules' the CSA exercised discretion in how it regarded such payments.

Deductions from earnings orders are calculated and applied in a slightly different way. At conversion any old arrears uncollected under the previous DEO may be included in a new one issued under the 'new rules'.

Certain non-resident parents with a maintenance assessment may make a deferred debt agreement under the **temporary compensation scheme**. This agreement may continue in force after conversion. If it is discharged the person with care may be eligible for a **deferred debt compensation payment** see p491).

A non-resident parent on income support (IS)/income-based jobseeker's **allowance (JSA)** will continue to have contributions for ongoing maintenance and arrears taken from benefit. When the case converts deductions may be taken under the new scheme – eg, at the flat rate. Non-resident parents on other benefits (eg, incapacity benefit or retirement pension) will have deductions taken for flat rate maintenance plus £1 for arrears (if applicable).

Deductions from earnings orders

Deductions made are based on the **normal deduction rate** and the **protected earnings rate**.

Chapter 21: Collection and enforcement
6. Existing 'old rules' and conversion cases

Normal deduction rate

The normal deduction rate is the amount that will be deducted each payday as long as net earnings are not brought below the protected earnings rate. The normal deduction rate can include current maintenance liability and amounts for arrears and interest due. No arrears or interest can be included if they would have brought the non-resident parent's disposable income, on the date the current assessment was made, below the protected income level (not the protected earnings rate) *minus* the minimum payment (see p223).[240] This does not apply where the current assessment is an interim maintenance assessment (IMA – see p399). See Chapter 15 for protected income level and disposable income.

Protected earnings rate

The protected earnings rate is the level below which earnings must not be reduced by the deductions. Unless a Category A or D IMA is in force, it is set at the exempt income level (see Chapter 12).[241] Where a Category A or D IMA is in force, the protected earnings rate is either:[242]

- if the CSA knows something of the non-resident parent's circumstances:
  - the IS single or couple personal allowance;
  - the IS personal allowance for any children under 16 living with him;
  - any relevant IS premiums (see Appendix 2); *plus*
  - £30; *or*
- otherwise, the IS adult personal allowance plus £30.

Where there is no assessment in force, the protected earnings rate is the exempt income level for the last assessment. If the non-resident parent satisfies the CSA that his circumstances have since changed, the protected earnings rate is the exempt income level he would have if his assessment were superseded.[243] Where the last assessment was a Category A or C IMA, the protected earnings rate is still worked out as for IMAs.

Administering a DEO

The rules are almost identical to those described in this chapter – ie, each payday the employer:

- should make a deduction from net earnings at the normal deduction rate. Where this reduces earnings below the protected earnings rate the deduction is adjusted and the unpaid amount is carried forward to the next payday;[244]
- may deduct up to £1 as an administrative charge. This can be made even where this would bring earnings below the protected earnings rate.[245]

However, in addition to these rules, if on any payday net earnings are below the protected earnings rate, then no deduction or charge can be made. When this occurs, the difference between net earnings and protected earnings is carried over and treated as additional protected earnings on the next payday.[246] For an illustration of how this operates in practice, see Example 18.1 of the 2001/02 edition of this *Handbook*.

Where two or more DEOs have been issued, the employer should deal with the earliest first.[247]

Temporary compensation payment scheme (deferred debt)

From 31 January 2001 a temporary compensation payment scheme was introduced to allow the CSA to reduce the arrears liability of a non-resident parent in certain circumstances.[248] In CSA terminology this means that the arrears are classed as a deferred debt.

The scheme only applies where a:[249]
- maintenance assessment was made before 1 April 2005;[250] *or*
- fresh maintenance assessment was made after a section 16 periodic review and the effective date of the assessment is on or before 6 December 1998; *or*
- fresh maintenance assessment was made after a section 17 review and the effective date of the assessment is on or before 1 June 1999; *or*
- fresh maintenance assessment was made after a section 18 or section 19 review and the effective date of the assessment is on or before 1 June 1999; *or*
- departure direction was made with an effective date before 1 June 1999 and the amount of the direction is higher than the current amount; *or*
- fresh maintenance assessment was made following an appeal tribunal against a decision by a CSO with an effective date before 1 June 1999.

To qualify, the non-resident parent must:[251]
- have more than six months' arrears of which at least three are due to unreasonable delay by the CSA/Secretary of State, through act or omission;
- be paying regular maintenance via the CSA;
- have no arrears under other maintenance assessments.

In these circumstances if a non-resident parent enters and keeps to an agreement to pay regular maintenance and repay the arrears, the CSA may reduce the amount of arrears to be repaid.[252] Throughout the period of the agreement the parent is still liable for the full amount. Therefore, if the agreement were broken, recovery action would be taken for the full amount outstanding.[253] Agreements can only be made before 1 April 2005 and must expire before 1 April 2006.[254] The agreement will set out the amount, method and payment interval;[255] this may be different than that for regular maintenance. The agreement is normally set for a period of 12 months or 52 weeks, though it can be set for a shorter or longer period of time.

Staff should identify cases where the scheme applies and offer it to non-resident parents as part of their normal debt recovery procedures. Where a non-resident parent believes the scheme may apply and he has not been offered it he should contact the CSA.

Where the non-resident parent keeps to the agreement for the full period of the agreement, the CSA may make a deferred debt compensatory payment to the person with care (see p491). While technically the deferred debt is not written off it will not be enforced by the CSA.

The non-resident parent defaults

If the non-resident parent defaults on the agreement within the period of the agreement, the entire deferred debt is recharged to the account unless the default was outside the non-resident parent's control (eg, bank error) or due to exceptional circumstances.[256] These circumstances include the death of an immediate family member or the unexpected hospitalisation of the non-resident parent. Because the deferred arrears may be large, a minor default by a non-resident parent with this type of agreement could have drastic consequences for him. Therefore, if he has this type of agreement and may be unable to make a payment, he should contact the CSA as soon as possible to explain the situation.

Deferred debt compensation to person with care

Where the CSA defers recovery of arrears under the temporary compensation scheme, the CSA can compensate the person with care. This is a discretionary decision, but CSA policy is normally to pay compensation once the non-resident parent has paid current child maintenance *and* kept to agreed arrears repayments for 52 weeks.[257] This compensation is worked out as follows:
- for any period the parent with care was not on IS/income-based JSA – all the arrears;
- for any period the parent with care was on IS/income-based JSA but would not have been if maintenance had been paid when due – the amount by which maintenance would have exceeded benefit.

Where the parent with care was on family credit during the period concerned see the 1999/2000 edition of this *Handbook*. No compensation is paid for any period when the person with care would still have been entitled to IS/income-based JSA even if child maintenance had been paid when due.

Before a compensation payment is made, the person with care must sign a form agreeing that, should the non-resident parent later default on the arrears agreement, the CSA can enforce the debt against him and keep any money collected.[258] If the person with care believes that she could lose money as a result of the CSA decision on deferring the debt, then before accepting the compensation she should seek legal advice about a judicial review (see p415). She could also complain to the Independent Case Examiner (see p19). However, this compensation scheme may encourage regular payments from the non-resident parent that would not have otherwise occurred.

Chapter 21: Collection and enforcement
Notes

1. s29(1) CSA 1991
2. s30(1) CSA 1991
3. Reg 3(3A) CSF Regs as revoked by reg 4 CS(CEMA) Regs

1. Payment of child maintenance
4. Reg 3 CS(C&E) Regs
5. Reg 2 CS(C&E) Regs
6. Reg 5 CS(C&E) Regs
7. Reg 4 CS(C&E) Regs
8. Reg 5 CS(AIAMA) Regs
9. Reg 6 CS(C&E) Regs
10. Reg 7(1) CS(C&E) Regs
11. Reg 7(2) CS(C&E) Regs
12. s29 CSA 1991; reg 2 CS(C&E) Regs
13. Maintenace direct
14. Non-maintenance direct
15. s29(1)(a) CSA 1991
16. Maintenance direct
17. s29(1)(b) CSA 1991
18. Changing the collection service
19. Maintenance direct
20. CSA statistical information, January 1999
21. Reg 8 CS(AIAMA) Regs
22. Letter from DSS to CPAG, 8 March 1993
23. Reg 3(1) CS(C&E) Regs
24. Reg 3(1A) CS(C&E) Regs
25. Non-maintenance direct
26. Reg 3(2) CS(C&E) Regs
27. Reg 6 CS(C&E) Regs
28. When to make Welfare of the Child decision; How to make Welfare of the Child decision
29. Non-maintenance direct
30. Payments made through the agency; reg 5(1) CS(C&E) Regs
31. s43 CSA 1991
32. s43 CSA 1991; Sch 9B SS(C&P) Regs
33. Sch 4 para 4(2) CSA 1991; reg 4 (2) CS(MCSC) Regs
34. Reg 4(3)(a) CS(MCSC) Regs
35. Reg 4(3)(b) CS(MCSC) Regs
36. Reg 35(l) SS(C&P) Regs; Sch 9B SS(C&P) Regs
37. Reg 4(1) CS(C&E) Regs
38. Reg 4(2) CS(C&E) Regs
39. Reg 6 CS(C&E) Regs
40. Reg 5(3) CS(C&E) Regs; Payment frequencies available to the PWC
41. Collection frequencies
42. Determining payment dates
43. CSA press release, 19 March 1996; Compensation payments
44. Client account statement
45. Reg 9 CS(AIAMA) Regs
46. Reg 10(1)(a) CS(AIAMA) Regs
47. Allocation rules
48. Reg 10 CS(AIAMA) Regs; Calculating the overpayment recovery schedule (Compensating the NRP)
49. Determine reason for unexpected receipt
50. Manually allocate unexpected receipt
51. Receipt intended as a gift
52. Refunds
53. Refunds; Compensation payments
54. Reg 10(1)(b) CS(AIAMA) Regs
55. Reg 10(3A)(b) CS(AIAMA) Regs
56. Reg 10(4) CS(AIAMA) Regs
57. Reg 10(2) and (3) CS(AIAMA) Regs; reg 3A(6) and 15D CSSCS(D&A) Regs
58. Reg 11 CS(AIAMA) Regs; reg 15C(6) SS&CS(DA) Regs
59. Regs 12, 13, 14, 15 and 16 CS(AIAMA) Regs; regs 3A(6), 6A(9) and 30A SSCS(D&A) Regs
60. s 41B CSA 1991
61. s 41B(1A) CSA 1991
62. Administration error
63. Reg 10A(1) CS(AIAMA) Regs; reg 10B CS(AIAMA) Regs
64. s41B(6) CSA 1991; reg 10A(2) CS(AIAMA) Regs; Overpayment of maintenance recovery

2. Collection of other payments
65. s30 CSA 1991; CS(CEOFM) Regs
66. s30(2) CSA 1991
67. Reg 5 CS(CEOFM) Regs
68. reg 2 CS(CEOFM) Regs
69. Regs 3 and 4 CS(CEOFM) Regs
70. s30(3) CSA 1991; Allocation rules
71. Receipt received for multiple cases
72. Reg 6(3) CS(CEMA) Regs
73. Negotiating other liabilities

3. Arrears
74. Notifying the NRP of the collection schedule
75. Reg 7 CS(C&E) Regs

493

Chapter 21: Collection and enforcement
Notes

76 Arrears negotiation
77 s28J CSA 1991 as inserted by s20 CSPSSA 2000
78 Reg 3(b) CS(VP) Regs
79 Reg 3(a) CS(VP) Regs
80 Payments made to the CSA
81 Regs 2(2) and 4(b) CS(VP) Regs; Payments made to the PWC
82 Reg 4(a) CS(VP) Regs
83 Conflicting evidence
84 Reg 5(10) CS(AIAMA) Regs
85 Arrears amount
86 Arrears amount
87 Suspending debt
88 Arrears amount
89 Non-maintenance direct
90 s41(2) and (2A) CSA 1991; reg 8 CS(AIAMA) Regs
91 s43 CSA 1991; S9B SS(C&P) Regs
92 Identify late/non-payment of liability
93 Investigate late/non-payment of liability
94 Contact client to investigate late/non-payment
95 Contact client to investigate late/non payment
96 Contact client to investigate late/non-payment
97 Suspend debt
98 Reg 2 CS(AIAMA) Regs
99 Investigating late/non-payment of Liability
100 Reg 2(4) CS(AIAMA) Regs
101 Suspend debt
102 s4A CSA 1991
103 s41A(2) CSA 1991
104 Late payment penalties (paper version of procedure)
105 Reg 7A CS(C&E) Regs
106 Late payment penalties (paper version of procedure)
107 Late payment penalties (paper version of procedure)
108 Calculating the amount of a late payment penalty (paper version of procedure)
109 Late payment penalties (paper version of procedure)
110 Reg 7(1A) CS(C&E) Regs
111 Reg 15C(7 and 8) SS&CS(DA) Regs
112 Reg 7A(4) CS(C&E) Regs
113 Negotiating other liabilities
114 Advance payment of maintenance
115 Misadministration
116 Advance payment of maintenance
117 Reg 4(1) CS(AIAMA) Regs

4. **Deduction from earnings orders**
118 s31 CSA 1991
119 Non-maintenance direct
120 Considerations before imposing a DEO
121 *R v CSA for Social Security ex parte Biggin* [1995] 2 FCR 595; [1995] 1 FLR 851
122 Arrears amount
123 Employer outside CSA jurisdiction
124 Sch 1 para 10 CS(NIRA) Regs
125 CSA(CA)O; Army Act 1955; Air Force Act 1955; Naval Forces Act 1947; Merchant Shipping Act 1970
126 s31(5) CSA 1991
127 s31(6) CSA 1991
128 s31(7) CSA 1991
129 s32(8)-(11) CSA 1991
130 Reg 9 CS(C&E) Regs
131 Reg 14(1) CS(C&E) Regs
132 Reg 14(2) CS(C&E) Regs
133 s32(8) and (11) CSA 1991; reg 25(aa) CS(C&E) Regs
134 Reg 1(3)(b) CS(C&E) Regs
135 s32(8) and (11) CSA 1991; reg 25(ab) and (b) CS(C&E) Regs
136 Reg 15(1) CS(C&E) Regs
137 Reg 15(2) CS(C&E) Regs
138 Reg 16(1) CS(C&E) Regs
139 Reg 16(2) CS(C&E) Regs
140 Reg 16(3) CS(C&E) Regs
141 Reg 13 CS(C&E) Regs
142 s8(2)(b) ERA 1996
143 s9 ERA 1996
144 s12(3)-(5) ERA 1996
145 Reg 8(3) and (4) CS(C&E) Regs
146 Reg 8(4)(a) CS(C&E) Regs
147 Reg 8(4)(b) CS(C&E) Regs
148 Reg 8(4)(f) CS(C&E) Regs
149 Reg 8(5) CS(C&E) Regs
150 Reg 9 CS(C&E) Regs
151 Regs 10(1) and 11(1) CS(C&E) Regs
152 Reg 9(d) CS(C&E) Regs
153 Reg 11(2) CS(C&E) Regs
154 Reg 12(6) CS(C&E) Regs
155 Reg 12(20) CS(C&E) Regs
156 Reg 12(4) CS(C&E) Regs
157 Reg 12(3A) CS(C&E) Regs
158 Reg 24(2)(a) CS(C&E) Regs
159 Reg 24(2)(b) CS(C&E) Regs
160 Regs 24(2)(a) and (3) CS(C&E) Regs
161 Reg 17 CS(C&E) Regs
162 Reg 18 CS(C&E) Regs
163 Reg 19 CS(C&E) Regs
164 Reg 20(1) CS(C&E) Regs
165 Reg 20(2) CS(C&E) Regs
166 Reg 21(1) CS(C&E) Regs
167 Reg 21(4) CS(C&E) Regs
168 Reg 21(5) CS(C&E) Regs
169 Reg 21(6) CS(C&E) Regs

Chapter 21: Collection and enforcement
Notes

170 Reg 22(1) CS(C&E) Regs
171 Reg 22(2) CS(C&E) Regs
172 Reg 22(3) CS(C&E) Regs
173 Reg 8(1) 'defective' CS(C&E) Regs
174 Rule 5 and form 6 AS(CSR)
175 Reg 22(4) CS(C&E) Regs
176 s32(6) CSA 1991
177 *Secretary of State for Social Security v Shotton* [1996] 2 FLR 241
178 ss48 and 49 CSA 1991; rule 6 AS(CSR)

5. Enforcement
179 Deciding if debt enforcement action is appropriate
180 Enforcement action not appropriate
181 Applying for a liability order
182 *DSS v Butler* [1995] 1 WLR 1528; [1995] 4 All ER 193
183 When to consider Welfare of the Child
184 Enforcement referral criteria
185 Reg 28(2) CS(C&E) Regs
186 s33 CSA 1991
187 s33(3) CSA 1991
188 s33(4) CSA 1991
189 HC Hansard, 2 February 1996, col 990
190 Reg 29 CS(C&E) Regs; rule 3 AS(CSR)
191 ss48 and 49 CSA 1991; rule 6 AS(CSR)
192 Reg 27 CS(C&E) Regs
193 NRP responds to the warning letter
194 Reg 28 CS(C&E) Regs
195 NRP responds to the warning letter
196 Reg 29(1) and Sch 1 CS(C&E) Regs
197 *Secretary of State for Social Security v Love* [1996] SLT 78
198 Rule 2 AS(CSR)
199 *Secretary of State for Social Security v Nicol* [1996] SLT 34
200 Forms 1-4 AS(CSR)
201 s35 CSA 1991
202 Reg 30(2) CS(C&E) Regs
203 Reg 30(4) and (5) CS(C&E) Regs
204 s35(3) and (4) CSA 1991
205 Reg 32 and Sch 2 CS(C&E) Regs
206 Reg 31 CS(C&E) Regs
207 s33(5) CSA 1991
208 s36 CSA 1991
209 ss38(1)(a) and 58(9) CSA 1991
210 Rule 4 and form 5 AS(CSR)
211 s38(1)(b) CSA 1991
212 Abolition of Poindings and Warrant Sales Act 2001
213 s39A CSA 1991
214 Is committal or disqualification from driving action appropriate
215 Deciding not to apply for committal to prison/Driving Licence Action
216 s40(1)-(11) CSA 1991; s39A(2) CSA 1991
217 s39A(3) CSA 1991
218 Reg 35(1) CS(C&E) Regs
219 s40(11) CSA 1991
220 s39A(4) CSA 1991
221 s39A(3) CSA 1991; Court hearing
222 s40A(1) CSA 1991
223 s40(5) and s40A(3) CSA 1991
224 s40(11) CSA 1991; s40A(8) CSA 1991; reg 35(2) CS(C&E) Regs
225 ss48 and 49 CSA 1991
226 ss40 and 40B CSA 1991
227 s40(5) and s40A(3) CSA 1991
228 s40(3) and s40B(1) CSA 1991
229 Sch 3 CS(C&E) Regs
230 s40(7) and s40A(5) CSA 1991
231 Reg 34(5) and (6) CS(C&E) Regs
232 Partial payment received committal/DFD proceedings; reg 35(3) CS(C&E) Regs
233 s40B CSA 1991
234 Reg 35(4)-(5) and Sch 4 CS(C&E) Regs
235 s40B(1) CSA 1991
236 s40B(5) CSA 1991
237 s40(7) CSA 1991
238 Bankruptcy England &Wales; Sequestration in Scotland
239 Is a warrant to imprison or an order for disqualification from driving appropriate

6. Existing 'old rules' and conversion cases
240 Reg 10 CS(C&E) Regs
241 Reg 11(2) CS(C&E) Regs
242 Reg 11(3) CS(C&E) Regs
243 Reg 11(4) CS(C&E) Regs
244 Reg 12(4) CS(C&E) Regs
245 Reg 12(2) CS(C&E) Regs
246 Reg 12(5) CS(C&E) Regs
247 Reg 24(1) CS(C&E) Regs
248 Reg 2(2) CSPSSA(Comm 13)O
249 s27 CSPSSA 2000 as modified by reg 2 CS(TCPS)(MA) Regs; reg 2 CS(TCPS) Regs
250 Reg 3 CS(TCPS) Regs as amended by reg 3 CS(TCPS)(MA) Regs
251 Reg 4 CS(TCPS) Regs
252 s27(3) CSPSSA 2000
253 s27(8) CSPSSA 2000
254 s27(5) CSPSSA 2000 as modified by reg 2 CS(TCPS)(MA) Regs
255 Reg 5 CS(TCPS) Regs
256 Missed payment exceptions
257 Deferred debt payable
258 Deferred debt payable – NRP compliant

Appendices

// Appendices

Appendix 1
Useful addresses

Child Support Agency (CSA)

Chief Executive
Doug Smith
Child Support Agency, DWP
Benton Park Road
Longbenton BP6201
Newcastle upon Tyne NE98 1YX
Tel: 0191 225 7743
Fax: 0191 225 3461

Face-to-face officers are in post at a number of sites within each of the Business Unit areas. Anyone wanting to arrange an interview should contact their Child Support Agency Centre (CSAC) to arrange an appointment.

Child Support Agency Centres (CSACs)

Hastings CSAC
(South East Business Unit)
Ashdown House
Sedlescombe Road North
Hastings
East Sussex TN37 7NL

Field operations (South East)
Offices covered:
Brixton, Lewisham, Hastings, Eastbourne, Tunbridge Wells, London Highgate, Ealing, Croydon, Bromley, Ilford, Canterbury, Edmonton, Colchester, Basildon, Gravesend

Plymouth CSAC
(South West Business Unit)
Clearbrook House
Towerfield Drive
Bickleigh Down Business Park
Plymouth
Devon PL6 7TN

Field operations (South West)
Offices covered:
Barnstaple, Basingstoke, Bristol East, Plymouth Crownhill, Exeter, Gloucester, Guildford, Hounslow, Isle of Wight, Poole, Portsmouth, Redhill, Southampton, Swindon, Taunton, Truro, Weymouth, Worthing

Dudley CSAC
(Midlands Business Unit)
Pedmore House
The Waterfront
Level Street
Brierley Hill
Dudley
West Midlands DY5 1XA
Postal address
2 Weston Road
Crewe CW98 1BD

Field operations (Midlands)
Offices covered:
Aylesbury, Birmingham Ladywood, Chester, Hanley, Lichfield, Stockport, West Bromwich, Worcester, Banbury, Milton Keynes, Shrewsbury, Telford

499

Appendix 1: Useful Addresses

Birkenhead CSAC
(Wales and North West Business Unit)
Great Western House
Woodside Ferry Approach
Birkenhead
Merseyside CH41 6RG
Postal address
2 Weston Road
Crewe CW98 1BD

Field operations (Wales and North West)
Offices covered:
NORTH WEST: Accrington, Ashton, Barrow-in-Furness, Birkenhead North, Blackpool North, Bolton, Burnley, Bury, Carlisle, Liverpool Cunard, Liverpool Huyton, Kendal, Liverpool Kirkby, Lancaster, Leigh, Liverpool City, Oldham, Penrith, Preston, Salford, Skelmersdale, Southport, St Helens, Whitehaven, Workington
WALES: Aberystwyth, Barry, Bridgend, Caernarfon, Caerphilly, Cardiff East, Cardiff West, Colwyn Bay, Cwmbran, Dolgellau, Ebbw Vale, Haverfordwest, Holyhead, Merthyr Tydfil, Newport, Newtown, Pontypridd, Rhyl, Swansea, Wrexham

Belfast CSAC (GB)

(Eastern Business Unit)
Great Northern Tower
17 Great Victoria Street
Belfast
Northern Ireland BT2 7AD

Field operations (Eastern)
Offices covered:
Ipswich, Lowestoft, Cambridge, Peterborough, Great Yarmouth, King's Lynn, Norwich, St Albans, Watford, Northampton, Wellingborough, Loughborough, Leicester – Yeoman Street, Leicester – Wellington Street, Nottingham David Lane, Lincoln, Grantham, Sutton-in-Ashfield, Sheffield, Doncaster, Rotherham, Barnsley, Huddersfield, Dewsbury, Bradford West, Halifax, Keighley, Hull West, Scarborough, Pontefract, Scunthorpe, Grimsby

Falkirk CSAC
(Scotland and North East England Business Unit)
Parklands
Callendar Business Park
Callendar Road
Falkirk FK1 1XT

Field operations – abolished

Local rate telephone lines

National enquiry line   08457 133133
(for general enquires on
CSA legislation and procedures)
Hastings CSAC   08456 090052
Plymouth CSAC   08456 090072
Dudley CSAC   08456 090062
Birkenhead CSAC   08456 090062
Belfast (GB) CSAC   08456 090092
Belfast (NI) CSAC   08456 080022
Falkirk CSAC   08456 090042
Welsh language
enquiry line   08457 138091

The Appeals Service (TAS)

The President
HH Judge Michael Harris
5th Floor
Fox Court
14 Grays Inn Road
London WC1 8HN
Tel: 020 7712 2600
www.appeals-service.gov.uk

Appendix 1: Useful Addresses

TAS Regional chairs

North East
Mr J W Tinnion
3rd Floor
York House
York Place
Leeds LS1 2ED
Tel: 0113 251 9500

North West
Mr Nick Warren
36 Dale Street
Liverpool L2 5UZ
Tel 0151 243 1400

South East
Mr R G Smithson
Copthall House
9 The Pavement
Grove Road
Sutton
Surrey SM1 1DA
Tel 020 8710 2900

Midlands and East Anglia
Mr R Martin
The Pearson Building
57 Upper Parliament Street
Nottingham NG1 6AZ
Tel 0115 909 3600

Wales and South West
Mr C B Stephens
Oxford House
Hills Street
The Hayes
Cardiff CF10 2DR
Tel 029 208 77200

Scotland
Mr W M Walker QC
Wellington House
134-136 Wellington Street
Glasgow G2 2XL
Tel 0141 354 8400

Offices of the Social Security and Child Support Commissioners

England and Wales
3rd Floor Procession House
55 Ludgate Hill
London EC4A 7JW
www.osscsc.gov.uk

Scotland
23 Melville Street
Edinburgh EH3 7PW
Tel: 0131 225 2201

Northern Ireland
1st Floor, Headline
10-14 Victoria Street
Belfast BT1 3GG
Tel: 028 9072 8731

Independent Case Examiner

PO Box 155
Chester CH99 9SA
Tel: 0151 801 8800
Minicom: 0151 801 8888
www.ind-case-exam.org.uk

Appendix 2
Income support premiums

Premiums are added to income support (IS) personal allowances and are intended to help with the extra expenses caused by age, disability or the cost of children. The premiums are used in the child support formula irrespective of whether the parent is in receipt of IS, although not all apply at each stage (the bereavement premium does not apply).

Family premium	£15.95
Disabled child premium	£42.49
Carer premium (per carer)	£25.55
Disability premium	
Single	£23.70
Couple	£33.85*
Severe disability premium	
One qualifies	£44.15
Two qualify	£88.30*
Enhanced disability	
Single	£11.60
Couple	£16.75
Child	£17.08
Pensioner	
Single (JSA only)	£49.80*
Couple	£73.65*

*These amounts are only ever used at the protected income stage.

Family premium

A person is entitled to this if her/his family includes a child, even if s/he is not the child's parent and that child has capital over £3,000. For IS purposes, a family includes a child where the claimant or partner receives child benefit for a child living in the same household. However, for child support purposes, a child is taken to be a member of the household where the adult has 'day-to-day care' of that child. If a child does not live in the household full time, a proportion of the family premium can be included in exempt income and protected income (see Chapter 16). Only one family premium is payable regardless of the number of children a person has.

The (transitional) lone-parent rate of family premium is not used in the child support calculation.

Where a child who is in the care of or being looked after by a local authority, or who is in custody, comes home for part of a week, a proportion of the premium is payable, according to the number of days the child is at home.

Disabled child premium

A person is entitled to a disabled child premium for each child who gets disability living allowance (DLA) or who is blind. A child is treated as blind if s/he is registered as blind and for the first 28 weeks after s/he has been taken off the register on regaining her/his sight. For how to qualify for DLA, see CPAG's *Welfare Benefits and Tax Credits Handbook*.

If DLA has stopped because the child is in hospital, this premium continues. But if the child ceases to be treated as a member of your family, the premium stops after 12 weeks. See CPAG's *Welfare Benefits and Tax Credits Handbook* for more details. If the child does not live in the household full time, a proportion of the premium is in exempt income and in protected income (see Chapter 16).

If a child has over £3,000 capital, there is no entitlement to this premium.

Carer premium

A person qualifies for this if s/he or her/his partner is getting carer's allowance (CA), or would get it but for the overlapping benefit rules – ie, because s/he is receiving another benefit paid at a higher rate. For example, a woman getting CA who at 60 is awarded retirement pension at a higher rate than CA, continues to qualify for the premium as long as the person being cared for continues to get the higher or middle-rate care component of DLA, or attendance allowance (AA).

A double premium is awarded where both the person concerned and her/his partner satisfy the conditions for it.

See CPAG's *Welfare Benefits and Tax Credits Handbook* for more details on the premium and conditions of entitlement for CA.

Disability premium

A person can get a disability premium if s/he is under 60 and one of the following applies to her/him (note that in the exempt income step of the child support formula, the age rule does not apply). S/he:
- is getting a qualifying benefit. These are DLA (or an equivalent benefit paid to meet attendance needs because of an injury at work or a war injury), disability or severe disability element of working tax credit, war pensioner's mobility supplement, incapacity benefit paid at the long-term rate or when terminally ill, or severe disablement allowance (SDA). A person or her/his partner must be getting the benefit for her/himself, not on behalf of someone else – eg, as a parent or an appointee. In some situations, entitlement to the premium continues after the person stops receiving the qualifying benefit – see CPAG's *Welfare Benefits and Tax Credits Handbook*;

Appendix 2: Income support premiums

- is registered as blind with a local authority (England and Wales) or regional or Islands council (Scotland); if sight is regained, s/he will still qualify for 28 weeks after s/he is taken off the register;
- has an NHS invalid trike or private car allowance because of disability;
- is 'incapable of work' (or exempt from the 'all-work test') and either entitled to statutory sick pay or has been incapable for at least:

196 days if certified as 'terminally ill' – ie, it can reasonably be expected that s/he will die within six months due to a progressive disease;

364 days in all other cases, provided s/he has claimed incapacity benefit (it is not necessary to send in medical certificates).

Breaks in incapacity/entitlement of up to 56 days (52 weeks if a 'welfare to work beneficiary') are included in these periods. For more on 'incapacity for work', see CPAG's *Welfare Benefits and Tax Credits Handbook*.

At the protected income stage of the child support calculation, couples will get the disability premium at the couple rate provided either of them qualifies under one of the first three of the above rules. But they will only get the premium under the last condition if the person who qualifies is the parent being assessed for child maintenance.

Pensioner premium

There are three pensioner premiums, all paid at the same rate:
- the pensioner premium if a person or her/his partner is aged 60-74 inclusive;
- pensioner premium (also known as an enhanced pensionr premium) if a person or her/his partner is 75-79 inclusive;
- higher pensioner premium if a person or her/his partner is aged over 80 or satifies other conditions detailed below.

Each of these can be paid at a couple rate if one partner fulfils the age condition. If a person or her/his partner is sick or disabled, check to see if the higher pensioner premium described below applies.

Enhanced disability premium

The enhanced disability premium applies if the person or a member of his/her family receives the highest rate of the DLA care component and is aged under 60.
The following people cannot qualify:
- children or young people with more than £3,000 in capital;
- a claimant who has been a hospital inpatient for more than six weeks; *or*
- either member of a couple, where each member of the couple has been a hospital inpatient for more than 52 weeks.

Higher pensioner premium

A person can get this if one of the following applies:
- a person or her/his partner is 80 or over; *or*

- a person was getting a disability premium as part of her/his IS at some time during the eight weeks (52 weeks for 'welfare to work beneficiaries') before s/he was 60 and has continued to get IS since the age of 60 (breaks of up to eight (or 52) weeks are ignored). Couples can qualify under this rule regardless of which partner meets the condition; *or*
- a person or her/his partner is aged 60-79 *and* either of them receives a qualifying benefit (as for the disability premium but including AA), is registered blind, or has an NHS trike or private car allowance. If a person stops getting IB or SDA to change to retirement pension, the higher pensioner premium still applies if there is a continuous entitlement (apart from breaks of eight weeks (52 weeks for welfare to work beneficiaries) or less) to IS.

Severe disability premium

The conditions for receipt are:
- a person is receiving AA (or the equivalent war pension or industrial injury benefit), or the higher or middle-rate care component of DLA (or extra-statutory payments to compensate for not receiving any of these). If s/he is part of a couple, they must both be getting one of these benefits or the partner who does not get AA/DLA must be registered or treated as blind; *and*
- no non-dependant aged 18 or over is living with her/him (see below); *and*
- no one is getting CA for looking after her/him.

A couple where both are severely disabled only get the single rate if someone is getting CA in respect of one of them or one of them qualifies only because they are registered or treated as blind.

Non-dependants aged 18 or over
The following people living with a person do not count:
- a partner (but s/he must be getting AA/DLA or be blind);
- anyone aged under 18;
- anyone staying in a person's home who normally lives elsewhere;
- a person (who may be her/his partner) employed by a charitable or voluntary body as a resident carer for a person or her/his partner if s/he pays for that service (even if the charge is only nominal);
- a person receiving AA or the higher or middle-rate care component of DLA;
- a person who is registered blind or treated as blind;
- a person, or her/his partner, who jointly occupies her/his home and is either a co-owner with the person or her/his partner, or jointly liable with them to make payments to a landlord in respect of occupying it;
- a person, or any member of her/his household, who is liable to pay on a commercial basis for occupying the dwelling (eg, tenant or licensee), unless s/he is a close relative;

Appendix 2: Income support premiums

- a person, or any member of her/his household, to whom a person or her/his partner is liable to make such payments on a commercial basis, unless s/he is a close relative.

If someone (other than those listed above) comes to live with a person in order to look after her/him or her/his partner, her/his severe disability premium will only remain in payment for the first 12 weeks.

For more detail of these rules, see CPAG's *Welfare Benefits and Tax Credits Handbook*.

Appendix 3
Child support 'old rules' formula

You do not have to do a calculation if the non-resident parent is on income support (IS) or income-based jobseeker's allowance (JSA).

The calculation is based on IS rates; the 2004/05 amounts are given at each stage. See pxii for the IS personal allowances for dependent children.

Calculation sheet 1 (see Chapter 11)
Step 1: Maintenance requirement
If the non-resident parent has to pay more than one person with care for different children, this step has to be carried out separately for each person with care.

Personal allowances
Adult:*   £55.65 if at least one of the children is under 11 years old
   or   £44.05 if at least one of the children is 11–13 years old
   or   £33.50 if at least one of the children is 14–15 years old
Children of the non-resident parent living with the person with care

Name _____   _____

Name _____   _____

Name _____   _____

Name _____   _____

Family premium* (£15.95)
Sub total
minus child benisit   − _____

MAINTENANCE REQUIREMENT   Box A
If both parents are non-resident and the person with care is only
applying for maintenance from one of the non-resident parents,
the maintenance requirement is halved:
                                                            Alternative Box A

*This is reduced if the person with care looks after children who have different non-resident parents

Appendix 3: Child support 'old rules' formula

Calculation sheet 2 (see Chapter 12)

Step 2: Exempt income of non-resident parent

If the parent has care of children for part of the week only, see Chapter 16.

Personal allowances
Parent £55.65

Children living with parent* (only count the parent's own child)

Name _____ _____

Name _____ _____

Name _____ _____

Premiums (if eligible – see Appendix 2)

Family* (£15.95) _____

Disabled child premium* (£42.49) _____

Disability premium (£23.70) _____

Enhanced disability (child) (£17.80) _____

Enhanced disability (adult) (£11.60) _____

Carer premium (£25.55) _____

Severe disability premium (£44.15) _____

Housing costs _____

Allowance for pre-April 1993 property settlement _____

Allowance towards travel-to-work costs _____

EXEMPT INCOME [   ] Box B

*These amounts may be halved if the child's other parent is the non-resident parent's partner and she can afford to help maintain the joint child

Appendix 3: Child support 'old rules' formula

CALCULATION SHEET 2 (CONTINUED)

Step 2: Exempt income of parent with care

Do not do this step if the parent with care is on IS, income-based JSA or working tax credit (WTC)
If the parent has care of any child for part of the week only, see Chapter 16.

Personal allowances

Parent £55.65

Children living with parent* (only count the parent's own child)

Name _____   _____

Name _____   _____

Name _____   _____

Name _____   _____

Name _____   _____

Premiums (if eligible)   _____

Family (£15.95)   _____

Disabled child premium* (£42.49)   _____

Disability premium (£23.70)   _____

Enhanced disability (child) (£17.80)   _____

Enhanced disability (adult) (£11.60)   _____

Carer premium (£25.55)   _____

Severe disability premium (£44.15)   _____

Housing costs   _____

Allowance towards travel-to-work costs   _____

EXEMPT INCOME   [   ]   Box C

*These amounts may be halved for any joint children of the parent and her partner, if the partner can afford to help maintain the joint child

Note: an allowance for a pre-April 1993 property settlement is included only where the parent with care was the non-resident parent at the time of the settlement.

Appendix 3: Child support 'old rules' formula

Calculation sheet 3 (see Chapter 13)

Step 3: Assessable income

Do not include income of any partner.

Non-resident parent		Parent with care (Do not do this if the parent with care is on IS/JSA/WTC – her assessable income is nil.)	
Net earnings	_____	Net earnings	_____
Income from benefits	_____	Income from benefits	_____
Income from capital	_____	Income from capital	_____
Other income	_____	Other income	_____
Children's income	_____	Children's income	_____
Net income	☐ Box D	**Net income**	☐ Box E
minus exempt income – (from Box B)	_____	minus exempt income – (from Box C)	_____
NON-RESIDENT PARENT'S ASSESSABLE INCOME	☐ Box F	**PARENT WITH CARE'S ASSESSABLE INCOME**	☐ Box G

If the non-resident parent has to pay maintenance to more than one person with care, the assessable income carried forward to step 4 is apportioned between the persons with care.

If the parent with care is claiming maintenance from more than one non-resident parent, the assessable income carried forward to step 4 is apportioned between the absent parents' calculations.

Calculation sheet 4 (see Chapter 14)

Step 4: Proposed maintenance

This is the amount which the non-resident parent will pay unless it is reduced by the protected income calculation (step 5).

If the non-resident parent has to pay maintenance to more than one person with care for different children, this step has to be carried out separately for each person with care using a proportion of assessable income.

If the non-resident parent looks after the child(ren) for part of the time, see Chapter 16.

To decide whether the 50% calculation applies:

Maintenance requirement	Box A
Non-resident parent's assessable income	Box F
Parent with care's assessable income	Box G

(if both parents are absent, include the other non-resident parent's assessable income in Box G)

Joint assessable income: add Box F and Box G	Box H
50% Box H equals	Box I

If Box I is smaller than (or equal to) Box A, do the 50% calculation

If Box I is larger than Box A, do the additional element calculation

50% calculation:

Proposed maintenance equals 50% Box F	Box J(i)

Now go to step 5 (unless proposed maintenance is £5.30 or less.

Appendix 3: Child support 'old rules' formula

CALCULATION SHEET 4 (CONTINUED)
Additional element calculation for proposed maintenance:

Basic element = ☐ × ☐ Box F = ☐
                Box A   Box H   Box K

Basic assessable income = ☐ × 2 = ☐
                         Box K   Box L

Additional assessable income = ☐ − ☐ = ☐
                               Box F   Box L   Box M

Additional element = ☐ × %* = ☐
                    Box M   Box N

* use 15% if there is one qualifying child, 20% if there are two, or 25% if there are three or more.

Proposed maintenance = ☐ + ☐ = ☐
                      Box K   Box N   Box J(ii)

Check this figure is below maximum   ☐
                                                Box J(iii)

The proposed maintenance is the smaller of the figures in Box J(ii) and Box J(iii)

Now go to step 5.

Appendix 3: Child support 'old rules' formula

Calculation sheet 5 (see Chapter 15)

Step 5: Protected income of non-resident parent

5a: Thirty per cent cap

Proposed maintenance from step 4 ☐ Box J(i), J(ii) or J(iii)

30% non-resident parent's net income ☐ × 30% = ☐ Box O
    Box D

Put whichever of Box J or Box O is lower into Box P
☐ Box P

5b: Basic protected income
If the non-resident parent has care of a child for part of the time, see Chapter 16.

Personal allowances
Single (£55.65) or couple (£87.30)

Children (all in the family)

Name _____ _____

Name _____ _____

Name _____ _____

Name _____ _____

Premiums
Family (£15.95) _____

Disabled child premium* (£42.49) _____

Disability premium (£23.70) _____

Enhanced disability (child) (£17.80) _____

Enhanced disability (adult) (£11.60) _____

Carer premium (£25.55) _____

Severe disability premium (£44.15) _____

Any applicable pensioner premium _____

Housing costs _____

Council tax (minus any CTB) _____

Travel-to-work costs _____

Standard margin £30.00

BASIC PROTECTED INCOME ☐ Box Q

Appendix 3: Child support 'old rules' formula

CALCULATION SHEET 5 (CONTINUED)
5c: Total family income

Non-resident parent's net income (Box D)*	_____
Partner's net income	_____
Child Tax Credit	_____
Child benefit	_____
TOTAL FAMILY INCOME	[ ] Box R

* Note that the rules about children's income are different and therefore an adjustment may need to be made.

5d: Total protected income

Excess family income = [ ] Box R − [ ] Box Q = [ ] Box S

Additional protected income = 15% of [ ] Box S = [ ] Box T

plus basic protected income (Box Q) + _____

TOTAL PROTECTED INCOME [ ] Box V

5e: Income above total protected level

Total family income (Box R)	_____
minus total protected income (Box V)	− _____
	[ ] Box W

5f: Maintenance payable

The maintenance payable is the smaller of Box P and Box W.

If the figure is less than £5.50, the non-resident parent pays the minimum payment of £5.50 a week (unless he is exempt).

Appendix 4
Statutes

A man is assumed to be the father of a child for child support purposes if he was found to be the father by a court in England or Wales in proceedings under:

section 42 of the National Assistance Act 1948
Affiliation Proceedings Act 1957
section 6 of the Family Law Reform Act 1969
Guardianship of Minors Act 1971
Children Act 1975
Child Care Act 1980
Children Act 1989
section 26 of the Social Security Act 1986
section 4 of the Family Law Reform Act 1987
section 105 of the Social Security Administration Act 1992

A maintenance order only prevents a section 4 or 7 application to the CSA if it was made in proceedings under:

Conjugal Rights (Scotland) Amendment Act 1861
Court of Session Act 1868
Sheriff Courts (Scotland) Act 1907
Guardianship of Infants Act 1925
Illegitimate Children (Scotland) Act 1930
Children and Young Persons (Scotland) Act 1932
Children and Young Persons (Scotland) Act 1937
Custody of Children (Scotland) Act 1939
National Assistance Act 1948
Affiliation Orders Act 1952
Affiliation Proceedings Act 1957
Guardianship of Minors Act 1971
Part II of the Matrimonial Causes Act 1973
Guardianship Act 1973
Children Act 1975
Supplementary Benefits Act 1976

Appendix 4: Statutes

Domestic Proceedings and Magistrates' Courts Act 178
Part II of the Matrimonial and Family Proceedings Act 1984
Family Law (Scotland) Act 1985
Schedule 1 to the Children Act 1989
Social Security Act 1986
Social Security Administration Act 1992

The court order usually states the legal provisions under which it was made.

Appendix 5
Information and advice

It is often difficult for unsupported individuals to get a positive response from the Child Support Agency (CSA). You may be more successful if you have taken advice about your rights or have an adviser assisting you. The following agencies may be able to help.
- Citizens Advice Bureaux (CABx) and other local advice centres provide information and may be able to represent you.
- Law centres can often help in a similar way to CABx or advice centres.
- Solicitors can give free legal advice to people on low incomes under the 'Legal help' or 'Claim 10' scheme. This does not cover the cost of representation at an appeal hearing but can cover the cost of preparing written submissions and obtaining evidence such as medical reports. However, solicitors do not always have a good working knowledge of the child support rules and you may need to shop around until you find one who does.
- Local authority welfare rights workers provide an advice and representation service for benefit claimants in many areas.
- Lone parent organisations may offer help and advice about child support. For details of your local group contact: Gingerbread (020 7336 8183); Single Parent Action Network (0117 951 4231); National Council for One Parent Families (0800 785026); One Parent Families Scotland (0131 556 3899).
- There are some local groups campaigning against the child support scheme who may be able to provide advice; for further details, write to NACSA News, PO Box 3159, Fishermead, Milton Keynes MK6 2YB.
- Many trade unions provide advice to members on child support.
- Local organisations for particular groups may offer help — eg, unemployed centres, claimants' unions, centres for people with disabilities.

If details of these agencies are not in the telephone book, the local library should have more information. Alternatively, CSA clients can write to the Child Support Practitioners' Group, c/o James Pirrie, The Family Law Consortium, 2 Henrietta Street, London WC2E 8PS for a list of advisers working in the field.

Representation at appeal tribunals

Some parents have been finding it difficult to obtain representation at appeal hearings. Although many parents, especially with the help of Chapter 20, will be perfectly able to present their own cases, it can be invaluable to obtain objective

Appendix 5: Information and advice

independent advice which draws on the legislation. An advice centre which has a copy of the legislation (see Appendix 6) and experience of representing at tribunals in other sorts of cases (eg, social security) should be able to provide a representative for a child support appeal to an appeal tribunal. Advisers can join the Child Support Practitioners' Group (see p517) for support and information.

Child Poverty Action Group

Unfortunately, CPAG is a small organisation and is unable to deal with enquiries either from advisers or directly from members of the public. Please do find local advice as we are unable to respond to individuals' enquiries.

CPAG runs training courses on child support. You can find useful information on our website (www.cpag.org.uk).

Appendix 6
Books and reports

Many of the books listed here will be in a main public library.

1. Legislation
Available from CPAG (including Sweet & Maxwell books if you are a CPAG member). See p521 for ordering information.

Child Support: The Legislation
E Jacobs and G Douglas (Sweet & Maxwell). The 6th edition main volume is available from September 2004, £72.

Welfare Benefits and Tax Credits CD-ROM
(CPAG) Includes: all social security legislation consolidated; tax credits legislation; over 1,900 commissioners' decisions, most with commentary; guidance; the *Welfare Benefits and Tax Credits Handbook* with links to the relevant legislation, decisions and guidance; CPAG's *Housing Benefit and Council Tax Benefit Legislation* (with commentary); significant housing benefit and council tax benefit circulars; transcripts of High Court judgments; the *Child Support Handbook* and child support regulations. Updated three times a year. Free trial disks are available from CPAG. The single user price for 2004, including updates, is £274 + VAT. Phone Liz Dawson on 020 7812 5212 for multi-user prices.

Social Security Legislation, Volume I: Non-Means-Tested Benefits
D Bonner, I Hooker and R White (Sweet & Maxwell). Legislation with commentary. 2004/2005 edition available from October 2004, £72.

Social Security Legislation, Volume II: Income Support, Jobseeker's Allowance, Pension Credit and the Social Fund
J Mesher, P Wood, R Poynter, N Wikeley and D Bonner (Sweet & Maxwell). Legislation with commentary. 2004/2005 edition available from October 2004, £72.

Social Security Legislation, Volume III: Administration, Adjudication and the European Dimension
M Rowland and R White (Sweet & Maxwell). Legislation with commentary. 2004/2005 edition available from October 2004, £72.

Social Security Legislation, Volume IV: Tax Credits and Employer-Paid Social Security Benefits
N Wikeley and D Williams (Sweet & Maxwell). Legislation with commentary. 2004/2005 edition available from October 2004, £72.

Social Security Legislation – updating supplement to Volumes I, II, III & IV
(Sweet & Maxwell) The March 2005 update to the 2004/2005 main volumes, £47.

CPAG's Housing Benefit and Council Tax Benefit Legislation
L Findlay, S Wright, C George and R Poynter (CPAG). Contains legislation with a detailed commentary. 2004/2005 edition (17th) available from December 2004, priced at £89 including Supplement. The 16th edition (2003/2004) is still available at £85 per set. This publication is also on the *Welfare Benefits and Tax Credits CD-ROM* (see above).

2. Periodicals

The *Welfare Rights Bulletin* is published every two months by CPAG. It covers developments in social security and tax credits law and updates CPAG's *Welfare Benefits and Tax Credits Handbook*. The annual subscription is £29 but it is sent automatically to CPAG Rights and Comprehensive members. For subscription and membership details cpntact CPAG. Many features of the *Bulletin* are also reproduced on the Welfare benefits & Tax Credits CD-ROM.

3. Child Support Agency publications

For guidance issued to CSA staff, see Appendix 7.

CSA leaflets and most other CSA publications can be obtained from the CSA National Enquiry line: 08457 133 133. The leaflet, *For Parents Who Live Apart*, is available in braille and on audio cassette, and in 13 languages.

CSA Charter (CSA 2047), November 1996

CSA Business Plan, CSA

CSA Performance Statistics are placed in the House of Commons library on a quarterly basis and can be obtained via an MP (these are different statistics from those published by the Government Statistical Service – see below).

4. Other publications – child support

This section lists only those publications referred to in footnotes. See the 1996/97 edition, Appendix 7, for other reports on child support.

Enquiries concerning HMSO and Stationery Office publications can be made on 0870 6005522 and orders can be fax on 0870 6005533.

White Paper, *Children Come First*, Volume 1, HMSO, October 1990

White Paper, *Children Come First*, Volume 2, HMSO, October 1990

White Paper, *Improving Child Support*, Cm 2745, HMSO, January 1995

House of Commons Social Security Committee, *The Performance and Operation of the Child Support Agency*, Second Report – Session 1995/96, HC 50, HMSO, 24 January 1996

House of Commons Social Security Committee, *Child Support: good cause and the benefit penalty*, Fourth Report – Session 1995/96, HC 440, HMSO, 26 June 1996 (£13.60)

Reply by the Government to the Fourth Report from the Select Committee on Social Security, Session 1995/96, Cm 3449, The Stationery Office, October 1996 (£1.55)

House of Commons Social Security Committee, *Child Support*, Fifth Report – Session 1996/97, HC 282, The Stationery Office, 12 March 1997 (£8)

House of Commons, Committee of Public Accounts, Child Support Agency: Client Funds Account 1996/97, Twenty-first Report – Session 1997/98, HC 313, The Stationery Office, 23 February 1998 (£8)

Appendix 6: Books and reports

Parliamentary Commissioner for Administration, Third Report – Session 1994/95, *Investigation of Complaints against the Child Support Agency*, HC 135, HMSO, 18 January 1995

Child Support Agency Annual Report and Accounts, 1996/97, HC 124, HMSO, 22 July 1997 (£16)

Parliamentary Commissioner for Administration, Third Report – Session 1995/96, *Investigation of Complaints against the Child Support Agency*, HC 20, HMSO, 6 March 1996

Annual Report of the Chief Child Support Officer, Central Adjudication Services, 1996/97, Stationery Office, October 1997 (£13)

The Requirement to Co-operate: a report on the operation of the 'good cause' provisions, DSS Social Research Branch, In-house report 14, April 1996

DSS Research Report No. 51, *Child Support Agency National Client Satisfaction Survey 1996*, HMSO (£22). (The 1993 and 1994 surveys are Research Report No. 29 and No. 39 respectively.)

DSS Research Report No 74, *Customer Views on Service Delivery in the Child Support Agency* (1998), Stationery Office (£27)

Child Support Agency Quarterly Summary of Statistics, DSS Analytical Services Division, Government Statistical Service (£5 a quarter)

Putting the Treasury First: the truth about child support, A Garnham and E Knights, CPAG, May 1994 (£7.95)

Child Support: issues for the future, F Bennett, CPAG, February 1997 (£5.95)

5. Other publications – general

Welfare Benefits and Tax Credits Handbook
2004/05 edition, April 2004, £32 (£7 for claimants)

Paying for Care Handbook
4th edition, September 2003, £16.95

Guide to Housing Benefit and Council Tax Benefit
July 2004, £21.50

Debt Advice Handbook
6th edition, Autumn 2004, £16.50

Disability Rights Handbook
28th edition, May 2004, £14.90

Fuel Rights Handbook
13th edition, Autumn 2004, £15.00

Council Tax Handbook
5th edition, November 2002, £13.95

Migration and Social Security Handbook: a rights guide for people entering and leaving the UK
3rd edition, October 2002, £17.95

For CPAG publications and most of those in Sections 1 and 5 contact:

CPAG, 94 White Lion Street, London N1 9PF, tel: 020 7837 7979, fax: 020 7837 6414. Order forms are also available at: www.cpag.org.uk. For postage and packing add a flat rate charge: for orders up to £10 in value add £1.30; for £10.01-£200 add £3.30; for £200.01+ add £5.30.

Appendix 7
Abbreviations used in the notes

AC	Appeal Cases
All ER	All England Reports
App	Appendix
Art(s)	Article(s)
CA	Court of Appeal
CCR	County Court Rules
Ch	Chapter
CMLR	Common Market Law Reports
col	Column
ECR	European Court Reports
FamD	Family Division
FCR	Family Court Reporter
FLR	Family Law Reports
HC	House of Commons
HL	House of Lords
para(s)	paragraph(s)
QB	Queen's Bench Reports
r(r)	rule(s)
Reg(s)	Regulation(s)
s(s)	section(s)
SCLR	Scottish Civil Law Reports
Sch(s)	Schedule(s)
SLT	Scots Law Times
Vol	Volume
WLR	Weekly Law Reports

(DC), (CA), (HL) and (ECJ) indicate decisions of the Divisional Court, Court of Appeal, House of Lords and European Court of Justice respectively.
(R) indicates a reported commissioner's decision.
Abbreviations relating to CSA guidance are covered at the end of this appendix, and details of reports can be found in Appendix 6.

522

1. The legislation

Acts and regulations may be ordered from the Stationery Office, PO Box 276, London SW8 5DR (tel: 0870 600 5522; fax: 0870 600 5533). Recent Acts and regulations are available on www.hmso.gov.uk.

A volume of annotated child support legislation by Douglas and Jacobs can be purchased from Child Poverty Action Group (see Appendix 6).

Acts of Parliament

AA 1976	Adoption Act 1976
A(S)A 1978	Adoption (Scotland) Act 1978
CA 1989	Children Act 1989
CSA 1991	Child Support Act 1991
CSA 1995	Child Support Act 1995
C(S)A 1995	Children (Scotland) Act 1995
CSPSSA 2000	Child Support, Pensions and Social Security Act 2000
DPMCA 1978	Domestic Proceedings and Magistrates' Courts Act 1978
ERA 1996	Employment Rights Act 1996
FL(S)A 1958	Family Law (Scotland) Act 1958
FLRA 1969	Family Law Reform Act 1969
HF&EA 1990	Human Fertilisation and Embryology Act 1990
HRA 1998	Human Rights Act 1998
ICTA 1988	Income and Corporation Taxes Act 1988
LR(PC)(S)A 1986	Law Reform (Parent and Child) (Scotland) Act 1986
MCA 1973	Matrimonial Causes Act 1973
MO(RE)A 1992	Maintenance Orders (Reciprocal Enforcement) Act 1992
SSA 1998	Social Security Act 1998
SSAA 1992	Social Security Administration Act 1992
SSCBA 1992	Social Security Contributions and Benefits Act 1992
TCA 1999	Tax Credits Act 1999
CSPSSA 2000	Child Support, Pensions and Social Security Act 2000

Statutory instruments (SI)

Each set of Regulations or Order of the Secretary of State or Lord Chancellor has an SI number and a year. Ask for them by giving their date and number.

AS(CSA)(AOCSCR)	The Act of Sederunt (Child Support Act 1991) (Amendment of Ordinary Cause and Summary Cause Rules) 1993 No.919
AS(CSR)	The Act of Sederunt (Child Support Rules) 1993 No.920
C(AP)O	The Children (Allocation of Proceedings) Order 1991 No.1677
CS(A:PD)	The Child Support (Applications: Prescribed Dates) Regulations 2003 No. 194

523

Appendix 7: Abbreviations used in the notes

CB&SS(FAR) Regs	The Child Benefit and Social Security (Fixing and Adjustment of Rates) Regulations 1976 No.1267
CS(AIAMA) Regs	The Child Support (Arrears, Interest and Adjustment of Maintenance Assessments) Regulations 1992 No.1816
CS(C&E) Regs	The Child Support (Collection and Enforcement) Regulations 1992 No.1989
CS(CATP) Regs	Child Support (Consequential Amendments and Transitional Provisions) Regulations 2001 No.158
CS(CEMA) Regs	Child Support (Collection and Enforcement and Miscellaneous Amendments) Regulations 2000 No.2001/162
CS(CEOFM) Regs	The Child Support (Collection and Enforcement of Other Forms of Maintenance) Regulations 1992 No.2643
CS(CI)(S) Regs	The Child Support (Civil Imprisonment)(Scotland) Regulations 2001 No.1236
CS(CMP&MA) Regs	The Child Support (Child Maintenance Premium and Miscellaneous Amendments) Regulations 2000 No.3176
CS(D&A)A 2000	The Child Support (Decisions and Appeals) (Amendment) Regulations 2000 No.3185
CS(D&A)A 2003	The Child Support (Decisions and Appeals) (Amendment) Regulations 2003 No.129
CS(IED) Regs	The Child Support (Information, Evidence and Disclosure) Regulations 1992 No.1812
CS(IEDMAJ)(A) Regs	Child Support (Information, Evidence and Disclosure and Maintenance Arrangements and Jurisdiction) (Amendment) Regulations 2000 No.2001/161
CS(MA) Regs	The Child Support (Miscellaneous Amendments) Regulations 2000 No.1596
CS(MA) Regs 2001	The Child Support (Miscellaneous Amendments) Regulations 2001 No.1775
CS(MA) Regs 2002	The Child Support (Miscellaneous Amendment) Regulations 2002 No.1204
CS(MA) Regs 2003	The Child Support (Miscellaneous Amendments) Regulations 2003 No.328
CS(MA) No.2 Regs 1999	The Child Support (Miscellaneous Amendments) (No.2) Regulations 1999 No.1047
CS(MAJ) Regs	The Child Support (Maintenance Arrangements and Jurisdiction) Regulations 1992 No.2645
CS(MAP) Regs	The Child Support (Maintenance Assessment Procedure) Regulations 1992 No.1813
CS(MASC) Regs	The Child Support (Maintenance Assessments and Special Cases) Regulations 1992 No.1815

Appendix 7: Abbreviations used in the notes

CS(MATP) Regs	The Child Support (Miscellaneous Amendments and Transitional Provisions) Regulations 1994 No.227
CS(MCP) Regs	The Child Support (Maintenance Calculation Procedure) Regulations 2000 No.157
CS(MCSC) Regs	The Child Support (Maintenance Calculation and Special Cases) Regulations 2001 No.155
CS(Misc) Regs	The Child Support (Miscellaneous Amendments) Regulations 1996 No.1945
CS(NIRA) Regs	The Child Support (Northern Ireland Reciprocal Arrangements) Regulations 1993 No.584
CS(TCPS) Regs	Child Support (Temporary Compensation Payment Scheme) Regulations 2000 No.3174
CS(TCPS)(MA) Regs	The Child Support (Temporary Compensation Payment Scheme)(Modification and Amendment) Regulations 2002 No.1854
CS(TP) Regs	The Child Support (Transitional Provisions) Regulations 2000 No.3186
CS(V) Regs	The Child Support (Variations) Regulations 2000 No.156
CS(V)(MSP) Regs	The Child Support (Variations)(Modification of Statutory Provisions) Regulations 2000 No.3173
CS(VP) Regs	The Child Support (Voluntary Payments) Regulations 2000 No.3177
CSA(CA)O	The Child Support Act 1991 (Consequential Amendments) Order 1993 No.785
CSA(Comm3)O	The Child Support Act 1991 (Commencement No.3 and Transitional Provisions) Order 1992 No.2644
CSA(JC)O	The Child Support Appeals (Jurisdiction of Courts) Order 1993 No.961 (L.12)
CSA(JOC) Regs	The Child Support Appeals (Jurisdiction of Courts) Order 2002 No.1915 (L.9)
CSC(P) Regs	The Child Support Commissioners (Procedure) Regulations 1999 No.1305
CSDDCA Regs	The Child Support Departure Direction and Consequential Amendments Regulations 1996 No.2907
CSF Regs	The Child Support Fees Regulations 1992 No.3094
CSPSSA(Comm3)O	Child Support, Pensions and Social Security Act 2000 (Commencement No.3) Order 2000 No.2994 (C.94)
CSPSSA(Comm 12)O	The Child Support, Pensions and Social Security Act 2003 No. 192 (C.11)
CSPSSA(Comm 13)O	The Child Support, Pensions and Social Security Act 2000 (Commencement No 13) Order 2003 No 346(Chapter 21)
CTB Regs	The Council Tax Benefit (General) Regulations 1992 No.1814

Appendix 7: Abbreviations used in the notes

FP(A)R	The Family Proceedings (Amendment) Rules 1992 No.295 (L.1)
FP(Am3)R	The Family Proceedings (Amendment No.3) Rules 1997 No.1893
FPC(CSA)R	The Family Proceedings Courts (Child Support Act 1991) Rules 1993 No.627 (L.8)
HB Regs	The Housing Benefit (General) Regulations 1987 No.1971
IS Regs	The Income Support (General) Regulations 1987 No.1967
JSA Regs	The Jobseeker's Allowance Regulations 1996 No.207
SS(C&P) Regs	The Social Security (Claims and Payments) Regulations 1987 No.1968
SS(C&P)A Regs	Social Security (Claims and Payments) Amendment Regulations 2001 No.18
SS(CMB) Regs	The Social Security (Child Maintenance Bonus) Regulations 1996 No.3195
SS(CMP)A Regs	The Social Security (Child Maintenance Premium) Regulations 2004 No.98
SS(CMPMA) Regs 2000	The Social Security (Child Maintenance Premium and Miscellaneous Amendments) Regulations 2000 No.3176
SS(CMPMA) Regs 2003	The Social Security (Child Maintenance Premium and Miscellaneous Amendments) Regulations 2003 No.231
SS(PAOR) Regs	The Social Security (Payments on account, Overpayments and Recovery) Regulations 1988 No.664
SSA1998(Comm7)O	The Social Security Act 1998 (Commencement No.7 and Consequential and Transitional Provisions) Order 1999 No.1510
SS&CS(DA) Regs	The Social Security and Child Support (Decisions and Appeals) Regulations 1999 No.991
SS&CS(MA) Regs	The Social Security and Child Support (Miscellaneous Amendments) Regulations 2000 No.1596
SS&CS(TC)CA Regs	The Social Security and Child Support (Tax Credits) Consequential Amendments Regulations 1999 No.2566
SSCS(D&A)(MA) Regs	The Social Security and Child Support(Decisions and Appeals)(Miscellaneous Amendments) Regulationss 2002 No.1379
TC(DCI) Regs	The Tax Credits (Definition and Calculation of Income) Regulations 2002 No.2006

2. Guidance for CSA staff

CSAG	*Child Support Adjudication Guide*, Central Adjudication Services, The Stationery Office (looseleaf binder updated)
CSG	*Child Support Guide* Volumes 1–9, CSA (updated)
DMG	*Decision Makers Guide for Child Support*
DDMG	*Departures Decision Makers Guide*
EFIG	*Effective Full Maintenance Assessments and Interim Maintenance Assessments Guide*, CSA
EG	*Enforcement Guide*, CSA
FOG	*Field Operations Guide*, CSA, 1996
FTFG	*Face to Face Guide*, CSA
PG	*Paternity Guide*, CSA (updated)
RCG	*Requirement to Co-operate Guide*, CSA (updated)
TG	*Tracing Guide*, CSA (updated)

The manuals produced by the CSA cannot be purchased, but – with the exception of Volume 9 of the CSG and the Enforcement Guide – they are public documents and can be viewed at a CSA office. If anyone is refused such a request, a complaint should be made to the Human Resources Director of the CSA (see Appendix 1) who has assured us this is the case.

Under the reformed scheme this paper system will largely be incorporated within the computer system so that staff may have direct access to relevant material. It is not clear whether this procedural guidance will be available to advisers either on-line or in CD format.

3. Guidance for Jobcentre Plus Staff

IS GAP	Income Support Guidance and Procedure manuals are a series of volumes produced by the DWP, there is an equivalent set for JSA. For ease of reference we refer to IS guidance only.
G & CI	Income Support Gateway and Case Intervention Guidance and Procedure is an additional volume in the series.

Like the CSA Guides these are public documents. Some local libraries may hold copies and they can be viewed at local Jobcentre Plus offices. If anyone is refused such a request a complaint should be made to the Jobcentre Plus.

Index

How to use this Index

Because the Handbook is divided into separate sections covering the different benefits, many entries in the index have several references, each to a different section. Where this occurs, we use the following abbreviations to show which benefit each reference relates to:

AA	Attendance allowance	I-JSA	Income-based jobseeker's allowance
CA	Carer's allowance		
CTB	Council tax benefit	JSA	Jobseeker's allowance
CTC	Child tax credit	MA	Maternity allowance
DLA	Disability living allowance	PC	Pension credit
HB	Housing benefit	SAP	Statutory adoption pay
IB	Incapacity benefit	SDA	Severe disablement alllowance
IIDB	Industrial injuries disablement benefit	SF	Social fund
		SMP	Statutory maternity pay
IS	Income support	SPP	Statutory paternity pay
C-JSA	Contribution-based jobseeker's allowance	SSP	Statutory sick pay
		WTC	Working tax credit

Entries against the bold headings direct you to the general information on the subject, or where the subject is covered most fully. Sub-entries are listed alphabetically and direct you to specific aspects of the subject.

16/17-year-olds
  nil rate maintenance 127
  qualifying for child support 27

A
abduction of children
  habitual residence for child support 34
abroad
  child support
    cancellation of maintenance calculation 39
accountants
  providing information to CSA 91
additional cases
  assests over £65,000 168
  effect of variation 181
  variation of maintenance 168
additional maintenance 37, 45
  collection by CSA 466
additional proposed maintenance 291
  more than one person with care 303
  parent with care has assessable income 294
  parent with care has no assessable income 292 292
  See also proposed maintenance

address
  CSA checking addresses 95
adoption
  child support 23, 25
    treatment of allowances for net income calculation 275
advance payments
  child support 475
advances/loans from employer
  exempt income calculation 244
  net income calculation 264
advisers
  child support issues 7
amendment
  applications for departure from child support formula 359
appeal tribunals
  child support 434
    membership 444
appeals
  child maintenance bonus 409
  child support 413
    appeal tribunals 434
    caselaw 440, 453
    change of circumstances 436
    child support commissioners 450

529

Index
appeals – assessable income

confidentiality of information 7
conversion decisions 207, 208
CSA submission 439
death of party to appeal 441
decisions that can be made 436, 447
deduction from earnings orders 482
deductions from benefit for child
    support 227
departure from formula 362, 374
evidence 440
expenses for attending hearing 445
from child support commissioners to
    courts 454
hearings 444, 445, 446
insufficient information 438
lapsed appeal 441
late appeals 438
late appeals to commissioners 451
notice of hearing 444
old rules cases 454
parentage disputes 25, 437
payment of child maintenance
    pending appeal 458, 470
postponement of hearing 444, 447
preparing an appeal 439
procedure 437
reduced benefit decisions 82
self-employed earnings 138, 270
setting aside decisions 449
striking out appeals 442
test case rules 427, 430
time limits 437, 444
variation of maintenance 180, 188
welfare of the child 31
who has right of appeal 436
withdrawing appeal 443
witnesses 445
applications for child support
    advance applications 50
    amending the application 52
    cancellation 53
    cancellation by Secretary of State 52
    delays in dealing with applications 382
    effective applications 51
    existing maintenance arrangements 44,
        45
    how to apply 47
    more than one person with care 43
    multiple applications 54
    old rules cases 56
    preventing applications to CSA 36, 44, 45
    priority between applications 54
    refusal of application by CSA 51
    section 4 applications 44, 47
    section 6 applications 44, 48
    section 7 applications 44, 47
    section 7 applications made by child 43
    when to apply 50

who can apply 43
withdrawing applications 52, 383
appointees
    child support 13
apportionment
    deductions from benefit for child support
        225
    exempt income calculation 240, 331, 332
    maintenance calculation
        more than one person with care 126
    maintenance requirement calculation
        230, 233, 235
    minimum child maintenance 223
    proposed maintenance
        both parents are non-resident 300
        more than one person with care 301
    protected income calculation 314
armed forces
    deduction from earnings orders 477
    exempt income calculation
        accommodation 244
    tracing a non-resident parent 95
arrears
    child support 467
        arrears agreement 469, 472
        arrears notice 472
        deductions from benefits for child
            support 225, 226
        default by non-resident parent 472
        delays in collection and enforcement
            475
        disqualification from driving 487, 488
        enforcement by person with care 476
        imprisonment 487, 488
        initial arrears 8, 468
        interest 476
        offsetting overpayments against
            arrears 464, 465
        payment of arrears 396, 470
        penalty payment 473
        recovery action 471
        suspending collection of arrears
            pending revision/appeal 470
        temporary compensation payment
            scheme 20, 491
        voluntary payments to avoid arrears
            8, 468
artificial insemination
    child support 24
assessable income 222, 229
    calculation 261, 281
    definition 261, 262
    parents receiving IS, income-based JSA
        or pension credit 261
    parents receiving working tax credit 262
    separated parents share care 333

530

Index
assessments of child support – carer premium

assessments of child support
  benefit upratings 221
  cancellation 392
  changes made to assessment
    departure direction 373
  effective date 400
  effects of changes to formula 221
  existing old rules cases 398
  insufficient information 403
  old rules cases 83
  phasing-in of assessments 404
    departure from child support formula 364
  termination 403
attendance allowance
  exemption from deduction for child maintenance 225
  exemption from payment of child maintenance 224
  net income calculation 271
authorisation to Child Support Agency
  requirement to give authorisation 5

B
backdating
  child support
    additional maintenance 38
    court orders for child maintenance 37
    date of receipt of maintenance application form 51
    deductions from benefit 225
bailiffs
  non-payment of child maintenance 485
bankruptcy
  child support arrears 488
basic protected income 313
benefit penalty
  old rules cases 84
benefit uprating
  child support assessments 221
benefits
  challenging child support decisions about benefit entitlement 415
  effect of maintenance calculation 394
  net income calculation 270
    benefits ignored in full 271
    benefits ignored in part 271
    deprivation of income by failing to apply for benefit 279
    increases for dependants 271, 277
    partner's income 271
bereavement allowance
  flat rate maintenance 127
biological parent 23
blood testing 105, 109
boarders
  net income calculation 268, 272

boarding school 29, 142, 327
  maintenance calculation 145
  variation of maintenance 165
bonus of wages
  net income calculation 263, 266
buildings insurance
  exempt income calculation 245
business
  use of home
    housing costs for exempt income 244
    net income calculation 273
business expenses
  net income calculation 268
Business Start-up Allowance
  net income calculation 268

C
calculation
  exempt income 239
  maintenance requirement 230
cancellation
  child support assessment 392
  deduction from earnings orders 482
  departure direction 373
  maintenance calculation 392, 431
  date of cancellation 393
  notification 394
capital
  child support
    net income calculation 262
  departure from child support formula
    under-use of assets 355, 356, 369
  deprivation of capital
    net income calculation 279
  net income calculation
    divided on divorce or separation 275
    income from capital 275
    jointly owned capital 275
caravans
  exempt income calculation 243
care
  children in care
    local authority shares care 153, 342
    maintenance requirement 231
    person with care 28
    treatment of payments for net income calculation 275, 277
care homes
  child support
    suspension of reduced benefit decision 81
  exempt income calculation
    housing costs 244
  nil rate maintenance 127
carer premium
  exempt income 240

531

Index
carer's allowance – children

carer's allowance
  exemption from deduction for child maintenance 225
  exemption from payment of child maintenance 224
  flat rate maintenance 127
case checks 424
case conversion date 200
caselaw
  child support appeals 440, 453
challenging a decision
  child support 415
    deductions from benefit 227
change of circumstances
  child support 383
    amending child maintenance enquiry form 99
    appeals 436
    cancellation of maintenance calculation 392
    changes to total family income 321
    duty to disclose 113, 418
    net income calculation 135, 266
    supersessions 323, 421, 422
charging order 486
charitable payments
  net income calculation 271, 276
child benefit
  determining the non-resident parent 143, 330
  maintenance requirement 230, 231
  net income calculation 271
  total family income 271, 312
child maintenance bonus 405
  amount 408
  appeals 409
  conditions for payment 406
  conversion 212
  payment 409
  person with care dies 408
  retired people 409
child maintenance enquiry form
  amending the form 99
  non-resident parents 97
child maintenance premium 395
  conversion 212
Child Support Agency 4, 5
  Child Support Agency Centres 12
  communicating with CSA 13
    online 15
    telephoning 14
    writing 13
  complaints 18
  disclosure of information 114, 115
    to other government departments 116
  enquiry line 14
  fees 467
  information seeking powers 87

local service bases 13
Northern Ireland 12, 382
offices 12
satellite processing centres 12
service targets and standards 17
structure 11
Child Support Agency Centres 12
child support commissioners 450
  appeals from commissioners to courts 454
  caselaw 453
  decisions 452
  error of law 450
  how to appeal 450
  oral hearings 452
  written procedure 452
child support formula
  changes to formula 221
  income support rates applicable 220
  maintenance payable 313, 317
  maximum child maintenance 296
  minimum child maintenance 223
  special cases 227
child support inspectors 11, 112
child support scheme
  changes in March 03 3
  issues for advisers 7
  representatives 13
child tax credit
  assessable income
    net income 272
    net income calculation 269
  net income calculation
    maintenance calculation 139
  total family income 312
  transferring from IS/JSA 62
childminders
  self-employed earnings
    net income calculation 268
children
  child support applications for additional children 56
  child's home for child support purposes 29
  children in care
    local authority shares care 153, 342
    maintenance requirement 231
    net income calculation 275
    person with care 28
  death of qualifying child
    cancellation of child support application 53
  dependency increases with benefit
    net income calculation 271, 277
  duty to maintain 4, 23
  exempt income calculation 238
    second families 255

532

Index
children – court orders for child maintenance

exemption from payment of child maintenance 224
habitual residence for child support 34
income of child
  net income calculation 263, 277
  total family income 312
nil rate maintenance 127
qualifying for child support 4, 26
section 7 applications for child support 43
treatment of maintenance paid for a child 277
  net income calculation 274
  total family income 312
christmas bonus
  net income calculation 271
clean-break maintenance orders/ agreements 36
close relatives
  responsibility for housing costs
    exempt income calculation 242
co-ownership scheme
  exempt income calculation 243
coastguard
  net income calculation 263
collection of child maintenance 458, 460, 466
  advance payments 475
  conversion decisions 213
  delays 464, 475
  fees and court costs 467
  non-resident parent on IS/income-based JSA 462
  payments made under court order 46, 466
  person with care receiving benefits 396, 460, 461
  requesting collection by CSA 460
  suspending collection of arrears 470
  suspension of collection 458
commission
  child support
    net income calculation 263, 266
community care
  direct payments
    net income calculation 276
compensation
  child support 20
  child support arrears
    temporary compensation payment scheme 491
  net income calculation
    loss of employment/unfair dismissal 264
    personal injuries 277
complaints
  child support 18
  to MP 19
  to Ombudsman 20
  Independent Case Examiner 19
confidentiality
  appeal hearings and papers 7, 446
  CSA 7
  disclosure of information by CSA 114, 115
consent orders 35
contact
  departure from child support formula for costs of contact 348
  variations for cost of contact 161
contents insurance
  exempt income calculation 243, 245
conversions 191
  conversion calculation 193
  conversion date 58, 191
  conversion decision 199
  departure directions 211
  early conversions 191
  further decisions 209
  grounds for revision, supersession or appeal 208
  linking rules 202
  non-resident parents on benefit 213
  outstanding decisions 207
  persons with care on benefits 212
  transitional phasing 194
  variations 211
council tax
  exempt income calculation 243
  protected income calculation 314, 315
council tax benefit
  child support
    effect of maintenance calculation 397
  net income calculation 271
  protected income calculation 314, 315
councillor's allowances
  net income calculation 263
couples
  definition for child support 32
  maintenance requirement 232
court orders for child maintenance 34
  additional maintenance 37
  backdating 37, 38
  collection of payments by CSA 46, 466
  consent orders 35
  effective date for maintenance calculation 389
  lump sum awards 38
  notification of maintenance calculation 37
  phasing-in of child support assessments 404
  phasing-in of maintenance calculation 387
  preventing applications to CSA 36, 45
  revocation 38, 46

533

Index
court orders for child maintenance – Department for Work and Pensions

variation 36, 38, 46
where CSA has no jurisdiction 38
courts
   appeals from child support
      commissioners 454
   collection and enforcement of court costs 467
   enforcing liability order for non-payment
      of child maintenance 485
      county court action 486
   parentage disputes 110
   proceedings in parentage disputes 108
   providing information to CSA 91
   role in child maintenance 34
   variation of maintenance arrangements 36
criminal offences
   failure to comply with deduction from
      earnings order 478
   failure to provide information to CSA 93
   obstructing child support inspectors 113
   unauthorised disclosure of information
      by CSA 116
croft land
   exempt income calculation 243
Crown employees
   providing information to CSA 91
Crown tenants
   exempt income calculation 243

D
Data Protection Act 115
day-to-day care 28, 326
   exemption from deduction for child
      maintenance 225
   exemption from excessive housing costs
      restriction 247
   maintenance calculation 141
death
   cancellation of child support application 53
   child maintenance bonus 408
   party to child support appeal 441
debt
   child support
      variation of maintenance 164
   departure from child support formula for
      debts of relationship 348, 353
decisions
   child support
      appeals 447
      challenging decisions on benefit
         entitlement 415
      challenging decisions which cannot
         be revised/superseded 415
      changing a child support decision 413
      commissioners 452
      departure from formula 359, 362

harm or undue distress 73
notification of appeal decision 448
notification of decision 437
requesting reasons for appeal
   decision 448, 450
requesting reasons for decision 437
revised decisions 420
standards of adjudication 7
superseded decision 424
test cases 427, 429
welfare of child 31
declaration of parentage 24, 108
deduction from earnings orders 477
   administration 480
      old rules cases 490
   amount of deduction 479
   appeals 482
   cancellation 482
   date of payment 478
   earnings defined 479
   enforcement in N. Ireland 477
   how deduction from earnings orders
      work 477
   information to be provided 478
   lapsed orders 482
   normal deduction rate 480
      old rules cases 490
   priority of orders 482
   protected earnings proportion 480
   protected earnings rate
      old rules cases 490
   revision 482
deductions from benefits
   child support payments 224, 226, 394, 462
   amount 225
   arrears 225, 226, 471
   backdating 225
   challenging a decision 227
   deductions from partner's benefit 224
   exemption from deductions 225
   maximum amount 226
   priority between deductions 226
   reduced benefit decision 77
default maintenance decisions 384
delays
   child support 8
      assessments 382
      compensation 20
      payments of child support 464, 475
      temporary compensationpayment
         scheme 491
   CSA 7
Department for Work and Pensions
   disclosure of information by CSA 116
   providing information to CSA 92

Index
departure from child support formula – earnings

departure from child support formula 220, 348
  additional cases 369
  additional cases grounds 355
  amending the application 359
  amending the direction 371
  appeals 362, 374
  applying for departure 358
  cancellation of assessment 373
  changes made to assessment 373
  consideration of case 362
  contact costs 348
  conversion calculation 197
  correction of errors 373
  debts of the relationship 348, 353
  decisions 359, 362
  direction 364
  disability or long term illness 348, 353
  disregards 348
  diversion of income 355, 356, 369
  effective date of direction 370
  factors to be taken into account 362
  financial commitments made before April 1993 348, 354
  grounds for departure 348
  housing costs 355, 357, 369
  information to be provided 360
  length of departure direction 371
  lifestyle inconsistent with income 355, 356, 369
  phased assessments 364
  procedure 359
  property/capital transfers 357, 367
  regular payments condition 360
  revisions/supersessions 361, 371, 372
  special expenses 348, 364
  stepchildren 348, 349
  travel to work costs 348, 352, 355, 357, 369
  under-use of assets 355, 356, 369
deprivation of capital
  net income calculation 262
deprivation of resources
  child support
    net income calculation 262, 279
director's remuneration
  net income calculation 263
disability
  additional maintenance for disabled child 38
  departure from child support formula 348, 353
  maintenance requirement for children with disabilities 232
disability living allowance
  exemption from deduction for child maintenance 225
  exemption from payment of child maintenance 224
  net income calculation 271
disability premium
  exempt income 240
disabled child premium
  exempt income 240
  second family 256
  shared care 331
  maintenance requirement 232
disabled children
  additional maintenance 38
  child support
    variation of maintenance 161, 163
  maintenance required 232
disablement benefit
  exemption from deduction for child maintenance 225
disposable income 312
  protected income
    calculating maintenance payable 317
  total family income 312
disregards
  child support
    net income 271
  departure from child support formula 348, 349, 352, 354
  housing benefit and council tax benefit maintenance 397
  net income
    child's income 278
    income from rent 272
    maintenance calculation 132
    other income 276
    student's income 273
diversion of income
  departure for child support formula 356
  variation of maintenance 170
divided families
  proposed maintenance 305
DNA testing 25, 105
  child support
    collection of test fees 467
    paternity disputes 100
  cost of testing 106
  ordered by courts 109
  results of test 107
driving
  disqualification for child support arrears 487
duty to provide information to Child Support Agency 5

E
earnings
  deduction from earnings orders 479
  exempt income calculation
    advances/loans from employer 244

535

Index
earnings – families

net income calculation
    advances/loans from employers 264
    calculating weekly earnings 265, 269
    child's earnings 277
    earnings from employment 133, 263
    earnings from self-employment 135, 266, 273
    maintenance calculation 133, 135
    net earnings 266
    relevant week 264
notional earnings
    net income calculation 278
weekly earnings
    maintenance calculation 134
educational maintenance allowances
    net income calculation 274
effective date
    child support assessments 400
    conversion decision 200
    departure directions 370
    interim effective date
        old rules 403
    interim maintenance assessments
        old rules 402
    maintenance calculation 388
        court order in force 389
    superseded child support decisions 425
employers
    providing information to CSA 90, 95, 111
    deduction from earnings orders 479
employment credits
    net income calculation
        maintenance calculation 139
endowment policy
    exempt income calculation 243, 245
enforcement of child maintenance 458, 483
    bankruptcy 488
    county court action 486
    court orders for child maintenance 46
    delays 475
    disqualification from driving 487, 488
    distress 485
    enforcement by person with care 476
    fees and costs 467
    imprisonment 487, 488
    liability order 484
    old rules cases 489
    Scotland 486
enquiry line
    Child Support Agency 14
errors
    correction of errors in departure direction 373
    error of law
        appeal to child support commissioners 450
        child support decisions 422

official error
    child support decisions 418
evidence
    child support
        appeals 440
        corroboration of evidence 111
        harm or undue distress 72
        incriminating 113
        investigations 111
        proof of harm or distress 73
        property settlements 250
        self-employed earnings 111, 138, 269, 270
ex gratia payments
    child support 20
excessive housing costs
    deprivation of capital/income
        net income calculation 280
    exempt income calculation 247
    protected income 314
exempt income 222
    calculation 239
    definition 238
    housing costs 241
    non-resident parents 239
    parent with care 239
    partner's expenses 238
    person with care 239
    property settlements 240, 249
    second families 238, 255
    separated parents share care 331
    travel costs allowance 240, 253
existing maintenance arrangements
    applications for child support 36
    phasing-in of child support assessments 404
    phasing-in of maintenance calculation 387
    preventing application to CSA 44, 45
    revocation by court 38, 46
    variation by court 36, 38, 46
expenses
    attending child support hearing 445
    business
        net income calculation 268
    net income calculation 263, 264
    voluntary work
        net income calculation 276
extension period
    qualifying for child support 27

F
failure to
    disclose material fact
        child support 418
    supply information to CSA 93
families
    definition for child support 32

Family Fund
    net income calculation 277
family premium
    exempt income 239
        second family 256, 257
        shared care 331, 332
    exemption from deduction for child maintenance 225
    exemption from payment of child maintenance 224
    maintenance requirement 230
    protected income
        shared care 336
fees
    CSA fees and court costs 467
feu duty
    exempt income calculation 243
firefighter
    net income calculation 263
fostering
    child support
        person with care 25
        treatment as family 33
        treatment of allowances for net income 275
fraud
    child support
        applications 72, 78
        fraudulent claims for benefit 54, 262
        false information given to CSA 93
frequency of payment
    child support payments 463
fuel costs
    ineligible housing costs
        exempt income calculation 246
full-time education
    child support 26
    exemption from payment of child maintenance 224

G
garnishee order 486
gateway intervention visits
    applications for child support 50
gay couples
    child support 33
        housing costs in exempt income calculation 241
good cause
    child support
        old rules cases 84
        opting out 7
    child support interviews 67, 68
    further benefit claims 74
    harm or undue distress 70
    new claims visit 64
    reconsideration of decisions 74

reduced benefit decision not made 75
refusal to co-operate with CSA 5
ground rent
    exempt income calculation 243
guardian's allowance
    net income calculation 271

H
habitual residence test
    child support 33
        children 34
        definition 33
harm or undue distress 7
    collection of child support payments after cancellation of maintenance calculation 461
    decisions 73
    definition 70
    evidence 72
    good cause for opting-out
        child support 70
    good cause interviews 67, 68
    reasonable grounds for believing risk exists 72
health benefits
    effect of maintenance calculation 397
    net income calculation 276
hearings
    child support appeals 444, 445
        conduct of hearing 446
        confidentiality 446
        travel expenses for attending hearing 445
        witnesses 445
hire purchase agreements
    exempt income calculation 243
holiday pay
    net income calculation 263
home
    child's home 29
    definition
        housing costs in exempt income calculation 244
home income plan
    net income calculation 277
Home Office
    disclosure of information by CSA 116
home visits
    child support interviews 16
hospital
    child support
        day-to-day care 29, 142, 327
        suspension of reduced benefit decision 81
    fares to hospital
        net income calculation 276
    maintenance calculation 145
    nil rate maintance 127

Index
houseboats – industrial disablement benefit

houseboats
    exempt income calculation 243
household
    definition for child support 29
housing benefit
    child support
        effect of maintenance calculation 397
        exempt income calculation 244
        net income calculation 271
housing costs
    departure from child support formula 355, 357, 369
    deprivation of income/capital 280
    exempt income calculation 238, 240, 244
        eligible housing costs 243
        excessive costs 247
        home defined 244
        ineligible housing costs 246
        mortgage payments 243, 245
        partner's housing costs 238, 241
        service charges 246
        two homes 244
        weekly amount 246
    protected income calculation 314

I
illness
    departure from child support formula 348, 353
improvement loans
    housing costs in exempt income calculation 243
in vitro fertilisation
    child support 24
incapacity benefit
    exemption from deduction for child maintenance 225
    exemption from payment of child maintenance 224
    flat rate maintenance 127
income
    changes to total family income
        maintenance payable 321
    departure from child support formula
        diversion of income 355, 356, 369
        lifestyle inconsistent with income 355, 356, 369
        under-use of assets 355, 356, 369
    net income calculation
        benefits treated as income 270
        child's income 277
        deprivation of income 279
        income from capital 275
        income other than earnings 139, 271
        maintenance calculation 132
        notional income 262
        rental income 272
        student's income 265, 273
        treatment of maintenance 274
    total family income
        child's income 312
    variation of maintenance
        diversion of income 170
        income not taken into account 170
        lifestyle inconsistent with declared income 171
income support
    applications for child support 44, 48
    child maintenance bonus 405
    child maintenance premium 395
    child support
        assessable income 261
        benefit claim ceases 80
        fraudulent claims 54
        new claims visit 64
        parents treated as applying 62
        requirement to co-operate 5
    collection of child support payments 396, 460, 461
        arrears 470
    departure from child support formula 347
    effect of maintenance calculation 394
    flat rate maintenance 128
    loss of entitlement to benefit 396
    mortgage interest payments
        effect of maintenance calculation 394
    non-resident parents 224
        exempt income 239
    parents with care
        exempt income calculation 239
        transferring to child tax credit 62
    payment of child maintenance 396
        non-resident parent receiving IS 462
    rates used in child support formula 220
    withdrawing applications for child support
        when benefit claim ends 53
income tax
    net income calculation 266, 268, 276
    taxation of child maintenance 398
increases for dependants
    net income 271, 277
incriminating evidence 113
Independent Case Examiner 19
Independent Living Funds
    exemption from deduction for child maintenance 225
    exemption from payment of child maintenance 224
    net income calculation 277
industrial disablement benefit
    exemption from deduction for child maintenance 225
    exemption from payment of child maintenance 224

Index
industrial injuries benefit – jury service

industrial injuries benefit
  flat rate maintenance 127
information
  child support
    appeals 438, 441
    confidentiality 7, 114, 115
    corroboration and verification of evidence 111
    deduction from earnings orders 478
    departure from formula 360
    disclosure by CSA 114, 115, 116
    disputing the information required 94
    duty to disclose change of circumstances 113
    duty to provide information 5, 51, 87
    further investigation by CSA 110, 112
    information that CSA can request 89
    inspectors 112
    old rules cases 117
    powers of CSA 87
    privileged information 113
    proof of harm or distress 73
    providing false information 93
    self-employed earnings 111, 138, 269, 270
    time limit for providing information to CSA 92
    unauthorised disclosure by CSA 116
    when CSA can ask for information 87
    who has to provide information to CSA 89
Inland Revenue
  providing information to CSA 92
insurance premiums
  exempt income calculation 243, 245
interest
  arrears of child maintenance 476
  late payments by Child Support Agency 464
  on savings treated as capital
    net income calculation 275
interim maintenance assessments 220, 399
  departure 347
  effective date
    old rules 402
  maintenance requirement 230
interim maintenance decision 177
interpreters
  child support
    appeal hearings 447
    interviews 16
interviews
  child support 16
    CSA request interview 16
    good cause interviews 67, 68
    travel expenses 17
    parentage disputes 101

  with non-resident parent 102
  with parent with care 103
investigations
  CSA 110, 112

J
Jobcentre Plus
  child support
    collecting information 63
    new claims visit 64
jobseeker's allowance
  applications for child support 44, 48
  child maintenance bonus 405
  child maintenance premium 395
  child support
    assessable income 261
    benefit claim ceases 80
    new claims visit 64
    parents treated as applying 62
    requirement to co-operate 5
  collection of child support payments 396, 460, 461
    arrears 470
  departure from child support formula 347
  effect of maintenance calculation 394
  flat rate maintenance 128
  fraudulent claims 54
  loss of entitlement to benefit 396
  mortgage interest payments
    effect of maintenance calculation 394
  non-resident parents 224
    exempt income 239
  parents with care
    exempt income calculation 239
    transferring to child tax credit 62
  payment of child maintenance 396
    non-resident parent receiving income-based JSA 462
  withdrawing applications for child support
    when benefit claim ends 53
joint income
  assessable income
    net income 263
joint occupiers
  exempt income calculation
    responsibility for housing costs 241
joint tenants
  exempt income calculation
    responsibility for housing costs 241
judicial review
  child support decisions 415
jury service
  allowances
    net income calculation 277

539

Index
jury service – maintenance calculation

L
lesbian couples
    child support 33
        housing costs in exempt income calculation 241
liability order
    non-payment of child maintenance 484
        enforcement of order 485
        notice to be given by CSA 484
        obtaining an order 484
        time limits 485
        Scotland 485, 486
licence to occupy home
    exempt income calculation 243
life assurance
    exempt income calculation 245
lifeboat crew
    net income calculation 263
linking rules
    old and new rules child support cases 202
living together
    cancellation of maintenance calculation 392
loans
    advances from employer
        exempt income calculation 244
        net income calculation 264
    business loans 137, 268
    housing costs in exempt income calculation 243, 245
    variation of maintenance 166
local authorities
    allowances for councillors
        net income calculation 263
    payments for welfare services
        net income calculation 276
    payments made for children in care
        net income calculation 275
    providing information to CSA 92
    shared care 153, 342
low income
    exemption from payment of child maintenance 224
    nil rate maintenance 127
    notional earnings
        net income calculation 278
lump sum maintenance awards 38, 275

M
Macfarlane Trusts
    net income calculation 277
maintenance
    additional maintenance 37, 45
    agreements made before 5 April 1993 44
        exempt income calculation 240
    basic rate 130
    clean-break arrangements 36

    collection and enforcement of payments by CSA 458, 466
    consent orders 35
    court's role 34
    existing arrangements 34
    flat rate 127
    initial maintenance decision 381
    lump sum awards 38, 275
    maximum amount 296
    nil rate 126
    parents treated as applying 62
    preventing applications to CSA 35, 36, 44, 45
    property/capital settlements
        departure from child support formula 357, 367
        exempt income 240, 249
        proposed maintenance calculation 301, 302
    reduced rate 128
    responsibility for child maintenance 4, 23
    shared care
        calculating maintenance 331
    spousal maintenance 38, 231, 466
        net income calculation 274
    stepchildren 37, 466
    taxation 398
    total family income calculation 312
    treatment for HB and CTB 397
    treatment for protected income 274
maintenance administration form
    completing the form 65
maintenance application form
    amendment 52
    backdating date of receipt 51
    completing the maintenance application form 48
maintenance calculation 125
    adjustments arising from overpayment 465
    applications
        after conversion date 204
        before conversion date 203
    basic rate 130
    cancellation 39, 392, 431
    conversion calculation 193
    date calculation takes effect 388
    effect on benefits 394
    effect on court orders 36
    effective date
        court order in force 389
        existing old rules assessment 391
        special cases 390
    flat rate 127
    maintenance period 391
    net income 132
    nil rate 126
    non-resident parent shares care

540

Index
maintenance calculation – non-advanced education

basic rate 146
flat rate 151
reduced rate 146
notification 37, 386
phasing-in 387
reduced rate 128
refusal to make calculation 384
suspended while paternity investigated 110
termination 391
maintenance enquiry form
old rules cases 118
maintenance period 391
maintenance requirement 221
both parents are non-resident 232
calculation 230
definition 229
interim maintenance assessments 230
more than one non-resident parent 230, 233
new partner 232
parent as carer element 230, 231, 234
parent with carer's contribution 229
separated parents share care 331
shared care
maintenance requirement met in full 342
two persons with care 230
maternity allowance
exemption from deduction for child maintenance 225
exemption from payment of child maintenance 224
flat rate maintenance 127
maximum child maintenance 296
parent with care has assessable income 297
parent with care has no assessable income 296
meals
ineligible housing costs
exempt income calculation 246
Member of Parliament
child support complaints 19
methods of payment
child support 461
milk tokens
net income calculation 276
minimum child maintenance 223
misrepresentation
revision of child support decisions 417, 418
mobile homes
exempt income calculation 243
modified amount
phasing-in of child support assessment 404

mooring charges
exempt income calculation 243
mortgage payments
exempt income calculation 243, 245
interest payments
effect of maintenance calculation 394
protected income calculation 314
variation of maintenance 166
mortgage protection policy
exempt income calculation 245
net income calculation 276
total family income 312
multiple applications for child support 54
additional children 56
before calculation is made 54
calculation in force 56
effective date 389, 401
more than one applicant 55
more than one person with care 55, 56, 328
maintenance calculation 144
old rules cases 57
same person applies more than once 54

N
national insurance contributions
net income calculation 266, 268
net earnings
net income calculation 266
net income
assessable income
benefits 270
capital 262, 275
child's income 263, 277
earnings from employment 263
earnings from self-employment 266
income other than earnings 271
joint income 263
maintenance 274, 275
notional income 278
partner's income 263, 271
spousal maintenance 274
student's income 273
exempt income calculation
partner's income 256, 257
maintenance calculation 132
income other than earnings 139
maximum amount 139
self employment 135
new claims visits
child support 64
New Deal
treatment of payments for net income calculation 274
NHS benefits
net income calculation 276
non-advanced education
child support 26

541

Index
non-dependants – overtime

non-dependants
  housing costs
    exempt income calculation 242
    protected income calculation 314
    treatment of payments
      net income calculation 272
non-resident parents
  applying to CSA 43
  applying to more than one non-resident parent 50
  arrears
    temporary compensation payments scheme 491
  compensation for arrears 20
  contact by CSA 97
  contacting a non-resident parent 94
  day-to-day care 327
  deduction from earnings orders 477
  definition 4, 29
  DNA testing 106, 109
  duty to maintain child 4, 23
  duty to provide information 90
  exempt income calculation 239
  exemption from payment of child maintenance 223
  grounds for departure
    special expenses 348
  interviews about parentage 102
  maintenance calculation
    shared care 145
  maintenance requirement
    both parents are non-resident 232
    more than one parent is non-resident 233
  more than non-resident parent
    maintenance requirement 230
  mother as non-resident parent 221
  parent with care treated as non-resident 142
  proposed maintenance
    both parents are non-resident 298
    more than one non-resident parent 306
  protected income 310
  receiving IS, income-based JSA or pension credit 224, 462
    assessable income 262
    exempt income 239
  receiving working tax credit
    assessable income 262
  separated parents share care 329
  tracing the non-resident parent 51, 66, 94
Northern Ireland
  Child Support Agency 12, 382
notice
  arrears
    child maintenance 472
  hearing of child support appeal 444

  liability order 484
  pay in lieu of notice
    net income calculation 263
notification
  cancellation of maintenance calculation 394
  child support decision 437
  conversion decision 201
  decision of child support appeal 448
  deductions of child support from benefit 226
  departure directions 362
  maintenance calculation 37, 386
  payments of child support 459
  revised child support decision 420
  superseded child support decision 426
  variation of maintenance 176
notional income
  failure to claim child maintenance 397
  net income calculation 262, 278
    deprivation of income/capital 279
    payments to third parties 280

O

occupational pensions
  net income calculation 139, 264, 266, 272
official error
  child support decisions 418
old rules child support cases
  appeals 454
  applications 56
  assessable income 261
  assessments of child support 83
  child support formula 219
  conversion to new rules 191
  departures 347
  enforcement of maintenance 489
  exempt income 238
  information required 117
  jurisdiction of CSA and courts 39
  maintenance assessments 398
  maintenance requirement 229
  proposed maintenance 286
  protected income 310
  revision and supersession 430
  shared care 326
ombudsman
  child support complaints 20
opting-in 83
opting-out 68
  good cause interview 68
  harm or undue distress 70
overpayments
  child support 464
    adjustments to payments 465
    recovery from person with care 465
overtime
  net income calculation 263

542

Index
overtime – person with care

P
parent as carer element
  maintenance requirement 230, 231, 234
parentage
  appeals 25, 437
  declaration of parentage 108
  disputes 25
    court hearings 109
    court proceedings 108, 110
    interviews 101
    investigations 99
    suspension of calculation 110
  DNA tests 25, 105
    fees 106, 467
    ordered by court 109
  interviews where parentage disputed
    with non-resident parent 102
    with parent with care 103
  legal costs 110
  old rules cases 118
  presumption of paternity 24
parentage statement 104
parental order
  child support 24
parental responsibility 25, 43
parents
  definition for child support 23
parents with care
  applying to CSA 43
  claiming IS/JSA 62
  definition 4, 29
  duty to maintain child 4, 23
  duty to provide information to CSA 87
  exempt income calculation 239
  fathers as parent with care 221
  interviews about parentage 103
  maintenance requirement 229
  maximum child maintenance
    assessable income 297
    no assessable income 296
  opting-out 68
  proposed maintenance
    assessable income 290, 294
    no assessable income 289, 292
  receiving IS, income-based JSA or
    pension credit
    assessable income 261
    exempt income 239
  receiving working tax credit
    assessable income 262
    exempt income calculation 239
  reduced benefit decision 75
  requirement to co-operate 5, 7
  treated as non-resident
    maintenance calculation 142

partner
  contribution to housing costs
    departure from child support formula
    355, 357, 369
  exempt income calculation 238, 255, 256, 257
  housing costs 241
  income of a partner
    assessable income calculation 263
    exempt income calculation 255
    net income 256, 257, 271
    proposed maintenance calculation 287
  maintenance requirement 232
  protected income calculation 311
pay in lieu of notice
  net income calculation 263
payment of child maintenance
  collection of payment by CSA 396
  delays in passing on payments 464
  direct to person with care 395
  method of payments 461
  non-resident parent on IS/income-based
    JSA 462
  notice of payments 459
  overpayments 464
  payment statements 464
  pending supersession, revision or appeal
    458, 470
  person with care receiving benefits 460
  persons with care receiving benefits 461
  regular payments condition 360
  timing of payments 463
  voluntary payments against initial
    arrears 468
  who is paid 459
payments in kind
  net income calculation 264, 276
  voluntary payments against arrears of
    child maintenance 468
penalties
  child support
    non-resident parents in arrears 473
pension credit
  child support
    assessable income 262
    departure from child support formula 347
    flat rate maintenance 128
    non-resident parents 224
      exempt income 239
    parents with care
      exempt income calculation 239
      reduced benefit direction ceases 82
pensioner premiums
  protected income 314
person with care
  applications for child support 43
  assessable income 261

543

Index
person with care – proposed maintenance

child maintenance bonus where person with care dies 408
definition 4, 28
direct payment of maintenance 395
duty to disclose change of circumstances 114
duty to provide information 90
enforcement of arrears of child maintenance 476
exempt income calculation 239
foster parents 25
maintenance calculation
   shared care 144
more than one person with care
   applications for child support 43, 55, 56
   maintenance calculation 144, 149
   maintenance payable 320
   maintenance requirement 230
   proposed maintenance 300
   shared care 328, 341
payment of child maintenance 460, 461
   person with care receiving benefits 394
providing information to trace non-resident parents 95
recovery of arrears deferred
   temporary compensation scheme 492
recovery of overpayments 465
taxation of child maintenance 398
three persons with care 341
personal allowances
   child support 220
   exempt income 239
      second family 255, 256
      shared care 331
   maintenance requirement 230, 231, 232
   protected income 313
personal equity plans
   exempt income calculation 243, 245
personal pensions
   exempt income calculation 243, 245
   net income calculation 139, 266, 268, 272
phasing-in
   child support assessments
      departure directions 364
      existing maintenance arrangements 404
      revision or supersession of decision 405
   maintenance calculations 387
   revision or supersession of decision 388
polygamous marriages
   child support 32
power of attorney
   child support 13
powers to enter
   child support inspectors 112

premiums
   child support 220
   exempt income 239
      second family 255, 256
      shared care 332
   maintenance requirement 230
   protected income 314
      shared care 336
prisoners
   contact by CSA 98
   exemption from payment of child maintenance 224
   net income calculation
      treatment of payments for prison visiting 276
      treatment of prisoner's pay 276
   nil rate maintenance 127
   non-payment of child maintenance 487
privileged information 113
profit-related pay
   net income calculation 266
property/capital settlements
   conversion calculation 197
   departure from child support formula 357, 367
   effect of variation 183
   exempt income calculation 240, 249
      evidence 250
      qualifying transfer 249
      qualifying value 251
   proposed maintenance calculation 301, 302
   variation of maintenance 166
proposed maintenance 222
   50 per cent calculation 287, 289
      parent with care has assessable income 290
      parent with care has no assessable income 289
   absent parent has no assessable income 288
   additional element calculation 287, 291
      more than one person with care 303
      parent with care has assessable income 294
      parent with care has no assessable income 292
   both parents are non-resident 298
   calculation 287
   definition 286
   divided families 305
   maintenance requirement met in full where shared care 342
   maximum child maintenance 296
   more than one non-resident parent 306
      parent with care has assessable income 307
   more than one person with care 300

544

Index
proposed maintenance – second family

additional element calculation 303
property settlements 301, 302
sharing proposed maintenance 301
separated parents share care 334
protected income 223
30 per cent limit 310
basic protected income 313
child benefit 271, 312
council tax 314, 315
definition 310
disposable income 312, 317
housing costs 314
maintenance payable 313, 317
    change of circumstances 321
    more than one person with care 320
separated parents share care 336
total family income 311
total protected income 311, 313, 315
travel to work costs 314, 315
treatment of child maintenance 274, 312

Q
qualifying child
death of qualifying child 53
definition 4, 26
hospital or boarding school 145

R
rape
harm or undue distress 72
rates
protected income calculation 315
reconciliation
cancellation of maintenance calculation 392
reduced benefit decision 7, 75
amount of reduction 77
appeals 82
further reduction imposed 82
length of reduction 80
number of reductions 79
process 75
reconsideration 78
reduction ceases 81
supersession 82
suspension 80
welfare of child 31
when reduction starts 79
when reductions cannot be imposed 77
reduced benefit direction
old rules cases 84
refusal to co-operate
fraud referrals 78
regular payment condition 178, 360
relevant child
definition 4, 30
relevant non-resident child
maintenance calculation 131

relevant week
net income calculation 264
maintenance calculation 134
rent
exempt income calculation 243
net income calculation 272
rental purchase
exempt income calculation 243
repairs
housing costs in exempt income calculation 243
requirement to apply for child maintenance 4
requirement to co-operate 5, 7
duty to provide information 51
resettlement benefit
net income calculation 276
residence order
treatment of allowances for net income 275
responsibility for child maintenance 23
retainer fee
net income calculation 263
retirement annuity contract
net income calculation 139, 268
retirement pension
flat rate maintenance 127
revision
child support 413
conversion decisions 207, 208
decisions which can be revised 416
deduction from earnings orders 482
deductions from benefit for child support 227
departure from formula 361, 371
late application for revision 417
notification of revised decision 420
old rules cases 430
payments pending revision 458, 470
phasing-in child support assessments 405
procedure for revising decisions 419
revised decision 420
time limits 372, 417
when decisions can be revised 417
variation of maintenance 184
rounding up
child maintenance rates 126
child support formula 220

S
school holidays
day-to-day care of child 327
school leavers
child support 26, 27
second family
exempt income calculation 238, 255
phasing-in of assessments 220

545

total family income
    change of circumstances 321
self-employment
    child support
        evidence of earnings 111
    child support assessments 8
    net income calculation
        calculating weekly earnings 269
        challenging amounts of earnings 138, 270
        director's remuneration 263
        earnings 266
        evidence of earnings 138, 269
        maintenance calculation 135
        period of assessment 137, 269
        rental income 273
sequestration
    child support arrears 488
service charges
    exempt income calculation 243, 246
service targets and standards
    Child Support Agency 17
severe disability premium
    exempt income 240
severe disablement allowance
    exemption from deduction for child maintenance 225
    exemption from payment of child maintenance 224
    flat rate maintenance 127
share fishermen
    net income calculation 269
shared care
    abatement 147
    day-to-day care 326
    definition 326
    local authority shares care 146, 342
    maintenance calculation 140
        day-to-day care 141
        local authority shares care 153
        non-resident parent shares care 145, 146
    maintenance requirement met in full 342
    more than one person with care 328
    parent and another person 337
        parent provides care for less time 337
        parent provides care for more time 339
    separated parents share care 328
    three persons with care 341
    treatment as non-resident parent 329
    two people not parents 341
site fees/rent
    exempt income calculation 243
social fund
    net income calculation 271
solicitors
    privileged information 113

special cases 227
special circumstances
    late applications for revision of child support decision 418
special expenses
    effect of variation 182
    grounds for departure 348, 364
    variation of maintenance 161
special reasons for late appeal 438
spousal maintenance 38, 231, 466
    net income calculation 274
statutory maternity pay
    exemption from deduction for child maintenance 225
    exemption from payment of child maintenance 224
    net income calculation 263
statutory sick pay
    exemption from deduction for child maintenance 225
    exemption from payment of child maintenance 224
    net income calculation 263
stepchildren
    court orders for additional maintenance 37
    departure procedure 348, 349
    exempt income calculation 222, 238, 255
    maintenance 25, 466
students
    child support
        net income calculation 273
    exemption from payment of child maintenance 224
    net income calculation 265
    nil rate maintenance 127
supersession
    child support 413
        change of circumstances 323, 421, 422
        conversion decisions 207, 208
        deciding whether to request supersession 427
        decisions which can be superseded 421
        deductions from benefit for child support 227
        departure from formula 361, 371, 372
        effective date of superseded decision 425
        error of law 422
        grounds for supersession 421
        notification of revised decision 426
        old rules cases 430
        payment of arrears pending revision 470
        payments pending supersession 458
        phasing-in child support assessment 388, 405

Index
supersession – variation of maintenance

procedure 423
reduced benefit decision 82
superseded decisions 424
when decisions can be superseded 421
variation of maintenance 184
surrogate parents
child support 24

T
temporary compensation payment scheme 20
tents
exempt income calculation 243
terminal date
child support 26
termination
assessments of child support
old rules 403
deduction from earnings orders 482
maintenance calculation 391
Territorial Army
net income calculation 263
test case rules
child support decisions 427
third party payments
net income calculation 280
payments to third parties treated as maintenance 460
voluntary payments against arrears of child maintenance 468
tied accommodation
exempt income calculation 243
net income calculation 264
time limits
child support
applications 50
backdating additional maintenance 38
child support appeals 437, 438, 444
from commissioners 454
to commissioners 450, 451
departure from child support formula
providing information to CSA 359
revisions/supersessions 371, 372
liability order 485
providing information to CSA 92
requesting reasons for child support decision 437
returning maintenance enquiry form 98
revision of child support decision 417, 418
supersession of child support decision 423
total taxable profits
net income calculation
maintenance calculation 135

tracing non-resident parent 94
trade disputes
net income calculation 264
training allowance
flat rate maintenance 128
net income calculation 274
training schemes
exemption from payment of child maintenance 224
transitional amount
phasing-in of child support assessment 404
transitional phasing 194
travel expenses
attending child support hearing 445
child support
contact costs 161
child support interviews 17
departure from child support formula 348, 355, 357, 369
contact costs 348
travel to work costs 352
exempt income calculation 240, 253
net income calculation 263
protected income calculation 314, 315
two homes
exempt income calculation 244

U
unfair dismissal
compensation
net income calculation 263

V
value added tax
net income calculation
self employed earnings 268
variation of maintenance 160
additional cases 168, 181
appeals 180, 188
applying for a variation 173
concurrent variations 183
contact costs 161
court orders 36, 38, 46
date variation ceases 186
date variation takes effect 184
debts 164
decision 180
disabled child 163
effect of variation 181
grounds for rejection 175
grounds for variation 160
interim maintenance decision 177
just and equitable 178
mortgage payments 166
notification of relevant parties 176
preliminary consideration 175
property/capital transfers 166, 183

547

Index
variation of maintenance – young people

regular payment condition 178
reinstating previous variation 186
revision or supersession 414
special expenses 161, 182
supersessions and revisions 184
violence
harm or undue distress 72
vitamins
net income calculation 276
voluntary maintenance arrangements
avoiding arrears 468
consent orders 35
phasing-in of child support assessments 404
phasing-in of maintenance calculation 387
preventing applications to CSA 36, 44
protected income 312
variation by court 36, 38
voluntary payments
net income calculation 276
voluntary unemployment
deprivation of income
net income calculation 280
voluntary work
net income calculation
expenses 276
notional income 278

W
war disablement benefit
exemption from deduction for child maintenance 225
exemption from payment of child maintenance 224
war disablement pension
flat rate maintenance 128
net income calculation 271
war pensions
flat rate maintenance 128
net income calculation 271
water charges
ineligible housing costs
exempt income calculation 246
welfare of child
duty to consider 31
reduced benefit decision not made 75
widow's pension
flat rate maintenance 127
widowed parent's allowance
flat rate maintenance 127
withdrawing applications for child support
52, 53, 383
departure directions 359
Secretary of State withdraws application 52

witnesses
allowances
net income calculation 277
child support appeal hearings 445
Work-Based Training for Young People
exemption from payment of child maintenance 224
net income calculation 274
nil rate maintenance 127
working tax credit
assessable income 262
net income 272
net income calculation 265, 269
departure from child support formula 347
net income calculation
maintenance calculation 138
non-resident parents
exempt income calculation 239
parents with care
exempt income calculation 239
written maintenance agreements
phasing-in of child support assessments 404
phasing-in of maintenance calculation 387
preventing application to CSA 44

Y
young people
exemption from payment of child maintenance 224
non-resident parents 99
qualifying for child support 26, 27